STOCK INDEX FUTURES

Innovative Finance Textbooks

The purpose of this series is to provide finance textbooks for optional, specialist or advanced courses. Published in hardback at paperback prices and written by acknowledged experts, Innovative Finance Textbooks are comprehensive and reliable. Each includes a range of learning aids to assist both lecturer and student.

Stock Index Futures
Third Edition

CHARLES M.S. SUTCLIFFE
The ICMA Centre, University of Reading, UK

ASHGATE

Published by
Ashgate Publishing Limited
Gower House
Croft Road
Aldershot
Hampshire GU11 3HR
England

Ashgate Publishing Company
Suite 420
101 Cherry Street
Burlington, VT 05401-4405
USA

Ashgate website: http://www.ashgate.com

British Library Cataloguing in Publication Data
Sutcliffe, Charles M.S.
    Stock index futures. - (Innovative finance textbooks)
    1. Stock index futures
    I. Title
    332.6'3228

Library of Congress Control Number: 2005935866

ISBN 0 7546 4192 9

Printed and bound in Great Britain by TJ International Ltd, Padstow, Cornwall.

Contents

PART 3 - PRICES

PART 4 - USES

This book is dedicated to Hanna and Josef and their futures

Acknowledgements

The following are thanked for their comments on earlier drafts of parts of the book: Professor John Board (University of Reading), Dr Peter Casson (University of Southampton), Brendan George (Ashgate Publishing), Professor George McKenzie (University of Southampton), Chris Royal (Liffe), Stuart Wheeler (IG Index), Professor Pradeep Yadav (Lancaster University) and an anonymous reviewer. Students taking the following degree programmes are thanked for acting as guinea pigs for the material in this book and for their comments: MSc in European Financial Analysis, University of Newcastle, MSc in International Banking and Financial Studies, University of Southampton, MSc in International Financial Markets, University of Southampton and the MSc in Finance and Economics, University of Southampton. In addition, I am grateful to the students who took the third year course Futures and Options at the University of Southampton.

I wish to thank the London School of Economics for allowing me to spend my sabbatical leave in a splendid office during the production of the second edition, and for the use of the BLPES library. This book could not have been written without the excellent assistance of the inter-library loans staff of the Universities of Newcastle and Southampton and the British Library Document Supply Centre at Boston Spa, West Yorkshire. Thanks are also due to the film industry for the names of the characters in the numerical examples. Finally, this book would not have been possible without drawing on the work of more than one thousand researchers, whose names appear throughout this book.

CMSS   2006

Preface

The purpose of this book is to present the theories and evidence available on index futures. The broad principles governing the trading of such futures are reasonably standard across futures exchanges; and so a single body of theories and empirical evidence can be drawn from a variety of countries. While many of the available studies are American, there is now a substantial body of empirical evidence from a wide range of countries, and so it is possible to form an international view on most of the major empirical issues.

The institutional details and numerical examples are based on the UKs FTSE 100 index future. The institutional details are those current at the time of writing, and may have altered subsequently.

The primary aim of this book is to analyze the market from the point of view of a user, and the orientation is away from broad economic questions concerning the welfare effects of the existence of futures markets, such as 'does the existence of futures markets raise economic welfare?' While these questions are interesting, they relate to every conceivable futures market, and are not specific to index futures.

This book uses the language and approach of finance to analyze the general properties of index futures markets, and seeks to provide a fundamental understanding of the economic forces at work. In places the book makes use of concepts from finance theory, e.g. portfolio theory, the capital asset pricing model, the efficient markets hypothesis and portfolio insurance. A brief explanation of these concepts is given in the book, and references are provided to where a more extended treatment can be found. The aim is to keep down the mathematical content.

There are a number of books aimed at those who wish to trade in financial futures markets, and these books contain a detailed description of the mechanics of the trading process. The objective of this book is different, although there is a chapter describing the mechanics of trading index futures.

While the primary audience of this book is students of finance, others , for example market participants or regulators, who seek an understanding of the operation of index futures markets will also benefit.

Changes in the Third Edition

Some text in the second edition has been removed to make way for new material. The section on the effects on share returns of inclusion of the company in an index has been removed from chapter 1, as has the appendix with details of some leading international stock indices. The old chapter 3 has also been deleted, as has the appendix to chapter 7 on the Samuelson hypothesis and spot-basis covariance. The old chapter 8 on returns and the risk premium has been moved to chapters 2 and 6, except for the detailed discussions of the distribution of returns and the mean-variance model of the demand for futures contracts, which have been deleted. The section on default risk has been relocated from the old chapter 13 to chapter 2. There is no longer an author index.

Some new areas have been added in this edition. The section on spread betting in chapter 2 has been expanded to include contracts for difference, while new sections on exchange traded funds and futures on individual stocks have been added to this chapter. A section on exchange trading hours has been included in chapter 11, and the section on the minimum tick size has been extended to included price clustering. Throughout the book a considerable amount of new empirical evidence has been included from the large number of recent articles on index futures. In addition, the size of the contract multipliers and names of exchanges have been updated throughout the book.

Abbreviations

ACCESS	American Computerized Commodity Exchange System and Services (Nymex)
ADR	American Depository Receipt
AFBD	Association of Futures Brokers and Dealers (UK, part of the SFA from April 1991)
AFFM	Australian Financial Futures Market
AFM	Amsterdam Futures Market
AIM	Alternative Investment Market (LSE, began on 19th June 1995)
AMEX	American Stock Exchange (New York)
AMVI	AMEX Market Value Index
AOI	All Ordinaries Index (Australia)
APS	Average Price System (CME)
APT	Automated Pit Trading (Euronext.Liffe; began in November 1989)
ARCH	Autoregressive Conditional Heteroscedastic model
ARIMA	Autoregressive Integrated Moving Average process
ARMA	Autoregressive Moving Average process
ASX	Australian Stock Exchange (Sydney)
ATOM	Automated Trading and Order Matching system (APT, Euronext.Liffe)
ATS	Automated Trading System (LCE, IFOX and NZFOE)
ATX	Austrian Traded Index (ÖTOB)
AUDIT	Automated Data Input Terminal (CBOT)
BBdeF	Bolsa Brazileira de Futuros
BDP	Bolsa de Derivados do Porto (Portugal)
BELFOX	Belgian Futures and Options Exchange (Brussels)
BFE	Baltic Futures Exchange (London, merger with London FOX on 2nd January 1991)
BIFFEX	Baltic International Freight Futures Exchange (Division of BFE)
BIS	Bank for International Settlements (Basle)
BM&F	Bolsa de Mercadorias & Futuros (Sao Paulo, Brazil)
Bobl	Bundesobligation
BOTCC	Board of Trade Clearing Corporation (CBOT)
BTP	Buoni del Tesoro Poliennali (Italian Government Bonds)
CAC	Compagnie des Agents de Change (France)
CAPM	Capital Asset Pricing Model
CAPS	Combined Actuarial Performance Services Limited (UK)

CAR	Cumulative Abnormal Residual
CATS	Computer Assisted Trading System (Toronto SE)
CBOE	Chicago Board Options Exchange
CBOT	Chicago Board of Trade
CD	Certificate of Deposit
CDR	Collateralized Depository Receipt
CFD	Contract for Difference
CFTC	Commodity Futures Trading Commission (US)
CIP	Capital International Perspective
CLOB	Central Limit Order Book (Singapore)
CME	Chicago Mercantile Exchange
COMEX	Commodity Exchange Inc. (New York, merged with NYMEX on 3rd August 1994)
CORES-F	Computer Assisted Order Routing and Execution System for Futures (Tokyo SE)
CPEN	Capital Protected Equity Note
CPPI	Constant Proportion Portfolio Insurance
CPS	Clearing Processing System (Euronext.Liffe)
CRSP	Centre for Research in Security Prices (Chicago)
CTA	Commodity Trading Adviser
CTG	Commodity Traders Group (UK)
CTX	Czech Traded Index (ÖTOB)
CUSUM	Cumulative Sum
DAR	Dollars At Risk (CME)
DAX	Deutscher Aktienindex (German stock index)
DIBOR	Dublin Interbank Offered Rate
DJIA	Dow Jones Industrial Average (US)
DOT	Designated Order Turnaround (NYSE)
DTB	Deutsche TerminBörse (Frankfurt)
E100	Eurotop 100 index
ECM	Error Correction Mechanism
ECOFEX	European Community Options and Futures Exchanges
ECU	European Currency Unit
EDSP	Exchange Delivery Settlement Price
EFP	Exchange For Physicals
EGARCH	Exponential GARCH
EMFA	European Managed Futures Association
EOE	European Options Exchange (Amsterdam)
ERISA	Employee Retirement Income Security Act 1974 (US)
ESP	Exchange Stock Portfolio (NYSE, introduced on 26th October 1989)
ETF	Exchange Traded Fund

FAST	Fast Automated Screen Trading (LCE)
FCM	Futures Commission Merchant
FCOJ	Frozen Concentrated Orange Juice
FEX	First European Exchange (OMLX and EOE)
FFM	Financial and Futures Market (Netherlands)
FIA	Futures Industry Association (US)
FINEX	Financial Instrument Exchange (Division of the NYCE)
FLI	Fifty Leaders Index (Australia)
FOF	Futures and Options Fund (UK)
FOM	Finnish Options Market
FORCE	Futures and Options Real-Time Computer Environment (Euronext.Liffe)
FOX	London Futures and Options Exchange (LCE from 1st July 1993)
FOX	Finnish Options Index
FSA	Financial Services Authority (UK)
FT-A	Financial Times - Actuaries All Share index (UK)
FTA	Financiële Termijnmarkt Amsterdam (Financial Futures Market, a division of EOE)
FTO	Financial Times Ordinary index (UK)
FT/S&P-AWI	Financial Times/S&P- Actuaries World Index (UK)
FTSE	Financial Times - Stock Exchange index (UK)
FUTOP	Guarantee Fund Danish Futures and Options Exchange (Copenhagen)
GARCH	Generalized Autoregressive Conditional Heteroscedastic model
GARCH-M	GARCH in Means
GDP	Gross Domestic Product
GEM	Growth and Emerging Markets (a division of the CME from 2nd December 1995)
GEMx	German Equity Market Index
GFOF	Geared Futures and Options Fund (UK)
GNMA	Government National Mortgage Association (US)
GRB	Guaranteed Return Bond
GSCI	Goldman Sachs Commodity Index (CME)
HIBOR	Hong Kong Interbank Offered Rate
HIPs	TSE 100 Index Participation Units (TSE, launched in October 1995)
HKFE	Hong Kong Futures Exchange
HTX	Hungarian Traded Index (ÖTOB)
IBIS	Integriertes Börsenhandels und Informationssystem (Integrated Stock Exchange Trading and Information System, Germany)
ICCH	International Commodities Clearing House

ICE	International Commodities Exchange (Atlanta)
IDB	Inter Dealer Broker
IDEM	Italian Equity Derivatives Market (Milan)
IFOX	Irish Futures and Options Exchange (Dublin)
IMM	International Monetary Market (Division of the CME)
INTEX	International Futures Exchange of Bermuda
IOM	Index and Options Market (Division of the CME)
IOSCO	International Organisation of Securities Commissioners
IPC	Índice de Precios y Cotizaciones (Mexico)
IPE	International Petroleum Exchange (London)
ISE	International Stock Exchange (renamed the LSE in 1991)
ISF	Individual Stock Futures
ISEQ	Irish Stock Exchange Equity index
JEC	Joint Exchanges Committee (UK)
JGB	Japanese Government Bond
JSE	Johannesburg Stock Exchange
KCBT	Kansas City Board of Trade
KLCE	Kuala Lumpur Commodity Exchange
KLSE CI	Kuala Lumpur Stock Exchange Composite Index
KLOFFE	Kuala Lumpur Options and Financial Futures Exchange
KOSPI	Korea Stock Price Index
LCE	London Commodity Exchange (London FOX until 1st July 1993) (merged with Liffe on 16th September 1996)
LCH	London Clearing House (subsidiary of ICCH until June 1991)
LEAPS	Long term Equity AnticiPation Securities (CBOE)
LIBOR	London Interbank Offered Rate
Liffe	London International Financial Futures Exchange to 23rd March 1992, and then London International Financial Futures and Options Exchange until 2001, when it became Euronext.Liffe
LME	London Metal Exchange
LOCH	London Options Clearing House
LOX	Large Order Execution (CME)
LSE	London Stock Exchange (formerly the ISE until 1991)
LTOM	London Traded Options Market (to 23rd March 1992, when it merged with Liffe)
MATIF	Marché à Terme International de France (Paris)
MCC	Modified Closing Call (CBOT)
MEFF RF	Mercado de Futuros Financieros Renta Fija (Barcelona)
MEFF RV	Mercado de Futuros Financieros Renta Variable (Madrid)
MERFOX	Mercado de Futuros y Opciones (Buenos Aires, Argentina)
MFA	Managed Futures Association

MIF	Mercato Italiano Futures (Italy)
MMI	Major Market Index (US)
MOFEX	Mercando de Opciones Financiero Espanol (Madrid)
MONEP	Marché des Options Négociables de la Bourse de Paris
MSCI	Morgan Stanley Capital International
NASDAQ	National Association of Securities Dealers Automated Quotation System (US)
NFA	National Futures Association (US)
NMS	Normal Market Size (LSE)
NPV	Net Present Value
NSC	Nouveau Systeme de Cotation (Paris Bourse and Matif)
NYCE	New York Cotton Exchange
NYFE	New York Futures Exchange
NYMEX	New York Mercantile Exchange (Merged with COMEX on 3rd August 1994)
NYSE	New York Stock Exchange
NZFOE	New Zealand Futures and Options Exchange
NZSE	New Zealand Stock Exchange
OARS	Opening Automated Report Service (NYSE)
OLS	Ordinary Least Squares regression
OMLX	London Securities and Derivatives Exchange (OM London until 1 April 1993)
OPALS	Optimized Portfolios As Listed Securities (Morgan Stanley, May 1993)
OSE	Osaka Securities Exchange (Japan)
OTC	Over the Counter
ÖTOB	Österreichische Termin und Optionenbörse (Austrian Futures and Options Exchange, Vienna)
PHBOT	Philadelphia Board of Trade
PHLX	Philadelphia Stock Exchange
PIBS	Permanent Interest Bearing Share
PSI	Portuguese Stock Index
PTX	Polish Traded Index (ÖTOB)
RAES	Retail Automatic Execution Service (CBOE)
S&P	Standard and Poors
SAEF	SEAQ Automated Execution Facility (LSE)
SAFE	Simulation Analysis of Financial Exposure (CBOT)
SAFEX	South African Futures Exchange (Johannesburg)
SEAQ	Stock Exchange Automated Quotations (LSE)
SEAQI	SEAQ International (LSE)
SEATS	Stock Exchange Automated Trading System (ASX)
SEATS	Stock Exchange Alternative Trading System (LSE)

SEC	Securities and Exchange Commission (US)
SEM	Simultaneous Equations Model
SETS	Stock Exchange Electronic Trading Service (LSE, 20 October 1997)
SFA	Securities and Futures Authority (UK, from a merger in April 1991 of AFBD & TSA)
SFE	Sydney Futures Exchange
SGX	Singapore Exchange
SIB	Securities and Investments Board (UK)
SIGNS	Stock Index Growth Notes
SIMEX	Singapore International Monetary Exchange (Singapore Exchange from 1 December 1999)
SMI	Swiss Market Index
SOFE	Swedish Options and Futures Exchange (Stockholm)
SOFFEX	Swiss Options and Financial Futures Exchange (Zurich)
SOM	Stockholms Optionsmarknad (Stockholm Options Market, or OM Stockholm)
SOM	Suomen Optiomeklarit Oy (Finnish Options Market)
SPAN	Standard Portfolio Analysis of Risk
SPDRs	Standard and Poors Depositary Receipts (Spiders, Amex from 29th January 1993)
SPI	All Ordinaries Share Price Index (Australia)
SRO	Self Regulatory Organisation (UK)
SURE	Seemingly Unrelated Regression Estimation
SYCOM	Sydney Computerized Overnight Market
TALISMAN	Transfer Accounting and Lodgement for Investors, Stock Management for Principals (LSE)
TAURUS	Transfer and Automated Registration of Uncertificated Stock (LSE, abandoned on 11th March 1993)
TFE	Toronto Futures Exchange
TGE	Tokyo Grain Exchange
TIFFE	Tokyo International Financial Futures Exchange
TIPs	Toronto 35 Index Participation Units (TSE, launched on 9th March 1990)
TOCOM	Tokyo Commodity Exchange
TOFS	The Futures and Options Society (UK)
TOPIC	Teletext Output of Price Information by Computer (LSE)
TOPIX	Tokyo Stock Price Index
TSA	The Securities Association (UK, part of SFA from April 1991)
TSE	Tokyo Stock Exchange
TSE	Toronto Stock Exchange
TRS	Trade Registration System (Euronext.Liffe)

UCITS	Units of Collective Investment in Transferable Securities (UK)
USDA	United States Department of Agriculture
USM	Unlisted Securities Market (LSE, replaced by AIM and ceased trading in 1996)
VAR	Vector AutoRegression
VLA	Value Line Arithmetic index (US)
VLCI	Value Line Composite Index (geometric) (US)
WEBS	World Equity Benchmark Shares (Amex)
WM	World Markets Company plc (UK)

PART 1

PRELIMINARIES

Chapter 1

Stock Market Indices

Introduction

Stock indices are fundamental to stock index futures, and so this initial chapter will be devoted to the construction and properties of these indices. Some readers, who are familiar with the concept and construction of stock indices, may prefer to omit this chapter and go straight to the subsequent chapters, which deal in detail with index futures.

1.1 The Need to Measure Market-wide Price Movements

An array of stock market indices has been developed to meet the strong demand for aggregate measures of stock market performance. These indices are designed to quantify widespread movements in stock market prices; either for the market as a whole or for major sections of the market. The usefulness of such market wide measures is increased if there is a generally positive correlation between the price changes of different shares. Such measurements are desired for a number of reasons. They can provide an historical comparison of the returns on money invested in the stock market as against investment in some other type of asset e.g. government debt or gold. They can be used as a simple standard against which to compare the performance of investment fund managers. Since the share price is often treated as a measure of the market's expectations of the cash flows from the company concerned, a market index provides a leading indicator of national economic performance. Furthermore, the news media have developed a need for a simple and convenient barometer of changes in financial markets, particularly when there are 'crashes' or 'booms'.

In recent years, the development of finance theories in which movements in the market as a whole assume a central role, has led to a demand for the measurement of such movements. Thus the market portfolio plays a vital role in the Capital Asset Pricing Model and the calculation of beta values for individual shares. It is also central to passive fund management, where the aim is to match the performance of the market as a whole via index funds. New financial instruments have been developed which are based on movements in the market rather than individual shares e.g. stock index futures, stock index options and options on stock index futures. The trading of these instruments is not possible without the existence of the relevant stock market index.

Therefore, the measurement of market-wide movements is an important activity, and is accomplished by the use of index numbers. There are numerous ways of constructing an index of movements in stock market prices, and each has its own advantages and disadvantages. Since an index number summarizes hundreds of price movements, it is unavoidable that much information is lost. Therefore, the choice of a stock market index is always a compromise, and this helps to explain why a variety of different indices are computed to quantify movements in a single stock market. An index that is appropriate for answering some questions is inappropriate for others.

Before discussing indices in detail, an important point about dividends will be mentioned. Almost all stock market indices measure changes in share prices, with no allowance for dividend payments. A major exception is the DAX index, which assumes that dividends are reinvested in the shares of the company concerned. When a share goes ex-dividend (i.e. a new owner does not buy the right to receive declared, but unpaid, dividends) the share price falls. If the shares of a number of large companies go ex-dividend on the same day this may cause a discernable decline in a market index. As well as causing small drops in the index on ex-dividend days, the omission of dividends means that movements in the index understate the long term rewards from holding shares by the amount of the dividends. Thus stock market indices are usually *price* indices rather than *returns* or *performance* indices. The dividends can usually be added back, because data are often provided separately for the rate of dividends on the shares in an index, although in the UK such data has only been available on an annual basis. As from 5 July 1993, daily total returns for the *Financial Times* indices have been published. The computation of returns uses closing prices and gross dividends, although prior to 11 July 1994 the net of tax dividend was used, FTSE Actuaries Share Indices Steering Committee (1995). The dividend and any associated tax credit are assumed to be reinvested immediately on the ex-dividend date without incurring any transactions costs, and it is assumed that the recipient pays no tax.

1.2 Types of Stock Market Index

Stock market indices can be classified using two criteria: the weighting system (market value weighted, price weighted or equally weighted) and the averaging procedure (arithmetic or geometric).

1.2.1 Weights

The simplest approach is to construct an index using the share prices directly without applying any weights. In such a price weighted index, movements in the share price of companies with a high share price are likely to dominate because they will tend to change by large absolute amounts.

Example. Suppose there are two companies, Dum and Dee, which are identical except for their capital structure. Dum has one million shares with a market price of 100p each, while Dee has 200,000 shares with a market price of 500p each. If there is a 10% rise in the value of the net assets of both Dum and Dee, the share price of Dum will rise by 10p while that of Dee will rise by 50p. Hence, Dee has a much greater influence on a price weighted market index than Dum purely because it has chosen to issue fewer shares, even though the total capitalization of the firms is the same (£1,000,000).

Another possibility is that the price of each share in the index is given an equal weight in the calculation of the index. Equal weight is achieved by considering the proportionate change in the price of each share relative to some base date, e.g. price relatives. While companies with a high share price do not have a disproportionate effect on the index, this method does not reflect differences in size between the companies. Thus, in an equally weighted index, the share price of a company with a market capitalization of £1 billion is given the same importance as the share price of a company with a market capitalization of £50 million.

A weighted index gives greater importance to the price of some shares, and hence less importance to the price of other shares. Weighting schemes usually award greater weight to the share prices of companies that constitute a big proportion of the value of the shares held by shareholders, and lesser weight to companies that account for only a small proportion of shareholders' portfolios. Such weights are generally market capitalization, i.e. the number of shares issued by the company multiplied by the share price at some specified time. The adoption of this particular weighting scheme has the considerable advantage that each share price is weighted in accordance with its importance in the average portfolio of shares. This means that, provided a suitable choice of averaging method is made, changes in the index measure changes in the value of the average portfolio, i.e. the market as a whole. Of course, if the objective is to measure changes in the value of an equally weighted portfolio, then an equally weighted index is more appropriate.

A capitalization-weighted index has the advantage of being harder to manipulate than most other weighting schemes, as the more liquid shares tend to get the higher weights. However there can be problems with capitalization-weighted indices. On 1st August 1995 46.3% of the value of the Finnish FOX index was accounted for by a single company, Nokia. Some indices put an upper bound on the weight which can be given to any single company to prevent the index being dominated by a few very large firms, e.g. the Amsterdam EOE index, the FOX and the Toronto Stock Exchange 35. In the last few years the major index providers (i.e. FTSE, MSCI and Dow Jones) have switched to using free float weights for their capitalization-weighted indices. The free float is the market value of shares in the company that are available for trading, and so is a more realistic measure of the investable market portfolio. The TOPIX index, which is a capitalization-weighted index, has the peculiarity that it can include both the parent company and its subsidiary. In which case the holding of the parent in the subsidiary is double counted (Kobayashi & Yamada, 2000).

Recently Arnott, Hsu and Moore (2005) argued that market cap weights give extra weight to overpriced stocks, and vice versa. They propose using fundamental weights such as sales, book value, cash flow, dividends or total employment.

1.2.2 Averaging

The prices (or price relatives) of individual shares must be aggregated to produce a single number; the value of the index. This is done in one of two ways: the arithmetic average or the geometric average. The arithmetic weighted average of three numbers (AW) is $AW = (w_1x_1 + w_2x_2 + w_3x_3)$, where the x_i are the numbers, and the weights (w_i) sum to one.

The geometric weighted average (GW) of a set of three numbers is $GW = (x_1{}^{w1}) \times (x_2{}^{w2}) \times (x_3{}^{w3})$. If each number is equally weighted (i.e. $w_i = 1/n$ for all i, where n is the number of shares in the index), the equally weighted (or unweighted) geometric mean (GU) becomes the nth root of the product of the numbers, or $GU = [x_1x_2x_3]^{1/3}$. The advantages and disadvantages of arithmetic and geometric averaging when computing indices are discussed in chapter 1.4.

1.3 Computation of Stock Market Indices

All market weighted and equally weighted indices have a base date. This is the time when the value of the index is usually set to unity, a hundred or a thousand. For price weighted indices the base date is of little importance, and the index is expressed in £ units, rather than as a ratio with respect to the base date. The value of a price weighted arithmetic index (AP) at time t is:-

$$AP_t = \sum_{i=1}^{n} P_{it}$$

Example. Morticia Addams decides to establish her own price weighted index, to be called the Zelig index. This will be based on the prices of four shares. The prices of these shares at times 0 and 1 are:

Share	Time 0	Time 1
Sydenham	100p	110p
Wimbledon	500p	490p
Dulwich	20p	25p
Surbiton	10p	9p
Totals	630p	634p

The value of the Zelig index at time 0 is 630, while by time 1 it has risen to 634.

Although any date can be chosen as the base, for market indices the first occasion the index is computed is often used as the base date.

The arithmetic weighted stock market index at time t with a base of time 0, denoted $AW_t{}^0$, can be expressed as the arithmetic average of the weighted price relatives, i.e. :-

$$AW_t{}^0 = \sum_{i=1}^{n} w_i R_i \qquad \text{where } R_i = P_{it}/P_{i0}, \text{ and } \Sigma w_i = 1$$

The geometric equally weighted stock market index at time t, with a base of time 0, denoted $GU_t{}^0$, is given by :-

$$GU_t{}^0 = (Z_t/Z_0)^{1/n}, \quad Z_j = P_{1j} \times P_{2j} \times P_{3j} \times \dots \times P_{nj}, \text{ where } j = 0 \text{ and } t.$$

1.4 Comparison of Geometric and Arithmetic Stock Market Indices

The merits of geometric and arithmetic indices will be considered by presenting the advantages and disadvantages of a geometric index relative to an arithmetic index.

1.4.1 Advantages of a Geometric Index

The advantages of geometric indices stem from a single property of such indices. This is the simple way in which the current value of the index can be decomposed. Thus

$$GU_t^0 = (Z_1/Z_0)^{1/n} \times (Z_2/Z_1)^{1/n} \times \ldots \times (Z_t/Z_{t-1})^{1/n}$$

which can be rewritten as :-

$$GU_t^0 = GU_1^0 \times GU_2^1 \times GU_3^2 \times GU_4^3 \times GU_5^4 \times \ldots \times GU_t^{t-1}$$

This leads to three advantages of geometric indices.

Changing the Base Date. The base date of a series of geometric index numbers can be changed very easily. If it is desired to change the base from time 0 to time r, since $GU_t^0 = GU_r^0 \times GU_t^r$, it follows that $GU_t^r = GU_t^0/GU_r^0$; and simple division rebases this index number. The previous values of the index can similarly be rebased from time 0 to time r by dividing the previous values through by GU_r^0.

Example. The following series of geometric index numbers based at time 0 can be rebased to time 2. Since $GU_t^2 = GU_t^0/GU_2^0$,

	Time 0	Time 1	Time 2	Time 3	Time 4
GU_t^0	1.00	1.04	1.08	1.12	1.20
GU_t^2	0.926	0.963	1.00	1.037	1.111

This simple rebasing property does not hold for an arithmetic index. However, while indices of consumer or producer prices are often rebased, stock market indices are seldom rebased (although the Italian Mibtel index is rebased to 10,000 every year).

Rates of Return Independent of the Base Date. The rate of return is independent of the choice of base date for a geometric index, but not for an arithmetic index. This property will be illustrated using a simple numerical example (in which the rate of return is arithmetic rather than logarithmic).

Example - Geometric Index. Suppose that the index comprises only two shares, A and B, and that the prices of these shares at two points in time are given below.

Share Prices

	Time 0	Time 1
Share A	£1.00	£1.5625
Share B	£1.00	£1.00

First, the percentage change in the value of an equally weighted geometric index using time 0 as the base will be computed. Second, this rate of return will be compared with that calculated if time 1 is used as the base. Using time 0 as the base date, the values of the index are:-

$$GU_0^0 = [(1 \times 1)/(1 \times 1)]^{1/2} = 1.00$$
$$GU_1^0 = [(1.5625 \times 1)/(1 \times 1)]^{1/2} = 1.25$$

Therefore, using time 0 as the base, the percentage increase is 1.25/1.00 = 25%.

If time 1 is used as the base, then:-

$$GU_0^1 = [(1\times1)/(1.5625\times1)]^{\frac{1}{2}} = \quad 0.80$$
$$GU_1^1 = [(1.5625\times1)/(1.5625\times1)]^{\frac{1}{2}} = 1.00$$

and the percentage increase is $1.00/0.80 = 25\%$, as before.

This result, that the rate of return on a geometric index is independent of the base date, is perfectly general. It follows from the definition of a geometric index that $GU_t^r = 1/GU_r^t$, i.e. there is a reciprocal relationship. The rate of return for the period r to t, using time r as the base, is given by $GU_t^r/GU_r^r = GU_t^r$, where $GU_r^r = 1$ because the value of an index at its base date is defined to be unity. Similarly, the rate of return using time t as the base is $GU_t^t/GU_r^t = 1/GU_r^t$. Since $GU_t^r = 1/GU_r^t$, it follows that the rates of return calculated using different base dates must be equal.

Using the same numerical example, changing the base date for an arithmetic index changes the rates of return. This means that, when an arithmetic index is rebased, the historic rates of return for all previous time periods will also be altered.

***Example* - Arithmetic Index.** Using the same share price data as for the geometric example, the percentage change in the value of an equally weighted arithmetic index will be calculated first when time 0 is the base date, and second, when time 1 is the base. With time 0 as the base:-

$$AU_0^0 = [1/1 + 1/1]/2 = \quad 1.0000$$
$$AU_1^0 = [1.5625/1 + 1/1]/2 = \quad 1.2815$$

Therefore the rate of return for this period using time 0 as the base is $(1.2815/1.00)-1.00 = 28.15\%$. Using time 1 as the base date :-

$$AU_0^1 = [1/1.5625 + 1/1]/2 = \quad 0.82$$
$$AU_1^1 = [1.5625/1.5625 + 1/1]/2 = \quad 1.00$$

and the rate of return is $(1.00/0.82)-1.00 = 21.95\%$, which is clearly different from the 28.15% computed using time 0 as the base.

Since stock indices are seldom rebased, this advantage of geometric indices is only rarely exhibited.

Share Substitution. The replacement at any time of one share in the index by another is easier when using a geometric than an arithmetic index. Since :-

$$GU_t^0 = (Z_1/Z_0)^{1/n}\times(Z_2/Z_1)^{1/n}\times \ldots \times(Z_t/Z_{(t-1)})^{1/n} \quad \text{where } Z_j = P_{1j}\times P_{2j}\times P_{3j}\times \ldots \times P_{nj}$$

if it is desired to change the identity of the second share in the index, then $(Z_t/Z_{t-1})^{1/n}$ can be replaced by $(Z_t^\#/Z_{t-1}^\#)^{1/n}$ when computing the index for time t, and earlier values of the index remain unchanged, Allen (1975, page 235). The computation of the Z terms is altered at the time of the substitution to use the prices of the new share; e.g. $Z_j^\# = P_{1j}\times P_{2j}^\#\times P_{3j}\times \ldots \times P_{nj}$, where the superscript # denotes the replacement share.

Example   **Share Prices**

	Time 0	Time 1	Time 2
Share A	£1.00	£1.5625	£1.00
Share B	£1.00	£1.00	£0.50
Share C	£0.80	£0.90	£2.00

Initially the equally weighted geometric index consists of shares A and B. At time 1, share B is replaced in the index by share C. Using time 0 as the base date, the values of the geometric index are:-

$$GU_0^0 = [(1\times1)/(1\times1)]^{\frac{1}{2}} = \qquad\qquad 1.00$$
$$GU_1^0 = [(1.5625\times1)/(1\times1)]^{\frac{1}{2}} = \qquad\qquad 1.25$$
$$GU_1^{0\#} = [(1.5625\times0.90)/(1\times0.80)]^{\frac{1}{2}} = \qquad 1.326$$
$$GU_2^{0\#} = [(1\times2)/(1\times0.80)]^{\frac{1}{2}} = \qquad\qquad 1.581$$

To prevent the index jumping at time 1 due to the change in its constituents, it could be multiplied by 1.25/1.326 so that $GU_1^{0\#} = 1.25$, and $GU_2^{0\#} = 1.4904$.

For an arithmetic index, share substitution is more complicated.

Information Asymmetry. Lien & Luo (1993d) specified three desirable features of a stock index: high trading volume, large profits for insiders and low expected losses for liquidity traders; and presented a theoretical model in which an equally weighted geometric index is generally superior to an market value weighted arithmetic index on each of these criteria when there is information asymmetry.

1.4.2 Portfolio Rebalancing

The arithmetic price and market value weighted indices considered in this chapter involve a buy-and-hold strategy, with no rebalancing of the portfolio of shares in the index. In consequence, there is an increase over time in the proportion of the portfolio invested in shares which have shown above average price rises. This can lead to the degree of diversification of the portfolio declining over time, with most of the money invested in a few very successful companies.

Latane, Tuttle & Young (1971) discuss an alternative form of arithmetic index where the portfolio is rebalanced periodically by hypothetically selling shares that have experienced large price increases and buying shares with low price rises so that the proportions of the investment in each company are returned to their initial levels. An equally weighted index achieves this result.

Example

	Share Prices		
	Time 0	**Time 1**	**Time 2**
Share A	£1.00	£1.5625	£1.00
Share C	£0.80	£0.90	£2.00

For simplicity, the initial investment proportions in the shares of companies A and C are 50% in each, the index is an equally weighted arithmetic index with a base date of time 0 and the initial sum invested is £1,000. The portfolio is rebalanced every time period. At time 0 the portfolio consists of 500 shares in company A and $(50/0.8)\times100 = 625$ shares in company C. The value of the index at time 0 is 1.00. At time 1 the value of this portfolio has risen to $(500\times1.5625)+(625\times0.9) = £1,343.75$ and the value of the index at time 1 is 1.34375.

The portfolio is now rebalanced. The revised number of shares in company A drops to $1343.75/(2\times1.5625) = 430$, while that in company C rises to $1343.75/(2\times0.9) = 746.53$. (Division by two occurs in these calculations because the portfolio is required to be equally balanced.) At time 2 the value of this rebalanced portfolio has risen to $(430\times1.0)+(746.53\times2.0) = £1,923.06$, i.e. the index at time 2 is 1.92306. Without any rebalancing the value of the portfolio at time 2 would have risen to only $(500 \times 1.0)+(625 \times 2.0) = £1,750$, i.e. an index value of 1.75.

None of the major arithmetic stock indices is periodically rebalanced, and the only important stock indices where rebalancing takes place are the geometric indices. In this case continuous rebalancing is implicit in the averaging procedure.

1.4.3 Disadvantages of a Geometric Index

1.4.3.1 Understate Price Rises. If the prices of all the shares in the index rise (or fall) by $x\%$, then an equally weighted geometric index will also rise (or fall) by $[(1+x)^n]^{1/n}$ $= (1+x) = x\%$. However, unless all share prices in the index rise (or fall) by exactly the same proportion, a geometric index will understate a rise and overstate the absolute size of a fall in share prices. The larger is the diversity of movement in the individual share prices, the greater is the degree of under or over statement. The criterion of the 'correct' change in share prices is the change in the market value of a portfolio of shares held throughout the period. The rates of return computed for the previous numerical examples can be used to illustrate the understatement of a price rise.

Example. Suppose Sally Bowles bought 1,000 shares in companies A and B at time 0 investing £1,000 in each company. The initial cost of this equally weighted portfolio is £2,000. At time 1 the value of this portfolio has risen to £1,000+£1,562.5 = £2,562.5. This represents a return of $(2,562.5/2,000)-1.00 = 28.13\%$, which is exactly the rate of return given by the equally weighted arithmetic index using time 0 as the base date. Hence, the arithmetic index (when the base date is the start of the time period for which it is desired to compute the return) correctly measures the rate of return on a portfolio held unchanged throughout the period. Since the percentage increase for the geometric index is 25% (regardless of the base date used), the geometric index understates the percentage increase in the value of a portfolio by 3.13%.

A numerical example will now be presented which illustrates that a geometric index overstates a price fall.

Example	**Share Prices**	
	Time 0	**Time 1**
Share A	£1.00	£0.50
Share B	£1.00	£1.00

The values of the equally weighted geometric index are :-

$GU_0{}^0 = [(1 \times 1)/(1 \times 1)]^{1/2} = \qquad 1.00$

$GU_1{}^0 = [(0.5 \times 1)/(1 \times 1)]^{1/2} = \qquad 0.7071$

and the percentage change in the geometric market index is a drop of 29.29%. (If time 1 had been used as the base date, the drop would also be 29.29%.) However, an equally weighted portfolio of £1,000 in each share, initially valued at £2,000, would have dropped in value to £1,000+£500 = £1,500, i.e. a drop of only 25%. (The return on an equally weighted arithmetic index with time 0 as the base is also

-25%.) Thus, the geometric index has overstated the price fall by 4.29%, relative to the change in value of a portfolio.

This result has important implications for measuring rates of return, and the real world magnitude of this bias will be considered in more detail in chapter 1.7. Arithmetic indices (where the base date is the date of the initial investment) correctly give the price rise or fall.

1.4.3.2 Zero Value. Since the computation of a geometric index involves the product of all the current share prices, if the price of any constituent share collapses towards zero, it must be removed before the index value becomes zero. This is not the case for an arithmetic index.

1.4.3.3 Non-Normality. If each of the shares in an arithmetic index has independent normally distributed arithmetic returns; arithmetic returns on the index must also be normally distributed. This is because the sum of independent normal variates is also normal. However, if these individual arithmetic returns are used to compute a geometric index, returns on this index will not be normal.

1.5 Details of the Computation of the FTSE 100 Index

As an illustration of the computation of a stock market index, details will be given of the computation of the FTSE 100 stock index, which is an arithmetic index using market capitalization weights. The value of this index at time t (I_t) is computed as:-

$$I_t = \lambda \sum_{i=1}^{100} C_i P_{it} / \sum_{i=1}^{100} C_i P_{ib}$$

where C_i is the number of shares issued by the ith company, P_{ij} is the price of shares in the ith company at time j and λ is an adjustment factor to ensure that the index is equal to 1,000 at the base date, and to allow for subsequent changes in the constituent companies and their capital structure. The base date, i.e. b, for this index is the 3rd January 1984. The formula can be rewritten as:-

$$I_t = \lambda \sum_{i=1}^{100} w_i (P_{it}/P_{ib}) / \sum_{i=1}^{100} w_i \qquad \text{where } w_i = C_i P_{ib}$$

Since every value of the index is divided by the constant, Σw_i, this number can be incorporated into the λ term, giving the equation:-

$$I_t = \lambda \sum_{i=1}^{100} w_i (P_{it}/P_{ib})$$

Apart from the inclusion of the λ term and the corresponding redefinition of the weights, this equation is equivalent to the earlier statement of an arithmetic weighted index, i.e. $AW_t^0 = \Sigma w_i R_i$.

Example. The following data is available for the computation of the FTSE 2 index; an index that will be computed in the same way as the FTSE 100 but containing only two shares.

Share Prices

	31st Dec	**31st Jan**	**28th Feb**	**31st Mar**
Multilever	300p	320p	340p	350p
Xoff	100p	90p	80p	120p

Throughout this period Multilever had an issued share capital of 10 million £1 shares, while the corresponding figure for Xoff was 5 million 50p shares. The base date is the 31st December.

I_{DEC} = 1.000 by definition, and so $1/\lambda$ = 3,500,000

I_{JAN} = [3,000m.(320/300) + 500m.(90/100)]/3.5m. = 1,042.9

I_{FEB} = [3,000m.(340/300) + 500m.(80/100)]/3.5m. = 1,085.7

I_{MAR} = [3,000m.(350/300) + 500m.(120/100)]/3.5m. = 1,171.4

1.6 Some Major Stock Market Indices

Some indices are categorized in table 1.1 according to two important characteristics: the weighting system and the averaging procedure. As can be seen, of the six possibilities only four are in use, and one (arithmetic, market weighted) is clearly the most popular.

Table 1.1: Classification of Some Major Stock Indices

	Market Weighted	Equally Weighted	Price Weighted
Arithmetic	CAC 40*	VLA*	DJIA
	DAX*	Amex Biotechnology	MMI*
	FT-A		Nikkei 225*
	FTSE 100*		Osaka 50 Kabusaki*
	Hang Seng*		
	IBEX 35*		
	Nikkei 300*		
	NYSE Composite*		
	SMI*		
	S&P500*		
	Topix*		
Geometric	-	FTO	-
		VLCI*	

* An index on which an index future has been traded.

1.7 Problems with Stock Market Indices

All stock market indices have problems, although some of these problems differ as between the various types of index. Therefore, one type of index may be superior in some situations, while other types of index may be preferable in other circumstances.

1.7.1 Long Term Downward Bias

It has been demonstrated above that, if share prices do not all change by the same proportionate amount, a geometric index (e.g. FTO or VLCI) will understate any price rise or overstate any fall. In reality share prices tend to rise in the long run, and they do so by differing amounts. Therefore, if the market index is an equally weighted geometric index, it can always be 'beaten' by the simple device of investing an equal amount in each share in the market index and holding this investment throughout the period, Cootner (1966).

While this downward bias of a geometric index will generally exist, it is only of practical importance if it has a material effect on calculated returns. Marks & Stuart (1971) investigated this question for the FTO index, which is an equally weighted geometric index. They took the share prices used in the computation of the FTO index, and calculated the values of the corresponding equally weighted arithmetic index. With the end of 1960 as the base date for these two indices, by the end of 1970 the FTO index had risen by 11.6%, while the arithmetic equivalent index was 41.2% higher than at its base date. Therefore, while the value of an equally weighted portfolio of the thirty shares in the index had risen by 41.2% over ten years, the FTO measured less than a third of this rise. This represents a serious understatement, and renders geometric indices unsuitable for measuring long term price movements.

1.7.2 Base Date

In the previous numerical examples, the base date was either the start or end of the time period for which the return was being computed. The importance of the chosen base date for the computed percentage change in the value of the index will be illustrated using a combination of the previous numerical examples, where base dates other than the start or end of the relevant period will be used.

Example	**Share Prices**			
	Time 0	**Time 1**	**Time 2**	**Time 3**
Share A	£1.00	£1.5625	£1.00	£1.00
Share B	£1.00	£1.00	£0.50	£1.00

The value of the equally weighted geometric and arithmetic indices for the three possible base dates (time 3 is ignored as the results are identical to time 0) are set out in table 1.2; together with the corresponding percentage changes in the index and the proportionate change in value of an equally weighted portfolio in table 1.3.

Table 1.2: Values of Various Indices for the Example

	Time 0	Time 1	Time 2	Time 3
GU^0	1.00	1.25	0.7071	1.00
GU^1	0.80	1.00	0.5657	0.80
GU^2	1.4142	1.7678	1.00	1.4142
AU^0	1.00	1.2813	0.75	1.00
AU^1	0.82	1.00	0.57	0.82
AU^2	1.50	1.7813	1.00	1.50

Table 1.3: Percentage Changes in the Indices for the Example

	Times 0 to 1	Times 1 to 2	Times 2 to 3
GU^0	25%	– 43.43%	41.42%
GU^1	25%	– 43.43%	41.42%
GU^2	25%	– 43.43%	41.42%
AU^0	28.13%	– 41.47%	33.33%
AU^1	21.95%	– 43.00%	43.86%
AU^2	18.75%	– 43.86%	50.00%
Portfolio	28.13%	– 43.00%	50.00%

These tables illustrate that: (a) the returns on a geometric index are independent of the base date, (b) relative to the market portfolio, a geometric index understates price rises and overstates price falls, (c) the arithmetic index only measures the percentage return on the market portfolio when the base date is the start of the period for which the return is being computed, and (d) depending on the base date chosen, the percentage change in the arithmetic index can be larger or smaller than that of the geometric index.

These results show that considerable caution is needed when using a stock market index to measure the change in value of a portfolio of shares. A geometric index is biased in a consistent direction, while the direction of bias in an arithmetic index varies. Thus, an arithmetic index with a base year other than the start of the investment period can over or understate the return on a portfolio, while a geometric index will always understate this return. By a suitable choice of start date and market index, a fund manager will often be able to claim to have 'beaten the market', when the reality is that the value of their fund has moved in line with the market.

1.7.3 Selection Bias

Some indices cover all shares traded on the exchange (e.g. NYSE Composite, AMVI, Topix and NASDAQ Composite) and there is no problem of selection bias. Before the widespread use of computers, calculation of an index in real time required the use of a smaller set of shares to enable the rapid and repeated calculation of the index. The inclusion of all the shares traded on an exchange still has the problem that small companies are thinly traded. If the coverage of the index is less than complete, the shares selected for inclusion in many stock market indices represent a biased sample of the market as a whole, e.g. FTSE 100, S&P500. This is for two reasons. First, since many indices are designed to contain only large leading companies, they are based on a biased sample because many relatively small companies are also traded on the stock market. Recent research has found that the performance of small firms tends to differ systematically from that of large companies; i.e. the size effect, see Dimson (1988).

A second source of bias concerns the way in which the identity of the shares in the index changes over time. Companies that have grown at a slow rate tend to be removed from the index, while companies that have shown rapid growth are added. Companies that are taken over or nationalized are removed from the index, while large newly privatized companies are added. Of the thirty original companies in the FTO in 1935, only five survived to 2001: Blue Circle Cement, GKN, ICI. Marconi and Tate & Lyle. This process tends to bias the index as it is based on companies with an above average historic performance, and so possibly an above average performance in future time periods.

There is also a potential problem which concerns the removal of shares from an index. Until 1992, if trading in a share was suspended, and then the share was removed from the FTSE 100 index before trading recommenced, it was deemed to have been withdrawn from the index at its suspension price, even if the suspended share proved worthless. This tended to give the index an upward bias as, by assumption, it was always able to liquidate suspended shares at the suspension price.

1.7.4 Averaging Bias

Suppose a time series of random numbers is used to produce a new time series by taking averages over short, non-overlapping time intervals of the initial series. Working (1960b), has shown that, even though changes in the original series are independent over time, changes in the averaged series will contain positive serial correlation. For example, let the daily closing values of a stock market index follow a random walk. If a new series is created by taking the weekly averages of the five daily closing values of the index, Working's result indicates that changes in this new series will have a positive first order serial correlation coefficient of 0.235.

Assuming that price changes follow a random walk, Board & Sutcliffe (1985) have shown that temporal averaging will introduce further distortions, in addition to serial correlation. The value of the variance of the averaged series will be two thirds that of the initial series, while the covariance between the averaged series and some other averaged series will be two thirds of the covariance between the unaveraged series. The mean of the averaged series will be biased down by one sixth of the value of the variance of the unaveraged series.

The introduction of positive serial correlation and the reduction of the variance, covariances and mean by averaging can occur in two ways. The first is when, for some reason, the published values of the market index are explicitly averaged. The second occurs when implicit averaging takes place in the calculation of the index. Each of these possibilities will be considered in turn.

1.7.4.1. Explicit Averaging. Some published values of stock market indices are, in fact, averages of a number of values of the index computed at different times. For example, the International Monetary Fund publication *International Financial Statistics* contains time series of stock market indices for a large number of countries. For a significant number of countries, the monthly stock index numbers published in *International Financial Statistics* are averages, e.g. the average of the Friday closing values for each calendar month.

This averaging will introduce (or increase) positive serial correlation in changes in the index, and will also lower the variance and mean of the stock market index; although not its covariance with individual shares. This can have important consequences. Board & Sutcliffe (1985) have investigated the effects of such averaging on the composition of portfolios constructed using historic data from *International Financial Statistics*. They demonstrate that using averaged data can considerably alter the portfolios in the efficient set, and that the biases introduced are non-trivial.

1.7.4.2. Non-Synchronicity. Market indices are usually calculated using the most recent transaction price of each share; although until 1997 the FTSE 100 index was based on quotations rather than the prices of actual trades. Since shares in the market index do not trade continuously, it is highly likely that some of the prices used in computing the index occurred a few minutes, or even a few hours previously, i.e. the prices used in computing the index did not occur at the same moment. This means that, implicitly, an index computed using such non-synchronized prices measures an average value of the 'true' index over the period to which the constituent prices relate.

For example, suppose the 'true' value of an equally weighted index has been rising steadily throughout the day because the 'true' prices of the constituent shares have been rising. Since share prices are trending upwards, an index computed using transactions that took place at different times throughout the day, will be lower than the current 'true' value of the index. In effect, it will be a weighted average of the 'true' values of the index during the day, where the weights depend on the times of the actual trades used in constructing the index (ap Gwilym & Sutcliffe, 1999, 2001).

Because of this implicit averaging over time in the calculation of stock market indices, there will be positive serial correlation in changes in value, even if the underlying share price changes are random. While the *Financial Times* indices were based on midprice quotations rather than the last traded prices, there may still have been a lagged response. Thus, changes in the daily closing values of the FT-A index for 1962-1988 have a first order serial correlation coefficient of approximately 0.20. Brealey (1970) attempted to measure the magnitude of the serial correlation introduced into UK market indices by non-synchronous trading. For 202 days in 1968 he used price quotations collected at 2 pm each day on the twenty nine shares in the FTO index (excluding Marks & Spencer) to compute an equally weighted arithmetic index. The first order serial correlation coefficient for this new index was 0.19. Brealey concluded that, after removing the positive first order serial correlation introduced by averaging, some positive correlation remained, i.e. the positive serial correlation was not entirely due to the non-synchronicity of the prices used to compute the FTO index.

A more recent study by Atchison, Butler & Simonds (1987) used transactions data on 280 shares quoted on the NYSE to investigate the magnitude of the non-synchronous trading bias, and found that it only accounted for about 15% of the positive autocorrelation in the index. MacKinlay & Ramaswamy (1988) argued that, as the length of the differencing interval is increased, so the effect of non-synchronous prices should diminish. They studied the S&P500 and found that, while an increase in the differencing interval from fifteen minutes to one hour led to a reduction in the positive autocorrelation, further increases in the differencing interval did not remove the remaining autocorrelation. They concluded there must be some cause for this residual autocorrelation other than non-synchronous prices.

Ahn, Boudoukh, Richardson & Whitelaw (2002) investigated daily data for 1982-99 on 24 indices from 16 countries. In 21 cases index returns had significantly more autocorrelation than returns on the corresponding index future. When volume was high the autocorrelation in index returns, but not index futures returns, dropped. This evidence points towards microstructure effects, such as stale prices, being a major cause of autocorrelation in indices.

1.8 Conclusions

Market indices differ in the way they are constructed, and this has implications for the properties of the resulting index values, and the relationship between the prices of the individual shares quoted on the exchange. Understanding the behaviour of stock market indices has important implications for the market in futures contracts on stock index futures.

Chapter 2

Introduction to Futures Trading

Introduction

A stock index future is, in essence, a bet on the value of the underlying index at a specified future date. They began in the US in 1982, and trading started in the UK in 1984 in FTSE 100 futures. Since they were launched, there has been very rapid growth in the volume and value of trading in index futures, and in the UK the value of trading in this index future is of the same order of magnitude as the value of transactions in the underlying shares. The growth of trading in index futures in the US and Japan has been even more dramatic than in the UK. This chapter provides a simple introduction to the trading of index futures, together a brief description of contracts for difference, spread betting, exchange traded funds and individual stock futures.

2.1 Forward and Futures Contracts

In micro-economics, there is much discussion of markets, demand curves, supply curves etc. Most of this discussion is of spot markets, i.e. markets where the entire transaction takes place immediately. However, in reality, the completion of many contracts is delayed, e.g. goods are ordered now but delivered and paid for at a later date. Such transactions are forward or futures contracts. Economic theorists argue that, while an intertemporal general equilibrium requires the existence of a complete set of markets in contingent commodities (i.e. a commodity which is contingent on a particular state of the world existing) or a complete set of insurance markets, a system of futures markets provides a good approximation to such an equilibrium, Allingham (1985), Arrow (1981) and Townsend (1978). While a futures market does not exist in every commodity, many transactions that involve an agreement now to buy or sell something in the future do take place.

A distinction will now be drawn between forward and futures contracts. Forward contracts must specify the price, a description of the item concerned, and the delivery date and conditions.

Example. Suppose Bruce Wayne goes to a garage wanting to buy a new motor car with pink bodywork and green upholstery. Since this is not in stock, he orders such a car for delivery in three months time. The price of the car is fixed at the time he places the order, but is not payable until the car is delivered. This agreement constitutes a forward contract.

Example. On Monday Clark Kent rings up his local greengrocer and, after finding out the price, orders 10 lbs of potatoes for delivery and payment on Friday. Again, this is a forward contract because the item concerned, its price, and the delivery date and conditions are all fixed at the time the contract is entered into, i.e. Monday.

Forward contracts can relate to any type of goods and services. They can also involve financial instruments e.g. foreign currency, stocks and shares and loans.

Example. Rhett Butler agrees with his bank to supply him with 15,000 pesetas on 1st July next year for his foreign holiday at a price of 150 pesetas per £1, irrespective of the exchange rate on 1st July next year. This constitutes a forward contract in a financial instrument (foreign currency).

Example. Michael J. Dundee is buying a house and agrees with a building society that, as from 15th October, they will lend him £30,000 at a specified interest rate etc. This is also a forward contract in a financial instrument (a mortgage).

A futures contract is very similar to a forward contract, but there are some important differences (Board & Sutcliffe, 2005a). Futures contracts are distinguished from forward contracts by being designed to be traded. For this to be possible there must be a standardised contract and well organized futures markets. This enables participants to buy and sell futures contracts freely, i.e. they are liquid. In contrast, forward contracts may be 'one off' deals between two people such as the example of Bruce Wayne's motor car. Houthakker (1982) identified five ways in which futures contracts are standardised: quantity (or contract size), quality, delivery date, delivery location and counterparty (the clearing house, see chapter 2.2.1). The differences between forward and futures contracts will be considered in more depth once we have covered the institutional background of futures markets.

Futures (and forward) contracts usually relate to an underlying asset, and these assets are 'produced' by a specialized group of suppliers, e.g. gold is mined, soyabeans are harvested, live cattle are reared, crude oil is pumped, gilts are issued by the government and stocks and shares are issued by the company concerned. However, a futures (or forward) contract in any of these underlying assets can be 'supplied' or sold by anyone. A trader does not have to own any of the underlying asset in order to sell a futures contract relating to that asset. Thus, the quantity of futures contracts that are outstanding can exceed the total world supplies of the underlying asset. Indeed, it is possible for a futures contract to be traded in an asset which does not exist, e.g. stock index futures and inflation rate futures.

Most of the remainder of this chapter is devoted to explaining the procedures that futures exchanges have developed for trading index futures.

2.2 The Mechanics of Futures Markets

In order to function successfully, futures markets have developed procedures and rules to govern the way trading is conducted. The main features of these procedures are common to most futures markets, although the details differ between exchanges and contracts within exchanges. The details also change over time for a given exchange or contract. In this section some of the most important features of futures markets will be briefly explained. The examples will largely be based on the FTSE 100 index future, which is traded on Euronext.Liffe (pronounced life). The treatment of the institutional details in this section does not include a development of the economic implications, and some of the issues raised will be pursued in greater detail in subsequent chapters.

2.2.1 The Clearing House

Every futures market has a clearing house. For each futures contract there must be both a buyer (i.e. long position) and a seller (i.e. short position). The clearing house then interposes itself between the buyer and seller, so that the buyer now has a contract with the clearing house not the seller, while the seller now has a contract with the clearing house not the buyer. The legal name for this process is novation. In this context 'buyer' and 'seller' refer to the members of the clearing house through whom the purchase and sale are cleared and not to the individual traders who are clients of these clearing house members, Edwards (1984), Bernanke (1990). This is illustrated in figure 2.1.

Buyer	Clearing House	Seller

[BUY -- SELL]

[BUY ----------------SELL] [BUY-------------- SELL]

Figure 2.1: Interposition of the Clearing House

This procedure, in which the clearing house always has a zero net position, greatly simplifies the administration of futures contracts, as every contract is with the clearing house. It also has the major benefit of standardizing and reducing the default risk of a futures contract. If there is any default by a member of the clearing house, the loss will fall on the clearing house, as all contracts are with the clearing house and not with other members. In consequence, futures traders are unconcerned about the credit risk of the other party with whom they deal. However, the clearing house does not protect a trader against default by his or her broker. The contracts of the clients of members of the clearing house are with the clearing house member not the clearing house, and this exposes clients to default risk, Jordan & Morgan (1990). This structure is illustrated in figure 2.2.

If a clearing house member defaults, the clearing house will seize the money in the clearing member's margin account with the clearing house to pay off the liabilities to other clearing house members. However, the clients of the defaulting member will not be paid by the clearing house, and will have to pursue a claim against the defaulting member. There has been only one default of a clearing member of Euronext.Liffe, and this was Drexel Burnham Lambert in 1990. Drexel was the fourth largest member of the London Clearing House, and on 14th February 1990 it failed to meet that morning's margin calls. There was no market disruption, and the settlement of Drexel's positions resulted in a net surplus of approximately $18 million which was paid to the company's administrators.

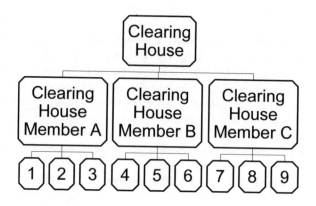

Figure 2.2: Structure of Default Risk

If a trader wishes to reduce the risk to them of default by their broker, they should consider choosing a broker whose clients have all taken an identical position in the futures markets. In this case there is a reduced risk of one client failing to pay money to the broker causing the broker to default on payments to another client, because there is perfect positive correlation between the payments for all clients, Jordan & Morgan (1990). When there is a favourable price movement there is no risk of default by clients or the broker because they are all recipients of money. If there is a violent adverse price movement sufficient to wipe out the maintenance margin, and the broker is pushed into default, none of the broker's clients will suffer as none of them is owed money by their broker. However, even when all a broker's clients have similar positions, some risk remains for clients since they have the required maintenance margin deposited with their broker, and this may be fraudulently removed.

Example. Rufus T. Firefly instructs his broker (broker A) to buy one futures contract. His broker agrees a trade with broker B, who is selling a futures contract on behalf of Eddie Felson. If there is a default by Rufus the clearing house will call on broker A, while if there is a default by Eddie the clearing house will call on broker B. However, neither Rufus nor Eddie can call on the clearing house in the event of a default by their broker.

Euronext.Liffe uses LCH.Clearnet, which was formed by the merger of the London Clearing House (LCH) and Clearnet in December 2003. From January 2004 the CBOT has used the CBOT/CME Common Clearing Link to the CME Clearing House Division; which also clears for the CME.

2.2.2 Delivery

At a specified date, the seller of a futures contract delivers the agreed asset to the buyer (via the clearing house). Very few financial futures contracts are held until the delivery date, and so very little actual delivery occurs. In the US in 1983 under 1% of futures contracts were delivered, Carlton (1984), while in 1989 only 3.6% of FTSE 100 futures contracts were held to delivery. Most futures contracts are liquidated or 'closed out' by an offsetting transaction before delivery is due. This procedure is facilitated by the standardized nature of futures contracts, so that any two contracts in the same futures contract with the same delivery date are perfect substitutes. This is not the case for forward contracts.

Example. Harry Lime, the manager of the Blakelaw Fund, who has bought some futures contracts (ten long gilt futures for delivery next December), sells an equivalent number of futures contracts (ten long gilt futures for delivery next December). The clearing house then offsets (i.e. cancels) all of these futures contracts because they relate to the same person.

For index futures, delivery is difficult because it would require the handing over of shares in 100 companies in the same proportions as are currently used in the computation of the FTSE 100 index. This runs into indivisibility problems, as well as generating substantial transactions costs. Martell & Salzman (1981) conclude that physical delivery of an index future would incur inordinately high delivery costs, and that cash settlement is preferable. However, the development of trading in baskets of shares (e.g. ETFs) may lead to a reduction in the costs of physical delivery (see chapter 2.2.2). Garbade & Silber (1983b), Jones (1982) and Paul (1985) also favour cash settlement, except when the index on which the EDSP (see chapter 2.2.4) is based is inaccurate, or subject to manipulation (see chapter 11.9 for a discussion of the manipulation of the EDSP). Therefore, if a contract is not 'closed out', settlement takes place in cash. An exception was the Osaka 50 Kabusaki index futures contract, traded on the Osaka Stock Exchange until March 1992, which could be settled either in cash or by the delivery of the underlying shares, i.e. physical delivery. (The possibility of physical delivery was because, when the contract was introduced in 1987, cash settlement was illegal in Japan, Brenner, Subrahmanyam & Uno, 1990b. Cash settlement was legalized by the Diet in May 1988, Semkow, 1989). The Argentinean Merval and Burcap index futures also offer the choice of either physical or cash settlement.

2.2.3 Quotation and Price

FTSE 100 futures are quoted in the same units as the underlying index e.g. 3,812.5, except that the number to the right of the decimal point can only be zero or five. This is because the minimum price movement (also known as a tick) for FTSE 100 futures is 0.5 index points. The price of a futures contract (i.e. contract size) is the quoted number (measured in index points) multiplied by the contract multiplier, which is £10 for the FTSE 100, e.g. 3,812.5×£10 = £38,125.00. Therefore the minimum price movement is £5.00. (Up to and including the March 1998 contract, the multiplier was £25 per index point.) The multiplier for S&P500 index futures is $250, while the minimum price movement is $2.50. As well as a minimum price movement, the Nikkei 225 also has a maximum price movement, Arai, Akamatsu & Yoshioka (1993).

The minimum price of a futures contract is zero, and so the maximum loss that can be sustained by a trader with a long position is the initial price of the contract. Since there is no maximum price, the potential loss of a trader with a short position is infinite.

2.2.4 Delivery Month and Price

For FTSE 100 futures there are four delivery months: March, June, September and December. At any one time there is trading in the four nearest delivery months, although the volume of trading in the 'far' month (i.e. the contract with the longest time to delivery) is very small. Thus, each contract is traded for twelve months. (Prior to 18th March 2002 only the nearest three contracts were traded.) Table 2.1 shows the four outstanding contracts each month during 2005.

Table 2.1: Outstanding Contracts by Month of the Year

Month	Contracts that are Traded			
Jan.05	Mar.05	Jun.05	Sep.05	Dec.05
Feb.05	Mar.05	Jun.05	Sep.05	Dec.05
Mar.05	Mar.05	Jun.05	Sep.05	Dec.05
Apr.05	**Mar.06**	Jun.05	Sep.05	Dec.05
May.05	**Mar.06**	Jun.05	Sep.05	Dec.05
Jun.05	**Mar.06**	Jun.05	Sep.05	Dec.05
Jul.05	**Mar.06**	**Jun.06**	Sep.05	Dec.05
Aug.05	**Mar.06**	**Jun.06**	Sep.05	Dec.05
Sep.05	**Mar.06**	**Jun.06**	Sep.05	Dec.05
Oct.05	**Mar.06**	**Jun.06**	**Sep.06**	Dec.05
Nov.05	**Mar.06**	**Jun.06**	**Sep.06**	Dec.05
Dec.05	**Mar.06**	**Jun.06**	**Sep.06**	Dec.05

For contracts expiring prior to November 2004, the EDSP was calculated over a twenty minute period (10.10 a.m. to 10.30 a.m.), with the price recorded every 15 seconds, i.e. 81 prices; of which the 12 highest and the 12 lowest values were discarded, and the remaining 57 were averaged. From November 2004 the EDSP became the value of the index computed using the prices established for each share by an intraday auction. At 10:10 am on the expiry day there is an auction call period which normally lasts 5 to 5.5 minutes, during which traders enter orders into SETS. If there are market imbalances for a stock, the auction period for that stock is extended for up to another 13.5 minutes, giving a maximum auction call period of 19 minutes. When the auction call period ends, the order matching process occurs, and crossed orders (i.e. buy price ≥ sell price) are executed. The resulting prices are used to compute the index, and this is used as the EDSP. The result is then rounded to the nearest 0.5.

Beginning with the September 1991 contract, the start of the period used for computing the EDSP was brought forwards by one hour to 10.10 a.m. to avoid any effects from the announcement of official economic statistics, which are usually made at 11.30 a.m. For the June 1992 and subsequent contracts, the last trading day of a futures contract moved to the third Friday in the delivery month, rather than the last day of the delivery month on which the exchange was open.

2.2.5 Open Interest

This is the total number of futures contracts which have not been 'closed out'. It is equal to the sum of either the outstanding long positions or the sum of the outstanding short positions. While there may be a large volume of futures transactions, open interest is usually much smaller. For example, the open interest in S&P500 futures on 31st December 1987 was only 1.1% of the total volume of transactions in this future during 1987. In 1989 the largest daily open interest for FTSE 100 futures was 3.4% of the annual volume.

Example. The following transactions take place in the December FTSE 100 futures contract:-
1. Peter buys 5 contracts sold by Paul
2. Mary buys 10 contracts sold by Bob
3. Paul buys 6 contracts sold by Peter
4. Carol buys 4 contracts sold by Mary
5. Ted buys 8 contracts sold by Paul
6. Alice buys 7 contracts sold by Mary

After each transaction the size of the open interest is :-

Table 2.2: Open Interest for the Example

	1	2	3	4	5	6
Peter	+5	+5	−1	−1	−1	−1
Paul	−5	−5	+1	+1	−7	−7
Mary	-	+10	+10	+6	+6	−1
Bob	-	−10	−10	−10	−10	−10
Carol	-	-	-	+4	+4	+4
Ted	-	-	-	-	+8	+8
Alice	-	-	-	-	-	+7
Open Interest	5	15	11	11	18	19

This example indicates that there are three possible effects of a futures trade on open interest. First, if each trader is creating a new position, open interest increases by the number of contracts traded. Second, if each trader is closing out an existing position, open interest decreases by the number of contracts traded. Finally, if one trader is opening a new position while the other is closing out an existing position, open interest is unchanged.

2.2.6 Marking to the Market and Variation Margin

To minimize the losses from any default, changes in the price of futures contracts are settled on a daily basis. At the close of trading each day the change in price of a futures contract during that day is calculated using the daily settlement price. The settlement price is based on the prices of those transactions that occur close to the end of the day's trading and is similar to the closing price. The other party to each contract is either paid this amount by the clearing house (it is placed in their account with the clearing house), or must pay this amount into the clearing house. These payments are called 'variation margin'. For the clearing house, these daily payments of variation margin will always sum to zero.

Example. Phileas Fogg buys (and Anna Karenina sells) one futures contract in the FTSE 100 index for £50,000 when the price of the contract, in terms of index points, was 5,000. The futures contract is due for delivery 3 days later and the contract multiplier is £10.

Table 2.3: Variation Margin Payments for the Example

Date	Price (Index Points)	Contract Settlement Price	Cash Flows	
			Phileas	Anna
−3	5,030	£50,300	+£300	−£300
−2	5,020	£50,200	−£100	+£100
−1	5,040	£50,400	+£200	−£200
0	5,050	£50,500	+£100	−£100
Totals			+£500	−£500

This example shows the zero sum nature of futures markets. Note that, while Phileas has made a profit of £500 (and Anna a loss of a similar amount) this amount in not paid as a lump sum on the delivery date. Because of the variation margin system, only £100 has to be paid on the delivery day.

While the norm is for variation margin payments to be requested at the end of trading each day, margin payments may be requested during the day. S&P500 futures were marked to the market 13 times during the day in October 1987, including three times on 19th October and twice on 20th October and 26th October, Fenn & Kupiec (1993). As from 1st March 1988, S&P500 futures switched from being routinely marked to the market once per day, to twice per day. MMI futures were always settled twice per day when listed on CBOT. The marking to the market process generates transactions costs, as each open position requires two cash payments for every time the EDSP changes.

As well as initiating an additional marking to the market during the day, exchanges may also simply require traders to place a specified additional sum in their margin accounts. For example, during the stock market crash of October 1987 three intra-day margin payments were required for FTSE 100 contracts: Monday 19th October £6,000 per long position, Tuesday 20th October £7,500 per long position and Thursday 22nd October £5,000 per contract for selected positions. On Monday 16th October 1989, fears of a stock market crash led to the holders of long positions in FTSE 100 futures being required to pay an additional £3,000 per contract into their margin accounts.

2.2.7 Initial Margin

There is a possibility that a member of the clearing house will default in making a payment to the clearing house of the variation margin. At the end of each day either the long or the short position will be showing a loss, and so has an incentive to default on paying the variation margin. Traders could open a futures position, and default if required to pay variation margin. To protect the clearing house against such behaviour, when a position is created (i.e. a futures contract is bought or sold such that it does not 'close out' some previous futures contract), an initial margin must be paid to the clearing house. The initial margin is not a part payment, but a good faith deposit that is paid by both the buyer and the seller and refunded on completion. The initial margin for FTSE 100 futures changes from time to time (see table 2.4 for initial margins when the contract multiplier was £25). In April 2004 the initial margin was £1,500, and this will be used in the examples in this book. This is approximately 3% of the price of a future, and is set to reflect the likely maximum daily change in the price of a FTSE 100 future. (Futures margins are usually set as sterling or dollar amounts, and not as percentages.) For a further discussion of setting margins, see chapter 11.1.

Table 2.4: FTSE 100 Futures Initial Margins

21 Jun. 1985	£750	1 Mar. 1991	£2,000
16 Oct. 1986	£1,000	11 Jun. 1991	£1,500
2 Oct. 1987	£1,500	4 Mar. 1992	£2,000
21 Oct. 1987	£5,000	24 Mar. 1992	£3,000
2 Nov. 1987	£7,500	23 Apr. 1992	£2,000
16 Nov. 1987	£5,000	15 Sept. 1992	£3,000
14 Dec. 1987	£4,000	19 Nov. 1992	£2,500
4 Feb. 1988	£3,000	26 Feb. 1993	£2,000
14 Jun. 1988	£2,500	4 Mar. 1994	£2,500
20 Feb. 1989	£1,500	30 May 1995	£2,000
17 Oct. 1989	£2,500	27 June 1995	£2,500
15 Jan. 1991	£4,000	25 Apr. 1996	£3,000

On 2nd April 1991 the LCH introduced SPAN for calculating the initial margins on options and futures. SPAN looks at the risks of the portfolio of options and futures positions held by the trader, some of which may be offsetting. SPAN simulates how a portfolio would react to changing market conditions, and the initial margin for the portfolio is the largest overnight loss that might reasonably occur. This is done by LCH.Clearnet specifying a range of possible price and volatility changes which the initial margin is required to cover. The 'scanning range' is the name given to the largest price movement in the underlying security for which the LCH.Clearnet requires cover. For example, in March 1993 the scanning range for FTSE 100 futures was 160 index points, or £2,000. Therefore, if the trader's only open position was in FTSE 100 futures, the initial margin was £2,000 per contract.

While variation margin must be paid to LCH.Clearnet in cash, clearing house members can choose to meet their initial margin obligations on Euronext.Liffe by depositing cash (Sterling, US dollars, yen, euros, Swedish, Danish and Norwegian krona, or Swiss francs), approved bank guarantees, a range of government bonds and bills for 14 countries, Sterling and US dollar CDs, and FTSE 100 equities (for equity futures and options only) with the clearing house. Except for cash and bank guarantees, the value of collateral is subject to a discount (or haircut) as LCH.Clearnet may only be able to sell it at below its current market value. For example, government bonds or bills may be subject to a discount of 5%. Interest is paid on cash deposits over £50,000, Bassett (1987). At times LCH.Clearnet may hold £billions, and this is put on overnight deposit in the London money market. LCH.Clearnet takes 25 basis points, and passes the remaining interest on to the depositors, Wilson (1995).

The margins required for the Nikkei 225 traded in Osaka have been set at much higher levels than those for index futures traded elsewhere. They are set as proportions of the price, rather than as absolute amounts. There is also a rule that a minimum proportion of the margin must be paid in cash, and no interest is paid on this cash deposit. In the early 1990s index margins and the minimum cash proportion were increased to restrict trading in index futures in Japan.

Every trade must be cleared through a member of the clearing house. The initial margin payments for a clearing house member can be calculated on the net position of all their clients, i.e. *net* margins, or on the separate positions of each of their clients i.e. *gross* margins.

Example. Daryl Van Horne, a broker, has two clients, one of whom has a long position of ten futures contracts and another who has a short position of five futures contracts in the same index future. This index future requires an initial margin of £1,500 per contract. If the exchange requires gross margins, the initial margin for these two positions is (10+5)×£1,500 = £22,500. If only net margins are required, the initial margin drops to (10−5)×£1,500 = £7,500.

LCH.Clearnet, which undertakes clearing for Euronext.Liffe, requires net margins to be paid by clearing house members. Gross initial margins are used by the CME (and so the S&P500 future has gross margins), Brady (1988). Since brokers collect margins for all their clients, i.e. on a gross basis, if they are only required to pay margins on a net basis to the clearing house they can invest the difference, and benefit from the interest earned.

2.2.8 Maintenance Margin

The variation margin payments are charged against the trader's initial margin. When the balance on this account drops below a specified level, called the maintenance margin, additional money must be paid in to restore the margin account to the level of the initial margin. Variation margin receipts can only be removed by the trader from the margin account to the extent that the balance exceeds the initial margin requirement. (For Nikkei 225 futures, no money can be withdrawn from the margin account until the position is closed, Chung, Kang & Rhee, 1994b.) The balance on such a margin account is illustrated in figure 2.3.

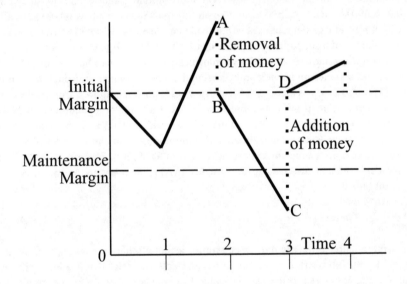

Figure 2.3: Example of the Balance on a Margin Account

Figure 2.3 shows that on day one there is an adverse price movement but, after removing the variation margin payment from the trader's margin account, the balance is still above the maintenance margin level, and so no further funds are required. The favourable variation margin on day two increases the balance in the margin account to point *A*. The trader chooses to immediately remove the excess above the initial margin from his margin account, i.e. *AB*. On day three there is an adverse price movement such that the payment of variation margin reduces the balance on the margin account to point *C*, which is below the maintenance level. Therefore, the trader must immediately pay in *CD* to restore his margin account to its initial level.

The required initial and maintenance margins may be reduced if the trader holds another asset whose price changes tend to be offsetting. For some futures, separate margins are specified for hedges, intramarket spreads and a wide range of likely intermarket spreads. See chapter 2.7.3 for a brief description of hedging and spreading, and chapters 6 and 9 for a fuller description. For Euronext.Liffe the maintenance margin is equal to the initial margin, and so every time the margin account drops below its initial level a margin call is issued to restore the account to its initial level. If a trader defaults on making the required margin payments, his or her position in the futures market can be immediately liquidated, so placing a lower limit on any losses. To illustrate the operation of a margin account where the initial margin differs from the maintenance margin, an example using the S&P500 index future will be presented.

Example. Rocky Balboa bought ten S&P500 index futures on Monday morning when the index stood at 1,000. Therefore, the nominal value of his purchase was $10 \times 1,000 \times \$250 = \$2,500,000$. The initial margin payment was $10 \times \$20,000 = \$200,000$. The settlement value of the index on Monday was 990, which generated a variation margin payment by Rocky of $10 \times (1,000-990) \times 250 = \$25,000$. This amount was removed from Rocky's margin account, leaving a balance of $175,000. Since the balance on this account exceeded the maintenance margin, $(10 \times \$16,000 = \$160,000)$, no payment into his margin account was required from Rocky. The settlement value of the index on Tuesday was 980, and this generated a variation margin payment of $10 \times (990-980) \times 250 = \$25,000$. When this amount was removed from Rocky's margin account, the remaining balance of $150,000 was below the maintenance margin requirement of $160,000. Therefore Rocky had to pay in a further $50,000 to restore his margin account to its initial level of $200,000.

2.2.9 Price Limits

Many futures are subject to daily price limits, although there are no daily price limits for FTSE 100 futures (however CONNECT rejects any price that is a long way away from the current market price, as it is probably a mistake). The exchange specifies the maximum upward and downward price movement permitted each day from the previous day's settlement price. If these limits are hit trading ceases until either traders are willing to trade within that day's price limits, or until the next trading day, when new price limits apply. If the day's trading has been halted by the price limits, that day's settlement price is the relevant price limit. A rationale for imposing daily price limits is presented in chapter 11.3. On 20th October 1988, a complicated system of shock absorber price limits was introduced for the S&P500 future. At the start of trading each morning, the price limits were very tight ($25), but after the first thirty minutes of trading wider limits applied ($150 and then $250). When a price limit was hit, trading was stopped for varying time periods (e.g. ten minutes to two hours). Subsequently, the details of these price limits have been varied frequently. Japanese index futures traded in Japan have been subject to a daily price limit of approximately 3% of the previous settlement price, Brenner, Subrahmanyam & Uno (1990b). The Japanese price limits have also been varied over time.

2.2.10 Position Limits

To prevent the market being manipulated by a few traders, some futures are subject to position limits. These restrict the number of contracts that can be held in a particular future by a single trader. For example, for S&P500 futures there is a position limit of 20,000 contracts net short or long in all delivery months combined. In Brazil, the BM&F has position limits for Ibovespa futures which depend on the size of the open interest in the particular contract month, Braga (1995). Position limits tend to be most important in metal and agricultural markets, while financial futures markets are usually more liquid, and so harder to manipulate. Euronext.Liffe has no position limits for any of its contracts. Some investors, e.g. US pension funds, may be subject to legal limitations on their open position, Binns (1989). A study by Pliska & Shalen (1991) investigated the effects of position limits. Using simulation, their theoretical model indicated that smaller position limits led to lower volume and open interest, and an increase in futures price volatility.

2.2.11 Payments to Brokers

The clearing house will only deal with its members, and not with the individual clients of its members. Therefore the payments of variation margin and initial margin only apply directly to clearing house members. However, clearing house members will require their clients to make similar payments to them. The precise size and timing of these payments is a matter for agreement between the clearing house member and client, although they cannot be lower than those payments required by the clearing house of its members. For example, in June 1990 a major broker required customers trading FTSE 100 futures to pay an initial margin of £3,000 per contract (compared with an exchange requirement of £2,500), and to maintain a minimum balance of £2,500 per contract in their margin account. Some brokers may pay interest to their clients on the initial margin payments of clients to the broker. Brokers are able to accept a wider range of securities as initial margin than are acceptable to the clearing house, Liffe (1992b).

2.2.12 Trading Process

Micro-economists often assume that competitive markets operate as a Walrasian auction, i.e. each time period the potential buyers and sellers meet, and an auctioneer calls out a price (assuming a price rather than a quantity adjustment process). The traders then announce the quantities they are willing to buy or sell at the announced price. Based on the degree of excess demand or supply, the auctioneer calls out another price. This process is repeated until demand equals supply. Then, and only then, the actual trades occur at this final equilibrium price. In figure 2.4 the initial price announced by the auctioneer is P_1, which leads to a supply of Q_s and a demand of Q_d. Since supply exceeds demand, the auctioneer revises the price downwards to P_2, etc., until the equilibrium is reached at P_E.

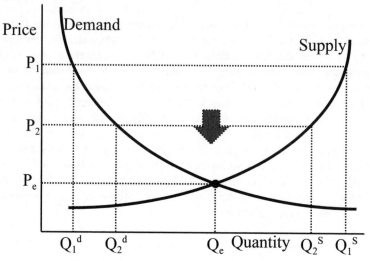

Figure 2.4: Walrasian Equilibrating Process

Futures markets function in a different way from this Walrasian ideal. First, they operate continuously, rather than periodically as does a Walrasian auction. Second, there is no auctioneer. Rather pit trading in futures markets is a double auction in which both buyers and sellers simultaneously call out bids and offers. After an initial bid (offer), subsequent bids (offers) must be higher (lower) than the previous bid (offer). A trade is executed as soon as a bid and an offer match. If those traders who have successfully bought or sold futures remain in the market (e.g. scalpers, see chapter 2.7.2), provided no new information arrives, the price will eventually converge to that which would have been produced by a Walrasian auction (although the average price will differ from that of a Walrasian market as trades will have occurred at prices other than the Walrasian equilibrium price). However, if successful traders immediately leave the market (e.g. position traders, see chapter 2.7.2), there is no reason to expect the price to converge to the Walrasian equilibrium price. In this case all that can be said is that transactions prices will be somewhere in the range between the highest price a buyer is prepared to pay and the lowest price a seller is prepared to accept, Monroe (1988).

The size of the crowd in the pit may affect the way the futures market behaves. Based upon empirical research, Baker (1984) identified three different crowd sizes. There may be a small crowd of a few people who act co-operatively, e.g. they all quote wide spreads. As the crowd size increases to say 15 to 30 participants the ideal of a highly competitive single market emerges. If the crowd size increases further, the market fragments into a number of submarkets. For example, there may be well over 400 traders in the S&P500 futures pit at the CME, and so many transactions can occur simultaneously, possibly at different prices. (Locke, Sarkar & Wu, 1994, report that in June-July 1987, the average daily number of floor traders who executed at least one trade in the S&P500 pit was 439.) Participants in a large crowd tend to trade only with those close to them because of the risks of mistakes in trading with those further away, and in some cases arbitrage may be possible by taking advantage of price differences between the various subgroups of the crowd.

Traders are attracted to volatile markets, and Baker found that large crowds have more volatile prices than do small crowds. Therefore, there is a tendency for crowds to increase in size. For a given order flow, an increase in the number of traders in the crowd tends to reduce the average trading volume of those already in the pit. Baker found that traders try to discourage those in other pits from joining in the crowd by failing to recognize the quotes of the incomers, so that they get no business. Alternatively, if the rules are such that the incomers are required to quote firm two-way prices, they may be forced to trade repeatedly on the same side of the market until their capital is exhausted.

FTSE 100 futures have been screen traded since 10th May 1999 using Euronext.Liffe's CONNECT trading system (see chapter 11.12 for further discussion of screen trading).

2.3 Interpreting the *Financial Times* Daily Reports

Each day the *Financial Times* publishes details of the previous day's trading in the near contract of FTSE 100 futures. An example of interpreting these daily reports will now be given.

Table 2.5: Daily Information in the *Financial Times*

	13 April 04 Jun	14 April 04 Jun	15 April 04 Jun
Open	4524.0	4502.5	4489.0
Sett	4523.0	4494.5	4508.0
Change	+33.0	−28.5	+13.5
High	4538.0	4509.0	4518.5
Low	4504.5	4463.5	4480.0
Est. Vol.	57,077	69,640	48,771
Open Int.	384,909	382,153	385,634
Spot open	4489.7	4515.8	4485.4
Spot close	4515.8	4485.4	4505.5

The spot values of the index, which appear elsewhere in the newspaper, have also been listed in table 2.5. Note that the opening price differs from the settlement price of the previous day, and that the changes are between the settlement prices. In addition, the daily high and low futures prices relate only to trade prices, and exclude quotations. The estimated volume and open interest are for the June contract, while the open interest is for the previous day. The variation margin for long positions on 14th April is the closing settlement price minus the opening settlement price times £10, i.e. −£285. The level of open interest in June FTSE 100 futures on 14th April 2004 had a nominal value of approximately £17.3 billion.

2.4 Payoff from a Forward Contract

This section presents diagrammatically the profits and losses from holding a forward contract, and shows that they are dependent on the value of the index at the delivery date. The diagrams are for forward rather than futures contracts, because marking to the market is ignored. The profit (loss) on a long forward contract is given by the spot price at the time of delivery (S_T) less the price of the forward (W), i.e. $S_T - W$. The profit (loss) on a short forward contract is $W - S_T$.

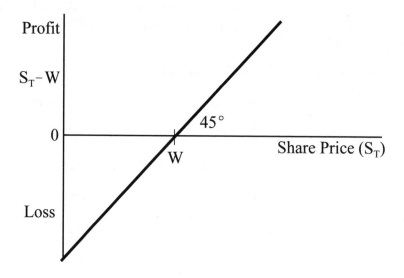

Figure 2.5: Payoffs from a Long Forward Position

As can be seen from figures 2.5 and 2.6, a forward contract is zero sum, i.e. the sum of the profits and losses is zero. It is also apparent that a rise or fall in the spot price at delivery (S_T) generates a rise or fall in a trader's profits of exactly the same amount, i.e. the slope of the line in the figures is 45°. Similar payoff diagrams also apply to a long (or short) position in shares, except that W is interpreted as the value at delivery of the purchase price of the shares, plus any dividends that accrued during the period of ownership.

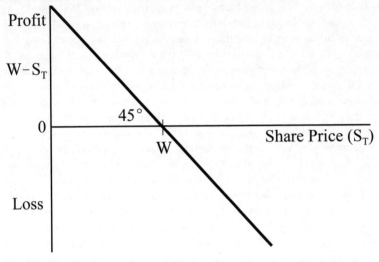

Figure 2.6: Payoffs from a Short Forward Position

2.5 Definition of Returns

The theoretical and empirical analysis of stock markets is based on the use of a rate of return to measure the benefits from holding an asset during a specified period. If a rate of return could also be defined for futures markets, futures could then be treated as an additional asset in portfolio and capital market theories, and the concept and tests of market efficiency could also be extended, in a straightforward manner, to futures markets. Unfortunately, there are difficulties in defining rates of return on futures.

2.5.1 The Problem

The arithmetic return on a futures contract might be expressed as the change in the price of the future during the period, i.e. $(F_{t+1} - F_t)$, divided by the initial investment (I_t). However, the definition of the sum invested (I_t) is problematic.

One possible definition of I_t is the initial margin payment, e.g. about 4% of the price of the future, (Bear, 1972, Brooks & Hand, 1988, Francis, 1991, Gressis, Vlahos & Philippatos, 1984, Levy, 1987, Niederhoffer & Zeckhauser, 1980, Panton & Joy, 1978, Robichek, Cohn & Pringle, 1972, Schrock, 1971, Turner, Houston & Shepherd (1992), Yau, Savanayana & Schneeweis, 1990), while Lukac, Brorsen & Irwin (1988a, 1988b), Hancock (2005) and Marshall & Herbst (1992) defined the investment as the initial margin plus the funds set aside to cover subsequent margin payments, i.e. the liquidity reserve. However, there are a number of problems with this approach. As Dusak (1973) and others have pointed out, the initial margin is not an investment, but a good faith deposit. This is illustrated by the way in which the initial margin payments do not flow from the buyer to the seller of a futures contract. Instead, both buyer and seller pay an initial margin, and these payments are held by the clearing house. If, nevertheless, the initial margin is used as I_t, the arithmetic return becomes $(F_{t+1}-F_t)$ $/(F_t m)$, where m is the proportion of the futures price that must be paid as an initial margin. The absolute values of these returns are about 25 times $(1/m)$ larger than the returns on the underlying shares, while the variance of these returns is about 625 times larger, i.e. $(1/m)^2$, than the variance of returns on the underlying shares.

Another definition of I_t is the initial value of the shares corresponding to one futures contract (i.e. S_t), so that arithmetic returns are calculated as $(F_{t+1}-F_t)/S_t$, Figlewski & Kon (1982). As with the purchase of a share, the maximum loss that can be suffered by someone who buys a futures contract is the initial price of the asset (S_t), since negative share prices are not possible. This definition of the sum invested has the advantage of producing returns that are roughly similar in size and dispersion to the returns on the underlying shares. However, at the time the futures contract is purchased there is no cash payment of S_t. Dusak (1973) has suggested interpreting $(F_{t+1}-F_t)/S_t$ as the excess return, i.e. the risk premium, rather than as an ordinary rate of return, see chapter 8.3.3 of Sutcliffe (1997). (Because it obviates the need to collect the spot as well as the futures prices, S_t has been replaced in some empirical work by F_t, e.g. Dusak, 1973.) Following Dusak (1973), Bodie & Rosansky (1980) also used $(F_{t+1}-F_t)/F_t$ as a measure of excess returns. (A similar position has been adopted by Taylor & Tari, 1989, and Taylor, 1992a & 1992b.) In addition, they defined a rate of return concept for direct comparison with the rate of return on shares. This was $(F_{t+1}-F_t)/F_t$, plus the interest at the risk free rate (R_F) on the average price of the futures contract during the period, i.e. $R_F(F_{t+1}+F_t)/2F_t$, to give $\{F_{t+1}(2+R_F)-F_t(2-R_F)\}$ $/2F_t$ as the measure of the return on a future.

Example. Jack Napier, the manager of the Hazlerigg Fund, purchased one FTSE 100 future for £45,000, when the spot value of the index was 4,400, and paid an initial margin of £1,500. He also set aside £3,000 to cover margin calls (denoted by C). A month later he closed out his long position when the futures price had risen to £46,300. The riskless interest rate during this month was 1%. Jack wishes to know the return on this investment. Four possible answers to this question will be presented.

a. $(F_{t+1}-F_t)/(F_t m) = (46,300-45,000)/1,500 = 86.7\%.$

b. $(F_{t+1}-F_t)/(F_t m+C) = (46,300-45,000)/(1,500+3,000) = 28.9\%.$

c. $(F_{t+1}-F_t)/S_t = (46,300-45,000)/44,000 = 3.0\%.$

d. $\{F_{t+1}(2+R_F)-F_t(2-R_F)\}/2F_t = \{(46,300\times2.01)-(45,000\times1.99)\}/(2\times45,000)$
$$= 3.9\%.$$

Black (1976) took the view that, since the initial margin is not an investment and there is no payment (receipt) of S_t, the sum invested is zero. In consequence, it is not possible to define a rate of return on a futures contract, and some other type of analysis must be used which does not require the use of the sum invested. While the logic of Black's view has been widely accepted, in practice many empirical studies have used some form of rate of return, although they may have given it another name. Thus they may refer to the percentage price change, or to the logarithm of percentage price changes.

2.5.2 Practical Solutions

All the proposed solutions to the problem of defining a return for futures contracts are open to objections. However, if standard finance theory is to be applied to futures, some definition must be chosen. Most authors have opted to study either price changes, i.e. $(F_{t+1} - F_t)$, or the change in the logarithm of prices, i.e. $\ln(F_{t+1}) - \ln(F_t)$, which can be rewritten as the logarithm of the price relative, i.e. $\ln(F_{t+1}/F_t)$. The advantages and disadvantages of these two measures will now be considered.

The analysis of price changes has the advantage of avoiding the need to define the sum invested. For example, it is possible to use a mean-variance approach to formulate a model of the demand and supply of futures in terms of price changes rather than rates of return which avoids the problems of defining returns for futures contracts, see chapter 7.4 of Sutcliffe (1997) and appendix 7.C to chapter 7 of Sutcliffe (1993). However, price changes are a scale dependent measure. The market index tends to rise over time, and this will cause the size and hence the variance of price changes to rise over time. Thus, a time trend and heteroskedasticity may be present in price change data. The change in the logarithm of prices has the advantage of being scale independent. Although the value of the market index will tend to increase over time, this need not cause the size and variance of this measure to rise. However, the usual arithmetic return is $(F_{t+1} - F_t)/F_t$, and so the price relative is equal to one plus the arithmetic return. Hence, the use of the change in the logarithm of prices implicitly assumes that F_t is the sum invested.

Example. Using the numbers from the Jack Napier example, the returns can be computed as $\ln(F_{t+1}/F_t) = \ln(46,300/45,000) = 0.0285$, i.e. 2.85%.

While the logarithm of the price relative is, in effect, a return; some authors have sought to overcome objections to defining F_t as the sum invested by calling $\ln(F_{t+1}/F_t)$ [or $(F_{t+1} - F_t)/F_t$] a "proportionate price change". These proportionate price changes are then treated as though they are returns.

If the conclusions from empirical studies employing different measures of return were the same, the definition of returns would not be an important issue. Yau, Savanayana & Schneeweis (1990) compared the results of forming portfolios of spot and futures (US treasury bonds) when three different returns measures were used (price change, percentage price change and return on the initial margin). The three returns measures gave very different results for risk-minimising hedging (see chapter 9) and when forming mean-variance efficient portfolios. And so, at least for treasury bonds, the definition of returns does matter.

2.5.3 Contract Linking

A related problem is that many empirical studies convert the price changes or returns on separate futures contracts into a single time series by linking together the prices of consecutive futures contracts. This requires choosing the time to switch from the near to the next near contract, and how to adjust for any differences in price level between the near and next near contracts (see ap Gwilym & Sutcliffe, 1999, pp 35-7). Ma, Mercer & Walker (1992) found that the way in which the price series are linked can have unpredictable effects on the conclusions of empirical studies. They examined the sensitivity of the mean, variance and serial correlation of price changes and returns for the S&P500, and four other futures. They also analyzed the effects on the day of the week effect (see chapter 8 for a discussion of this anomaly). Six alternative ways of linking together the daily prices between 1982 and 1989 were used, and some substantial differences in the results were observed. Thus, the linking procedure adopted may affect the conclusions reached.

Geiss (1995) set out six criteria to be met by a price index that links the price series of different futures contracts. Only one class of price index meets these conditions - a weighted average of the prices of the outstanding contracts, where the weights are a function of time. Linking the price levels of the near contract by an additive or multiplicative adjustment does not meet these criteria. While many possible patterns of weights are possible, Geiss considers only a two price index, where the weight on any one price level is tent-shaped. Thus, the initial weight on the price of a particular contract is zero. It increases over time in a linear manner to 100%, and then declines to zero as the next contract is included in the price index. In this way the price of each contract gradually enters and then leaves the price index before the contract expires, and so there is a smooth seamless splice. Rougier (1996) adopted a similar approach, and derived a set of weights for the prices of the outstanding contracts, where the weights are a function of time. For two outstanding contracts, the weighted average price has a fixed maturity equal to the time between contract maturities (v), the weight on the near contract is m/v, and that on the far contract is $(v-m)/v$, where m is the maturity of the near contract. Thus, as for Geiss (1995), the weights on a particular contract are tent-shaped. For three outstanding contracts, three alternative sets of weights are permissible, with fixed maturities varying from v to $v(4/3)$.

Example. Seth Brundle wishes to construct a series of futures prices for the period from January to June that are not subject to any maturity effects. The prices of the near and next near contracts (all arbitrage free) are available in table 2.6, along with the spot price.

Seth decides to compare the use of the near contract with a weighted average of the prices of the near and next near contracts using the weights m/v and $(v-m)/v$ respectively, where v is the time between contract maturities (i.e. 3 months), and m is the maturity of the near contract (3, 2 or 1 months).

Table 2.6: Futures and Spot Prices for the Example

	March	June	Sept.	Spot
January	£94,340	£96,236	-	£92,500
February	£94,775	£96,683	-	£93,750
March	£95,192	£97,114	-	£95,000
April	-	£98,204	£100,217	£96,250
May	-	£96,059	£97,997	£95,000
June	-	£93,930	£95,813	£93,750

Table 2.7 shows that, because the near contract is subject to maturity effects, the ratio between the near and spot prices varies systematically with maturity, while this is not the case for the weighted average price, which has a constant maturity of 3 months.

Table 2.7: Comparison of Near Futures Prices and Weighted Futures Prices

	Near Contract	Weights		Weighted Average	Near ÷ Spot	Weighted Av. ÷ Spot
Jan.	£94,340	1	0	£94,340	1.02	1.02
Feb.	£94,775	2/3	1/3	£95,410	1.01	1.02
Mar.	£95,192	1/3	2/3	£96,473	1.00	1.02
Apr.	£98,204	1	0	£98,204	1.02	1.02
May	£96,059	2/3	1/3	£96,705	1.01	1.02
Jun.	£93,930	1/3	2/3	£95,185	1.00	1.02

Because of the problems and pitfalls of linking price series, methodologies which avoid this are preferable, e.g. a separate analysis of the price series for each maturity. Another alternative is to link returns computed using the same contract, not prices.

A related question is how to deal with prices that are limit up or limit down. Sutrick (1993) considered the effects of four ways of dealing with limit moves in empirical studies: drop them, keep them, use a longer differencing interval to reduce the effects of limit moves, and replace them with the estimated equilibrium price. He concludes that using the estimated equilibrium price is preferable.

2.6 Distribution of Price Changes or Returns

The way in which returns are defined can have important consequences for the distribution of returns. Thus, if the investment is defined as the initial margin, the variance of the resulting returns will be several hundred times larger than if the spot price was used as the investment. The nature of the distribution of futures price changes (or returns) is of interest for a number of reasons. First, parametric significance tests of hypotheses involving price changes (or returns) rely on the variable concerned following some tabulated distribution, e.g. the normal distribution. Second, it is sometimes of interest to know if price changes (or returns) have a symmetric or skewed distribution (e.g. a skewed distribution would mean that the risk of margin calls differs between long and short positions). Third, the nature of the distribution of price changes (or returns) may provide evidence concerning the nature of the stochastic process generating futures prices.

There is very strong evidence that the distributions of stock index futures returns are leptokurtic, i.e. a sharp peak at the mean value, with fat tails. There is also weaker evidence of skewness. For evidence on the returns distribution and discussion of the various explanations for the non-normality, see Sutcliffe (1997, chapter 8.2).

2.7 Classification of the Trading Process

The trading process can be categorized in a number of ways, e.g. type of trader (principals and agents), location of the principal (on or off the floor of the exchange), trading strategy (hedging, speculating, spreading and arbitraging) and trading style (scalping, day trading and position trading). Any particular trade can be classified under each of these headings.

Example. Felix Unger is a floor trader who undertakes an arbitrage transaction. Using the above categories, the trading strategy is arbitrage, the trading style is position trading, the trader is the principal, and the principal is located on the floor of the exchange.

Clearly there will be strong interactions between the categories, e.g. almost all arbitrage trades will involve position trading. The various ways of classifying the trading process will now be considered in more detail.

2.7.1 Type and Location of the Trader

The users of index futures traded by open outcry (e.g. S&P500 futures) can be divided into those who trade on the floor of the exchange and those who do not. Floor traders can be split into those who trade on their own account (proprietary traders) and those who trade on behalf of others (brokers), Jones (1984). (In the US, brokers are also called futures commission merchants, or FCMs.) In general, floor traders can act both on their own account and as an agent for someone else, i.e. they have dual capacity. The choice between dual and single capacity is considered in chapter 11.13.

Proprietary floor traders (or locals) benefit from low transactions costs due to acting for themselves, the ability to gather information by participating in the trading process and the possibility of responding very rapidly to market opportunities. Brokers trade futures contracts on the floor of the exchange on behalf of others, and independent brokers fill orders for a range of different customers in return for a commission, while other brokers are employees of firms, and act only for their employer. Off-floor traders (e.g. private individuals, companies, investment funds, pension funds and insurance companies) are those users of futures markets who place their trades through brokers.

Euronext.Liffe is now screen based, as are most futures exchanges; and so the location of the trader is unimportant. However, there is still a distinction between those who are screen traders with direct access to the market, and those who have to trade via someone else.

2.7.2 Trading Style

A key group of proprietary floor traders are scalpers. They act as market makers, standing ready to buy or sell futures contracts as required, so helping to provide the liquidity that is essential to a successful futures market. They trade large volumes of contracts, making money from the bid-ask spread, i.e. the difference between the bid price, at which they are ready to buy, and the ask price, at which they are willing to sell. Wiley and Daigler (1998) found that 50% of MMI index futures trading was accounted for by scalpers.

Scalpers hold their positions for only a few minutes, and close out all contracts by the daily close of trading. The trading activity of a typical scalper in NYSE Composite index futures was analyzed by Silber (1984). He found that, on average, a position of 2.9 contracts was held open for only 116 seconds. It was also found that the scalper's profits were due, very largely, to the bid-ask spread, and were not caused by favourable price movements. Thus, scalpers did not outperform the market due to any superior knowledge or forecasting skills.

Kuserk & Locke (1993) used transactions data from July 1990 to September 1990 to study the trading behaviour of over 150 S&P500 traders they identified as scalpers. On average they traded 2.1 contracts, and their average daily gross profit from scalping in S&P500 futures was $1,256. They did little trading outside S&P500 futures, and made few trades on behalf of others. The average realised bid-ask spread (the difference between the prices at which the scalper bought and sold) for S&P500 futures during this period was 0.0116%. Across twelve different futures, Kuserk & Locke (1993) found that, as the average daily profit of scalpers rose, so did the variability of scalper profits. Thus, there was a risk-return trade-off for scalping in different futures.

In screen-based markets there are traders who fulfil the market making function of scalpers or locals by posting both buy and sell orders on the screen throughout the trading period.

Day traders initiate trades rather then standing ready to form the other side of trades initiated by others, as do scalpers. Day traders take long and short positions for a few hours, and close out all their positions before the close of trading. In America, established day traders are not required to pay initial margin on positions that are closed out within the day, Brady (1988). Similarly, in the UK, if a position is closed out in the same day there is no margin requirement.

Position traders are willing to hold their positions for more than one day and so accept the risks of holding a position open overnight and over days when the market is closed, e.g. weekends and bank holidays. Moser (1994) used daily data for S&P500 futures from April 1982 to January 1990 to examine the effects of the 1987 crash on the relationship between open interest and volume. He found that before the crash a 1% increase in open interest led to a 0.16% increase in volume, while after the crash this rose to 0.98%. Thus, after the crash there was a substantial increase in trading involving overnight positions, i.e. position trading.

2.7.3 Trading Strategy

Four types or trading strategy are usually recognised: speculation, spread trading, arbitrage and hedging; and each will be briefly described. Index futures can be used for taking large positions (long or short) in the market as a whole for the purposes of speculation on a general rise or fall in share prices. This is accomplished with low transactions costs, minimal capital and little adverse price response. Spread trading involves the simultaneous purchase of one future and the sale of another, where each element of a spread is called a leg. Spreads are designed to take advantage of anticipated changes in the relative price of two futures, and are considered in more detail in chapter 6. Arbitrage involves exploiting pricing anomalies between the spot and futures markets to produce a riskless profit, and will be considered in detail in chapters 3, 4 and 5. Hedging is the purchase or sale of futures contracts to offset possible changes in the value of assets or liabilities currently held, or expected to be held at some future date. It will be examined in chapter 9.

2.8 Comparison of Forward and Futures Markets

Now that the basic mechanics of futures markets have been briefly explained, a number of points of difference between forward and futures markets will be listed, Carroll (1989), Miskovic (1989).

1. Size and Unit of Trading. Futures. The contract precisely specifies the underlying instrument and price. Forward. There is an almost unlimited range of instruments, with individually negotiated prices.

2. Delivery Dates and Delivery Procedures. Futures. These are standardised to a limited number of specific dates per year, at approved locations. Forward. Delivery can take place on any individually negotiated date and location.

3. Delivery. Futures. Delivery is not the objective of the transaction, and less than 2% are delivered. Forward. Delivery is the object of the transaction, and over 90% are delivered.

4. Common Price. Futures. The price is the same for all participants, regardless of transaction size. Forward. The price varies with the size of the transaction, the credit risk etc.

5. Method of Trading. Futures. Trading is on the exchange's computer screen, or by open outcry auction on the trading floor of the exchange. Forward. Trading takes place by telephone, telex or computer screen between individual buyers and sellers.

6. Marketplace and Trading Hours. Futures. Trading is centralised on the computer screen or exchange floor, with worldwide communications, during hours fixed by the exchange. Forward. Trading is 'over the counter' worldwide, 24 hours per day with telephone, telex or computer access.

7. Price Dissemination. Futures. Prices are disseminated publicly. Forward. Prices are not publicly disseminated.

8. Best Price. Futures. Each transaction is conducted at the best price available at the time. Forward. There is no guarantee that the price is the best available.

9. Security Deposit and Margin. Futures. The exchange rules require an initial margin deposit and the daily settlement of variation margins. Forward. The collateral level is negotiable, with no adjustment for daily price fluctuations.

10. Clearing Operation. Futures. A central clearing house is associated with each exchange to handle the daily revaluation of open positions, cash payments and delivery procedures. Forward. There is usually no separate clearing house function.

11. Volume. Futures. Volume (and open interest) information is published. Forward. Volume data is not available.

12. Daily Price Fluctuations. Futures. There is a daily price limit (although the FTSE 100 future is unlimited). Forward. There are no daily price limits.

13. Market Liquidity and Ease of Offset. Futures. There is very high liquidity and ease of offset with any other market participant due to standardised contracts. Forward. The limited liquidity and offset is due to the variable contract terms. Offset is usually with the original counterparty.

14. Credit Risk. Futures. The clearing house assumes the credit risk. Forward. The market participant bears the risk of the counterparty defaulting.

15. Regulation. Futures. Futures trading is centrally regulated, usually by a government agency, such as the Financial Services Authority in the UK. Forward. These markets are self-regulating.

2.9 Some Advantages of Stock Index Futures

Trading index futures has a number of important advantages over trading the portfolio of shares corresponding to the index.

1. *Easy Short Selling*. Short selling shares involves various difficulties, e.g. the costs of borrowing shares, and SEC rule 10a-1 in the US (the uptick rule) which prevents shares being sold short unless the last price movement was up. In the UK only market makers (including equity options market makers) can borrow UK shares, they must do so via money brokers and are required to pay a fee of roughly 1% per annum of the value of the shares, Quality of Markets Unit (1991). In consequence, short selling shares is not widespread. However, exactly half the trades in index futures involve taking a short position, i.e. a short position is easy for futures but not for shares.

2. *Low Transactions Costs*. The transactions costs are lower than for trading a diversified portfolio of shares. Indeed, Kling (1986) has argued there is no reason for

the existence of financial futures if they do not have lower transactions costs. Transactions costs for trading futures comprise: commission, the bid-ask spread, market impact (adverse price movement), the opportunity cost of the funds used in paying the initial margin and which are set aside to meet variation margin, and taxes, if any. Greer & Brorsen (1989) suggest that transactions costs should also include an allowance for the risk of 'slippage' or execution risk, i.e. the difference between the price at which the trade is executed and the price at which the order was intended to trade. (For index futures denominated in a foreign currency, e.g. the CME Nikkei 225, there is also the currency bid-ask spread.) Unlike shares, no stamp duty has ever been payable on futures transactions in the UK. Instead of buying (or selling) shares in 100 or 500 separate companies, buying (or selling) index futures requires only a single transaction. As an example of the low costs of trading futures, in June 1990 a major US futures broker charged £22 (plus £3.30 value added tax) per round turn or trip (establishing and liquidating the position) per FTSE 100 futures contract.

Liffe (1990) and Norman & Annandale (1991) estimated the round trip transaction costs in table 2.8. This shows that the transactions costs for trading shares are more than ten times larger than for trading the equivalent value of index futures. These calculations ignore any market impact costs, which are probably substantially lower for futures than for shares.

Table 2.8: Estimated Round Trip Transactions Costs

| | Liffe (1992b) | | Norman & Annandale (1991) | |
| | UK Alpha | FTSE 100 | FTSE 100 | FTSE 100 |
	Shares	Futures	Shares	Futures
Bid-ask spread	1.10%	0.05%	0.80%	0.083%
Stamp duty	0.50%	0	0.50%	0
Commission (twice)	0.40%	0.05%	0.40%	0.033%
Total Cost	2.00%	0.10%	1.70%	0.116%

Arai, Akamatsu & Yoshioka (1993) have estimated the round trip costs of trading 10 Nikkei 225 futures contracts, and the equivalent basket of shares, in August 1992. Table 2.9 shows that the transactions costs for index futures in Japan were about twenty times smaller than for shares.

Yadav & Pope (1992b) examined pairs of bid and ask quotations which were within sixty seconds of each other for FTSE 100 futures. Using data for 1986-90, they found the median spread for the near contract had dropped from about 0.12% in 1986 to about 0.05% in 1990, while the corresponding figure for the next near contract had fallen from about 0.34% in 1986 to roughly 0.14%. Berkman, Brailsford & Frino (2005) used trade and quote data for 2000 to compare the effective and realized spreads for FTSE 100 futures with those of very large trades in FTSE 100 stocks. These spreads were 15 to 16 times larger for the equity block trades than for the futures trades. Since the permanent price impact of futures trades was about a quarter of the effective spread, this implies that most of the futures spread was due to temporary liquidity costs, rather than to permanent information effects. A study of the bid-ask spread for S&P500 futures by Wang, Moriarty, Michalski & Jordan (1990) found that it is generally very small (i.e. equal to the minimum allowed price change or tick size), although during the stock market crash of October 1987 it rose by seven or eight times. Smith & Whaley (1994a, 1994b) also found that the S&P500 traded bid-ask spread was one tick. Bortoli, Frino & Jarnecic (2004) found that for 1998-2001 the average commission charged for trading SPI futures was 0.003%. These commissions were a positive function of price volatility and the bid-ask spread, and a negative function of order size and trading via screens. These results (in conjunction with table 2.9) indicate that the bid-ask spread for shares is markedly larger than for index futures.

Table 2.9: Estimated Round Trip Transactions Costs for the Nikkei

	Nikkei Basket of Shares	Nikkei Futures
Commission	2.232%	0.142%
Consumption tax	0.067%	0.004%
Loss of interest on margin	0	0.039%
Share transfer tax	0.299%	0
Exchange tax	0	0.002%
Bid-ask spread	1.006%	0
Total cost	3.604%	0.187%

Rubinstein (1989) and Stoll (1987) argue this is because a market maker in particular shares is exposed to greater risk than a scalper (effectively a market maker) in index futures. The open position of a market maker in stock index futures is only subject to systematic (or market) risk, as unsystematic risk is diversified away by holding a position in a widely diversified portfolio. A market maker in a particular share is exposed to both systematic and unsystematic risk, as the unsystematic risk is not diversified away. If, as in the UK, the market makers make a market in a number of different shares, they will have the benefit of some degree of diversification, while if they are part of a large integrated financial firm, this will also provide some diversification.

It is more likely that an investor has access to information which is not yet reflected in the price of a particular share, rather than that he or she has access to information affecting all share prices. Hence, adverse information costs are greater for shares than index futures. Stoll (1989) estimated that 43% of the spread for individual shares was caused by adverse information costs. Since trading is frequent in index futures markets, an uninformed scalper can expect to rapidly unwind their position, so minimising the period of time for which they are exposed to the arrival of adverse information. A study by Followill & Rodriguez (1991) found that the major determinant of the size of the daily bid-ask spread for S&P500 futures was daily futures volume. As volume rose the bid-ask spread declined, and this is consistent with higher volume reducing the period for which a scalper must hold a position, so reducing the risks of supplying liquidity.

There is an additional explanation of the smaller bid-ask spreads for index futures. Because short selling shares is more costly than sales from a long position, market makers in shares may choose to hold, on average, a net long position in shares. This will tie up capital and expose them to risk. However, because short selling index futures is no more costly than closing out a long position, futures market makers have no reason to hold a long position in index futures.

Because of the additional risk, due to lack of diversification, adverse information and the need to hold inventory, the market maker in a particular share will require a larger bid-ask spread.

Futures market makers have two other advantages over equity market makers in some countries. They need not be present in a particular pit all the time, and so can switch their activity between a number different futures contracts, depending on circumstances. If they are trading futures via a computer screen, they can switch to trading a different security; although such switching is also possible for screen-based equity traders. Furthermore, futures market makers usually have dual capacity, enabling them to switch between market making and acting as a broker for clients, Grossman & Miller (1988).

3. *High Leverage*. For an initial margin of (say) £1,500, it is possible to acquire a market position in the FTSE 100 index of roughly £10×5,000 = £50,000, i.e. 33:1. Because of marking to the market, the trader will also need to set aside a sum of money to cover payments of variation margin, see chapter 11.2 for a discussion of the size of this cash balance.

4. *Liquid Market*. The market for index futures is much more liquid than the market for shares in individual companies. The turnover in FTSE 100 futures in 2004 was 20,772,878 contracts valued at roughly £1,000 billion, while a single trade of 4,966 FTSE 100 contracts (worth over £200 million) was conducted in 2000 (Berkman, Brailsford & Frino, 2005). Therefore rapid investment or disinvestment of large sums of money in the stock market via index futures is less likely to have an adverse price effect. Harris, Sofianos & Shapiro (1994) estimated that the price effect of a programme trade (buy, sell, index arbitrage or non-index arbitrage) on the NYSE in the years 1989 and 1990 of $10 million was only 0.03 index points, while for 1990-91 Hasbrouck (1996) estimated this effect at 0.024 index points.

Often liquidity (or market impact) is proxied by volume. However, there is some evidence that, at least over long periods, volume may be a poor proxy for liquidity. Park & Sarkar (1994) studied transactions data for S&P500 futures for 2 months in 1987 and 2 months in 1991. The total volume in 1991 was about half that in 1987 and, after controlling for bid-ask bounce, adverse selection costs and the number of active floor traders, they found that for both years the market impact of a trade was unaffected by this drop in volume. Therefore, they conclude that since a halving of volume failed to have a significant effect on market impact (liquidity), volume is an unsuitable proxy for liquidity.

5. *Known Price*. If an investor wishes to buy a widely diversified portfolio of shares (e.g. 500) it is probable that the transactions will be conducted over a period of time at prices which were unknown in advance. However, if index futures are purchased, the position is taken (effectively in all the shares in the index) by a single transaction.

6. *Taxation*. There may be differences in the way profits and losses on futures are taxed, relative to the taxation of shares. For example, in the UK stamp duty is payable on share transactions, but stamp duty has never been charged on futures contracts. Pension funds in the UK are exempt from any taxation on their profits from futures trading, but are only tax exempt for profits on share transactions when they are not deemed to be trading in shares (Liffe, 1993). One factor discouraging US mutual funds from participating in the futures markets is that, if they earn more than 30% of their annual gross income from the sale of securities held for less than three months, all of the income of the mutual fund becomes liable to taxation, Miller (1988).

7. *Regulations*. Since futures are different financial instruments from shares and traded on different exchanges, they are subject to different laws and regulations. For example, in the US in 1986 insider trading in futures was not illegal, while insider trading in shares was illegal, Scarff (1985), Grossman (1986). [In late 1993 the CFTC approved regulations which made it a criminal offence for employees or board members of a US futures exchange to trade on the basis of inside information.] In the UK the Companies Securities (Insider Dealing) Act 1985 made insider trading in stock index futures illegal, White (1992, p. 295).

8. *Longer Trading Hours*. Some futures exchanges may have longer trading hours than the underlying spot market; while the development of screen-based trading for futures permits long trading hours (e.g. the 24 hour Globex system).

2.10 Contracts for Difference and Spread Betting

As an alternative to trading futures (or forward) contracts, a number of private companies (for example, City Index and IG Index) in the UK offer a betting service on the prices of a wide range of stock indices, currencies, interest rates and individual shares. Bets on the value of the underlying instrument (the index) are called contracts for difference and are equivalent to swapping an interest bearing security for the basket of shares underlying the index; while bets on the value of the futures contract are called spread bets.

The client places a bet with the company that the price of a specified index (or index future) will rise or fall. The bookmaker quotes continuous buy and sell prices for the index (or index future), and clients can choose to buy or sell at these prices. At a subsequent time of the client's choosing, they can close out their position. Contracts for difference have no fixed end date, while spread bets end when the futures contract reaches its delivery date. The bookmaker makes money from the bid-ask spread that is charged when the bet is opened and closed. Clients with long positions in a contract for difference are charged interest on the value of their outstanding position, while those with short positions receive interest. If the underlying shares declare a dividend, this is paid to those with long positions in a contract for difference, and charged to those with short positions.

Although the bookmaker takes the opposite side to every bet, they are exposed to little risk. This is because many bets cancel out, i.e. some clients bet on the index (or index future) rising while others bet on it falling. To the extent that bets are not offsetting, the bookmaker hedges (or lays off) the remaining risk in the relevant futures market.

The advantages of this form of participation in futures markets are: small bets are possible (e.g. for the FTSE 100, the contract multiplier is only £1 per index point); above the minimum bet size (e.g. one contract) clients can deal in fractions of a contract; all bets are subject to cash settlement, including those for currencies, interest rates, and individual shares, where the futures are subject to physical not cash settlement; betting is possible in sterling on indices for which no futures contract has a sterling contract multiplier; betting is available on some indices in which futures markets do not exist; betting on the index is possible when the futures market is closed; and bookmakers offer the facility for stop-loss orders that operate even when the index jumps through the chosen price.

Contracts for difference have the additional advantages that the bet has no fixed expiry date; and since the bet is based on the spot price not the futures price, any interest rate and dividend risk is excluded from the bet. Spread bets held to maturity do not incur any additional bid-ask spread on delivery.

In the UK such contracts are legally betting not futures trading, and so profits and losses are taxed in a completely different way from profits and losses on futures contracts. Individuals are exempt from paying UK capital gains tax, income tax and value added tax on any winnings, although the company (bookmaker) pays betting duty.

The disadvantages are that large positions are beyond the resources of the bookmaker at times of the day when he cannot hedge; margins are larger than for futures (e.g. £3,000 for the FTSE 100); margin payments can usually only be made by cheques drawn on a UK bank; and there is always the risk that the company (bookmaker) will go into liquidation. However, financial bookmakers are regulated by the Financial Services Authority, and clients are protected by a compensation scheme. Thus, contracts for difference and spread betting are more appropriate for individuals, while direct participation in the futures market is usually more appropriate for large corporate traders.

2.11 Exchange Traded Funds (ETFs)

In the last decade, a new form of security has emerged that is similar in many ways to index futures. They are called exchange traded funds, but have many different brand names (SPDRs or Spiders, Diamonds, QQQs (or qubes), Vipers, iUnits, TIPs, HIPs, iShares (formerly Webs), iFTSE 100 and Leaders). They began in Canada in 1990 as Toronto Index Participations (TIPs), the US in 1993 and Europe in 2000, Kostovetsky (2003).

The index basket of shares is purchased by the promoter of the exchange traded fund, and depositary receipts on this portfolio are traded in the secondary market (such as the London Stock Exchange). They are similar to index futures in that:-

- They are traded continuously.
- The price of the depositary receipts corresponds very closely to the current value of the underlying basket of shares. This is because institutional traders are able to create or redeem large blocks of depositary receipts if prices diverge too far. The largest gap for iShares on the FTSE 100 has been 19 basis points, or 0.19%.
- No stamp duty for trading in the depositary receipts.
- The depositary receipts can be sold short.
- They have very low transactions costs (e.g. 9.5 basis points).

However, there are a couple of ways in which exchange traded funds differ from an index future and resemble the index basket of shares:-

- Dividends are paid on the depositary receipts corresponding to those on the index basket.
- Infinite life.

2.12 Futures on Individual Stocks

Futures on individual stocks provide an alternative to trading the underlying stocks, and have the advantages of lower transactions costs (for example in the UK they would avoid the payment of stamp duty of 0.5%), easy short selling, and high leverage (Lascelles, 2002). With the exception of the absence of dividends, the payoffs on individual stock futures (ISFs) resemble those from equity trading on an exchange with a long settlement period, and so ISFs can be used as an alternative to direct equity trading for those wishing to trade for long settlement. In some countries ISFs are cash settled, while in others there is physical settlement.

Trading in ISF in the USA was blocked for twenty years under the Shad-Johnson Accord of 1982. This ban was caused by a lack of agreement on whether ISFs should be regulated by the SEC or the CFTC, and because of a fear that the ISF settlement price (i.e. the underlying share price) would be manipulable. However the Commodities Futures Modernization Act (2000) lifted this ban, with the regulation of ISFs being shared between the CFTC and the SEC. This Act also outlawed insider trading and manipulation in the markets for ISFs and options on ISFs, so reducing fears of manipulation.

In the US, ISFs are margined differently to index futures. The required margin is a fixed percentage of the nominal value of the contract, and so varies with the price of the future, but not with its riskiness. Dutt & Wein (2003b) show that the margin collection period (e.g. 1 to 4 days) can be varied to adjust for differences in risk.

Brailsford & Cusack (1997) found that Australian ISFs are generally priced in accordance with the no-arbitrage condition presented in chapter 3, and mispricings decline as delivery approaches. However, a study of two Russian individual stock futures (Lukoil and RAO EES) from 1996 until 1998, when the market ceased operation, found considerable mispricings, Chetverikov (2000).

ISF in Australia switched from cash to physical settlement, and Lien & Yang (2004) and Lien & Tse (2005) found that the spot and futures markets became more volatile; while hedging effectiveness increased. ISFs in other countries also offer physical settlement, and so what works for an index of shares appears not to apply to individual shares.

Lien & Yang (2003a) examined the relationship between Australian ISF and the underlying shares. Using daily data from 1994-8, and in contrast to the studies of index futures reported in chapter 6, he found that the spot market led the futures market. This finding is attributed to the much higher volume of trading in the shares (150 to 2,000 times larger). The switch from cash to physical settlement increased the strength of the price discovery role of the stock market.

Lien & Yang (2003b) investigated daily data for 1991-2000 on Australian stocks with an ISF. They found that for some stocks the introduction of an ISF led to a reduction in the elevated volume and returns volatility which occurred when equity options on these stocks expired.

2.13 Conclusions

Futures trading can play an important role in providing the full range of markets necessary for economic efficiency. Futures are standardised commodities traded on liquid markets according to well specified rules and procedures, and differ from forward contracts in a number of important respects. While the definition of a rate of return for a future creates conceptual problems, the practical solution is to use either price changes or the logarithm of the price relatives. The distribution of price changes or returns on index futures has often been found to be leptokurtic. Index futures have a variety of attractive features for a trader who wishes to trade a portfolio of shares corresponding to the index. Finally there are a number of new products (ETFs, CFDs, spread betting and ISFs) which fulfil a similar function to index futures.

PART 2

ARBITRAGE

Chapter 3

Arbitrage and the Valuation
of Stock Index Futures

Introduction

An arbitrage argument, based on some simplifying assumptions, will be used to derive a formula for the valuation of a stock index futures contract. This valuation formula (or no-arbitrage condition) is then restated in various ways. Next, the arbitrage process for over and underpriced futures is examined. Then the early or delayed unwinding of an arbitrage position is considered. Finally, there is a brief consideration of synthetic futures, followed by coverage of other forms of index arbitrage.

3.1 Assumptions

The derivation of the formula for valuing stock index futures relies on the assumptions which are discussed in detail in chapter 5; where the consequences of their relaxation for the valuation of index futures are explored.

3.2 Derivation of the No-Arbitrage Condition

Arbitrage is a fundamental economic concept, and the theorems of Modigliani & Miller on the cost of capital and dividends can be viewed as an application of arbitrage, as can the Black-Scholes option pricing model and the arbitrage pricing theory of Ross. If there are two identical products, the possibility of arbitrage requires them to have an identical price. If not, arbitrageurs will buy the cheap product and sell it as the dear product. Such action will raise the price of the cheap product and lower the price of the dear product, so equalising prices and eliminating the arbitrage opportunity.

Arbitrage has proved useful for valuing complicated financial instruments because, if the new instrument can be replicated by combining existing instruments whose individual values are known, the value of the new instrument must be equal to that of the replicating strategy, Varian (1987). If not, an arbitrage opportunity exists. In finance, arbitrage is viewed as the simultaneous purchase of one asset against the sale of the same or equivalent asset from zero initial wealth to create a riskless profit due to price discrepancies. Thus, arbitrage is riskless, requires zero wealth and so can be of arbitrary scale. Hence, only a few rational traders are required to remove arbitrage opportunities. Arbitrage is more general than 'the law of one price', Dybvig & Ross (1992). The law of one price only applies to identical assets, and not to situations where the return on one asset dominates another, but may do so by different amounts in different states of the world.

Consider two alternative strategies for owning 'one unit' of the market index, i.e. a long position, between now (time 0) and time T (the delivery date of the future). The first strategy uses spot transactions in the underlying asset and debt markets, while the second strategy uses futures contracts and debt markets. The same pair of alternative strategies of spot and debt or futures and debt also apply to acquiring a short position of one unit of the index. For the spot and futures markets to be in simultaneous equilibrium, i.e. a no-arbitrage situation, these alternative strategies must all have the same cost at time 0. Otherwise an arbitrage profit will be available.

3.2.1 Dividends

The owner of shares in the index receives dividends, while the holder of a long or short futures position in the corresponding index future does not. This difference must be allowed for in any arbitrage trade, and this is done by computing the present value of the dividends on the index basket of shares.

Ownership of the index basket of shares confers the right to receive those dividends for which the ex-dividend date occurs during the period of ownership, e.g. between now (time 0) and time T. Note that few dividends will be received in the early part of the period of ownership, as there is a time lag between the ex-dividend date and payment of the dividends; while dividends will continue to be received for some time after the shares have been sold. Let £D be the present value of this expected dividend stream, discounted at the riskless rate of interest. This can be specified as:-

$$D = \sum_{t=1}^{m} D_t/(1+\varphi)^t$$

where the time between now and receipt of the last dividend payment is divided into m short periods, the riskless interest rate for each of these short periods (compounded each time period) is φ, and the value of dividends paid during period t is D_t. Figure 3.1 shows the relationship between the ex-dividend dates and the payment dates for four dividends. For the owner of the shares between time 0 and time T, the relevant dividends are A, B and C. Dividend D is not included because the ex-dividend date occurs after time T.

Ex-Dividend Dates

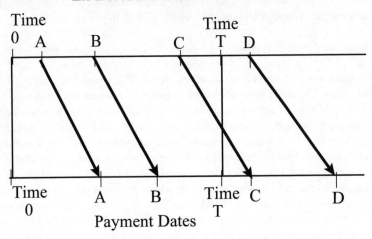

Figure 3.1 Relevant Dividends

3.2.2 Spot and Debt

At time 0 the arbitrageur purchases one unit of a fund that consists of shares in the market index, for £S. At the same time the arbitrageur borrows the sum £D now, and uses the subsequent dividends (plus interest) from the basket of shares to repay this loan (plus interest) at time T. (This effectively removes the dividends from consideration). The total net cost at time 0 of this strategy for owning one unit of the market index (excluding the dividends) between time 0 and time T is $£S-D$.

Example. On 1st January (time 0) Gordon Gekko, the manager of the Blaydon Fund, buys shares corresponding to one unit of the Bull index at a cost of £50,000. Owning these shares until 30th June (time T) will entitle him to the following dividends: January 0, February 0, March £50, April £200, May £300, June £100, July £200, August £166.36. No dividends are received in January and February, while dividend receipts continue into July and August because of the time lag between a share going ex-dividend and the actual payment. Note that the calculation of D requires a knowledge of the risk free rate of interest for the two months after delivery. The riskless monthly rate of interest (φ) (compounded monthly) is 0.8% and, assuming the dividends are received on the last day of each month, the present value of these dividends on 1st January is given by $D = 50/(1.008)^3+200/(1.008)^4+300/(1.008)^5+100/(1.008)^6+200/(1.008)^7+166.36/(1.008)^8 = £971.40$. Therefore, Gordon borrows £971.40 at a monthly interest rate of φ and uses the subsequent dividends (and the interest earned from investing them at the monthly interest rate of φ) to repay the loan plus interest at time T. The present value of the repayment of the loan plus interest at time T is £971.40. Thus, the net cost to Gordon on 1st January of owning one unit of the index between 1st January and 30th June is $50,000-971.40 = £49,028.60$.

3.2.3 Futures and Debt

The arbitrageur buys a futures contract at time 0 for $£F_L$ deliverable at time T for one unit of the index. The arbitrageur also buys riskless government debt that will mature at time T to yield $£F_L$. The price (present value) of this debt is $£F_L/(1+r)$, where r is the riskless rate of interest for the period between time 0 and T (which is probably *not* a year), i.e. $r = (1+\varphi)^m - 1$, where r is compounded every m time periods. For example, if the monthly riskless rate of interest is 1% compounded monthly, the value of r for a futures contract with a remaining life of three months is $(1.01^3-1)\times100 = 3.03\%$. This definition of the riskless rate of interest (r) can be thought of as the return on a riskless bond that matures at time T. At time T the government debt will mature to yield $£F_L$, which will exactly pay for the futures contract. The total cost at time 0 of this strategy for owning one unit of the market index between time 0 and time T is $£F_L/(1+r)$.

Example. Gordon Gekko, of the Blaydon Fund, buys one futures contract on 1st January on the Bull index for delivery on 30th June at a price of £51,430. On the same date he also invests £49,028.60 in a riskless bond that will mature on 30th June to yield £51,430. This is based on a riskless interest rate (r) of 4.897% over the six months, i.e. $\{(1.008)^6-1\}\times100 = 4.897$, where the monthly rate of interest is 0.8%. Thus, Gordon must invest £49,028.60 on 1st January to own one unit of the index (excluding dividends) over the next six months.

Since the purchaser of a long position in the futures market can always replicate this position by the use of a long position in the spot market at a cost of $£S-D$, he or she will never be prepared to pay more than this for a future, i.e. $S-D \geq F_L/(1+r)$, or $F_L \leq (S-D)\times(1+r)$. Hence, the possibility of arbitrage puts an upper limit on the price of a long position in the future. This upper bound on the futures price is illustrated in table 3.1 which uses the cash flows at time 0 and time T, where S_T is the value of the basket of shares at time T.

Table 3.1: Cash Flows for Long Positions in Futures and Shares

	Time	
	0	**T**
Future (long)	0	$S_T - F_L$
Shares (long)	$-(S-D)$	S_T
Differential Cash Flows	$S-D$	$-F_L$

The advantage of using futures, rather than shares, to establish a long position is given by the present value (PV) of the difference in the cash flows, and this differential cash flow is certain. Computed using the riskless discount rate, this is $PV = S-D-F_L/(1+r)$. This present value must be non-negative for long positions in futures to be attractive relative to shares, and so $F_L \leq (S-D) \times (1+r)$, i.e. the futures price cannot exceed the cost of the replicating portfolio, which is to borrow money and use it to buy a long position in the shares corresponding to one unit of the market index (adjusted for any dividends on the shares).

In a similar manner, an arbitrage bound can also be established for a short position of one unit in the market index. At time 0 the arbitrageur sells short one unit of a fund that consists of shares in the market index, for £S. Dividends will be payable on the underlying shares between now and time T. Let £D be the present value of this expected dividend stream, discounted at the riskless rate of interest (r). The arbitrageur invests the sum £D now at the interest rate r, and uses the repayment of this money (plus interest) to pay the subsequent dividends. (This effectively removes the dividends from consideration.) The total net receipts at time 0 of this strategy from having a short position of one unit of the market index between time 0 and time T are £$S-D$.

The arbitrageur sells a futures contract for one unit of the index at time 0 for £F_S deliverable at time T. The arbitrageur also borrows £$F_S/(1+r)$, (on which he or she must pay interest at the rate r over the life of the future), i.e. at time T the arbitrageur must repay £F_S. The total receipt at time 0 from this strategy for having a short position of one unit of the market index (excluding dividends) between time 0 and time T is £$F_S/(1+r)$.

Since a short position in the futures market can always be replicated by the use of a short position in the spot market with the receipt of £$S-D$, a trader will never be prepared to sell a future for less than this, i.e. $S-D \leq F_S/(1+r)$, or $F_S \geq (S-D) \times (1+r)$. Hence, the possibility of arbitrage puts a lower limit on the price of a short position in the future. This lower bound on the futures price is illustrated in table 3.2 which uses the cash flows at time 0 and time T.

Table 3.2: Cash Flows for Short Positions in Futures and Shares

	Time	
	0	**T**
Future (short)	0	$-S_T+F_S$
Shares (short)	$S-D$	$-S_T$
Differential Cash Flows	$-(S-D)$	F_S

The present value of the certain differential cash flows computed using the riskless discount rate is $PV = -(S-D) + F_S/(1+r)$. This present value must be non-negative for establishing a short position using futures to be attractive, rather than using shares; and so $F_S \geq (S-D) \times (1+r)$, i.e. the futures price cannot be less than the cost of the replicating portfolio, which is to short sell the shares corresponding to one unit of the market index (adjusted for any dividends on the shares), and invest the proceeds at the riskless rate of interest.

3.2.4 No-Arbitrage Condition

The price at which traders are prepared to sell futures must be the same as that at which other traders are prepared to buy futures, i.e. $F_S = F_L = F$. Therefore the equilibrium condition for a future on an arithmetic index is that $F \leq (S-D) \times (1+r)$ and $F \geq (S-D) \times (1+r)$, and so the price of a future is given by the no-arbitrage condition:-

$$F = (S-D) \times (1+r)$$

For the futures and stock markets to be in simultaneous equilibrium, the above condition must be met. If it is not met, stock index arbitrage is possible. The procedures for undertaking arbitrage are described in chapter 3.4. While this condition will be called the no-arbitrage condition, it is also known as the 'fair value' or the 'theoretical value' of the futures contract. It is also called the cost of carry futures value because it is equal to the cost of carrying an equivalent spot position until delivery at time T.

3.3 Restatements of the No-Arbitrage Condition

The above no-arbitrage condition uses the present value of future dividends (D) and the risk free interest rate for the remaining life of the future (r). Some authors have restated this no-arbitrage condition using alternative definitions of the terms representing the risk free interest rate and the dividends on the shares in the index. There are two alternative ways of treating the interest rate: the rate for the remaining life of the future and the annual rate; while there are four alternative ways of dealing with dividends: the present value, the terminal value, the rate for the life of the future and the annual rate. (Continuous compounding of interest and the continuous payment of dividends is considered in appendix A of chapter 5). While these restatements are mathematically equivalent to the no-arbitrage condition presented above, they will be argued to be inferior.

Terminal Dividends. In this case the dividends are compounded forwards to give their value at the delivery date (D^*), and the no-arbitrage condition becomes $F = S(1+r) - D^*$, Sultan, Hogan & Kroner (1995).

Example. Continuing the Gordon Gekko example used earlier in this chapter, Gordon decides to compute the no-arbitrage futures price as $F = S(1+r) - D^*$. Since $D^* = 971.40 \times 1.04897 = £1,019$, $F = 50,000 \times 1.04897 - 1,019 = £51,430$.

Dividend Rate Until Delivery - A. One variant of the no-arbitrage condition, which has been employed by many authors (e.g. Blake, 1990; Figlewski, 1987; Fink & Feduniak, 1988, p. 512; Furbush, 1989; Gould, 1988; Moriarty, Phillips & Tosini, 1981; Petzel, 1989, page 96; Silk, 1986; Solnik, 1988, p. 243; Stoll, 1987; and Stoll & Whaley

1987, 1988a, 1988b, 1993) uses the dividend rate (d) instead of the present value of dividends (D). This gives the no-arbitrage condition $F = S(1+r-d)$, where d is the dividend rate for the remaining life of the futures contract, i.e. $d = D(1+r)/S$. Thus, d is the value of the dividends at time T divided by the 'investment' at time 0, i.e. $£S$.

Example. Gordon Gekko reconsidered his arbitrage decision using the dividend rate for the six month period, i.e. $d = (971.40 \times 1.04897)/50,000 = 0.02038$. The no-arbitrage price of the future is $F = S(1+r-d) = 50,000(1+0.04897-0.02038) = £51,430$.

Dividend Rate Until Delivery - B. Dumas & Allaz (1995) have suggested using a somewhat different definition of the dividend rate until delivery, $\chi = D/(S-D)$. This gives the no-arbitrage condition $F = S(1+r)/(1+\chi)$.

Example. For the Gordon Gekko example, $\chi = D/(S-D) = 971.40/(50,000-971.40) = 0.019813$, and so $F = S(1+r)/(1+\chi) = (50,000 \times 1.04897)/1.019813 = £51,430$.

Annual Dividend Rate. Instead of the dividend rate over the life of the future, dividends may be expressed as an annual dividend yield (ψ), where $\psi = 1-(1-D/S)^{1/h}$, where h is the time in years remaining until delivery. Thus the no-arbitrage condition becomes $F = S(1+r) \times (1-\psi)^h$. This use of ψ implicitly assumes that dividends are paid as a constant amount per time period, where the time period is the shortest period used in defining h, e.g. a day.

Example. For Gordon Gekko $\psi = 1-(1-D/S)^{1/h} = 1-(1-971.40/50,000)^2 = 0.038486$, and so the no-arbitrage futures price is $F = S(1+r) \times (1-\psi)^h = 50,000 \times 1.04897 \times (1-0.038486)^{0.5} = £51,430$.

Annual Interest Rate. Another modification to the no-arbitrage condition involves the redefinition of the risk free rate of interest on to an annual basis. If η is the annual riskless rate of interest such that $\eta = (1+r)^{1/h}-1 = (1+\varphi)^m-1$, then the no-arbitrage condition can be stated as $F = (S-D) \times (1+\eta)^h$. Typically h will be less than one year, and so this no-arbitrage condition assumes that interest is compounded at least every h years. Since h will change as the maturity of the contract shortens, it is assumed that interest is compounded at the end of the shortest time period used in defining h, e.g. a day.

Example. Using the numbers from the Gordon Gekko example considered above, $\eta = (1+\varphi)^{12}-1 = (1.008)^{12}-1 = 0.10034$. Therefore, the no-arbitrage futures price is $F = (S-D) \times (1+\eta)^h = (50,000-971.40) \times (1.10034)^{0.5} = £51,430$.

Terminal Dividends and an Annual Interest Rate. In this case the terminal value of the dividends is combined with an annual interest rate to give $F = S(1+\eta)^h - D^*$. This formulation has been used by Daigler (1993a, 1993b) and Johnson & Giacotto (1995).

Example. For Gordon Gekko, $F = S(1+\eta)^h - D^* = 50,000 \times (1.10034)^{0.5} - 1,019 = £51,430$.

Dividend Rate and an Annual Interest Rate. The dividend rate for the remaining life of the future may be used, instead of the present of terminal value of dividends, in conjunction with an annual interest rate. Thus $F = S[(1+\eta)^h - d]$, Watsham (1993).

Example. For Gordon Gekko, $F = S[(1+\eta)^h - d] = 50,000[1.10034^{0.5} - 0.02038] = £51,430$.

Annual Dividend Rate and an Annual Interest Rate. Some traders may be more comfortable working with the annual risk free interest rate and the annual dividend yield. Thus, $F = S(1+\eta)^h \times (1-\psi)^h$, CBOT (1989).

Example. Again, using the Gordon Gekko example, the no-arbitrage price of the future is $F = S(1+\eta)^h \times (1-\psi)^h = 50,000(1.10034)^{0.5} \times (1 - 0.038486)^{0.5} = £51,430$.

3.3.1 Constant Dividend Rate

While the various approaches are mathematically equivalent, the use of D (the present value of dividends) emphasises the explicit computation of the present value of a particular set of cash flows, while the use of d, χ or ψ (the dividend rate or annualized dividend yield) suggests some constant rate of dividends per time period. Since the flow of dividends is uneven throughout the year, the assumption of a constant dividend rate or yield is incorrect. This is shown for the shares in the FTSE 100 index in table 3.3 taken from Robertson (1990, p 26). In addition, in the UK shares usually went ex-dividend on the first day of a stock exchange account, so introducing a further small lumpiness. As from the introduction of rolling settlement in the UK on 18th July 1994, shares have generally gone ex-dividend on any Monday, and this has roughly doubled the number of ex-dividend days, so reducing this lumpiness.

Table 3.3: Dividends on the Shares in the FTSE 100 Index During 1988

Month	% of total	Month	% of total
January	1.2%	July	7.0%
February	9.2%	August	11.3%
March	13.9%	September	13.7%
April	7.9%	October	4.7%
May	8.2%	November	6.8%
June	5.5%	December	10.6%

Dividends on the shares in the S&P500 index and the DJIA are also unevenly distributed throughout the year, Gastineau & Madansky (1983) and Kipnis & Tsang (1984a). In Finland companies generally pay only one dividend per year, usually in the Spring, and so there is a clustering of dividend payments into a couple of months, Puttonen (1993a). For the CAC 40, about 80% of the dividends for the year 1990-91 occurred in the two months of June and July (Fitzgerald, 1993, p. 87), while two thirds of the dividends for the DAX are declared in the months of April, May and June, Bamberg & Röder (1994b).

Therefore, while these alternative statements of the no-arbitrage condition are equivalent to the initial no-arbitrage condition, they invite errors in the measurement of the dividend term. There may also be a slight simplification in the use of r, rather than η as the interest rate. For this reason, from now onwards the no-arbitrage condition will be stated as $F = (S-D) \times (1+r)$, rather than one of the restatements offered above.

3.4 The Arbitrage Process

This section describes the transactions by which an arbitrageur can lock in a riskless profit now if the future is not priced in accordance with the no-arbitrage condition.

It is important to draw a distinction between mispricings and arbitrage opportunities. The proportionate mispricing is the current futures price less the no-arbitrage futures price, all divided by the current futures (or spot) price. While mispricings are small, they are seldom exactly zero, and so mispricings exist most of the time. An arbitrage opportunity only exists when the mispricing exceeds the transactions costs of an arbitrage trade, and this is rare.

Stock index arbitrage can be divided into two different cases; when the futures price is *high* relative to the spot, and when it is *low* relative to the spot. These two situations will be considered separately.

3.4.1 Relatively High Futures Price

If $F > (S-D) \times (1+r)$ arbitrageurs will sell the overpriced asset, i.e. futures on the stock index, for £F, and buy the underpriced asset, i.e. shares in the index, for £S. The arbitrageur will also borrow £D, the present value of the future dividends, using the dividends to repay this loan. Such arbitrage is called cash and carry arbitrage because it involves carrying a long spot position to delivery. The net cost of the shares in the index at time 0 is £$S-D$. and the present value of the receipts from selling the stock index futures contract is £$F/(1+r)$. Therefore the profit at time 0, for zero initial capital, is £$F/(1+r)-(S-D)$ per futures contract. Given the assumptions of certain dividends, a constant riskless rate of interest and no marking to the market, these arbitrage profits are riskless. Therefore, the arbitrageur will attempt to trade as many futures contracts as possible. This form of arbitrage ensures that the price of a stock index futures contract cannot exceed $(S-D) \times (1+r)$, i.e. that the condition $F \leq (S-D) \times (1+r)$ will always be met.

Example. The value of the FTSE 100 index on 1st July is 5,400.0, while the price of a futures contract on this index for delivery six months later is 5,600 index points. Annie Hall, the manager of the Blythe Fund, calculates that the present value of the dividends to be paid on the shares in the index over the next six months is £1,500. The riskless rate of interest for the six month period until delivery is 5%. The no-arbitrage price of the future is given by $(5,400 \times 10 - 1,500) \times 1.05 = £55,125$. This is £875 less than the current price of a futures contract, and so an arbitrage profit of $\pi = F/(1+r) - (S-D) = (56,000/1.05) - (5.400 \times 10 - 1,500) = £833.33$ per contract at 1st July is available. Annie promptly sells one FTSE 100 December future for £56,000, buys a basket of shares corresponding to one FTSE 100 contract for 5,400×10 = £54,000 and borrows £54,000 to pay for these shares. Thus, her net cash outflow on 1st July is zero. During the next six months she invests the dividends on the shares at the riskless rate to produce 1,500×1.05 = £1,575 on 31st December. On this date she sells the shares for £z and receives £56,000−z as her gain on the short position in the futures contract. She also repays the loan of £54,000 plus interest, i.e. £54,000×1.05 = £56,700. This adds up to a net cash inflow of £875 on 31st December. This gain has a present value on 1st July of £875/1.05 = £833.33.

The arbitrage profit is independent of z, the value of the index at maturity, and requires only that the position be held until maturity. In this example Annie Hall made no initial margin payments, nor was any consideration given to the sum of money she had available for arbitrage purposes. A more complicated example follows which includes initial margin payments which earn interest, recognizes that the arbitrageur may be subject to an upper borrowing limit and deals with the indivisibility of futures contracts.

Example. The price of one FTSE 100 stock index futures contract (F) is 5,300 index points (or £53,000), while the value of the index is 5,100, giving a value for the index basket (S) of £51,000. This futures contract has three months to maturity and the initial margin (M) is £1,500 per contract. The present value of the dividends (D) on the index during the life of the futures contract is £1,000, while the risk free rate of interest (r) over the period of the next three months is 2.411% (i.e. 10% per year, compounded every quarter). Lawrence Garfield, an arbitrageur employed by the Brandling Bank, wishes to borrow approximately £100 million (excluding any loan to be repaid from the dividends) for the period of the life of the near contract, which is approximately three months. Letting x be the number of futures contracts to be traded then, assuming the full price of the shares has to be paid immediately, the cost of the shares and the futures margins must be set equal to the loan plus the present value of the dividends that will be received on the shares. Thus, $Sx+Mx = 100,000,000+Dx$, which becomes $51x+1.5x = 100,000+1x$, and so $x = 1,941.7476$. Rounding up the number of futures contracts traded to 1,942, Lawrence Garfield borrows £100,013,000. The interest payable on this loan will be £2,411,313 (i.e. 2.411%, or 10% per year).

Lawrence then sells 1,942 FTSE 100 stock index futures contracts at £53,000 each, i.e. 53,000×1,942 = £102,926,000, paying an initial margin of 1,942×1,500 = £2,913,000. It will be assumed that this initial margin earns interest at the risk free rate of 2.411% for 3 months i.e. £2,913,000×0.02411 = £70,232. He buys shares corresponding to 1,942 units of the index at a cost of 1,942×51,000 = £99,042,000. Lawrence also borrows £1,942,000, to be repaid using the dividends on these shares. It is assumed that there are no payments of variation margin. At the delivery date Lawrence sells the shares at the then market price for a total of £z. The delivery price of the futures is also £z (since at delivery $F=S$). The loan plus interest is repaid, as is the initial margin plus interest.

Thus the initial cash flows at time 0 are

Loan	+100,013,000
Dividend loan	+1,942,000
Share purchase	−99,042,000
Initial margin	−2,913,000
Net cash flow	0

The cash flows at delivery (time T) are :-

Repayment of loan	−100,013,000
Interest on loan	−2,411,313
Delivery of futures	−z
Refund of Initial margin	+2,913,000
Interest on Initial margin	+70,232
Selling shares	+z
Proceeds from future	+102,926,000
Net cash flow at delivery	+£3,484,920
Present value of the cash flow at delivery	+£3,402,876

Consistency check. The instant arbitrage profit per futures contract is given by $F/(1+r)-(S-D)$ i.e. $53,000/1.02411-(51,000-1,000)=£1,752.253$. Therefore, the total arbitrage profit from trading 1,942 futures contracts is $1,942 \times 1,752.253 = £3,402,876$, which gives the same result as the more detailed treatment above. Thus Lawrence Garfield makes an instant and riskless profit of £3.3 million before transactions costs.

3.4.2 Relatively Low Futures Price

If $F < (S-D) \times (1+r)$ arbitrageurs will buy the underpriced asset, i.e. futures contracts on the stock index, for £F, and sell the overpriced asset, i.e. shares in the index, for £S. The arbitrageur will also invest £D at time 0 to provide for the subsequent dividends on the shares in the index. The net receipts from selling the shares in one index basket are £S−D, while the present value of the cost of a stock index futures contract is £F/(1+r). Therefore the riskless profit at time 0 is $£(S-D)-F/(1+r)$ per futures contract. The first example below ignores initial margin and any position limits on the arbitrageur, while the second example includes these features.

Example. On 1st March the value of the Bull index is 5,500, while the price of a September contract on this index is 5,600 index points. The value on 1st March of the dividends to be paid on the shares in the index during the next six months is £1,300. The riskless rate of interest for the next six months is 6%. Montgomery Brewster, an employee of the Brunswick Fund, calculates the no-arbitrage futures price as $F = (5,500 \times 10 - 1,300) \times 1.06 = £56,922$. This implies an arbitrage profit of £922 per contract on 30th September, or $922/1.06 = £869.81$ on 1st March. Montgomery buys one futures contract at a price of £56,000 and sells shares equivalent to one futures contract for $5,500 \times 10 = £55,000$ on 1st March. At the same time, Monty invests £1,300 to provide the money to pay the dividends on the shares he has sold short. These transactions produce a net cash inflow of £53,700, which Monty invests at 6% to produce 53,700×1.06 = £56,922 on 30th September. When the futures contract ends on 30th September he buys the shares he has sold short for £z and makes a gain on the future of £z−56,000. This results in a net cash inflow on that date of £922, which is equivalent to a gain of 922/1.06 = £869.81 on 1st March.

The next example incorporates initial margin payments (which earn interest) and trading limits.

Example. The current value of the FTSE 100 stock index is 5,000 and so the price of one unit of the index basket (S) is 5,000×10 = £50,000, while the current price of a FTSE 100 stock index futures contract for delivery in nine months (F) is also £50,000. The riskless rate of interest for a nine month period (r) is 8%, and the present value of the dividends on the shares in the index during this period (D) is £3,000. The no-arbitrage condition implies that the price of this futures contract should be (5,000×10−3,000)×1.08 = £50,760. Hence, this futures contract is under priced by £760, relative to the price of the underlying shares.

Scarlet O'Hara, the manageress of the Byker Fund, sells short £12 million worth of the shares (her trading limit) in the index, in proportion to their index weight. This is assumed to generate an immediate payment of £12 million which she invests at the risk free interest rate to give £960,000 by the delivery date. She then buys 12,000,000/(5,000×10) = 240 FTSE 100 index futures contracts. She must pay an initial margin of 240×1,500 = £360,000 which is assumed to bear interest at the risk free interest rate of 8% over nine months, i.e. £28,800. In order to finance the dividend payments on the shares she has sold, Scarlet borrows 240×3,000 = £720,000, which will cost £57,600 at the risk free interest rate. It is assumed there are no payments of variation margin.

At delivery Scarlet buys the shares she has sold short at the then market price (£z). The delivery price of the futures contracts is also £z, i.e. a net payment of $(S_T−F)$ per contract, or £z−(50,000×240) = £z−£12,000,000. She repays the loan plus interest taken out to cover the cost of dividends (i.e. £777,600), and receives repayment of her investment of £12 million plus interest and her initial margin plus interest (i.e. £388,800). She pays back the loan plus interest taken out to cover the initial margin i.e. £388,800.

The initial cash flows are:-

Share sale	+£12,000,000
Investment	−£12,000,000
Initial margin	−£360,000
Loan for initial margin	+£360,000
Dividend payments	−£720,000
Loan for dividend payments	+£720,000
Net cash flow	0

The cash flows at delivery are:-

Share purchase	−£z
Sale of futures contracts	+£z

Cost of futures contracts	-£12,000,000
Repayment of investment	+£12,000,000
Interest on investment (12,000,000×0.08)	+£960,000
Repayment of initial margin	+£360,000
Interest on initial margin (360,000×0.08)	+£28,800
Repayment of loan for initial margin	-£360,000
Interest on initial margin loan (360,000×0.08)	-£28,800
Repayment of dividend loan	-£720,000
Interest on dividend loan (600,000×0.08)	<u>-£57,600</u>
Net cash flow at delivery	+£182,400
Present value of the cash flows	+£168,889

Check. The instant arbitrage profit available from trading one FTSE 100 stock index futures contract is $(S-D)-F/(1+r)$ = (50,000-3,000)-50,000/1.08 = £703.7037. If 240 futures contracts are traded, the total arbitrage profit is 240×703.7037 = £168,889.

3.5 Early Unwinding of an Arbitrage Position

If at any time during the life of the arbitrage position the no-arbitrage condition is met, there is no need to wait until delivery to close out the arbitrage transactions. This means that some arbitrage positions may be closed out before delivery, so reducing the volume of potentially destabilising transactions on the stock market when the futures contract matures, see chapter 12.4.2 for a discussion of expiration effects. Rather than closing out the initial arbitrage position, an early unwinding can be viewed as establishing an equal and opposite arbitrage position to that taken initially, as shown in table 3.4. These two arbitrage positions then cancel out.

Table 3.4: Early Unwinding as the Sum of Two Arbitrage Trades

	Futures	Shares
Arbitrage the Initial **Over**pricing	Short	Long
Arbitrage the Subsequent **Under**pricing	Long	Short
Net Position	0	0

Example. Consider the above example of arbitrage involving Scarlet O'Hara. Three months after she established her arbitrage position, the FTSE 100 index has moved to 5,050, the risk free interest rate for the remaining period of the contract is 5.233% (and so the interest rate for the first three months is 1.08/1.05233-1.00 = 2.6294%), the present value of the dividend payments is £2,000 and the price of the futures contract has risen to its no-arbitrage value, i.e. (5,050×10-2,000) ×1.05233 = £51,038. Scarlet can choose to unwind her arbitrage transaction after three months and get the same profit as if she waited until delivery in six months time. It is assumed in this example, as it was in the derivation of the no-arbitrage condition, that the profit (or loss) from trading futures contracts is not realized until delivery. If the arbitrageur can realise their arbitrage profit earlier than at delivery, they can invest the proceeds to make a small additional profit, McMillan (1991). The initial cash flows are, as before:

Share sale	+£12,000,000
Investment	-£12,000,000
Initial margin	-£360,000
Loan for initial margin	+£360,000
Dividend payments	-£720,000
Loan for dividend payments	+£720,000
Net cash flow	0

The cash flows from closing out the short position in shares after three months are:-

Share purchase (5,050×10×240)	-£12,120,000
Repayment of investment	+£12,000,000
Interest on investment (2.6294%)	+£315,528
Repayment of dividend loan	-£720,000
Interest on dividend loan (2.6294%)	-£18,932
Unpaid dividends (2,000×240)	+£480,000
Net cash flow at three months	-£63,404

The cash flows at delivery from the two offsetting futures positions:-

Sale of futures contracts (51,038×240)	+£12,249,120
Cost of futures contracts	-£12,000,000
Repayment of initial margin	+£360,000
Interest on initial margin (8%)	+£28,800
Repayment of loan for initial margin	-£360,000
Interest on initial margin loan (8%)	-£28,800
Net cash flow at delivery	+£249,120

The net present value of these cash flows is $-£63,404/1.026294 +£249,120/1.08 = £168,887$. Allowing for rounding error, the profit from this early unwinding is the same as that from holding the arbitrage position to delivery. By unwinding early Scarlet has avoided the risk of being unable to close out the share position at the delivery price.

In the Scarlet O'Hara example, the arbitrage was unwound when the futures contract price moved to its no–arbitrage level. Early unwinding raises the possibility of making a profit from an arbitrage position, over and above the riskless arbitrage profit that was locked in initially. At any time before delivery the initial mispricing (which led to the creation of the arbitrage position) may be reversed, and a mispricing occur in the opposite direction. If this situation arises, early unwinding of the arbitrage position will lead to an additional riskless profit.

Suppose the initial arbitrage position involves an overpricing, with a long position in shares and a short position in futures. If there is subsequently an underpricing, this can be arbitraged by selling shares and buying futures. Assuming these two arbitrage positions are of equal size, arbitraging the underpricing effectively closes out (or unwinds early) the initial arbitrage position, i.e. the shares are sold and the short futures position is closed out by buying futures. Thus, an initial position is taken at time t and it is unwound at time u; the present value of the arbitrage profit per contract at the time of the initial arbitrage transaction is $\pi_t + \pi_u \times [(1+r_u)/(1+r_t)]$, where $\pi_t = F_t/(1+r_t) - (S_t - D_t)$, r_u is the riskless rate of interest between the time of the early unwinding and the delivery date, $\pi_u = F_u/(1+r_u) - (S_u - D_u)$ and the subscripts t and u denote variables at times t and u respectively.

Figure 3.2 shows that if the arbitrage of an overpricing in the near contract is unwound early at time A, the total arbitrage profit is the profit from the initial arbitrage (given by the distance OX at time 0) plus the profit from the arbitrage of an underpricing in the near contract at time A (i.e. AB at time A).

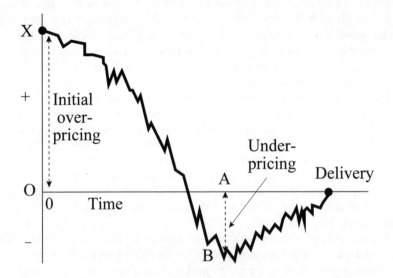

Figure 3.2: Early Unwinding

Example. Consider the Scarlet O'Hara example above of early unwinding. After three months, the FTSE 100 index has risen to 5,050, but the price of an index future is above its no-arbitrage price of £51,038 and is now £52,000. In this case an early unwinding will produce an additional profit as at the time the initial position was opened for N contracts of $N[F_t/(1+r_t) - (S_t - D_t)] \times [(1+r_u)/(1+r_t)]$ = $240 \times [52,000/1.05233 - (5,050 \times 10 - 2,000)] \times (1.05233/1.08) = £213,777$, making a total profit of £382,664.

3.5.1 Transactions Costs, Embedded Options and Risky Arbitrage

The main reason why early unwinding is beneficial is that the transactions costs are lower than for two separate arbitrage positions; primarily because the shares need only be traded once. For example, a person with an arbitrage position that is long in shares and short in futures (e.g. Lawrence Garfield) can take advantage of a subsequent relative undervaluation of futures contracts merely by liquidating their long position in shares and their short position in futures. There is no need for them to incur the transactions costs of creating (and subsequently liquidating) a short position in shares. The total transactions costs from an early unwinding are those for a single arbitrage transaction, and half the bid-ask spread for futures (as the futures position will be liquidated at either the bid or ask price, while delivery would have used the EDSP). Therefore, such arbitrageurs face lower transactions costs for a subsequent reversal of the initial mispricing than do other potential arbitrageurs.

In effect, the creation of the initial arbitrage position gives the arbitrageur the side benefit of an embedded option (American style, since it can be exercised at any time during the life of the futures contract) to arbitrage subsequent reverse mispricings at much reduced transactions costs. This leads to the problem of when to exercise the early unwinding option as, by delaying, the reverse mispricing may increase in size. Assuming that the mispricing follows a Brownian bridge, Duffie (1990) derived an early unwinding boundary for reverse mispricings. When the size of the reverse mispricing reaches this boundary (which drops to zero as delivery nears), the arbitrage should be unwound early. He also pointed out that it may be sensible to gradually unwind early. Bühler & Kempf (1994) demonstrate that the value of this early unwinding option increases with the time to maturity, and with the difference in transactions costs between establishing a new arbitrage position and unwinding an existing position. Kempf (1998) specified a model for making the early unwinding decision by assuming that mispricings follow a random walk, and that arbitrage trades have a linear effect on the mispricing. This model incorporates differential transactions costs for over and under pricings.

The presence of this embedded option opens up the possibility of risky arbitrage, i.e. the initiation of an arbitrage position when the current mispricing is insufficient to cover transactions costs, in the expectation that the mispricing will subsequently be reversed and can be unwound early at a net profit.

A further benefit of early unwinding occurs when the total size of the positions taken by an arbitrageur is limited by the amount of capital available to them for such purposes (Brennan & Schwartz, 1988). Early unwinding frees up capital for use in another arbitrage transaction, so raising the annual rate of return on such capital.

3.5.2 Empirical Evidence on Early Unwinding

USA.   Brennan & Schwartz (1990) examined the profitability of a strategy to unwind arbitrage positions early, where the presence of the early unwinding option affects the initial decision to initiate an arbitrage position. This might occur when the initial mispricing was not quite large enough to cover transactions costs, but the trader decided to open a (risky) arbitrage position in the expectation that the initial mispricing would be reversed and the combined profits from the initial arbitrage and the early unwinding would be sufficient to more than offset the total transactions costs. Brennan & Schwartz used prices every fifteen minutes on the S&P500 from 1983 to 1987, and found that their trading strategy produced an average profit (after transactions costs) of one index point per futures contract in the initial arbitrage position.

Merrick (1988b) used daily closing prices for the S&P500 from 1982 to 1986. He tested the performance of two simple trading rules for the establishment and early unwinding of arbitrage positions. Relative to a strategy of holding the arbitrage positions to delivery, the early unwinding strategies produced an increase in profits of 52% and 78%.

Finnerty & Park (1988a) considered the profits (before transactions costs) from the early unwinding of arbitrage positions in the MMI, and found that if an arbitrage was unwound when the initial mispricing was reversed, the profits were considerably larger than if the arbitrage position was held until delivery.

Habeeb, Hill & Rzad (1991) considered data at 5-minute intervals for the S&P500 from December 1987 to June 1990. An arbitrage was entered when the mispricing was sufficient to cover the transactions costs of a buy and hold arbitrage plus the required entry profit. Early unwinding occurred when the mispricing reversal was large enough to cover the additional transactions costs plus the required exit profit. In each case the trading signal had to persist for two consecutive 5-minute periods. They found that the highest returns came from requiring an entry profit of 0.8 to 0.9 S&P500 index points, and an exit profit of 0.2 to 0.4 index points. This study highlights the need for arbitrageurs to set entry and exit profit levels.

Sofianos (1993) studied 1,442 trades establishing an index arbitrage position in the S&P500 over the period January to July 1990. He found that the average expected arbitrage profit, after allowing for transactions costs, was negative at −5.7 index basis points. On average, the mispricing was reversed within one day, and two thirds of the arbitrage positions were unwound early. Since the average arbitrage profit, after deducting transactions costs, was 4.7 index basis points, the early unwinding option was worth at least 10.4 index basis points.

Neal (1995) analyzed 837 arbitrage trades on the NYSE in the first three months of 1989. Only 7 arbitrage trades were liquidated at the delivery of the March 1989 contract. Using minute by minute data, he estimated a logit regression model, where the occurrence of an arbitrage trade was explained by the current absolute mispricing, the largest mispricing reversal over the next 24 hours, the number of days to delivery and the current bid-ask spread for the S&P500 basket. He obtained significantly positive coefficients for the absolute mispricing and the mispricing reversal, but a significantly negative coefficient for the number of days to delivery. The results for the mispricing reversal support the view that, when the volatility of the mispricing is high, the early unwinding option is more valuable, and so arbitrageurs are more likely to initiate an arbitrage position.

Germany.   Based on some simplifying assumptions, Kempf (1998) developed a model of the early unwinding problem which can be solved numerically to give the quantity of index baskets to trade in each time period, and so solves the problem of precisely when to unwind early. He tested this model on quote data every 5 minutes for the DAX from 1990-92.

Finland.   Puttonen (1993a) used daily data on the Finnish FOX index from May 1988 to December 1990. He found low additional profits (6% of arbitrage profits) from unwinding early. However, this finding may be due to the strategy of not requiring any exit profit.

These empirical studies have shown that early unwinding can be very valuable, which suggests that it should be an important market phenomenon. This is conformed by Sofianos (1991, 1993) who reported that in the first half of 1990, two-thirds of the arbitrage transactions in S&P500 futures were unwound early.

3.5.3 Path Dependence in Mispricings

As well as increasing the profits of individual arbitrageurs, early unwinding by many arbitrageurs can tend to reduce or eliminate reverse mispricings. It is likely that early unwinding will tend to eliminate reverse mispricings before the transactions cost boundary is crossed and it becomes worthwhile establishing new arbitrage positions. This introduces path dependence into the mispricing series, in that once a mispricing has become sufficiently large to overcome transactions costs, the early unwinding of the resulting arbitrage positions will tend to prevent a large mispricing in the opposite direction, i.e. history matters. This is illustrated in figure 3.3 for positive mispricings (an equivalent diagram could be drawn for negative mispricings).

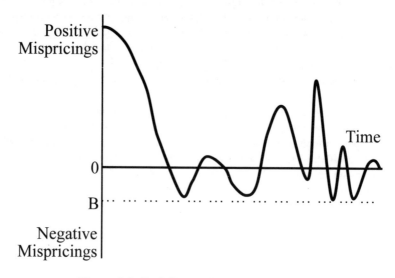

Figure 3.3: Path Dependence of Mispricings

Figure 3.3 shows that, since the initial mispricing was positive, when this mispricing is reversed as far as B, some of the initial arbitrageurs will unwind early, so tending to push the mispricing back towards zero. As a result, the mispricing will not become more negative than B so long as arbitrageurs remain with positions they can unwind early. However, once all such positions have been unwound, the reverse mispricing can then increase to the level given by the transactions costs of a new arbitrage position. Such behaviour may create arbitrage thresholds, which are examined in chapter 5.6.

This path dependence has been examined empirically by MacKinlay & Ramaswamy (1988) using data on the S&P500 from April 1982 to June 1987. They computed a series of mispricings (before transactions costs) every fifteen minutes and investigated the tendency for a particular contract to have either mostly violations of the upper bound of the no-arbitrage band, or mostly violations of the lower boundary. They found there was a strong tendency for mispricings in excess of the transactions costs to be either all overpricings, or all underpricings, so providing clear evidence in favour of path dependence. For the DAX, Kempf (1998) also found evidence supporting path dependence.

3.6 Delayed Unwinding (or Rollover) of an Arbitrage Position

In a standard arbitrage transaction, the share holding is liquidated when the futures contract matures. However, instead of liquidating the share position at maturity, if one of the futures contracts that remain outstanding (e.g. the far contract) is mispriced in the same direction as the initial arbitrage, a new arbitrage position can be established by closing out the initial futures position and replacing it with a position of similar size and direction in the far contract. Since there is no need to trade shares, the only transactions costs involved in this new arbitrage position are those for trading the futures. Thus, establishing an arbitrage position gives the additional embedded option to delay unwinding by rolling over the arbitrage at maturity with very low additional transactions costs.

Table 3.5 shows that the arbitrage of an over-pricing in the near contract can be converted into an arbitrage of an over-pricing in the far contract without the need to trade any shares; as the initial long position in shares is also appropriate for arbitraging the over-pricing in the far contract. All that is required is to close out the short position in the near contract, and establish a short position in the far contract.

Table 3.5: Delayed Unwinding of an Over-pricing

	Near Future	Far Future	Shares
Initial **Over**-pricing in the Near	Short	0	Long
Unwind the Near Arbitrage	Long	0	*Short*
Arbitrage the Far **Over**-pricing	0	Short	*Long*
Net Position	0	Short	Long

Example. Charlie Allnutt, the manager of the Caversham Fund, had an arbitrage position which involved a long position in the shares of the FTSE 100 index. At the delivery date for the futures in this arbitrage (28th June), these shares had a market value of £12 million, while the value of the index was 4,800 index points. On this date, the September contract was overpriced by £60 per contract, while the transactions costs of arbitrage (buying and subsequently selling the shares, and selling the futures) were £100 per contract. Therefore, no arbitrage opportunity in the September contract existed for a trader who had to incur a full set of transactions costs. However, provided the cost of trading a futures contract was less than £60, Charlie could profitably arbitrage the September contract by selling 12,000,000/(4,800×10) = 250 September contracts and retaining the £12 million share portfolio.

A delayed unwinding can occur at maturity; but usually the initial arbitrage is unwound early, generating an additional profit or loss. This is illustrated in figure 3.4 which shows that at time B the initial overpricing of OX in the near contract has reversed to become an underpricing of BC, while at time B there is an overpricing in the far contract of AB. Therefore, if an arbitrageur rolls over their arbitrage position into the far contract (i.e. closes out their short position in the near contract, and establishes a similarly sized short position in the far contract) they will make a total arbitrage profit of OX at time O, and AB + BC = AC at time B. This is made up of the initial arbitrage (OX), the gain from arbitraging the reverse mispricing (BC) at time B (early unwinding), and the profit from arbitraging the far contract at time B (AB).

If the initial mispricing has been reversed, while the far contract is mispriced in the same direction as the initial mispricing, an early unwinding and rollover will be profitable, before transactions costs, as in figure 3.4. If the initial mispricing has not been reversed and the far contract is mispriced in the same direction as the initial mispricing, provided the mispricing of the far contract is larger than the current mispricing of the contract used in the arbitrage, an early unwinding and rollover will be profitable, before transactions costs. This is illustrated in figure 3.5, which indicates that if the initial arbitrage of the overpricing is rolled into the far contract at time C, the arbitrageur will make an additional profit of AB at time C. This is made up of a loss of BC from an early unwinding of the arbitrage position in the near contract, and a profit of AC from the arbitrage of the overpricing in the far contract.

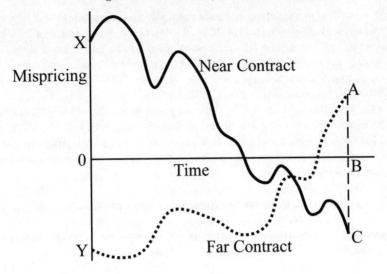

Figure 3.4: Rollover 1

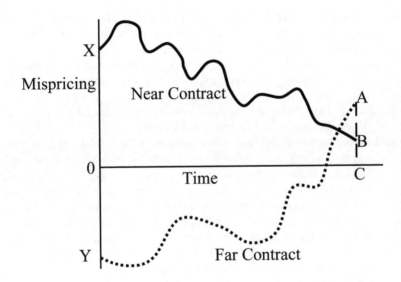

Figure 3.5: Rollover 2

Example. On 11th February the value of the FTSE 100 index was 4,700, while the price of March futures was 4,800 index points. Since the interest rate until delivery in March was 1.5% and the present value of the dividends on the shares corresponding to one futures contract was £300; the no-arbitrage value of a March contract on 11th February was $(4,700 \times 10 - 300) \times 1.015 = £47,400$. Thus, the March contract was overpriced. If the present value of the transactions costs of an arbitrage for overpriced futures (i.e. long in shares and short in futures) was £200 per contract, the net arbitrage profit was $(48,000/1.015) - (4,700 \times 10 - 300) - 200 = £390.64$ per contract.

On 11th February Rose Sayer, the manageress of the Charvil Fund, sold twenty FTSE 100 March contracts at £48,000 each, and invested $20 \times 4,700 \times 10 = £940,000$ in a basket of shares corresponding to the FTSE 100 index. By 1st March the index had risen to 4,750, and the data for the three nearest outstanding contracts were as follows:-

Table 3.6: Data for the Rose Sayer Example - 1st March

Futures Contract	Dividends	Interest Rate	Market Price	No-arbitrage Price	Mispricing
Mar.	£200	1%	4,750	£47,773	-£273
Jun.	£800	4%	4,900	£48,568	£432
Sep.	£1,400	7%	5,000	£49,327	£673

On 1st March Rose considered three alternative strategies: (a) hold the existing arbitrage position to delivery, (b) unwind the existing arbitrage and roll it over into the June contract, or (c) unwind the existing arbitrage and roll it over into the September contract. Rose did not consider the December contract, as the volume of trading was too low. The present values of these strategies, as at 11th February, were:-

(a) $£390.64 \times 20 = £7,813$ net profit, after allowing for the transactions costs of selling the futures, and buying and selling the shares.

(b) The extra gross profit from the early unwinding $= N[(S_u - D_m) - F_m/(1+r_m)]$ $\times [(1+r_m)/(1+r_t)] = 20 \times [(4,750 \times 10 - 200) - 47,500/1.01] \times (1.01/1.015) = £5,379$. S_u is the spot price at the time of the early unwinding, D_m, D_j and D_s are the present values at the time of the early unwinding of the dividends from holding one unit of the index until the March, June or September delivery date, F_m, F_j and F_s are the prices of the March, June and September futures contracts at the time of the early unwinding, r_m, r_j and r_s are the riskless interest rates between the time of the early unwinding and the March, June and September delivery dates. If the extra transaction costs payable on trading the futures is £40 per contract, the net increase in profit is $£5,379 - (20 \times 40) = £4,579$.

The extra gross profit from rolling over into the June contract $= N[F_j/(1+r_j) - (S_u - D_j)] \times [(1+r_m)/(1+r_t)] = 20 \times [49,000/1.04 - (4,750 \times 10 - 800)] \times (1.01/1.015) = £8,267$. If the transactions costs of trading a futures contract are £40, the net profit as at 11th February is $8,267 - (20 \times 40) = £7,467$. This gives a total net profit of $7,813 + 4,579 + 7,467 = £19,859$.

(c) The extra gross profit from rolling over into the September contract = $N[F_s/(1+r_s) - (S_u - D_s)] \times [(1+r_m)/(1+r_f)]$ = $20 \times [50,000/1.07 - (4,750 \times 10 - 1,400)] \times (1.01/1.015) = £12,517$. If the transactions costs of trading a futures contract are £40, the net profit is $£12,517 - (20 \times 40) = £11,717$. This gives a total net profit as at 11th February of $7,813 + 4,579 + 12,517 = £24,909$.

Rose concluded that her most profitable policy was to unwind her existing arbitrage, and rollover into an arbitrage on the September contract. She did not consider the possibility that, if she waited, an even more profitable strategy may become available.

The are two final situations when early unwinding or rollover is not attractive. Figure 3.6 shows a situation where unwinding the initial arbitrage early results in a loss of AC, which is partially offset by a profit of BC on arbitraging the far contract. The result is a net loss of AB. In figure 3.7 there is a loss on both unwinding the initial arbitrage early and on arbitraging the far contract. In each of these cases, the trader may choose to leave the initial arbitrage position intact, and initiate an unrelated arbitrage in the far contract if the mispricing exceeds their transactions costs for a new arbitrage.

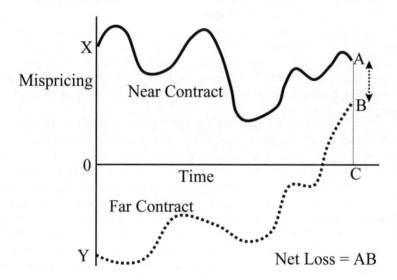

Figure 3.6: Do Nothing 1

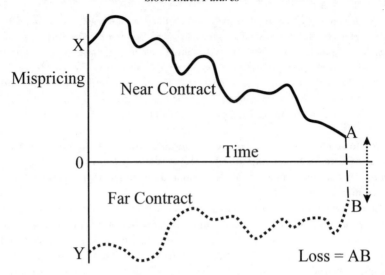

Figure 3.7: Do Nothing 2

The decision at any moment in time whether to unwind early, rollover or do
nothing is summarized in figure 3.8. (Note that for each outcome in figure 3.8 at the
end of this chapter, the arbitrageur should also consider a new arbitrage position in the
far contract, unconnected with the initial position established in the near contract.) In
addition, the arbitrageur has to deal with the dynamic problem that, although a current
early unwinding or rollover is profitable, profits may be higher if the decision is
delayed. Of course early unwinding or rollover could also become less profitable if the
arbitrageur delays action.

UK.   Yadav & Pope (1990) used daily data on the FTSE 100 from 1984
to 1988 to simulate the profits on four different trading rules: arbitrage, arbitrage with
early unwinding, arbitrage with rollover and arbitrage with both early unwinding and
rollover. They found the option to unwind early or rollover was usually exercised, and
led to a considerable increase in arbitrage profits, after allowing for transactions costs.
They also investigated risky arbitrage, where arbitrage positions are entered at a loss
in the expectation that the profits from either early unwinding or rollover will more
than compensate for this loss. Using data for the FTSE 100, they discovered that risky
arbitrage can lead to a substantial reduction in the size of mispricing required to show
an expected net profit, e.g. by 60%. Such returns appear to be large enough to offset
the likely risks.

Yadav & Pope (1994) used hourly data for the FTSE 100 from April 1986 to
March 1990 to replicate their earlier paper which simulated the profits from four
different trading rules. They examined two alternative levels of transactions costs for
arbitrage that is held to delivery: 0.25% and 0.75%. The initial arbitrage position was

also required to show an entry profit of at least 0.25%, as was any subsequent early unwinding or rollover. They also allowed for a one hour trading lag, as well as producing results with no trading lag. Table 3.7 gives the average profit, after transactions costs, from an arbitrage position involving one futures contract. This shows that early unwinding or rollover can lead to a substantial rise in arbitrage profits, e.g. for transactions costs of 0.75% and a one hour trading lag, rollover increased profits by 123%. Yadav & Pope (1994) also found that, when early unwinding and rollover are considered, only 3% of arbitrage positions were held to delivery. In consequence, arbitrage is unlikely to create any increase in spot volatility when the EDSP is calculated, see chapter 12.4.2 for a discussion of increases in volatility at delivery. Table 3.7 shows that the introduction of a one hour trading lag reduces, but does not eliminate, arbitrage profits.

Table 3.7: Average Profit per Futures Contract from Four Alternative Arbitrage Strategies

Arbitrage Strategy*	No Lag	One Hour Lag
Transactions Costs of 0.25%		
Hold to Delivery	£544.4	£278.7
Unwind Early	£728.3	£367.9
Rollover	£1,006.7	£417.2
Unwind Early & Rollover	£988.3	£414.8
Transactions Costs of 0.75%		
Hold to Delivery	£154.5	£52.0
Unwind Early	£220.1	£91.7
Rollover	£286.9	£116.1
Unwind Early & Rollover	£281.5	£119.3

* Allowance was made for the additional transactions costs of early unwinding and rollover.

Yadav & Pope (1994) used their hourly data to repeat their earlier simulation of risky arbitrage. They considered initiating an arbitrage when the proportionate mispricing exceeded a threshold (0.5% or 1.0%), while the trader's transactions costs for an arbitrage held to delivery were in excess of their threshold by 0.25%, 0.50%, 0.75% or 1.00%, that is, a potentially negative entry profit. In each case the arbitrage strategy included early unwinding or rollover as soon as the additional profit from early unwinding or rollover made the arbitrage profitable, after allowance for the additional transactions costs. Thus, the required exit profit was set equal to the loss on entry. Profits were made because the data was hourly and, when the position was unwound or rolled over, the price had usually moved some way beyond its break even level. Table 3.8 gives the average profit per futures contract traded, as well as the percentage of occasions on which the risky arbitrage was profitable. This reveals that, even when the arbitrageur's transactions costs exceeded the mispricing by 1%, over 70% of the risky arbitrage trades were profitable. It should be noted that table 3.8 presents the average profit per trade, and there will be more simulated trades in a given time period when there is risky arbitrage. Yadav & Pope (1994) concluded that risky arbitrage reduced the size of the no-arbitrage band by over 60%.

Table 3.8: Profitability of Risky Arbitrage[*]

	Transaction Costs in Excess of Threshold			
	0.25%	0.50%	0.75%	1.00%
Average Profit per Futures Contract				
0.5% threshold	£508.7	£367.3	£241.7	£69.3
1.0% threshold	£172.8	£138.4	£107.1	£91.3
Percentage of Profitable Trades				
0.5% threshold	96.9%	93.1%	84.0%	72.9%
1.0% threshold	99.5%	96.3%	88.6%	83.6%

* Allowance was made for the additional transactions costs of early unwinding and rollover.

Strickland & Xu (1993) considered hourly data on the FTSE 100 from January 1988 to December 1989. They examined the extra profits from unwinding early when the reverse mispricing covered the additional transactions costs, and from rollover when the difference in the mispricing of the two contracts covered the additional transactions costs. The profits, which are much larger than those obtained by Yadav & Pope (1994), are shown in table 3.9. Three levels of transactions cost for buy and hold arbitrage were used: 0.5%, 1.0% and 1.5%. Again, the additional profits from early unwinding and rollover are substantial, and were sometimes more than double the average profit from a buy and hold arbitrage.

Table 3.9: Average Profit per Contract from Four Alternative Arbitrage Strategies

Arbitrage Strategy[*]	Transactions Costs		
	0.5%	1.0%	1.5%
Hold to Delivery	£1894.8	£1169.5	230.3
Unwind Early	£2956.3	£1430.3	£366.8
Rollover	£3223.8	£2481.0	£1516.3
Unwind Early or Rollover	£3923.3	£2495.3	£1516.3

* Allowance was made for the additional transactions costs of early unwinding and rollover.

Finland.   Puttonen (1993a) calculated the additional profit from rollover in the last week of the life of FOX futures contracts over the period May 1988 to December 1990. Using daily data, substantial profits were found to exist (about two thirds the size of the pure arbitrage profit), even though no exit profit was required.

3.7 Synthetic Futures Contracts

Futures contracts can always be replicated using the spot market and riskless borrowing and lending, provided the assumptions listed in chapter 5 apply. Thus, buying one unit of the underlying asset (the index) at time 0 for £S and simultaneously borrowing £S at the interest rate r for repayment at time T, means that the trader has one unit of the underlying asset at time T and must pay £$S(1+r)$ at that time. As dividends are received on the shares in the index, they are invested in riskless bonds to produce £$D(1+r)$ at time T. Hence the net cost of this strategy at time T is £$S(1+r)-D(1+r) = (S-D) \times (1+r)$. This is equivalent to buying a futures contract at time 0 for delivery at time T and, by arbitrage, this should cost £$(S-D) \times (1+r)$. The delivery date T is not restricted to the delivery dates of the futures contract, and can be chosen to suit the needs of the trader. It is also possible to create synthetic futures contracts using options. Therefore, even if the relevant futures market does not exist, portfolio managers can still use futures in the management of their portfolios by the construction of synthetic futures. Of course, all the assumptions underlying the derivation of the no-arbitrage condition may not apply, and so synthetic futures will only be approximations to actual futures. In which case, some of the advantages of using futures may be lost.

3.8 Other Forms of Arbitrage

Arbitrage relationships exist between index futures and any other relevant security, or set of securities.

3.8.1 Futures-Options Arbitrage

As well as spot-futures arbitrage, arbitrage is also possible between the futures and options markets. The well known put-call parity relationship for European style index options is that $C = P - K/(1+r) + S - D$, where C and P are the prices of European style call and put options on the index respectively, and every option has a strike price of K. The current value of the index basket of shares is S, the interest rate between now and expiry is r, while D is the present value of the dividends on the index over the period between now and expiry. The no-arbitrage price of an index future that expires at the same time as the index options is $F = (S-D)(1+r)$. This gives the no-arbitrage condition between the futures and options markets: $F = (C-P)(1+r)+K$. Note that dividends do not appear in this condition, and this facilitates its empirical examination.

This form of arbitrage does not suffer from short selling restrictions, and the complication of a tax timing option is usually absent.

USA.   This arbitrage relationship was studied by Lee & Nayar (1993) using transactions data from November 1989 to June 1991 for S&P500 futures and S&P500 European style index options. They analysed 1,900 synchronous observations for both markets and found that, if allowance is made for a trading lag of longer than one minute, there were no futures-options arbitrage profits (after transactions costs), and so these two markets were highly integrated.

In a study of 701 daily closing prices for the S&P500 in 1993, Fung & Chan (1994) also found no evidence of mispricings, relative to a transactions cost threshold of 0.5%.

Sternberg (1994) used transactions data for the S&P500 for two months in 1983. After allowing for delays in the time stamping of trades, he still found a large number of mispricings that exceeded any likely transactions costs. Similarly Figlewski (1988), who used closing prices for the 1983-84 period for the NYSE Composite, found substantial arbitrage opportunities. However, the data for these two studies was generated shortly after index futures started trading, and the arbitrage opportunities may have been due to inexperience.

Hong Kong   Fung & Fung (1997) used transactions data on the Hang Seng for 1993-95 and studied triplets of European style call and put options and futures trades within the same minute. After allowing for transactions costs they found some arbitrage opportunities, particularly in longer maturity, away-from-the-money options. However, these opportunities were not economically significant.

Fung, Cheng & Chan (1997) also used one-minute triplets of European style call and put options and futures trades for the Hang Seng for 1993-95. Allowing for transactions costs and a trading lag, they did not find evidence of profitable arbitrage opportunities.

As previously, Cheng, Fung & Pang (1998) used one-minute triplets of European style call and put options and futures trades for the Hang Seng for 1993-95. Allowing for transactions costs, they found no arbitrage profits. When they introduced the early unwinding option, there were a small number of modest arbitrage profits for trades conducted with a trading lag of 5 minutes or less.

Bae, Chan & Cheung (1998) compare the arbitrage opportunities for the Hang Seng revealed using bid-ask data and trade data from 1993-94. They argue that bid-ask quotes avoid the bias inherent in trade prices, and find a dramatic reduction in the number of arbitrage opportunities. However, a similar study by Fung & Mok (2001) using data for 1994-95 found that the switch to bid-ask quotes increased the number of arbitrage opportunities. This difference may be due to Bae, Chan & Cheung (1998) using a price matching interval of ten minutes, while Fung & Mok (2001) used only one minute. Using similar data, Fung & Mok (2003) found that introducing the early unwinding option increased arbitrage profits by 50%.

Cheng, Fung & Chan (2000) looked for arbitrage opportunities during the Asian crisis of 1997-98 and the intervention by the Hong Kong government in the stock market in August 1998. They used trade data for the Hang Seng from 1996-98, and analysed one-minute triplets of European style call and put options and futures trades. They found that even during these periods of increased volatility, while mispricings increased in magnitude, after allowing for transactions costs and a trading lag, there were few arbitrage opportunities.

These findings are supported by Cheng & White (2003) who looked at arbitrage opportunities during volatile periods. Using one-minute triplets of trade prices in the Hang Seng for 1993-98, they found that when the market is volatile, the time between trades increases and the number and size of arbitrage opportunities also increase. But when allowance is made for trading lag, the increase in arbitrage opportunities is counteracted by the increase in the trading lags, and minimal arbitrage profits are achieved.

UK. Liouliou (1995) used synchronous daily closing prices from February 1992 to February 1995 on FTSE 100 futures and FTSE 100 European style options. The options prices were split into three levels of 'moneyness' using the definition $M_t \equiv S_t/K_t$, where S_t is the spot price, and K_t is the strike price. For call options, at-the-money was $0.95 \leq M_t < 1.05$, in-the-money was $0.85 < M_t < 0.95$, and out-of-the-money was $1.05 \leq M_t < 1.15$. For put options, the definitions of moneyness for in-the-money and out-of-the-money options were reversed. She allowed for transactions costs of between 0.2% and 0.7%. For transactions costs of 0.7%, the proportion of observations outside the no-arbitrage band for the near futures contract (and matching options contract) were 36% for in-the-money options (mostly due to the futures being relatively overpriced), 15% for at-the-money options, and 73% for out-of-the money options (mostly due to the futures being relatively underpriced). There was a strong maturity effect, with most of the mispricings occurring before the final delivery month. Exploitable violations of the no-arbitrage condition only occurred with any frequency for out-of-the-money options, and may have been due to thin trading in these options. These violations appear to have decreased over time.

Draper & Fung (2002) matched the European style put and call and futures prices for the FTSE 100 contracts to within one minute, using data for 1991-98. After allowing for transaction costs and trading lags, they found a small number of arbitrage opportunities. These were concentrated in at-the-money options and disappeared within about 3 minutes. They found that the early unwinding of a futures-options arbitrage was sometimes profitable.

Spain. Balbás, Longarela & Pardo (2000) used 1 minute returns for 1997 on Ibex 35 futures and European style options on Ibex 35 futures. They found some arbitrage opportunities during a period when the market was stable, and substantially more opportunities during a more volatile period.

3.8.2 Spread Arbitrage

Where two (or more) exchanges trade a future on the same index, it may be possible to arbitrage between the two futures, Board & Sutcliffe (1996), see chapter 11.11.

3.9 Conclusions

This chapter has used arbitrage (and some powerful assumptions) to derive a formula for the valuation of index futures. Various restatements of this no-arbitrage condition were also presented. Then, trading strategies to take advantage of under and overpriced futures were considered. The possibilities of early and delayed unwinding of arbitrage positions were examined, and finally some other forms of arbitrage were explained.

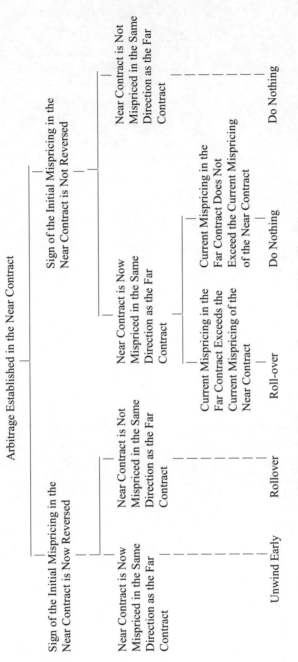

Figure 3.8: The Early Unwinding or Rollover Decision

Chapter 4

Arbitrage in Practice

Introduction

The theory of arbitrage pricing contains a number of predictions about market behaviour. These include predictions that the no-arbitrage condition should generally apply, and when it ceases to apply this should promptly trigger index arbitrage transactions which rapidly eliminate the deviation from the no-arbitrage condition. Since their introduction in 1982, there has been a steady flow of empirical studies of index arbitrage, and these studies will be considered in the first two sections of this chapter. The first section is a review of the empirical evidence on the degree to which actual futures prices deviate from the theoretical prices given by the no-arbitrage condition of chapter 3. This is followed by a discussion of the available evidence on the speed and size of the arbitrage response to a violation of the no-arbitrage condition. The third section considers the link between mispricings and spot volatility. Finally, there is a discussion of some of the practicalities of arbitrage.

4.1 Over or Underpriced Futures?

The evidence on the extent to which actual index futures prices depart from the values predicted by the no-arbitrage condition generally supports the view that economically significant departures do exist. Before considering the empirical studies, some of the terms used will be explained. If the actual futures price is less than the no-arbitrage futures price, the future is said to be underpriced, and the arbitrageur buys futures and sells shares. If the actual futures price exceeds the no-arbitrage futures price, the future is overpriced and the arbitrageur sells futures and buys shares. In addition, many studies use the term 'mispricing'. While the definition of a mispricing differs between authors, it usually refers to the actual less the no-arbitrage futures price, and is often deflated by either the spot price or the no-arbitrage futures price. In a few cases the mispricing incorporates transactions costs. If the mispricing (not allowing for transactions costs) exceeds the relevant transactions costs, an arbitrage opportunity exists.

4.1.1 Empirical Results

The empirical evidence presented below is classified by country.

USA. For the S&P500 index for 1982, the no-arbitrage condition was found by Cornell & French (1983a, 1983b) to overpredict the actual price of index futures contracts, and so the future was underpriced. A subsequent study by Cornell (1985a) analyzed the values of ten S&P500 contracts for the period 1982-3, and found no general pattern of underpricing. He concluded that the no-arbitrage condition is supported by the empirical evidence, and that the earlier underpricing may be explained by the newness of the market and the inexperience of the participants, or by the tax timing option becoming unimportant. (The tax timing option is described in chapter 5.4.)

Kipnis & Tsang (1984b) analyzed the S&P500 index for 1982-3 and, after allowing for transaction costs, found a considerable number of departures from the no-arbitrage condition, with both over and underpricing being present. Overall, they found a greater tendency to underpricing.

Figlewski (1984a) used data on the S&P500 index for 1982-3. He found underpricing for the first third of his data period, and overpricing for the remainder. For the entire period he found that, on average, the no-arbitrage condition was approximately correct.

Billingsley & Chance (1988) analyzed weekly data for 1982-6 for the S&P500 index. In contrast to the findings of Cornell (1985a) and Figlewski (1984a), they found that for April 1982 to September 1983 there was overpricing, while for October 1983 to January 1986 there was underpricing. For the entire period, Billingsley & Chance (1988) found overpricing.

Merrick (1987) studied daily data on the S&P500 and NYSE Composite indices. He also found that, for 1982-6, there was underpricing.

Arditti, Ayaydin, Mattu & Rigsbee (1986) argued that, in the initial years of trading, S&P500 index futures were underpriced. They compared the actual returns on sixty US mutual funds for the three year period (1982-84) with the returns that would have been made if a specified strategy for investing in S&P500 futures had been followed. This strategy was to devote 20% of the fund to buying futures when they were underpriced by a specified amount; closing out these futures positions when the futures were overpriced by the same amount. For all but two of the sixty mutual funds, this strategy increased returns over the three year period, suggesting that prices deviated from the no-arbitrage condition.

Bhatt & Cakici (1990) considered daily closing prices for the S&P500 for 1982-7. They found that futures tended to be overpriced, and that the average size of the mispricing tended to drop over time. This study appears not to have allowed for transactions costs.

MacKinlay & Ramaswamy (1988) used data on the S&P500 to compute a series of mispricings at fifteen minute intervals for 1982-7. They found that, on average, the futures were overpriced by 0.12% (before allowing for transactions costs).

Klemkosky & Lee (1991) studied transactions data on the S&P500 for 1983-7. They allowed for marking to the market, transactions costs (which differed between institutions and members, and between long and short positions) and for capital gains, income and futures taxes. This produced a no-arbitrage band, which depended on the status and tax position of the arbitrageur. Klemkosky & Lee looked for a mispricing every ten minutes and found that, even for the arbitrageurs with the largest no-arbitrage band (taxed institutional investors), the no-arbitrage band was violated 5% of the time. The frequency and degree of overpricing of the future was much larger than for underpricing. They also found that, if a trading lag of ten minutes was incorporated, arbitrage remained profitable for all classes of arbitrageur.

Chen, Cuny & Haugen (1995) used daily synchronous prices for the S&P500 for 1986-90. The mispricings were, on average, negative, indicating underpricing.

Neal (1995) analyzed 837 S&P500 arbitrage trades on the NYSE in the 3 month period of January to March 1989. Roughly two thirds of the trades were buying shares and selling futures, and one third were selling shares and buying futures. The average gross profit per trade (ignoring the time value of money, and assuming no trading lag and that the position was held to delivery) was 0.31% for overpricings, and 0.32% for underpricings. For these arbitrage trades to have been profitable implies that transactions costs were very low. During this period the average bid-ask spread for the S&P500 index basket was 0.64%, and so the gross arbitrage profit was just half the bid-ask spread. Thus the expected profits which triggered these arbitrage trades were very small.

Dwyer, Locke & Yu (1996) used minute to minute prices on the S&P500 for 1982-90. Unlike most previous studies, they managed to compute mispricings without estimating dividends and interest rates. They specified the no-arbitrage condition as $F = Se^{(\pi-\omega)h}$, where ω, is the continuous dividend rate, π is the continuously compounded annual risk free rate of interest, and h is the time in years until delivery. If the actual futures price is $F_A = Se^{(\pi-\omega)h}m$, where m is the proportionate mispricing $(F_A-F)/F-1$. Taking logarithms of the equation for the actual futures price gives $\ln F_A = \ln S + (\pi-\omega)h + \ln m$. Within the course of a day the entitlement to dividends and interest payments will be unchanged, and so the term $(\pi-\omega)h$ is constant (k). If it is assumed that over each day the average proportionate mispricing is zero, then the expected value of $\ln m$ is zero. In which case the expected log futures price for each day is given by $E[\ln F_A] = E[\ln S] + k$. Substituting for k, the log proportionate mispricings can now be written as $\ln m = (\ln F_A - E[\ln F_A]) - (\ln S - E[\ln S])$. Therefore, if the expected futures and spot prices are measured by their means, the proportionate mispricings can be estimated using only the actual futures and spot prices, making the analysis much easier. They found evidence that the distribution of mispricings (after allowing for autocorrelation, but not transactions costs) was symmetric around zero. This supports the view that over and underpricings are equally likely.

On 24th June 1997, the NYSE reduced its minimum price change for stocks from an eighth of a dollar to a sixteenth. Henker & Martens (2005) examined arbitrage trades involving S&P500 futures for the six months before and after this rule change. The reduction in the tick size for stocks led to a decline in stock spreads; and this lowering of transactions costs affected arbitrage activity. The average size of each arbitrage trade fell from $16.5 million to $13.8 million, while the number of stocks per arbitrage rose from 355 to 379. The reduction in trade size may be due to the drop in market depth after the tick change; while the increase in the number of stocks is probably due to the reduction in transactions costs for small trades. Allowing for higher market volatility after the tick size reduction, the average mispricing required to trigger an arbitrage trade fell; while the mean reversion in mispricings became stronger. Therefore the size and duration of mispricings was reduced by this regulation-induced drop in transactions costs.

Morse (1988) looked for mispricings of S&P500, NYSE Composite and MMI index futures using daily closing prices for 1986-8. For 1986, each of the three index futures was underpriced, while for 1987 and 1988 only the MMI was significantly underpriced. He also considered the relationship between mispricings of index futures and mispricings of S&P 100 index options, and discovered a contemporaneous correlation between changes in the futures mispricing for each of the three index futures and changes in the mispricing of S&P 100 options.

The MMI was studied by Finnerty & Park (1988a), who found that profitable arbitrage opportunities existed and, while they did not explicitly consider transactions costs, that the arbitrage profits were large enough to cover such costs.

Chung (1991) analyzed transactions data for the MMI future and its twenty constituent shares for 1984-6. Every second he used the latest futures and share prices to compute the size of any deviations from the no-arbitrage condition. If a mispricing exceeds one of three different levels of transactions costs, this constituted a signal to engage in arbitrage. Many previous studies have assumed it is possible to establish an arbitrage position at the prices used to compute the mispricing. This is unrealistic, and Chung considered trading lags of twenty seconds, two minutes and five minutes. The inclusion of such trading lags makes the arbitrage risky, as the mispricing at the time the arbitrage position is established is unknown when the decision to trade is taken. He found that the number of mispricing signals has declined substantially over time. Allowance for trading lags led to clear reductions in the average arbitrage profit, and these profits were risky, e.g. many of the realized profits were negative. Over time, these arbitrage profits have become riskier, and their average size has declined. Chung found that only 7% of the mispricing signals indicated an underpricing of the future, and he interpreted this as evidence against the presence of a tax timing option (see chapter 5.4 for a discussion of the tax timing option), which would lead to an increase in the number of underpricings. He also investigated the effects of the uptick rule when the future is underpriced, and found that arbitrage involving short positions in shares was less profitable and much riskier than arbitrage with a long share position. He concluded that the uptick rule is a serious constraint to arbitraging futures underpricings.

Daigler (1993a, pp 195-198, 1993b, pp 110-114) used data every five minutes for the S&P500, the NYSE Composite and the MMI for 1987-8. Allowing for transactions costs, he examined the effect of trading lags on the arbitrage profits. He found that the large arbitrage profits which existed for no trading lag were much reduced when allowance was made for trading lags of five and fifteen minutes.

Cakici, Harpaz & Yagil (1990) used daily closing prices for the VLCI for 1982-7 to test the Eytan & Harpaz (1986) no-arbitrage condition for geometric index futures (see chapter 5.10). They estimated γ (the extra term that appears in the no-arbitrage condition of a geometric index), using the returns for the most recent twenty days, and found the resulting estimate was reasonably stable over time at an annual rate of 5.77%. For all years, except 1987, VLCI futures were overpriced. Although they did not allow for transactions costs directly, Cakici, Harpaz & Yagil concluded that some of the deviations were sufficiently large to represent profitable arbitrage opportunities.

Thomas (1995) studied daily data on VLCI and VLA futures. He used the Eytan & Harpaz (1986) no-arbitrage condition (see chapter 5.10) for the geometric VLCI (1982-8), and the usual no-arbitrage condition for the arithmetic VLA (1988-91). The difference in price between futures on arithmetic and geometric versions of an index is given by γ (see chapter 5.10). Past average values of the arithmetic and geometric versions of the Value Line were used to give estimates of γ, and these lay between 0.0210 and 0.0287. For 1982-6 the mispricings of the VLCI were predominantly overpricings. After allowing for transactions costs of 0.75%, a substantial number of arbitrage opportunities existed. However, from 1986 onwards there was a roughly equal number of over and underpricings, and few arbitrage opportunities. Thomas then investigated why the substantial overpricings of the VLCI ended in 1986. He hypothesized that until 1986 the market had wrongly been using the no-arbitrage condition for arithmetic indices for the geometric VLCI. This was changed in 1986 by the publication of the correct no-arbitrage condition for geometric indices by Eytan & Harpaz, and the entry of well capitalized and sophisticated traders.

This hypothesis was tested in two ways. First, Thomas computed mispricings for 1982-6 using the incorrect arithmetic no-arbitrage price (i.e. $\gamma = 0$), rather than the correct Eytan & Harpaz price. He found a roughly equal number of under and overpricings, and a much reduced number of arbitrage opportunities. This supports the hypothesis that the market was using the wrong no-arbitrage condition. Second, he investigated intracommodity spreads (see chapter 6.10). If the riskless interest rate exceeds the dividend yield then the price of the far contract, less that of the near contract, is always positive for an arithmetic index. However, for a geometric index, the introduction of γ into the no-arbitrage condition means that this spread may be positive or negative. This implies that, if the VLCI was priced using the correct Eytan & Harpaz condition, there may be a mixture of positive and negative intracommodity spreads from 1982-8. However, what Thomas found was that for 1982-6 the intracommodity spreads were strongly positive, while for 1986-8 they were very largely negative. This switch in 1986 is consistent with the hypothesis that until this date traders were wrongly using the arithmetic no-arbitrage condition.

Canada.   Park & Switzer (1995b) computed daily proportionate mispricings for Toronto 35 futures for 1988-92, and found the futures were underpriced throughout this period. The mispricings (before transactions costs) were generally small, and became very small after the introduction of TIPs (a form of ETF) on 9th March 1990.

Japan.   Brenner, Subrahmanyam & Uno (1989a, 1990a) studied deviations from the no-arbitrage condition for trading in two Japanese indices; the Nikkei 225 (traded on SGX) and the Osaka 50 Kabusaki index traded on the OSE. Using daily data for 1987-8, after allowing for transactions costs of 0.5% to 1%, they found a substantial degree of underpricing for the Nikkei 225 futures, i.e. 42% of the time there was an underpricing in excess of the estimated transaction costs. Overpricing (after allowing for transaction costs) was found only 3% of the time. For Osaka 50 Kabusaki index futures, there was overpricing (after allowing for transactions costs) 40% of the time, and underpricing (after allowing for transactions costs) 27% of the time. The magnitude of the deviations from the no-arbitrage price dropped over time for both indices. By the end of the data period the average of the absolute proportionate deviations was down to 0.6% for the Osaka 50 Kabusaki, and 0.5% for the Nikkei 225.

Brenner, Subrahmanyam & Uno (1989b, 1990a) studied daily closing prices on the Nikkei 225 and the corresponding future traded on SGX for 1986-8. The mispricings were predominantly negative, i.e. futures were underpriced, and their size declined over time. Allowing for 1% transactions costs meant that only a small number of the mispricings became arbitrage opportunities, and few of these corresponded to overpricings.

Brenner, Subrahmanyam & Uno (1990b) used daily closing prices for 1988-9 on the Nikkei 225 (traded on both the OSE and SGX) and Topix to look for arbitrage opportunities. After allowing for transactions costs of 0.5%, they concluded that until early in 1989 there was clear evidence of all three futures being overpriced. However, in the Spring of 1989 the Japanese Ministry of Finance relaxed some of the restrictions on arbitrage, and from then onwards the mispricings declined substantially, so that there were very few arbitrage opportunities by the end of the data period.

Bailey (1989) analyzed daily data on the Nikkei 225 traded on SGX and the Osaka 50 Kabusaki for 1986-7. Like Brenner, Subrahmanyam & Uno (1989a, 1990a) he found overpricings for the Nikkei 225, and underpricings for the Osaka 50 Kabusaki. For both indices, he concluded that these mispricings were insignificant. However, this conclusion, which differs from that of some previous studies, may be due to looking at average, rather than individual, mispricings.

Lim (1992a and 1992b) analyzed the Nikkei 225 and the corresponding future traded on SGX. For twenty days spread over 1988 and 1989, he computed spot and futures returns for five minute periods. After allowing for transactions costs, he concluded that very few arbitrage opportunities remained. However, this conclusion is unreliable as it appears to be based on the daily average mispricing, rather than individual mispricings.

Arai, Akamatsu & Yoshioka (1993) considered minute-by-minute prices for 1991 for the Nikkei 225 traded in Osaka. Allowing for the transactions costs of TSE members, they found that arbitrage was possible for the near contract about 56% of the time. During the first five months of 1992 the number of arbitrage opportunities computed using minute-to-minute data declined to 16% of the time.

Vila & Bacha (1994) used daily closing prices for the Nikkei 225 in Osaka and Singapore for 1986-91. They found a substantial number of mispricings, particularly overpricings, in both markets after allowing for transactions costs. On SGX arbitrage opportunities existed in the near contract 40% of the time, while the corresponding figures for Osaka was 50%.

Lim & Muthuswamy (1993) analyzed data for five minute periods on the Nikkei 225 traded on SGX. The no-arbitrage bounds allowed for transactions costs, including the cost of short selling shares, and for Japanese taxation of 20% on interest, dividends and capital gains. They also allowed for trading lags of 5, 10 and 15 minutes. In contrast to most of the previous studies, there was an almost total absence of arbitrage opportunities. This is not due to the inclusion of taxation because the number of arbitrage opportunities rose from only one to two when a tax rate of zero was used.

Chung, Kang & Rhee (1994b, 2003) studied prices every minute for 1988-91 on the Nikkei 225 and the corresponding futures traded in Osaka. After allowing for the transactions costs payable by brokers, arbitrage opportunities existed about 26% of the time, with an average profit of 0.41%. Over 96% of these arbitrage opportunities were overpricings. The introduction of trading lags of 5, 10 and 15 minutes reduced these average profits to 0.36%, 0.34% and 0.34% respectively, while the proportion of profitable arbitrage trades fell from 100% to 80%, 75% and 74%. During the period studied, on 14% of days there was no trading in at least one of the stocks in the Nikkei 225. This indicates that the index is affected by stale prices, and suggests that on some days it may be difficult to trade the full index basket. Chung, Kang & Rhee propose that the frequent arbitrage opportunities they found could not be exploited because they are, in part, due to stale prices and an inability to trade the index basket.

Hong Kong. Silk (1986) considered daily mispricings of the Hang Seng for the first three months after trading in index futures began (May to July 1986). After allowing for transactions costs, he found that futures were overpriced in the first half of May 1986, but thereafter there were no arbitrage opportunities.

Mispricings of Hang Seng index futures were also studied by Yau, Schneeweis & Yung (1990) using daily closing prices for 1986-8. Allowing for transactions costs, futures were overpriced in the period before the October 1987 crash, while after the crash there were few mispricings.

Ho, Fang & Woo (1992) used minute-to-minute data on the Hang Seng for 17 days in 1991. After allowing for transactions costs, they concluded that mispricings were uncommon, and more likely to be overpricings than underpricings.

In August 1998 the Hong Kong government purchased 7.3% of the Hong Kong stock market, set a floor of 7,850 to the Hang Seng, and indicated it was willing to buy over 30% of the market if necessary. The government also changed the rules to maker short selling harder. Using quotes, and allowing for dividends and transactions costs, Draper & Fung (2003) found that Hang Seng futures became substantially underpriced, with arbitrage opportunities existing for the next month. These arbitrage opportunities are attributed to the risks and difficulties of engaging in short selling during this period.

Korea. On 3rd May 1996 index futures began trading in Korea on the KOSPI index. Using daily synchronous data for the next two years, Gay & Jung (1999) found evidence of underpricing; with a substantial number of arbitrage opportunities for exchange members. This was partly attributed to the difficulty of borrowing stock, and the risks of having the borrowed stock recalled with 5 days notice (making the arbitrage risky).

Australia.   Twite (1998) studied daily mispricings of the Australian AOI for 1983-8. The no-arbitrage condition allowed for both taxes and transactions costs. With no additional transactions costs for short selling, a substantial number of mispricings existed. If an extra 5% had to be paid for short selling shares, most of the underpricings disappeared. The absolute size of the mispricing declined as delivery approached.

Hodgson, Kendig & Tahir (1993) used 15 minute returns for the Australian AOI from February 1992 to September 1992 and, allowing for a 15 minute trading lag, found that arbitrage opportunities only existed for traders with transactions costs of under 0.5%. For such traders, arbitrage opportunities existed for 26% of the time, and were larger on Mondays, but did not vary by time of day.

UK.   Using daily data for the FTSE 100 for 1984-8 Yadav & Pope (1990) examined proportionate mispricings, i.e. the mispricing divided by the current spot price. They found that the average gross proportionate mispricing fell from an underpricing of 0.5% before Big Bang, to an underpricing of 0.2% after Big Bang. When they allowed for four different levels of transactions costs, they concluded that many potential opportunities for profitable arbitrage remained. The introduction of a trading lag of half a day reduced, but did not eliminate, these arbitrage profits.

Yadav & Pope (1994) analyzed hourly data on the FTSE 100 for 1986-90. They found there were frequent proportionate mispricings in excess of transactions costs, and that the average size of the proportionate mispricings did not drop over this four year period. Some contracts were, on average, overpriced; while for others the average price was too low. Overall, there was no clear pattern of over or underpricing. The proportionate mispricings for the next near contract were larger than those for the near contract, which is consistent with arbitrage being riskier for longer maturities. The near and next near contracts were generally mispriced in the same direction, and by a roughly similar amount.

Strickland & Xu (1993) studied hourly data on the FTSE 100 for 1988-90. The no-arbitrage condition allowed for the effect of stock exchange accounts in delaying the payment for shares. After subtracting transactions costs of 0.5%, the future was overpriced 6% of the time, and underpriced for 46% of the observations. Hence, arbitrage opportunities were common, particularly underpricings.

Theobald & Yallup (1996) started with the continuous time version of the no-arbitrage condition (see appendix A to chapter 5). They re-expressed this as $(F-S)/S = (\pi-\omega)h$, where π is the continuously compounded annual risk free rate of interest, ω is the continuously compounded annual dividend rate, and h is the fraction of a year until delivery. They then added terms to allow for the UK settlement system, taxes on the index basket of shares, and non-synchronous prices. Using daily data for the FTSE 100 for 1984-95, they regressed $(F-S)/S$ on their explanatory variables and found that the UK settlement system, and the non-synchronicity proxies had a significant effect, while taxes on shares did not. They concluded that there was little deviation from no-arbitrage pricing, particularly in the early 1990s.

Germany.   Grünbichler & Callahan (1994) computed proportionate mispricings for DAX futures for 1990-1. Since the DAX is a performance index, they used a modified no-arbitrage condition (see chapter 5.11). For proportionate mispricings (before transactions costs) calculated every 5 minutes, about 90% were underpricings. Since the vast majority of mispricings were smaller than 1%, it was concluded that profitable arbitrage opportunities did not exist. For proportionate mispricings computed every 15 minutes, Grünbichler & Callahan only considered overpricings (16% of the total). This was because the short selling difficulties in Germany (it is not officially permitted, London Stock Exchange, 1994b), were thought to rule out any arbitrage opportunities for underpricings. After allowing for transactions costs of just 0.5% only 1.6% of the overpricings remained. Again, this indicated an absence of profitable arbitrage opportunities.

Bühler & Kempf (1995) analyzed transactions data on the DAX for 1990-2. They assumed that dividends were taxed at the 36% rate assumed in the computation of the DAX index, and found that the vast majority of mispricings were underpricings - overall the DAX was underpriced 79% of the time. After allowing for transactions costs (including a risk premium of 0.25%), they found that arbitrage opportunities existed 5% of the time, and 99.5% of these arbitrage opportunities were underpricings. Allowance for a trading lag of 15 minutes resulted in a small reduction in the arbitrage profits.

Bamberg & Röder (1994a) studied mispricings for the DAX every minute for 1991-2. These were computed using a modified no-arbitrage condition which allowed for the re-investment of dividends after paying a corporate tax rate of 50%. After deducting transactions costs (which included a charge for stock borrowing when appropriate) and allowing for a trading lag of one or two minutes, they found virtually no overpricings. However, there were a large number of profitable underpricings. This result is consistent with the view that the costs of short selling stock in Germany are greater than the allowance made in this study, or that an absence of short selling does create arbitrage opportunities. Using the same data, Bamberg & Röder (1994b) found that the profitable underpricings were concentrated in the June contracts. Since two thirds of the dividends on shares in the DAX are declared in the months of April, May and June, the concentration of mispricings in these months suggests that the transactions costs of rebalancing the portfolio of shares to replicate the index basket are substantial.

Finland.   Puttonen & Martikainen (1991) considered daily closing prices of the Finnish FOX index for 1988-90. Allowing for transactions costs, they found that most of the mispricings were underpricings. Puttonen (1993a) reported similar results, and observed that the prevalence of underpricing may be due to the absence of short selling in Finland. Puttonen also found that the number of mispricings increased over the 1988-1990 period.

Switzerland.   Stulz, Wasserfallen & Stucki (1990) studied daily data on Swiss Market Index futures traded on an OTC market run by the Leu Bank from January to October 1989. The largest mispricing of 1.3% was barely sufficient to cover transactions costs, and so they concluded that the no-arbitrage condition was not violated.

Netherlands.   Berglund & Kabir (1994) used Wednesday closing prices on the EOE index for 1991-3. The mispricing was defined as the logarithm of the actual futures price, less the logarithm of the no-arbitrage futures price, and throughout the period the average mispricing was negative, i.e. there was underpricing.

4.1.2 Explanations for the Empirical Results

Although many of the studies of US index futures ignored transactions costs, some of the deviations from the theoretical prices were sufficiently large to cast doubt on the conclusion of Cornell (1985a) that the no-arbitrage condition is supported by the evidence. The relevant question is not 'is the *average* deviation from the no-arbitrage condition significantly different from zero?', but 'are there *sometimes* deviations from the no-arbitrage condition that are large enough to cover transactions costs?' Those US studies which have allowed for transactions costs have also found evidence of arbitrage opportunities. Therefore, the evidence supports the view that, over the periods studied, profitable arbitrage opportunities existed for the S&P500. However, the study of the MMI by Chung (1991) found evidence that by 1986 the arbitrage opportunities had been largely eliminated.

The results for Australian, British, Canadian, Dutch, Finnish, Hong Kong and Japanese index futures, which generally allowed for transactions costs, suggest that arbitrage opportunities also existed in these markets, although some studies of Germany and Switzerland have concluded that arbitrage opportunities did not exist. Some of the more recent studies, which have been able to use a longer data set, have found evidence that the absolute size of mispricings has declined over time. However, Schwarz & Laatsch (1991) have questioned whether there has been a steady improvement in efficiency, and suggest that efficiency fluctuates over time, while Puttonen (1993a) found an increase in the number of mispricings over time.

The suggested explanations for the existence of arbitrage opportunities split into two groups:-

(a) While the empirical tests reveal an arbitrage opportunity, it cannot be profitably exploited. This may be due to a variety of factors, including the invalidity of the assumptions used in deriving the no-arbitrage condition. For example, the use of stale prices in the computation of the index, the use of non-synchronous closing prices, the use of prices that are constrained by a price limit, inadequate allowance for transactions costs, regulatory restrictions (such as the US uptick restriction on short selling shares, which limits arbitrage aimed at removing an underpricing of futures contracts), time lags in trading the portfolio of shares corresponding to the index, the presence of arbitrage risk (the arbitrage transaction is not riskless due to uncertain dividends, uncertain interest rates, uncertain transaction costs, failure to unwind the share position at the EDSP, marking to the market, etc), or because the model used to compute the no-arbitrage prices is incorrect (e.g. not allowing for the potential effects of price limits, see chapter 11.3).

(b) There are real arbitrage opportunities and these remain because of institutional inertia, the inexperience of traders in a new market, or because of an insufficient volume of arbitrage transactions to move prices to their no-arbitrage levels, possibly due to an inadequate supply of arbitrage capital (e.g. Nick Leeson risk).

Twite (1991) tested two of these possible causes of mispricings using daily closing prices for the Australian AOI between 1983 and 1988. He rejected stale prices as a cause, but found some support for arbitrage risk as an explanation of mispricings. The presence of restrictions on short selling shares encourages the underpricing of index futures, but the empirical evidence has not found that underpricing is the dominant form of mispricing.

Some studies of US index futures have found a predominance of underpricings; while others have found a predominance of overpricings. Of the non-US studies, many found mostly underpricing; while others found no under or overpricings; and Yadav & Pope (1994) found roughly equal amounts of under and overpricing. These mixed results suggest that short selling restrictions are not the main cause of mispricings. In chapter 5.13, the effects on arbitrage of difficulties in short selling are considered further.

Some evidence on the influence of trading lags is provided for the USA, the UK, Japan, Germany and Australia by the empirical studies. They generally found that allowance for a trading lag reduced, but did not eliminate, the arbitrage profits; and so the presence of arbitrage opportunities cannot be explained by short delays in trading.

4.2 Dynamics of the Arbitrage Response

As well as looking at the size and direction of mispricings, it is also possible to consider the time series properties of mispricings. Temporal patterns in mispricings may be induced by arbitrage activity. For example, a mispricing may lead to trading by arbitrageurs to exploit a profitable opportunity. This raises the questions of how quickly do the arbitrageurs respond, how fast is the reduction in the size of the mispricing, and is this accomplished by a change in the futures or spot prices?

4.2.1 Properties of Mispricings

A number of studies have examined the properties of mispricings over time. It has been universally found that the number and magnitude of mispricings declines as delivery approaches, see table 4.1. This result is consistent with a drop in dividend and interest rate risk as the time to delivery decreases, as well as a decline in the risk of tracking the index basket with a partial basket of stocks. It is not consistent with an early unwinding option that decreases in value as delivery approaches. Bhatt & Cakici (1990) have also found that the absolute size of mispricings declines as the dividend yield increases.

Table 4.1: Relationship Between Absolute Mispricings and Time to Delivery

Study	Index	Relationship
MacKinlay & Ramaswamy (1988)	S&P500	Positive
Bhatt & Cakici (1990)	S&P500	Positive
Klemkosky & Lee (1991)	S&P500	Positive
Chung, Kang & Rhee (1994b, 2003)	Nikkei SA (Osaka)	Positive
Twite (1998)	SPI	Positive
Yadav & Pope (1990)	FTSE 100	Positive
Yadav & Pope (1994)	FTSE 100	Positive
Strickland & Xu (1993)	FTSE 100	Positive
Theobald & Yallup (1993)	FTSE 100	Positive
Puttonen (1993a)	FOX	Positive
Grünbichler & Callahan (1994)	DAX	Positive
Bühler & Kempf (1995)	DAX	Positive
Kempf (1998)	DAX	Positive
Lafuente & Novales (2003)	Ibex 35	Positive

Such a decline in the absolute size of mispricings as delivery approaches is illustrated in figure 4.1.

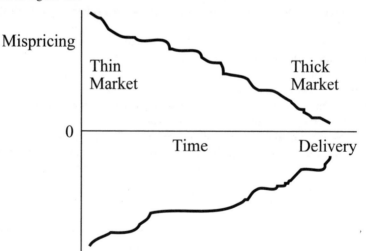

Figure 4.1: Mispricings and Maturity

It was argued in chapter 3.5 that early unwinding can induce path dependence into mispricings, and various studies have considered the time series properties of mispricings. This has been done in a number of empirical studies by computing the first order autocorrelation of mispricings and changes in mispricings.

USA. MacKinlay & Ramaswamy (1988) studied mispricings (before transactions costs) of the S&P500, computed every fifteen minutes. They discovered that the first order autocorrelation of the mispricing series was 0.93, indicating that mispricings tended to persist over time, e.g. a few hours. However, the first order autocorrelation of first differences of the mispricing series was −0.23, and this suggests that mispricings tend to be partially reversed within fifteen minutes.

Vaidyanathan & Krehbiel (1992) argued that, if the assumptions underlying the no-arbitrage condition are met there should be no dependence over time in mispricings. They used the data from the MacKinlay & Ramaswamy (1988) study to look for nonlinear dependence over time in the percentage mispricings of the S&P500. Using analytical techniques from chaos theory, they found evidence of nonlinear dependence, although the form of this dependence is not known.

Dwyer, Locke & Yu (1996) studied minute by minute mispricings for the S&P500 for 1982-90. They found evidence that mispricings tended to persist over time, and that mispricings which exceeded transactions costs led to a reduction in the size of the mispricing that was twice as fast as when the mispricing was inside the transactions cost threshold. The reduction in the mispricing lasted for about 20 minutes, and was achieved primarily by movements in the spot price; although there was also some adjustment in the futures price.

Neal (1995) analyzed 837 S&P500 arbitrage trades on the NYSE in the 3 month period of January to March 1989. He plotted the average mispricing for the 10 minutes before and after the submission of an arbitrage trade. For both over and underpricings, there was evidence that the submission of an arbitrage trade was associated with a statistically significant reversion of the mispricing towards zero.

Miller, Muthuswamy & Whaley (1994) used transactions data on the S&P500 for 1982-91. They were concerned with the time series behaviour of changes in the basis (which is $F-S$), rather than mispricings, over 15, 30 and 60 minute intervals. Over short periods of time during which expected dividends and interest rates are be assumed to be unchanged, the change in the mispricing (ΔM) is equal to the change in the basis (ΔB) minus the change in the spot price times the interest rate (ΔSr), that is $\Delta M = \Delta B - \Delta Sr$. Therefore, since r is very small over a few minutes, studying changes in the basis is very similar to studying changes in the mispricing.

They found there was significant negative autocorrelation in changes in the S&P500 basis of −0.369 for 15-minute changes, −0.396 for 30-minute changes and −0.380 for 60-minute changes. The corresponding correlations for the VLCI from September 1982 to March 1988 were −0.182, −0.273 and −0.233 respectively. Previous studies have attributed negative correlation in mispricings to arbitrage activity. However, Miller, Muthuswamy & Whaley argue that this negative autocorrelation could be a statistical illusion. Lengthening the differencing interval does not reduce the size of this negative autocorrelation, and arbitrage-induced negative correlation would be expected to diminish as the differencing interval is lengthened. When they excluded observations where the S&P500 mispricing exceeded 0.25%, the negative first order autocorrelation of changes in the basis dropped only slightly. This supports the view that the negative autocorrelation in basis changes is not produced by arbitrage activity, as mispricings under 0.25% are unlikely to lead to profitable arbitrage.

Miller, Muthuswamy & Whaley assume that observed changes in the index can be represented as $\Delta S_t = \varphi \Delta S_{t-1} + (1-\varphi)e_t$, where $0 \le \varphi \le 1$ and φ measures price staleness ($\varphi = 0$ implies no staleness); and e_t (the true change in the index) has zero mean and is serially uncorrelated and homoskedastic. Observed changes in the futures price are assumed to follow a MA (1) process and $\Delta F = a_t + \Theta a_{t-1}$, where $-1 \le \Theta \le 0$ and Θ measures the degree of futures bid-ask bounce ($\Theta = 0$ implies no bid-ask bounce); a_t (the true change in the futures price) is a zero mean serially uncorrelated homoskedastic variable. Given these assumptions, they show that if some of the prices used in computing the index are stale (that is $\varphi > 0$), and if there is some bid-ask bounce in the futures price (that is $\Theta < 0$), observed futures price changes have a higher variance than observed spot price changes, even though their true variances are identical.

Miller, Muthuswamy & Whaley also demonstrate that if there is no futures bid-ask bounce ($\Theta = 0$), there are stale spot prices ($\varphi > 0$), the variances of changes in the true index and futures prices are the same, and the correlation between changes in the true index and futures prices is perfectly positive, then the first order autocorrelation of observed changes in the basis is $(\varphi - 1)/2$, which is always negative. When φ is small the autocorrelation in observed basis changes becomes more negative, and so strong negative autocorrelation can be observed when the stale price effect is very small. Thus, they argue that the finding of negative autocorrelation in the basis need not be due to arbitrage activity, merely a small degree of stale prices.

He & Wu (2001) develop the work of Miller, Muthuswamy & Whaley by pointing out that, in addition to infrequent trading inducing negative autocorrelation in the basis, the use of non-synchronous prices in the construction of an index also has this consequence. For trade data from 1985-1999 for the S&P500, they find that allowing for both infrequent and non-synchronous trading considerably reduces the negative autocorrelation of changes in the basis; and conclude that mean reversion is a statistical phenomenon.

Monoyios & Sarno (2002) argue that, rather than a set of discrete thresholds, there is a smooth boundary between arbitrage and no arbitrage. Beyond some minimum size, mispricings become increasingly mean reverting. They fitted the exponential smooth transition autoregressive (ESTAR) model to daily values of the basis for 1988-98 for the S&P500 and FTSE 100. Then, using dynamic stochastic simulation, large mispricings were found to have a half life of a few days; while small mispricings had a half life of one to two weeks. Therefore, there is no discrete threshold and, as expected, the speed of the adjustment to a mispricing is a positive function of its size.

Tse (2001) used 5 minute returns for DJIA futures for 1998-9 and found that changes in the mispricing had an autocorrelation of -0.45, while very small changes in the basis had a negative autocorrelation of -0.27 to -0.48. This later result is unlikely to have been be caused by arbitrage activity. Tse argues that arbitrageurs are heterogeneous due to differences in transactions costs, capital constraints, perception of risk, the presence or otherwise of the early unwinding option, and trading lags. Tse then uses the exponential smooth threshold autoregressive (ESTAR) model to simulate mispricings and, when allowance is made for heterogeneous arbitrageurs, finds negative autocorrelation in the mispricings. Therefore, mean reversion in mispricings can be explained by the presence of heterogeneous arbitrageurs.

Taylor (2004b) analyzed 5 minute data for 2001-2. The futures prices were for both S&P500 futures and S&P500 E-mini futures, while the spot prices were for S&P500 iShares (an ETF). He fitted three basic models to the data - the threshold autoregressive model (TAR), the smooth transition autoregressive model (STAR), and the augmented STAR model, where there are differences between arbitrageurs and these differences change over time as transactions costs and execution risk vary during the day. The data supported the augmented STAR model; and the propensity to arbitrage was found to be highest at the start of the day, and lowest at the close.

Japan.   Brenner, Subrahmanyam & Uno (1989a, 1990a) studied deviations from the no-arbitrage condition for trading in the Nikkei 225 (traded on SGX) and the Osaka 50 Kabusaki index traded on the OSE. Using daily data for 1987-8, they found strong positive autocorrelation for lags of up to four days in the mispricings (before transactions costs) for both indices. This suggests that, rather then being promptly eliminated by arbitrage, the mispricings (before transactions costs) tended to persist for a number of days.

Brenner, Subrahmanyam & Uno (1989b, 1990a) studied daily closing prices on the Nikkei 225 and the corresponding future traded on SGX for 1986-8. They found a strong positive first order correlation in the mispricings of around 0.80 (as did Yadav & Pope, 1990, for the UK).

Lim (1992a, 1992b) analyzed the Nikkei 225 and the corresponding future traded on SGX. For twenty days spread over 1988-9, he computed spot and futures returns for five minute periods. For both spot and futures returns, there was no significant autocorrelation, suggesting that stale prices were not a problem for the index. There was a high (over 0.80) first order positive autocorrelation in the mispricings (before transactions costs), while the fourth order autocorrelation was still significantly positive (at about 0.40). This implies that mispricings (although not necessarily arbitrage opportunities) tended to persist for over twenty minutes.

Vila & Bacha (1994) computed the autocorrelation of daily mispricings for the Nikkei 225 traded in Osaka and Singapore. They found that for Singapore there was substantial positive first order autocorrelation, although this declined as from the beginning of 1990. The authors suggest this reduction in the autocorrelation of mispricings may be because mispricings have increased in size from 1990 onwards, and this has attracted arbitrage activity which has quickly removed the mispricing.

Lim & Muthuswamy (1993) considered the basis every five minutes for Nikkei 225 futures on SGX. As argued above, over short periods of time changes in the basis are equivalent to changes in the mispricing. Their data covered 25 days in 1988-91, and the first order autocorrelation for changes in the basis was negative on 18 of the 25 days, with values between −0.2 and −0.5.

Hong Kong.   Ho, Fang & Woo (1992) used minute-to-minute data on the Hang Seng for 17 days in 1991. They found significant positive autocorrelation in the mispricings. Changes in the basis were negatively correlated over time, although not significantly. Following the arguments of Miller, Muthuswamy & Whaley (1994), this lack of significance may be due to an absence of a stale price effect, as evidenced by a lack of autocorrelation in spot returns.

UK.   Using daily data for the FTSE 100 for 1984-8 Yadav & Pope (1990) found that proportionate mispricings persisted over time, with a first order serial correlation coefficient of 0.80 for proportionate mispricings computed using closing prices. Yadav & Pope (1994) analyzed hourly data on the FTSE 100 for 1986-90, and again found that the direction of the mispricing tended to persist over time.

Yadav & Pope (1992c) considered two data sets: 15-minute observations on the S&P500 for 1983-7 (the data used by MacKinlay & Ramaswamy, 1988), and hourly data on the FTSE 100 for 1986-90. Mispricings were defined as the natural logarithm of the actual futures price minus the natural logarithm of the no-arbitrage futures price. They found that, for both the UK and the USA, the change in the mispricing depended on the level of the mispricing in the previous period. If the previous mispricing was positive (the future was overpriced), then the change in the mispricing tended to be negative (the overpricing declined), and vice versa. Thus, mispricings were a mean reverting process. This mean reversion effect became stronger in both countries as delivery approached, and this is consistent with arbitrage becoming less costly and less risky as maturity declines. Yadav & Pope then divided the mispricings by size into one of 5 categories and found that the mean reversion effect was strongest in the USA and UK when the absolute value of the mispricing in the previous period was largest. This supports the results of Pope & Yadav (1992) (reported in chapter 5.6) that there are a number of groups of arbitrageur, each facing different transactions costs.

Theobald & Yallup (2001) generalize the Miller, Muthuswamy & Whaley (1994) model by allowing for the partial adjustment of the spot and futures markets, which is shown to represent a separate cause of negative autocorrelation in the basis. Using 5 minute returns for the FTSE 100 for 1999, they found that, even after removing the effects of infrequent trading, the basis still exhibited negative autocorrelation. Using estimators of the partial adjustment coefficients from Theobald & Yallup (1998), they found the futures market adjusted fully within 5 minutes. The spot market adjustment was only 27% within 5 minutes, and it was only after about 30 minutes that the spot market had fully adjusted. Therefore, in contrast to Miller, Muthuswamy & Whaley, they conclude that mean reversion in the basis is not just a statistical artefact.

Garrett & Taylor (2001) applied the TAR model to 1 minute returns on the FTSE 100 for 1998 to investigate the Miller, Muthuswamy & Whaley (1994) findings. The first-order serial correlation of changes in the mispricing was − 0.080. When the data was purged of microstructure effects in the way suggested by Miller, Muthuswamy & Whaley (1994); the first order serial correlation became more negative at − 0.093. The first order serial correlation of mispricing changes was − 0.43 when the transactions costs threshold was exceeded, and zero when it was not. They concluded that it is arbitrage and not microstructure effects that creates the first order negative serial correlation in mispricing changes.

Germany. Grünbichler & Callahan (1994) found that proportionate mispricings for the DAX, calculated every 5 minutes for 1990-1, exhibited strong positive first order serial correlation of about 0.9. They also found that the first order serial correlation for changes in the proportionate mispricings was negative, at about − 0.2, which indicates some reversal of mispricings within 5 minutes.

For 5 minute returns on the DAX for 1990-92, Kempf (1998) found that the average mispricing was negative, and increased with time to maturity. He also found mean reversion in the mispricings, and presented evidence that this reversion is due to arbitrage trading. Kempf & Korn (1998) used 1 minute returns on the DAX for 1995-6, and found mean reversion in the mispricings.

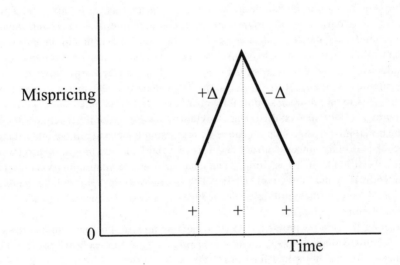

Figure 4.2: Autocorrelation in Mispricings

The general finding is that the first order serial correlation of mispricings is positive and high, while the corresponding figure for changes in mispricings is usually negative. Such a pattern is shown in figure 4.2. This indicates that mispricings are not immediately eliminated by an arbitrage response, but that the size of the mispricing is reduced over time, which Miller, Muthuswamy & Whaley (1994) argue could be due to stale prices. However, the evidence of Neal (1995) and Dwyer, Locke & Yu (1993) is that mispricings which exceed the transactions cost threshold are associated with both arbitrage activity and a reduction in the mispricing.

4.2.2 Speed of the Arbitrage Response

If futures are mispriced, this will lead to arbitrage transactions, and these will tend to remove the initial mispricing by pushing the spot and futures prices back into line. This suggests that mispricings can be used to predict subsequent spot and futures price movements.

USA.   Swinnerton, Curcio & Bennett (1988) used transactions data on the S&P500 for 1986, and found that the mispricing was a modest predictor of movements in the spot price over the next five minutes, particularly when futures were overpriced.

Furbush (1989) used data for five minute intervals on the S&P500 index for 14th, 15th, 16th, 19th and 20th October 1987 - the period of the stock market crash and the few days just before. He examined whether a mispricing triggered index arbitrage transactions within a few minutes. He regressed the volume of programme trades classified as index arbitrage, where positive values indicate buying shares and negative values denote selling shares, on the actual futures price less the no-arbitrage futures price. (For a definition of programme trades, see chapter 4.4.4). Using data for concurrent five minute periods, he found that for 14th, 15th 16th and the morning of 19th October, there was a highly significant positive relationship between the volume of index arbitrage and the size of the mispricing. Lagging the mispricing variable by five minutes weakened this relationship, suggesting that the primary reaction of arbitrageurs to an arbitrage opportunity occurs within five minutes.

Furbush (1989) also studied the extent to which arbitrage activity reduces the size of the initial mispricing. This was done by regressing the change in the mispricing of the S&P500 index on the current and lagged values of the volume of programme trades classified as index arbitrage. The data was for five minute intervals for 14th, 15th, 16th, 19th and 20th October 1987. The results were not clear cut, but generally supported the view that index arbitrage reduces the size of the mispricing within about fifteen minutes.

During the first six months of 1990, using one minute spot and futures prices for the S&P500, Sofianos (1993) found that arbitrage opportunities lasted for just 3 to 5 minutes. This result applied for transactions costs between 40 and 200 index basis points.

In a study of mispricings every five minutes for the MMI, Chan & Chung (1993) found that, for 1984-5, absolute mispricings persisted for about ten minutes. This suggests that the major arbitrage response occurs within about ten minutes.

Eagle & Nelson (1991) used minute-by-minute observations on the S&P500 for 1985-9 to compute mispricings. This relied on the assumption that, within each day the average mispricing was zero. They examined the relationships between two variables; the size of the initial mispricing and the change in the mispricing over a given time interval (that varied from one to twenty minutes). They found evidence of a small reduction in the mispricing after a minute, with larger and larger reductions as the response time was extended to twenty minutes.

Harris, Sofianos & Shapiro (1994) found that index arbitrage programme trades are clustered in time. Using data from the NYSE for 1989-90, the average number of such trades in each cluster was 2.5, while the average duration of a cluster was 2.3 minutes. This indicates that the typical arbitrage response involved two or three arbitrageurs, and that they all submitted their orders at approximately the same time.

Neal (1993b) studied programme trades during the first three months of 1989 on the NYSE. He found that for five minute periods where one or more index arbitrage trades occurs, the average period contains 1.84 index arbitrage trades. He also found that the first order serial correlation of the signed volume of index arbitrage trading in each five minute period was 0.31. These results suggest that arbitrage trades occur in clusters, and that these clusters last for longer than five minutes.

UK. Pope & Yadav (1992) used hourly data for the FTSE 100 for 1986-8 to investigate the speed with which a mispricing is reversed. They found that the main response occurs within the first hour.

Conclusions. The evidence from the available studies suggests that arbitrage begins within about five minutes of a mispricing, and this produces some reduction in the size of the mispricing. In some situations, while there is evidence of a mispricing which exceeds transactions costs, traders may be reluctant to initiate arbitrage positions, Conrardy (1993). At the opening of trading stock prices are particularly likely to be stale, and so the apparent arbitrage opportunity may not lead to arbitrage trades. When movements in the stock market are close to triggering circuit breakers, e.g. the 50 point DJIA "collar", arbitrageurs may be reluctant to trade as they risk being caught by uptick and downtick rules, and restrictions on the use of DOT, see chapter 11.3.3. Finally, when volume is low in the spot and futures markets, arbitrageurs may be less willing to trade because of the lack of liquidity.

4.2.3 Size of the Arbitrage Response

Adachi & Kurasawa (1993) report that during eleven weeks in September to November 1991, the average value of index arbitrage trading (buys plus sells) on the Tokyo Stock Exchange was 183 billion yen (£800 million) per week, while the average share position due to index arbitrage was 1,303 billion yen (£5,700 million). This indicates that substantial sums of money are devoted to index arbitrage. From November 1989 to March 1991, 4.4% of trading on the NYSE was due to index arbitrage, and in some weeks this rose to 9.7%, Miller, Muthuswamy & Whaley (1994).

4.2.4 Arbitrage and Changes in Futures and Spot Prices

The reduction in the mispricing can be disaggregated into two components:

movements in the price of the futures contract, and movements in the prices of the underlying shares. Figure 4.3 shows three possibilities: all the adjustment occurs in the futures price, all the adjustment occurs in the index (where S^* represents the current value of the index adjusted for dividends and interest, i.e. $S^* = (S-D)(1+r)$), and both the futures price and the index adjust.

Furbush (1989) tested these different responses by separately regressing the change in the futures price and changes in the index on current and lagged values of the volume of programme trades classified as index arbitrage. The results were mixed, and this may be due to the presence of another powerful factor (the 1987 stock market crash) during the data period. The general level of futures and spot prices tend to move together, and this effect was particularly marked in October 1987 when there were large downward price movements. Therefore, any small, equilibrating, and opposite movements in the spot and futures prices may have been swamped by the very strong positive correlation between these two prices induced by the Crash.

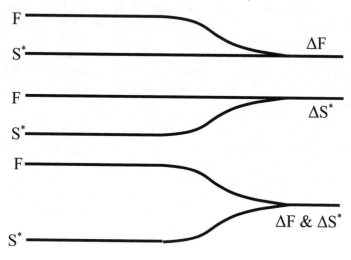

Figure 4.3: Does F or S Adjust?

A study by Harris, Sofianos & Shapiro (1994) of programme trading on the NYSE in 1989-90 found evidence that index arbitrage programme trading occurs when the basis (the difference between the futures and spot prices, see chapter 6.1) is wide, and that the basis closed to its usual level within about ten minutes of the submission of the programme trades. This is consistent with the earlier study by Furbush (1989) that arbitrage reduces the mispricing in fifteen minutes. This is also the conclusion reached by MacKinlay & Ramaswamy (1988). Because all the arbitrage trades in response to a particular mispricing are submitted more or less concurrently, Harris, Sofianos & Shapiro (1994) found little difference in the price response between the first and subsequent arbitrage programme trades in each cluster. For both over and underpricings, the spot and futures price response to index arbitrage was of equal and opposite size. Thus, prices in both markets adjust equally to remove the mispricing.

Using one minute data on 37 S&P500 stocks for 1990-1, Hasbrouck (1996) investigated the effect of index arbitrage programme trades on stock prices. He found that, after controlling for the effects of futures returns and mispricings, index arbitrage trades had a significantly smaller effect on the S&P500 index than did other trades (0.019, rather than 0.024 index points). This lower price impact is consistent with these trades being viewed as informationless, which makes them less effective than other trades in moving share prices back to their no-arbitrage level.

In October 1997 trading in FTSE 100 stocks became possible using a new screen-based trading system (SETS), and this led to a substantial drop in the costs of trading the index basket. Taylor, Van Dijk, Frances & Lucas (2000) found that this drop in transactions costs speeded up the response of the futures and spot prices to shocks. Pre-SETS the futures market adjusted more quickly, but post-SETS both markets adjusted with the same speed.

The evidence from the small number of studies suggests that arbitrage activity causes a substantial reduction in the mispricing within about fifteen minutes. This empirical evidence of an arbitrage response to mispricings supports the view that the negative first order autocorrelation in changes in mispricings is caused by arbitrage, rather than stale prices (as suggested by Miller, Muthuswamy & Whaley, 1994). Finally, it appears that arbitrage opportunities are removed by roughly equal movements in spot and futures prices.

4.3 Mispricings and Spot Volatility

Chen, Cuny & Haugen (1995) have suggested that investors may attach a 'customization value' to holding stocks in their portfolio due to hedging benefits (see chapter 9), bullish private information, or potential tax timing benefits (see chapter 5.4 for a discussion of the tax timing option). In the derivation of the no-arbitrage condition, these benefits are assumed not to exist. When stock market volatility rises, such investors will be less willing to sell their stocks, and more likely to hedge the risk using stock index futures (see chapter 10.1.1 for an explanation of using index futures to control portfolio risk). Thus an increase in stock market volatility leads to an increase in the demand for short positions in index futures, and this tends to push down their price, relative to that of the underlying index basket of shares and the no-arbitrage price. Therefore, the mispricing decreases, while the basis (futures price less the spot price) widens. In addition, since the number of traders who wish to hold short positions in index futures has increased, open interest increases when spot volatility increases.

USA. Chen, Cuny & Haugen (1995) used daily synchronous prices for the S&P500 for 1986-90. Market volatility was measured by the implied volatility of put and call options on S&P500 index, and also by the variance of S&P500 returns for the 10 days centered on the observation. They found that the mispricings fell when spot

volatility rose, and that the size of this effect increased as the time to delivery increased. They also discovered that open interest rose as spot volatility increased.
Netherlands.   Berglund & Kabir (1994) used Wednesday closing prices on the EOE index for 1991-3 to test the Chen, Cuny & Haugen (1995) hypothesis that an increase in spot volatility is associated with a drop in the value of mispricings and an increase in the size of the open interest. Spot volatility was measured as the implied volatility of EOE index options, while the mispricing was defined as logarithm of the actual futures price, less the logarithm of the no-arbitrage futures price. Berglund & Kabir found a negative relationship between the EOE mispricing and spot volatility, and that the impact of spot volatility on the mispricing was related to the maturity on the futures contract. The longer the time until delivery, the greater was the drop in the mispricing for a given increase in spot volatility. They also found some evidence of a concave relationship between interest rates and mispricings, as predicted by the no-arbitrage condition of Hemler & Longstaff (1991), see chapter 5.27. Finally, Berglund & Kabir found that open interest in EOE futures increased as spot market volatility increased.

These results for the USA and the Netherlands are consistent with the hypothesis of Chen, Cuny & Haugen (1995) that shares have a customization value. However, large mispricings tend to be followed by arbitrage activity. An arbitrage trade (indeed, any programme trade) 'refreshes' spot prices, so that the last transaction prices of stocks in the index are current rather than stale. In addition, an arbitrage trade means that all the transaction prices used in computing the index are either at the ask or the bid, depending on the direction of the mispricing. Usually, the last trade prices are a random mixture of trades at both the bid and the ask, giving an average of the midquote. For these two reasons (removing the stale price effect, and pushing all the prices in the index to either the bid or the ask), an arbitrage trade will *appear* to increase spot price volatility.

4.4 Some Practicalities of Arbitrage Transactions

Having considered the empirical evidence on mispricings, some of the practicalities of arbitrage transactions will now be discussed.

4.4.1 The Arbitrage Portfolio

Even if it were possible to use all the shares in the index in an arbitrage transaction, e.g. when $F > (S-D) \times (1+r)$ and short selling shares is not required, arbitrageurs often choose to use an alternative approach. This is to construct a much smaller portfolio (e.g. 15 to 100 shares, rather than 500 or 1,700 shares) which is designed to track the full index, i.e. an arbitrage portfolio. This has a number of advantages. Restrictions on short selling particular shares can be circumvented by excluding them from the arbitrage portfolio, and the small number of transactions required both lowers transactions costs and increases the speed of the arbitrage transaction. The disadvantage of using an arbitrage portfolio is that the arbitrage transaction is no longer risk free because, at delivery, the value of the arbitrage portfolio may differ from that of the index. This will result in an unpredictable profit or loss, in addition to the certain arbitrage profit that motivated the trade. Thus, there is an optimal arbitrage portfolio which maximizes the benefits from reduced transactions costs and increased arbitrage speed, less the costs of the arbitrage risk. The popularity of using less stocks in the arbitrage than are in the index suggests that the advantages more than compensate for the risk that the value of the arbitrage portfolio will deviate from the index at delivery.

The following example shows that there may be a dividend mismatch between the arbitrage portfolio and the index, and that there is a risk that the arbitrage portfolio will not exactly replicate the index.

Example. The CYROX index currently stands at 200 index points and has a multiplier of £600 per index point, so that the index basket is worth £120,000. Kathy Burgess aims to arbitrage this index using an arbitrage portfolio of only three shares.

Stock	Number of Shares	Current Price	Value (£000)	w_i %	Beta	$w_i \times$ Beta
Orpington	20,000	200p	40	⅓	0.8	0.267
Teddington	10,000	400p	40	⅓	1.0	0.333
Islington	8,000	500p	40	⅓	1.2	0.400
Total			120	1		1.000

If the beta values turn out to be correct, this arbitrage portfolio will exactly replicate the CYROX index. Suppose that June CYROX futures are currently trading at 210 index points, that the riskless interest rate between now and June is 5% and the present value of dividends on the index basket between now and June is £3,000, while that for the arbitrage portfolio is £5,000. $F = (S-D)(1+r) = (120,000-3,000)(1.05) = £122,850$. Therefore CYROX futures are currently overpriced by $(210 \times 600 = £126,000)$ £126,000 - 122,850 = £3,150. Buy shares and sell futures. Suppose that during the period of the arbitrage the CYROX index rises by 20%, the value of the arbitrage portfolio will also rise by 20% because the arbitrage portfolio has a beta of 1.

Trades	Now	Delivery
Buy the arbitrage portfolio (120,000×1.2)	-120,000	144,000
Sell 1 CYROX June futures (200×1.2-210)600	-	-18,000
Debt (borrow to buy the shares) (120,000×1.05)	120,000	-126,000
Dividends at expiry (5,000×1.05)	-	5,250
Net cash flow	0	5,250

The additional arbitrage profit of $(5,250-3,150 =)$ £2,100 is caused by a higher dividends on the arbitrage portfolio than the index basket. When an arbitrage portfolio is used the mispricing computation should allow for any difference in dividends. If the actual betas for the period differ from the forecasts, the use of an arbitrage portfolio is risky.

Stock	Number of Shares	Current Price	Value (£000)	w_i %	Beta	$w_i \times$Beta
Orpington	20,000	200p	40	⅓	0.7	0.2333
Teddington	10,000	400p	40	⅓	0.9	0.3000
Islington	8,000	500p	40	⅓	1.1	0.3667
Total			120	1		0.9000

Trades	Now	Delivery
Buy the arbitrage portfolio (120,000×1.2×**0.9**)	−120,000	129,600
Sell 1 CYROX June futures (200×1.2−210)600	-	−18,000
Debt (borrow to buy the shares) (120,000×1.05)	120,000	−126,000
Dividends (5,000×1.05)	-	5,250
Net cash flow	0	−9,150

In this case the use of the arbitrage portfolio leads to a loss on the arbitrage.

Arbitrage is easier for interest rate or currency futures markets than for index futures because, in these other markets, the underlying asset can be purchased or sold in a single transaction. For market indices based on a small number of shares, e.g. the MMI with only twenty shares, arbitrage using all the shares in the index is much easier than for indices like the NYSE Composite, which comprises about 1,700 shares. A futures contract was traded on the FTA in an index called the Dutch Top 5 which consisted of just five shares (AKZO, KLM, Royal Dutch Shell, Philips and Unilever). This suggests that the size of the departures from the no-arbitrage condition will be a positive function of the number of shares in the index.

Arbitrage restores the no-arbitrage condition by increasing the demand for the underpriced asset and increasing the supply of the overpriced asset. However, if the arbitrage portfolios tend to contain roughly the same sub-set of shares, there will be little direct pressure on the prices of the remaining constituents of the index. This may lead to a distortion in relative prices as between the shares used in the arbitrage process and other shares. It is also possible that the shares chosen for inclusion in the arbitrage portfolio are those which have a high price elasticity. The choice of such shares will increase the profits of the arbitrageurs, as the adverse price movement (which helps to restore the no-arbitrage condition) will be minimized. To the extent that a two-tier market in shares develops, i.e. between shares in the arbitrage portfolio and the rest, traders may seek to exploit any perceived price differential between the two groups by trading shares, and this will tend to restore price relativities.

Sofianos (1993) studied the establishment of 1,442 arbitrage positions in the S&P500 during the first six months of 1990. He found that, for arbitrage involving a long position in shares (overpricings), approximately 400 of the 500 S&P500 stocks were traded. For an arbitrage involving a short position in shares (underpricings), only 140 stocks were traded. The much smaller number of stocks for short positions is probably due to difficulties with short selling (the uptick rule and higher transactions costs).

Neal (1995) analyzed 837 S&P500 arbitrage trades on the NYSE in the 3 month period of January to March 1989. He found that for the arbitrage of overpricings, the average number of stocks was 427. The arbitrage of underpricings was split into situations where the arbitrageur sold shares they already held (direct sell arbitrage), and those where short selling was required. Neal found that 28% of the arbitrage of underpricings did not involve short selling, as the arbitrageurs simply sold stocks they already held, and so were not constrained by the uptick rule. In addition, due to a misunderstanding of the regulations, arbitrage that involved short selling may, in practice, have been unconstrained by the uptick rule. In 1986 the SEC issued a statement exempting certain arbitrage trades from the uptick rule, provided the NYSE member retained a net long position in aggregate across all their customer accounts. While this statement was intended to apply only to liquidating trades, it was widely interpreted as applying to trades establishing arbitrage positions. The SEC position was clarified in April 1990.

Direct sell arbitrage (which was conducted almost entirely by institutional investors) involved the sale of 484 stocks, while for arbitrage involving short selling (which was carried out almost entirely by NYSE member firms) only 183 stocks were sold short. Neal discovered that the distribution of the number of stocks sold short by member firms was bimodal. 22% of trades used more than 405 stocks, while the median number of stocks for the remaining 78% of trades was only 85. He attributes this pattern to the confusion which then prevailed over short selling restrictions.

4.4.2 Arbitrage in the UK

In the UK in 1989 under 1% of the shares traded on the UK stock market were part of an index arbitrage transaction, while the corresponding figure for the NYSE for July to December 1989 was about 5%, Quality of Markets Unit (1989). (In Japan, the corresponding figures for arbitrage involving the Nikkei 225 in 1991 and the first five months of 1992 were 7% and 11.2%, Arai, Akamatsu & Yoshioka (1993).) Index arbitrage in the UK has been hampered in the past by the lack of a mechanism (such as DOT in the US) to speed up the process of trading a basket of shares, the requirement to pay stamp duty and insufficient liquidity to cope with large arbitrage trades without an adverse price movement, Price (1988).

In 1989 index arbitrage in the UK was conducted by a very small number of financial institutions (about six) on their own account, with only three or four institutions engaging in index arbitrage on a regular basis. These arbitrageurs are also market makers in a large proportion of the shares in the FTSE 100 index, and so they can buy and sell shares 'in-house' to and from the firm's own market makers. As market makers they have a number of important advantages. They (and charities) avoid paying stamp duty of 0.5% (1% prior to Big Bang) on purchases of shares that are sold within seven days. Market makers (and some members of Euronext-Liffe) also have special stock borrowing privileges which permits taking a short position in shares. Market makers have access to the inter dealer broker (IDB) systems, and are exempt from a duty to stop trading when in possession of inside information, Office of Fair Trading (1995). Since the share trades are 'in-house', the commission charges on dealing in the shares are notional. Therefore, these market makers have considerably lower transactions costs than other potential arbitrageurs. Since as market makers they already hold a position in almost all the stocks in the index basket, there is no need to use a subset of the index stocks, while such 'in-house' trading also reduces execution risk.

Yadav & Pope (1994) considered the suggestion that, when the index is rising, market makers run down their holdings of the shares in which they make a market, and when the index is falling they increase their holdings of such shares. Arbitrageurs, who are also market makers in many of the index stocks, tend to buy and sell shares 'in-house'. When the market making arm of the company has run down its holdings, in-house arbitrage of overpricings (which involves 'buying' shares from the market maker) will be possible only to a limited degree. Conversely, when the market making arm has increased its holdings, in-house arbitrage of underpricings (which involves 'selling' shares to the market maker) may be unattractive. Similar difficulties will be faced by arbitrageurs who are not also market makers. This implies that futures will tend to be overpriced in a rising market, and underpriced in a falling market. Yadav & Pope (1994) used hourly data for the FTSE 100 index from April 1986 to March 1990 to examine whether there was a connection in the UK between index returns and mispricings. They found a significant positive relationship, as predicted, but concluded that it was not of economic significance.

There has been effectively no involvement of UK funds in index arbitrage. This is for a number of reasons. First, there is the issue of taxation. Uncertainty over the tax position deterred some funds, but clarification by the 1990 Finance Act has removed this barrier; and this has encouraged these institutions to participate in futures markets to a greater extent than previously. Second, institutions must pay stamp duty of 0.5% when they buy shares. Third, the rules governing the investment policy of a fund may prohibit the use of futures contracts, so preventing the fund from engaging in arbitrage. Fourth, the fund may lack the accounting systems and performance measurement techniques to incorporate futures, so discouraging their use. Finally, the management of the fund may be unfamiliar with futures trading, and be cautious about engaging in arbitrage transactions. See chapter 10.3 for further discussion of the barriers to the use of index futures by institutional investors. The changes to the taxation of futures do not mean that pension funds and unit trusts will become major participants in index arbitrage; and market makers remain well placed to execute index arbitrage transactions.

4.4.3 Computer Trading

To discover arbitrage possibilities in the FTSE 100 index it is necessary to keep track of the prices of the 100 shares in the index, i.e. $£S$, as well as the present value of the expected dividends before delivery for each of these 100 shares, i.e. $£D$, for each of the three outstanding delivery dates. In addition, the price of the futures contract, i.e. $£F$, for the three delivery dates, the cost of borrowing funds (r) for the three periods and the transactions costs must also be considered. Since the analysis of this data must be performed in real time, traders use computers. As well as searching for arbitrage opportunities, computers can also be used to initiate programme trades. In the US, shares can be traded on the NYSE via computer orders to the exchange's DOT system. This sends such orders electronically and simultaneously to many market makers, and so speeds up taking a position in the shares of many different companies. Harris, Sofianos & Shapiro (1994) estimated the time lag in June 1989 between the submission of a programme trade and the shares being purchased on the NYSE at about two minutes for a market order, and longer for tick-sensitive orders. In the UK brokers can execute smaller trades (up to half the stock's normal market size) using the SEAQ Automatic Execution Facility (SAEF) at the best price available on SEAQ.

4.4.4 Programme Trading

Programme trading is the simultaneous trading of a basket of shares as part of a strategy or plan, and it predates trading using computers (Board & Sutcliffe, 2005b). The NYSE definition of a programme trade requires the simultaneous trading of at least 15 stocks with a total value of over $1 million. The most important form of programme trading is the buying and selling of shares as part of index arbitrage. Harris, Sofianos & Shapiro (1994) found that, during the years 1989 and 1990, for the 29,186 index arbitrage programme trades on the NYSE, the average trade was valued at $5.9 million and involved shares in 201 stocks for buy trades, and 154 stocks for sell trades. For the first six months of 1990, Sofianos (1993) found that the average S&P500 index arbitrage position involved 280 stocks, and was valued at $7 million. Neal (1995) studied 837 arbitrage trades on the NYSE in the first three months of 1989, and found that the average value per trade was about $9 million. Other forms of programme trading include portfolio insurance (see chapter 12.2).

Programme trading has attracted much criticism, especially after the stock market collapses in October 1987 and October 1989. Although the profit per contract from arbitrage is small, because riskless profits are available, a very large volume of transactions will be initiated, and this is claimed to destabilize financial markets, see chapter 12. A number of studies, e.g. Furbush (1989), have found little evidence to substantiate the claim that programme trading was a major factor in the 1987 stock market crash.

Duffee, Kupiec & White (1992) report that 97% of programme trading on the NYSE between July 1988 and November 1989 was handled by thirteen firms, with

43% of programme trading handled by just three firms (Morgan Stanley, Kidder Peabody and Merrill Lynch). About two thirds of programme trading was on behalf of clients, while the remaining third was by these thirteen firms for their own account. Four firms (Morgan Stanley, Kidder Peabody, Susquehanna and Bear Stearns) dominated trading by firms on their own account, and were responsible for initiating about a quarter of all programme trading on the NYSE.

4.5 Conclusions

While futures prices are usually very close to their no-arbitrage levels, arbitrage opportunities have been found in all the markets so far tested. These arbitrage opportunities are typically no more than one or two percent of the spot price. There are a number of explanations for these results, but it is not yet clear which explanations are correct. Studies of the dynamic behaviour of mispricings have found that the absolute size of mispricings declines as delivery approaches. It has also been found that mispricings tend to persist over time (e.g. a few hours or a few days), but to reduce in size within say 15 minutes. These results may be due to arbitrage activity; although it has been suggested that stale prices may be responsible. Finally, there is some evidence of a negative link between the levels of volatility and mispricings.

Chapter 5

Arbitrage and Relaxing the Assumptions

Introduction

In this chapter, the assumptions underlying the derivation of the no-arbitrage condition in chapter 3 are considered in detail. The assumptions used in chapter 3 will be analyzed from two viewpoints. First, if an assumption is dropped, can a different no-arbitrage condition be derived? If it can, is the assumption concerned a simplifying assumption, and gross violations of the assumption encompassed by a more general formula? Second, to what extent is the assumption met in reality, and how large is the effect of violation on the validity of the no-arbitrage condition? If the effects are large, and a more general no-arbitrage condition relaxing the assumption cannot be derived, the validity of the no-arbitrage condition is conditional on the relevant assumption.

5.1 No Marking to the Market

The derivation of the no-arbitrage condition relates to a forward rather than a futures contract as marking to the market is ignored. This implies that any gains or losses on the futures contract are not received until delivery. Cox, Ingersoll & Ross (1981) have shown that, if riskless interest rates are certain (and the other assumptions apply), despite the presence of marking to the market for futures contracts, futures and forward contracts have an identical price. Appendix A to chapter 5 of Sutcliffe (1993) contains a proof of this result. Thus, if the no marking to the market assumption is replaced with an assumption that riskless interest rates are certain, the no-arbitrage condition in chapter 3 for futures prices still applies. In chapter 5.3 it is shown that the assumption of a riskless interest rate can also be relaxed.

Assuming no marking to the market rules out any effects from price limits on the no-arbitrage futures price, except when the price limits affect the final settlement price, see the Chance model in chapter 11.3.2.

5.2 Single Riskless Interest Rate

The derivation of the no-arbitrage condition requires that the risk free borrowing and lending rates are equal. That the arbitrageur can lend money at the riskless rate of interest appears sensible, but it is more questionable to assume that he or she can also borrow at the riskless rate (although if the marginal arbitrageur is a large financial institution, the assumption may be reasonable). The justification for this assumption is that the arbitrage transaction is riskless, and so repayment is guaranteed. However, in reality all the assumptions that underlie riskless arbitrage will not be met, and so there will always be some risk. The derivation of a no-arbitrage condition relies on the use of the capital market to move the cash flows arising from the arbitrage transaction through time so that they are non-negative in all time periods, and positive at least once. If the capital market is imperfect such that the lending rate exceeds the borrowing rate, the results of the arbitrage argument may vary, depending on whether cash is being moved forwards in time at the lending rate, or backwards in time at the borrowing rate. In this situation, whether an arbitrage transaction is attractive or not depends on the time preferences of the arbitrageur, and it is not possible to state a general no-arbitrage condition.

If an arbitrageur's borrowing rate (r_b) exceeds the riskless lending rate (r_l), then a no-arbitrage band will be created, and small overpricings will now lie inside this no-arbitrage band. Thus $(S-D)(1+rl) \leq F \leq (S-D)(1+r_b)$.

5.3 Constant Riskless Interest Rate

If there is no marking to the market, variations in the riskless interest rate have no effect on the no-arbitrage condition. This is because the arbitrageur locks in the interest rate when the arbitrage position is initiated, and subsequent variations are irrelevant. However, since marking to the market is a universal feature of futures contracts, the simultaneous relaxation of both the no marking to the market and the constant riskless interest rate assumptions will be examined.

In the presence of marking to the market, provided the changes in the riskless interest rate are known with certainty, while the proof becomes more complicated, the no-arbitrage condition remains valid. Levy (1989), Flesaker (1991) and Sercu & Uppal (1995, pp. 155-9) have shown that assuming the changes in the riskless interest rate are known (and that contracts are divisible, Polakoff, 1991), is equivalent to assuming that each day the traders know the next day's risk free interest rate with certainty. While interest rates until delivery are not known with certainty, the risk free rate for the following day can be predicted with considerable accuracy. This implies that any differences between forward and futures prices will be inconsequential. Jabbour & Sachlis (1993) pointed out that the dynamic strategy for replicating the terminal cash flow of a forward contract using futures generates considerable transactions costs, while the forward contract itself will probably have much smaller transactions costs. This implies that differences between forward and futures prices can emerge, provided they do not exceed the difference in transactions costs.

An obvious way to examine whether marking to the market in the presence of stochastic interest rates leads to a difference between futures and forward prices, is to compare actual futures and forward prices for the same asset. However, this approach encounters two problems. First, for many assets (e.g. stock market indices) there is either a futures market or a forward market, but not both; and so a direct comparison is not possible. Second, if a difference is found this may be due to a range of factors besides marking to the market with stochastic interest rates, e.g. default risk, liquidity, the greater ease of exercising the early unwinding option in futures rather than forward markets, regulation etc, (see chapter 2.8 for a list of differences between futures and forward markets). Therefore, a simple comparison of the futures and forward prices of those assets where trading exists in both, is not an adequate test.

However, an alternative method for investigating this problem, which overcomes both of these difficulties, has been provided by Cox, Ingersoll & Ross (1981). They derived the theoretical result that positive (negative) correlation between the risk free interest rate and percentage changes in futures prices implies that the futures price is greater (smaller) than the forward price. Given the validity of this theoretical result, the size and direction of this correlation for existing futures can be used to draw inferences about the effect of marking to the market on futures prices. However, there are problems in determining the proportion of any price differential that is due to marking to the market and stochastic interest rates. There have been a number of empirical studies of various assets where both futures and forward markets exist. These are largely based on the idea that the correlation of changes in spot and futures prices with stochastic interest rates differs between commodities, and so the importance of marking to the market will also differ. Some studies of commodities other than index futures are summarized in appendix 5.B of Sutcliffe (1993), and generally confirm the theory of Cox, Ingersoll & Ross (1981).

USA. A study of the MMI by Chang, Loo & Chang (1990) analyzed the difference between futures and forward prices using a test which differs from that proposed by Cox, Ingersoll & Ross (1981). Since no forward contract exists on the MMI, they used a synthetic forward contract based on MMI call and put options. Using daily data for 1984-5, they found that the covariance between the riskless rate of interest and the rate of return on the spot asset had a statistically significant positive effect on the futures price. This test supports the view that marking to the market with stochastic interest rates can have a small but measurable effect on futures prices.

Cakici & Chatterjee (1991) examined daily closing prices for the S&P500 for 1982-7, and compared the mispricings calculated using a no-arbitrage condition which allowed for stochastic interest rates, and one which did not. The model with stochastic interest rates assumed that interest rates followed a mean-reverting process, and that the correlation between changes in interest rates and changes in spot prices was zero (which is questionable). The mispricings for 1986 and 1987 were significantly larger when no allowance was made for stochastic interest rates, but there was no difference for 1982 to 1985. A simulation analysis, in which the correlation between changes in interest rates and changes in spot prices was not constrained to be zero, found that stochastic interest rates only affected the no-arbitrage price when strong mean-reverting movements were expected. Such movements were expected when the current interest rate was well above or below its long run mean, and there was a high degree of reversion each time period. They concluded that the importance of allowing for stochastic interest rates varies over time, depending on whether or not large changes in interest rates are expected.

Modest (1984) also made use of a no-arbitrage condition to test the effects of marking to the market in the presence of stochastic interest rates on the prices of index futures. He used stochastic simulation to examine the no-arbitrage price of the S&P500, and found there to be little effect.

Japan.   Bailey (1989) analyzed daily data on the Nikkei 225 traded on SGX for 1986-7, and on the Osaka 50 Kabusaki for 1987. He used a no-arbitrage condition which allowed for stochastic interest rates, and found this had very little effect on the results.

Australia.   Only one of the six studies of the effects of marking to the market on index futures, (Twite, 1992), has used the Cox, Ingersoll & Ross results. Twite (1992) examined daily data on the Australian AOI for 1983-6 and found a significantly positive correlation between futures returns and the riskless rate of interest. This implies that forward prices exceeded futures prices, i.e. that marking to the market and stochastic interest rates reduced the futures price. Twite concluded that there is limited support for marking to the market having an effect on futures prices.

UK.   Yadav & Pope (1992b, 1994) investigated the effects of marking to the market on the profits from arbitrage positions held unchanged until delivery. Using daily data on the FTSE 100 for 1986-90, the effects were usually small, with a mean of 0.014% of the spot price. Thus, the average effect of marking to the market was an additional profit of about £8 per contract. The consequences for arbitrage risk were also generally small, and 88% of the cases fell within the range 0.1% to -0.1% (that is an extra profit or loss of about £60 per contract). However, there were a few outliers with values of over 0.4%, and so marking to the market occasionally had an important effect on arbitrage profits.

It appears that the effect of marking to the market with stochastic interest rates is generally rather small, can vary as between futures (depending on the sensitivity of their price to movements in interest rates) and may also vary over time for the same future. Polakoff & Diz (1992) have argued that the assumption that futures contracts are divisible, which underlies the Cox, Ingersoll & Ross model, is unrealistic. They demonstrate that when futures are indivisible, even if movements in futures prices can be predicted and interest rates are constant (and so there is zero correlation between futures prices and interest rates), futures and forward prices will differ. Thus the Cox, Ingersoll & Ross result is changed, and forward and futures prices will differ, even when there is zero correlation between futures prices and interest rates. Polakoff & Diz have also shown that indivisibility will induce autocorrelation in futures-forward price differences. They studied sterling, Deutschmark, yen and Swiss franc futures-forward price differences and found evidence of autocorrelation, which they interpreted as caused by futures contract indivisibility. Such autocorrelation may invalidate the significance tests in the previous empirical studies of the futures-forward price differential.

Empirically, the assumption of constant interest rates has usually been found to be an acceptable approximation. Therefore, while Cornell & French (1983a & 1983b) have derived a generalized no-arbitrage condition for the case when interest rates are stochastic and there is marking to the market, it is of little practical interest.

If the effects of marking to the market are thought to be substantial, these can be reduced by tailing the futures position used in the arbitrage. A change in the futures price generates an immediate payment or receipt of variation margin, which must be borrowed or invested until delivery. Therefore, a change in the futures price now of ΔF leads to a cash flow of $\Delta F(1+r)$ at delivery, where r is the riskless interest rate between now and delivery. To allow for tail risk, the number of futures contracts used in the arbitrage is reduced to $1/(1+r)$ times the initial number of contracts. Each day the value of r declines, and so the futures position should be recomputed each day. (Tailing is discussed further in chapter 9.10, in the context of hedging.)

Example. Consider the Lawrence Garfield example from chapter 3. He used a short position of 1,942 contracts in his arbitrage. If he wishes to tail his position, he will hold only $1,942 \times (1/1.02411) = 1,896$ contracts at the start of his arbitrage. When there is only one month before delivery, the riskless interest rate until delivery is 0.80%, and so the tailed futures position is $1,942 \times (1/1.008) = 1,927$ contracts. On the day the arbitrage position is established, the price of FTSE 100 futures rises from £53,000 to £53,500. Subsequently, (and unrealistically) the futures price is unchanged, so that the delivery price is also £53,500. Without tailing his futures position, Lawrence must bear the additional cost of financing the payment of variation margin of $(53,500-53,000) \times 1,942 = £971,000$ for the next three months, i.e. $971,000 \times 0.02411 = £23,411$. If he tails his position, the cost of financing the payment of variation margin falls to $(53,500-53,000) \times 1,896 \times 0.02411 = £22,856$. Thus tailing has avoided interest charges of £555 on variation margin payments. As maturity approaches, he steadily increases his short position in futures, so that at delivery he has 1,942 contracts.

5.4 No Taxes

The introduction of taxes may, or may not, affect the no-arbitrage condition. If capital gains, interest and dividends are taxed at the same rate ($x\%$) payable at delivery, and the tax on dividends is computed on their present value at the start of the arbitrage, the no-arbitrage condition is unaffected. Note that losses generate tax credits received at delivery. The resulting cash flows from matching long positions in shares and futures are shown in table 5.1, which is based on table 3.1.

Table 5.1: Cash Flows (Including Tax) for Long Positions in Futures and Shares

	Time		
	0	**T**	**Tax at T**
Future (long)	0	(S_T-F)	$-(S_T-F)x$
Shares (long)	$-S$	S_T	$-(S_T-S)x$
Dividends	D	-	$-Dx$
Differential Cash Flows	$S-D$	$-F$	$(F-S)x+Dx$

Discounting by the post-tax risk free interest rate $r(1-x)$ and setting the result equal to zero, i.e. no arbitrage profits, gives $S-D-(F-(F-S)x-Dx)/(1+r-rx) = 0$. This can be rearranged to give $F = (S-D)(1+r)$, as before. Note that the tax rate x can differ between arbitrageurs, and they will all still agree on a common no-arbitrage price.

However, if the assumptions are changed, taxation may well affect the no-arbitrage condition. For example, in the US, until 1986, all gains and losses on futures contracts were taxed at the long term rate of tax, while gains and losses on shares held for less than six months were taxed at the higher short term rate. In consequence, while the gross gains and losses on the futures contracts and shares in an arbitrage transaction were equal, the net gains and losses were not, Schwarz, Hill & Schneeweis (1986, pp 105-106). Thus, while the gross profit on an arbitrage transaction may be zero, because of differential taxation of the profits and losses on futures and shares, the net profit may be positive or negative. This will alter the trader's no-arbitrage condition. Similarly, if the trader's transactions costs are tax deductible, the no-arbitrage condition will be altered.

There is also the question of the taxation of dividends on the shares in the index. While the recipient of dividends may be taxed, those who have sold shares short (and must therefore pay, or manufacture, dividends to the buyer) may not receive an equivalent payment, or tax credit. Even if they do, the timing of the tax payments by the recipient of dividends may differ from that of the tax payments to those making dividend payments. In this case the present value of the dividends will differ, depending on whether they are being received or paid, and the no-arbitrage condition becomes a no-arbitrage band: $(S-D_P)\times(1+r) \leq F \leq (S-D_R)\times(1+r)$, where D_R is the present value of dividends received, and D_P is the present value of dividends paid on shares sold short. This band only exists if $D_P > D_R$.

5.4.1 Tax Timing Option

As well as differential tax rates, the timing of tax payments may also differ. The 'tax timing option' is available for shares but not futures in the US and UK. With daily marking to the market, the capital gains and losses on an index futures contract are realized every day and the owner has no discretion over their timing, i.e. shifting capital gains and losses between tax years. For shares, capital gains and losses are only recognized when the share is sold, and this is directly under the owner's control. For this tax timing option for shares to be valuable, the marginal tax payer must not be tax exempt (e.g. not be a pension fund), and must be capable of holding the shares into the next tax period (e.g. not be an arbitrageur or market maker). Thus the presence of a valuable tax timing option is an empirical issue.

USA.   Cornell & French (1983a, 1983b) included different income and capital gains taxes on futures and shares in their no-arbitrage condition, incorporated the tax timing option and also allowed for stochastic interest rates. They found that allowing for the tax timing option (as well as stochastic interest rates and different income and capital gains tax rates) in the no-arbitrage condition resulted in the no-arbitrage prices of the S&P500 moving much closer to the actual prices for 1982 than if no such adjustments were made to the no-arbitrage condition. However, a later study by Cornell (1985a) found that the mispricing for the S&P500 was no longer present, and he concluded that the tax timing option had become unimportant.

If the tax timing option is valuable, its value will increase as index volatility increases. Since a valuable tax timing option increases the value of the spot (relative to the future), an increase in spot volatility will lead to futures becoming underpriced (relative to the theoretical futures price which ignores the tax timing option), i.e. there will be a negative relationship between the mispricing and spot volatility, as found in chapter 4.3.

UK.   Using hourly data for the FTSE 100 for 1986-90, Yadav & Pope (1994) found a *positive* relationship between mispricings and spot volatility (measured using the implied volatility from FTSE 100 call option prices). Hence, for the UK, the tax timing option appears to be of no value.

5.5 Certain Dividends

FTSE 100 futures have a maximum life of twelve months, and most of the volume occurs in the last four months of the contract's life. Given the short period to maturity, there may be little remaining dividend uncertainty. For example, in the UK the average period between the ex-dividend date and payment of the dividend is fifty three days, while the dividend is announced a few weeks before the ex-dividend date, Yadav & Pope (1994). Yadav & Pope (1990) investigated the assumption that the dividends on the shares in the index during the arbitrage period are known. They found that a 50% variation in dividends led to only a 0.3% change in the no-arbitrage futures price of the FTSE 100 index. Yadav & Pope (1994) examined the effects of two different sources of dividend risk; the size of the dividend, and the payment date. Dividends were estimated using last year's dividend plus 0% or 20%, and the resulting error in the proportionate mispricing was usually under 0.1%. They also found that an error of eight weeks in the date of payment led to an average error in the proportionate mispricing of only 0.01%. Hence, the no-arbitrage futures price is highly insensitive to the estimate of dividends used in the calculation, and the dividend certainty assumption is innocuous. If it is necessary to make allowance for uncertain dividends, Cornell & French (1983b) have derived the corresponding no-arbitrage condition. For performance indices, such as the DAX, there is no risk concerning the size and timing of dividends, Bühler & Kempf (1995).

5.6 No Transactions Costs

In reality, arbitrageurs incur transactions costs, and some estimates of the round trip transactions costs involved in stock index arbitrage are set out in table 5.2.

Table 5.2: Round Trip Transactions Costs for Index Futures Arbitrage

Author	Index Future	Round Trip Costs[††‡]
Billingsley & Chance (1988)	US futures	1%
Robertson (1990)	FTSE 100	1.85% institutions
		0.90% market makers
Yau, Schneeweis & Yung (1990)	Hang Seng	1.96%
Liffe & LTOM (1991) &	FTSE Eurotrack 100	1.67%[1]
Liffe (1991)		2.42%[2]
Chung, Kang & Rhee (1994b)	Nikkei St. Av. (Osaka)	2.7% institutions
		0.8% brokers

[†] Percentage of the value of the shares traded, [‡] The bid-ask spread is only paid once if the future is held to delivery and liquidated at the EDSP, [1] Buying shares and selling futures, [2] Selling shares and buying futures

It is possible to modify the no-arbitrage condition to cover the case in which transactions costs are present, Modest & Sundaresan (1983) and Klemkosky & Lee (1991). Instead of an equality, a no-arbitrage band emerges within which the prices of the spot and future can move without creating index arbitrage opportunities. This band is: $[(S-D)+(C_{SL}+C_{FN})] \geq F/(1+r) \geq [(S-D)-(C_{SN}+C_{FL})]$; where C_{SL} is the transactions cost of being long in the spot index i.e. buying shares in the index, C_{FN} is the transactions cost of being short in the future i.e. selling a futures, C_{SN} is the transactions cost of being short in the spot index i.e. selling short every share in the index and C_{FL} is the transactions cost of being long in the future i.e. buying a future. These transactions costs are expressed as present values at the date the arbitrage is initiated. It is likely the transactions costs of being short differ from those of being long i.e. $C_{SL} \neq C_{SN}$, and $C_{FN} \neq C_{FL}$. Some transactions costs differ between traders, and the relevant transactions costs for the no-arbitrage band are those faced by the marginal trader, usually the market makers in the underlying shares.

If futures are overpriced (after allowing for transactions costs), arbitrageurs will sell futures and buy shares, and so eliminate the initial overpricing. Therefore, the upper bound of the no-arbitrage band includes the transactions costs of selling futures and buying shares, while the lower bound involves the transactions costs of buying futures and selling shares. If all the transactions costs are zero, this condition collapses back to the previous no-arbitrage equality. This no-arbitrage band is illustrated in figure 5.1. Provided the futures price lies somewhere within this band, there are no arbitrage opportunities.

Sofianos (1993) analyzed 1,442 S&P500 index arbitrage positions in the first six months of 1990. He found that the expected arbitrage profit for overpricings was a loss of -20.2 index basis points, while the corresponding figure for underpricings was a profit of 21.1 index basis points. This difference of 41.3 index basis points in the expected profit means that the no-arbitrage band is not symmetrical, as larger underpricings are required before arbitrage is triggered. This asymmetry is probably due to the higher transactions costs and risks associated with short selling.

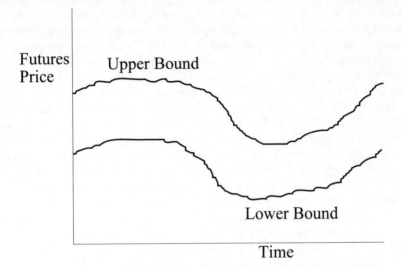

Figure 5.1: No-Arbitrage Band Due to Transactions Costs

The presence of transactions costs is responsible for a number of features of the trading of index futures. First, without the presence of substantial transactions costs for trading the index basket, the early unwinding and rollover options (see chapter 3.5) would be of little value. Second, if index futures were subject to physical delivery, as was the Osaka 50 Kabusaki, the transactions costs (and the increase in trading volume) of liquidating the arbitrage portfolio at delivery would be avoided, Stoll (1987).

5.6.1 Transactions Costs Risk

In many countries a substantial part of the transactions costs of an arbitrage transaction are unknown when the arbitrage is initiated, making the arbitrage risky. This risk can occur because the bid-ask spread and brokers' commission when unwinding the spot position at delivery vary with the value of the index basket. In addition, there may be a transactions tax which also varies in proportion to the index, e.g. an arbitrageur in the UK who buys the index basket at delivery must pay 0.5% stamp duty. However, in this situation it is possible to remove the transactions cost risk by departing from the usual one-to-one ratio for the size of the spot and futures positions. Adams & Van Deventer (1992) propose that when the arbitrageur is buying shares and selling futures, for every one futures contract sold, the arbitrageur should buy $1/(1-p)$ index baskets, where p is the proportion of the value of the index basket that must be paid in transactions costs at delivery. When selling shares and buying futures, the arbitrageur should sell $1/(1+p)$ index baskets for every futures contract bought. This removes the transactions cost risk from the arbitrage. In this case, the no-arbitrage band can be restated as $[(S-D+C_1)/(1-p)] \geq F/(1+r) \geq [(S-D-C_2)/(1+p)];$ where C_1 is the fixed transactions cost at the time the arbitrage is initiated of buying the index basket and selling a future, while C_2 is the fixed transactions cost at the time the arbitrage is initiated of selling the index basket and buying a future. In the above formula, it is assumed that there are no costs for unwinding the futures position, while all the costs of unwinding the spot position are proportional to the index at delivery.

Example. The Dagenham Fund, which is managed by Archie Rice, wishes to arbitrage the FTSE 100. The current value of this index in September is 3,700 points, while the December FTSE 100 future is priced at 3,539 index points. The present value of dividends on the index between September and December is £1,400, while the riskless rate of interest for this period is 2%. This gives a no-arbitrage futures price of £36,312. Therefore, ignoring transactions costs, the futures are underpriced by £922. The relevant transactions costs today for selling the index basket now and buying a future (C_2) are £400, while the transactions costs for buying the index basket at delivery in December are 0.7% of the value of the shares at that time. There will be no charge in December for settling the futures contract, and no fixed transactions costs for unwinding the spot position. The risk is that, for every 100 index points that the FTSE 100 rises between now and December, the transactions costs rise by £17.50.

To remove the transactions cost risk, Archie Rice uses the ratio $1/(1+p)$, where $p = 0.007$, and ignoring indivisibilities, sells 0.993049 index baskets, and buys one December FTSE 100 future. His arbitrage profit at delivery is as follows:

Shares short	$(S(1+r)-S_T)/(1+p) =$	$-0.993049S_T+£37,478$
Dividends	$-D(1+r)/(1+p) =$	$-£1,418$
Futures long	$S_T-F =$	$S_T-£35,390$
Transactions costs	$-C_2(1+r)/(1+p) -pS_T/(1+p) =$	$-£405-0.00696S_T$

The terms involving S_T (the spot price at delivery) cancel out, and so the total arbitrage profit at delivery is £265. This profit is independent of the value of S_T, and so is riskless.

5.6.2 Alternative Equilibrating Mechanisms

So far arbitrage has been considered as the equilibrating mechanism. This process generates two sets of round trip transactions costs: buying and selling the underlying shares and buying and selling the risk-free asset, as well as the cost of acquiring the futures position. Elton, Gruber & Rentzler (1984) and Stoll & Whaley (1993, pp. 109-111) identify three additional ways in which the spot and futures prices may be brought back into line - swaps, trade-the-cheapest and treasury bill substitution. (Kawaller (1991) has also identified similar mechanisms.) While arbitrage is open to any investor, these three alternative strategies, which will now be explained, are open to only a limited number of investors.

a. Swaps.   First, an investor who holds a long position in shares which are overpriced can sell them and buy the relatively underpriced index future, i.e. a swap or stock replacement. (Such investors have been called substituters, Gammill & Marsh, 1988.) This will generate lower transactions costs than arbitrage as it requires only one sale of shares and one purchase of futures; assuming that the investor would have closed out his or her long position in shares at the delivery date anyway, or is content to roll over the long futures position until they would otherwise have sold their share portfolio. It should prove attractive to investors who, for other reasons, wish to have an investment in the market index. This strategy will be profitable until the sum of the transactions costs of selling the existing share portfolio and buying the index future (including the rollover costs, if any) exceeds the deviation from the no-arbitrage condition.

Example Lex Luthor holds a portfolio of shares corresponding to ten FTSE 100 futures. He aims to hold these shares for another year. The riskless interest rate for the life of the far contract is 5%, while the present value of the dividends on the portfolio during this period is £8,570. The current value of the portfolio of shares is £480,000, and so the no-arbitrage price of the far contract is $(48,000-857)1.05$ = £49,500. The current market price of the far contract is only £49,000. Lex sold the share portfolio for £480,000 and bought ten FTSE 100 futures at a price of £49,000 each. The profit at delivery before transactions costs, relative to continuing to hold the portfolio of shares, was $10[(S-D)\times(1+r)-F]$ = £5,000. Given that the alternative strategy is to continue to hold the portfolio of shares, this profit is independent of the value of the index at delivery, and so is riskless. At delivery, he bought another ten index futures for delivery at the end of the year, the date when he would otherwise have liquidated his share portfolio. The additional transactions costs of this swap strategy are to buy ten index futures (twice), and it is only attractive if these are less than £5,000. (Note that the costs of liquidating the share position are not relevant.)

b. Trade-the-Cheapest.   Second, investors who have decided they wish to take an open position in the market index must choose between using shares or futures, Kawaller (1987). Presumably, they will choose the cheapest method and the cumulative market impact of these trades will tend to alter the relative prices of shares and futures towards conforming with the no-arbitrage condition. Similarly, those who wish to end an open position in the market can do so, initially, by taking an offsetting position in the other asset, (futures or shares), as well as by liquidating their position directly. Again, they are presumed to choose the most advantageous alternative, and this will tend to restore the no-arbitrage condition. Of course, this process is still subject to transactions costs, but these may be just the cost of buying (selling) either a future or the underlying shares. The deviations from the no-arbitrage condition that cannot be removed in this way should not exceed the difference in transactions costs between the alternative strategies, i.e. trading futures or the underlying shares.

Example Leonard H. McCoy owns a portfolio of shares corresponding to twenty FTSE 100 futures, which he decides to sell. The data are the same as in the Lex

Luthor example, i.e. S = £48,000, D = £857, r = 5% and the no-arbitrage price of the future is £49,500. The only difference is that the actual futures price is £50,000. Instead of selling the share portfolio now for £960,000, he opens a short position of twenty FTSE 100 contracts. At delivery the shares are sold to give a profit (relative to that obtained by immediately selling the portfolio of shares) before transactions costs of $20[F-(S-D)\times(1+r)]$ = £30,000. This profit is independent of the value of the share portfolio at delivery. The additional transactions costs were only for selling twenty index futures.

Miller (1993) has explained how foreign brokers in Japan made profits from index futures trading, in terms of trading the cheapest and differential transactions costs. The transactions costs for a Japanese investor buying an index basket of shares were 30 to 50 times greater than for members of the TSE. The transactions costs for trading index futures were small for both groups. This created an opportunity for 'commission arbitrage'. The foreign brokers bought an index basket of shares at a price of A, and sold an equivalent number of futures to Japanese investors at a price of D (equivalent to a no-arbitrage spot price of B), where $B > A$. Thus the foreign brokers made a profit of $B-A$ on each contract. These transactions give the appearance that the foreign brokers are arbitraging an overpricing of index futures. Japanese investors were willing to engage in this trade because B was lower than C, the price they would have had to pay for the basket of shares. Therefore, investors who wished to buy a portfolio of shares made a saving of $C-B$ per index basket by using index futures instead.

c. Treasury Bill Substitution.   If a trader wishes to hold a long position in treasury bills, this can be achieved either by buying treasury bills directly, or by buying the index basket and simultaneously selling the corresponding index futures - synthetic treasury bills. The net position is riskless and, if the no-arbitrage condition applies, will have a return equal to the risk free rate. However, if the index futures are overpriced, this strategy will give a higher return than the riskless rate. It is very similar to arbitrage, except that the trader starts with an initial sum of capital, and so there is no need to borrow to finance the arbitrage.

Thus, the no-arbitrage condition can be tested with respect to four alternative trading strategies: arbitrage, swaps, trade-the-cheapest and treasury bill substitution. Assuming the no-arbitrage condition is correct in the absence of transactions costs, these transactions costs set upper and lower bounds on the departures from this condition that can occur in a competitive market. The weakest test of conformity with the no-arbitrage condition uses the bounds set by the transactions costs of arbitrage. Since this strategy generates riskless profits and is open to anyone, it should always be met. Treasury bill substitution is very similar to arbitrage, except there is no need to borrow the initial capital required. The swap strategy provides a more demanding test as the transactions costs will be lower. However, it is only open to those who already hold the overpriced asset and so relies on this group of investors trading sufficient assets to move the relative prices of the shares in the index and index futures back into line. Finally, the trade-the-cheapest strategy provides the tightest bounds on the deviations from the no-arbitrage condition in the absence of transactions costs, as the relevant transactions costs are the difference between those for buying (or selling) futures and the underlying shares. Provided a sufficiently large flow of investors are taking new positions in the market, this trade-the-cheapest strategy will effectively restore the no-arbitrage condition.

Neal (1995) analyzed 837 arbitrage trades on the NYSE in the first three months of 1989. If there is a single no-arbitrage band, then the moment the mispricing exceeds the threshold, arbitrage trades will be submitted and the mispricing will move back towards zero. However, Neal found a wide dispersion in the mispricings that were current when arbitrage trades were submitted. This could be due to submission lags having a random effect on the size of the mispricing that was current when the arbitrage was actually submitted, variation in the value of the early unwinding option, and a range of no-arbitrage bands due to variations in costs between potential arbitrageurs.

Arago, Corredor & Santamaria (2003) studied daily closing prices for the Ibex 35 for 1996-97. In January 1997 there was a dramatic reduction in the transactions costs of trading Ibex 35 index futures. As expected, the correlation between the spot and futures prices increased, as did volatility spillovers between these two markets. A range of other possible explanations (a decrease in small trades reducing the influence of noise traders, an increase in volume reducing the stale price problem, and the Asian Crisis creating large correlated moves in the variables) were ruled out. This leaves a narrowing of the no-arbitrage band as the explanation.

5.6.3 Differential Transactions Costs and Threshold Effects

Pope & Yadav (1992) argued that potential arbitrageurs can be divided into groups, each with a different level of arbitrage transactions costs. Every group has a limited amount of money available for arbitrage transactions (possible due to self-imposed position limits). In this case, the supply of arbitrage services is a step function, with a large increase in arbitrage supply occurring when the mispricing is just large enough to cover the transactions costs of a new group of arbitrageurs. This sequence of potential arbitrageurs, in order of increasing transactions costs, is known as 'the queue', Conrardy (1993).

USA.   Yadav, Pope & Paudyal (1994) looked for arbitrage thresholds using data on the March 1987 contract of the S&P500. For prices sampled every 15, 30 and 60 minutes, they concluded that there were thresholds, that these thresholds were small (e.g. 0.1% to 0.3%) and that overpricings had a lower absolute threshold than underpricings (possibly due to the costs of short selling shares when arbitraging underpricings).

Martens, Kofman & Vorst (1995) also looked for such threshold effects in the mispricings of S&P500 futures. They used 1-minute log returns for seven months of 1993, and identified four thresholds for each month. Using an ECM, they found some evidence that the mean reversion in mispricings was weaker for those mispricings lying close to zero, i.e. below the smallest positive threshold and above the smallest negative threshold. This accords with an absence of arbitrage in this range, with the weak mean reversion being due to stale prices, as proposed by Miller, Muthuswamy & Whaley (1994).

Dwyer, Locke & Yu (1996) used minute to minute mispricings for the S&P500 for 1982-90 to look for threshold effects in arbitrage activity caused by transactions costs. Using a threshold ECM approach, they found a threshold effect at transactions costs of about 0.13%. This was argued to be consistent with the threshold used by arbitrageurs who allow for the benefits of the early unwinding option.

UK.   Pope & Yadav (1992) tested their threshold model using hourly data on the FTSE 100 for 1986-8, and found about two or three steps (or transactions cost thresholds) ranging between 0.1% and 1.6%. In consequence they accepted the hypothesis of a step function for the supply of arbitrage services. This conclusion is supported by the results of Yadav & Pope (1992c), which are discussed in chapter 4.2.1.

5.6.4 Exchange Traded Funds (ETFs)

Since they offer a way of trading the index basket of shares with lower transactions costs, Park & Switzer (1995b) investigated the effect of the introduction of TIPs on 9th March 1990, see chapter 2.11. The found that the volume of trading in TSE 35 futures increased after March 1990, while volume in the TSE 35 stocks did not increase. Futures and TSE 35 volume were adjusted by deflating by the volume of trading in shares in the TSE 300 index (excluding the TSE 35 stocks). This suggests that the introduction of TIPs led to an increase in futures arbitrage using TIPs rather than shares. A GARCH analysis of daily proportionate mispricings found that they decreased in size after the introduction of TIPs, again supporting the view that TIPs facilitated arbitrage.

The creation of ETFs in the early 1990s meant that a trading the underlying basket of shares became quicker, cheaper and easier. Switzer, Varson & Zghidi (2000) studied arbitrage between S&P500 futures and Spiders (the ETF on the S&P index) for 1990-96. They found that the introduction of Spiders on 29th January 1993 resulted in a small but significant reduction in the magnitude of the mispricings.

On 10th March 1999, an ETF (called QQQ or Qubes) based on the NASDAQ 100 index began trading. Using trade data for 1998-99, Kuron & Lasser (2002) found that the introduction of Qubes led to a reduction in the magnitude and frequency of violations of the no-arbitrage boundary. These arbitrage opportunities also disappeared faster than previously (i.e. within two minutes). This conclusion cannot be explained by changes in price volatility or futures volume.

5.7 No Initial Margin

The derivation of the no-arbitrage condition can be generalized to include the case where initial margin payments are required. Provided the margin payments earn interest at the risk free rate, the resulting no-arbitrage condition is unaltered. This is illustrated in the earlier examples of arbitrage by Lawrence Garfield and Scarlet O'Hara in chapter 3. For FTSE 100 futures, clearing house members can choose to meet their initial margin obligations by depositing a wide range of financial assets (see chapter 2.2.7), while interest is paid by the clearing house on cash deposits over £50,000. In the UK, private investors generally do not receive interest from their brokers on the balance in their margin accounts. However, retail clients are most unlikely to be arbitrageurs.

5.8 No Continuous Compounding

Each of the ways of expressing the no-arbitrage condition considered in chapter 3.3 allows for compound growth, but not for continuous compounding. It is possible to modify these various statements of the no-arbitrage condition to allow for continuous compounding. Ways in which this can be done are set out in appendix A to this chapter, where it is shown that the introduction of continuous compounding leads to more complicated no-arbitrage conditions than otherwise.

Real world interest rates are quoted in discrete rather than continuous terms. Therefore, although statements of the no-arbitrage condition which use continuous compounding are common in the academic literature, they are not used in this book; which uses $F = (S-D) \times (1+r)$.

5.9 Index Weights

The arbitrage arguments used in chapter 3 were based on the idea that, by holding a portfolio of the shares in the index with the same weights as the index, the price of this portfolio must converge at delivery to that of the index future. This applies for a market capitalization weighting system, and for a price average, but not for an index that uses equal weights. So, while it is possible to construct a fixed index-replicating portfolio for market value weighted indices, such as the FTSE 100 and the S&P500, and for price weighted indices, such as the Nikkei 225, the DJIA and the MMI, it is not possible for equally weighted indices, such as the VLA. The arbitrage portfolio for equally weighted indices must be continuously rebalanced if it is to exactly track the index, because the change in any single share price requires all the constituent shares to be traded to restore equality. This requirement results in high transactions costs because of the many trades required to rebalance the arbitrage portfolio, and also generates tracking risk due to the temporary mismatches between the index and the arbitrage portfolio before rebalancing can take place. This may explain why index futures have only been traded on one equally weighted arithmetic index - the VLA.

5.10 Arithmetic Index

The construction of a fixed index-replicating portfolio is also not possible for a geometric index. It is a property of geometric indices that they understate price rises and overstate the absolute size of price falls of a portfolio of shares, see chapter 1.4.3.1. Hence, it is not possible to replicate the movements in a geometric index with an unchanging portfolio of shares. While most of the indices on which index futures are traded are arithmetic indices, (e.g. S&P500, NYSE and FTSE 100), from 1982 to 1988 futures on a geometric index, the VLCI, were traded on the Kansas City Board of Trade. From 9th March 1988, this future was replaced by one on the Value Line Arithmetic index, which is the arithmetic equivalent of the VLCI.

Modest & Sundaresan (1983) have shown that the no-arbitrage condition for futures on a geometric index is different from that for an arithmetic index. For the zero transaction costs case they derived an inequality $F \leq (S-D) \times (1+r)$. Therefore, it is not possible to use this condition to argue that a future is underpriced, only that it is overpriced, see figure 5.2. This makes it difficult for traders to recognize arbitrage possibilities involving a future on a geometric index when the future is underpriced, and may account for the replacement of the geometric VLCI future by its arithmetic equivalent.

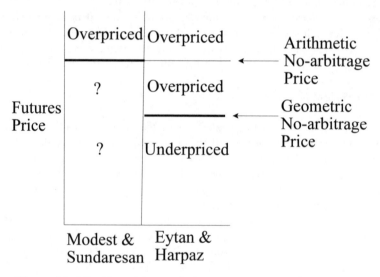

Figure 5.2: The No-arbitrage Price for Geometric Index Futures

Eytan & Harpaz (1986) derived a no-arbitrage condition for geometric indices covering both under and overpricing. If the no-arbitrage condition for an arithmetic future is written as $F = Se^{(\pi-\omega)h}$ (see appendix A to this chapter), the corresponding condition for a geometric index is $F = Se^{(\pi-\omega+\gamma)h}$, where π is the continuously compounded interest rate, ω is the continuous dividend rate and h is the time in years until delivery. The geometric no-arbitrage condition contains an extra term (γ), where γ is half the difference between the average of the variances of the instantaneous returns on the shares in the index $(\bar{\sigma}^2)$ and the variance of the instantaneous return on the index (σ^2_e), i.e. $\gamma = (\bar{\sigma}^2 - \sigma^2_e)/2$. The term γ must be non-negative, and so the no-arbitrage price for futures on a geometric index is lower than for the corresponding arithmetic index. This is illustrated in figure 5.2. While there is an exact no-arbitrage price for futures on geometric indices, it requires the calculation of γ, and this may be difficult and cause the arbitrage to be risky.

5.11 Price Index

Almost all the major indices on which futures are based are price indices, and so ignore dividend payments. However, the Ibovespa and DAX indices are performance indices and assume dividends are immediately reinvested in the shares of the company concerned, increasing the weight of that company in the index. Provided the arbitrageur immediately reinvests the dividends received, the value of the basket of shares and the index will converge at delivery. Given this immediate reinvestment strategy, it is possible to derive a simple no-arbitrage condition for performance indices. This strategy assumes that the rate of dividend tax used in computing the index $(1-x)\%$ is the rate paid by the arbitrageur. Let the gross value of the reinvested dividends at maturity be $D^{\ddagger}$, then table 3.1 becomes:

Table 5.3: Cash Flows for Long Positions in Futures and Shares

	Time	
	0	**T**
Future (long)	0	$S_T + xD^{\ddagger} - F$
Shares (long)	$-S$	$S_T + xD^{\ddagger}$
Differential Cash Flows	S	$-F$

where S_T represents the value at delivery of the initial basket of shares with no reinvestment of dividends. To rule out a risk free profit the present value of the differential cash flows must be zero, i.e. $S = F/(1+r)$, and so the no-arbitrage condition for a performance index is simply $F = S(1+r)$, which is the previous condition, but excluding the dividend adjustment to the index basket. Grünbichler & Callahan (1994). If the future is underpriced, this no-arbitrage condition not only implies an ability to short sell the index basket of shares, but also a slightly different arbitrage strategy. The arbitrageur pays out the dividends to the purchaser of the shares, less the arbitrageur's assumed tax credit of $(1-x)\%$; i.e. xD at time 0, where D is the present value of the dividends on the index basket of shares. The arbitrageur also short sells shares at time 0 for this amount, i.e. the arbitrageur receives xD at time 0 and pays $D^{\ddagger}$ at delivery.

If the tax rate on dividends payable by the arbitrageur differs from that assumed in the computation of the index, then dividends reappear in the no-arbitrage condition. For example, if the index assumes a $(1-x)\%$ tax on dividends, while the arbitrageur pays $(1-y)\%$, the above no-arbitrage condition becomes $F = S(1+r)+(x-y)D^{\dot{t}}$. Since $D^{\dot{t}}$ is uncertain, because it depends on the returns achieved on the reinvested dividends, this is not a riskless strategy and so is inappropriate for arbitrage. If the arbitrageur reinvests $x\%$ of the dividends in shares, and invests the remainder at the riskless rate, the riskless no-arbitrage condition is $F = (S+(x-y)D)\times(1+r)$. Note that this no-arbitrage condition involves D, not $D^{\dot{t}}$. When the future is underpriced, it is assumed the arbitrageur receives a tax credit of $(1-y)\%$ of the amount of dividends paid to the purchaser.

Example. Dr. Hannibal Lecter, manager of the Shiremoor Fund, decided to open an arbitrage position in the PAX. The PAX is an arithmetic capitalization-weighted performance index which consists of only two shares - Eltham and Feltham. On 28th December 1995 the PAX index stood at 100, while the prices and issued capital of Eltham and Feltham were 100p and 40 million shares, and 200p and 30 million shares respectively. The multiplier for PAX index futures is £100, and no dividends had been declared by either company since the weights were reset to remove the effects of previous dividends. Therefore, the index weights on 28th December 2005 were: Eltham $(40\times100)/(40\times100+30\times200) = 0.4$; and Feltham $(30\times200)/(40\times100+30\times200) = 0.6$; while the index basket was valued at $100\times£100 = £10,000$. Hannibal sold ten March 2006 PAX futures at a price of £10,100 each, and bought ten lots of the index basket of shares: $(0.4\times£10,000)/100p = 4,000$ shares in Eltham and $(0.6\times£10,000)/200p = 3,000$ shares in Feltham. The delivery date for the PAX contract was 16th March 2006.

In January 2006 Eltham declared a dividend of 5p per share, payable on 1st March 2006, with the shares going ex-dividend on 5th January. In February 2006 Feltham declared a dividend of 15p per share, payable on 1st April 2006, with the shares going ex-dividend on 9th February. The computation of the PAX index assumes that the present value of dividends (less 36% taxation) is reinvested on the day the shares go ex-dividend. Hannibal is exempt from taxation on dividends from Eltham and Feltham. The risk free interest rate is 0.026% per day (compounded daily) throughout this period.

The after-tax present value of the dividend on Eltham shares on 5th January was $0.64(4,000\times5p/1.00026^{55}) = £126.18$. Thus, on this day, since the price of Eltham shares was then 126p each, the index basket of shares changed to include an additional 100 shares in Eltham. On 5th January, as well as buying another 100 shares per index basket in Eltham, Hannibal also invested the dividend tax, from which he is exempt, at the riskless rate for 70 days to give £70.98$\times1.00026^{70} = $ £72.28 per index basket at delivery. The after-tax present value of the Feltham dividend on 9th February is $0.64(3,000\times15p/1.00026^{51}) = £284.21$. And so on this day, when the price of a Feltham share was 284p, the number of Feltham shares in the index basket increased by 100. On 9th February Hannibal invested in another 100 Feltham shares per index basket. He also invested the dividend tax, which he does not have to pay, at the riskless rate for 35 days producing £159.87$\times1.00026^{35}$ = £161.33 per index basket at delivery.

At delivery the price of Eltham shares was 130p, and that of Feltham shares was 300p. Therefore the value of the PAX index was $(4,100 \times 130p + 3,100 \times 300p)/£100 = (£5,330 + £9,300)/£100 = 146.3$. Hannibal's arbitrage profit per contract is given by:

Gross profit on each index basket of shares (£14,630–£10,000)	£4,630.00
Payment of interest on the money invested in the shares $(10,000 \times 1.00026^{78})$	–£204.80
Loss per futures contract (£10,100–£14,630)	–£4,530.00
Value of the tax exemption at delivery (£72.28 + £161.33)	£233.61
Arbitrage profit per contract at delivery	£128.81

This arbitrage profit can be checked using the no-arbitrage formula. Since $F = (S-0.36D) \times (1+r)$, the arbitrage profit per contract on 28th December is $0.36D+F/(1+r)-S$. The value of D is $£200/1.00026^{63} + £450/1.00026^{94} = £635.89$, and so the arbitrage profit per contract on 28th December is $0.36 \times £635.89 +10,100/1.00026^{78}-£10,000 = £126.22$. The value of this profit at delivery is $£126.22 \times 1.00026^{78} = £128.81$.

5.12 Current Prices

Many market indices are computed using the most recent transaction price for each share. However, this may not be the price that would prevail if the share were traded now. Clearly, an arbitrageur will be concerned with the prices at which he or she could trade now, rather than with historic prices. If the index is computed using 'stale' prices, it is possible that the no-arbitrage condition appears to be violated, although if current prices were used in computing the index there would be no violation. This problem is of considerable empirical importance when testing the no-arbitrage condition and a number of authors have tried to control for this effect. Even if the index is computed using midquotes, there may be a short lag in computing and disseminating the index and before market makers adjust their price quotations. Therefore, mispricing in the UK may be due, in part, to such lags. There is also likely to be trading lag, and this is discussed as part of the simultaneous trading assumption in chapter 5.15.

5.13 Short Selling

When $F < (S-D) \times (1+r)$ arbitrage requires selling all the shares in the index. In the UK short selling after a downward price movement is allowed, Bank of England (1988). A distinction can be made between short selling and stock borrowing. In the UK any trader can sell shares they do not currently possess, although they are required to deliver these shares a few days later to the purchaser. To meet this obligation the short seller can roll over their short position by buying for cash the shares to deliver, and simultaneously selling the shares for a new settlement period (called 'reverse cash and new', London Stock Exchange, 1994b), or by borrowing shares. Alternatively, the short seller can fail to deliver the shares on the due date, London Stock Exchange,

1994b. Since reverse cash and new will incur substantial transactions costs, it is only by borrowing shares that a trader can hold a short position over the long term.

Short selling has been banned in a number of countries [Norway (Bradbery, 1992), Singapore (London Stock Exchange, 1994b), Australia until the mid-1980s (Bowers & Twite, 1985), Sweden until August 1991 and Malaysia until 30th September 1996]; and was a criminal offence in Hong Kong (Yau, Schneeweis & Yung, 1990). In Finland there was no institutional framework for short selling until 22nd May 1995, and so it was impossible in practice before that date (Puttonen, 1993b). In Germany the banks are prevented from lending shares to their customers for use in a short sale, and this makes short selling difficult, Grünbichler & Callahan (1994).

In the US a share can only be sold short if its last price movement was upwards (an uptick). This condition is unlikely to be met for all the shares in an index, particularly those indices based on many shares, e.g. S&P500, VLA and NYSE Composite. For such widely based indices, it is often not possible to short sell the index. However, if the arbitrageur already holds a long position in those shares which cannot be sold short, short selling these shares can be replaced by the liquidation of some or all of the arbitrageur's existing long positions. This restricts arbitrage requiring the short selling of shares to those traders who initially hold long positions in many of the shares in the relevant index, e.g. large market makers or institutional investors. If the underlying asset cannot be sold short, or the arbitrageur does not hold stocks which can be sold, arbitrage for the case when the futures price is relatively low is not possible and the no-arbitrage condition becomes $F \leq (S-D) \times (1+r)$. Some arbitrageurs may be prepared to short sell only some of the shares in the index. While this may overcome restrictions, such as the US uptick rule, the performance of the arbitrage portfolio is not guaranteed to perfectly replicate the index, and so the arbitrage is no longer riskless.

In the USA short selling can be achieved by submitting tick-sensitive orders to overcome the uptick rule. However, such orders take longer to execute. In consequence, the mispricing has to be larger to compensate for the execution risk, and this was found to be the case by Sofianos (1993) in a study of 1,442 index arbitrage trades in the S&P500 in the first six months of 1990. The expected arbitrage profit for tick-sensitive sell orders was 38.3 index basis points, while the average for all arbitrage trades was a loss of 5.6 index basis points, i.e. 43.9 index basis points lower.

Following the 1987 stock market crash, the NYSE introduced an amendment to rule 80a on 1st August 1990. When the NYSE moves down (up) by more than fifty points, selling (buying) shares (not just short selling) as part of an index arbitrage transaction can be executed only if the last price movement was up (down). This rule, in effect, disconnects the spot and futures markets when there are large price movements. Miller (1992) reports that, when rule 80a is operative, arbitrage volume drops by over one third. An NYSE report in 1991, quoted by Santoni & Liu (1993), found that when rule 80a was triggered the execution times for arbitrage orders increased from 1.5 minutes to 30 minutes. This considerably increased the execution risk of arbitrage transactions. However, there is no evidence that this leads to a delinking of spot and futures prices. Further empirical evidence on the operation of the amended rule 80a is presented in chapter 11.3.3.

The UK had a system of stock exchange accounts until 18th July 1994, each of which lasted for two (occasionally three) weeks. Transactions during an account were all settled on the same day: the second Monday following the end of the account. This meant that short selling shares for any period within a stock exchange account did not require stock borrowing. Therefore, the arbitrage of underpricings (which requires short selling shares) was opened up during the stock exchange account which included the delivery date to traders who could not usually short sell. This provided an opportunity to test the effect on arbitrage of the short selling difficulties which otherwise exist.

Pope & Yadav (1994) examined hourly data on the FTSE 100 for 1986-90. They compared the average mispricing in the near contract during the stock exchange account which included the delivery date, with that in the next near contract for the same period, and with that for the near contract in previous stock exchange accounts. They found that the average proportionate mispricing was very significantly larger in the stock exchange account which included the contract's delivery date, than otherwise. This result strongly supports the hypothesis that underpricing (i.e. negative mispricings) have been reduced for the near contract during the stock exchange account which includes the delivery date. This implies that short selling difficulties led to a widening of the no-arbitrage band by permitting greater underpricings. Pope & Yadav (1994) also examined the hypothesis that short selling within the stock exchange account is more attractive at the start of a three week account than otherwise. They found that the mean mispricing during the first five days of a three week account was significantly larger than for other mispricings. This is consistent with the view that during this period it was easier to arbitrage underpricings, so increasing the value of the average mispricing. On 18th July 1994, the UK moved to rolling settlement on a $T+10$ basis, on 26th June 1995 the settlement period for institutional investors was reduced to $T+5$, while on 5th February 2001 it moved to $T+3$; and so short selling without stock borrowing has become more difficult in the UK. This should have led to a drop in the value of the average mispricing.

A possible way round the problem that only large investors are in a position to borrow stock, is for investors to replace short selling the index basket by entering into a short 'contract for differences' in the OTC market, see chapter 2.10. It is possible to use options and debt to replicate the short selling of a share by writing a call option, buying a put option, both on the same stock with the same expiration date and strike price, and borrowing the present value of the common strike price. These trades produce a cash inflow now equal to the current price of the share, and requires a cash payment equal to the market price of the share at expiration. This result assumes the trader can borrow funds at the risk free rate, that the options concerned are correctly priced and that liquid markets exist in put and call options on the stock concerned (Euronext-Liffe does not trade options on all of the shares in the FTSE 100). This method for replicating short sales will incur the transactions costs of trading two options and borrowing funds.

In January 1994 members of the Hong Kong stock exchange were allowed to short sell 17 of the 33 constituents of the Hang Seng index; while on March 1996 they were allowed to short sell all the shares listed on the exchange and the uptick rule was abolished. Fung & Draper (1999) found that the progressive removal of short selling constraints reduced the mispricings and speeded up market adjustment, especially for underpricings; while arbitrage opportunities were largely absent.

5.14 Proceeds of Short Sales

The derivation of the no-arbitrage condition assumed that all the proceeds of selling shares short are immediately available to the vendor. However, this is unlikely to be the case. Payment of some (e.g. half) the proceeds may be delayed until the vendor has completed his or her side of the bargain and delivered the relevant shares. Arbitrage involving buying shares is unaffected, and so the no-arbitrage condition that $F \geq (S-D) \times (1+r)$ remains valid. However, arbitrage transactions involving taking a short position in shares (i.e. when $F < (S-D) \times (1+r)$) are altered, Brenner, Subrahmanyam & Uno (1990a). If only the proportion f of the short sales proceeds is paid immediately, with the remainder being paid at the delivery date of the futures contract, the terminal value of the cash flows from arbitrage involving short selling shares is reduced to $S(1+rf)-D(1+r)$, and the no-arbitrage condition becomes the no-arbitrage band $S(1+rf)-D(1+r) \leq F \leq (S-D)(1+r)$. The width of this band is $Sr(1-f)$, and so it widens as the spot price increases, as illustrated in figure 5.3.

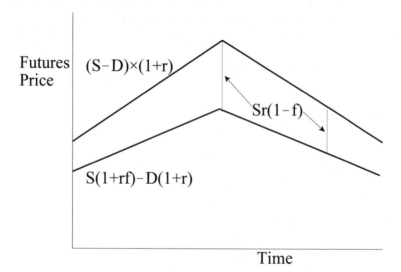

Figure 5.3: No-arbitrage Band with a Delay in the Receipt of Short Sales Receipts

Example. The current value of the FTSE 100 index is 4,400, while the current price of one FTSE 100 index future for delivery in six months is £44,150. The present value of dividends on the shares in the index during the next six months is £1,000, and the riskless rate of interest for six months is 5%. Therefore the no-arbitrage price of the future is $(S-D) \times (1+r) = (4,400 \times 10 - 1,000) \times 1.05 = £45,150$. Hence, the future is underpriced by £1,000. Lee Winters, the manageress of the Corbridge Fund, is considering engaging in index arbitrage, but has discovered she will initially receive only half of the proceeds from short selling shares, i.e. $f = 0.5$. In this case her no-arbitrage futures price is $S(1+fr) - D(1+r) = (4,400 \times 10 \times 1.025)$ $-(1,000 \times 1.05) = £44,050$. Since the futures price is currently £100 above this level, there is no arbitrage opportunity for Lee, even though the current futures price is £1,000 below the no-arbitrage value.

USA.   Modest & Sundaresan (1983) examined data on S&P500 index futures for 1982. They studied the effects of variations in the use of the proceeds of short selling (zero use, 50% use and full use) on mispricings. They found that when arbitrageurs did not receive more than half the short sales proceeds, there were no arbitrage opportunities; but when they immediately received the full proceeds, arbitrage opportunities existed. This result suggests that an allowance for delays in the receipt of short sales proceeds in the no-arbitrage condition may be appropriate.

5.15 Simultaneous Trading

It has been assumed that, if an arbitrage opportunity arises, it is possible to immediately trade index futures and the corresponding basket of shares. This may not be possible for two reasons: trading lag and trading impossibility.

5.15.1 Trading Lag

Trading a basket of 100 or more shares may take some time (i.e. there is a trading lag), and during this period prices may move from those at which the arbitrage transaction was initiated, and the futures position established, i.e. there is execution risk. Daigler (1993a, p. 195) and Daigler (1993b, p. 110) states that some brokers offer to acquire a share portfolio at a guaranteed price, so removing the execution risk, in exchange for a higher commission. Vila (1993) argues that execution risk makes index arbitrage risky, and this will decrease the amount of such arbitrage. When the stock market is illiquid, execution risk is increased, and so index arbitrage is disproportionately discouraged during illiquid periods. Vila (1993) also points out that once the arbitrage becomes risky, one-to-one values of the spot and futures arbitrage positions is no longer the most appropriate arbitrage strategy. The arbitrage has become equivalent to a risky hedge (see chapter 9), and the value of the futures position is slightly smaller than that of the spot position.

An arbitrageur may deliberately establish one leg of an arbitrage before the other, i.e. legging into the arbitrage, BoBS (sections 3.41 and 3.65, 1995). This is done when short term favourable movements are expected in the price of the delayed leg, and such trading amounts to speculation. Sofianos (1993) studied the differences in time between the submission of the orders to create the spot and futures legs of S&P500 index arbitrage positions. Using data for the first six months of 1990 on 1,442 positions, he found that 63% of the orders were submitted synchronously, i.e. within the same minute. For 22% of these arbitrage positions, the order to establish the futures leg was submitted before the spot leg, while the reverse was the case for the remaining 15% of trades. The overall profitability of legging into arbitrage positions was around zero.

Neal (1995) found that 81% of the legs of NYSE arbitrage trades in the first three months of 1989 were submitted synchronously, the futures leg was submitted first in 16% of cases, and the stock leg was submitted first for 3% of trades. Neal (1995) suggests that the futures leg may be submitted first because the futures price is more volatile than the spot price (see chapter 12.1.1), and so arbitrageurs place greater importance on locking in the futures price.

5.15.2 Trading Impossibility

Another way in which the simultaneous creation of the arbitrage position in both the spot and futures markets may not occur is when only one of these markets is open. In which case the no-arbitrage condition is undefined, and arbitrage transactions are impossible. A related problem is that many empirical studies use closing prices and, if the closing times differ between the spot and futures markets, the closing prices from the spot and futures markets will not be directly comparable and need not obey the no-arbitrage condition. Finally, it is possible that either the spot or the futures market is subject to a price limit or trading halt, so making arbitrage trading impossible (see chapter 11.3).

5.16 No Delivery Price Risk

Since index futures use cash settlement, riskless arbitrage requires that, if a long (short) position has been taken in shares they must be sold (bought) at the delivery price of the corresponding index future, i.e. z in the Annie Hall, Lawrence Garfield, Montgomery Brewster and the Scarlet O'Hara examples in chapter 3. The arbitrage profit is independent of the price at which the shares are finally sold (bought), provided this is the delivery price of the future used for the arbitrage. Therefore, arbitrage can lead to the sale or purchase of very large blocks of shares, irrespective of the price, in the few minutes when the delivery price is determined. This is argued to have a potentially destabilizing effect on the stock market. This problem is amplified if other financial instruments also expire at the same time. For example, until 1987, four times per year the US had a 'triple witching hour'. At this time the S&P500 index future, options on the S&P500 index, options on futures on the S&P500 index and some options on individual stocks all expired. Because this was thought to increase volatility, in June 1987 the expiry times were altered to avoid this triple witching hour, Stoll & Whaley (1991), see chapter 12.4.2 for further discussion of the triple witching hour and expiration volatility.

For the FTSE 100, arbitrageurs cannot guarantee they will be able to trade the shares in the index at the delivery price. This is because the EDSP is the average value of the index over a twenty minute period. For ISEQ futures this problem was even more marked. The EDSP for the ISEQ was calculated as the simple average of seven values of the index: the four values for the penultimate day and three values at 10.30, 12.30 pm and 4.30 pm on the last trading day. Thus, the EDSP was the average price over two days, and this permitted considerable delivery price risk, unless the arbitrageur unwound one seventh of the index basket at each of the relevant times. Similar problems apply to other index futures.

In practice, at least in the UK, delivery risk is small. First, as reported in chapter 3.6, Yadav & Pope (1994) found that 97% of their simulated arbitrage positions were unwound early, and so there was no delivery risk in most cases. Second, Yadav & Pope (1994) estimated that the variance of the FTSE 100 index over a 10 minute period between 11 am and 12 noon was 0.05%, which is very small. Finally, any arbitrageur who has not unwound early and who wishes to avoid the small delivery risk can pay a market maker to close them out at the EDSP, Yadav & Pope (1994).

5.17 No Changes in the Definition of the Index

It is possible that, during the life of an arbitrage transaction, there is a change in the way the index is computed, e.g. the identity of the shares in the index is altered, the mechanics of the index computation are changed or the weights attached to the shares in the index computation are revised. There is a steady stream of deletions and additions to the shares comprising the FTSE 100 index. For example, during the three years 1987, 1988 and 1989, there were 34 changes in the constituents of the FTSE 100 index, Robertson (1990). During the eleven year period 1973-83, there were 228 changes in the composition of the S&P500 index, Harris & Gurel (1986), although for the ten year period 1980 to 1989 inclusive, there were only eight changes in the constituents of the Nikkei 225. Over the seventy years 1929-1988 there were only 37 changes in the DJIA, Beneish & Gardner (1995).

From time to time a subtle change may be made to the details of the computation of the index. If there is a change in the definition of the index during the life of an arbitrage transaction, the portfolio of shares (long or short) must be immediately adjusted to reflect the new definition of the index. If not, the arbitrage is no longer riskless.

Example. Consider an index that contains the hundred largest publicly quoted UK companies. On 1st July futures on this index were substantially overpriced, and Mary Poppins, the manageress of the Cramlington Fund, sold an index future, and purchased the basket of shares in the index costing £60,000 in exactly the same proportions as used in computing the index. If the computation of the index was

138

unchanged until delivery Mary need do nothing until delivery. However, after three months the UK government privatized the telephone industry, and it was decided that this newly quoted company, British Telecoms, should be included in the index with a weight of 0.10. At the same time Metal Bashers Ltd, a company with a weight of 0.005, was removed from the index to keep the total number of companies at 100. Therefore the weight of each of the other 99 shares fell from an average of 1.005% to 0.909%. To maintain her riskless arbitrage, Mary was required to instantly sell her holding in Metal Bashers Ltd, buy shares in British Telecoms to bring her holding up to 10% of her portfolio and sell part of her holding in each of the other 99 companies to reduce their average weight in her portfolio to 0.909%.

The DAX is a performance index, and dividends are assumed to be reinvested in the company concerned, so increasing the weight of that company in the index. This requires the rebalancing of the arbitrage portfolio each time a dividend is paid. In addition, each year, after the delivery of the September contract, all the weights of the DAX index are reset to remove the effects of any dividends paid during the previous year. This requires a major rebalancing of arbitrage portfolios.

5.18 Perfect Asset Divisibility

In order to construct an arbitrage transaction where the number of futures exactly offsets the basket of shares in the index, it is necessary to be able to hold shares or futures in fractional quantities, which is not possible. This indivisibility problem will tend to be smaller if each futures contract has a small nominal value, and the total value of the arbitrage transaction is very large.

Example. Sarah J Connor, an employee of the Cullercoats Bank, is considering an arbitrage transaction in either the maxi VL index future or the mini VL index future. Maxi futures on the VL index are currently priced at £65,000, while the price of mini futures on the VL index is, by definition, one fifth of the maxi VL price, i.e. £13,000. The current value of the basket of shares corresponding to one futures contract is £60,000 for the maxi VL, and £12,000 for the mini VL. There are a thousand companies in the VL index, each of which is currently priced at £2.75 per share. Sarah J Connor can engage in an arbitrage transaction worth a maximum of either £105,000 or £5 million. There are four arbitrage possibilities open to Sarah J Connor involving: (a) the maxi VL index and £5 million, (b) the maxi VL index and £105,000, (c) the mini VL index and £5 million and (d) the mini VL index and £105,000. These are summarized in table 5.4.

The last line of table 5.4 shows the extent to which indivisibilities have caused an imbalance between the value of futures and shares in the arbitrage transaction. As can be seen, these are all fairly small, and in practice the lack of asset divisibility is not a major problem, although it does mean that a completely riskless arbitrage transaction may be impossible. The transactions costs for trading round lots of shares (e.g. 100 shares) may be lower than for odd lots. This was not considered in the above example, and will increase the costs of arbitraging an index which contains many companies. The Toronto 35 index uses modified market value weights, so that the number of shares in each company required to form the arbitrage portfolio is rounded to the nearest hundred. This reduces the costs of arbitraging this index as the trading of odd lots of shares is never required. The Osaka 50 Kabusaki index future, which initially required physical delivery, normally had as the underlying asset a basket of 1,000 shares in each of the fifty companies in the index, Millers (1992). This facilitated the physical delivery of the index basket, but made each contract worth about £250,000.

Table 5.4: Example of the Effects of Asset Indivisibility

	a	b	c	d
Desired no. of contracts	83.3	1.75	416.7	8.7
No. of contracts traded	83	1	416	8
Desired total no. of shares per co.	1,810.9	21.8	1,815.3	34.9
No. of shares per co. traded	1,811	22	1,815	35
Underspend due to rounding (£1,000)	20	45	8	9
Arbitrage imbalance	£250	£500	£750	£250

5.19 No Price Effect Except in Aggregate

This assumption is that the prices of assets are unaffected by a single arbitrage transaction. The markets for the major index futures and the shares included in the underlying indices are usually highly liquid, and so there is likely to be little adverse price movement for all but the largest arbitrage transactions. Harris, Sofianos & Shapiro (1994) estimated that the price effect of an index arbitrage programme trade on the NYSE in the years 1989 and 1990 of $10 million was only 0.03%. However, the aggregate amount of arbitrage activity must be sufficiently large to bring the prices of shares and a stock index future on those shares into some equilibrium relationship. Given the other assumptions, arbitrage is riskless, requires zero wealth and so can be of arbitrary scale. Therefore this requirement should be met.

5.20 Shares are Paid for Immediately

The purchaser of shares usually receives a short period of interest-free credit due to settlement lag. In some markets, e.g. the UK or France, this could amount to three or four weeks. This delayed cash flow alters the net present value of an arbitrage transaction which involves buying shares. The effect of settlement lag can be represented by reducing the risk free rate used for the spot price from r to rg, and the no-arbitrage bound for buying shares and selling futures becomes $F \leq [S(1+rg)-D(1+r)]$. If there are also delays in the receipt of the proceeds from short selling shares (see chapter 5.14), assuming $f \leq g$, the full no-arbitrage band becomes

$[S(1+rf)-D(1+r)] \leq F \leq [S(1+rg)-D(1+r)]$. The difference between the upper and lower bounds is $Sr(g-f)$, and so the size of the no-arbitrage band increases as S increases. Note that this no-arbitrage band will lie below the no-arbitrage price given by $F = (S-D) \times (1+r)$ by the distance $Sr(1-g)$, see figure 5.4. A computer spreadsheet supplied by Liffe (1991), which computes the FTSE Eurotrack 100 no-arbitrage futures price, offers the facility to allow for settlement lag, while Yadav & Pope (1992a, 1994) and Pope & Yadav (1994) allowed for settlement lag in their calculation of FTSE 100 no-arbitrage prices.

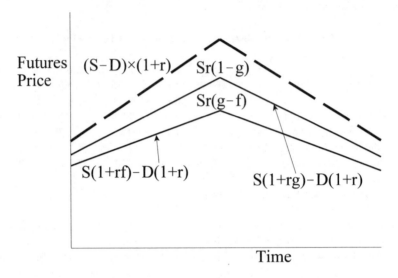

Figure 5.4: Settlement Lag and Short Sale Proceeds Lag

5.21 Capital Gains or Losses are Paid at Liquidation

The derivation of the no-arbitrage condition in chapter 3 relied upon the payment of the capital gains or losses on the shares at the liquidation of the position. (The payment of profits or losses on futures positions is dealt with by marking to the market.) This assumption will normally be met for long positions in shares, but for short positions the potential losses are infinite and, if there has been a substantial rise in the index, a short seller may be required to put up additional funds before delivery. For example, in the UK a market maker who borrows shares must immediately pay the market value of the borrowed shares (plus a margin of about 5%) to the intermediary who arranged the stock lending. The value of the stock that has been borrowed is revalued every day, and adjustments made to restore an equivalence between the value of the stock that has been lent and the payment made, London Stock Exchange (1994a). Thus, in the UK, the borrower pays any losses (and receives any profits) as they occur. This cash flow (effectively variation margin payments on shares) will have to be financed (or invested), so altering the net present value of the arbitrage transaction.

5.22 No Risk of Default

If a person trading futures contracts fears that the contract will not be honoured by the counter party, they will require a default premium, Bailey & Ng (1991). This will tend to reduce the price that a trader is prepared to pay for a long position, and increase the price required for a short position. Thus, default risk is analogous to transactions costs in creating a gap between the no-arbitrage buy and sell prices. If Υ is the default premium, then the no-arbitrage price becomes a no-arbitrage band: $(S-D)(1+r)-\Upsilon \leq F \leq (S-D)(1+r)+\Upsilon$. One of the few defaults occurred on 5th October 1994 when the Board of Exchange in Moscow went bankrupt because clients were unable to pay the 21.3 billion roubles they owed to the clearing house. The Board of Exchange cleared for the Moscow Central Stock Exchange, which traded foreign currency futures. Another default was in 1983 when the Kuala Lumpur clearing house failed after all its members defaulted on palm oil contracts, Gemmill (1994). Although the regulatory systems for futures markets have generally prevented defaults, the probability of a default must always exist to some small (and variable) degree. The omission of a default premium from the no-arbitrage condition is probably of little consequence for futures traded on established and well regulated exchanges.

5.23 Common Currency for Shares and Multiplier

The contract multiplier must be in the same currency as the underlying shares. If not, the arbitrage involves a small amount of exchange rate risk, see chapter 11.11.

5.24 Zero Value of Voting and Other Rights

Owning a long position in an index future enables the trader to participate in price changes of the shares in the index. However, he or she is not legally the owner of any shares and so does not receive dividends, and cannot vote. The lack of dividends is reflected in the no-arbitrage condition, while the absence of voting rights is not. When the trader owns a small proportion of the voting shares the lack of voting rights may be an insignificant loss but, as the proportion of the company's shares held by the trader rises, the voting rights start to become valuable. Since it is the larger companies that are included in stock indices (and the smaller the company the lower its weight), the omission of a value for the voting rights is probably not important, except possibly for the VLA index, which is an equally weighted index covering some 1,700 companies. Share owners also get various benefits such as copies of the annual report and accounts, the right to lend shares for a fee to someone who wishes to sell short, the right to attend, speak and propose motions at the annual general meeting, shareholder discounts on the firm's product etc. The value of these rights is not included in the no-arbitrage condition.

5.25 Immoral Investments

By buying an index future, the arbitrageur has indirectly invested in all the shares in the index. Some of the shares in the index may be objectionable on moral grounds to the customers (or potential customers) of institutional investors, e.g. pension funds, investment trusts and insurance companies. It is possible that such customers will not be concerned by an indirect holding via an index future, Martin (1988), Luskin (1987, pp 343-344). This possible benefit of index futures (which is likely to be very small) is ignored by the no-arbitrage condition.

5.26 Costless Storage

Apart from financing costs, which are included in the no-arbitrage condition, it is assumed the underlying asset, i.e. the shares which comprise the index, can be stored costlessly and does not depreciate with storage. While this would be a restrictive assumption for many commodity futures, e.g. live cattle or frozen concentrated orange juice, this appears to be a reasonable assumption for shares. Therefore, there is no need to include such holding costs in the no-arbitrage condition.

5.27 Independence of the Index

The derivation of the no-arbitrage condition for futures prices assumes that the value of the index is given. Hemler & Longstaff (1991) relaxed this assumption, and constructed a general equilibrium model in which the index, the volatility of returns on the index, the price of the index future and the (stochastic) risk free rate of interest are determined simultaneously. This continuous time model finds that the price of index futures depends on the volatility of returns on the index, as well as on the spot price, dividend yield, the risk free rate of interest and the time to delivery. One implication of this general equilibrium model is that market volatility is added to stochastic interest rates as an additional reason for being unable to specify the direction of the relationship between forward and futures prices, as discussed in chapter 5.3.

Hemler & Longstaff derived a number of empirical predictions of their general equilibrium model that differ from those of the no-arbitrage model. Using monthly data on the NYSE Composite index for 1983-7, these predictions were tested. They fitted the regression equation $L_t = \alpha + \beta r_t + \gamma V_t + \varepsilon_t$, where $L_t = \ln[(F_t + D)/S_t]$, V_t is the volatility of returns on the index, r_t is the riskless interest rate, α, β, and γ are parameters, and ε_t is a disturbance term. The no-arbitrage model predicts that $\alpha = \gamma = 0$, and $\beta = \tau$ (where τ is the maturity of the contract, measured in years), while the general equilibrium model predicts that $\beta > \gamma$, $\beta > 0$, $\beta > \tau$, $\gamma \neq 0$ and $\alpha \neq 0$. Their empirical results largely supported the predictions of the general equilibrium model, rather than those of the no-arbitrage model. Thus, α and γ were significantly different from zero, while $\beta > \tau$. The need to include stock market volatility in the pricing equation for index futures may account for the apparent mispricings indicated by the no-arbitrage condition, particularly when the market is volatile, when the general equilibrium model would not indicate a mispricing. To test this possibility, Hemler & Longstaff computed mispricings from January 1986 to November 1987 using both models, and compared the results. When October 1987 is included, the general equilibrium pricing model produces smaller mispricings, which is consistent with the need to allow for market volatility. However, when the October 1987 observation is removed, this conclusion is reversed; which indicates that, except in highly volatile periods, the no-arbitrage model is preferable.

The Hemler & Longstaff model was used with daily data for the KOSPI index by Gay & Jung (1999) and for individual stock futures by Brailsford & Cusack (1997). In each case, the Hemler & Longstaff model had reasonable explanatory power, but was not superior to the cost of carry model.

5.28 Conclusions

A consideration of the assumptions underlying the no-arbitrage condition found that for most existing stock index futures many are valid, or that the deviations are of little empirical consequence. For the remaining assumptions, it was possible to generalize the no-arbitrage condition. Therefore, it is concluded that there are no assumptions which are invalid, cannot be relaxed by using a more general no-arbitrage condition, and where violations of the assumption have an important effect. However, it is possible that, while the assumptions underlying the no-arbitrage condition may be reasonable for most existing stock index futures, this is not the case for other, as yet unlisted, index futures.

APPENDIX A: No-Arbitrage Conditions with Continuous Compounding

Suppose £100 is invested at an annual rate of 10%. If interest is compounded annually the outcome at the end of the year is £110, while if interest is compounded continuously, the result is $100e^{0.10} = £110.52$. If η is the annual riskless rate of interest, r is the risk free rate of interest for the period between now and delivery and h is the time in years until delivery, and interest is continuously compounded at an annual rate of π, then $\pi = ln(1+\eta)$ or $\pi = ln(1+r)/h$. The no-arbitrage condition becomes $F = (S-D)e^{\pi h}$, where S is the spot price and D is the present value of the dividends. Such a formulation has been proposed by Hull (2005). To be consistent, continuous compounding must also be used in the computation of the present value of the dividend stream. Thus :-

$$D = \sum_{i=0}^{T} (d_i^+ e^{-\pi(i/365)})$$

where d_i^+ represents the dividends received on day i.

A5.1 Terminal Dividends

Some authors, e.g. Brennan & Schwarz (1990), Brenner, Subrahmanyam & Uno (1989a, 1989b, 1990b), Chan & Chung (1993), Chance (1991), CBOT (1990), Cornell (1985a), Cornell & French (1983a), Chung, Kang & Rhee (1994b), Lim (1992a, 1992b) and Stoll & Whaley (1993), have used the value of the dividend stream at time T, rather than 0, i.e. $D^* = De^{\pi h}$. In which case the no-arbitrage condition becomes $F = Se^{\pi h} - D^*$.

Example. The Gordon Gekko example from chapter 3 will be used to illustrate this no-arbitrage condition. On 1st January the spot price of shares corresponding to one unit of the Bull index was £50,000. On that day, the present value of the dividends from owning these shares until 30th June was £971.40. The riskless rate of interest for the six month period from 1st January to 30th June was 4.897%, while the annual riskless rate of interest was 10.034%. Thus, the continuously compounded annual risk free rate of interest (π) was $\pi = \ln(1 + \eta) = \ln(1 + 0.10034) = 0.095619$ (or $\pi = \ln(1 + r)/h = \ln(1.04897)/0.5 = 0.095619$). $D^* = De^{\pi h} = 971.40 \times 1.0489708 = £1,018.97$. Since $e^{\pi h} = e^{0.095619/2} = 1.0489708$, the no-arbitrage futures price is $F = Se^{\pi h} - D^* = 50,000 \times 1.0489708 - 1,018.97 = £51,430$. The formula $(S - D)(1 + r)$ gives the same answer.

A5.2 Continuous Dividends

Another way of specifying the no-arbitrage condition has been used by a number of authors, e.g. Bailey (1989), Bhatt & Cakici (1990), Billingsley & Chance (1988), Cakici & Chatterjee (1991), Canina & Figlewski (1995), CBOT (1990), Cornell & French (1983a), Daigler (1993a, p. 181, 1993b, p. 94), Dwyer, Locke & Yu (1996), Hull (2005), Johnson & Giaccotto (1995), MacKinlay & Ramaswamy (1988), Stoll & Whaley (1990b, 1993), Strong (1994), Tang (1990), Tse (1995), Vaidyanathan & Krehbiel (1992), Watsham (1992) and Yau, Schneeweis & Yung (1990). They assume that dividends are paid continuously at the rate ω, where $\omega = \ln(S/(S - D))/h$. This results in the no-arbitrage condition $F = Se^{(\pi - \omega)h}$. Where a continuously compounded dividend rate is used and it is expressed as a compound growth rate for the spot price (S_t), it implies that dividends are reinvested in the share portfolio rather than at the riskless rate of interest, Stoll & Whaley (1993, p. 107). This invites the use of an incorrect figure for the dividend rate which assumes reinvestment of dividends in the share portfolio, not in the risk free asset.

Example. Making use of the Gordon Gekko numbers, the continuous dividend yield is $\omega = \ln(S/(S - D))/h = \ln(50,000/(50,000 - 971.40))/0.5 = 0.039238$. Therefore the no-arbitrage condition is $F = Se^{(\pi - \omega)h} = 50,000e^{(0.095619 - 0.039238)/2} = £51,430$.

This no-arbitrage condition in the futures and spot prices has been converted into a no-arbitrage condition for logarithmic rates of return by Stoll & Whaley (1990b). Since $F = Se^{(\pi - \omega)h}$, then $\ln(S_t/S_{t-\mu}) = \ln(F_t/F_{t-\mu}) + (\pi - \omega)\mu$, where μ is the period of time (in years) over which the rates of return are computed. While a no-arbitrage condition stated in terms of rates of change is not very useful for spotting arbitrage opportunities, it does represent an interesting implication of the link between spot and futures rates of return in an arbitrage-free market.

Example. Using the numbers from the Gordon Gekko example, if the spot price rises by 2% over the next month, the rise in the no-arbitrage futures price is given by $\ln(1.02) = \ln((F_t/F_{t-\mu})+(0.095619 - 0.039238)/12$, and so $\ln((F_t/F_{t-\mu}) = 1.51041\%$. Therefore $F_t = 1.0151041 \times 51,430 = \pounds 52,207$. Thus, over the month, the spot logarithmic return (excluding dividends) plus the continuously compounded dividend yield equals the futures logarithmic return plus the continuously compounded interest rate, i.e. $1.98026\% + 0.32696\% = 1.51041\% + 0.79681\%$.

A5.3 Annual Dividend Yield

Cornell & French (1983b) and Leuthold, Junkus & Cordier (1989) define the no-arbitrage condition using τ, the annual value of the dividends paid on the shares corresponding to one future. These dividends are assumed to be paid continuously during the remaining life of the future. Thus, $\tau = \pi D e^{\pi h}/(e^{\pi h}- 1)$, and so the no-arbitrage condition becomes $F = Se^{\pi h}- (\tau/\pi) \times (e^{\pi h}- 1)$.

Example. For the Gordon Gekko numbers, $\tau = \pi D e^{\pi h}/(e^{\pi h}- 1) = [(0.09562) \times(971.40)\times(1.0489708)] /(1.0489708 - 1) = \pounds 1,989.61$. Therefore $F = Se^{\pi h}- (\tau/\pi) \times (e^{\pi h}- 1) = 50,000 \times 1.0489708 - (1,989.61 /0.09562)\times(1.0489708 - 1) = \pounds 51,430$.

A5.4 Continuously Compounded Annual Dividend Yield

Duffie (1989) expressed the annual dividend yield as a continuously compounded rate (θ), and so $\theta = \tau/S$, and the no-arbitrage futures price is $F = S(e^{\pi h} - \theta(e^{\pi h}- 1)/\pi)$. [This equation can be rearranged as $F = S[e^{\pi h}(1 - \theta/\pi)+\theta/\pi]$, Cornell & French (1983b).]

Example. Using the Gordon Gekko data, the continuously compounded dividend yield is $\theta = \tau/S = 1,989.61/50,000 = 0.0398004$. Therefore, the no-arbitrage futures price is $F = S(e^{\pi h}- \theta(e^{\pi h}- 1)/\pi) = 50,000\{1.0489708 - 0.0398004 \times (1.0489708 - 1) /0.095619\} = \pounds 51,430$.

While all the above no-arbitrage conditions (and those in chapter 3) result in the same no-arbitrage futures price, e.g. £51,430, they have used a wide range of interest and dividend rates. The interest rates used were $\varphi = 0.800\%$, $r = 4.897\%$, $\eta = 10.034\%$ and $\pi = 9.562\%$; while the dividend terms used were $D = \pounds 971.40$, $d = 2.0380\%$, $\psi = 3.8486\%$, $\omega = 3.9238\%$, $\theta = 3.9800\%$ and $\tau = \pounds 1,989.61$. Clearly, there is considerable room for confusion. Continuous compounding leads to more complex no-arbitrage conditions, while the continuous payment of interest and dividends is a less realistic assumption than payments at fixed intervals.

PART 3

PRICES

Chapter 6

Basis, Spreads and the Risk Premium

Introduction

Various price relationships are investigated in this chapter. First, the difference between the current spot and futures prices (the basis) is studied. Second, the difference between the current prices of two futures contracts (spreads) is analysed. Finally, the relationship between the current futures price and the expected spot price at delivery (the risk premium) is considered.

6.1 The Basis

The basis is defined as the current price of a future minus the spot price of the underlying asset, i.e. basis $\equiv F-S$. (It is sometimes defined in the reverse manner, i.e. basis $\equiv S-F$.) Given the no-arbitrage condition derived in chapter 3, the basis is determined by two factors of opposite sign. Thus, $F = (S-D)(1+r)$ can be rearranged as: $F-S = Sr-D(1+r)$, and the basis is equal to the difference between two terms, Sr and $D(1+r)$. These two terms which determine the basis will now be considered.

(a) Sr.   Futures contracts do not require any carrying costs, as any loss of interest on money invested in margins is ignored, and so the futures price is higher than the spot price by £Sr, the interest foregone by tying up £S in the stock market.

(b) $D(1+r)$.   Holding the shares in the index also gives the right to dividends, making the spot price higher than the futures price by the present value of the dividends (D), plus the interest on this sum (Dr).

Since both Sr and $D(1+r)$ are non-negative, the basis for a stock index can be positive or negative, depending on the relative magnitudes of $D(1+r)$ and Sr. The values of D and r for different maturities may be such that the basis is positive for some maturities, and negative for others.

Asset pricing theory leads to the expectation that the returns on the market index (capital gains plus dividends) exceed the risk free rate of interest. It is also generally true that the risk free rate exceeds the rate of dividends on the market index (d). If this is the case, and it can easily be investigated empirically, the restated no-arbitrage condition $F = S(1+r-d)$ gives the result that the basis for a stock index is positive, i.e. $F > S$, Figlewski (1984b).

Example Hawkeye Pierce wishes to disaggregate the basis for the outstanding FTSE

100 contracts into two parts: the dividend effect $[D(1+r)]$ and the foregone interest effect $[Sr]$. The current value of the FTSE 100 index is 4,500, while the present value of dividends on shares corresponding to one FTSE 100 index future is £1,000 for the June contract, £1,500 for the September contract and £2,500 for the December contract. The March contract is not considered as volumes were very low. The riskless rate of interest for the period to delivery is 3% for the June contract, 6% for the September contract and 9% for the December contract. In which case, the following table can be computed by Hawkeye. In this example, the foregone interest exceeds the dividends foregone, and the basis for each contract is positive.

Table 6.1: Components of the Basis for the Example

Delivery Month	Sr	D(1+r)	Basis
June	£1,350	£1,030	£320
September	£2,700	£1,590	£1,110
December	£4,050	£2,725	£1,325

6.2 Basis Speculation

Investors may have a view, not about subsequent movements in the level of the futures or spot price, but about relative movements in these prices, i.e. the basis. Such a person may choose to speculate on movements in the basis. A long position in the basis, defined as $F-S$, (which is rather confusingly called 'short the basis') is achieved by short selling shares corresponding to the index basket and buying an index future. Since $F-S = Sr-D(1+r)$ when the no-arbitrage condition applies, changes in the basis can be caused by movements in S, D and r. Partially differentiating this equation with respect to each of these variables in turn gives:-

$$\delta(F-S)/\delta S = r > 0$$
$$\delta(F-S)/\delta D = -(1+r) < 0$$
$$\delta(F-S)/\delta r = S-D-(1+r)\times(\delta D/\delta r) > 0$$

It has been implicitly assumed above that $\delta S/\delta D = 0$, which accords with the Miller-Modigliani (1961) result that the share price is unaffected by dividend policy. The trading implications of these partial derivatives are that if the spot price or the risk free interest rate is expected to rise, $F-S$ gets bigger (i.e. the basis weakens) and, if $F > S$, the basis widens. If dividends are expected to rise, $F-S$ gets smaller (i.e. the basis strengthens) and, if $F > S$, the basis narrows. Note that when a share goes ex-dividend this should have no effect on the price of the index future because both S and D will fall by the same amount (the present value of the dividend). However, the basis will weaken when a share in the index goes ex-dividend because the futures price is unaffected, while the spot price falls, Schwarz (1991). A given change in the annual interest or dividend rate will have a larger effect on the basis, the longer is the time to maturity of the future.

Example. Bash Brannigan, the manager of the Dunston Fund, formed the view that dividends on equities were about to rise and so the excess of the no-arbitrage price of an index future (F) over the spot price of the shares in the index (S) would reduce, i.e. the basis will narrow. On 4th July the FTSE 100 index stood at 4,400 while the risk free interest rate for the period to the end of March (r) was 8%, and the present value of the dividends on the shares in the index (D) was £1,500. The price the March index future was equal to the no-arbitrage value of $(4,400 \times 10 - 1,500) \times 1.08 = £45,900$. Thus the basis was $45,900 - 44,000 = £1,900$ (or 190 index points). Bash Brannigan had no views about the direction of movement of spot or futures prices. If the present value of the dividend stream rose to £2,500, while at the same time the value of the index fell by x points, the no-arbitrage futures price would be $[(4,400 - x) \times £10 - £2,500] \times 1.08 = £44,820 - 10.8x$, and the basis would become $£44,820 - 10.8x - 44,000 + 10x = £820 - 0.8x$. If this happens the basis will fall by $£1,900 - (£820 - 0.8x) = £1,080 + 0.8x$. Provided the index does not unexpectedly rise by more than $1,080/0.8 = 1,350$ index points (31%), a most unlikely event, Bash Brannigan will make a profit from speculating on the basis. So he sold ten futures in the index and bought ten index baskets. When the estimate of D changed to £2,500 and the index fell to 4,000 (i.e. $x = 9.1\%$), he liquidated his positions in futures and shares. He made a loss of £40,000 from his long position in shares, but this was more than offset by his profit of £54,000 from his short futures position. Thus, overall, he made a gross profit of $10(1,080 + 0.8 \times 400) = £14,000$.

Basis speculation is profitable primarily because of a change in one or more of the variables determining the spot or futures prices. However, it is possible to make a small profit even if none of the three variables (S, D and r) deviate from their expected values implicit in the no-arbitrage futures price. This is because the profits on the futures position are paid when the basis speculation is unwound, rather than at delivery of the futures contract (as assumed by the no-arbitrage condition). In consequence, the speculator makes a small profit equal to the present value at the unwinding date of the interest earned between then and delivery of the future. This profit can be expressed as $\Delta(F - S) = r_2 \Delta F / (1 + r_2)$, where $\Delta(F - S)$ is the change in the basis by the unwinding date, ΔF is the change in the futures price by the unwinding date, and r_2 is the risk free rate of interest from the unwinding date to delivery. If the spot price is unchanged, this equation simplifies to $\Delta(F - S) = \Delta F = r_2(D_1(1 + r_1) - S_1 r_1)$, where S_1 is the spot price at the start of the basis speculation, D_1 is the present value of dividends receivable on the index basket during the period the position is held, and r_1 is the risk free rate for the same period. Depending on the relative magnitudes of $D_1(1 + r_1)$ and $S_1 r_1$, ΔF can be positive or negative. As argued above, ΔF is more likely to be positive. When $D_1(1 + r_1) > S_1 r_1$ the speculator should 'short the basis' and sell shares and buy futures, and when $D_1(1 + r_1) < S_1 r_1$ the speculator should 'long the basis' and buy shares and sell futures.

Example. On 4th January, Han Solo, who manages OPM Holdings, bought ten FTSE 100 September futures at a price of 4,310×£10 = £43,100, when the index was 4,300. At the same time he sold ten index baskets of shares, i.e. long the basis. By 4th March, when he closed out both positions, the index was unchanged at 4,300, while the price of September futures had risen to £43,336. The present value on 4th January of the dividends receivable on the index basket of shares between then and 4th March was £1,088.24, while that for dividends from 4th March to delivery was £1,282,05. The risk free rates were 2% for 4th January to 4th March, and 4% from 4th March to delivery in September. At all times the futures were priced in accordance with the no-arbitrage condition. Thus on 4th January F = (4,300×£10−£1,088.24 −£1,282.05)×1.02×1.04 = £43,100, while on 4th March F = (4,300×£10−£1,282.05×1.02)×1.04 = £43,360. Although the initial expectations of S, D and r implicit in the no-arbitrage price have been fulfilled, Han has made a small profit, as at 4th March.

Futures profit 100(4,336−4,310)	£2,600
Shares 100(4,300−4,300)	0
Dividends paid 10×£1,088.24×1.02	−£11,100
Interest received on proceeds of share sale 10×£43,000×0.02	£8,600
Profit	£100

Alternatively, the profit can be computed as the interest over the period from 4th March until delivery on the profit from the futures position. This is $r_2\Delta F/(1+r_2)$ = 100(4,336−4,310) ×0.04/1.04 = £100. The profit from basis speculation when the initial market expectations of S, D and r are fulfilled will usually be insufficient to cover the round trip transactions costs.

The above analysis assumes the basis is affected by only S, D and r. However, if the assumptions underlying the derivation of the no-arbitrage condition are not met, other factors may also cause changes in the basis. For example, the presence of transactions costs may mean that the basis can change within the appropriate no-arbitrage band, while mispricings and changes in taxation may also affect the basis. See chapter 5 for a discussion of the assumptions underlying the derivation of the no-arbitrage condition.

6.3 Basis and Maturity

The approach of delivery has a predictable effect on the absolute size of the basis. As delivery approaches r (the riskless rate of interest for the remaining life of the future) tends to zero, as does D (the present value of the dividends payable). In consequence, the basis tends to zero, irrespective of whether it is positive or negative. At delivery $F = S$, because a future for immediate delivery is equivalent to the spot, and the basis is zero. This convergence is illustrated in figure 6.1.

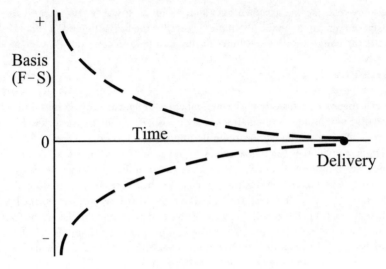

Figure 6.1: Convergence of the Basis

Using daily data on the S&P500 and the MMI for 1985-91 Beaulieu (1998) found that the variance of the basis dropped as maturity approached. Low, Muthuswamy, Sakar & Terry (2002) examined the weekly log-basis of the Nikkei 225 for 1986-96 and found the basis declined in a linear manner as the time to delivery dropped.

Example Using the numbers from table 2.6 for the FTSE 100 index future in April
2004:-

Table 6.2: Values of the Basis ($F-S$) for the FTSE 100 June Contract

Date	Opening Basis	Closing Basis
13 April 04	+34.3	+7.2
14 April 04	- 13.3	+9.1
15 April 04	+3.6	+2.5

From this table the basis is positive (apart from the open on 14th April).

The convergence of the basis to zero at maturity implies that changes in the basis tend to exhibit positive first order autocorrelation. However, since the convergence is due to changes in dividends and interest, this first order autocorrelation is only present for overnight changes in the basis, which is when dividend entitlements and interest obligations change, Miller, Muthuswamy & Whaley (1994).

Hemler & Longstaff (1991) have developed a general equilibrium model for pricing index futures, in which the futures price depends on stock market volatility, see chapter 5.27. One implication of this model is that, because market volatility and the riskless interest rate are assumed over time to revert towards their mean values, no clear statements can be made about movements in the basis. Indeed, it is possible for the basis to change sign several times during the life of a contract.

6.4 Basis Risk

Basis risk means variations in the numerical value of the basis, i.e. variations in $(F-S)$. The relative magnitude of fluctuations in the basis, $(F-S)$, the futures price (F) and the spot price (S) is a matter of considerable importance for some users of futures, e.g. hedgers, see chapter 9 for a discussion of hedging. The variance of the difference between two numbers $(F$ and $S)$, i.e. σ_{F-S}^2, is equal to the variance of F, i.e. σ_F^2, plus the variance of S, i.e. σ_S^2, minus twice the covariance between F and S, i.e. $2\sigma_{F,S}^2$, or $\sigma_{F-S}^2 = \sigma_F^2 + \sigma_S^2 - 2\sigma_{F,S}^2$. In effect, the basis is a portfolio of two securities, one long and the other short. If the basis risk, i.e. σ_{F-S}^2, is to be smaller than the risk of the spot (σ_S^2) and the future (σ_F^2), there must be a substantial positive correlation between the spot and futures prices. For example, if the futures and spot prices have an equal variance, i.e. $\sigma_F^2 = \sigma_S^2 = \sigma^2$, and the correlation between movements in the spot and futures prices is zero, i.e. $\sigma_{F,S}^2 = 0$, then $\sigma_{F-S}^2 = 2\sigma^2$ and the basis risk, i.e. variance of $(F-S)$, is twice that of either the spot price or the futures price. However, a zero correlation is unlikely and, if the correlation between the spot and futures prices is 0.8 (i.e. $\sigma_{F,S}^2 = 0.8\sigma^2$), then the variance of the basis is only 40% of that of either the spot or futures prices, i.e. $\sigma_{F-S}^2 = 0.4\sigma^2$. This illustrates the general property that basis risk is usually considerably smaller than the risk attached to either the spot or future alone. Arbitrage, by confining spot and futures prices to a no-arbitrage band, increases the correlation between these two prices, and this is formally proved by Lien (1992a).

As delivery approaches, the basis converges to zero. Therefore it is plausible to expect that the basis risk will also drop to zero as delivery approaches, as illustrated in figure 6.2.

Castelino & Francis (1982) prove this result for the case considered by Samuelson (1965), see appendix A to chapter 8 of Sutcliffe (1993) for details of Samuelson's model. The intuition is that, as delivery approaches, the future slowly turns into the spot. The arrival of new information is more likely to affect spot and futures prices in the same way (so reducing basis risk) if it arrives closer to delivery. Low, Muthuswamy, Sakar & Terry (2002) carried out an empirical study of the relationship between basis risk and maturity for the Nikkei 225, and found that the variance of the log-basis dropped in a linear manner as delivery approached.

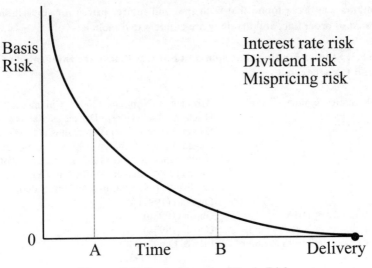

Figure 6.2: Convergence of Basis Risk

6.5 Cointegration of Spot and Futures Prices

There have been a number of investigations of the order of integration of spot and futures prices for stock indices and, given they have the same order of integration, whether they are cointegrated. There are various reasons for expecting the order of integration of spot and futures prices to be one i.e. $I(1)$, and that they are cointegrated.

A random walk with drift is a reasonable model for most security prices. This fits with the concept of an efficient market in which the current price (P_t) reflects the available information. Prices rise each period by θ due to factors such as inflation. New information (ε_t) is random, and when it arrives the price immediately adjusts. In which case, prices follow a random walk with drift $(P_t = P_{t-1}+\theta+\varepsilon_t)$. The first differences of a random walk $(P_t-P_{t-1} = \theta+\varepsilon_t)$ are stationary, and so prices are integrated of order one (or $I(1)$). Since spot and futures prices are linked by a no-arbitrage relationship, they will move together in the long run. Therefore, a linear combination of the spot and futures prices can be chosen such that the result is stationary (i.e. $E[F_t-\alpha S_t]=0$, where α is the spot price weight), and spot and futures prices are cointegrated. Since the basis changes with contract maturity, as r and D decline as delivery approaches, the relationship between spot and futures prices alters slightly over the life of each contract. If the no-arbitrage condition applies, the cointegrating coefficient (α) is given by $\alpha=(1+r)(1-d)$, where $d=D/S_t$. The effect of changes in α is small in relation to fluctuations in the levels of spot and futures prices, and creates a cycle that is repeated every few months. Thus, in the long run, the value of α converges to a value that is close to unity.

Authors who have found that both spot and futures prices for stock indices are integrated of order one, and that they are cointegrated include:-

Table 6.3: Studies Finding that Spot and Futures Prices are Integrated of Order One and Cointegrated

S&P500 futures & index	Alizadeh & Nomikos (2004), Chiang (2003), Chu, Hsieh & Tse (1999), Darrat & Rahman (1999), Dwyer, Locke & Yu (1996), Ghosh (1993a, 1993b), Hogan, Kroner & Sultan (1997), Koutmos & Tucker (1996), Lien & Luo (1993c), Martens, Kofman & Vorst (1995), Mercer (1997), Pizzi, Economopoulos & O'Neill (1998), Sarno & Valente (2000), Wahab & Lashgari (1993)
S&P500 futures & DJIA	Ghosh (1993b)
S&P500 futures & NYSE Comp.	Ghosh (1993b)
NYSE Composite futures & index	Lien & Luo (1993c)
MMI futures & index	Lien & Luo (1993c)
DJIA futures & index	Tse (1999b)
IPC futures and spot	Zhong, Darrat & Otero (2004)
Nikkei (SGX) futures & index	Chiang (2003), Choudhry (2003), Chou, Denis & Lee (1996), Ghosh & Clayton (1996), Lien & Tse (2000b), Tse (1995)
Nikkei (Osaka & SGX) futures & index	Covrig, Ding & Low (2004), Frino & West (2003)
Nikkei futures (Osaka & SGX)	Shyy & Shen (1997)
Nikkei 500 index & Nikkei 225 futures	Choudhry (1997)
Nikkei 300 futures & index and AOI index & SPI futures	Sim & Zurbruegg (1999)
Hang Seng futures & index	Choudhry (1997, 2003), Raj (1995), So & Tse (2004), Fung & Jiang (1999)
KOSPI 200 futures & index	Sim & Zurbruegg (2001b)
Taiwan (MSCI & Taifex) futures & indices	Roope & Zurbruegg (2002), Wang & Low (2003
Taiwan MSCI & Taifex futures	Hsieh (2004), Chou & Lee (2002)
AOI index & SPI futures	Bhar (2001), Brailsford, Corrigan & Heaney (2001), Choudhry (1997, 2003), Eldridge, Peat & Stevenson (2003), Yang (2003), Yeh & Gannon (2000)
AOI index, SPI futures & SPI futures volume	Hodgson, Masih & Masih (2005)
11 Australian stocks & individual stock futures	Lien & Yang (2003, 2004)
Forty futures & index	Raj (1995)
FTSE 100 futures & index	Alizadeh & Nomikos (2004), Antoniou & Garrett (1989, 1992), Antoniou & Holmes (1995a), Brooks, Henry & Persand (2002), Brooks, Rew & Ritson (2001), Choudhry (2003), Frino & McKenzie (2002a),

	Ghosh & Clayton (1996), Holmes (1996b), Sarno & Valente (2000), Wahab & Lashgari (1993)
DAX 30 futures & index	Booth, So & Tse (1999), Choudhry (2003), Ghosh & Clayton (1996)
CAC 40 futures & index	Chiang (2003), Ghosh & Clayton (1996). Green & Joujon (2000), Shyy, Vijayraghavan & Scott-Quinn (1996)
CAC 40 futures & index basket midquotes	Shyy, Vijayraghavan & Scott-Quinn (1996)
FOX futures & index	Booth, Martikainen & Puttonen (1993), Martikainen, Perttunen & Puttonen (1995a), Martikainen & Puttonen (1994b), Puttonen (1993b)
Ibex 35 futures and index	Lafuente & Novales (2003)
MIB 30 index & futures	Pattarin & Ferretti (2003)
FTSE-ASE-20 futures & index	Alexakis, Kavussanos & Visvikis (2002), Floros & Viougas (2004)
FTSE-ASE Mid-40 futures & index	Alexakis, Kavussanos & Visvikis (2002), Floros & Viougas (2004)
JSE Industrial 25 futures & index	Beelders & Massey (2002), Choudhry (2003)
JSE All Share futures & index	Beelders & Massey (2002)
JSE Gold shares futures & index	Beelders & Massey (2002)

Kim, Szakmary & Schwarz (1999) found no cointegration between S&P500, MMI and NYSE Composite futures. They also failed to find cointegration between the S&P500, MMI and NYSE Composite indices. Booth, Martikainen & Puttonen (1993) found that there was no cointegration between the S&P500 spot or futures, and the FOX spot or futures. They also, rather surprisingly, found a lack of cointegration between S&P500 futures and spot. Lim (1996) considered 5 minute returns on the Nikkei 225 for 20 days in 1989-9, and found a lack of cointegration between spot and futures. This negative result is probably due to the use of 5 minute returns. Lin, Chen & Hwang (2003) considered 5 minute returns on Taiex index futures and the corresponding index for 1999-2000. While these series were globally cointegrated, when attention was focused on movements within the no-arbitrage band, they were not cointegrated. Thus futures and spot prices were only cointegrated when the mispricing exceeded a transactions costs threshold.

Arshanapalli & Doukas (1997) investigated cointegration between the S&P500 index and index futures for each day in October 1987 using one minute trade data. They found the two series were cointegrated each day, apart from Friday 16th October and Monday 19th October. The lack of cointegration on Friday 16th October is evidence that the 1987 Crash originated in the US on the Friday.

Using daily closing prices for 1985-98, Bilson, Brailsford & Evans (2005) found cointegration between S&P500 and SPI futures, and between SPI and FTSE 100 futures. However, there was no significant cointegration between S&P500 futures and FTSE 100 futures.

If spot and futures prices are cointegrated, and individually *I(1)*, then Granger's representation theorem requires that either spot prices lead futures prices, futures prices lead spot prices, or both, Cuthbertson, Hall & Taylor (1992, pp. 133-4). This is because, if spot and futures prices are to return to their long run relationship with each other, short run deviations must be corrected. Thus, investigations of leads and lags for indices and index futures are predicted to find something other that a completely contemporaneous relationship.

6.6 Information, Adjustment Speed and Price Discovery

In chapter 3 a no-arbitrage equation was derived for the relationship between the spot and futures prices of a market index. In a dynamic world, the relevant information set underlying this no-arbitrage condition is continually changing, leading to continuous movement in the no-arbitrage spot and futures prices. One of the important roles attributed to futures markets is that of 'price discovery', i.e. the futures market reflects new information before the spot market.

6.6.1 Price Discovery

The creation of a futures market will attract investors to trade the future who did not already trade the spot, Cox (1976). For example, investors might be attracted by the advantages of a highly liquid market, low transactions costs, easily available short positions, low margins and rapid execution. The information held by these new investors about the expected spot price at the futures delivery date will be revealed in the futures price. This additional information is then available to traders in the spot market. Therefore, the introduction of futures will increase the amount of information reflected in the spot price.

Grossman (1977) constructed a different model in which there are informed and uninformed traders. The spot price reveals only part of the information possessed by informed traders because the spot price is also influenced by random disturbances. In these circumstances, a futures market may convey some more of the information possessed by the informed, to the uninformed, traders. The result is the same as for Cox, i.e. the introduction of a futures market increases the amount of information reflected in the spot price.

Green (1986) has argued that, in the absence of a market in index futures, traders without an initial long position in shares cannot reveal any bad news they may possess about share returns because short selling shares is difficult. If there is a market in index futures, such traders can take a short position by selling futures, thereby impounding their information about bad news into the futures price.

Covey & Bessler (1995) argued that the creation of a futures market for a storable asset, such as shares, will not improve price discovery because no new information is provided. However, for non-storable assets a futures market will reveal information not included in the spot price concerning the future demand and supply conditions of the asset.

Cooper & Mello (1990) present a model in which the introduction of a market in index futures causes share prices to be less, rather than more, informative. They argue that the creation of a market in index futures diverts volume that is not primarily based on information about a specific company away from the stock market, and so the remaining trades in shares are more information-based than before. This causes the market makers in shares to widen their bid-ask spreads, to protect themselves in their dealings with better informed traders. Because of this increase in transactions costs, the profits from exploiting company-specific information in the stock market decline. This leads to a drop in the amount of company-specific information collected, and a decline in stock market volume. Thus, share prices reflect less information than before the introduction of index futures. This argument ignores a number of factors that will tend to operate in the opposite direction. For example, index arbitrage will create a substantial increase in uninformed share trading, the holders of shares (e.g. market makers) can hedge some of the risk via index futures, and index futures permit the revelation of bad news (of a general nature) by adopting a short position.

Given the large amount of data already impounded in share prices, and that few well informed investors will be induced to trade index futures who did not already trade shares, the increase in information reflected in share prices is likely to be small. There is also the problem that the futures market price reflects a market index, while equity traders deal in individual shares, Miller (1990a). Thus, the futures price reflects predominantly market-wide information, while each share price reflects information specific to that company; as well as systematic (or market-wide) factors. Ultimately, the effect of the introduction of index futures on the information content of share prices is an empirical matter.

USA. Froot & Perold (1995) document a decline in the first order serial correlation of 15-minute returns on the S&P500 index from +0.35 in 1983, to −0.05 in 1987. They argue that this decline is due to share prices more rapidly reflecting market-wide information. Since trading in S&P500 futures began in 1982, this effect could be due to price discovery by the futures market.

Fleming, Kirby & Ostdiek (1998) analysed daily data for 1983-95 for S&P500 futures, US Treasury bond futures and US Treasury bill futures. Using GMM, they found that volatility movements across the three futures were strongly positively correlated, which implies that information is reflected within a day in all three markets.

Chu, Hsieh & Tse (1999) analysed transactions data for the S&P500 index and futures and S&P depositary receipts for 1993. They found that the dominant price discovery role was played by the futures market; with the depositary receipts contributing much less, and the spot market contributing the least.

Hasbrouck (2003) used transactions data for 3 months in 2000 to investigate the relative price discovery of S&P500 futures, S&P500 e-mini futures and S&P depositary receipts (SPDRs). He found that about 90% of the price discovery was attributable to e-mini futures, with about 5% each to S&P500 futures and SPDRs. For the NASDAQ 100 index, the corresponding price discovery shares were similar. The S&P MidCap 400 has no e-mini contract, and here the price discovery is split approximately equally between S&P MidCap 400 futures and the S&P MidCap 400 exchange traded fund. The e-mini contracts are smaller contracts which are screen traded, and this may explain their dominance. Hasbrouck also investigated the relative price discovery of SPDRs and the nine sector exchange traded funds; and found that the sector funds made only a modest contribution to price discovery.

Tse (1999b) analysed one minute returns for the DJIA for 1997-8. He found that DJIA futures accounted for 88% of the price discovery, while the index managed only 12%.

Chou & Chung (2004) considered the effect of the decimalization of ETF trading on price discovery by S&P500 e-mini futures, Nasdaq 100 e-mini futures, DJIA futures, and their corresponding ETFs. Using 5 minute returns for 2000-1, they found that decimalization led to a drop in ETF spreads. The proportions of price discovery, relative to the ETF, accounted for by the futures contracts changed as follows: S&P500 - 93% to 95%, Nasdaq 100 - 88% to 81%, and DJIA - 82% to 75%. The increase in information share for the Nasdaq 100 and DJIA ETFs was attributed to the transactions cost reduction caused by decimalization.

Kurov & Lasser (2004) studied trade data at 1 second intervals on 86 days in 2001 for S&P500 and Nasdaq 100 futures, and the corresponding e-mini futures. The information shares of the e-mini futures were 99% for the S&P500, and 97% for the Nasdaq 100. They also found that e-mini prices responded to large floor trades about 15-20 seconds before floor prices; primarily because locals used trading screens next to the pit to trade e-mini futures. This indicates that, while the e-mini futures dominate price discovery; institutional trading of standard contracts on the exchange floor is an important source of information to the market.

Ates & Wang (2005) used data at 5 second intervals for 1997-2001 to investigate the relative importance of full sized S&P500 futures and S&P500 e-mini futures in the price discovery process. By 2000, the screen-based e-mini futures had an information share of about 88%, leaving just 12% for floor-traded S&P500 futures. A similar analysis for 1999-2001 found that by 2000 the screen-based Nasdaq 100 e-mini futures had an information share of about 93%, while floor-based standard size Nasdaq 100 futures managed just 7%. When the analysis was broadened to include the underlying index, the S&P500 index had an information share of about 5%; while the Nasdaq 100 index had an information share of only 4%. A time series regression found that the information shares for both S&P500 and Nasdaq 100 e-mini futures increased as their market share of trading increased; and as their realized bid-ask spread, relative to that of the standard contracts, decreased. This supports the view that e-mini futures have a dominant information share because there are screen-based, leading to greater liquidity and lower transactions costs.

Japan.   Craig, Dravid & Richardson (1995) studied the extent to which Nikkei 225 futures traded on the CME reflect information relevant to the Nikkei index released during the Japanese non-trading period. Using data from 1991-2, they found that CME Nikkei futures captured a lot of the overnight returns of the Nikkei index. They also found no evidence of contagion from the NYSE to CME Nikkei futures.

Contagion occurs when mistakes in setting prices in one market are transmitted to another.

Covrig, Ding & Low (2004) compared the price discovery of the Nikkei 225 spot market, the domestic futures market in Osaka, and the foreign futures market in Singapore. Using quotes for three months in 2000, they found that 21% of price discovery was in the spot market, 46% in the domestic futures market and 33% in the foreign futures market.

Hong Kong.   So & Tse (2004) used transactions data for 1999-2002 to compare the relative contribution to price discovery of the Hang Seng index, Hang Seng index futures and a Hang Seng tracker fund created by the government as a response to the sharp fall in the index in the autumn of 1998. They found that 75%-80% of the price discovery was by the futures market, 20%-25% by the spot market, and nothing by the tracker fund.

Taiwan.   Roope & Zurbruegg (2002) considered transactions data for four months in 1999 on Taiwan MSCI futures in Singapore, Taifex futures in Taiwan, and the two underlying indices. By considering pairwise information shares, they concluded that price discovery was dominated by Taiwan MSCI futures in Singapore. Hsieh (2004) reconsidered this question and, using transactions data for 1998-2001, analysed the change in information shares around each of five regulatory changes in Taifex futures trading. Each regulatory change made futures trading in Taiwan more attractive, and the final four rule changes led to an increase in price discovery by Taifex futures. The biggest increases in price discovery were for a halving of the transfer tax and a doubling of the position limit. While Taiwan MSCI futures dominated price discovery in the earlier periods, by 2001 Taifex futures had a slightly larger share.

Australia.   Frino, Harris, McInish & Tomas (2004) considered the relative contribution to price discovery by locals and non-locals trading AOI futures for 5 months in 1997. They found that by observing the order flow, locals contributed 73% of the price discovery, as against 27% for trades executed without the involvement of a local. This price discovery by locals is based on the information contained in the futures order flow generated by others. This result contrasts with that of Fong & Zurbruegg (2003), who found that for 1997-98, locals contributed only about one third of the price discovery.

UK.   Holmes & Tomsett (2004) analysed daily data on FTSE 100 futures for 1992-6, and concluded that it was consistent with the mixture of distributions hypothesis, and that futures volume is driven very largely by informed traders, rather than noise traders. This supports the view that information is exploited in the futures market, and so the futures market is an important mechanism for price discovery.

Germany.   So, Booth & Loistl (1997) employed 5 minute returns on DAX-30 futures, options and index for 1992-4. They found that 5 and 15 minute returns for spot, futures and options reacted differently to market wide information. However, 30 minute returns displayed a common volatility process, indicating that it took about 30 minutes for information to be impounded into all three markets.

Booth, So & Tse (1999) studied transactions data for DAX 30 futures, options and the DAX 30 index for 1992-4. They found that 50% of the price discovery was by the index, 48% by the futures and only 2% by the index options.

6.6.2 Leads and Lags

As well as studying information shares, there have been a considerable number of studies looking at leads and lags between futures and spot markets. If the index futures market reflects new information before the spot market, futures prices will lead spot prices. Because of the ease of trading in futures, index futures may reflect new information faster than spot markets (i.e. they provide a leading indicator of share price movements). There are a number of reasons for expecting the prices of index futures to adjust faster than the spot price, i.e. the market index.

First, when new information is received, traders can choose whether to exploit this knowledge in the futures or spot markets. For information that affects the share price of only a few companies (unsystematic information), traders will probably choose to buy or sell individual shares (or their options) rather than index futures because the movement in the index will be very much smaller than that in the share prices of the affected companies. However, traders may prefer to use the futures market to exploit information which relates to the economy in general (systematic information) rather than to particular companies. This is because trading futures has the advantages of a highly liquid market, low transactions costs, easily available short positions, low margins and rapid execution (often aided by screen trading). Therefore, the futures price will respond first to information of a general, or market-wide, nature, while information specific to a few companies will have little impact on the index or the futures price. However, when new information causes movements in the prices of a few companies, and this results in a change in the index, the spot price may lead the futures price.

This conclusion is subject to the exception that, if futures are overpriced relative to the spot, bullish market-wide information may be exploited by buying shares, not futures. This may happen when the mispricing exceeds the extent to which the transactions costs are increased by buying the index basket, rather than futures. Corresponding conditions can be derived for cases involving underpricing and bearish information. Thus, even if there is generally an incentive for futures prices to lead spot prices, this may not always be the case, even for market-wide information.

Second, even if traders choose to trade mainly in the spot market, there is likely to be a delay in the response of the spot market to the arrival of information of a general nature. If a new piece of information arrives which is bullish, traders will immediately increase the price of futures, e.g. the next trade should fully reflect the new information. For the spot price (i.e. the index) to fully respond, if the index is computed from actual rather than quoted prices, there must be a trade in every share in the index, e.g. 500 or 1,700 shares, and then the index must be recomputed. This suggests some delay in the response of the index (spot price) to new information due to the 'stale prices' effect. In the UK, until 20th October 1997 the FTSE 100 index was based on quotations from SEAQ rather than transactions prices, and so the index was likely to be a more accurate reflection of the current state of the equity market.

Finally, since short selling shares may be difficult, e.g. due to the uptick rule in the US, bad news may be reflected first in the futures market, and only later in the stock market.

The index and the future differ in respect of the times at which they value the basket of shares in the index, and this can be a source of additional information. A stock index represents the market's estimate of the present value of the subsequent cash flows expected from the constituent companies, while the current price of a futures contract on an index for delivery at time T represents the market's estimate of the present value at time T of the subsequent cash flows. Therefore the additional information contained in the futures price, over and above that contained in the spot price, is the value of the cash flows from owning the index between now and time T, Carlton (1984).

6.6.3 Empirical Studies of Leads and Lags

The results of a substantial number of studies of the leads and lags between spot and futures prices will be considered to see if the theoretical prediction that futures prices usually lead spot prices is supported and, if so, to see how long is the lag before spot prices catch up with futures prices.

USA.   Kawaller, Koch & Koch (1987, 1988) examined the S&P500 index for leads and lags between the spot and futures prices using transactions data for 1984-1985. They found that, in general, these two prices move very closely together. However, they did find some evidence that the price of index futures leads the spot price (S&P500 index) by some 20 to 45 minutes.

Kawaller, Koch & Koch (1993) used minute-by-minute data on S&P500 futures for the last quarter of 1986. They argued that the nature of the lead-lag relationship between the spot and futures markets may change over time. For example, when there is no mispricing, only hedgers and speculators are trading, but when there is a mispricing arbitrageurs will enter the market to ensure the movement of futures and/or spot prices to remove the mispricing. Seemingly unrelated regression estimation (SURE) was used to fit four equations - one for each of Geweke's four feedback measures - to the minute-by-minute price changes. This was repeated for each day. This provided four Geweke feedback measures for each day. A strong contemporaneous link between spot and futures prices was found, as well as a weaker finding that futures prices led spot prices. The daily feedback measures were then regressed on three daily volatility measures (the daily range, the daily variance of minute-to-minute changes in the basis and the frequency of stock index arbitrage opportunities each day), two daily spot volume measures, a time trend and day of the week dummies. It was found that the daily range had a significantly positive effect on the Geweke feedback measures. Hence, increased price volatility strengthens the link between futures and spot prices, and large price movements do not cause a breakdown in the price relationship between these markets.

Herbst, McCormack & West (1987) analysed price changes over ten second periods to examine the lead-lag relationship between the spot and futures markets for both the S&P500 and VLCI indices. They found that, for each index, the futures market led the spot market by a few minutes, and that there was a strong contemporaneous relationship between spot and futures returns. For the S&P500 the lead was between zero and eight minutes, with an average lead of 0.7 minutes. For the VLCI, the lead was zero to sixteen minutes, with an average of 0.9 minutes.

Furbush (1989) studied movements in the spot and futures prices of the S&P500 index over five minute periods in October 1987. He regressed the change in the spot price on the change in the futures price for the previous five minute period and found a positive and highly significant relationship.

Kutner & Sweeney (1991) studied minute-by-minute data for the S&P500 between August and December 1987. After pre-whitening the series of spot and futures prices, they looked for Granger causality (see chapter 7.4 for a discussion of Granger causality) between these series, and found that futures prices led spot prices by about twenty minutes.

Stoll & Whaley (1990b, 1993 pp 114-116) analysed returns (logarithm of the price relative) over five minute intervals for the S&P500 and MMI index futures and indices for 1982-7. They fitted an autoregressive moving average (ARMA) model to the share price data and the indices to remove the effects of bid-ask bounce (in the absence of new information, the transaction prices for a security will fluctuate between the bid and the ask prices, depending on whether the trade was initiated by a buyer or a seller) and infrequent trading (or stale prices). Therefore, any remaining lead of the futures price over the spot price is due to either new information being reflected first in the futures market (i.e. price discovery), or to recording and reporting lags for the index. They found that, while the main relationship is contemporaneous, the returns on the S&P500 and MMI futures lead those on the underlying index by about five minutes, and attribute this to a price discovery role for index futures.

Cheung & Ng (1990) analysed fifteen minute returns for the S&P500 for 1983-7. They made allowance for a stale price effect in the index (by including a first order moving average process), and used a GARCH(1,1) model to control for autocorrelation in the variance of the disturbances. They found that futures returns led spot returns by at least fifteen minutes, although there was also a strong contemporaneous correlation between spot and futures returns.

Chan, Chan & Karolyi (1991) fitted a bivariate GARCH model to the S&P500 from 1984 to 1989. Using returns computed over five minute intervals, they found that futures returns led spot returns by about five minutes.

Fleming, Ostdiek & Whaley (1996) looked for leads and lags between the spot, futures and options markets. They argued that, since the transactions costs of trading the S&P500 index basket of shares were roughly five times larger than for a corresponding trade in index options, and about 30 times larger than for a similar trade in index futures, traders with market-wide information will choose to use the futures or options markets, rather than the spot market. They used 5-minute log returns on the S&P500 index, the S&P 100 index, S&P500 futures and S&P 100 options for 1988-91. The returns on the index implied by the S&P 100 options prices were computed using midquotes and the previous day's implied volatility. To purge the observed values of the S&P500 and S&P 100 indices of spurious autocorrelation due to stale prices, an ARMA process was fitted to the spot returns for each day. The S&P500 futures returns were simply the log returns computed using transactions prices. They found that the futures price led both indices (purged of their autocorrelation) by up to 20 minutes, and that the strength of the contemporaneous relationship between spot and futures prices has grown over time. They also found a strong contemporaneous relationship between futures and options prices. While there was evidence that futures prices led options prices, and that options prices led futures prices, the futures lead over options was the stronger relationship.

Wahab & Lashgari (1993) studied daily data on the S&P500 for 1988-92. Using an error correction mechanism (ECM) framework, they found bidirectional causality between spot and futures returns.

Using an ECM approach, Ghosh (1993a) analysed 15-minute returns on the S&P500 for 1988, and found that futures prices led spot prices by 15 minutes.

Mercer (1997) applied an ECM approach to one minute returns for the 1987 crash and 5 days in 1988, He concluded that the inclusion of the error correction term was beneficial, and that S&P500 futures led spot.

De Jong & Nijman (1997) developed a way of using irregularly spaced data to compute covariances which avoids non-trading bias. This was applied to data for the S&P500 for the last three months of 1993. They found that futures led spot by 11 minutes, while spot led futures by 2 minutes.

Using one minute returns for 1987 on the S&P500, Pizzi, Economopoulos & O'Neill (1998) found bidirectional causality with the futures market leading the spot market by 20 minutes, and the spot market leading the futures market by 3 or 4 minutes.

Chatrath, Christie-David, Dhanda & Koch (2002) analysed 15 minute returns for the S&P500 for 1993-6 to investigate the circumstances under which futures lead spot. When the index was rising, volatility high, and the market was not at the open or close; the futures lead was strongest. Leadership by the spot market was most apparent in the opposite circumstances. The authors argue that these findings are caused by commercial traders choosing to trade futures in a rising market, and equities when the market is falling.

For each change in the value of the MMI, Finnerty & Park (1987) regressed the natural logarithm of S_t/S_{t-1} on the immediately preceding natural logarithm of F_t/F_{t-1}; where S_t is the spot value of the index at time t and F_t is the value of the future on the MMI at time t. The futures price changes used in this study were argued to precede the spot price changes by roughly one minute, although this has been disputed; Gordon, Moriarty & Tosini (1987) and Herbst & Maberly (1987). Finnerty & Park concluded that futures prices lead the spot market by about one minute, although the size of this effect is small.

These results are supported by those of Laatsch & Schwarz (1988). They used minute-to-minute data to fit a simultaneous equations model of the determination of spot and futures prices for the MMI. Using data for the near and next-near futures contracts for 1984-6, they found clear support that futures prices lead spot prices by one minute. The only other lag for which they tested was 24 hours, and there was no clear lead-lag relationship in this case.

Schwarz & Laatsch (1991) again used a simultaneous equations model, and applied it to data for the MMI from 1985 to 1988. They measured price changes over periods of one week, one day, five minutes and one minute, and concluded that the relationship between spot and futures prices has varied over time. Initially, the spot market led futures but, by the end of the data period, the futures market led the spot.

Using transactions data for the MMI for 1986, Swinnerton, Curcio & Bennett (1988) found that the change in futures prices over the last five minutes had some predictive power for the change in the index over the next five minutes.

Chan (1992) considered transactions data on the twenty shares in the MMI for two periods; 1984-5, and 1987. He also used transactions data on MMI futures for the same periods. For spot and futures returns over five minute periods, he found evidence that futures returns led spot returns by up to fifteen minutes, as well as a strong contemporaneous relationship. Chan then tested various explanations for this result. Adjusting for stale prices reduced, but did not eliminate, the lead by futures prices; while restrictions on short selling shares were rejected as an explanation. Market-wide information appeared to be a cause of futures prices leading spot prices. Finally, there was no evidence that the lead-lag relationship was affected by the relative intensity of trading in the futures and spot markets.

Ng (1987) used daily data (1981-6) on the near contract for the S&P500 and VLCI indices to look for Granger causality between spot and futures prices. She found that, for both the stock indices the futures price led the spot price by one day; the only lag considered. There was also a strong contemporaneous relationship between spot and futures prices. However, the correlations between current changes in the spot price and lagged changes in the futures price were low.

If new information leads to a move in the futures price before the spot price, the basis will change prior to a change in the spot price. Zeckhauser & Niederhoffer (1983a) examined the rank correlations between the basis and the change in the spot price over the next one and three days for the S&P500 and VLCI indices. They found evidence of a positive relationship between the basis and subsequent changes in the spot price for both indices. This provides evidence that rises (falls) in the futures price precede rises (falls) in the spot price by one to three days. Zeckhauser & Niederhoffer (1983b) also found that the basis for the VLCI could be used to predict movements in the spot price over the next three days.

Kim, Szakmary & Schwarz (1999) studied 5-minute returns from 1986-91 for the S&P500, MMI and NYSE Composite indices and futures. They concluded that

S&P500 futures lead the other two futures by five minutes, while the MMI index leads the other two indices by about five minutes.

Brooks, Garrett & Hinich (1999) used the Hinich test, which allows for non-linearities and non-stationarities, to examine daily returns on the S&P500 (1983-93) and FTSE 100 (1985-93). They found no evidence of leads and lags for the S&P500; and only a short period in 1992 when futures led spot for the FTSE 100. They concluded that most of the previous tests for leads and lags, which have assumed linearity and stationarity, are biased.

Chou & Chung (2004) considered 5-minute returns on S&P500 e-mini futures, Nasdaq 100 e-mini futures, DJIA futures, and their corresponding ETFs for 2000-1. They found that for each index, futures led spot by about 30 minutes.

Canada.   Beaulieu, Ebrahim & Morgan (2003) analysed 15 minute returns (adjusted for missing values) for the three months in 1991 around the reduction in tick size for the ETF (TIPS) on the TSE 35 index. The lower tick size for TIPS resulted in a sharp drop in their effective and quoted spreads. Before the reduction in tick size TSE 35 futures led the TSE 35 index by 15 minutes, while there were no leads and lags between the index and the ETF. After lowering the tick size, futures returns led the index by 30 minutes, and the ETF now led the index by 15-45 minutes. This shows the importance of transactions costs in determining lead-lag relationships.

Mexico.   Zhong, Darrat & Otero (2004) investigated daily data on the IPC index for 1999-2002. Using an EC-GARCH model that found that futures returns led spot returns.

Japan.   Lim (1992a, 1992b) studied the Nikkei 225 (SGX) on twenty days in 1988 and 1989. For price changes over five minutes, he found no evidence from cross correlations that futures prices led spot prices, or that spot prices led futures prices. For most of the observations, Nikkei futures were traded in Japan, as well as Singapore, and the volume in the Japanese market was much larger than for SGX. Thus, prices on SGX may not have had a measurable effect on the index.

Vila & Bacha (1995) used daily opening and closing prices for 1986-92 for the Nikkei 225. The spot is traded in Tokyo, and the futures markets in Singapore and Osaka trade synchronously with the spot market; while the futures market in Chicago only opens after Tokyo has closed. The overnight futures returns for Singapore and Osaka led the following day's trading return on the spot market, and the Chicago trading returns led the spot trading returns for the following day, but the effect was small. These results indicate that the futures markets led the spot market by a number of hours.

Hiraki, Maberly & Takezawa (1995) used transactions data for Nikkei 225 futures traded in Osaka for 1988-91. Until 2nd October 1990, the futures were traded for 15 minutes longer than the spot, while after this date (until 7th February 1992) futures were traded for 10 minutes beyond the cessation of spot trading. Information that arrives after the close of the spot market, but before the close of the futures market, ought to be reflected in futures returns for this 'end of the day' period, and in the overnight return for the spot market. Hiraki, Maberly & Takezawa (1995) found that unexpected end of the day futures returns had a positive effect on the subsequent overnight spot return, while the variance of unexpected end of the day futures returns also had a positive effect on the conditional variance on the subsequent overnight spot return. These results accord with the simultaneous impounding of information into the spot and futures markets. However, they also discovered that end of the day futures returns had a positive effect on spot returns for the next two days; implying that futures prices led spot prices by several days.

Tse (1995) analysed daily data on Nikkei 225 futures traded on SGX and the underlying index for 1988-93. Using the ECM approach, the spot price was found to be influenced by the spot and futures prices up to two days previously, while the futures price was not affected by past spot or futures prices. This finding that futures prices lead spot prices cannot be explained by stale prices, as the lead is up to two days.

Iihara, Kato & Tokunaga (1996) used 5-minute log returns on Nikkei 225 futures traded in Osaka, and the underlying index for 1989-91. They found that futures returns led spot returns by up to 20 minutes, while spot returns led futures returns by up to 5 minutes. There was also a strong contemporaneous relationship between spot and futures returns.

Chung, Kang & Rhee (1994a) analysed 5-minute returns for 1988-91 on Nikkei 225 futures in Osaka, and the index. To purge the data of the effects of stale prices and bid-ask bounce, only innovations in the spot and futures returns were analysed. They found a strong contemporaneous relationship between spot and futures returns, that futures returns led spot returns by up to 20 minutes, and that spot returns led futures returns by up to 15 minutes. The coefficients for the lead by futures returns were larger than those for the lead by spot returns.

A high level of spot volume will tend to reduce any stale price effects that remain after prewhitening, so reducing the extent to which futures returns lead spot returns. Alternatively, a high level of spot volume may overload the trading system for Japanese equities, leading to trading lag and an increase in the extent to which futures returns lead spot returns. Chung, Kang & Rhee found that spot returns led futures returns only when there was high spot volume, supporting the stale prices argument. When spot volume was high relative to futures volume, spot returns led futures returns by 5 minutes, and the futures lead over spot returns was weaker than otherwise. Thus, spot volume, and spot volume relative to futures volume, can affect leads and lags.

Macroeconomic news that changes the prices of equities in the same direction will tend to be exploited first in the futures market, causing futures returns to lead spot returns; while firm-specific information will tend to cause spot returns to lead futures returns. Chung, Kang & Rhee measured the extent to which the prices of Nikkei stocks moved together each day, with high values indicating the arrival of macroeconomic news. They found only a slight effect, with the futures lead being stronger on days when there was macroeconomic news, as expected.

Next they examined whether the cost of short selling equities was responsible for futures leading spot. Short selling is of relevance when there is bad news, and so the hypothesis is that the futures lead over spot will be stronger when there is bad news. Good news was defined as occurring when daily spot returns were high, and bad news arrived when daily spot returns were low. The results did not support the hypothesis. Finally, during the data period there were three increases in futures margin, and higher margins may discourage the use of the futures market. However, there was no clear evidence of such an effect.

Shyy & Shen (1997) used transactions data for two months in 1994. They found bidirectional causality between Nikkei 225 futures in Osaka and Singapore, with leads and lags of a few minutes.

Covrig, Ding & Low (2004) used quotes for the Nikkei 225 in 2000, and found bidirectional Granger causality between the spot market, the Osaka futures market and the Singapore futures market.

Frino & West (2003) studied 1-minute returns for 30 days in 1998 on Nikkei 225 futures in Osaka and Singapore and the underlying index. After allowing for the effects of stale prices, they found strong contemporaneous effects, and also that Singapore futures led Osaka futures by up to 5 minutes, which in turn led the index by up to 3 minutes. The lead by Singapore over Osaka is explained by their lower transactions costs.

Sim & Zurbruegg (1999) considered 10 minute returns on Nikkei 300 futures for 1997, and found bidirectional causality between the spot and futures markets.

Hong Kong. Tang, Mak & Choi (1992) used daily closing prices for the Hang Seng and found that the futures leads the spot. However a study of minute-to-minute returns on 17 days in 1991 by Ho, Fang & Woo (1992) found no evidence of leads and lags of 3 minutes or less for the Hang Seng.

Raj (1995) used daily data on the Hang Seng for 1992-3. Using an ECM approach, he found bidirectional causality between spot and futures returns, i.e. futures returns led spot returns, and spot returns led futures returns.

Fung & Jiang (1999) examined the effects of relaxing the short-selling restrictions in January 1994 and March 1996 on leads and lags for the Hang Seng. Using transactions data for 1993-6, they found that futures led spot by 25 minutes before any relaxation on short sales; while this lead dropped to ten minutes after the relaxations. Similarly the 20 minute lead of spot over futures dropped to only five minutes after the relaxations. Jiang, Fung & Cheng (2001) examined the same problem and found that futures led spot by 15 minutes before any relaxation of the short-selling restrictions, and this lead dropped to nine minutes after the relaxations; while the contemporaneous correlation strengthened. In all periods, spot led futures by three minutes.

Chiang & Fong (2001) analysed 5 minute data for the Hang Seng in 1994. After removing serial correlation from the index, they found bidirectional causality; with futures leading spot by up to 15 minutes, and spot leading futures by up to 5 minutes. They also looked for leads and lags between each of the index constituents and the futures. The larger the company, the smaller the futures lead over the spot.

Korea. Min & Najand (1999) studied 10 minute returns for the KOSPI 200 index for five months in 1996. They found that futures led spot by up to 30 minutes.

There was also some evidence that spot led futures by up to 20 minutes.

Taiwan.   In May 2000 the transactions tax on futures traded on Taifex was halved, including the tax on futures on the Taiwan Stock Exchange weighted index. Futures on the MSCI Taiwan stock index were also traded in Singapore. Chou & Lee (2002) used transactions data for 1999-2000 to analyse the change in leads and lags between these two futures contracts. Before and after the tax reduction there is bidirectional Granger causality with leads and lags of 4 to 5 minutes, with Singapore as the more dominant market. However, after the tax reduction on Taifex, the size and significance of Taifex futures on SGX futures has increased. This is attributed to the reduction in transactions costs for Taifex.

Australia.   Twite (1991) studied daily closing prices for the Australian AOI for 1983-8, and found that, while the strongest relationship between spot and futures returns was contemporaneous, there was also evidence that futures returns led spot returns by one day.

   Hodgson, Kendig & Tahir (1993) used 15 minute data for 1992 for the AOI. They found that for two contracts futures returns led spot returns by up to thirty minutes, while for the third contract, spot returns led futures returns by fifteen minutes. They concluded that the lead-lag relationship was not stable.

   Frino & West (1999) considered transactions data on the AOI and SPI futures for 1992-7. After removing the effects of stale prices and bid-ask bounce from the index, they found that the contemporaneous relationship was dominant, In addition, futures led spot by 20-25 minutes, while spot led futures by 5 minutes. They also found that by 1997, the futures lead had shortened to 15 minutes and the spot lead had disappeared. This may have been due to the halving of stamp duty on equities in July 1995.

   Sim & Zurbruegg (1999) considered 10 minute returns on SPI futures and the AOI index for 1997, and found that the spot led the futures market.

   Between 3 September 1990 and 1 October 1990 most trading of the shares in the AOI moved from floor to screen. Brailsford, Frino, Hodgson & West (1999) used 5 minute returns for 1989-92 on the AOI and the corresponding futures contract to investigate the effects of this change on lead-lag relationships. They found that before the move to screens, futures led spot by 25 minutes; and spot led futures by 15 minutes. However, after the switch to screen trading, the contemporaneous relationship became stronger, as did the 5 and 10 minute lagged effects of futures returns on spot returns, while the longer lags now had less effect. Therefore, the interaction between these two markets was compressed into a shorter time frame by the introduction of screens.

   Frino, Walter & West (2000) used 1 minute returns for the AOI and SPI futures for 1995-6. After removing the effects of stale prices and bid-ask bounce from the AOI, they found that futures led spot by 18 minutes, while spot led futures by 4 minutes. Within 30 minutes of the release of a major piece of macroeconomic news, the first six minutes of the futures lead over spot was strengthened. This is consistent with the futures market being used to exploit market-wide news. Within 30 minutes of the announcement of significant items of company-specific news, the leads and lags between the spot and futures markets were unchanged, although, as suggested by the theory, there was some slight evidence of a weakening of the futures lead. Both macroeconomic and firm-specific news led to a weakening of the contemporaneous relationship.

In & Lim (2003) applied wavelet analysis to daily data on the AOI and SPI futures for 1988-2001. There found bidirectional Granger causality with leads and lags in both directions extending of over 256 days.

Eldridge, Peat & Stevenson (2003) considered 5 minute returns on the AOI and SPI futures for 1995-6. When the spot and futures returns were transformed to remove the autocorrelation in the level and volatility of returns, the leads and lags between futures and spot disappeared. There was also no clear evidence of nonlinear Granger causality in these transformed returns. The authors concluded that, when the effects of stale prices etc. are properly allowed for, there are no leads and lags of 5 minutes or more.

Chng & Gannon (2003) looked for leads and lags between the volatility of SPI futures returns, and the volatility of returns on SPI futures options. Using half hour data for 1994, they found that options' volatility led futures volatility.

Hodgson, Masih & Masih (2005) studied 15-minute data on AOI and SPI returns and SPI volume for 1992-3. They found that during bear markets there were no long run leads and lags between spot returns, futures returns and futures volume; while in bull markets stock returns led both futures returns and futures volume in the long run. In the short run futures returns led spot reruns in both bear and bull markets, while futures volume was exogenous. Overall, they concluded that futures returns led spot returns in both bear and bull markets, after allowing for any futures volume effects.

New Zealand. Raj (1995) analysed daily data on the Forty index for 1992-3. Using an ECM framework, he found that futures returns led spot returns by up to two days. Forty index futures are traded electronically, and stocks have been traded electronically in New Zealand since June 1991.

UK. Wahab & Lashgari (1993) studied daily data on the FTSE 100 for 1988-92. Using an ECM framework, they found there was bidirectional causality between spot and futures returns.

Theobald & Yallup (1993) analysed data on the FTSE 100 for 1984-91. They regressed daily spot returns on futures returns for the current, preceding and subsequent days and found a strong contemporaneous relationship, and also that futures returns led spot returns by one day.

Abhyankar (1995) analysed hourly returns on the FTSE 100 for 1986-90. Innovations in spot returns (the residuals after fitting an AR(2) model to returns) were regressed on leading and lagging innovations in futures returns using the generalized method of moments. It was found that there was a strong contemporaneous relationship between spot and futures returns, and that futures returns led spot returns by one hour. The use of innovations should have removed the effects of stale prices and bid-ask bounce, and so these are unlikely to be the causes of the futures lead.

Abhyankar then investigated the sensitivity of this result to variations in transactions costs, good or bad news (size of return), spot volume and spot volatility. In the post Big Bang period spot transactions costs fell, and this was associated with a reduction in the strength of the futures lead. Therefore, the low transactions costs of trading futures may be a cause of the futures lead. The futures lead was strongest during periods of neither good nor bad news. When there was bad news, the futures lead over the spot was less pronounced than when there was average news, while there was no lead when there was good news. This suggests that, while difficulties with short selling may have some role in the futures lead over spot, it is not very large. The futures lead was insensitive to variations in spot volume. An AR(2) EGARCH(1,1) model was fitted to spot and futures returns to give time series of the estimated volatilities, and during periods of high and low volatility futures market returns led spot market returns.

Abhyankar (1998) studied 5-minute returns on the FTSE 100 for the four near contracts traded in 1992. The spot and futures returns were filtered using an AR(n)-EGARCH(1,1) model to remove non-stationarities, and it was found that futures led spot by 5-15 minutes. He then applied the Baek & Brock test (as modified by Hiemstra & Jones) to the residuals from the linear regressions, and this revealed bidirectional non-linear causality, in addition to the linear causality from futures to spot.

Ap Gwilym & Buckle (2001) studied hourly returns on the FTSE 100 for 1993-6. After removing the effects of stale prices, they found strong contemporaneous relationships, and that futures led spot by one hour; while there was a bidirectional relationship between the futures and American style options markets, with leads and lags of one hour.

Frino & McKenzie (2003) used 5 minute returns for the five months in 1999 around the move of FTSE 100 futures trading to the CONNECT screen-based system, so that both spot and futures became screen traded. CONNECT reduced the strength of the futures lead over spot, and strengthened the contemporaneous relationship. This outcome is puzzling as CONNECT improved the attractiveness of using the futures market to exploit information, and this should have increased the futures lead over spot.

Germany.   The earlier studies analysed situations where neither the shares nor the futures were traded on screens. However, with the creation of screen-based futures exchanges in the 1990s (e.g. DTB, OM, OMLX, Soffex, ÖTOB, Meff RV, SOM, NZFOE, BDP, Korea Stock Exchange, IDEM), there were many situations where the futures are traded on screens, and the underlying shares were floor-traded. Grünbichler, Longstaff & Schwartz (1994) argued that, if futures trading is screen-based while stock trading is not, the futures lead over the spot market will tend to lengthen. This is because screen-based trading will further lower the transactions costs and speed up the execution of futures trades. In addition, informed traders may be encouraged by the anonymity that is usual in screen-based trading to be more active.

Grünbichler, Longstaff & Schwartz studied the leads and lags between DAX index futures, which are screen-traded, and the DAX index, whose shares are floor-traded.

They used 5 minute returns for 1990-1. To remove the effects of stale prices and bid-ask bounce, an AR(3) process was fitted to the index returns. The innovations in the resulting spot returns were then regressed on futures returns (with lags of +5 to -5). They found that futures returns led spot returns by 15 minutes, while there was some weak evidence that spot returns led futures returns by 5 minutes. There was also a strong contemporaneous relationship between spot and futures returns. In the USA, where both futures and shares are floor-traded, futures returns lead spot returns by less than 5 minutes. Grünbichler, Longstaff & Schwartz argue that the longer lead in Germany is consistent with screen-based trading speeding up the price discovery process in the futures market.

Kempf & Korn (1998) used 1 minute returns for the DAX 30 for 1995-6. After controlling for stale prices, they found that futures led spot more strongly than spot led futures. In each case the lead was a few minutes.

France. Green & Joujon (2000) used an ECM framework to analyse daily data on the CAC 40 for 1989-93. The data was split into three sub-periods, and they found that spot returns led futures returns in the first period. In the second period there was bidirectional causality, and in the final period futures led spot. Since CAC 40 futures were introduced in August 1988, these results may be due to the markets learning how to use index futures.

Shyy, Vijayraghavan & Scott-Quinn (1996) studied one minute data on the CAC 40 for August 1994. They looked for leads and lags between the prices of CAC 40 futures trades and the CAC 40 index, and found that futures led spot by 3 to 5 minutes. However, this result may be due to the use of stale prices in the computation of the index. To reduce this stale price problem, they switched to using midquotes for CAC 40 futures and the 40 constituent shares in this index. In this case, the direction of 'causality' was reversed, and the spot price led futures by 3 minutes. Trading on the Paris Bourse was screen-based, while Matif was open outcry, and they suggest that this may have allowed spot market quotes to react faster to news than recorded futures quotes, which depend on pit observers.

Sweden. The trading of both stocks and index futures in Sweden is screen-based. Niemeyer (1994) analysed transactions data on the OMX index for 1991-3. To control for bid-ask bounce and stale prices he used an OMX index computed from midquotes, as well as the published OMX index, which is based on last transaction prices. OMX futures were thinly traded, with almost three quarters of the five minute periods between December 1991 and July 1992 having no futures trading. Since OMX options were traded more frequently, Niemeyer also analysed the prices of synthetic futures constructed using OMX put and call options. Using returns for 5, 10 and 15 minutes, he found that during some periods, spot returns led futures returns by up to 60 minutes, while at other times futures returns led spot returns by a similar interval. There was also a strong contemporaneous relationship between spot and futures returns.

Finland. Puttonen (1993b) considered the leads and lags between returns on the FOX index and FOX index futures (using midquote prices) for 1988-90. Using daily data and an ECM, he found that spot returns were explained by futures returns for the previous two days, while spot returns could not be used to predict futures returns. Thus futures prices led spot prices by two days. He then investigated the sensitivity of this result to changes in volume and short sales restrictions. It was insensitive to variations in the level of spot and futures volume. There was some suggestion that the futures lead was reduced when spot volatility was high. In Finland, short selling was impossible in practice, and so bad news should strengthen the futures lead, and this is what was found.

A study by Östermark & Hernesniemi (1995) which used daily open, close, high and low price data, for FOX futures and the FOX index for 1988-91 found support for futures prices leading the index.

Martikainen, Perttunen & Puttonen (1995a) studied daily closing prices on the FOX index, FOX index futures and 22 stocks in the FOX index for two years from May 1988. Using Granger causality, they found that returns on both index futures and the index led returns on the individual stocks by 3 days, and that index futures were a better predictor of individual stock returns than the index. Since many of the shares in the FOX index were subject to thin trading, the finding that index futures and index returns lead those of constituents of the index may be due to stale prices. To examine this possibility, the 22 stocks were formed into four equally weighted portfolios on the basis of the proportion of days on which there was no trading in the stock. This varied between the four portfolios from not trading on 22% of days to not trading on 1% of days. The Granger causality tests were then repeated for these four portfolios, and there was little difference in the results as between the four portfolios. Thus, stale prices do not appear to be an important cause of index futures and index returns leading returns on individual stocks.

Östermark, Martikainen & Aaltonen (1995) analysed daily data on the FOX index for 1988-91 and found that futures returns tended to lead spot returns by two days.

Hietala, Jokivuolle & Koskinen (2000) used daily data on the FOX index for 1988-94, during which time short selling shares was not possible. They found that futures led spot by one day.

Switzerland.   Braund & Gibson-Asner (1998) examined trade data on the SMI and SMI futures for 1991-3, and found that futures returns led spot returns by about 20 minutes.

Netherlands.   De Jong & Donders (1997) studied the Amsterdam EOE stock index (AEX), and futures and options on this index using transactions data for 1992-3. They found that futures led both the index and index options by 5-10 minutes; while there was no systematic leadership between the index and index options.

Greece.   Alexakis, Kavussanos & Visvikis (2002) analysed daily returns on the FTSE-ASE-20 and FTSE-ASE Mid-40 indices and futures for 1999-01, and found that futures returns led spot returns by one or two days.

Conclusions.   For index futures there is clear evidence that the futures price leads the spot price by a few minutes, while for lags of a day the evidence is much weaker. Such lags may be consistent with an absence of arbitrage opportunities if they are caused by traders choosing to exploit information in the futures market, and the resulting movement in the futures price does not place it outside the no-arbitrage band because the transactions costs are not exceeded, allowing for the fact that the prices at which the shares in the index basket could now be traded incorporate the market-wide information. In addition, a delay in the response of the calculated index, i.e. stale prices, may be responsible for the futures price appearing to lead the index. Before October 1997 the lag for the UK may have been shorter, because quotations were used to compute the index.

Many of the studies reported above have focused on leads and lags, and tended to downplay the strength of the contemporaneous relationship between spot and futures prices. The available evidence, summarized above, is that this contemporaneous relationship is considerably stronger than any leads or lags. Therefore, most of the reaction of the spot and futures markets to the arrival of information occurs simultaneously.

There is a debate over the appropriate statistical procedures to use for estimating contemporaneous and lead-lag relationships: e.g. vector autoregression (VAR), simultaneous equations models (SEM), ECM, etc, Koch (1993) and Chan & Chung (1995). More recently, a number of authors have argued that the tests should allow for nonlinear and nonstationary relationships.

6.6.4 Leads and Lags Between Countries

Index futures are traded around the world, e.g. America, Europe and the Far East. If one market is dominant, returns for that market will lead those for other markets and enable satellite market returns to be predicted.

USA and Canada. Racine & Ackert (2000) studied daily data for 1988-93 on S&P500, NYSE Composite and Toronto 35 futures and indices. Using an M-GARCH model with dummies for weekends and bank holidays, they found that the correlations between contemporaneous futures returns volatilities between the Toronto 35 and the two US futures were about 0,66. While they did not investigate leads and lags in volatility, these results show a very strong contemporaneous relationship between the US and Canadian futures markets, at least at the daily frequency.

USA, Japan and UK. Becker, Finnerty & Tucker (1993) investigated this question using opening and closing prices for the S&P500 (Chicago), the FTSE 100 (London) and the Nikkei 225 (Singapore) index futures for 1983-9. Apart from a short overlap between the end of trading in London and the start of trading in Chicago, the futures markets studied do not trade simultaneously. If a piece of information arrives during trading in Japan, it will be reflected in the closing value of the Nikkei 225, will then be incorporated into the value of the FTSE 100 when London opens, and subsequently into the value of the S&P500 when Chicago starts trading. Thus, the returns during trading on each market are likely to lead the closed market returns for the other markets, and this is what Becker, Finnerty & Tucker found, except that the Nikkei 225 did not lead the FTSE 100. They went on to consider whether the return during trading on one market leads the return during trading on the other markets. They found a significant negative correlation between returns during trading for the S&P500 and the subsequent returns during trading for the Nikkei 225. However, this relationship was not economically significant. Returns in London are not influenced by the previous Nikkei returns, while Chicago returns have a positive correlation with the preceding returns on Nikkei futures, but this is not economically significant. Hence, semi-strong efficiency is supported.

Booth, Chowdhury & Martikainen (1996) analysed daily data on the S&P500, Nikkei 225 and FTSE 100 futures for 1988-91. They found that returns on the S&P500 led those on both the Nikkei 225 and the FTSE 100, and that there was a single common factor generating volatilities in all three markets.

Booth, Chowdhury, Martikainen & Tse (1997) studied daily data on S&P500, Nikkei 225 and FTSE 100 futures for 1988-94 and looked for the presence of heat waves (volatility in a country persists, but is unconnected to volatility in other countries), or meteor showers (volatility in a country precedes volatility in another country, as well as being persistent). They discovered bidirectional intermarket volatility spillovers (meteor showers) between the US and UK, while Japanese volatility was not affected by the other two markets (heat wave).

USA and Japan.   Aggarwal & Park (1994) studied leads and lags between the Nikkei 225 (SGX) and the S&P500. Using daily opening and closing prices for 1987-9, they confirmed the results of Becker, Finnerty & Tucker (1993). There were no significant leads or lags between open market returns for the two countries, while returns during trading for each market led the closed market returns for the other market.

Pan & Hsueh (1998) investigated daily data on S&P500 and Nikkei 225 futures for 1989-93, and found that Japanese returns led US returns, while US volatility had a negative spillover effect on the Japanese market, and vice versa. (Note the objections of Board, Sandmann & Sutcliffe (2001) to including non-dummy variables in the conditional variance equation; see chapter 12.1.2).

Fung, Leung & Xu (2001) studied daily data on Nikkei 225 futures for 1991-2000 traded in both Osaka and Chicago. There were bidirectional leads and lags in both returns and return volatility. This conflicts with the expectation that information for pricing Nikkei 225 futures arrives primarily during Japanese business hours, and price discovery occurs mainly in Osaka. It is possible that the bidirectional leads and lags were due to US information influencing the Nikkei 225. This was supported by the finding that returns on S&P500 futures had twice the influence on Chicago Nikkei 225 futures than the reverse.

USA and Hong Kong.   Gannon & Choi (1998) used 15 minute returns on Hang Seng futures and index for 1993-4, and found that futures volatility led spot volatility. In addition, the volatility of S&P500 returns had a positive effect on subsequent Hang Seng futures return volatility.

Gannon & Au-Yeung (2004) considered daily data on the Hang Seng index and futures, and S&P500 futures for 1994-2001.They fitted a GARCH (1,1) model which included a measure of the volatility of the S&P500 index, relative to that of S&P500 futures, in the conditional variance equation. (Note the objections of Board, Sandmann & Sutcliffe (2001) to including non-dummy variables in the conditional variance equation; see chapter 12.1.2). Only when the unconditional volatility of the S&P500 was used were there any spillover effects on the Hang Seng index.

Gannon (2005) used 15 minute returns on the Hang Seng index and futures for 1993-4. The volatility of S&P500 futures had a significant effect on only the volume of Hang Seng futures; although its inclusion led to a striking reduction in the significance of other variables explaining the volatility of Hang Seng spot and futures returns.

USA and Australia.　　　Using 15 minute data for 1992-3, Hodgson (1994) found that the immediately previous daily return on the S&P500 index had a significant and positive effect on the price of AOI futures, and that this effect was concentrated at the opening of trading in Sydney. This is consistent with market efficiency.

Fong & Martens (2002) considered 5 minute returns for 1994-8 on S&P500 futures and synchronous returns on SPI futures traded overnight on SYCOM. They found that S&P500 futures returns led SPI returns by up to 10 minutes, with a contemporaneous correlation of 0.32. (A small US lead is expected, since these observations occurred during US business time.) While the correlation between daily returns in the US and Australia using closing prices for the same calendar day was approximately zero; when synchronous prices were used, the daily correlations rose to about 55%.

USA, Australia and UK.　　Bilson, Brailsford & Evans (2005) examined daily closing prices for S&P500, SPI and FTSE 100 futures for 1985-98. They found bidirectional spillovers of mispricings between all three countries, which indicates that these markets are linked.

USA and UK.　　　　Gannon (1995) only looked for contemporaneous links between the volatility of FTSE 100 and S&P500 futures. Contemporaneous 15 minute futures returns for 1992-3 were analysed in two different ways. First, he fitted GARCH(1,1) models to FTSE 100 and S&P500 futures returns, with the volatility of the other future (measured by the logarithms of the squared changes in futures prices) in the conditional variance equation. (Note the objections of Board, Sandmann & Sutcliffe (2001) to including non-dummy variables in the conditional variance equation; see chapter 12.1.2). He found that the volatility of each future had a positive effect on the volatility of the other future, i.e. both markets were volatile at the same time. Second, he fitted a regression equation containing an ECM to explain the volatility of each future. He found that FTSE 100 futures volatility had a negative effect on that of S&P500 futures, while the volatility of S&P500 futures had no effect on that of FTSE 100 futures. Thus, the two approaches gave conflicting results.

Kofman & Martens (1997) considered 1 minute returns on FTSE 100 and S&P500 futures for 1993. S&P500 returns led those on the FTSE 100 by a couple of minutes, while S&P500 volatility led that of the FTSE 100 by 1 to 7 minutes.

Wu, Li & Zhang (2005) studied tick data in 1995 on the FTSE 100 and S&P500 futures during the 1 hour 40 minutes each day when trading took place simultaneously in both countries. After removing intraday patterns in returns, they fitted a bivariate MA(1)-GARCH(1,1) model, which allowed for asymmetric volatility effects, to 5 minute returns. They found no leads or lags in returns, but they did find bidirectional spillovers in volatility; and concluded that there are "heat waves" in returns; but 'meteor showers' in volatility.

USA, UK, Finland and the World.   Martikainen & Puttonen (1992) examined the correlations between returns on the stock markets of the UK, USA and the world (the FT Actuaries World index), and returns on the Finnish FOX index and FOX index futures. They used daily data for 1988-90, and found a significant positive correlation between the returns on FOX index futures and the current and lagged returns on the UK stock market. For the US (whose stock markets open roughly when the Helsinki Stock Exchange closes) and the world index, there was a significant positive correlation with returns on FOX index futures only with lagged values of US and world index returns. There were no significant correlations between Finnish stock returns and current or lagged stock returns for the UK, USA or the world. These results suggest that (allowing for the differences in trading hours between markets), information from foreign stock markets is reflected in the Finnish index futures market within a few hours, but not in the underlying spot market. This supports semi-strong efficiency for the Finnish futures market, but not the Finnish stock market.

USA and Finland.   Booth, Martikainen & Puttonen (1993) considered links between FOX spot and futures prices, and S&P500 spot and futures closing prices for 1988-90. Using an ECM approach, they found that S&P500 spot and futures returns led FOX futures returns by one day, and that S&P500 and FOX futures returns led FOX index returns by one day. This indicates that the USA leads Finland, that FOX futures lead the FOX index, and that there are no leads or lags between S&P500 spot and futures.

Japan and Australia.   Sim & Zurbruegg (1999) investigated 10 minute returns for 1997 on Nikkei 300 futures and spot, and AOI and SPI futures. They found that Nikkei 300 spot and futures returns led AOI and SPI returns. There were also volatility spillovers from the Japanese spot and futures markets to SPI futures.

UK, Germany and France.   Antoniou, Pescetto & Violaris (2003) employed daily data for 1990-8 on the spot and futures markets for FTSE 100, DAX-100 and CAC-40 indices. They found bidirectional leads and lags between spot and futures returns in both the UK and France; while futures returns led spot returns in Germany. There were also many leads and lags between the future and spot returns in different countries. These leads and lags in returns did not provide a profitable trading rule. For the volatility of returns, they found bidirectional leads and lags between spot and futures in Germany and France; while futures volatility led spot volatility in the UK. In addition, there were many other leads and lags between spot and futures volatility in the different countries. When the cross-country effects were eliminated from the model, this mis-specification led to different estimates of the coefficients and different conclusions on price leadership, demonstrating the importance of allowing for cross-country effects.

Finland and the World. Martikainen & Puttonen (1994b) studied daily closing prices on the FOX index, FOX index futures and the FT-Actuaries World index (in US$) for 1988-90. Using SURE regressions, they found that returns on the world index the previous day had a positive effect on FOX futures returns, and the previous day's futures returns had a positive effect on spot returns, while returns on the world index two days ago did not. Thus, it appears that world news affects the Finnish stock market, via the futures market, with a lag of two days.

6.7 The Basis and the October 1987 Crash

There is much casual evidence that, during the stock market crash in October 1987, the futures market crashed first and then dragged the spot market down. The basis (futures price less the spot price) was larger than usual and, on 19th October in the US it became negative (i.e. the futures price was well below the value of the index). However, a number of empirical studies of the US and UK during the 1987 crash have found that the futures market did not drag the spot market down.

USA. Bassett, France & Pliska (1989) studied the basis of the MMI on Monday 19th October 1987 using minute-to-minute data. They found that much of the large negative basis in the first one and a half hours of trading was due to the use of stale prices from Friday 16th October in computing the index. Subsequently, the futures price led the spot price by five to ten minutes and, at a time of rapid price movements, this resulted in a large negative basis.

Harris (1989a) and Moriarty, Gordon, Kuserk & Wang (1990) studied the basis of the S&P500 during the crash and also found that the large negative basis was substantially reduced when allowance was made for stale prices, and that the futures price led the spot price by a few minutes (even after allowing for the stale prices effect). The widening of the basis during the crash, over and above that accounted for by stale prices, is attributed to restrictions and delays in the trading of shares.

These conclusions have been confirmed in a more extensive study by Kleidon & Whaley (1992) and Kleidon (1992). If the futures market was responsible for dragging down the spot market, shares outside the index (e.g. non-S&P500 shares) would be much less affected. It is generally agreed that up to about 11 am on Monday 19 October 1987 the large negative basis was caused by the delayed opening of many shares, that is, non-trading. The problem is to explain the subsequent large negative basis when almost all shares were open for trading. They considered two different explanations for the delinkage of the S&P500 spot and futures markets during the 1987 crash. The first of these is the view of Blume, MacKinlay & Terker (1989) that the spot market, particularly shares in the S&P500 index, suffered from illiquidity in the face of very high volumes, and this led to an excessive fall in their prices. (See chapter 12.4.2 for further discussion of this study.) The alternative explanation is that the prices of non-S&P500 shares declined less sharply than those in the index because they reflected information more slowly. This may have been due to the long delays in the submission and execution of spot trades caused by the overloading of the NYSE order routing system, which were longer for non-S&P500 shares. When trades were finally executed they did not fully reflect the information then available. Thus the prices were stale, not because the transaction took place some time ago (non-trading), but because the price was based on out-of-date information. Using 5-minute returns for 1 to 15 October 1987, they concluded that the negative basis after 11 am on Monday 19 October was primarily due to stale prices, particularly physical delays in the processing of spot transactions, and not to illiquidity.

Jones, Nachtmann & Phillips-Patrick (1993) studied minute-to-minute returns on S&P500 and non-S&P500 shares during the crashes of October 1987 and 1989. They used the returns on a portfolio of twenty public utilities in the S&P500, and a matched portfolio of twenty public utilities which were not in the S&P500. During the two crash periods, when the strains on the market were high, the returns on these two portfolios were cointegrated. This implies that there was no breakdown in the linkage between the prices of shares in the S&P500 and other NYSE shares during these periods.

Arshanapalli & Doukas (1994) used 5 minute returns on the S&P500 for the month of October 1987. They adjusted the spot returns to alleviate the stale price effect by regressing current returns on four spot lagged returns, and using the residuals from this regression in the subsequent analysis. They found that on every day in October 1987 (except Monday 20th October) spot returns followed an ARCH process, while futures returns followed on ARCH process on every day of this month. They then tested whether S&P500 spot and futures returns followed the same ARCH process, e.g. whether the conditional variance of spot returns was a linear transformation of the conditional variance of futures returns. They found that this was not the case, and that a single factor was not driving the spot and futures ARCH effects during this period. This means that the basis involved two ARCH processes, because both the spot and futures ARCH effects were involved, and that the risk minimizing hedge ratio (see chapter 9) was time varying, since the two ARCH effects did not cancel out.

Wang & Yau (1994) studied 5-minute data on S&P500 spot and futures for 14th October to 23rd October 1987. Because of the severe non-trading problem for many stocks during the 1987 crash, they reconstructed the S&P500 index using the only the prices of stocks that did trade. They found that, after first differencing, both futures and spot prices were stationary, and then tested for cointegration between these price series. For 14th, 16th and 22nd October they found support for cointegration, while for 15th, 19th, 20th, 21st and 23rd October they did not. They conclude that index arbitrage activity was sufficient to maintain the links between the spot and futures prices on 14th, 16th and 22nd October, but not on the other days studied. These results were confirmed by fitting the Garbade & Silber (1983a) model to the data.

UK.   Antoniou & Garrett (1993) analysed one minute data on FTSE 100 spot and futures for Monday 19th and Tuesday 20th October 1987. To allow for the problem of stale prices, they fitted a Kalman filter to the index data, and the resulting adjustments to the index were small for both days. Spot and futures prices were found to be cointegrated on both days, and so an ECM approach was appropriate. Antoniou

& Garrett argued that, since the cointegrating vector on Monday was not the basis, the arbitrage relationship between the spot and futures markets had broken down. It was restored on Tuesday. They fitted GARCH(1,1) regressions, including an ECM, to spot and futures price changes for each of the days. These revealed that on Monday the change in the index during the previous minute had a large positive effect on current changes in the futures price, while changes in futures prices over the previous 10 minutes had a positive effect on current changes in the spot price. Thus, futures led spot, and spot led futures. On Tuesday, the pattern was different. Futures price changes over the previous minute had a small positive effect on changes in spot prices, while past changes in spot prices had no effect on current changes in the futures price. Therefore futures led spot.

6.8 Leads and Lags in Price Volatility

As well as leads and lags in the level of prices, there may also be leads and lags in price volatility.

USA. Kawaller, Koch & Koch (1990) have investigated whether any leads or lags exist between the volatility of futures and spot prices. They used transactions data on the S&P500 for 1984-6, and measured volatility as the natural logarithm of the variance of the minute-to-minute price changes. A Granger causality test was used to examine whether futures volatility leads spot volatility, or vice versa, and no systematic pattern was found.

Cheung & Ng (1990) used 15 minute returns on the S&P500 for four years. Allowing for stale prices and GARCH effects, they found that the volatility of futures returns led that of spot returns by fifteen minutes. There was also some evidence that spot volatility led futures volatility by 15 minutes.

Chan, Chan & Karolyi (1991) used a bivariate GARCH model to study the relationship between five minute spot and futures returns for the S&P500 for 1984-9. They found evidence of strong intermarket volatility linkages. Information that arrives in either market can be used to predict subsequent volatility rises in both the spot and futures markets.

Lee & Linn (1994) used 10-minute log returns on the S&P500 for 1983-7 to study leads and lags in volatility. Volatility was measured as the absolute deviation of the log return from the median log return. A Granger causality test found clear evidence that futures volatility leads spot volatility; and that sometimes spot volatility leads futures volatility.

Koutmos & Tucker (1996) analysed daily data on S&P500 spot and futures for 1984-93. They fitted a bivariate EGARCH model with an ECM to futures and spot returns. The error correction term used was simply the lagged basis times minus one, i.e. $(S_{t-1} - F_{t-1})$. The ECM played a significant role in explaining spot and futures returns, and there was strong volatility persistence. The point of interest was the volatility spillovers between the spot and futures markets. The previous day's futures volatility had a significant positive effect on today's spot volatility. These volatility spillovers were asymmetric, in that bad news in the futures market increased spot volatility by about 60% more than did good news in the futures market. This asymmetry can be explained by the leverage effect: when the price of a share falls, and the value of the firm's outstanding debt is fixed, the ratio of debt to equity rises, i.e. its leverage rises. This makes returns on the share more risky, reinforcing the rise in volatility caused by the bad news. For good news the rise in volatility caused by the good news is offset by the fall in volatility due to the drop in leverage. The previous day's spot volatility had no effect on today's futures volatility. Thus, futures volatility leads spot volatility by one day.

Chatrath, Christie-David, Dhanda & Koch (2002) used 15 minute returns on the S&P500 for 1993-6. A bivariate GARCH model found strong bidirectional volatility effects between spot and futures for a lag of 15 minutes.

Tse (1999b) fitted a bivariate EGARCH(1,1) model to one minute returns on the DJIA for 1996-7. They found that futures volatility led spot volatility by about three minutes, with little evidence that spot volatility led futures volatility.

Darrat, Rahman & Zhong (2002) considered monthly data on the S&P500 for 1987-97. They found that, after allowing for the effects of the volatilities of industrial production, the risk premium, the term structure, inflation and the budget deficit; spot volatility led futures volatility, while futures volatility did not lead spot volatility.

Mexico.   Zhong, Darrat & Otero (2004) investigated daily data on the IPC index for 1999-2002. Using an EC-GARCH model they that found that futures return volatility led spot volatility, and vice versa.

Japan.   Iihara, Kato & Tokunaga (1996) analysed 5-minute log returns on Nikkei 225 futures traded in Osaka and the corresponding index for 1989-91. They fitted a bivariate GARCH (1,1) model to this data, and concluded that the variance of futures returns led that of spot returns by 5 minutes.

Korea.   Min & Najand (1999) studied 10 minute returns for the KOSPI 200 index for five months in 1996 and found limited support for bidirectional Granger causality in spot and futures volatilities.

Australia.   Brailsford, Frino, Hodgson & West (1999) studied 5 minute returns on the AOI and SPI futures for 1989-92, and found no leads or lags in volatility.

UK.   Abhyankar (1995) fitted an EGARCH model to hourly returns for the FTSE 100 index and futures for 1986-90. The resulting estimated hourly conditional volatilities were then tested for leads and lags. There were no systematic patterns. Separate analysis of periods of good or bad news, and high and low spot volume did not find any significant patterns.

Frino & McKenzie (2003) used 5 minute returns on the FTSE 100 for five months in 1999, and found that futures volatility led spot volatility by 10-20 minutes.

Germany.   Grünbichler, Longstaff & Schwartz (1994) used 5 minute returns on the DAX for 1990-91. After fitting an AR(3) process to spot returns, the squared deviations were regressed on squared futures returns (with lags of +5 to -5). Futures volatility led spot volatility by 20 minutes, while there was little sign of spot volatility leading futures volatility.

Spain.　　　　　Lafuente (2002) considered hourly data on the Ibex 35 for 1993-6. He fitted a bivariate ECM with GARCH disturbances, and found that futures returns led spot returns, but there was bidirectional causality between spot and futures volatilities.

Finland.　　　　Martikainen & Puttonen (1994a) fitted a GARCH(1,1) model to daily returns on FOX index futures for 1988-90. They then used the squared errors from this model for the previous day as explanatory variables in the conditional volatility equation of a GARCH(1,1) model of daily returns on the FOX index. They found that this term had a significant and positive effect on spot volatility. Thus, spot volatility is predictable using the previous day's innovation in futures market returns.

Greece.　　　　Alexakis, Kavussanos & Visvikis (2002) used daily data on the FTSE-ASE-20 and FTSE-ASE Mid-40 indices and futures for 1999-01, and found that volatility in futures returns led that in spot returns.

Conclusions.　　The results are mixed. The strongest finding is that futures volatility leads spot volatility, but there is also some weak evidence that, on occasion, spot volatility leads futures volatility, i.e. bidirectional causality. Koutmos & Tucker (1996) found asymmetric volatility effects for good and bad news for the S&P500, while Abhyankar (1995) found no such asymmetries in the UK.

6.9 Spread Trading

Spread trading involves the simultaneous purchase of one future and the sale of another. Each of the elements of a spread is called a leg. Spreads are designed to take advantage of anticipated changes in the relative prices of two futures. Spreads in futures are also called straddles although, in the context of traded options, straddle has a different meaning. Spreads can be divided into intracommodity spreads and intercommodity spreads. Intracommodity spreads involve different contracts of the same future, e.g. selling the December 2004 future and buying the March 2005 future in the FTSE 100 index on Liffe. This is also called a time spread, a horizontal spread, an intermonth spread, an interdelivery spread or a calendar spread. Intercommodity spreads can be subdivided into: (a) intermarket spreads where the two futures in the spread are traded on different exchanges, e.g. Euronext-Liffe and the CME, and (b) spreads consisting of different futures traded on the same exchange, e.g. the FTSE 100 index future and the long gilt future, both traded on Euronext-Liffe.

Spreads have a number of features which are attractive to some traders, Schwager (1984, p. 492-493). While each individual futures position may be highly risky, holding both long and short positions in the same or similar assets means that most of these risks cancel out because of the strong negative correlation in the profits from the two positions. Therefore spreads are usually less risky than a position in a single futures contract. A consequence of the lower risk is that many futures exchanges require lower margins for spreads than for single positions. The initial margin for an intracommodity spread in FTSE 100 index futures was £35 in August 2004, compared with an initial margin of £1,500 in April 2004 for a single (speculative) position. This is because the expected daily losses are much smaller because the variation margin payments on the long and short futures contracts are likely to be offsetting. Spreads may be expected by some traders, e.g. those who have views on subsequent movements in relative spot and futures prices but not price levels; to have a superior risk-return performance to single positions in futures.

6.10 Intracommodity Spreads

For traders who want a low risk futures position, an intracommodity spread may be attractive.

Example. On the 5th September Harry Palmer, the manager of the Earley Fund, took an intracommodity spread on the FTSE 100 index. The two legs of the intracommodity spread were to sell September for £60,500, and buy March for £61,650. The price difference was £1,150. The following day, when the price difference had widened to £2,125, Harry liquidated his intracommodity spread. This was accomplished by the trades of buying September for £59,900, and selling March for £62,025. The result was a profit of $2,125 - 1,150 = £975$, with an initial margin of only £100. [This profit ignores transaction costs].

The determinants of the profit on an intracommodity spread will now be considered. Let F_F be the current price of the far contract, F_N be the current price of the near contract, and define the spread basis as $\pi \equiv F_F - F_N$. It is assumed that each futures contract is priced according to the no-arbitrage condition, i.e. $F = (S-D) \times (1+r)$. The near contract price is $F_N = (S-D_N) \times (1+r_N)$, and the price of the far contract is $F_F = (S-D_F) \times (1+r_F)$, where the N subscripts on D and r denote the dividends and riskless interest rate for the near contract, and the F subscripts indicate the far contract. Letting $(1+r_F) \equiv (1+r_N) \times (1+r')$ and $D_F \equiv D_N + d'$, then $F_F = (S-D_N-d') \times (1+r_N) \times (1+r')$. Therefore, the no-arbitrage condition for an intracommodity spread, expressed in terms of the spread basis, is: $\pi = (1+r_N) \times [(S-D_N-d')r'-d'(1+r')]$. Partially differentiating this equation with respect to each of the variables gives the marginal effect of changes in that variable on the spread basis (π). It will be assumed that the trader is long in the far contract and short in the near contract, i.e. a bull spread. (The results below are reversed if the trader is long in the near contract and short in the far contract, i.e. a bear spread.)

$$\delta\pi/\delta S = (1+r_N)r' \qquad > 0$$
$$\delta\pi/\delta D_N = -(1+r_N)r' \qquad < 0$$
$$\delta\pi/\delta d' = -(1+r_N) \times (1+2r') \quad < 0$$
$$\delta\pi/\delta r' = (1+r_N) \times (S-D_N-2d')-(1+2r') \times (1+r_N) \times (\delta d'/\delta r') > 0 \qquad \text{where } \delta d'/\delta r' < 0$$
$$\delta\pi/\delta r_N = (S-D_F)r'-d'(1+r')-r'(1+r_N) \times (\delta D_N/\delta r_N)$$

An increase in the spot price of the index (S) will tend to increase π, while an increase in dividends (for either the near or far contracts) will tend to reduce π. An increase in the risk free rate of interest for the period after the delivery of the near contract and before the delivery of the far contract (r') will increase π. The direction of the effect of an increase in r_N on π is not clear cut. If $r' > d'/\{S-D_F-d'-(1+r_N) \times (\delta D_N/\delta r_N)\}$, π increases, while if $r' < d'/\{S-D_F-d'-(1+r_N) \times (\delta D_N/\delta r_N)\}$, π decreases.

The trading implications of this analysis are: (a) if the spot price is expected to rise, buy the far contract and sell the near contract, (b) if dividends on the index for the period after the near contract is delivered are expected to rise, or if the dividends on the near contract are expected to rise, sell the far contract and buy the near contract, (c) if the risk free rate of interest for the period between the delivery of the near and far contracts is expected to rise, buy the far contract and sell the near contract, and (d) the implications of a change in r_N depend on the value of r'.

6.10.1 Normal and Inverted Markets

Since intracommodity spreads are concerned with the relative prices of different delivery months for the same future, the pattern of prices for different delivery months is of interest to a spread trader. A normal market occurs when the current prices of contracts for different delivery months are higher, the more distant is the delivery month. This is illustrated in figure 6.3. Provided the riskless interest rate exceeds the dividend rate, the no-arbitrage price for an index future on an arithmetic index will increase, the more distant is the delivery month. (This does not apply to geometric indices, Thomas, 1995.)

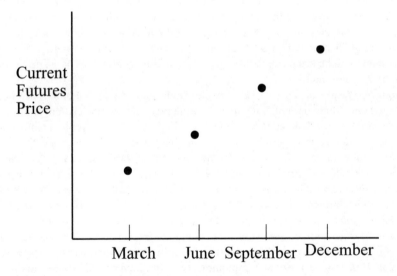

Figure 6.3: A Normal Market

An inverted market exists when the opposite occurs, i.e. the current price is lower, the more distant is the delivery month. This is illustrated in figure 6.4.

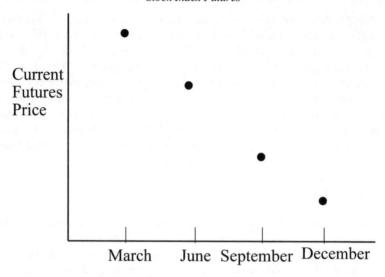

Figure 6.4: An Inverted Market

6.10.2 Butterfly Spread

A special form of intracommodity spread is called a butterfly spread. This is a combination of two spreads, one a bull spread and the other a bear spread. Such a spreading strategy is useful when the price of the middle contract is out of line with the prices of the near and far contracts, and the trader is not able to predict whether the adjustment will be primarily in the price of the middle contract, or in the prices of the near and far contracts.

Example. The prices of the FTSE 100 index futures are March £60,000, June £62,500 and September £63,000. Sam Spade, the manager of the Elswick Fund, notices that the price of the June contract looks high relative to March and September, as in figure 6.5. He is uncertain whether the June price will fall or the March and September prices will rise, and decides to open a butterfly spread. Any movement to correct the overpricing of the June contract will lead to the difference between the June and March futures prices $(F_J - F_M)$ falling, and that between the September and June futures prices $(F_S - F_J)$ increasing. Thus Sam opens a bear spread for March and June, and a bull spread for June and September. This is done by buying one March contract and selling one June contract, and buying one September contract and selling one June contract. Suppose that futures prices adjust to March £60,500, June £61,500 and September £62,500. Sam's profit on the June-March bear spread is £1,500, while his profit on the September-June bull spread is £500, making a total gross profit of £2,000.

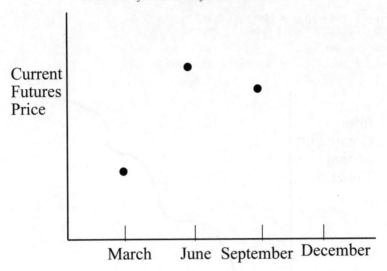

Figure 6.5: Butterfly Spread -Middle Contract is Relatively High

6.10.3 Volatility and the 'Length' of the Intracommodity Spread

As the delivery dates of the two contracts in the spread get further apart the correlation in their price movements will become weaker, and the volatility of the spread basis will increase. Given the Samuelson (1965) model, Castelino & Vora (1984) prove this result, which is illustrated in figure 6.6.

6.11 Intercommodity Spreads

These spreads are attractive to traders who have views on the relative movement of the prices of two different futures, but are unable to forecast movements in the price level of either future. Such traders may be able to forecast changes in the relative spot prices of the underlying assets, the present values of the dividends on the shares in the indices or the relevant risk free interest rates. The determinants of the profit on an intercommodity spread will now be analysed. If F_L is the price of the index future in which a long position is taken, while F_S is the price of the index future in which a short position is adopted, the intercommodity spread basis is: $F_L - F_S = (S_L - D_L) \times (1 + r_L) - (S_S - D_S) \times (1 + r_S)$. If the two contracts have an equal maturity, $r_L = r_S$ and the spread basis becomes $F_L - F_S = (S_L - D_L - S_S + D_S) \times (1 + r)$. The effect of a change in the relative spot prices, the present values of dividends and the risk free interest rate on the spread basis is given by partially differentiating this equation with respect to $(S_L - S_S)$, D_L, D_S and r to get:

$$\delta(F_L-F_S)/\delta(S_L-S_S) \;=\; (1+r) \qquad > 0$$
$$\delta(F_L-F_S)/\delta D_L \qquad\;\; =\; -(1+r) \qquad < 0$$
$$\delta(F_L-F_S)/\delta D_S \qquad\;\; =\; (1+r) \qquad\;\; > 0$$
$$\delta(F_L-F_S)/\delta r \qquad\;\; =\; S_L-S_S-D_L+D_S-r(\delta D_L/\delta r-\delta D_S/\delta r)$$

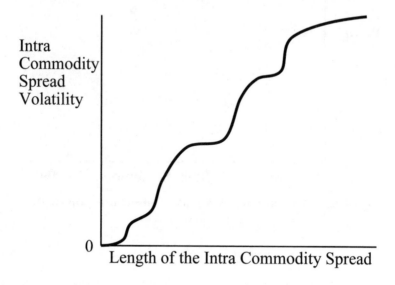

Figure 6.6: Intracommodity Spreads and the Length of the Spread Period

The effect of an increase in the difference in the spot prices or an increase in the dividends on the asset in which a short futures position has been taken is (given $F_L>F_S$) a widening of the difference between the prices of the underlying assets. If the dividends on the long asset increase, assuming $F_L>F_S$, there will be a narrowing of the price difference between the underlying assets. The direction of the effect of a change in the risk free interest rate depends on the relative sizes of the relevant coefficients.

6.12 Spread Ratios

The discussion so far has implicitly assumed that both the long and the short legs of the spread involve an equal number of contracts. However, this need not be the case; and there are situations in which a spread with a different number of contracts in each leg may be preferable. The ratio between the number of contracts in the two legs of a spread can be termed 'the spread ratio' (denoted ρ), and has so far been unity. Let the spread ratio be defined as $\rho \equiv$ (number of contracts in the short leg)/(number of contracts in the long leg) = N_s/N_l.

An obvious case for a spread ratio other than unity occurs with an intercommodity spread. Since the legs are in different futures, the size and price of the contracts will differ. In this case, buying and selling an equal number of contracts for each leg may lead to an unbalanced spread. Thus, even if the relative prices of the two legs are unchanged, the spread trader will record a gain or loss when the level of futures prices changes. To avoid this, the trader must buy and sell different numbers of contracts in each future, so that the two legs are of equal value. In this case, the spread ratio (ρ) equals the price of the future in which a long position is taken (F_l), divided by the price of the future in which a short position is taken (F_s), i.e. $\rho = F_l/F_s$. (This is because equalizing the value of the long and short positions requires that $N_l F_l = N_s F_s$, and so $\rho = N_s/N_l = F_l/F_s$.)

Example. Lois Lane, the manageress of the Fenham Fund, has no views about the general level of futures prices for the commodities she is considering trading, but does have a view about relative price movements, in that she expects the price of kryptonite futures to rise relative to that of phlogiston futures. She wishes to initiate a spread by going long in kryptonite futures (currently priced at £50,000 each for one ton for delivery in twelve months) and short in phlogiston futures (currently priced at £10,000 each for 1,000 lbs for delivery in twelve months). Lois is considering two alternative strategies:- (a) buy and sell an equal number of contracts in each commodity, e.g. ten contracts with a spread ratio of unity and, (b) buy and sell an equal value of contracts in each commodity, e.g. ten in kryptonite and fifty in phlogiston, and a spread ratio of five. If the futures prices for both commodities fall by 10%, the first strategy will result in Lois losing $10 \times (50,000 \times 0.10 - 10,000 \times 0.10) = £40,000$, while the latter strategy will produce zero profit because it is unaffected by changes in the general level of prices, $[10 \times 50,000 \times 0.10 - 50 \times 10,000 \times 0.10 = 0]$. Lois will only make a profit or loss under the second strategy when there are changes in relative prices.

This example assumes that the prices of kryptonite and phlogiston futures respond by equal proportionate amounts to a change in the general level of market prices, and this may not be the case. For example, when the market index rises by 10% kryptonite futures prices may increase by 20% (i.e. a ratio of two), while the price of phlogiston futures may increase by only 5%, (i.e. a ratio of a half). (For a discussion of models of the relationship between changes in the market index and the price of an asset, see chapter 6.18, and chapter 9.6 of Sutcliffe (1997).) The spread ratio can be adjusted to allow for this differential response to a change in the level of market prices. Let $\mu = \beta_l/\beta_s$, where β_l and β_s are the ratios of changes in the prices of the long and short positions respectively to the change in the market index, then the adjusted spread ratio is $\rho = \mu F_l/F_s$ or $F_l\beta_l/F_s\beta_s$. In effect, μ measures the change in the price of the long position (kryptonite), divided by the change in the price of the short position (phlogiston). The question of measuring the response of the futures market to changes in the rate of return on the market portfolio will be considered further in chapter 6.18.

Example. Continuing with the Lois Lane example, suppose that she still expects the price of kryptonite futures to rise relative to that of phlogiston futures (ignoring the effects of any general price movements on their relative prices), and she has no views about general price movements. Given that an increase in general prices of 10% causes a 20% rise in the price of kryptonite futures and only a 5% rise in the price of phlogiston futures, the spread ratio which ensures that Lois is unaffected by the differential response of kryptonite and phlogiston futures prices to changes in the general level of prices is twenty, $F\beta_k/F_s\beta_s = 50\times2/10\times0.5 = 20$. Let the general price level fall by 10%, leading to a fall in the price of kryptonite futures of 20% and of phlogiston futures of 5%. Lois will make a loss on her long position in kryptonite futures of $10\times50,000\times0.20 = £100,000$, and a profit on her short position in phlogiston futures of $200\times10,000\times0.05 = £100,000$. Thus, she is protected against general movements in prices, and will only be affected by movements in the relative prices of kryptonite and phlogiston futures, over and above those caused by general price movements.

The above discussion has shown that an intercommodity spread requires the choice of a spread ratio, and that the choice of this ratio depends on the purpose of the spread. For example, the spread ratio may be unity, the ratio of the contract values, the ratio of contract values adjusted for responsiveness to the general level of market prices or by some other factor.

If the trader is concerned about the effects of marking to the market on a spread (intracommodity or intercommodity), he or she may consider tailing the spread (tail risk and tailing is considered at greater length in chapter 9.10). Tailing a futures position means that it is reduced by multiplying the initial position by $1/(1+r)$ each day, where r is the riskless interest rate over the period to delivery. If both futures involved in the spread have the same delivery date, they will each be multiplied by $1/(1+r)$, and the spread ratio is unaffected by tailing. For intracommodity spreads the delivery dates differ, and tailing each position will lead to a change in the spread ratio (Kawaller, 1997).

6.13 Synthetic Index Futures

In chapter 3.2 it was demonstrated that spot and debt can be used to replicate a futures contract. A weighted spread, i.e. a spread with a spread ratio other than unity, in two index futures can be used to create a new synthetic index future. An intercommodity spread between two index futures, where the shares in one index are a subset of the shares in the other index, represents a futures contract on the shares that are in one index but not the other.

Example. Annie Oakley, the manager of the Gosforth Fund, wishes to create an index future in smaller US companies. The S&P500 index, which covers most of the largest 500 firms quoted on the NYSE, accounts for roughly 80% of the market value of all shares quoted on the NYSE. (It will be assumed in this example that the S&P500 index covers only large shares quoted on the NYSE, although in actuality the S&P500 index includes some over-the-counter shares.) The NYSE Composite index covers all shares (about 1,700 US and 400 overseas shares) quoted on the NYSE. The current cost of one S&P500 index future is 1,200×250

= $300,000, while one NYSE Composite index future costs 7,000×50 = $350,000. Annie Oakley buys 15 NYSE contracts and sells 14 S&P500 contracts, both with the same delivery date, i.e. a spread ratio of 14/15 = 0.933. The net effect of these transactions is to establish a long position of $1,050,000 in a synthetic index future which comprises the smaller (and overseas) shares quoted on the NYSE which are not in the S&P500 index. In effect, each NYSE Composite index futures contract costing $350,000 comprises two parts (a) $280,000 of the S&P500 index and (b) $70,000 of the shares of the 1,200 smaller US companies and 400 overseas companies. So, 15 NYSE contracts gives 15×280,000 = $4,200,000 of the S&P500 index future, which can be offset by selling 14 futures in the S&P500 index, i.e. 14×300,000 = $4,200,000. This leaves a net position of 15×70,000 = $1,050,000 long in a synthetic index future of the smaller US companies (and overseas companies) quoted on the NYSE.

In the above example, the weighting used was 0.9333 S&P500 contracts for every one NYSE contract. The general value of this ratio is given by pF_I/F_s, where F_s is the current price of one S&P500 index future, i.e. $300,000, F_I is the current price of one NYSE Composite index future, i.e. $350,000, and p is the proportion of the market value of the shares quoted on the NYSE that is accounted for by companies in the S&P500 index, i.e. 0.80.

In the UK long (short) positions in both the FTSE 100 and FTSE Mid250 futures can be used to create a synthetic future on the largest 350 UK shares. Since there is no overlap in the shares underlying these two indices, it is not possible to create a synthetic future on a subset of the shares in one of these indices.

6.14 Empirical Studies of Spreads

The data from the CFTC (1995) indicates that in the US only about 1% of the open positions in index futures are spreads, while the corresponding figure for the FTSE 100 is probably lower. Therefore, spreads are of little importance for index futures, and this may explain why there has been only a few empirical studies of the pricing of spreads in index futures.

USA. Billingsley & Chance (1988) used the no-arbitrage condition for an individual future to give a no-arbitrage condition for an intracommodity spread by differencing the no-arbitrage conditions for the constituent futures contracts. Weekly data on the S&P500 index future for 1982-6 was used. They found that, after allowing for transactions costs of about 1%, the no-arbitrage condition for intracommodity spreads was met. They also considered intercommodity spreads between the S&P500 and NYSE index futures contracts of the same maturity using weekly data for 1983-6. Again, they found that, after allowing for transactions costs, the no-arbitrage condition for an intercommodity spread was met. Therefore, the relative prices of index futures appear to be set in accordance with the no-arbitrage condition, adjusted for transaction costs.

Australia. Twite (1998) tested the no-arbitrage condition for intracommodity spreads using the Australian AOI, and found some mispricings in excess of transactions costs.

UK.   Yadav & Pope (1992d) studied hourly data on the near and middle FTSE 100 futures contracts for 1986-90. When the spread basis was sufficiently non-zero to cover the estimated transactions costs, simulated spread arbitrage transactions were initiated. Where the middle contract was overpriced, relative to the near contract, one middle contract was sold and one near contract purchased. At the delivery of the near contract, the index basket of shares was bought and held until the delivery of the middle contract. The long and short positions in this arbitrage process were reversed when the initial mispricing was an underpriced middle contract. Spread arbitrage profits were found, although there was little benefit to be gained by unwinding early, and hence risky spread arbitrage was unattractive. The relaxation of short selling restrictions just before delivery had a powerful effect, while the tax timing option had no value. Finally, the spread mispricings were mean reverting. These results are consistent with the previous studies of the FTSE 100 by Yadav & Pope of mispricings between spot and futures prices.

Butterworth & Holmes (2002) considered daily data on the FTSE 100 and FTSE Mid 250 futures for 1994-6. They investigated the profitability of intercommodity spreads between these two futures, and after allowing for transactions costs, their trading strategy was not profitable.

6.15 The Risk Premium

A long-standing issue in futures markets is whether the return includes a premium for risk bearing, i.e. what is the relationship between the current futures price, and the expected price of the underlying asset at delivery, see Kamara (1984), Leuthold, Junkus & Cordier (1989, pp 108-113) and Teweles & Jones (1987, pp. 109-116 and 308-324). In the case of the risk premium, the differences between other futures and index futures are sufficiently large that the results for other futures are not very informative about index futures.

6.16 The Expected Spot Price

Since at delivery (time T) the price of a futures contract (F_T) must equal the spot price (S_T), i.e. $F_T=S_T$, this suggests a relationship between the current (time t) futures price (F_t) and the spot price at delivery (S_T). In the absence of transactions costs for trading futures and assuming no risk aversion or preference, the current price of a futures contract for delivery at time T in a competitive market will equal today's expectation of the spot price at time T, i.e. $F_t=E[S_T]$. If this were not the case and $F_t<E[S_T]$, a trader who bought a futures contract now and held it to delivery would, on average, make a profit of $E[S_T]-F_t$. Similarly, if $F_t>E[S_T]$ a trader who sold a futures contract now and held it to delivery would expect to make a profit of $F_t-E[S_T]$. This result has implications for the current value of the basis. Earlier in this chapter, the determinants of the basis were shown to be $S_t R_F$ and $D(1+R_F)$, rather than expectations of the spot price at delivery. However, if risk neutral investors are not to be able to make profits from speculating on the stock market (and assuming the no-arbitrage condition also applies), it is required that $E[S_T] = F_t = (S_t - D) \times (1+R_F)$, and so $F_t - S_t = E[S_T] - S_t$. Thus, the current basis is equal to the expected increase in the spot price by delivery.

6.17 Backwardation, Normal Backwardation and Contango

Although the terms backwardation, normal backwardation and contango are particularly relevant to commodity futures, they are also applicable to index futures. The terms were defined by Keynes (1923, 1930), and used by Hicks (1946, p 138), as follows. Backwardation occurs when $S_t > F_t$, i.e. the basis is negative, while contango occurs when $F_t > S_t$, i.e. the basis is positive. Normal backwardation occurs when the expected spot price at delivery (time T) exceeds the current futures price (time t), i.e. $E[S_T] > F_t$. Thus, the above condition that $F_t = E[S_T]$ is violated when normal backwardation exists. These definitions by Keynes of backwardation and normal backwardation are illustrated in figure 6.7.

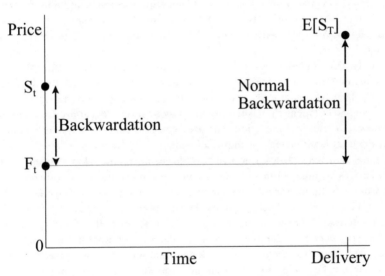

Figure 6.7: Backwardation and Normal Backwardation

Backwardation or contango can be calculated using current market prices, while normal backwardation requires the use of the expected delivery price, which is not directly observable. Subsequently, other authors have used the terms backwardation, contango and normal backwardation in ways other than as defined by Keynes, which has led to some confusion.

6.18 The Risk Premium for Index Futures

The aim of this section is to use capital market theory to obtain an expression for the risk premium of an index future. There are three different views on the presence of a risk premium. The view of Keynes (1930), Hicks (1946) and Houthakker (1968) is that the usual situation for a futures market is one of normal backwardation, i.e. $F_t < E[S_T]$. This is explained by relaxing the previous assumption of risk neutrality. If there were not an expectation that the spot price at delivery will be higher than the current price of the futures contract, it is argued that the number of those who wish to hold a short position (e.g. producers of the underlying physical asset hedging their risks) would exceed the number who wish to hold a long position in the futures contract, e.g. speculators assuming the producers' price risk. In order to increase the demand for long positions there has to be the expectation of a profit from holding the futures contract, i.e. a risk premium of $E[S_T] - F_t$.

Telser (1960) argued that, in aggregate, speculators do not require compensation for risk bearing. He split speculators into professionals and amateurs. The amateurs are gamblers who enjoy the risks, and so do not require compensation for risk bearing. Indeed, they lose money. Overall, the losses of the amateurs tend to offset the compensation for risk bearing required by the professionals, and there is no risk premium.

Finally, Dusak (1973) pointed out that, instead of considering total risk, attention should be focused on the increase in risk bourn by a speculator with a well diversified portfolio. If the systematic risk (beta) of a futures contract is zero, the increase in risk is zero, and no compensation is required for risk bearing. This approach is considered in more detail later in this section. The presence or absence of a risk premium in any futures market is ultimately an empirical matter.

Kipnis & Tsang (1984a) argued that the usual relationship between spot and futures prices during the life of a futures contract is represented in figure 6.8. It can be seen from this figure that the contango is measured by $(F_t - S_t)$, while the normal backwardation, $(E[S_T] - F_t)$, represents the risk premium, i.e. the profit required to compensate traders for assuming the risk of fluctuations in the spot price at delivery.

There is a very considerable literature on the risk premium in stock markets. This will be used to analyse the issue of a risk premium for index futures, and to derive an expression for the risk premium for an index future. The capital asset pricing model (CAPM), see Sharpe (1970), splits the total risk from owning an asset into two components; systematic (or market) risk and unsystematic (or non-market) risk. Systematic risk is associated with movements in the market as a whole, while unsystematic risk is due to events which affect only one or a few assets, not the entire market. An important aspect of the CAPM is the security market line.

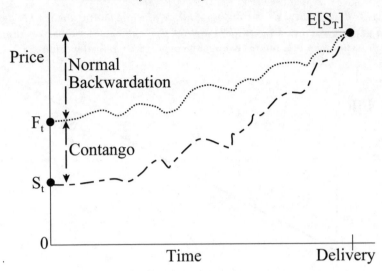

Figure 6.8: The Usual Relationship Between Spot and Futures Prices

Given various assumptions, the security market line requires a linear relationship between the systematic risk of an asset and its expected return. This linear relationship can be stated as $E[R_i] = R_F + \{E[R_M] - R_F\}\beta_i$, where $E[R_i]$ is the expected return on the asset, $E[R_M]$ is the expected return on the market portfolio (usually proxied by a stock market index) and R_F is the risk free interest rate. The systematic risk of the ith asset is measured by $\beta_i^2\sigma_M^2$, where σ_M^2 represents the variance of returns on the market portfolio. Therefore, given the risk of the market portfolio (σ_M^2), systematic risk is determined by the β_i coefficient, which quantifies the extent to which returns on the asset are correlated with those of the market, i.e. $\beta_i = Cov(R_i, R_M)/Var(R_M)$. Thus, β_i is the correlation between R_i and R_M multiplied by the standard deviation of R_M and divided by the standard deviation of R_i. The security market line (SML) is illustrated in figure 6.9.

Unsystematic risk can be avoided by holding a well diversified portfolio so that, by definition, the unsystematic risk of its components cancels out. Therefore, there is no reward, in terms of additional return, for bearing the unsystematic risk of assets and the only type of risk that matters in markets dominated by well diversified investors is systematic risk, measured by beta.

The security market line is usually stated in terms of rates of return but, as discussed in chapter 2.5, the notion of a rate of return for futures has proved problematic. The requirement to define a rate of return on futures can be avoided because the security market line can be expressed in terms of price levels using the procedures proposed by Black (1976) and Duffie (1989), which are contained in appendix 7.B to chapter 7 of Sutcliffe (1993). Black obtains the result that $E[F_{t+1} - F_t]$

$= (E[R_M] - R_F)\beta^*_i$, where β^*_i is $Cov([F_{t+1} - F_t], R_M)$, while Duffie obtains $E[F_T - F_t] = (E[E_T] - F_t^M)\beta_\zeta$, where $\beta_\zeta = Cov(E_T, F_T)/Var(E_T)$, E_T is aggregate terminal wealth and F_t^M is the price at time t of a futures contract on aggregate terminal wealth.

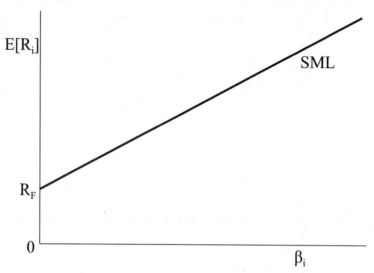

Figure 6.9: The Security Market Line

The security market line was also restated by Dusak (1973). She pointed out that since, in equilibrium, futures and spot prices are related by a no-arbitrage condition, the existence of a risk premium can be investigated using either spot or futures prices. Ignoring dividends, she restated the security market line in terms of spot prices as: $\{E[S_{t+1}] - S_t(1+R_F)\}/S_t = (E[R_M] - R_F)\beta_i$, where β_i is the beta value of the asset underlying the future (i.e. the index basket), with respect to the market portfolio. (If the present value of dividends, D, is included, then $\{E[S_{t+1}] - (S_t - D) \times (1+R_F)\}/S_t = (E[R_M] - R_F)\beta_i$.) She then used a no-arbitrage condition to introduce futures prices. Setting $F_t = S_t(1+R_F)$, (which becomes $F_t = (S_t - D) \times (1+R_F)$ if dividends are included), and recognizing that at delivery $S_T = F_T$, she derived

$$(E[F_{t+1}] - F_t)/S_t = (E[R_M] - R_F)\beta_i$$

which is unchanged if dividends are included. (Figlewski & Kon (1982) implicitly assumed that $\beta_i = 1$.) Note that the risk free term, R_F, does not appear as a separate term in the above equation because no capital is invested in a futures contract.

She then argued that $(E[R_M] - R_F)\beta_i$ is the risk premium per unit of the underlying asset, and that this can be measured using either spot prices, $\{E[S_{t+1}] - S_t(1+R_F)\}/S_t$, or futures prices, $(E[F_{t+1}] - F_t)/S_t$. Dusak opted for using futures prices, and approximated excess returns, $(E[F_{t+1}] - F_t)/S_t$ by $(E[F_{t+1}] - F_t)/F_t$ in her empirical work as this avoided having to collect the spot prices. Stoll & Whaley (1993, pp 66-7) derived a different version of the above equation where the return on the future is defined with F_t, rather than S_t, as the denominator, i.e. $(E[F_{t+1}] - F_t)/F_t = (E[R_M] - R_F)\beta_S$. In this case there is a distinction between the asset beta (β_i) and the futures beta (β_S).

Dusak's result is in terms of the futures price today (time t) and the futures price tomorrow (time $t+1$), while the risk premium is usually discussed in terms of the expected delivery price (S_T). Her result can be restated to cover the situation where returns are computed over the time period between now (t) and delivery (T): $(E[S_T] - F_t)/S_t = (E[R_M] - R_F)\beta_i$.

These results imply that a perfectly hedged portfolio of shares produces the riskless rate of return. Consider a portfolio which consists of a short position of one index future, and a long position in the basket of shares corresponding to one index future. If the assumptions used in chapter 3 when deriving the no-arbitrage condition apply, the expected return on this portfolio between now (time t) and delivery (time T) is given by $E[R_p] = \{E[S_T] - S_t + D(1 + R_F)\}/S_t - (E[S_T] - F_t)/S_t$. Notice that the investment in this portfolio is taken to be S_t, which implies zero additional investment in the future. This equation can be rearranged so that the term $E[S_T]$ disappears, giving $E[R_p] = \{F_t - S_t + D(1 + R_F)\}/S_t$. If the no-arbitrage condition applies at time t, i.e. $F_t = (S_t - D) \times (1 + R_F)$, the expected return on the portfolio is equal to the risk free rate, i.e. $E[R_p] = R_F$, Grant (1982b). This result is not surprising since the portfolio is perfectly hedged, i.e. riskless (see chapter 9 for a discussion of hedging). Thus, the expected return on the basket of shares in the index is given by $E[R_i] = \{E[S_T] - S_t + D(1 + R_F)\}/S_t$, and so $E[R_p] = E[R_i] - (E[S_T] - F_t)/S_t = R_F$. That is, the return on a fully hedged index basket of shares is equal to the return on the index basket, less the return on the futures, which is equal to the risk free rate.

Dusak's result can be rearranged as $E[S_T] = S_t(E[R_M] - R_F)\beta_i + F_t$. Provided $\beta_i > 0$, then $E[S_t] > F_t$, normal backwardation exists for index futures, and the risk premium is given by $S_t(E[R_M] - R_F)\beta_i$. If β_i is unity, then $E[R_M] - R_F = (E[S_T] - F_t)/S_t$ and the normal backwardation (or risk premium) per basket of shares is equal to the excess return on the market.

If the no-arbitrage condition applies, in theory there is no difference between the beta value of the index basket of shares with respect to the market portfolio, and the beta value of an index future with respect to the market portfolio (β_F), and $\beta_i = \beta_F$. However, since they can differ empirically, it is helpful to draw a distinction between β_i and β_F.

Example. On 1st January the value of the FTSE 100 index was 5,600, while the arbitrage-free price of a September FTSE 100 future was £57,000. The riskless interest rate for the period until the end of September was 6%, while the expected return on the market for this period was 10%. Vicki Vale, the manageress of the Heaton Fund, estimates the value of β_i for this period to be 0.9. She wishes to know the estimate of the expected value of the FTSE 100 index at the end of September that is implicit in these numbers. This is given by $E[S_T] = 5,600 \times 10 \times 0.9 \times (0.10 - 0.04) + 57,000 = £60,024$.

The conclusions produced by this theoretical analysis might be tested empirically by fitting the equation $S_T = \alpha + \beta_1 S_t (R_M - R_F) \beta_i + \beta_2 F_t + \varepsilon_t$ to historical data. Using the actual values of S_T and R_M rather than their expectations assumes that these expectations are unbiased and, on average, the actual values are equal to their expected values. The hypothesis to be tested is that $\alpha = 0$ and $\beta_1 = \beta_2 = 1$. Brooks (1994) fitted the equation $S_T = \alpha + \beta_2 F_t + \varepsilon$ to monthly data for Australian AOI futures and found that, as expected, $\alpha = 0$ and $\beta_2 = 1$. He then went on to discover that β_2 varied over time. Buckle, Clare & Thomas (1994) used monthly data for the S&P500 and FTSE 100 futures to find that futures returns varied over time. There was evidence from fitting a GARCH-M(1,1) model that these variations in futures returns were due to fluctuations in risk, i.e. a time varying risk premium.

6.19 Conclusions

Investors can speculate on movements in aggregate dividends, the riskless interest rate or the index with less risk if they hold offsetting positions in futures and the underlying shares. In line with theoretical expectations, futures prices were found to lead the index by a few minutes. Intracommodity spreads provide a low risk method for speculating on changes in aggregate dividends and the riskless interest rate, while intercommodity spreads permit low risk speculation on relative aggregate dividends and index values. Spreads also allow the creation of synthetic index futures. Capital market theory implies that, for index futures, there is a risk premium, and that it will be roughly equal to the stock market risk premium.

Chapter 7

Maturity, Price Volatility and Volume

Introduction

This chapter considers the pairwise relationships between three measures of trading activity over a short period of time, e.g. one day, for a particular futures contract. The three measures are price volatility, the maturity of the futures contract, i.e. the length of time remaining until delivery of the contract, and the volume of trading in the futures contract. For each of the three pairwise relationships, see figure 7.1, the theoretical predictions about the nature of the relationship is examined, and then the empirical studies testing these theories is considered.

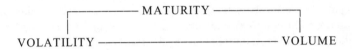

Figure 7.1: Pairwise Relationships Between Maturity, Volatility and Volume

7.1 Measurement of the Variables

In order to test the rival theories, it is necessary to define maturity, volume and price volatility in ways that can be measured. The definitions of maturity and volume are relatively straightforward.

It should be noted that the maturity variable differs between the contracts traded at any moment in time. For example, on 1st May 2004 four different FTSE 100 index futures contracts were traded: June 2004, September 2004, December 2004 and March 2005. While the price volatility and volume variables for transactions on the 1st May 2004 could be defined with respect to all the contracts outstanding on that day; if their relationship with maturity is to be analyzed, it is necessary to disaggregate the volume and volatility data into sub-sets with a common maturity. This implies splitting the data for each time period, e.g. day, into that relating to the individual outstanding futures contracts.

7.1.1 Maturity

If daily data is available, maturity is the number of calendar days remaining until delivery of the futures contract takes place. It would also be possible to use the number of trading days remaining, but this has not been done by researchers. The use of calendar rather than trading time may be because interest accrues in calendar time, and information arrives during non-trading periods (although possibly at a slower rate than in trading time). With transactions data the possibility exists of shortening the time period used, e.g. to hours, and measuring maturity by the number of hours to delivery.

7.1.2 Volume

Volume is usually measured as the total number of contracts traded during the specified time period, e.g. day. Some other measures of volume used in empirical studies are (a) the value of contracts traded, Telser & Higinbotham (1977), (b) the level of open interest, Grammatikos & Saunders (1986), (c) the level of open interest multiplied by the price, Telser & Higinbotham (1977) and (d) the number of contracts traded in all the outstanding delivery months, not just the delivery month whose prices are being used, e.g. Cornell (1981), Martell & Wolf (1987).

Holmes & Rougier (2001) point out that volume contains periodic spikes due to rollover. This means that, if volume is used as a proxy for information arrival, it is contaminated by these rollover cycles. To deal with this problem, Holmes & Rougier derive an upper bound on the rollover volume using open interest. Using data for S&P500 futures for 1996-2000, they show that removing the estimated rollover volume produces a volume series with no apparent spikes.

7.1.3 Price Volatility

The measurement of price volatility is a considerably more difficult task, and over 20 different measurement procedures have been employed. These can be subdivided into those which have used historical volatility, and those which have used a forecast of the volatility between now and maturity. These forecast volatilities have been estimated using the implied volatility, which is the instantaneous variance of the percentage changes in futures prices implicit in the price of options on the futures contract.

The definition of historical price volatility employed in any particular study depends on the frequency of the available observations (e.g. transactions data, closing prices, etc) and the length of period for which the volatilities are to be computed, (e.g. days, months, etc). It is often taken as the variance of the natural logarithm of the daily price relatives. This has the advantage that, as the level of prices alters over time, the variance of the logarithm of the price relatives is more likely to be stationary than is the variance of the alternatives. Many studies have used daily closing prices, but this data is vulnerable to the effects of daily price limits. The recorded price may be a disequilibrium price constrained by the limit, leading to an underestimate of the variance.

If only daily data is available, the historical volatility estimates rely on a small number of observations. For example, if an estimate of the volatility for each day is required, the sample size is one. To overcome this problem Parkinson (1980) devised an estimator of the variance of price changes (ΔX) that uses the high and low prices during the time period $t\text{-}1$ to t. This is $Var\{\Delta X\} = 0.361(X_{high} - X_{low})^2$. Parkinson suggested that, since the natural logarithm of prices is the more normally distributed, his formula applies to $\ln F_t$ rather than F_t. His variance estimator for the logarithms of futures price changes (i.e. log returns) is $Var\{\ln\Delta F_t\} = 0.361(\ln F_{high} - \ln F_{low})^2$.

Garman & Klass (1980) developed Parkinson's work by considering an additional piece of information - the closing price - when estimating the variance. Given that the only available pieces of information are the high, low and closing prices; they derived the minimum variance unbiased estimator of $Var\{\ln\Delta F_t\}$, which is more efficient than the Parkinson estimator. The equation for this new estimator is $Var\{\ln\Delta F_t\} = 0.511(\ln F_{high} - \ln F_{low})^2 - 0.019[(\ln F_t - \ln F_{t-1}) \times (\ln F_{high} + \ln F_{low} - 2\ln F_t) - 2(\ln F_{high} - \ln F_t) \times (\ln F_{low} - \ln F_t)] - 0.383(\ln F_t - \ln F_{t-1})^2$. With minimal loss of efficiency, the Garman & Klass estimator can be approximated by $Var\{\ln\Delta F_t\} = 0.5(\ln F_{high} - \ln F_{low})^2 - 0.39(\ln F_t - \ln F_{t-1})^2$, which is the weighted average of the Parkinson estimator and the 'classical' estimator. Garman & Klass defined the classical estimator of $Var\{\ln\Delta F_t\}$ as $[\ln\Delta F_t]^2$, which is equivalent to applying the formula $\Sigma(x_i - \bar{x})^2/n$, where $x = \ln\Delta F_t$, $\bar{x}$ (i.e. the mean of $\ln\Delta F_t) = 0$, and $n = 1$.

The Parkinson and Garman & Klass estimators of volatility have been used in a number of the empirical studies considered below, e.g. Grammatikos & Saunders (1986), Chamberlain (1989), Board & Sutcliffe (1990) and Serletis (1992a). They rely on assuming that the logarithm of futures prices follows a random walk, and that futures prices are continuously generated and recorded. Since futures prices are not generated continuously (i.e. there are time gaps between transactions), and prices move in discrete steps (i.e. the tick size), these estimators are biased downwards. Garman & Klass provided a table of factors to adjust upwards the values of their estimator which requires knowing the number of transactions per time period. When the number of transactions per time period (e.g. day) is five hundred their estimator understates the true variance by about 11%. As the number of transactions per time period drops the understatement increases, e.g. for ten transactions per time period the understatement is about 49%.

Beckers (1983) used daily data on 208 US shares for 7.25 years (1973-80) to test the performance of the Parkinson and classical estimators and, since it is the weighted sum of these two estimators, the Garman & Klass estimator. The relationship between these two estimators was found to be unstable across shares and over time, suggesting that the fixed weighting scheme used in the Garman & Klass estimator may not be optimal in reality. Beckers showed that a linear combination of past and present values of the Parkinson and classical estimators produced superior estimates of the present and future values of $[\ln\Delta F_t]^2$. These estimates of the value of the classical estimator can then be used in the Garman & Klass estimator. Whether these results for shares are applicable to index futures contracts is an open question.

Wiggins (1992) studied the performance of modified versions of the Parkinson and Garman & Klass estimators using data for S&P500 futures for 1982-9. S&P500 futures were chosen for investigation because they are frequently traded and have a small tick size (relative to daily price movements), and so the assumption that prices are continuous is approximately correct (when the futures market is open). He concluded that both these estimators exhibited little downward bias, and were much more efficient than the classical estimator in estimating the close to close volatility for the next period.

Many more recent studies have used a variety of GARCH models to estimate the variance. Speight, McMillan & ap Gwilym (2000) studied 5 minute returns on FTSE 100 futures for 1992-5 to investigate the appropriateness of GARCH models. They found that volatility contained both temporary ARCH effects (lasting up to about half a day), and long run ARCH effects. For a data frequency of half a day or longer, the standard GARCH models were appropriate, but for shorter frequencies this was not the case as temporary ARCH effects were important.

7.2 Price Volatility and Maturity

A knowledge of the negative (or positive) relationship between volatility and maturity has a number of important implications. The desired margin size is a positive function of the volatility of futures prices. Therefore, if volatility rises as delivery approaches, margins are also required to increase as delivery approaches. As volatility increases, the cash balances held by traders to cover margin calls will also rise, see chapter 11.2. Exchanges may wish to alter any daily price limits as volatility changes. In addition, there are implications for hedging. If the volatility of futures prices rises as delivery approaches, this suggests the correlation between spot and futures prices declines. In consequence, the hedging strategy must be adjusted, see chapter 9. If traders are risk averse, as volatility increases, the size of any risk premium will also tend to increase. Finally, since volatility is one of the factors determining the price of an option, an understanding of the determinants of futures price volatility helps in pricing options on the future.

7.2.1 The Theory

Samuelson (1965) has argued that, as the delivery date of a futures contract approaches, the volatility of its price will increase, i.e. volatility is a negative function of the time to delivery (or maturity). The positive relationship between volatility and time is illustrated in figure 7.2.

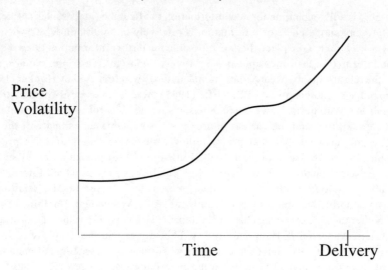

Figure 7.2: Positive Relationship Between Price Volatility and Time

This figure can be redrawn with the time to delivery on the horizontal axis to show the negative relationship between volatility and maturity.

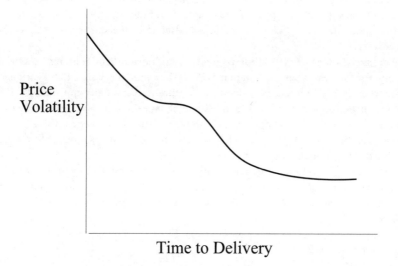

Figure 7.3: Negative Relationship Between Price Volatility and Maturity

The intuition behind this result is that, when there is a long time to the delivery date, there is still much time for new information to affect the final delivery price, and therefore any single piece of information is relatively unimportant. However, when delivery is about to take place there is little time for further information to arrive, and so the information that does appear is relatively important. This intuitive argument about the relationship between volatility and maturity was first used by Hooker (1901). In appendix 8.A to chapter 8 of Sutcliffe (1993) there is an example demonstrating Samuelson's hypothesis. However, Samuelson's argument is not conclusive, and relies on the assumption that the current futures price is an unbiased estimate of the spot price at delivery and that spot prices follow a first order autoregressive process, Kamara (1982), Ball & Torous (1986). Rutledge (1976) presented an alternative example (see appendix 8.B to chapter 8 of Sutcliffe, 1993) in which futures price volatility decreases as the delivery date approaches. Therefore, the relationship between volatility and maturity is an empirical issue, Anderson & Danthine (1983).

Another theory explaining changes in futures price volatility is the 'state variables' hypothesis, Anderson & Danthine (1983). This argues that the volatility of futures prices will be relatively high during periods when substantial amounts of uncertainty over the levels of demand or supply for the underlying asset are resolved. This theory conflicts with the Samuelson hypothesis. For example, any resolution of uncertainty at the maturity of the near contract will affect all the outstanding contracts. In which case, there will be cycles in the volatility of a particular contract as a sequence of near contracts reach maturity, Bessembinder, Coughenour, Seguin & Smoller (1995b).

Bessembinder, Coughenour, Seguin & Smoller (1995b) argue that a negative correlation between the spot price and the basis (defined as $F-S$) is necessary for Samuelson's result, see the appendix to chapter 9 of Sutcliffe (1997). The assumption that the current futures price is an unbiased estimate of the spot price at delivery is unnecessary.

Hemler & Longstaff (1991) used a general equilibrium model to derive a pricing equation for futures prices, see chapter 5.27. If their model is correct, the variance of futures returns may increase or decrease as the delivery date approaches. If the covariances between changes in the index and changes in interest rates, and between changes in the index and changes in the volatility of stock exchange returns are zero, then the volatility of futures price changes will fall as delivery approaches, i.e. the opposite of the Samuelson hypothesis.

Hong (2000) developed a general equilibrium model, and showed that when the information asymmetry between traders is small, the Samuelson hypothesis holds. However, when the information asymmetry is large, the Samuelson hypothesis need not hold.

7.2.2 Empirical Studies

Since the relationship between maturity and price volatility cannot be resolved theoretically, the empirical studies which have examined this relationship for index futures will now be summarized.

USA. Park & Sears (1985) used daily closing prices of futures contracts and call options on the NYSE Composite and S&P500 indices. The data period was January to June 1983. An important feature of this study was the use of the daily prices of call options on the outstanding contracts for each index to calculate the implicit market estimates of the subsequent price volatility for each of the outstanding contracts. The purchase of a call option on a futures contract gives the owner the right to acquire a long position in the futures contract at a set price (the exercise or strike price) during (or at the end of) a specified time period. The pricing model for options on futures contracts developed by Black (1976) contains the variance of the percentage changes in futures prices as a parameter. If the cost of carry (dividends and interest rate) depend only on time, the volatility of the futures price is the same as the volatility of the underlying asset. Therefore, the implied volatility of call options on the index can be used. Given the market price of the option is known, the equation can be solved to give the implied estimate of this variance. This is an ex ante estimate of the variance and reflects the market's expectations, while many other studies used an ex post estimate based on past price movements.

Using data for each of the individual futures contracts, Park & Sears used regression (allowing for autocorrelation) to fit the equation $V_t^{1/2} = \alpha + \beta M_t + \mu_t$, where V_t is the implied variance, and M_t is the number of days to delivery. The estimated equations were:-

NYSE Composite $\quad V_t^{1/2} = 0.0401 + 0.0021 M_t \qquad\qquad n = 307, \bar{R}^2 = 0.24$
$$(35.5)^* \quad\quad (9.9)^*$$

S&P500 $\qquad\qquad V_t^{1/2} = 0.0451 + 0.0012 M_t \qquad\qquad n = 285, \bar{R}^2 = 0.05$
$$(27.0)^* \quad\quad (3.9)^*$$

where the figures in brackets are *t*-values, and * denotes significance at the 1% level. These results show a significant positive effect of maturity on volatility, and this contradicts the Samuelson hypothesis of a negative effect. These contrary results using implied volatilities may be due to the form of option pricing model used, or they may reveal a difference between ex ante and ex post prices in measuring price volatility.

Park & Sears compared these results with those obtained using a different estimate of daily price volatility. This was the standard deviation of the logarithms of the daily price relatives between day *t* and delivery (*T*), converted to a monthly equivalent, i.e. $[Var\{\ln(F_t/F_{t-1})\}365/12]^{1/2}$, where $t = 1 \ldots T$. Thus, the estimated variance for day *i* was computed using the price relatives for every day between then and delivery. When there were less than thirty days to delivery, no further daily volatility estimates were computed. Instead of measuring volatility for a sequence of non-overlapping periods, e.g. days, as have previous authors, Park & Sears calculated volatility for the remaining period to delivery. For both indices, they found significant positive correlation between the daily measures of volatility based on options prices and the actual daily price relatives. This indicates that, using alternative measure of volatility, the positive relationship between maturity and volatility remained, and the second measure of volatility also resulted in a contradiction to the Samuelson hypothesis.

Han & Misra (1990) studied daily data on the S&P500 index for 1987-8. Daily implied volatility estimates were obtained from the closing prices of options on index futures. Because there are up to seven outstanding maturities at any one time, the total number of observations was over two thousand. Observations for the last six days before maturity were dropped, as was the period around the October 1987 stock market crash. They regressed each of the daily implied standard deviations (σ_t) on the number of days to maturity, (M_t), i.e. $\sigma_t = \alpha + \beta M_t + \varepsilon_t$. The results are summarized in table 7.1, where * denotes significance at the 1% level.

Table 7.1: Han and Misra's Estimates of Beta

Futures Contract		β	t-statistic
September 1987		0.02824	0.24
December 1987	Pre crash	−0.08026	−3.64*
	Post crash	0.48314	4.56*
March 1988		0.67239	3.55*
June 1988		0.32511	6.33*
September 1988		0.23004	4.05*

They concluded that volatility is a positive function of maturity, in contradiction of the Samuelson hypothesis, particularly after the stock market crash in October 1987.

Sherrick, Irwin & Forster (1992) used the prices of S&P500 futures options to compute the implied volatility of the price of S&P500 futures. Using transactions data from January 1984 to September 1988, the following regression equation was separately estimated for each of ten futures contracts: $V^{1/2}_t = \alpha + \beta M_t + \varphi F_t + \varepsilon_t$, where $V^{1/2}_t$ is the implied standard deviation of futures prices at time t, M_t is the number of days to maturity, F_t is the futures price at time t and ε_t is a disturbance term. The level of the futures price was included to control for the possibility that, as the futures price rises, its variance also rises. All the regressions found that β was positive and highly significant. This provides a contradiction of the Samuelson hypothesis. The estimation procedure allowed for a switch of regime in the parameters (α, β and φ), and such a switch was found for each contract about fifty days before expiration. In every case the estimate of β was markedly higher for the period closer to delivery, i.e. volatility declines at a faster rate in the fifty days just before delivery.

Yang & Brorsen (1993) studied daily log returns on nearby S&P500 futures for 1983-8, and nearby NYSE Composite futures and Value Line futures (1984-8). They fitted a GARCH(1,1) regression to futures returns, and the number of days to delivery was included in the conditional variance equation. For each of these futures there was a significant negative coefficient, which supports the Samuelson hypothesis.

Houthakker (1994) studied the standard deviation of daily log price changes for the S&P500 and the NYSE Composite futures from when trading began until the early

1990s. The standard deviation for each contract, e.g. near, mid and far, was computed and the results compared. Houthakker deliberately included the period right up to delivery, on the grounds that Samuelson's hypothesis partly relies on the effects of such technical factors. There was no apparent change in volatility for the nearer contracts, which does not support the Samuelson hypothesis.

Kawaller, Koch & Peterson (1994) analysed minute-to-minute returns on S&P500 futures for the last three months of 1988. They did not find any relationship between maturity and the daily volatility of futures returns, nor maturity and the daily average implied volatilities.

Bessembinder & Seguin (1992) investigated a different but related question - does a decline in futures maturity lead to a rise in *spot* volatility? Using daily data for the S&P500 from 1978 to 1989, they found no evidence of any such maturity effect.

Galloway & Kolb (1996) considered data on the S&P500 (1982-92), MMI (1985-92) and the NYSE Composite (1982-92). Using the monthly variance of daily settlement prices to estimate volatility, they found the MMI supported the Samuelson hypothesis, while there was no maturity effect for the other two futures.

Akin (2003) used daily data on S&P500 futures (1982-2000), S&P Midcap futures (1992-2000) and Nikkei 225 futures (1990-2000). By including maturity in the conditional variance equation of a GARCH model, she tested whether maturity affected volatility. There was no effect for any of the three futures.

Japan. Chen, Duan & Hung (1999) examined the Samuelson hypothesis using daily data on the Nikkei 225 for 1988-96. Contrary to this hypothesis, they found that futures volatility decreases as delivery approaches. They also found that, since volatility increases with maturity, the risk-minimising hedge ratio and hedging effectiveness decrease with maturity.

Australia. Twite (1990b) studied daily closing prices for the Australian AOI for 1983-6. The daily volatility of futures prices (V_t) was measured in two alternative ways: the absolute value of the daily return and the square of the daily return. Spot and futures returns were computed as the natural logarithm of the daily price relatives. He fitted a regression equation (expressed in first differences) of the form $(\ln V_t - \ln V_{t-1}) = \beta_1 (M_t - M_{t-1}) + \beta_2 (\ln W_t - \ln W_{t-1}) + \varepsilon_t$ where W_t is the daily variance of returns on the index, measured in the same way as V_t, and M_t is maturity. Twite found that, for both measures of volatility, β_1 was significantly positive, i.e. maturity had a positive effect on futures volatility, in contradiction of the Samuelson hypothesis. When he split the data into two sub-periods, he found that β_1 was only significantly positive during the first sub-period, i.e. the maturity effect is not stable over time. He also found, as expected, that spot volatility had a very powerful positive effect on futures volatility.

UK. Chamberlain (1989) used daily data on the high and low prices of the FTSE 100 index futures contracts ending in 1985-6. Volatility was defined as the variance of the natural logarithm of the daily closing prices, $Var(\ln \Delta F_t)$, and estimated using Parkinson's equation. Unlike many previous studies, Chamberlain did not pool the observations for the separate contracts on each commodity. For each individual contract he fitted the regression equation: $V_t = \alpha + \beta (\ln M_t) + \mu_t$, where V_t is the estimated variance for day t and M_t is a time dummy representing maturity, i.e. the number of days remaining until the delivery of the contract. While the values of α, (which represents an estimate of the volatility of the spot market), were expected to be positive, in general they were not significantly different from zero. According to the Samuelson hypothesis, the values of β were expected to be negative. However, for Chamberlain's data, this was generally not the case.

The estimated equations for the two FTSE 100 index futures contracts studied were:-

March 1985 Contract $V_t = 0.7077 + 0.4061 \ln M_t$ $R^2 = 0.015$, n = 82
                            (1.23)   (1.09)

June 1985 Contract $V_t = 1.9252 - 0.7895 \ln M_t$ $R^2 = 0.225$, n = 100
                           $(7.97)^*$ $(-5.33)^*$

where the figures in brackets are the t-statistics, and * denotes significance at the 1% level. The above equations show that the results for FTSE 100 index futures were mixed. The results for the June 1985 contract were in accordance with the expectations of a positive α and a negative β, but those for the March 1985 contract indicate no relationship.

Board & Sutcliffe (1990) studied transactions data for the FTSE 100 index for 1984-9. The daily volatility was estimated in six different ways: the Garman-Klass estimate of $Var\{\ln\Delta F_t\}$, $F_{high} - F_{low}$, $|\ln(F_t/F_{t-1})|$, $(F_t - F_{t-1})^2$, $[\ln(F_t/F_{t-1})]^2$ and $|F_t - F_{t-1}|$. The data for each of twenty futures contracts maturing during the data period was analyzed separately. Studies to be discussed in chapter 7.3 have found a positive relationship between volatility and volume, and the 'causality' studies discussed in chapter 7.4 do not rule out the possibility that, on some occasions, changes in volume 'cause' changes in volatility. This implies that allowance must be made for the effects of changes in volume on price volatility when studying the volatility-maturity relationship. This was done by regressing the natural logarithm of volatility on maturity (M_t), a weekend dummy (D_t) and a proxy for the rate of information arrival (Φ_t), i.e. $\ln V_t = \beta_4 + \beta_5 M_t + \beta_6 D_t + \beta_7 \Phi_t + \varepsilon_t$. Two information arrival proxies were used: spot volatility and futures volume, as well as omitting the information arrival proxy from the regression equation. Only when volatility was measured by the Garman & Klass method or the daily range was there evidence that maturity had a negative effect on volatility. For the other volatility measures the Samuelson hypothesis was not supported when the rate of information arrival was proxied by volume. However, when spot volatility was used as the proxy, there was some evidence of a maturity effect. The proxy for the rate of information arrival (volume or spot volatility) had a positive effect on all measures of volatility, as predicted; particularly when spot volatility was used as the proxy. The weekend was associated with an increase in volatility, in accordance with expectations.

These results suggest that the use of spot volatility as the proxy reveals a clearer maturity effect than when volume is used as the proxy. When the information proxy was omitted from the equation the number of significant negative maturity effects increased for all measures of volatility, particularly Garman & Klass and the daily range. This suggests that, when explaining volatility, the inclusion of a proxy for the rate of information arrival affects the estimation of the coefficient on maturity. When analyzed by time period there was some evidence that, for the regressions including a proxy for information (futures or spot volatility), the overall negative maturity effect on volatility was weaker for contracts maturing after the stock market crash in October 1987. This is consistent with the results of Han & Misra (1990). When the information proxy was dropped, the difference between the pre and post-crash results disappeared.

Bessembinder, Coughenour, Seguin & Smoller (1995b) have argued that, for the Samuelson hypothesis to be valid, there must be a negative correlation between the spot price and the basis. Bessembinder, Coughenour, Seguin & Smoller (1995a) found that for the S&P500 there was no relationship between spot prices and the basis, where the basis is the risk free rate, less the rate of net benefits from owning the underlying asset, e.g. for index futures; the dividend rate. For a constant stream of dividends, as the share price rises, the dividend rate will fall, giving a negative relationship for stock indices between the spot price and net benefits. In the long run, equity prices rise, while the dividend rate remains fairly constant, giving little correlation between spot prices and net benefits. In contrast, for real assets a positive correlation between spot prices and net benefits is more likely; and this may be induced by harvests and business cycles. Therefore, the prediction is that agricultural commodity futures and crude oil (and to a lesser extent precious metal futures) will exhibit a rise in volatility as delivery approaches, in accordance with the Samuelson hypothesis, while financial futures will not. Conformity with the Samuelson hypothesis is due to a positive correlation between spot prices and the net benefits of ownership.

Using daily data for 1982-91, Bessembinder, Coughenour, Seguin & Smoller (1995b) found that for crude oil and five agricultural commodity futures, the Samuelson hypothesis was strongly supported. For three precious metals there was limited support for the Samuelson hypothesis, while for the two financial futures (S&P500 and treasury bonds) there was no relationship between futures volatility and maturity. These results accord with the predictions using the spot-basis correlations.

7.2.3 Conclusions

Park & Sears, Sherrick, Irwin & Forster and Han & Misra (all using implied volatilities) and Twite (using historic closing prices to estimate volatility) found evidence contradicting the Samuelson hypothesis. Houthakker, and Kawaller, Koch & Peterson found no support for the Samuelson hypothesis. Chamberlain (using a simplified version of Garman & Klass) found some limited support for the Samuelson hypothesis. Board & Sutcliffe found evidence supporting the Samuelson hypothesis for index futures, but this occurred only when the high and low prices were used in the volatility measure. Finally, the study by Yang & Brorsen supported Samuelson, while

Bessembinder, Coughenour, Seguin & Smoller found no support for the Samuelson hypothesis. These results may be criticized for the imposition of linear relationships, and the omission of relevant variables (such as the level of speculative activity, the concentration of positions etc.).

Since studies of the volatility-maturity relationship for other assets, particularly non-financial assets, have found much more support for the Samuelson hypothesis (even when the high and low prices are not used in measuring volatility), this suggests there may be something different about the volatility-maturity relationship for index futures. Houthakker suggests that the Samuelson hypothesis does not apply to any financial future, as do Bessembinder, Coughenour, Seguin & Smoller. The available evidence does not provide clear support for the Samuelson hypothesis for index futures, and the studies using implied volatilities suggest that volatility declines as delivery approaches - the opposite of the Samuelson hypothesis.

7.3 Price Volatility and Volume

7.3.1 The Theory

There are a number of theoretical models of asset markets which lead to predictions about the relationship between volume and volatility. The leading theories are the 'mixture of distributions hypothesis' and the 'sequential information arrival' model. These theories predict a positive relationship between daily volume and volatility, as illustrated in figure 7.4.

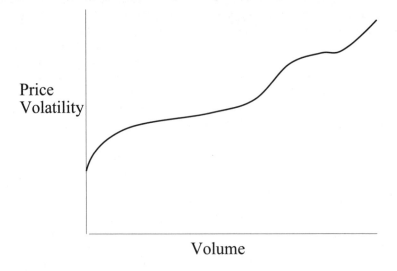

Figure 7.4: Positive Relationship Between Price Volatility and Volume

Mixture of Distributions Hypothesis. This is based on a distinction between price changes over equal periods of calendar time; and over an equal number of information arrivals, termed 'event' time. It relies on the idea that the passage of time by itself does not cause prices to change, and futures prices only change when information arrives. Since the arrival of information cannot be directly observed, it may be proxied by the observance of the trading activity stimulated by the information arrival. Therefore it is hypothesized that, rather than evolving at a constant speed in calendar time, futures prices evolve at a constant speed in event time. In the language of Clark (1973), futures prices are a subordinated stochastic process, where the directing process (also called the mixing or conditioning variable) is information arrival. The implications of the mixture of distributions hypothesis for the distribution of price changes calculated over equal periods of calendar time are considered in chapter 8 of Sutcliffe (1997). The predictions for the relationship between volume and volatility will now be considered. There are three important papers in the application of the mixture of distributions hypothesis to futures prices, and these will be considered in turn.

a. Clark (1973). He assumed that, given the arrival of information, the values of the consequential price change and volume of trading are distributed independently from each other, and that each variable is independently and identically distributed over a series of information arrivals. It is also assumed that the number of arrivals of information per time period varies. If information arrived at a constant rate in calendar time, the approaches using calendar time and event time would be identical.

Some of the implications of this model are, Harris (1987):-

1. Provided the number of information arrivals is sufficiently large, the central limit theorem can be used to argue for normality in the distributions of price changes (over a given number of information arrivals), and volume (over a given number of information arrivals). (The mixture of distributions hypothesis is sometimes called the 'mixture of normals hypothesis' when the subordinated stochastic process and the directing process are assumed to have a normal, or lognormal, distribution.)

2. For a given number of information arrivals, there is zero correlation between volatility and volume. For example, if the number of transactions is used as a proxy for the arrival of information, there should be zero correlation between volatility and volume computed using transactions data.

3. For a given time period, there is a positive correlation between volatility and volume. This is because both are positive functions of the rate of arrival of information during the time period.

4. There will be leptokurtosis in the distribution of price changes computed over equal time periods, see chapter 8 of Sutcliffe (1997).

b. Tauchen & Pitts (1983). They developed a model in which average daily volume and the variance of daily price changes are positive functions of the daily flow of information, the extent to which traders disagree, and the number of traders. For a fixed number of traders, they derived the result that the covariance of squared daily price changes and daily volume is a positive function of the variance of the directing or mixing variable, and this relationship is expected to have a heteroskedastic disturbance term. Their model can be viewed as an amplification of Clark (1973).

c. Epps & Epps (1976). They presented a theoretical model of the determination of the equilibrium asset price following the release of a piece of information. Both volume and the absolute value of the change in price are assumed to be a positive function of the amount of disagreement between traders. Assuming the new equilibrium price is instantly established, they derived an expression for the change in price between transactions. This led to the derivation of an expression for the relationship between the variance of transaction to transaction changes in the logarithm of price, i.e. $Var\{\log(P_i/P_{i-1})\}$, and transaction volume, Vol_i, i.e. $Var\{\log(P_i/P_{i-1})\} = BVol_i^\beta$. Hence, a positive relationship between volume and price volatility for transactions data is predicted based on both being positive functions of the amount of disagreement amongst traders. This also implies a positive relationship between volume and volatility for fixed intervals of time, as argued by Clark (1973).

Sequential Information Arrival.   Copeland (1976) developed a simple model of the effects of the arrival of a single piece of information on price and volume. The key assumption of his model is that the information is received by one trader at a time, and each recipient trades on the basis of this information before it becomes known to anyone else. Thus, Copeland postulates a sequence of temporary market equilibria, ending when every trader is aware of the information. If the information increases the demand for long positions in the asset by some traders, and decreases the demand for a long position by others, the adjustment path will depend on the sequence in which optimists and pessimists receive the information. Hence, the dynamics of the market reaction are probabilistic, depending on the actual sequence in which optimists and pessimists receive the information.

Using computer simulations, Copeland showed there will be a positive correlation between price volatility, as measured by the absolute value of price changes, $|\Delta P|$, and volume. He also demonstrated that volume is a positive function of the logarithm of the number of traders, and a positive function of the logarithm of the strength of the information, i.e. the size of the shift in a trader's demand curve. In addition, Copeland argued that, if the information is simultaneously received by all traders, there will be a negative correlation between volume and the absolute value of price changes. Thus, it is the sequential rather than the simultaneous arrival of information that leads to the prediction of a positive relationship between volume and volatility.

The Clark version of the mixture of distributions hypothesis and the sequential information arrival model provide complementary theoretical arguments for a positive relationship between price volatility and volume. As Karpoff (1987) pointed out, these models of the relationship between volume and volatility assume a symmetric effect for price increases and price decreases. While this assumption is questionable for shares due to short selling difficulties, it is more acceptable for futures contracts.

7.3.2 The Evidence

There are a number of studies of the volatility-volume relationship for index futures.

USA.   Kawaller, Koch & Koch (1990) used transactions data on S&P500 index futures for 1984-6. For minute to minute data, they computed the natural logarithm of the variance of price changes for each day. Using a simultaneous equations model, they regressed this measure of volatility on its own lagged values, lagged values of the volatility of the spot value of the S&P500 index, three volume measures, a maturity variable and day of the week dummies. Amongst other things, they found that the daily volume of trading in the S&P500 futures contract had a significantly positive effect on the volatility of the corresponding future, as predicted. There was no maturity effect, but this finding is not in conflict with the Samuelson hypothesis because the test was conducted using transactions data. There was no day of the week effect.

Locke & Sayers (1993) considered minute-to-minute logarithmic returns on S&P500 futures for April 1990. Assuming the expected return each minute was zero, they used the squared return for each minute to measure the variance. These volatility estimates were regressed on an information arrival proxy (volume, number of transactions, number of price changes, or order imbalance) and twenty lagged values of the dependent variable to allow for ARCH effects. They found that the information arrival proxies (including volume) had a highly significant positive effect on volatility, and that there was also an ARCH effect, that is, some unexplained variance persistence remained.

Kawaller, Koch & Peterson (1994) analysed minute-to-minute returns on S&P500 futures for the last three months of 1988. They found that daily futures volume had a significant positive effect on the daily volatility of minute-to-minute futures returns, but no effect on the daily average implied volatility. Thus, results for historic volatility are in accordance with theoretical expectations. Since the theory is concerned with current volatility, not the forecast volatility between now and expiration of the option, it is no surprise that futures volume is unconnected with implied volatility.

Kocagil & Shachmurove (1998) examined daily data on S&P500 futures for 1982-95. As expected, there was a significant positive relationship between volume and volatility, and no relationship between volume and returns. They also found bidirectional leads and lags between price volatility and volume, but no leads and lags between returns and volume.

Wang & Yau (2000) studied daily data on S&P500 futures for 1990-4. They found that contemporaneous volume had a strong positive effect on price volatility, while the previous day's volume had a small negative effect.

Daigler & Wiley (1999) used daily data on MMI futures for 1986-8 with three alternative measures of daily volatility. They were able to identify the daily volume of four types of trader, enabling them to show that the strong positive relationship between volume and volatility was driven by the general public. This result is consistent with uninformed traders (the general public) being unable to differentiate between liquidity and informational trading.

Irwin & Yoshimaru (1999) explored daily data on S&P500 and NYSE Composite futures for 1988-9. The S&P500 daily net (long–short) trading by commodity pools tended to decrease S&P500 futures volatility (as measured by the Parkinson estimator); although total trading by commodity pools (long+short) had no effect. For NYSE Composite futures, trading by commodity pools had no effect on NYSE Composite futures volatility, and the authors concluded that the results for the S&P500 were due to chance, and volume did not affect volatility.

Kawaller, Koch & Peterson (2001) looked at the effects of switching the trading pits of the near and next near S&P500 futures each quarter, which results in a surge in volume for the next near contract, and a drop in volume for the near contract. Using daily data for 1983-98, they documented the positive relationship between volume and futures price volatility. After controlling for this positive relationship, they found the volume changes associated with the switch of pits led to a drop in volatility for the next near contract, and a rise in volatility for the near contract, i.e. a negative relation between volume and volatility. This may be because the (informed) market makers stay in the same pit, and switch their activity from one contract to another. In consequence, the negative relation is due to the increase in informed traders of the next near contract, and the drop in informed traders of the near contract.

Wang (2002) considered weekly data on S&P500 futures for 1993-2000 and found a strong positive relationship between volume and futures price volatility. When he disaggregated trading demand (long open interest minus short open interest) by trader type, he found that the effect of unexpected trading demand on price volatility differed by type of trader. For large speculators, it had a negative effect, for large hedgers it had a positive effect, while for small traders it had no effect. Large speculators are the most informed traders, and their trades were volatility reducing, while large hedgers are uninformed and their trades were volatility increasing.

Pan, Liu & Roth (2003) studied daily data on S&P500 futures for 1993-2000. They found that, depending on the measure of volatility used and whether long or short positions were considered, it sometimes had a positive effect on weekly open interest.
Japan. The correlation between absolute spot price changes and futures volume for the Nikkei 225 and the Osaka 50 Kabusaki was analyzed by Bailey (1989). Using daily data for 1986-7 for the Nikkei, and from June to October 1986 for the Osaka 50 Kabusaki, he found some evidence of a positive relationship for both indices.

Using data on the Nikkei 225 traded in Osaka and Singapore, Vila & Bacha (1994) regressed the daily futures volume for each exchange on a range of variables, including the daily volatility of futures prices traded on the same exchange. The daily price volatility was estimated using the daily high and low prices. For both SGX and Osaka, price volatility had a significant positive effect on volume, as expected.
Australia. The relationship between futures volume and volatility for SPI futures was studied in two different ways by Gannon (1995) using 15 minute returns for 1992. First, he used GARCH(1,1) with current futures volume in the conditional variance equation, to estimate the effect of contemporaneous futures volume on the volatility of futures returns. (Note the objections of Board, Sandmann & Sutcliffe, 2001, to including volume in the conditional variance equation; see chapter 12.1.2..

Second, he fitted a regression equation containing an ECM to futures volatility, measured by the logarithms of the squared changes in futures prices. Both of these analyses found a strong positive association between futures volume and volatility.

Ragunathan & Peker (1997) examined daily data on SPI futures for 1992-4. Unexpected (but not expected) volume had a positive effect on futures volatility.

UK. The data used by Board & Sutcliffe (1990) is described above in chapter 7.2.2. They used Pearson partial correlation coefficients for each of the twenty contracts, with maturity and the weekend dummy held constant, to examine the degree of daily comovement in volume and volatility (measured in six different ways). On average, a small positive correlation between these variables was found and, (excluding Garman & Klass), this was significantly positive for over half of the twenty contracts. The Garman & Klass volatility estimator had a lower correlation than the other volatility measures, but was still generally positive. Thus, the hypothesis of a positive association between volatility and volume was supported, even when the effects of maturity and weekends were removed.

Ap Gwilym, McMillan & Speight (1999) studied data on FTSE 100 futures for 5-minute periods covering 1992-9. After allowing for macro-economic announcements, they found a strong contemporaneous relationship between volume and volatility. They also found evidence of bidirectional leads and lags of 60 minutes.

Spain Illueca & Lafuente (2003c) analyzed hourly data on Ibex 35 futures for 1993-6. They found that, while unexpected and total volume was associated with a rise in futures volatility, expected volume was not. This is consistent with theoretical expectations. In addition, futures volume (total, expected or unexpected) had no effect on futures returns, i.e. the response to volume was symmetric.

Finland. Due to the higher costs of short selling shares than buying shares, there is a positive relationship between volume and returns for shares, Karpoff (1987, 1988). However, since there is no asymmetry in the costs of buying and selling futures, no such relationship is expected for index futures. Östermark, Martikainen & Aaltonen (1995) examined the relationship between the volume of trading in FOX futures and spot and futures returns. As predicted, they found no significant relationship.

7.3.3 Conclusions

These results clearly support the theoretical prediction of a positive relationship between volume and price volatility.

7.4 'Causality' Between Price Volatility and Volume

7.4.1 The Theory

There have been a number of studies which have investigated whether any 'causal' relationship can be established between volume and volatility. Some of the theoretical papers suggest that changes in both volatility and volume are caused by the arrival of new (private) information, and there is no causative relationship between volume and volatility. This is illustrated in figure 7.5 which shows both volume and volatility being caused by the arrival of new information.

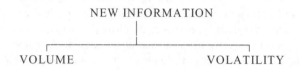

Figure 7.5: New Information Driving Volume and Volatility

Causality is Granger causality, which is based on the idea that, if past values of the variable X improve predictions of the current value of variable Y, relative to predictions made using just the past values of Y, while past values of Y cannot improve on the predictions of the current value of X made using past values of X, X 'causes' Y, in the special sense that X leads Y. There are five possibilities: (i) X 'causes' Y, and Y does not 'cause' X, (ii) Y 'causes' X, and X does not 'cause' Y, (iii) X 'causes' Y, and Y 'causes' X, (iv) X does not 'cause' Y, and Y does not 'cause' X and (v) X and Y are contemporaneously related (Sims test only). There are two main tests for the presence of 'causal' relationships; the Granger test and the Sims test, and they examine the leads and lags between the variables concerned.

7.4.2 The Evidence

The only study of 'causality' for index futures is by Merrick (1987). He used daily data for the spot and futures prices of the S&P500 and NYSE Composite indices for the period 1982 to 1986. Data was only recorded for the near contract, excluding the delivery month, because volume was low in the deferred contracts and in the near contract during the delivery month. This left 526 observations for the S&P500, and 479 observations for the NYSE Composite. Volatility for futures prices was measured as the square root of the absolute value of the natural logarithm of the daily price relatives, multiplied by 252, e.g. $[252(|\ln(F_t/F_{t-1})|)]^{1/2}$. Volume was measured as the logarithm of the number of futures contracts traded each day in the near contract. Merrick also considered the absolute deviations from the no-arbitrage price, i.e. $A_t = |F_a - F_t|$, where F_a is the futures price actually observed, and F_t is the no-arbitrage futures price calculated from $F_t = (S-D) \times (1+r)$, but with continuous compounding.

He used the following general equation to test for 'causality':-

$$Y_t = a + bt + ct^2 + \sum_{i=1}^{4} d_i Y_{t-i} + \sum_{i=0}^{2} e_i X_{t-i} + \sum_{i=0}^{2} f_i Z_{t-i} + \mu_t$$

where t is a time dummy, Z is another variable that may 'cause' or be 'caused' by Y, μ_t is a disturbance term and a, b, c, d_i, e_i and f_i are the coefficients to be estimated. This equation can be used to investigate whether variable X 'causes' Y (given the values of variable Z, if Z is included in the regression), and whether variable Y (given the values of variable X, if variable X is included in the regression). When the Z variables were included in the equation, Merrick called it a test of conditional 'causality', while if the current values of X (and Z) were included in the equation, Merrick termed it a test of instantaneous 'causality'. Linear and quadratic time trends were included to control for the upward trend in volume.

The following tests were conducted for each index, both with and without the current values of X and Z included in the regression equation:-

1. Volatility is 'caused' by A, or volume, or A given volume, or volume given A.
2. A is 'caused' by volume, or volatility, or volume given volatility, or volatility given volume.
3. Volume is 'caused' by A, or volatility, or A given volatility, or volatility given A.

He found evidence for both indices that the logarithm of volume was 'caused' by volatility, but not by deviations from the no-arbitrage condition. The values of A_t were 'caused' by volatility and not volume for both indices. There was evidence of volume 'causing' volatility in the NYSE Composite, but not in the S&P500. However, the instantaneous 'causality' tests revealed a strong contemporaneous relationship between volatility and both volume and A_t. This study found evidence for the S&P500 and the NYSE Composite index futures that volume is 'caused' by volatility, that arbitrage opportunities are 'caused' by volatility, and that volatility is 'caused' by volume for the NYSE Composite but not the S&P500.

7.4.3 Conclusions

While Merrick (1987) found evidence of strong 'causality' for index futures, studies for a wide range of other futures have not found strong 'causality' in either direction between volume and volatility. A lack of 'causality' accords with the view that both volatility and volume are caused by the arrival of information.

7.5 Volume and Maturity

7.5.1 The Theory

If price volatility increases as delivery approaches, and price volatility increases as volume increases, it is implied that volume increases as delivery approaches. This is illustrated in figure 7.6.

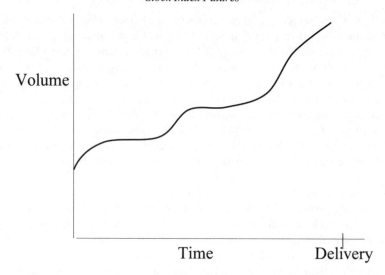

Figure 7.6: Positive Relationship Between Volume and Time

This can be restated as a negative relationship between volume and maturity.

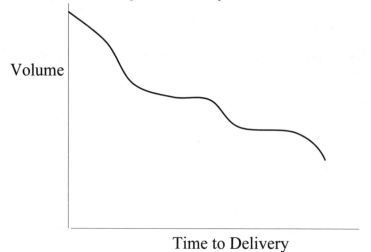

Figure 7.7: Negative Relationship Between Volume and Maturity

It is also possible to construct an independent argument for a negative relationship between volume and maturity. In chapter 11.8 there is a discussion of a number of factors that favour the use of short maturity contracts (i.e. dividend risk, interest rate risk and mispricing risk) for hedging, so leading to a rise in volume as delivery approaches.

7.5.2 The Evidence

The data used by Chamberlain (1989) has already been described in chapter 7.2.2. Volume was measured separately for each outstanding futures contract by the number of contracts traded during the day. He fitted the following regression equation separately to the observations for each futures contract: $\ln Vol_t = \alpha + \beta(\ln M_t) + \mu_t$, where Vol_t represents the volume for day t, and M_t is the maturity on day t, i.e. the number of days left until delivery. For the FTSE 100 the relationship between volume and maturity appeared negative, as expected. The estimated regression equations for the two FTSE 100 index futures contracts studied were:-

March 1985 Contract $\quad \ln Vol_t = 2.4704 - 0.1376 \ln M_t \qquad R^2 = 0.011, \; n = 82$
$$(0.86) \quad (-0.94)$$

June 1985 Contract $\quad \ln Vol_t = 3.2970 - 0.8183 \ln M_t \qquad R^2 = 0.282, \; n = 100$
$$(15.34)^* \quad (-6.20)^*$$

where the figures in brackets are the t-statistics, and * denotes significance at the 1% level.

The data used by Board & Sutcliffe (1990) has been described above in chapter 7.2.2. They regressed the natural logarithm of daily volume on maturity (M_t), a weekend dummy (D_t) and a proxy for the rate of information arrival (Φ_t), i.e. $\ln Vol_t = \beta_0 + \beta_1 M_t + \beta_2 D_t + \beta_3 \Phi_t + \mu_t$. Information arrival was proxied by daily futures and spot volatility estimated in one of six different ways. There was strong support for maturity having a negative effect on volume, i.e. volume rises as delivery approaches. There was also some evidence that the rate of information arrival (as proxied by futures or spot volatility) had a positive effect on volume, particularly when volatility was estimated using the daily range. The weekend had no effect on volume. These conclusions were the same for all the volatility measures and for spot and futures volatility.

7.5.3 Conclusions

An inspection of the data on various index futures reveals a strong negative relationship between volume and maturity, i.e. most of the trading is in the near contract. The two empirical studies of index futures confirm this finding.

Chapter 8

Market Efficiency

Introduction

The aim of this chapter is to examine the degree of efficiency with which futures are priced. Market efficiency has been defined by Jensen (1978) as follows. 'A market is efficient with respect to information set θ_t if it is impossible to make economic profits by trading on the basis of information set θ_t'. Thus, efficiency is defined relative to a particular information set, and a market can be both efficient with respect to one information set and inefficient with respect to another. The literature has recognised three different information sets, (a) all past prices (weak efficient), (b) all public information (semi-strong efficient) and (c) all information, both public and private (strong efficient). As a result of forty years of research, it has been established that actively traded shares listed on thriving stock exchanges are priced with a high degree of efficiency. Unlike stock markets, futures markets are a zero sum game (excluding transactions costs) since any profit made by one trader represents an equivalent loss for another trader. Therefore, to the extent that a trader is able to use some information set to 'beat the market', other traders, in total, must consistently lose out. After examining the efficiency of index futures, the considerable evidence on time related anomalies in index futures is discussed. In the absence of a satisfactory economic explanation, these anomalies contradict weak form market efficiency.

8.1 Weak Efficiency

Samuelson (1965) has argued that, even if the spot price of the underlying asset follows a strong time trend (e.g. seasonality) and so is predictable, the expected value of changes in futures prices is zero, i.e. there is *no* time trend in futures prices. This is because, as argued in Sutcliffe (1997, ch. 8), in the absence of risk aversion and transactions costs, the current price of a futures contract for delivery at time T in a competitive market will equal today's expectation of the spot price at time T, i.e. $F_t = E[S_T]$, where F_t represents the price of a future at time t, for delivery at time T. Tomorrow the futures price will be given by $F_{t+1} = E[S_T]$. Provided the new information acquired each day and used in forming $E[S_T]$ is uncorrelated over time (and there is no reason to expect any such correlation), it follows that $E[F_i - F_j] = 0$ for all $0 < j < i \leq T$. This result is illustrated using an example in appendix A to chapter 9 of Sutcliffe (1993). If investors are risk averse, the expected change in the futures price is no longer zero, i.e. there will be a risk premium. In consequence there will be a predictable trend in futures prices, but it will not be possible to profit from this trend because the gain will be offset by the risk.

Hemler & Longstaff (1991) have used a general equilibrium model to derive a pricing equation for index futures, where the futures price depends on the volatility of stock market returns, see chapter 5.27. The dynamics of the changes in stock market volatility assumed in this model imply first order autocorrelation in futures returns (or price changes). Thus, the expected returns on futures may be varying over time due to changes in stock market volatility, and this feeds through to autocorrelation in futures returns. Such a situation need not indicate an inefficiency because the required return varies with the level of risk, Fama (1991).

There is a number of ways of testing whether it is possible to use past prices to forecast future prices, e.g. trading rules, runs tests, spectral analysis and serial correlations. When testing weak efficiency, if a pattern is found in prices that can be used to generate profits, unless some economic rationale can be provided for the pattern which makes the use of the trading rule unattractive, weak efficiency has been disproved. However, if no such pattern is found, this does not prove the market is weak efficient. It may be that a profitable trading rule exists but has not been identified.

8.1.1 Trading Rules

One way of testing for weak efficiency in futures markets is to examine whether trading rules based on past prices are capable of generating profits. There is a number of features of testing such trading rules which can lead to difficulties:-

(a) The performance of the trading rule must be compared with some alternative use of the money. There are a number of realistic alternatives from which to choose, and these include buy-and-hold, a market index, random selection and zero profit. Leuthold (1976) has argued that, because there is no investment, the appropriate benchmark for futures trading is zero profit.

(b) Trading inevitably generates transactions costs (including the bid-ask spread), and these must be allowed for when evaluating the performance of the trading rule and the benchmark strategy. These costs may not be a simple proportion of the value or number of trades.

(c) If the trading rule and the benchmark strategy do not involve portfolios of equal risk, allowance must be made for this when comparing their profits. This may require the use of a model which prices risk, e.g. the CAPM, and so the null hypothesis is the joint hypothesis that there is no information content in past prices and that the model used to allow for differences in risk is correct. Since the beta value for index futures is around unity (see Sutcliffe, 1997, ch. 8), the risk of a futures position for investors with a well diversified portfolio is the same as for other investors.

If there is a time varying risk premium, it may be possible to predict its size, e.g. using macroeconomic variables. In which case a trading rule that relies on this predictive model to invest in the market only when the risk premium is expected to be high will produce large returns, relative to a benchmark that does not allow for this high risk. However, these large returns are due to taking high risks, rather than outperforming the market.

Taylor (1983, 1986) argues that a trading rule which can adopt either zero or long positions (of a specified size) will be less risky than a buy-and-hold strategy because the trader owns risky futures for a shorter period. Therefore, if the trading rule produces higher profits, it is to be preferred.

(d) Trading large blocks of futures contracts may only be possible at a less attractive price than is currently being quoted for small trades. Any study of a trading rule must consider allowing for such market impact costs.

(e) It is often assumed that the same amount of capital is invested in each transaction. However, given the indivisibility of futures contracts, this may not be possible.

(f) Proportionate transactions costs, market impact costs and indivisibility problems vary with the absolute size of the trade, while a particular sum of money must be specified for investment in the benchmark strategy. Therefore, it is necessary to specify a capital sum to be committed to the trading strategy. This can considerably complicate the strategy as it is not possible to accept all the opportunities identified by the rule. Difficult sequential decisions must be made to turn down marginally attractive opportunities in the hope that a more attractive possibility will arise subsequently.

(g) Allowance must be made for a time delay between the receipt of the past share or futures price data and undertaking a consequential trade, i.e. a trading lag. For example, Daigler (1993a, 1993b) found that allowance for trading lag eliminated the profitability of a trading rule.

(h) The use of transactions data rather than closing prices alters the nature and performance of many trading rules.

(i) The gains or losses must be expressed in terms of either price changes, i.e. profits, or returns. Each of these ways of quantifying the gains or losses is problematic, (see chapter 2.5).

(j) For parametric statistical tests of the significance of the results, a knowledge of the distribution of the profits or returns from the trading strategy (as well as the benchmark strategy) is required, and this may often be unknown, Cargill & Rausser (1975).

(k) If a trading rule generates significantly negative gross returns, this suggests that reversing the long-short decisions in the trading rule will lead to significantly positive gross returns, and possibly to significantly positive net returns.

(l) If a data set is used to optimize the choice of parameters for the trading rule, the same data set cannot be used to test the performance of the rule. Part of the data set must be held back for use in the testing. If the same data is used both to derive and to test the trading rule, it will always be possible to find a rule that is, ex post, profitable.

(m) Trading rules are generally tested in isolation, whereas a trader may rely on the simultaneous use of a battery of indicators.

(n) Trading rules are applied to the test data to provide buy or sell decisions for the entire data period, whereas traders may only rely on the trading rule at certain times.

Sutcliffe (1997, pp. 225-228) describes a number of trading rules including filter rules, price channels, moving averages with percentage price band and double moving average crossovers. In addition, many traders have devised their own trading rules. Some empirical tests of trading rules will now be considered.

USA.   Maberly (1986) examined the opening and closing prices of S&P500 index futures for two and a half years. He analyzed price changes while the market was closed and found a profitable trading rule existed. If there is a big (the largest 10% or 50%) fall (rise) in the futures price during the non-trading period, buy (sell) the future at the start of the next trading period. The profits from following this rule were largest for trades on Monday morning based on price movements over the weekend. However, Maberly did not allow for transactions costs or risk. Nor did he conduct any test of whether his profits were significantly positive.

Arditti, Ayaydin, Mattu & Rigsbee (1986) studied the S&P500 for 1982-4, and found that a simple trading rule, which was described in chapter 4.1.1, enabled them to make profits on all but two of sixty occasions.

Brorsen & Lukac (1990) and Lukac & Brorsen (1990) used daily data on S&P500 futures for 1982-6. The average monthly return, after allowing for transactions costs, from applying 23 trading rules to this data was -1.2403%, while the return on just the price channel rule was -2.0160%. Hence, the application of trading rules to index futures was not profitable.

Trippi & DeSieno (1992) used a system of six neural networks to produce a composite trading rule based on their predictions. These networks were trained on past values of the S&P500 index for 1986-90 and tested for 1990-1. After allowing for transactions costs, the composite rule appeared to generate substantial profits and to outperform a random trading strategy.

Farrell & Olszewski (1993) used daily log returns on the S&P500 for 1982-9 to estimate the parameters of trading rules, which were then tested over 1989-91. Their two rules did not outperform a buy and hold strategy, although three other rules proposed by other authors were found to give a profit, after allowance for transactions costs. There was no allowance for risk, and Farrell & Olszewski's results are consistent with weak efficiency.

Grudnitski & Osburn (1993) analyzed monthly values of the S&P500 for 1982-90. They trained their neural network to use four inputs (monthly growth in the money supply, the change in the monthly value of the S&P500 index, the standard deviation of the values of the S&P500 for the last month and the net percentage commitments of S&P500 futures traders) to forecast the average value of the S&P500 for the next month. After adjusting for transactions costs, the neural network-based rule did not generate profits in excess of the risk-adjusted rate.

Buckle, Clare & Thomas (1994) used monthly returns on S&P500 futures for

1983-93. They found that futures returns could be predicted using lagged values of spot returns, the bond equity yield ratio and the term structure. However, a trading rule based on this predictive model was unsuccessful in making money, before transactions costs.

Olszewski (1998) used daily data on S&P500 futures for 1986-93 to investigate the profitability of a momentum trading rule, where the V statistic is used to filter trading signals. This generated large losses.

Karjalainen (1998) examined the performance of genetic programming in forecasting the price of S&P500 futures. He used daily data for 1983-93, and found the trading rule produced modest profits, after allowing for transactions costs. He also concluded that the rule remained profitable, after making allowance for the slightly higher risk.

Tsaih, Hsu & Lai (1998) applied a hybrid of an expert system and a neural network to predict the direction of S&P500 futures price changes. Using daily data for 1984-93, their trading rule outperformed buy-and-hold, after allowing for transactions costs.

Wang (2000) investigated the ability of genetic programming to forecast S&P500 futures prices. Using daily data for 1983-98, he found that the net risk-adjusted performance of the trading rule varied from year to year, and overall did not outperform buy and hold.

Lin, Onochie & Wolf (1999) considered daily data on the S&P500, MMI, NYSE Composite, Value Line and Mini Value Line futures for 1988-92. Each day the winners (relative to an equally weighted index of the five futures) on the previous day were sold, and the losers bought, i.e. a contrarian strategy. Over the following day this strategy generated significant profits before transactions costs.

Simon & Wiggins (2001) used three indicators of market sentiment - the volatility index, the put-call volume ratio and the NYSE trading index - as part of a trading rule. For daily data on S&P500 futures for 1989-99, they found that net risk-adjusted returns were positive from buying when a high level of fear was indicated.

Miffre (2001b) analyzed monthly data on S&P500 and NYSE Composite futures for 1982-96. She found that during the trough of an economic cycle investors should buy these futures, and sell them at the peak of an economic cycle. However, there was no allowance for transactions costs, nor any out-of-sample testing of this trading rule,

Grant, Wolf & Yu (2005) studied one minute returns on S&P500 futures for 1987-2002. After large overnight price movements they found a significant overreaction during the first 1.5 to 4 hours of trading after the open (except for Mondays, when there was price continuation). However, after allowing for transactions costs, the gross profits largely disappeared, and the results were consistent with weak efficiency.

Japan. Brenner, Subrahmanyam & Uno (1989a) considered the profits to be derived from two trading strategies. The first trading strategy was to use the deviations from the no-arbitrage condition to take an intercommodity spread position in the Nikkei 225 and Osaka 50 Kabusaki futures contracts. (Spreads are discussed in chapter 6.) The trading rule was to sell the futures contract with the largest over pricing or, if both contracts were under priced, to sell the futures contract with the smallest under pricing, and buy an equivalent number of contracts in the other futures contract. (Note that it is the number of contracts rather than the value of the position that is being equated.) This trading rule was profitable (after transactions costs) on about 95% of the occasions that an intercommodity spread was opened.

The second trading strategy dispensed with the no-arbitrage condition and relied on two ratios; the historic value (over the previous three months) of the ratio of the spot values of the Nikkei 225 and Osaka indices (S_N/S_O), and current value of the ratio of the futures prices of the two indices (F_N/F_O). When $(S_N/S_O) > (F_N/F_O)$ this rule requires buying Nikkei 225 futures and selling Osaka 50 Kabusaki stock index futures, and vice versa. Trading was only initiated when there was a substantial difference between these ratios. This strategy was profitable (after transactions costs) about 75% of the time, and was deemed inferior to the first trading strategy.

Becker, Finnerty & Tucker (1993) found a negative correlation between open to close returns on S&P500 futures and the subsequent open to close return on Nikkei 225 futures (traded on SGX). This suggested that a trading rule may be profitable. They considered the rule of buying (selling) Nikkei 225 futures at the open and selling them at the close when S&P500 futures have fallen (risen) by more than 1.5% in the previous trading session. For falls of over 1.5% in S&P500 futures, the average rise in the Nikkei 225 was 0.191%, while for rises in the S&P500 of over 1.5%, the average fall in the Nikkei 225 was 0.130% (significant at the 10% level). They concluded that any profits from following this rule would be consumed by transactions costs.

Hong Kong.   Raj & Thurston (1996) applied two trading rules to opening prices for Hang Seng futures for 1989-93. They found that the moving average oscillator did not produce higher returns than buy and hold, while the trading range break out rule did generate superior returns. However, in the absence of any allowance for transactions costs, it is not clear whether this rule generated a significant net profit.

Li & Lam (2002) developed their own trading rule, which was then applied to daily data on Hang Seng futures for 1987-99. After allowing for transactions costs, the return for the trading rule was substantially worse than buy and hold.

Fung & Lam (2004) used mispricings to identify overreactions in Hang Seng futures prices for 1993-2000. After allowing for transactions costs, trading lag and risk, they found the trading rule was profitable.

Australia   Yeh & Gannon (2000) employed daily data on the SPI and AOI for 1988-96. The risk minimizing hedge ratio was computed in five different ways, and the resulting profit or loss on the hedged portfolio (after transactions costs) computed. The bi-variate GARCH (1,1) with day-of-the-week dummies was clearly the most profitable.

Fong & Martens (2002) considered 5 minute returns for 1994-8 on S&P500 futures and synchronous returns on SPI futures traded overnight on SYCOM. If the overnight return on the SPI is above 1% (below -1%), sell (buy) the SPI at the open and close out the position 40 minutes later. This strategy generated profits after allowing for the transactions costs of locals.

UK. Buckle, Clare & Thomas (1999) used monthly returns on FTSE 100 futures for 1984-93. They found that futures returns could be predicted using lagged values of spot and futures returns and a January dummy. However, this predictive model was unable to generate profits, even before transactions costs.

Brooks, Rew & Ritson (2001) analyzed 10-minute returns on the FTSE 100 for 1996-7, and found that futures led spot by 10-minutes. Futures returns were then used to forecast spot returns over the next 10 minute period. After allowing for transactions costs, this trading rule was unable to beat the benchmark.

France. Clare & Miffre (1995) used weekly data for CAC 40 futures for 1990-3, and found that CAC 40 futures returns could be explained using lagged values of seven variables: returns on CAC futures, the French stock market and the S&P500 index, the price earnings ratio of the French stock market and the S&P500 index, the US term structure and the dividend yield on the French stock market. Using 12 rolling one step ahead forecasts, they found that their simple trading rule produced higher gross profits than holding the CAC 40 index basket or a long position in CAC 40 futures. However, since they did not allow for transactions costs, it is not clear whether this trading rule generated positive net profits during the 12 week test period. Even if it did produce net profits, this may be because of a time varying risk premium, rather than market inefficiency.

Germany. Clare & Miffre (1995) repeated their analysis of the CAC 40 for DAX futures using weekly data for 1991-3. They found that DAX futures returns could be explained by lagged values of four variables: returns on DAX futures, the German stock market and the S&P500 index; and the German term structure. Using 12 rolling one step ahead forecasts, a simple trading rule under-performed the DAX index basket and DAX futures. Allowance for transactions costs would only strengthen the conclusion that the trading rule was not profitable.

Spain. Rubio (2004) considered daily data on Ibex 35 futures for 1992-2000 and applied three trading rules; none of which was superior to buy and hold.

Conclusions. These results indicate that trading rules for index futures may sometimes outperform a naïve benchmark, after allowing for transactions costs and risk, and this implies weak inefficiency. This is somewhat surprising, given the evidence that trading rules do not work for stock markets. A partial explanation for the many studies that have found trading rules appear to work is 'publication bias' - studies which contradict the accepted wisdom are more likely to be written up and published than studies which confirm the accepted orthodoxy.

8.1.2 Futures Funds

There have been some studies of the performance of US futures funds. A futures fund raises money from investors, which is then pooled and invested in futures contracts and interest bearing securities. Each futures fund has a manager, and trading decisions are usually based on (undisclosed) trading rules. Therefore, a study of the performance of these futures funds represents an indirect test of the ability of trading rules to beat the market. A number of such studies are summarized in table 8.1.

Table 8.1: Empirical Studies of the Profitability of Futures Funds

Study	Futures	Criterion	Costs	Conclusion
Brorsen & Irwin (1985)	20 Funds	RAR	TC	WE
Murphy (1986)	11 Funds	B&H	TC	WE
Elton, Gruber & Rentzler (1987)	85 Funds	ER	TC	WE
Elton, Gruber & Rentzler (1990)	91 Funds	ER	TC	WE
Irwin, Krukemyer & Zulauf (1993)	186 Funds	ER	TC1	WE
Irwin, Krukemyer & Zulauf (1993)	186 Funds	ER	TC2	WI
Edwards & Park (1996)	361 Funds	RAR	TC	WE

B&H = Buy and hold, ER = Return above the riskless rate, RAR = Risk adjusted return, TC = Transactions costs, TC1 = TC for retail investors, TC2 = TC for institutional investors, WE = Weak efficiency, WI = Weak inefficiency.

The studies in table 8.1 indicate that the use of trading rules by futures funds does not lead to superior performance after transactions costs. However, there is an extra component of transactions costs for futures funds - the fees, incentive payments and expenses of the fund manager, and these can be both substantial and variable, Irwin & Brorsen (1985) and Cornew (1988). Such management charges may reflect the 'creaming off' of excess profits generated by the fund, leaving a net performance that is not superior to the market. This is consistent with the finding by Irwin, Krukemyer & Zulauf (1993) that institutional investors, who are able to negotiate much lower transactions costs, are able to earn excess returns from futures funds. These results for futures funds conform with the studies of funds which invest in equities (e.g. mutual funds, investment trusts and unit trusts), which have been found not to outperform the stock market.

8.1.3 Other Tests for Weak Efficiency

As well as trading rules, a variety of tests have been conducted which looked for dependence over time in futures prices or returns. These tests, which include autocorrelation, runs tests and spectral analysis, are designed to detect non-random behaviour. They are not a direct test of weak efficiency as they usually do not allow for transactions costs, trading lags, price impact, etc. In addition, some of the tests (e.g. autocorrelation) assume the process generating futures prices or returns is linear, which may not be the case, Taylor (1985), Heaney (1990) and Hsieh (1989). However, these tests do provide a different approach, and this has a number of advantages. The sampling distribution of the autocorrelation coefficient is known, as is that of the runs test, and so significance tests can be conducted. The runs test is a non-parametric test that does not use the size of price movements, only their direction, and is insensitive to data errors and distributional assumptions. Spectral analysis is a non-parametric method in the frequency domain, rather than the time domain.

There have been various studies of randomness in stock index futures, and these will now be summarized.

USA. Zeckhauser & Niederhoffer (1983b) examined price changes in VLCI futures over half hour periods for March to June 1982. They applied a runs test to these futures price changes, and concluded that independence could not be rejected, i.e. their results support weak efficiency.

Goldenberg (1988) studied transactions data for futures on the S&P500 index for about four hundred days in 1983-4 (648,300 transactions prices). Because transactions data is unequally spaced over time, he also analyzed a minute-to-minute price series, which involved dropping about three quarters of the transactions data. He considered two alternative models of transactions price movements, both of which led to negative autocorrelation. One possibility is the presence of reflecting barriers, and these may be due to bid-ask bounce or to the clustering of limit orders at specific price levels. Another possibility is that transactions prices follow a mean reverting process, and the greater is the departure from the mean price, the greater is the probability of a move towards the mean. Goldenberg found significant negative first and second order autocorrelation in price changes between transactions, and interpreted this as consistent with both reflecting barriers due to limit orders, and with mean reversion. (Bid-ask bounce was ruled out as an explanation because the price movements were markedly larger than the bid-ask spread.) He then examined the equally spaced data and found that, as the differencing interval was increased from one to ten minutes, the evidence of reflecting barriers disappeared, while there was no evidence of mean reversion, even in the one minute data. These results indicate that changes in transactions prices are non-random but, since transactions costs and risk were not considered, it is not clear whether these results are inconsistent with weak efficiency.

Goldenberg (1989) also studied transactions data for S&P500 futures for 1983-4. A series of price changes over ten second intervals was constructed for use in the analysis. He found significant negative first and second order autocorrelation, and that the best representation of these price changes was an ARIMA model.

Cheung & Ng (1990) analyzed fifteen minute returns on S&P500 futures for 1983-7. The average first order correlation was -0.03, and this may be due to bid-ask bounce inducing a small amount of negative correlation. While the authors did not consider the efficiency implications, this result appears consistent with weak efficiency.

Blank (1991a) studied daily data on S&P500 futures for 1982-7 using chaos analysis. The basic approach is to use linear methods to remove any linear relationships from the data, and then to look for any non-linearities. His results suggest that this market is characterized by deterministic chaos, i.e. nonlinear relationships exist between current and lagged prices. Again, since transactions costs were not considered, no conclusions can be reached regarding weak efficiency.

Lee & Huh (1991) used daily data for five technical indicators over the past hundred days as input to a neural network. This was used to forecast whether the price of S&P500 futures would rise or fall during the next day. The data set was then rolled forward one day and the exercise repeated. Using data for the September contract, 100 forecasts were generated, and these were found to have predictive ability, according to the Henriksson-Merton test.

Rao & Ma (1991) used rescaled range analysis to compare the degree of dependence in the spot and futures prices of the S&P500. Using the daily 3 pm prices, they found that for 1978-86 there was significant positive dependence in the spot price. However, for futures prices for 1983-6 there was no dependence in futures prices. Using minute to minute prices they again found significant positive dependence in spot prices, but significant negative dependence in futures prices. They then used daily data to investigate the effect of the introduction of futures trading in April 1983 on the dependence of spot prices. They discovered that spot dependence increased in the post-futures period. Rao & Ma hypothesize that this effect was due to futures trading changing the nature of spot traders. In particular, it decreased the degree to which spot traders responded simultaneously to new (macro) information.

Fung, Lo & Peterson (1994) analyzed minute-to-minute log returns on S&P500 futures for twelve days in 1987-8. Variance ratios (adjusted for heteroskedasticity) computed for one to twelve minute periods found evidence of both positive and negative dependence over time in futures returns. The authors also looked for longer term dependence using modified rescaled range analysis and autoregressive fractionally integrated moving averages. However, within each day, there was no evidence of longer term dependence.

Barkoulas, Labys & Onochie (1999) also fitted an autoregressive fractionally integrated moving average process to daily data on S&P500, NYSE Composite and Value Line futures for 1982-93. In each case the estimated parameter was unity, which implies there is no long term memory in the series.

Gao & Wang (1999) analyzed daily returns on S&P500 futures for 1984-93, looking for nonlinear dependencies. They found such evidence; and that the GARCH (1,1) model was dominated by the threshold autoregressive (TAR) and autoregressive volatility models. There was no evidence of deterministic chaos.

Crato & Ray (2000) studied daily data on S&P500 futures for 1982-97 and applied three different tests for long term memory in returns and the variance of returns. There was no evidence of dependence in returns, but strong evidence for dependence in the variance of returns.

Fung, Mok & Lam (2000) used trade data on S&P500 and Hang Seng index futures for 1993-6. After a large overnight return, they found price reversals at the open. After allowing for transactions costs and execution lag, this yielded a small profit, so contradicting weak efficiency.

Koutmos (2002) postulated that the interaction of utility maximizing and positive feedback traders leads to negative time-varying autocorrelation in futures returns. This prediction was supported by daily data on S&P500, Nikkei 225, DAX and CAC 40 futures. Therefore, even though there is negative autocorrelation in futures returns, this is consistent with weak efficiency.

Japan　　　　　Wang (2005) considered 5 minute returns on Nikkei 225 futures for 1993-4. Using Markov chains, returns were non-random over 5 and 10 minute periods, but not over longer periods. This highlights the way in which predictability can vary with the differencing interval. A market may be predictable over very short periods, but not over longer periods. Such markets may be weak efficient, even over short periods, because the transactions costs outweigh any gross profits from trading based on the return predictability.

Hong Kong　　　　Mok, Lam & Li (2000) show that, if returns follow a random walk, the daily high and low prices are more likely to occur near the open or close, than in the middle of the day. Transactions data on S&P500 futures for 1993-6 and Hang Seng futures for 1994-6 was analyzed, and the actual times of the daily high and low compared with the theoretical times. For S&P500 futures the distribution of daily high-low times is strongly U-shaped, and accords with the theoretical probabilities given by a random walk. For Hang Seng futures, the daily high-low times are more U-shaped than the theory predicts, and this suggests weak inefficiency may exist.

Australia.　　　　　Heaney (1990) studied daily close to close returns on SPI futures for 1983-7. Using autocorrelation, runs and spectral analysis tests (which assume a linear relationship) he found little evidence of non-random behaviour. However, using a test which does not impose linearity, he found evidence of non-randomness.

Hodgson, Keef & Okunev (1993) analyzed daily closing prices for SPI futures. Regressing the changes in futures prices on the level of futures prices, they found evidence of weak mean reversion. A similar result was also obtained for the index, although the mean reversion was somewhat weaker than for futures prices. Depending on the level of transactions costs, trading risk etc., this dependence over time may or may not be consistent with weak efficiency. However, the result that the mean reversion is stronger for futures is consistent with arbitrageurs having a larger effect on futures than on spot prices.

Brooks & Michaelides (1995) examined the predictability of absolute futures returns, raised to some power d, i.e. $|r|^d$. When $d = 1$ they were looking for dependence in absolute returns, and when $d = 2$ they were looking for dependence in squared returns. Using daily data for SPI futures for 1989-94, they found that the strongest autocorrelation existed for values of d in the region of unity, i.e. big price changes tended to follow big price changes, and small price changes tended to follow small price changes. Such ARCH effects need not contradict market efficiency.

Brooks & Lee (1997) studies daily data for 1989-94 for SPI futures. They fitted a wide range of ARCH (p) and GARCH (p,q) models to the various contracts, and found that ARCH (1) was the most common best fit.

UK.   Miffre (2001a) used monthly data for 1984-99 to examine the ability of a multi-factor model to predict the FTSE 100 futures return one month ahead. After allowing for variations over time in the risk premia and factor sensitivities, movements in FTSE 100 futures returns were largely explained. This result supports weak efficiency.

Ap Gwilym, Brooks, Clare & Thomas (1999) considered 5 minute returns on FTSE 100 futures for 1992-5. The only non-linear dependence they found was ARCH; with no evidence of chaos.

France.   Lee, Gleason & Mathur (2000) examined daily data on CAC 40 futures for 1988-97. The application of variance ratio tests, unit root tests and serial correlation tests was unable to detect any signs of weak inefficiency.

Spain.   Lee & Mathur (1999) analyzed daily data on Ibex 35 futures for 1992-5. Variance ratio tests, unit root tests and serial correlation tests were all consistent with weak efficiency.

Conclusions.   Some of the evidence from these tests suggests that index futures markets may not be weak efficient, and this conflicts with theoretical expectations.

8.2 Semi-Strong Efficiency

This section examines the possibility of using all publicly available information to forecast futures prices. If the market is semi-strong efficient, there will be no information content in any particular type of public information, including the past prices of the future concerned. Thus, if a market is not weak efficient, it cannot be semi-strong efficient.

8.2.1 Econometric Models

There have been studies which have compared the spot price forecasts from econometric models with the spot price forecasts implicit in futures prices. Since the econometric models use public information, if the futures market is at least semi-strong efficient, they should not produce forecasts that are superior (allowing for transactions costs) to those from the futures market.

USA.   De Roon, Nijman & Veld (2000) used fortnightly data on the S&P500 and Value Line for 1986-94 to examine whether hedging pressure (the imbalance between short and long hedging demand) could be used to predict futures returns. After controlling for systematic risk, there was no evidence of predictive ability.

8.2.2 Event Studies

There are only three event studies for index futures.

USA. Ma, Dare & Donaldson (1990) looked for evidence of over or under-reaction to new information in S&P500 and VLCI futures prices. They used the daily closing prices of the near contract for 1982-8, and defined returns as the logarithm of price changes. Instead of collecting data on specific major events to which the market responds, they used the returns to calculate proxies. This was done by fitting an ARIMA model to the returns series, and then regarding residuals which are significant at the 5% level as indicating the date of an event. For the period after each event, they computed the cumulative abnormal residuals (CARs). For positive events (i.e. large price rises) the CARs for the S&P500 were significantly positive for the next five days, indicating a delayed response due to an initial under reaction. For negative events the S&P500 and VLCI CARs were significantly negative for the next five days, again indicating an initial under reaction. While this study provides evidence of some predictability in the response to important events, in the absence of any consideration of transactions costs, it does not necessarily demonstrate semi-strong inefficiency.

Becker, Finnerty & Friedman (1995) studied the effects of announcements of macroeconomic news in the USA and UK on FTSE 100 and S&P500 futures returns. Using data for 1986-90, they found that, on days when there was a US announcement, the variance of FTSE 100 returns for the 30 minutes period after the announcement was 5.5 times higher than otherwise. They also found that the level of FTSE 100 futures returns responded to surprises in US announcements of the consumer price index, the producer price index, merchandise trade and nonfarm payrolls. FTSE 100 futures returns also responded to surprises in UK announcements of the public sector borrowing requirement, visible trade and the current account. Overnight S&P500 returns responded to surprises in US announcements of the producer price index and merchandise trade, and also to FTSE 100 futures returns, but not to surprises in UK announcements. These results generally support the view that FTSE 100 and S&P500 futures are semi-strong efficient.

UK. Chalk (1993) studied the effect of changes in the UK government's base rate of interest on the price of FTSE 100 futures. While an increase in interest rates is expected to have a negative effect on stock prices, what matters is not the announced change in base rate, but the unexpected component of this announcement. The 'news' component of base rate announcements was measured by the reaction of the price of 3 month Sterling futures traded on Euronext-Liffe. An increase in the price of 3 month Sterling futures indicated an unexpected fall in interest rates, and should be associated with a fall in the price of FTSE 100 futures. Chalk analyzed daily data for 1984-93, during which period there were 72 changes in the base rate. Changes in base rate of under 3% were excluded from the analysis. He studied movements in the FTSE 100 futures price from 4 days before the announcement to 6 days afterwards, relative to the average daily movement in the FTSE 100 futures price from 7 days after the last announcement to 5 days before the present announcement. For announcements where the price of 3 month Sterling futures rose, the price of the FTSE 100 futures also rose on the announcement day. When the 3 month Sterling futures price fell, the price of FTSE 100 futures fell on the announcement day. These results are consistent with semi-strong efficiency in the markets for FTSE 100 and 3 month Sterling futures.

Buckle, ap Gwilym, Thomas & Woodhams (1998) analyzed 5-minute FTSE 100 futures returns for 1992-3, and found that macroeconomic announcements led to a rise in both volume and price volatility, which is consistent with semi-strong efficiency.

Australia. Frino & Hill (2001) examined the response of SPI futures to 132 scheduled Australian macroeconomic announcements over 1995-7. Using data for 10 second periods, they found that the volatility of futures returns was raised from 10 seconds before each announcement until about four minutes after the announcement. There was a strong price response in the minute after each announcement; but with some overreaction, which conflicts with semi-strong efficiency. The number and size of trades increased for four minutes immediately after each announcement, while the quoted bid-ask spread widened for 20 seconds before each announcement until 30 seconds afterwards.

Conclusions. There have been over 50 tests of the effect of public information on other futures prices. They generally looked for a rapid price response in the appropriate direction to the release of unexpected price sensitive information. While the majority of these studies are consistent with semi-strong efficiency, about one third are not. The few results for index futures also tend to support semi-strong efficiency.

8.2.3 Forecasting Ability of Traders

Since futures markets are a zero sum game (ignoring bid-ask spreads, commissions and taxes), every profitable trade is matched by an unprofitable trade. This raises the question of whether there is some systematic difference between winners and losers. The available data only permits studying a few different forms of classification of traders: e.g. large or small open interest, commercial or non-commercial trader, long or short, hedger, spreader or speculator, frequent or infrequent holder of overnight positions. The relevant studies (none of index futures), have found that traders with large open positions made significant profits before transactions costs, and suggests that large traders possess superior forecasting skills. Alternatively, the profits achieved by large speculators could be due to normal backwardation. There have been four studies of this hypothesis using data on open positions, and three found that large speculators possessed forecasting skill. It is not clear what information set is used by large traders to forecast prices, and so the degree of market efficiency being tested is uncertain. However, it is likely that large traders were using public information (and possibly some inside information). Therefore, the results for commodity futures suggest that these markets were not semi-strong efficient. However, this conclusion may not apply to index futures.

8.2.4 Arbitrage Opportunities

An absence of arbitrage opportunities can be regarded as a requirement of market efficiency, in that the current price should fully reflect the chosen information set.

Instead of forecasting subsequent price movements, public data on the corresponding spot price, the riskless interest rate and dividends is used to make instantaneous (and riskless) profits using zero capital. The absence of arbitrage represents a test of the joint hypotheses that both the spot and the futures markets are efficient; and the presence of arbitrage opportunities may be due to inefficiencies in either the spot market, the futures market, or both markets. Such studies of index futures have been discussed in chapter 4, where it is concluded that arbitrage opportunities exist, but they are becoming smaller and less frequent over time. In similar vein, the pricing of intra and inter commodity spreads or the basis could be tested to see if some information set can be used to generate profits. If so, this implies inefficiency in one or more of the markets involved.

8.2.5 Risk Neutrality and Efficiency

Some tests of efficiency are a joint test of efficiency and unbiasedness. Assuming risk neutrality and no transactions costs; semi-strong efficiency implies that $S_T = F_t + \varepsilon_t$, where S_T is the spot price at time T, F_t is the current price of a future for delivery at time T, and ε_t is a disturbance term with zero mean. Rejection of this equation linking the current futures price with the delivery price implies the presence of a risk premium, semi-strong inefficiency or the presence of transactions costs.

UK.　　　　　　Antoniou & Holmes (1995a) tested the validity of the equation $S_T = F_t + \varepsilon_t$ using daily data for FTSE 100 futures for 1984-93. First, spot and futures prices must be co-integrated if the above equation is to be valid. Second, it is necessary for the long run validity of the equation that it has a zero intercept ($\alpha=0$), and F_t has a co-efficient of unity ($\beta=1$). Finally, if the equation is to be valid in the short run, errors must be corrected within one period.

Antoniou & Holmes used the log of monthly prices and found that for 1, 2, 3, 4, 5, and 6 months to delivery, S_T and F_t were co-integrated. The second condition ($\alpha=0$ and $\beta=1$) was valid for 1, 2, 4 and 5 months to delivery, but not for 3 and 6 months to delivery. This failure is attributed to the expiry of the near contract, which happens with 3 and 6 months to delivery, and may be due to the presence of a risk premium, market inefficiency or transactions costs. To investigate the short run validity of the equation, they included an ECM for the four months (1, 2, 4 and 5) that passed the test for long term validity. For 1 and 2 months to delivery the error correction term had a co-efficient of - 1, as well as $\alpha=0$ and $\beta=1$, which supports the short run validity of the equation. For 4 and 5 months to delivery the error correction term was higher than - 1, α was positive and β was less than one, which indicates that the equation is not valid in the short run. This may be due to the presence of a risk premium, inefficiencies or transactions costs.

Antoniou & Holmes also applied a variance bounds test to daily log prices for 1, 4 and 20 day periods to provide an alternative test of the above equation. If it is valid, since the covariance between F_t and ε_t is zero, $Var(S_T) = Var(F_t)+Var(\varepsilon_t)$, and because $Var(\varepsilon_t) \geq 0$, the variance of futures prices must be less than the variance of spot prices.

Because this test is only valid if the two variances are finite, which is not the case if they are non-stationary, Antoniou & Holmes transformed this test by subtracting a lagged value of S_T from each variable. For 1 and 2 months to delivery the variance bounds test supported short run validity, while for 3, 4 and 5 months to delivery there were some failures.

Overall, Antoniou & Holmes found support for semi-strong efficiency and the lack of a risk premium and transactions costs for the 1 and 2 months before delivery. For longer periods to delivery, the evidence suggested the presence of a risk premium, market inefficiencies or transactions costs. These results are consistent with the risk premium only becoming significant for periods longer than 2 months. They also fit with the evidence that mispricings decrease in size and frequency as delivery approaches (see chapter 4.2.1).

8.3 Strong Efficiency

Strong efficiency requires the market price to reflect all relevant information, both public and private. Strong efficiency is a more stringent requirement than weak or semi-strong efficiency, and includes them both as special cases. Thus, the negative results for weak and semi-strong efficiency imply that futures markets will also fail the tests for strong efficiency. Perhaps this is one of the reasons why there have been few studies of strong efficiency for futures markets, and none for index futures.

8.4 Time-related Anomalies

Even if futures markets are weak efficient, there may be time related patterns in futures prices. Many studies have found time related anomalies (e.g. weekend effect, January effect), in stock market indices. For example Board & Sutcliffe (1988) have documented a weekend effect (lower return over the weekend than for the other days of the week) in the Financial Times All Share index. However, Samuelson (1965) has shown that, even if the spot price of an asset is predictable, the price of a futures contract on such an asset will have a zero expected change. Therefore, although there is a small degree of predictability in the index, e.g. a weekend effect, (as well as the predictability due to the effects of non-synchronous trading), there is no reason (other than the arbitrage linkage) to expect this to cause a time related anomaly in index futures prices. In the remainder of this chapter studies of various time related anomalies in index futures will be presented. These are classified by the time period (day, week, month, quarter, year) and the object of study (mean price changes or returns, volatility of price changes or returns, volume, basis, and intercommodity spread).

8.4.1 The Weekend Effect

There have been a large number of studies of the weekend effect in index futures. *Returns.* The primary focus of research has been on looking for an abnormally low return over the weekend. The empirical studies of the weekend effect in futures markets are summarized in table 8.2.

Table 8.2: Empirical Studies of the Weekend Effect in the Returns on Index Futures

Study	Index	Returns	No. of Months	Week-end	Conclusions
Cornell (1985b)	S&P500	R	27	FC-MO	No
	S&P500	R	27	MO-MC	No
	S&P500	R	27	FC-MO	No
Dyl & Maberly (1986a)	S&P500	ΔP	36	FC-MO	Yes
	S&P500	ΔP	36	MO-MC	No
	S&P500	ΔP	36	FC-MC	No
Dyl & Maberly (1986b)	S&P500	R	44	FC-MO	Yes
	S&P500	ΔP	44	FC-MO	Yes
Junkus (1986)	S&P500	R	24	FC-MC	No
	VLCI	R	24	FC-MC	No
	NYSE	R	24	FC-MC	No
Keim & Smirlock (1987, 1989)	S&P500	ΔP	57	FC-MO	Yes
	S&P500	ΔP	57	MO-MC	No
	S&P500	ΔP	57	FC-MC	No
	VLCI	ΔP	57	FC-MO	No
	VLCI	ΔP	57	MO-MC	No
	VLCI	ΔP	57	FC-MC	No
Maberly (1987)	VLCI	R	46	FC-MO	Yes
	VLCI	R	46	MO-MC	No
Finnerty & Park (1988b)	MMI	R	24	FC-MO	No
	MMI	R	24	MO-MC	No
	MMI	R	24	FC-MC	No
Pieptea & Prisman (1988)	S&P500	R	39	FC-MC	No
Maberly, Spahr & Herbst (1989)	S&P500	R	52	FC-MO	Yes
	S&P500	R	52	MO-MC	No
	S&P500	R	52	FC-MC	No
	VLCI	R	52	FC-MO	Yes
	VLCI	R	52	MO-MC	No
	VLCI	R	52	FC-MC	No
Cinar & Vu (1991)	S&P500	R	73	FC-MC	No

	VLCI	R	73	FC-MC	No
Najand & Yung	S&P500	R	81	FC-MO	No
(1994)	S&P500	R	81	MO-MC	No
	S&P500	R	81	FO-MC	No
Szakmary &	Value Line	R	120	FC-MC	Yes
Kiefer (2004)	S&P 400	R	108	FC-MC	Yes
	Russell 2000	R	108	FC-MC	Yes
Kamara (1997)	S&P500	R	140	FC-MC	No
Chamberlain, Cheung & Kwan (1988)	TSE 300	ΔP	36	FC-MC	Yes
Bailey (1989)	Nikkei-SGX	R	7	FC-MC	No
	Nikkei-SGX	R	7	FC-MO	No
	Osaka 50	R	5	FC-MC	No
	Osaka 50	R	5	FC-MO	No
Ziemba (1990)	Nikkei-SGX	R	24	Unspecified	No
	Osaka 50	R	16	Unspecified	Yes
Twite (1990b)	SPI	R	48	FC-MC	No
Heaney (1990)	SPI	R	57	FC-MC	No
Yadav & Pope	FTSE 100	R	47	FC-MO	No
(1992a)	FTSE 100	R	47	MO-MC	Yes
Martikainen & Puttonen (1996)	FOX	R	24	FC-MC	Yes
Lee & Mathur (1999)	Ibex 35	R	37	FC-MC	Yes

FC= Friday close, MO = Monday open, MC = Monday close, R = Returns, ΔP = Price Changes, No=No weekend effect, Yes= Weekend effect

The results in table 8.2 are mixed, and many studies have failed to find a weekend effect. This may be because any weekend effect is small, and has disappeared in recent years. There have also been a number of studies of other futures, and these suggest that lower returns over the weekend are a general feature of futures markets.

Bank holidays are, in some ways similar to weekends, as they are periods when the market is predictably closed for a day or so. Fabozzi, Ma & Briley (1994) looked for a bank holiday effect in the returns of 28 US futures contracts (none of which were index futures). Of the futures studied, 16 were traded primarily in the US, while 12 were traded internationally. Although US holidays may be important for domestic futures, they might have less impact on futures that continue to be traded in other countries. A reduction in the volume on the day before a bank holiday was found for the 16 domestic futures, while there was an increase in volume on the day following a bank holiday. After controlling for other possible time related anomalies (January, turn of the month and day of the week effects) as well as allowing for heteroskedasticity, there were higher returns for domestic futures on the day before a bank holiday. These results are consistent with an inventory adjustment argument.

Traders are reluctant to increase their open positions, particularly short positions, on the day before a bank holiday. As a result volume drops and prices rise. After the bank holiday volume increases to compensate for its earlier reduction. These effects only apply to domestic futures, as trading in international futures is still possible on many US bank holidays (e.g. presidents day, memorial day, fourth of July, labour day, election day and thanksgiving day).

Some Explanations of a Weekend Effect in Returns. While no fully satisfactory explanation exists for either the weekend effect in futures (or shares) some suggestions have been made to account for the weekend effect in index futures.

1. Maberly (1986) and Dyl & Maberly (1986a, 1988) argue that the preponderance of large price changes with a negative sign during the weekend closure is consistent with bad news being released over the weekend. However, there is some degree of circularity in using negative price changes to indicate bad news, which is then used to explain negative price changes. Yadav & Pope (1992a) did not find such an effect for the UK.

2. Phillips-Patrick & Schneeweis (1988) suggest that a partial explanation for the negative returns on index futures over the weekend closure is the additional loss of interest. The equilibrium price of an index futures contract at time t for delivery at time T is given by $F_t = (S-D) \times (1+r_t)$. Assuming for simplicity that S and D are unchanged during the period under consideration (j days), the only variables in this equation that change with the passage of time are F_t and r_t (the riskless rate of return for the period t to T). Letting i represent the annual riskless rate of return, the above equation can be rewritten as $F_t = (S-D) \times (1+i(T-t)/365)$, where $r_t = i(T-t)/365$ and $F_{t+j} = (S-D) \times (1+i(T-t-j)/365)$. Therefore, over a period of j calendar days, the change in the equilibrium futures price due to the interest rate effect is a drop of $F_{t+j} - F_t = -ij(S-D)/365$. Over the weekend j equals three, while overnight j equals one. Therefore, over the weekend the drop in the futures prices due to this interest rate effect is three times larger than the overnight change for Tuesday to Friday price changes, i.e. $(F_{t+3} - F_t)/(F_{t+1} - F_t) = 3$. When they controlled for the interest rate effect, Yadav & Pope (1992a) still found weekend anomalies in the UK. This may be because, in the UK shares go ex-dividend on Mondays, leading to a drop in the index over the weekend.

The Variance of Returns. If futures markets operate in calendar time, the variance of returns from Friday close to Monday close will be three times larger than the variance of the close to close returns for the other days of the week. For returns calculated from close to open, the extent to which the weekend variance exceeds the overnight variance depends on the length of time the market is open each day (x). This ratio is given by $(72-x)/(24-x) \geq 3$, and the longer the market is open the greater is the ratio. Some empirical studies of the ratio of the variance of index futures returns over the weekend to that for the other days of the week are summarized in table 8.3. These results suggest that the increase in the variance for index futures is much lower than the 200% increase the calendar time hypothesis predicts. This result, of only a slightly higher variance over the weekend, is also found for other futures.

Table 8.3: Empirical Studies of the Weekend Effect in the Variance of Index Futures

Study	Index	Returns	No. of Months	Week -end	Conclusions
Dyl & Maberly (1986a)	S&P500	ΔP	36	FC-MO	86%
Maberly (1987)	VLCI	R	46	FC-MO	75%
Finnerty & Park (1988b)	MMI	R	24	FC-MO	47%
Pieptea & Prisman (1988)	S&P500	R	39	FC-MC	-20%
Chamberlain, Cheung & Kwan (1988)	TSE 300	ΔP	36	FC-MC	8%
Bailey (1989)	Nikkei-SGX	R	7	FC-MC	1%
Bailey (1989)	Osaka 50	R	5	FC-MC	-57%
Lauterbach & Monroe (1989)	S&P500	R	9	FC-MC	25%
Ziemba (1990)	Nikkei-SGX	R	24	Unspecified	-58%
Ziemba (1990)	Osaka 50	R	16	Unspecified	-35%
Heaney (1990)	SPI	R	57	FC-MC	23%
Ekman (1992)	S&P500	R	71	FC-MO	61%

FC= Friday close, MO = Monday open, MC = Monday close, R = Returns, ΔP = Price Changes

Variance of Returns and Information Arrival.   In an efficient market prices move in response to the arrival of information. Therefore, since information arrival (public or private) is generally larger during business hours, the variance of open market returns (per hour) is expected to exceed the variance of closed market returns. An implication of this is that, for dual listed futures, the variance of returns should be largest during the trading hours of the underlying asset, which need not correspond with the trading hours of the futures contract. (Dual listed contracts are discussed further in chapter 11.11.) This has been confirmed in a number of studies covering markets in the USA, UK and Japan.

For the S&P500 Becker, Finnerty & Tucker (1993) found that the ratio of the variances of close-close returns to close-open returns was 6.4, while for the FTSE 100 and the Nikkei 225 the corresponding figure was only about 1.4. This suggests that the price sensitive information which arrives during US business hours has a major impact on share prices, not only in the US, but also in the UK and Japan. However, the price sensitive information that arrives during business hours in the UK and Japan has a much smaller effect on US share prices.

Craig, Dravid & Richardson (1995) considered open to close and close to open returns on Nikkei 225 futures traded on the CME for 1991-2. They found that the variance of closed market returns was 3.3 times larger than that for open market returns. This accords with most of the relevant information arriving during Japanese, rather than US, business hours.

Booth, Lee & Tse (1996) studied the open and close prices of Nikkei 225 futures in Osaka, Singapore and Chicago for 1990-4. They found that the three price series of futures prices were cointegrated with a single stochastic trend. The trading variances (per hour) for Singapore and Osaka were similar, and much higher than their common non-trading variance. For Chicago, the reverse was the case and the trading variance (per hour) was much smaller than the trading variance. Finally the variance per hour when Singapore and Osaka are closed is similar to the variance per hour when Chicago is open. This suggests that Nikkei 225 prices are driven by a single set of information (probably public) that arrives when Osaka and Singapore are open and Chicago is closed.

The Basis. If there is a similar weekend effect in both the spot and the futures markets, there may not be a weekly pattern in the basis, i.e. *(F - S)*. This issue has been investigated for both US and Canadian index futures, and there was some indication of a small pattern.

USA. Cornell (1985b) analyzed changes in the basis (logarithm of the futures price minus the logarithm of the spot price) for the S&P500 index. He found that over the weekend (Friday close to Monday open) the change in the basis was positive, while that for the other days of the week was negative. Dyl & Maberly (1986) discovered a number of errors in Cornell's data set of futures prices and, when they repeated his tests for day of the week effects in returns, obtained a different result. However, they did not replicate Cornell's study of the basis. Kamara (1997) considered the basis *(F - S)* for the S&P500 over the weekend for 1982-93, and found a positive effect.

Canada. Chamberlain, Cheung & Kwan (1988) studied the daily changes in the close to close basis *(F - S)* of the TSE 300 index future. Like Cornell, they found a positive change over the weekend, and a negative change for the other days of the week. However, these changes in the basis were not significantly different from zero.

8.4.2 The Turn-of-the-Year Effect

For shares it has been found that there is a rise in returns for the end of December and the first few days of January, and this is called either the turn-of-the-year effect, or the January effect.

Returns. There has been only one major study of the turn-of-the-year-effect for index futures, and this was Keim & Smirlock (1987, 1989). This study analyzed the S&P500 and VLCI index futures. They defined the turn-of-the-year as the last trading day in December and the first four trading days in January, and found no significant effect on price changes in either index future.

An explanation proposed for the turn-of-the-year effect in shares, for countries with a tax year that coincides with the calendar year, is the tax loss selling hypothesis. In December assets, whose current value is less than the purchase price, are sold to realize a tax loss. This loss can then be offset against capital gains made elsewhere during that tax year. If desired, the assets sold at a loss in December can be repurchased in January. This strategy effectively brings forward the tax benefits of losses, while leaving the timing of the tax on gains unaltered. The US Economic Recovery Act (1981) changed the taxation of futures contracts entered into after 23rd June 1981 in such a way as to remove any incentive for the tax loss selling of futures contracts. So, if tax loss selling was responsible for the turn-of-the-year effect, it should disappear after June 1981. This is just what Gay & Kim (1987) found for US Commodity Research Bureau price index futures.

Spreads.   For equities it has been found that the size effect (see Sutcliffe, 1992) is concentrated around the turn-of-the-year. Therefore an intercommodity spread between futures based on the share prices of small and large firms may be profitable if held over the turn-of-the-year.

USA.   Keim & Smirlock (1987, 1989) studied the seasonality of a spread between the VLCI and S&P500 index futures (VLCI price minus S&P500 price). Since the S&P500 contains large firms while the VLCI is argued to represent small firms, this spread is influenced by the seasonality in any size effect in futures prices. There appears to be a positive turn-of-the-year effect (last trading day in December and the first four trading days in January) for daily open to close price changes, i.e. the price of VLCI futures rises relative to that of S&P500 futures.

Clark & Ziemba (1987) propose a trading strategy based on the positive change in the spread between the Value Line and S&P500 index futures over the turn-of-the-year. They suggest adopting a short position in S&P500 futures and a matching long position in Value Line futures between 15th and 17th December, and closing out these positions on 15th January. Ziemba (1994) extended the analysis of Clark & Ziemba (1987) to include another four years of data. The new results strengthened the earlier findings of a size effect in futures prices around the turn-of-the-year. Hensel & Ziemba (2000) updated the earlier studies to 1998, and found that, while there continued to be a size effect in the second half of December, it was no longer present in January. Rendon & Ziemba (2005) updated the study to include data to 2000 for Value Line futures with a $500 multiplier; and to 2005 for Value Line futures with a $100 multiplier. While the Value Line - S&P500 spread trade remained profitable, it was not statistically significant. This lack of significance is due to lower liquidity in Value Line futures in recent years, which has made this trade very risky. Rendon & Ziemba (2005) also examined spreads between Russell 2000 and S&P500 futures for 1993-2005. This spread also generated profits, particularly if it was liquidated three days before the year end; although these profits are not statistically significant.

Szakmary & Kiefer (2004) found that for 1982-93, Value Line futures had a turn of the year effect, while for 1993-2000 S&P Midcap 400 and Russell 2000 futures lacked such an effect.

Conclusions.   The US evidence supports the existence of a turn-of-the-year effect in spreads, with index futures on smaller companies having relatively higher returns.

8.4.3 The Turn-of-the-Month Effect

A few studies of equities have found that returns for the last day of the previous calendar month and the first half of the current month are higher than those for the rest of the current month (excluding the last day).

Returns. There have been a number of studies looking for a turn-of-the-month effect in index futures.

USA. Keim & Smirlock (1987, 1989) studied the S&P500 and the VLCI index futures. They defined the turn-of-the-month as the last day of the previous month and the first four trading days of the current month, and found that, while a few months (April and November) had significantly different average price changes, there was no consistent pattern. Therefore they conclude that there is no turn-of-the-month effect in price changes.

Cinar & Vu (1991) found that daily futures returns for 1982-8 on the S&P500 and VLCI were higher in the first half of each calendar month.

Hensel, Sick & Ziemba (1994) defined the turn-of-the-month as the last day of the previous month and the first four days of the new month. Using daily data on log returns for 1982-92, they found a significant positive turn-of-the-month effect for both the S&P500 futures and Value Line futures (they joined up the data on the VLCI and the VLA). When the data was disaggregated, the turn-of-the-month effect was significantly positive for the Value Line in January, February and March.

Szakmary & Kiefer (2004) found that over the 1993-2002 period, Russell 2000 futures had a turn of the month effect, while S&P Midcap 400 futures did not. For the period 1982-93 Value Line futures lacked a turn of the month effect.

Japan. Ziemba (1990) found evidence suggesting a turn-of-the-month effect in futures on two Japanese stock indices - the Nikkei 225 (traded on SGX), and the Osaka 50 Kabusaki (traded on the Osaka Securities Exchange). However, the positive returns appear a few days earlier than on the spot market. For Nikkei 225 futures the positive effect is five to eight days before the turn on the month, while the corresponding figure for Osaka 50 Kabusaki futures is five to seven days.

Finland. Martikainen, Perttunen & Puttonen (1995b) used daily returns on FOX futures, and found they were significantly higher some 2 to 3 days before the turn-of-the-month. They argue that this anticipation of the turn-of-the-month effect is consistent with the couple of days lead that Finnish futures returns have over spot returns. They rule out expiration effects and any quarterly effects as causes of this turn-of-the-month effect in Finnish futures.

Conclusions. There is some evidence for a turn-of-the-month effect, but in Japan and Finland it occurs a bit earlier than in the corresponding stock market.

Spreads. Since there appears to be a size effect at the turn-of-the-year, perhaps there is a size effect at the turn-of-the-month. Keim & Smirlock (1987, 1989) studied spreads between VLCI and the S&P500 index futures. However, there was no clear turn-of-the-month effect (defined as the last day of one month and the first four days of the next month) in this spread.

8.4.4 The Month-of-the-Year Effect

For equities there have been many studies looking for patterns in share prices, depending on the month-of-the-year. The main anomaly found in share prices is of higher returns in January - the January, or turn-of-the-year effect. It is possible that seasonal patterns (in addition to the January effect) exist in futures prices.

Returns.   Keim & Smirlock (1987, 1989) looked at daily price changes for the S&P500 and the VLCI index futures for 1982-6 (as well as the values of the spread between these two futures). Some marginally significant departures from the average were found for some months, but overall there did not appear to be any clear patterns.

   Cinar & Vu (1991) studied daily data on the S&P500 and VLCI for 1982-8, and found no evidence for a statistically significant month of the year effect in either future.

Volatility.   Agricultural commodities with an annual harvest are prone to changes in return volatility, depending on the month-of-the-year, and clear seasonal patterns in futures price volatility have been found. For three US index futures (S&P500, MMI & NYSE Composite) using daily data for 1982-92 Galloway & Kolb (1996) found evidence of differences in volatility between months.

The Basis.   Because dividends are seasonal, according to the no-arbitrage condition, the size of the difference between the spot and futures prices should fluctuate during the year, CBOT (1990). However, there are no empirical studies for index futures.

8.4.5 Intraday Patterns in Returns

Using transactions data, researchers have found various intraday patterns for shares, e.g. returns (excluding Monday morning), volume and volatility all follow a U-shaped daily pattern, as does the first order autocorrelation coefficient of returns. There are two explanations for such intraday patterns in volume (and also in volatility and bid-ask spreads). The first explanation is that if both liquidity and informed traders have discretion over when they trade, they will all choose to trade at the same time as each other, so that their trades have the minimum price impact, Admati & Pfleiderer (1988). These periods of high volume are likely to be at the open and close because non-discretionary traders will tend to increase volume at these times.

   The second explanation is that the optimal portfolio to be held over a non-trading period is different from that which is optimal for an open market period. Therefore, there is an increase in volume at the open and close due to portfolio rebalancing trades, Brock & Kleidon (1992). These explanations for intraday patterns in stock markets are also applicable to futures markets. A number of studies have looked for such daily patterns in futures markets.

USA.   Lauterbach & Monroe (1989) used transactions data for the S&P500 index future for nine months in 1988. This data period is rather short, but an analysis of the minute-to-minute returns (natural logarithm of the price relative, adjusted for the elapsed time between observations to convert the return to a one minute basis) revealed that they rose in the first half hour of trading on Monday morning, and this rise was larger than that for any other day of the week. This result is in contrast to the finding for equity markets of a sharp fall on Monday mornings when trading begins.

Ekman (1992) analyzed transactions data on S&P500 futures for 1983-8, and found that logarithmic returns were negative on Monday mornings, in contrast to the other days of the week and to Lauterbach & Monroe (1989).

Andersen & Bollerslev found no intraday patters in S&P500 futures 5 minute returns for 1986-9.

Australia. Aitken, Frino & Jarnecic (1997) considered 10 minute returns on SPI futures for 1992-4, and were unable to find any intraday patterns.

UK. Yadav & Pope (1992a) used hourly data on FTSE 100 index futures, and analyzed returns. They found that returns declined throughout the day, particularly on the first Monday of a stock exchange account. In support of Lauterbach & Monroe (1989), the returns during the first hour of trading on the first Monday of a stock exchange account were significantly positive. They found a drop in returns between 2.00 pm and 3.00 pm, which coincides with the opening of the NYSE. Futures prices rose only when the market was closed, while the index rose only when the market was open.

Buckle, ap Gwilym, Thomas & Woodhams (1998) studied 5-minute FTSE 100 returns for 1992-3, and found no intraday patters in returns.

Abhyankar, Copeland & Wong (1999) analyzed 5-minute returns on FTSE 100 futures for 1991-3, and found no pattern in returns during the day (apart from a small drop from 2:30 to 3 pm). Ap Gwilym, Buckle & Thomas (1999) also failed to find any intraday patterns in 5-minute returns on FTSE 100 futures returns for 1992-3, while Lequeux (1999) failed to find any pattern in 15-minute FTSE 100 futures returns for 1987-97.

Conclusions. The studies are divided as to whether returns rise or fall on Monday mornings. Otherwise no consistent pattern emerges in returns.

8.4.6 Intraday Patterns in Volatility

USA. Kawaller, Koch & Koch (1990) analyzed transactions data for S&P500 index futures for the fourth quarters of 1984 to 1986 and found that the volatility of the futures price follows a U-shaped pattern each day.

Froot, Gammill & Perold (1990) studied returns over 15 minute intervals on S&P500 index futures for 1988 and 1989 and found a U-shaped daily pattern in volatility, with high variances at the start and end of the day.

Cheung & Ng (1990) analyzed 15 minute returns on S&P500 futures for 1983-7. After controlling for a GARCH (1,1) effect, the variance of returns exhibited a U-shaped pattern within each day.

Chan, Chan & Karolyi (1991) found that the variances of five minute returns on S&P500 futures for 1984-9 followed a U-shaped pattern within each day.

Ekman (1992) discovered that the volatility of 15-minute logarithmic returns for S&P500 futures followed a U-shaped pattern within each day.

Park (1993) measured the volatility of returns on the MMI over 30 minute periods for 1984-6 in two different ways: the variance of returns, and the Cho & Frees (1988) estimator. In the first case there was evidence of a U-shaped pattern during the day in futures and spot volatilities, while in the second case there was not.

Lee & Linn (1994) used 10-minute log returns on S&P500 futures for 1983-7. They found that within each day, volatility followed a U-shaped pattern.

Herbst & Maberly (1992) examined the variance of S&P500 futures returns over a short period of the trading day. They considered futures returns between 4.00 pm (when the NYSE closes) and 4.15 pm (when futures trading ceases), and found highly significant differences between the days of the week, with the largest variance on Fridays, and the smallest on Wednesdays. They concluded that the flow of information is a function of the day of the week.

Chang, Jain & Locke (1995) analyzed transactions data for S&P500 futures. The spot market closes 15 minutes earlier than the futures market. Futures price volatility (measured using the Parkinson estimator) for the last 15 minutes of NYSE trading exceeded that for the final 15 minutes of futures trading (except on Fridays). While the spot market was open the volatility of futures prices was U-shaped. In the first five minutes after the closure of the spot market, futures volatility fell, and it fell further in the next five minutes, only to rise to a very high level for the last five minutes of futures trading. Thus, over the whole day, futures price volatility followed a W-pattern.

Wang, Michalski, Jordan & Moriarty (1994) analyzed transactions data for S&P500 futures for the December 1987, June 1988 and September 1988 contracts. After controlling for the effects of information arrival (proxied by the volatility of treasury bill futures and the lagged number of trades), the mean bid-ask spread and the lagged number of market makers in the pit; they found that price volatility followed a daily U-shaped pattern.

Kawaller, Koch & Peterson (1994) analyzed minute-to-minute returns for S&P500 futures for the last three months of 1988. The standard deviations for 40 minute periods exhibited a daily U-shaped pattern. After controlling for lagged spot returns, the number of futures and options quotes and a time trend, futures volatility rose throughout the day. Implied volatilities did not exhibit any daily patterns.

Chang, Pinegar & Schachter (1997) used daily data for S&P500 futures for 1983-90 and found that volatility followed an inverted U-shape.

Kofman & Martens (1997) considered one minute returns for S&P500 futures in 1993, and found that volatility was U-shaped within each day.

Andersen & Bollerslev (1997) studied 5 minute returns on S&P500 futures for 1986-9, and found a U-shaped pattern for return volatility while the spot market was open, followed by another U-shaped pattern after the spot market closed.

Daigler (1997) considered one minute returns on S&P500 and MMI futures for 1988-9, and found that each day the volatility of returns for these futures followed a U-shape.

Tse (1999b) used one minute returns on DJIA futures for 1997-9, and found a *U*-shape in daily volatility.

Japan.　　　　　Kim, Ko & Noh (2002) used trade data to study Nikkei 225 futures for 1993-6. They found that volatility was *U*-shaped within each day.

Shiyun, Guan & Chang (1999) used Markov chains to study the intraday volatility of Nikkei 225 futures prices for 1993-4, and found a *U*-shape.

Ding & Charoenwong (2003) studied quote and trade data for 1995-9 on three futures listed on the SGX that were thinly traded - Nikkei 300, Dow Jones Thailand and MSCI Hong Kong indices. They found that the volatility of prices was crudely *U*-shaped.

Hong Kong.　　　Tang & Lui (2002) studied 15 minute data on the Hang Seng for 1994-6. Within each day, the volatility of 15 minute returns for both spot and futures returns followed an *L* shape.

Taiwan.　　　　Huang (2002) analyzed the volatility of 5-minute returns on futures on the Taiwan index traded on Taifex and the SGX for 1997-2000. There were three *U*-shapes; one for the open, another for the close, and a third for the period between the open and the close.

Australia.　　　Gannon (1994) studied 15-minute log returns on SPI futures for three months to March 1992, and failed to find a *U*-shaped daily pattern for volatility (measured by squared log returns).

UK.　　　　　Yadav & Pope (1992a) used hourly FTSE 100 futures data. The number of returns in the top and bottom deciles and quartiles of the data set suggested that the volatility of returns may be *U*-shaped within each day.

Abhyankar, Copeland & Wong (1999) analyzed 5-minute returns on FTSE 100 futures for 1991-3.They measured volatility as the mean absolute deviation, and found it followed a *U*-shaped pattern within each day. There was an upward spike at 1.30 pm which is when trading begins on the NYSE. Relative volatility (futures/spot) varied between 1.5 times at the open, and 4.5 times at 1.30 pm. This ratio then declined to about 2.5 at the close, and so follows an inverted *U*-shape during the day.

Kofman & Martens (1997) analyzed one minute returns for FTSE 100 futures in 1993, and found that volatility was *U*-shaped within each day, with a spike at 11:30 corresponding to the release of UK macroeconomic information.

Buckle, ap Gwilym, Thomas & Woodhams (1998) studied 5 minute FTSE 100 futures returns for 1992-3, and found daily volatility to be *U*-shaped.

Ap Gwilym, Buckle & Thomas (1999) considered 5-minute returns on FTSE 100 futures for 1992-3, and found that volatility was *U*-shaped within each day. The same result was obtained for 1992-9 by ap Gwilym, McMillan & Speight (1999).

Lequeux (1999) analyzed 15-minute returns on FTSE 100 futures for 1987-97, and found that volatility was *U*-shaped within each day, while kurtosis followed an inverted *V*-shape.

Tse (1999a) analyzed 5 minute returns on the FTSE 100 for 1995-6, and found a *U*-shape for volatility each day, with a spike at 1:30 when US news is announced before the open of the NYSE.

If futures returns are assumed to follow a random walk, the daily high and low prices are about four times more likely to occur at the beginning and end of the day than in the middle of the day. In an analysis of trade prices for FTSE 100 futures for 1992-5, Acar, Lequeux & Ritz (1996) found that the proportion of daily highs and lows that occurred at the beginning of the day was about 50% higher than expected. This finding is consistent with higher volatility at the start of the day.

Spain   Lafuente (2002) and Lafuente & Novales (2003) studied hourly Ibex 35 returns for 1993-6, and found that volatility was U-shaped within each day.

Conclusions.   There is pervasive evidence for the USA, Japan and UK that the volatility of futures returns follows a U-shaped pattern within each day.

8.4.7 Intraday Patterns in Volume

The relationship between either the number of trades or the volume of trading during the day has been investigated for the USA (Chang, Pinegar & Schachter, 1997, Ekman, 1992, Taylor, 2004b); Japan (Kim, Ko & Noh, 2002; Vila & Sandmann, 1995); Australia (Gannon, 1994); Taiwan (Huang, 2002); UK (Abhyankar, Copeland & Wong, 1999, ap Gwilym, Buckle & Thomas, 1999, ap Gwilym, McMillan & Speight, 1999, Buckle, ap Gwilym, Thomas & Woodhams, 1998, Chng, 2004a, Tse, 1999a); Netherlands (De Jong & Donders, 1997). Every study found a daily U-shaped pattern for volume or the number of trades.

8.4.8 Intraday Patterns in Autocorrelation, Mean Reversion, Bid-Ask Spread etc

USA.   Ekman (1992) found that for S&P500 futures the negative autocorrelation of one minute logarithmic returns rose rapidly from -0.04 at the opening to a peak of approximately -0.12 at about 11 am, and then fell until roughly 2 pm, returning to its opening level. It then rose sharply until the close, reaching about -0.13. Ekman termed this an S-shaped pattern.

Wang, Moriarty, Michalski & Jordan (1990) studied transactions data for S&P500 futures for the December 1987, June 1988 and September 1988 contracts. They measured the traded bid-ask spread as the mean of the absolute price changes that were price reversals, and found a daily U-shaped pattern.

Wang, Michalski, Jordan & Moriarty (1994) analyzed transactions data of S&P500 futures for the December 1987, June 1988 and September 1988 contracts. They found a daily U-shaped pattern for the number of market makers in the pit, the average number of contracts per trade, and the bid-ask spread (as well as price volatility). They then showed that, after controlling for the daily U-shaped patterns in the number of active market makers, price volatility and trade size; the U-shaped pattern in the bid-ask spread disappeared.

Taylor (2004b) found that mispricings for the S&P500 in 2001-2 followed a U-shaped pattern each day.

Japan.   Kim, Ko & Noh (2002) considered quote data for 1993-6 for Nikkei

225 futures. They found that the quoted bid-ask spread was *U*-shaped within the day. When they disaggregated the bid-ask spread into its three components, they found that the adverse information cost was *L*-shaped, the inventory holding cost followed an inverted *U*-shape, while order processing costs were flat.

Shiyun, Guan & Chang (1999) used Markov chains to study the intraday bid-ask spread of Nikkei 225 futures prices for 1993-4, and rejected a *U*-shape.

Ding & Charoenwong (2003) studied quote and trade data for 1995-9 on three futures listed on the SGX that were thinly traded - Nikkei 300, Dow Jones Thailand and MSCI Hong Kong indices. They found that quoted bid-ask spreads were rather flat each day, although spreads narrowed on days when there was trading. The number of quote revisions was also flat on days without trading, but became *U*-shaped on days with trading.

UK.   Yadav & Pope (1992c) analyzed 15-minute data for the S&P500 and hourly data for the FTSE 100. Mispricings were found to be a mean reverting process, and the strength of this mean reversion varied during the day, being strongest at the start and end of the day in both the UK and the USA. They also found that the mean reversion effect was weaker on Mondays than otherwise.

Buckle, ap Gwilym, Thomas & Woodhams (1998) studied FTSE 100 futures prices for 15-minute intervals for 1992-3, and found a reduced level of price reversals at the open.

Abhyankar, Copeland & Wong (1999) analyzed 5-minute returns on FTSE 100 futures for 1991-3. The bid-ask spread followed an inverted *U*-shape each day, with an upward spike at 1.30, when the NYSE opens. The volatility of the bid-ask spread was very high at the open. The intraday mispricings followed a *U*-shaped pattern, with overpricings at the open and close, and underpricings around 3 pm.

Tse (1999a) analyzed 5 minute returns on the FTSE 100 for 1995-6, and found an inverted *U*-shape each day for bid-ask spreads.

8.5 Conclusions

While stock markets rapidly reflect public information, the evidence for the efficiency of futures markets is less clear. Although there are fewer empirical studies of index futures, there is an appreciable amount of evidence of weak inefficiency. There is considerable evidence of the presence of time related anomalies in index futures prices, e.g. a drop in prices during the weekend, only a slight rise in the variance over the weekend, and *U*-shaped daily patterns in price volatility. There is also evidence of *U*-shaped daily patterns in volume, autocorrelation and the bid-ask spread.

PART 4

USES

Chapter 9

Hedging

Introduction

Although hedging is the major reason for trading index futures, (see chapter 3.3 of Sutcliffe. 1997), the objective of hedging has proved controversial. This chapter sets out the alternative views of the purpose of hedging and, following the previous literature, the primary concern is with the risk-minimising hedge. However, consideration is also given to the more recent view that hedging can be viewed as an aspect of the construction of a portfolio of many spot assets and futures. In addition, a number of alternatives to the risk-minimising hedge are briefly mentioned. Discussion of the choice of futures contract is followed by ways of measuring the effectiveness of a hedge. The risk-minimizing hedge ratio is then restated using the CAPM beta. It may be necessary to hedge several different spot positions using a range of futures, and the more complicated hedge ratios this involves are presented. It is shown how the risks induced by marking to the market and dividend payments can be allowed for in the hedging decision. Whether the risks of a company should be hedged, and whether this should be done by the company or its shareholders are discussed. Finally, the problems associated with alternative ways of estimating the risk-minimising hedge ratio are covered; followed by a summary of the available empirical evidence.

9.1 The Purpose of Hedging

The origin of the term hedging is unclear, but appears to derive from the use of hedges to form a protective or defensive barrier around property. There are three views of the nature and purpose of hedging: risk minimisation, profit maximization and reaching a satisfactory risk-return trade-off using a portfolio theoretic approach, Rutledge (1972). Each of these interpretations will be considered in turn.

9.1.1 Risk Minimization

This is the traditional view of hedging. It refers to someone who is exposed to a risk, and wishes to reduce or remove this exposure, i.e. the objective of hedging is taken to be risk minimisation. This is accomplished by undertaking an additional investment whose risk cancels out, or offsets, the initial risk (rather then just liquidating, e.g. selling, the initial position in a risky asset). Hedging converts spot price risk into basis risk (risk that the spot and futures prices will not move in unison). In this traditional view of hedging, the holdings of both the initial asset and the security used to offset the risk of this asset are of equal magnitude. In this case the hedge ratio, i.e. the number of futures contracts bought or sold divided by the number of spot contracts whose risk is being hedged, is one-to-one (or unity). Later in this chapter, it will be shown that requiring the hedge ratio to be unity is an unnecessary restriction that may well reduce the effectiveness of the hedge. However, the traditional view of hedging uses a one-to-one hedge ratio.

Example. Danny Zucco runs the Ashington pension fund which receives a one-off payment of £20 million from its property investments. Three months later, this sum of money must be paid out again. Instead of incurring the transactions costs of buying shares worth £20 million, and then selling them again, Danny decides to lend the £20 million for the three months. However, this leaves the fund exposed to market risk on the shares worth £20 million that would otherwise have been bought. To remove this risk Danny buys index futures worth £20 million.

Because futures are marked to the market daily, a small amount of risk remains, i.e. the difference in returns between buying shares worth £20 million, as opposed to lending the £20 million and selling index futures. Daily fluctuations in the price of the index future will generate variation margin payments, and these are unlikely to have a present value of zero. Hence, some risk remains unhedged, although this 'tail risk' can be hedged by a 'tail hedge', which is explained later in this chapter. (A forward contract is not subject to this problem.)

Example. Sandy Olsson has a life assurance policy, where all the funds are invested in a well diversified portfolio of UK shares. She is due to retire in six months, at which time her policy will mature and she will be paid a lump sum based on the current market value of the underlying shares. Sandy wishes to avoid the risk of possible changes in the value of her lump sum between now and retirement. So she hedges this risk by selling FTSE 100 index futures. Then, if the stock market falls, her smaller lump sum is offset by gains on the index futures, while if the market rises, her larger lump sum is offset by losses on her index futures.

If the hedge involves a long position in the future (as in the Danny Zucco example), this is a long hedge, while if the hedge involves a short position in the future (as in the Sandy Olsson example), this is a short hedge. Short positions in index futures can be used to hedge the share holdings of underwriters, market makers in shares and in options, equity issuers and block positioners. This reduces their risk and thereby reduces the charges they make for their services, e.g. commission or bid-ask spread, Stoll & Whaley (1988a & 1988b), Tosini & Moriarty (1982). Index futures can also be used by financial bookmakers to 'lay off' any imbalance in bets on the index, and by OTC traders to hedge their positions.

A perfect hedge occurs when the risk of the additional investment exactly offsets the initial risk, so eliminating all of the initial risk. Such a hedge is very difficult to find. For example, if a person owns an asset and wishes to hedge the risk of fluctuations in its price by selling a futures contract on this asset, this will not eliminate all risk because, due to basis risk, the spot and futures prices will not move in unison. Because basis risk is argued to drop to zero as delivery approaches (see chapter 6.4), hedgers can reduce basis risk (and hence the risk of the hedged position) by using the near contract.

While the minimization of risk is usually taken to be the objective of hedging, other views have been expressed. The most extreme alternative is that the aim of hedging is to maximize profits.

9.1.2 Profit Maximization

Working (1953) has argued that a hedge (e.g. long in the spot and short in the future) may be viewed as a spread between the futures contract and the corresponding spot asset. Under this interpretation, the objective of a hedge is not to minimize risk, but to make a profit from movements in the relative prices of the futures contract and the spot asset, i.e. speculation on the basis, (see chapter 6.2 for a discussion of speculation on the basis). Houthakker (1968, p. 197) has endorsed this view that 'traders hedge not to reduce their risk (although this may be an incidental effect), but to increase their profits.'

A view of hedging that is increasing in popularity, is that both risk minimisation and profit maximization are objectives of hedgers.

9.1.3 Portfolio Approach

Based on earlier work by Johnson (1960) and Stein (1961), Ederington (1979) argued that a portfolio approach to hedging is superior to both the traditional one-to-one risk-minimizing and Working's profit maximizing interpretations, encompassing them as special cases. The portfolio approach for the case of a fixed spot position will now be explained. It is assumed that the size of the spot position to be hedged is known with certainty, and this may not always be the case. For example, the spot position to be hedged may be a share portfolio whose value is not known at present (perhaps because the exact contents of a relative's will are secret until it is read). The analysis is for a single period, rather than for multiple periods. Howard & D'Antonio (1991) have argued that, for share portfolios, a single period analysis is sufficient because the main purpose is to hedge an existing spot holding.

Let X_s and X_f be the quantities (in terms of units of the index) of the spot asset and the futures contract respectively that are held by the investor. Let S_t and F_t be the prices of the spot asset and the futures contract at time t, respectively, while D^*_{t+k} is the value at time $t+k$ of any dividend entitlements received during the period t to $t+k$. Time $t+k$ is the date when the hedge is planned to end (i.e. the horizon date), and may well differ from the delivery date of a futures contract. The profit at time $t+k$ (P_{t+k}) on a portfolio of X_s units long of the index and X_f units long of the stock index future, held over the period t to $t+k$, is $P_{t+k} = X_s(S_{t+k} - S_t + D^*_{t+k}) + X_f(F_{t+k} - F_t)$. (There is no interest charge for the money invested in the shares at time t, i.e. $X_s S_t$, because it is assumed that these shares will be held anyway, while payments of variation margin are ignored for the moment.) Let the hedge ratio be defined as $b \equiv -X_f/X_s$. This hedge ratio is not confined to the zero-one range, and may be greater than one or less than zero. However, since hedging usually involves balancing a long position with a short position, b will generally be positive. [Note that the profit at time $t+k$ has been defined in terms of long positions in both spot and futures. Given there is usually a positive price correlation between an asset and the futures used in the hedge, the hedge ratio will typically be negative, e.g. long in the spot and short in the future.] Substituting for X_f gives $P_{t+k} = X_s\{S_{t+k} - S_t + D^*_{t+k} - b(F_{t+k} - F_t)\}$.

Risk can be measured by the variance of the profit at time $t+k$ on the hedged position, $Var(P_{t+k})$. Since an anticipated change in the profit on the hedged position does not represent risk, the calculation of the variance should allow for any predictable change in profit, i.e. the conditional rather than the unconditional variance of profit is required. In consequence, the deviations used in calculating the variances and covariances are from the predicted levels of the relevant variables. (This has implications, which will be considered later in this chapter, for the estimation of the hedge ratio.) Because the values of X_s and b are taken as fixed during the hedge, $Var(P_{t+k}) = X_s^2\{\sigma_{\Delta s}^2 + b^2\sigma_{\Delta f}^2 - 2b\sigma_{\Delta s \Delta f} + \sigma_d^2 + 2\sigma_{\Delta sd} - 2b\sigma_{\Delta fd}\}$, where $\sigma_{\Delta s}^2$ and $\sigma_{\Delta f}^2$ are the estimated variances of the spot and futures price changes between t and $t+k$, $\sigma_{\Delta s \Delta f}$ is the corresponding covariance, σ_d^2 is the variance of D^*_{t+k} and $\sigma_{\Delta sd}$ and $\sigma_{\Delta fd}$ are the covariances between dividends and spot and futures price changes, respectively. If it is assumed that dividends are certain (and so dividend risk is not being hedged), the expression for the variance of profit simplifies to $Var(P_{t+k}) = X_s^2\{\sigma_{\Delta s}^2 + b^2\sigma_{\Delta f}^2 - 2b\sigma_{\Delta s \Delta f}\}$. Since the values of S_t and F_t are known, this expression can be restated in terms of the price levels at time $t+k$, i.e. $Var(P_{t+k}) = X_s^2(\sigma_s^2 + b^2\sigma_f^2 - 2b\sigma_{fs}) = X_s^2(Var(bF_{t+k} - S_{t+k}))$, where σ_s^2 and σ_f^2 are the estimated variances of the spot and futures prices at time $t+k$, σ_{fs} is the corresponding covariance, and $Var(bF_{t+k} - S_{t+k})$ is the variance of the basis at time $t+k$, except that the futures price is multiplied by the hedge ratio (b).

If the asset underlying the futures contract is the spot asset whose risk is being hedged (e.g. a portfolio of shares that is identical to the appropriate market index) and the hedge is held until delivery, then the hedge ratio is unity, the value of $Var(bF_{t+k} - S_{t+k})$ is zero (i.e. no basis risk), and the hedge is an arbitrage and is riskless (i.e. a perfect hedge), Castelino (1992). In this case the hedger will make a certain profit (loss) at delivery equal to the initial basis ($F_t - S_t$) when hedging a long (short) position in the underlying asset. Most hedges will not be lifted at delivery, and so are subject to basis risk (i.e. uncertainty over the value of $bF_{t+k} - S_{t+k}$). Thus, hedging an asset substitutes basis risk for spot risk. If it is assumed that the no-arbitrage condition applies at all times (and dividends and interest rates are known) then, even though the hedge is not ended at the delivery date of the future, there will be no basis risk. This is because the basis is always given by $F - S = SR_F - D(1 + R_F)$.

Having derived expressions for the profit and risk of the hedged position, the hedging decision can be formulated as a portfolio selection problem and solved. The Markowitz portfolio problem for the two asset case can be stated as: Maximize

$x_1E[R_1]+x_2E[R_2]-\lambda(x_1^2\sigma_1^2+x_2^2\sigma_2^2+2x_1x_2\sigma_{12})$, subject to the constraint that $x_1+x_2=1$, where $E[R_i]$ is the expected return on the ith asset, σ_i^2 is the variance of returns on the ith asset, σ_{ij} is the covariance of returns on assets i and j, λ is the risk aversion parameter and x_i is the proportion of funds to be invested in the ith asset; see Levy & Sarnat (1984). When the portfolio model is applied to hedging, the resulting model differs from this usual formulation because the holding of the underlying asset (X_s) is taken as fixed, and because there is no budget constraint, i.e. $x_1+x_2=1$.

The portfolio model of hedging may be stated as: Maximize $X_s\{E[S_{t+k}-S_t+D^*_{t+k}] -bE[F_{t+k}-F_t]\}-\xi X_s^2 Var(bF_{t+k}-S_{t+k})$, subject to X_s being constant. The efficient frontier (i.e. feasible combinations of expected profit and risk which, for each level of risk, have maximum profit), can be found by repeatedly solving this portfolio problem (which is a quadratic programming problem) for a wide range of values of ξ, the risk aversion parameter. The resulting efficiency frontier is illustrated in figure 9.1. Since hedgers may well have different levels of risk aversion, i.e. different values of ξ, they will select different points on the efficiency frontier and different hedge ratios. If ξ equals zero, the profit maximizing solution is obtained, i.e. point C, while if ξ is infinite, the risk-minimizing solution is found, i.e. point M. Any hedge which does not plot on this efficiency frontier is inefficient, e.g. point I, and therefore a superior hedge exists.

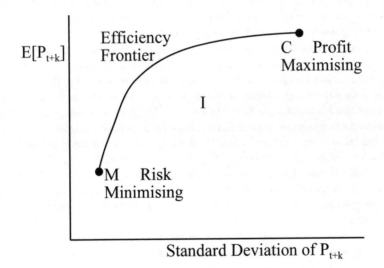

Figure 9.1: Efficiency Frontier for Hedged Positions

In the case of hedging a spot asset whose magnitude (X_s) is variable, it is possible to derive an expression for the utility-maximizing hedge ratio that is independent of ξ, the risk aversion parameter. Heifner (1972), Kahl (1983). This hedge ratio is $b_{var}= (\mu_f\sigma_s^2-\mu_s\sigma_{fs})/(\mu_s\sigma_f^2-\mu_f\sigma_{fs})$, where $\mu_s=E[S_{t+k}-S_t]$ and $\mu_f=E[F_{t+k}-F_t]$. The value of ξ still affects the values of X_s and X_f, but not their ratio, b_{var}.

9.2 Risk Minimization and the Portfolio Approach

The portfolio approach to hedging permits a wide range of hedge ratios to be efficient (i.e. all the hedge ratios underlying the points on the efficiency frontier in figure 9.1), depending on the trader's risk aversion (ξ). Following Anderson & Danthine (1980, 1981), Duffie (1989, pp 91-96) and Leuthold, Junkus & Cordier (1989, page 99), have shown that the demand for futures contracts by a utility-maximizing trader in a mean-variance framework can be split into the sum of the speculative and hedging components, (see appendix C to chapter 7 of Sutcliffe, 1993). The speculative demand is given by $z = (E[F_{t+k}] - F_t)/2\xi\sigma_f^2$, where σ_f^2 is the variance of F_{t+k}, and the hedging demand is given by $b = -Cov(e_{t+k}, F_{t+k})/\sigma_f^2$, where $Cov(e_{t+k}, F_{t+k})$ is the covariance of e_{t+k}, the trader's terminal wealth at time $t+k$ from all sources other than the futures under consideration, and F_{t+k}. However, the hedging literature has largely ignored the speculative demand and concentrated on the risk-minimizing hedge, i.e. point M in figure 9.1.

Duffie (1989, pp 214-215) has proposed two reasons for focusing on the risk-minimizing hedge. First, the expected speculative gain may be difficult to estimate. Second, given the spot position, the speculative position depends on each trader's risk aversion parameter (ξ) and so will differ from trader to trader, while the risk-minimizing position need not. Benninga, Eldor & Zilcha (1983, 1984) and Lence (1995) have provided a theoretical justification for the use of the minimum risk hedge ratio that does not require the trader to be highly risk averse (i.e. have a very large value of ξ). They investigated the consequences of assuming that the current futures price is an unbiased predictor of the spot price at delivery, i.e. time T. Thus, it is assumed that $F_t=E[S_T]$, $F_{t+k}=E[S_T]$, and so $F_t=E[F_{t+k}]$. (This assumption conflicts with the notion of a risk premium and normal backwardation, see chapter 6.18.) Given this unbiasedness assumption, and assuming that F_{t+k} and ε_{t+k} are independently distributed, where $S_{t+k}=a+bF_{t+k}+\varepsilon_{t+k}$, then $X_f E[F_{t+k}-F_t] = 0$, and so $E[P_{t+k}] = X_s E[S_{t+k}-S_t+D^*_{t+k}]$. Therefore, the expected profit on the portfolio is independent of the hedging decision. This removes speculation from the objective function, leaving only risk minimisation. In consequence, the portfolio problem has collapsed to finding the risk-minimizing hedge ratio.

The risk-minimizing value of b (i.e. point M) is found by differentiating $Var(P_{t+k})$ with respect to b, and setting the result equal to zero. This gives $\delta Var(P_{t+k})/\delta b = 2bX_s^2\sigma_f^2 - 2\sigma_{fs}X_s^2 = 0$, and so the risk-minimizing hedge ratio is :-

$$b = \sigma_{fs}/\sigma_f^2$$

which is independent of the risk aversion parameter, ξ, Kahl (1983). As the hedge ratio departs from b the risk of the hedged position will rise, as shown in figure 9.2

The equation for the risk-minimizing hedge ratio shows that, apart from a hedge which is terminated at delivery, this ratio is unity only if $\sigma_{fs} = \sigma_f^2$, and there is no reason to expect this to be the case. Since $\sigma_{fs} = \rho_{fs}\sigma_s\sigma_f$ (where ρ_{fs} is the correlation between S_{t+k} and F_{t+k}), the risk-minimizing hedge ratio can be rewritten as $b = \rho_{fs}(\sigma_s/\sigma_f)$. The value of b is seen to be determined by the closeness of the correlation between spot and futures prices at the horizon and the standard deviation of the spot price at the horizon, relative to that of the futures price. The position in futures contracts required by a risk-minimizing hedge is $-X_s b$, i.e. the number of units of the spot asset multiplied by the hedge ratio, where the minus sign indicates a short position. Substituting $b = \sigma_{fs}/\sigma_f^2$ into the expression for $Var(P_{t+k})$ gives an equation for the risk of the profit from the risk-minimizing hedge, i.e. minimum $Var(P_{t+k}) = X_s^2 \sigma_s^2 (1-\rho_{fs}^2)$. Since the slope coefficient of an ordinary least squares (OLS) regression of S_t on F_t is given by σ_{fs}/σ_f^2, regression provides an obvious way to estimate risk-minimizing hedge ratios in practice, and this will be discussed in more detail later in this chapter.

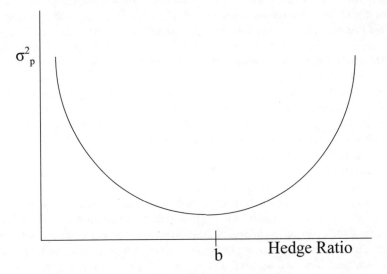

Figure 9.2: The Hedge Ratio and Risk

Example. The Dolphin Company wishes to minimize the risk of its well diversified share portfolio (with weights equal to the FTSE 100) between now (2nd July) and 5th September. The current market value of this portfolio is £65 million, while the value of the FTSE 100 index on 2nd July is 2,600. This means the current value of the portfolio is equal to the current price of 65,000,000/(2,600×25) = 1,000 'units' of the index, where a unit of the index is the basket of shares underlying one index futures contract (i.e. $X_S = 1,000$). Dolphin's finance director, Max Bialystock, expects the correlation between the value of one thousandth of his portfolio (i.e. one unit of the index) and the price of the September FTSE 100 futures contract on 5th September to be +0.8, while the price variances on that day will be £4,900 and £10,000 respectively. The risk-minimizing hedge ratio is given by $b = \sigma_{fs}/\sigma_f^2$ $= \rho_{fs}\sigma_s/\sigma_f = (0.8\times70)/100 = 0.56$. Thus, Max should take a short position of

1,000×0.56 = 560 FTSE 100 contracts.

It is important to realize that the variances and covariances used in determining the risk-minimizing hedge ratio are determined by the risks at the time the hedge is lifted, e.g. time $t+k$. The risks when the hedge is initiated are irrelevant. If σ_f^2 and σ_{fs} are constant over time, the date when the hedge is ended is unimportant when choosing the hedge ratio. However, since basis risk is present before delivery and will drop to zero by the delivery date, it is clear that basis risk must change over the life of a futures contract. The Samuelson hypothesis is that the price volatility of a futures contract (i.e. σ_f^2) increases as delivery approaches, see chapter 7.2.1. Castelino & Francis (1982) have produced both theoretical and empirical evidence that basis risk declines as delivery approaches (see chapter 6.4). If this is correct, the risk-minimizing hedge ratio depends on the maturity of the contract when the hedge is ended, but not on the maturity of the contract when the hedge is initiated. As the date when the hedge is lifted becomes closer to the delivery date, the risk-minimizing hedge ratio increases towards one, Castelino (1992).

There is a different reason why the risk-minimizing hedge ratio will change with the maturity of the future at the end of the hedge. If there is no basis risk and the no-arbitrage condition applies at all times, the risk-minimizing hedge ratio is $b = 1/(1+r_{k,T})$, where $r_{k,T}$ is the interest rate from the date the hedge ends (k) until the delivery date of the future (T), Merrick (1988b), Herbst, Kare & Marshall (1993). If the daily interest rate (i) is constant during this period, $b = 1/(1+i)^{T-k}$. This hedge ratio clearly varies with the maturity of the future when the hedge ends (that is time $T-k$). As the gap between the end of the hedge and delivery ($T-k$) gets shorter, so the risk-minimizing hedge ratio rises towards one.

Lien (1992b) has shown that, if the spot and futures prices are assumed to be cointegrated, and any maturity and interest rate effects are ignored, the risk-minimizing hedge ratio for a one period hedge will usually be smaller than that for a multi-period hedge. Thus, the risk-minimizing hedge ratio is not independent of the length of time for which the hedge will be held, and becomes larger as the duration of the hedge lengthens. This is because the assumption of cointegration implies that differences between the spot and futures prices follow an autoregressive process. In consequence, futures and spot prices are correlated over time, and the risk (and hence the risk-minimizing hedge ratio) of a multi-period hedge is affected by these correlations. Over a short period the spot and futures prices may diverge, but in the long run they are linked by an arbitrage relationship, and so will be highly correlated. That cointegration leads to risk-minimizing hedge ratios that increase towards one as hedge duration increases, is also shown by Geppert (1995).

The variance of the profit on a hedged position was initially stated in terms of price changes rather than price levels and, if desired, it is possible to express the risk-minimizing hedge ratio using price changes, i.e. $b = \sigma_{\Delta s \Delta f}/\sigma_{\Delta f}^2$, where $\sigma_{\Delta s \Delta f}$ is the covariance between spot and futures price changes over the period of the hedge, and $\sigma_{\Delta f}^2$ is the variance of futures price changes over the period of the hedge. The hedge ratio computed using price changes over the period of the hedge is equivalent to the use of spot and futures price levels when the hedge is lifted as $\sigma_{\Delta s \Delta f} = \sigma_{sf}$ and $\sigma_{\Delta f}^2 = \sigma_f^2$ because the opening spot and futures values are certain.

The hedging problem can also be restated in terms of share returns and proportionate changes in futures prices, Brown (1985), Chance (1991) and Duffie (1989, p. 243),. Letting $r = (S_{t+k} - S_t + D^*_{t+k})/S_t$ and $q = (F_{t+k} - F_t)/F_t$, it can be shown that the risk-minimizing hedge ratio is given by $b = (S_t/F_t) \times (\sigma_{qr}/\sigma_q^2)$, where σ_{qr} is the covariance of r and q, and σ_q^2 is the variance of q. (If the 'return' on futures is redefined as $Q = (F_{t+k} - F_t)/S_t$, then $b = \sigma_Q/\sigma_Q^2$, Figlewski, 1984a, 1985b.) If log returns are used, an assumption concerning the distribution of spot and futures returns is required; while the risk minimizing formula becomes considerably more complicated, Terry (2005).

Chang, Chang & Fang (1996) derived the risk-minimizing hedge ratio using different assumptions from those used above. They assumed that the spot and futures prices and the basis exhibit unexpected jumps, that the frequency of these jumps in prices and the basis varies over time, and that the basis is mean-reverting. The resulting formula is considerably more complex than $b = \sigma_{fs}/\sigma_f^2$, and the results of an empirical test of a simplified version of this hedge ratio are reported chapter 9.14.

9.3 Alternative Hedge Ratios

Rather than assume that the objective of hedging is risk minimisation, a number of authors have used a variety of other objectives, all of which introduce expected returns in some way.

1. Howard & D'Antonio (1984, 1987) (and also Nelson & Collins, 1985, Chen, Lee & Shrestha, 2003) have derived an alternative to the risk-minimizing hedge ratio, based on rates of return for situations where the spot position is fixed (see Yau, Savanayana & Schneeweis, 1992). This relies on the assumption that the trader's objective is to maximize Sharpe's reward-to-variability ratio, Sharpe (1966), but applied to a portfolio of shares and futures, see figure 9.3. This is defined as $(p-c)/\sigma_p$, where p is the return over the period t to $t+k$ on the hedged portfolio, so that $p = (X_s S_t r + X_f F_t q)/X_s S_t$, c is the risk free rate of interest and σ_p is the variance of p. This can be shown to give the hedge ratio $b^* = (S_t/F_t) \times (\sigma_r(\lambda - \rho_{pr})/\sigma_q(1 - \lambda\rho_{pr}))$, where $\lambda = q\sigma_r/\sigma_q(r-c)$, σ_r^2 is the variance of r, and ρ_{pr} is the correlation between r and p. This more complicated hedge ratio depends on the expected values of q, r and c; and on σ_q, σ_r and ρ_{pr}, as well as S_t and F_t, but it does not directly involve the covariance term, σ_{qr}.

2. Hammer (1988) has derived a hedge ratio for the case when the trader wishes to maximize the ratio of the expected return on the hedged portfolio to its variance (i.e. p/σ_p^2), and applied it to currencies.

3. Chang & Fang (1990) (see also Chang, Chang, Loo & Fang, 1991) have derived a utility-maximizing hedge ratio when there is marking to the market and stochastic interest rates. The resulting equation requires the estimation of fifteen parameters, and so is difficult to apply in practice.

4. The portfolio theoretic approach to hedging is, in effect, goal programming with

two goals: risk and return. Sharda & Musser (1986) have extended this, and proposed a goal programming model of hedging with four goals: risk, transactions costs, margin payments and margin opportunity costs.

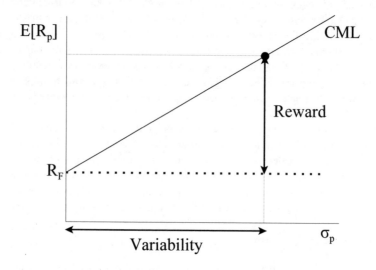

Figure 9.3: Sharpe's Reward to Variability Ratio

5. Wu, Sheu & Lee (1990) have proposed that the objective of hedging is to create a portfolio with a risk that is no larger than some tolerable level, and have devised an iterative procedure for calculating the corresponding hedge ratio.

6. Lien & Tse (1998, 2002) (see also Chen, Lee & Shrestha, 2003) suggested measuring risk using the lower partial moment. This is based on deviations below some target return, raised to the integer power n, where n depends on the investor's risk aversion.

7. Hemler & Longstaff (1991) proposed the use of a general equilibrium model to price index futures, see chapter 5.27. In this model the price of the index future depends on the volatility of stock market returns, and so, even if the objective is risk-minimisation, the hedge ratio may well be different from that derived above using the no-arbitrage condition.

8. Cheung, Kwan & Yip (1990) proposed the use of Gini's mean difference as a measure of risk. This measure is consistent with first and second degree stochastic dominance, and avoids any reliance on normality or mean-variance utility functions. Subsequently, Hodgson & Okunev (1992), Kolb & Okunev (1992, 1993), Shalit (1995), Chen, Lee & Shrestha (2003) and Lien & Tse (2002) suggested the use of the extended mean Gini coefficient to measure risk when calculating hedge ratios.

9. Howard & D'Antonio (1994) recognize that hedging involves two types of cost: the fixed transactions costs of the hedging trades, and the reduction in expected return on

the hedged portfolio associated with the reduction in risk. Assuming no mispricings, and ignoring futures margins, they show that as the degree of risk reduction (measured by the percentage reduction in the standard deviation of returns) increases, the cost of hedging increases at an increasing rate. They suggest that the rapidly increasing cost will lead to hedging stopping before the risk-minimizing hedge is reached. Assuming that the CAPM is valid, and that hedging will occur until the risk-return trade-off is equal to the market price of risk, Howard & D'Antonio are able to specify an optimal hedge ratio where the benefits of further hedging are outweighed by the costs. This optimal hedge ratio increases as the correlation between spot and futures returns increases, and the correlation between spot and market portfolio returns decreases.

These alternative hedge ratios indicate that, once the hedger moves away from risk-minimisation (where risk is measured using the variance), a large number of possibilities open up. Since these hedge ratios involve both risk and return, or more complex ways of computing risk, they are generally more complicated than the simple minimisation of risk. So far, none of these alternative hedge ratios have achieved much popularity.

9.4 Choice of Futures Contract and Cross Hedging

In order to create a hedge, the trader must select a particular futures contract for use in offsetting the initial risk. The objective of this choice is generally taken to be to select that futures contract which produces a hedged position with the lowest risk. If a future exists on the spot asset whose risk is to be hedged, it is usually best to use this future in the hedge. Often there is no futures market in the asset whose risk it is desired to remove. Therefore, hedgers use that future whose price has the highest correlation (positive or negative) with the spot price of the asset concerned. This cross hedging introduces cross hedging risk, i.e. the risk that the spot price of the asset whose future is being used and the spot price of the asset concerned do not move together exactly. Because there is a difference between the spot asset and the asset underlying the futures contract used in the hedge, cross hedging risk, unlike basis risk, does not tend to zero at delivery. While cross hedging provides an extra source of risk in addition to basis (and dividend) risk, the risk-minimizing hedge ratio for a cross hedge is still given by $b = \sigma_{fs}/\sigma_f^2$. The composition of share portfolios will not usually correspond exactly to that of an index underlying an index future, and may differ substantially. Therefore, hedging share portfolios will generally involve a cross hedge. In this case the cross hedging risk is the unsystematic risk of the share portfolio.

When cross hedging, there will probably be a difference in the units of measurement between the asset being hedged and the asset underlying the futures contract used in the hedge. In this case, the size of the hedge ratio becomes arbitrary, and depends on the relative units chosen to measure the spot asset (X_s) and the futures contract (X_f). This is not a problem, although it can lead to unusual hedge ratios.

Example. Lorenzo St Du Bois owns shares in only one company, Springtime Productions, and these are currently worth £10 million. He wishes to hedge the risk of this share holding between now and 5th September using FTSE 100 index futures. Treating his share holding as a single entity (i.e. X_S), Lorenzo estimates that the correlation between the total value of his share holding and the price of the September contract on 5th September is +0.75, while the price variances on that day are £144 million for the entire share holding and £10,000 for one FTSE 100 future. Therefore, the risk-minimizing hedge ratio is $b = \sigma_{fs}/\sigma_f^2 = \rho_{fs}\sigma_s/\sigma_f = (0.75\times12,000)/100 = 90$. Since Lorenzo holds one unit of the share holding in Springtime, he should sell ($X_s b = 1\times90$) ninety FTSE 100 September contracts, which correspond to shares with a current nominal value of $90\times2,600\times25 = £5.85$ million, where the current spot value of the FTSE 100 index is 2,600.

The same result could have been reached using a different definition of the units of Lorenzo's investment in shares. The current value of the share holding corresponds to the spot equivalent of $10,000,000/(2,600\times25) = 153.84615$ FTSE 100 futures contracts (i.e. $X_s = 153.84615$). Lorenzo's estimate of the variance of one unit of his share holding (i.e. shares with a current price of $10,000,000/153.84615 = £65,000$) is £6,084. Therefore $b = \sigma_{fs}/\sigma_f^2 = \rho_{fs}\sigma_s/\sigma_f = (0.75\times78)/100 = 0.585$, and so Lorenzo should take a short position in FTSE 100 September contracts of $153.84615\times0.585 = 90$ contracts.

The convention used in defining X_s (the number of units of the spot asset) is to calculate the total spot value of the assets to be hedged, divided by the spot price of the assets underlying one futures contract, e.g. $10,000,000/(2,600\times25) = 153.84615$. The value of X_f is simply the number of futures contracts.

Not only must the hedger select a future for use in the hedge, he or she must also choose a particular delivery date (i.e. maturity). The choice of future and delivery date are interrelated and, in effect, each available futures contract is a rival to every other futures contract for use in the hedge. Because basis risk is thought to decline as delivery approaches, the risk of the hedge may be minimized by using the contract whose delivery date is the first following the planned end of the hedge, or by using the nearby contract, which is then rolled over until the hedge is ended. When a position is rolled over, the open position in the near contract is liquidated and, simultaneously, a new position of equivalent size and direction is opened in a far contract. This process can be repeated for as long as the hedged position is desired.

Example 1. Leo Bloom wishes to hedge the risk of his UK share portfolio between 5th July and 5th September. Since at this time there is only one index future on UK shares (the FTSE 100 index future) the only choice Leo has to make is which available contract to use (September, December or March). Since it is likely that the September contract will be the most liquid and have the lowest basis risk on 5th September, Leo chooses to use a short position in the September FTSE 100 futures contract.

Example 2. Franz Liebkind wishes to hedge the risk of a portfolio of US shares between 5th September and 5th April the following year. There are a number of US index futures from which to choose (e.g. S&P500, NYSE Composite, MMI and Value Line Arithmetic). In addition, since the hedge will last for seven months, the choice of contract is not straightforward (e.g. using the near contract will require an initial position in the September contract of the chosen index future, which is then rolled over on chosen dates into the December, March and June contracts). The choice of hedging strategy will depend on the forecast risk of the hedged positions, and on the transactions costs of rolling the hedge forwards.

Shalen (1989) has considered the issue of the choice of maturity for use in a hedge. Since hedging is the main motive for trading futures and most volume occurs in the near contract; this implies that most hedging is in the near contract. As mentioned earlier in this chapter, if there is no dividend or interest rate risk and the no-arbitrage condition applies at all times, the risk-minimizing hedge ratio is $1/(1+r_{k,T})$. In which case the choice of maturity is arbitrary. Because the hedge ratio rises as $(T-k)$ (the time period from the end of the hedge to the delivery of the future) decreases, if hedgers choose at random the maturity of the contracts they use, the volume of trading in near contracts will tend to be slightly larger than in far contracts.

Example. On 1st October Hudson Hawk, the manager of the Belsay Fund, wants a hedge for one month, and must choose between the near contract that expires on 31st December and the far contract that expires on 30th June the following year. The interest rate is 10% per annum (or 0.0261% per day), and there is no basis risk. For the December contract the risk-minimizing hedge ratio is $1/1.000261^{61} = 0.9842$, and for the June contract it is $1/1.000261^{243} = 0.9386$. Thus, if Hudson chooses to use the December rather than the June contract, the volume he must trade will be 4.9% higher.

This example demonstrates that the change in the hedge ratio due to the decrease in $(T-k)$ is insufficient to explain the large differences in volume between the near and far contracts noted in chapter 3 of Sutcliffe (1997). Therefore the preference for near contracts must be due to the presence of basis risk.

If the only source of basis risk is dividend uncertainty, since dividend risk declines as delivery approaches, a hedger will tend to choose the contract that is the next to expire after the horizon date of the hedge. Some traders may have the freedom to quickly vary their demand for hedging, and this flexibility gives these traders a fairly short time horizon for their hedges. Such hedgers will tend to use the near contract. If the only source of basis risk is stochastic interest rates, as delivery approaches it is likely that risk declines. Therefore, hedgers will choose to use the contract that expires immediately after the horizon date of their hedge. This will again tend to produce hedging in the near contract. Thus, there are three factors tending to favour hedging in the near contract; the higher risk-minimizing hedge ratio, and the lower dividend and interest rate risk for near contracts for hedgers with a short time horizon. Once a dominance by a particular maturity is established, it will tend to be reinforced by a desire to trade in the most liquid delivery months.

Some hedgers, with a long term commitment, may wish to hedge using an index futures contract with a delivery date several years away. This would remove the necessity to repeatedly rollover the position (saving on transactions costs). It would also eliminate the price risk when closing out a position in one delivery date and opening a position in another. This risk may occur because the prices of the futures concerned may deviate from the no-arbitrage condition, or (for a contract with physical delivery) someone has cornered the market. However, index futures contracts with a long life do not exist. This is probably because the demand for long hedges is low (which implies low liquidity in a market for such futures), and because the increases in transactions costs and price risk from rolling the hedge forwards are small, Gardner (1989).

9.5 Measuring Hedge Effectiveness

The effectiveness of a risk-minimizing hedge (E) is measured as the reduction in the variance of profits due to the hedge, i.e. the variance of profits without the hedge [$Var(U)$] less the variance of profits with the hedge [$Var(P)$], expressed as a proportion of the variance of profits without the hedge [$Var(U)$], Ederington (1979). Thus $E = [Var(U) - Var(P)]/Var(U)$, where $Var(U) = X_s^2 \sigma_s^2$ and $Var(P) = X_s^2 \{\sigma_s^2 + b^2\sigma_f^2 - 2b\sigma_{fs}\}$. Since $b = \sigma_{fs}/\sigma_f^2$, it can be shown that $E = \sigma_{fs}^2/\sigma_f^2\sigma_s^2$, and so:-

$$E = \rho_{fs}^2$$

i.e. the square of the correlation between S_{t+k} and F_{t+k}. This squared correlation can be estimated by the R^2 (or coefficient of determination) of the regression equation $S_t = a + bF_t + \varepsilon_t$. In this regression equation the value of the spot price at time t is given by a constant (a) plus a slope coefficient (b) times the price of the future at time t (F_t), plus a disturbance term (ε_t). For example, given Max Bialystock's estimate of ρ_{fs} as 0.8, $E = 0.64$, while the value of E for Lorenzo St Du Bois is $0.75^2 = 0.5625$. Note that the R^2 from the regression $(S_{t+k} - S_t) = a + b(F_{t+k} - F_t) + \varepsilon_t$ corresponds to a different definition of E, i.e. $E = [Var(\Delta U) - Var(\Delta P)]/Var(\Delta U)$, where $Var(\Delta U) = X_s^2\sigma_{\Delta s}^2$ and $Var(\Delta P) = X_s^2\{\sigma_{\Delta s}^2 + b^2\sigma_{\Delta f}^2 - 2b\sigma_{\Delta s\Delta f}\}$.

Lindahl (1989, 1990) has pointed out that E measures the *proportionate* reduction in risk. Therefore, while E can be used to compare the effectiveness of different futures contracts in hedging a particular spot asset held until a particular date, other comparisons are inappropriate, e.g. different spot positions and different futures contracts. However, such comparisons are often made, and care must be exercised in their interpretation.

Lien (2005a) considered the widespread use of E to compare the in-sample performance of OLS hedge ratios with hedge ratios estimated using some other technique. He showed that OLS hedge ratios have a superior E because they choose the hedge ratio which minimizes the unconditional variance of the hedged portfolio, and so cannot be beaten. For out-of-sample hedging effectiveness OLS can be beaten, but only if the in-sample size is large, the out-of-sample size is small, or there is a structural change between the in and out-of-sample periods. E relies on the unconditional variance while, as argued above, hedge ratios should be chosen to minimize the conditional variance. Therefore, E is unsuitable for measuring the hedging effectiveness of non-bivariate OLS hedge ratios. If another hedge ratio is used, E can be redefined using the conditional variance from a correctly specified econometric model.

The effectiveness measure E is only appropriate for risk-minimizing OLS hedges. Once other objectives are introduced, a wide variety of effectiveness measures become possible and the choice between such measures depends, in part, on the objectives of the user. Gjerde (1987) proposed a simple effectiveness measure based on returns, rather than variances. The ex ante version of his measure is the maximum expected return on a hedged portfolio with the same risk as the spot asset, divided by the expected return on the spot asset. (A similar measure was used by Board & Sutcliffe, 1991.) Howard & D'Antonio (1987) have developed a different measure of hedging effectiveness which corresponds to their assumption that hedgers maximize $(p-c)/\sigma_p$ which is, in effect, a reward to variability ratio. Their effectiveness measure is $(c+\Theta\sigma_r-r)/\sigma_r$, where c is the risk free rate of interest, r is the expected spot return, σ_r is the standard deviation of spot returns, and Θ is the slope of the line from the risk free asset to the hedged position, in standard deviation-return space. The Howard & D'Antonio measure has been simplified by Kuo & Chen (1995), while Satyanarayan (1998) showed that the second order conditions are less restrictive that previously thought. The Howard & D'Antonio measure has been extended to the case of multiple spot assets and futures markets by Lien (1993a).

Hammer (1990) has also proposed an effectiveness measure based around a risk-return ratio, i.e. $E[Q]\sigma_r^2/(E[r]\sigma_Q^2(C_p-2b))$, where C_p is the hedge ratio and the other terms are as previously defined. Chang & Fang (1990) (see also Chang, Chang, Loo & Fang, 1991) have also derived an effectiveness measure based on reward to variability, corresponding to their hedge ratio.

Hsin, Kuo & Lee (1994) developed a measure of hedging effectiveness for utility maximizing hedgers with a mean-variance utility function. Their measure is the certainty equivalent returns of the hedged portfolio, less the certainty equivalent returns of the spot position. This can accommodate situations where the excess returns on the spot position are negative.

Lindahl (1991) argued that effectiveness measures which use deviations from the returns on the spot asset (e.g. Howard & D'Antonio, 1987) are unsuitable for appraising share portfolio hedges. If the hedge of a share portfolio is perfect, making the risk-minimizing hedge ratio unity and the hedged portfolio riskless, it follows from the CAPM that the rate of return on the hedged portfolio must be the risk free rate. Therefore, Lindahl proposed that the benchmark for the returns on a fully hedged (i.e. $b = 1$) share portfolio be the risk free rate. She put forward a two part effectiveness measure: $E[\Omega_t]$ and $Var(\Omega_t)$, where Ω_t is the return on the fully hedged portfolio for period t less the risk free interest rate for period t. The lower the values of the mean and variance of Ω_t, the better is the hedge. If the risk free rate of interest is constant, $Var(\Omega_t)$ is the variance of returns on the hedged portfolio. When the hedge ratio is not unity, the risk free rate is replaced by the weighted sum of the risk free rate (R_F) and the return on the spot portfolio (R_S), i.e. $(b \times R_F)+(1-b)R_S$.

Instead of relying on means and variances to measure effectiveness, Cheung, Kwan & Yip (1990) have suggested the use of Gini's mean difference. It is computed as the covariance between P_i and $g(P_i)$, where $g(P_i)$ denotes the probability density function of P_i, and P_i is the ith element of the probability distribution of profit from the hedged position.

The effectiveness measures considered so far have been concerned with hedging a single spot asset using a particular futures contract. However, the trader may hold a portfolio of both spot assets and futures contracts, and the effectiveness of a futures contract ceases to be a well defined concept for two reasons. First, as the spot asset is no longer homogeneous, the hedging effectiveness of a futures contract depends on the nature of the spot portfolio being hedged, and this leads to an infinite number of effectiveness measures (one for each different spot portfolio). Second, if a number of different futures contracts are being used in a composite hedge (see chapter 9.8), allocating the total risk reduction amongst the contributing futures is problematic. Lien (1990) suggests that the first problem can be solved by considering all possible sets of portfolio weights for the spot assets (ignoring the possibility of new spot assets entering the portfolio), and calculating the maximum and minimum values of E. To deal with the second problem, Lien proposes that attention be focused on the marginal contribution of the future under consideration to risk reduction. Thus, when calculating E, the variance of the unhedged portfolio is replaced by the variance of the portfolio hedged using all futures contracts except that under consideration. When the spot portfolio consists of more than one asset, the maximum and minimum values of E are again computed.

If the spot-futures correlation changes over time, the effectiveness measure for a previous period will be a biased estimate of the effectiveness of a new hedged position, Daigler (1993). Since $b = \sigma_{fs}/\sigma_f^2 = \rho_{fs}\sigma_s/\sigma_f$, and $E = \rho_{fs}^2$, it follows that this bias is given by $E_2 - E_1 = (b_2^2 - b_1^2) \times (\sigma_f^2/\sigma_s^2)$. The bias can be positive or negative, and it increases in size as the change in b becomes larger.

Brailsford, Corrigan & Heaney (2001) compared three measures of hedging effectiveness on the same set of data - daily observations on the SPI for 1990-9. The standard deviation, Howard and D'Antonio (1989) and Lindahl (1991) measures gave different rankings of hedging effectiveness, which is not surprising as they are based on different objectives.

9.6 Restatement of the Hedge Ratio Using Betas

The analysis of the risk-minimizing hedge ratio will now switch from using covariances, e.g. σ_{fs} or σ_{is}, to using beta values from the CAPM (where beta is calculated with respect to the market portfolio) with which traders may be more familiar, Merrick (1990, pp 157-158). For example, they may know the beta value of their share portfolio, and wish to control it using index futures (which is discussed more fully in chapter 10). Using the CAPM, the expected rate of return on the share portfolio can be stated as $E[r] = R_F + (E[R_M] - R_F)\beta$, where $r = (S_{t+k} - S_t + D^*_{t+k})/S_t$, β is the beta value of the portfolio with respect to the market portfolio, R_F is the risk free rate of interest, and R_M is the return on the market portfolio. If the return on the future is defined as $Q = (F_{t+k}-F_t)/S_t$ (rather than $q = (F_{t+k}-F_t)/F_t$, as in chapter 9.2), then $E[Q] = (E[R_M]-R_F)\beta_F$, where β_F is the beta value of the index future with respect to the market portfolio. This definition of β_F does not allow for any maturity effects. Note that the risk-free term, R_F, does not appear as a separate term because there is no capital invested in a futures contract. It follows that $E[r] = R_F + E[Q]\beta/\beta_F$, and the risk-minimizing hedge ratio for a share portfolio $(b = \sigma_{Qr}/\sigma_Q^2)$, is equivalent to:-

$$b = \beta/\beta_F$$

When hedging a share portfolio, it is possible to distinguish between the value of the spot asset underlying the index future (i.e. the index, I_t) and the price of a unit of the share portfolio (S_t), and this permits a restatement of the risk-minimizing hedge ratio, b. Since $F_{t+k} \equiv I_{t+k}+F_{t+k}-I_{t+k} \equiv I_{t+k}+B_{t+k}$, where B_{t+k} is the basis at time $t+k$, the risk-minimizing hedge ratio can be rewritten as $b = (\sigma_{is}+\sigma_{sb})/(\sigma_i^2+\sigma_b^2+2\sigma_{bi})$, where σ_{is}, σ_{sb} and σ_{bi} are the covariances between the spot price and the index, the spot price and the basis and the index and the basis respectively, and σ_i^2 and σ_b^2 are the variances of the index and the basis. If the hedge ends at the same time as the delivery of the index future there is no basis risk (although cross-hedging risk remains) and $\sigma_{sb} = \sigma_{bi} = \sigma_b^2 = 0$. In which case, $b = \sigma_{is}/\sigma_i^2$ and the risk-minimizing hedge ratio can be estimated by β, Figlewski (1984a, 1985b). Therefore, when there is no basis risk the portfolio's beta value from the CAPM is equal to the risk-minimizing hedge ratio; and the aim of the hedge is to remove the portfolio's systematic risk. If the index and the spot portfolios are identical, and there is no basis risk, then $\sigma_{is} = \sigma_i^2$, and $\beta=1$.

This analysis can also be conducted in terms of β_w (the beta value of the futures contract with respect to the share portfolio), where β_w is defined in the equation $E[Q] = (E[r]-R_F)\beta_w$, Watsham (1992). If desired, the analysis can also be restated using $q = (F_{t+k}-F_t)/F_t$ as the definition of futures returns. In this case, if $E[q] = (E[R_M]-R_F)\beta_{Fq}$, then $E[r] = R_F+E[q]\beta/\beta_{Fq}$, and the risk-minimizing hedge ratio for a share portfolio is $b = (S_t/F_t)\times(\sigma_{qr}/\sigma_q^2) = (S_t/F_t)\times(\beta/\beta_{Fq})$, Kolb (1988, appendix to ch.9, pp. 310-311), Peters (1986), Fabozzi & Peters (1989).

There have been a small number of empirical studies of the beta value of index futures, with respect to the market portfolio.

USA.　　　　　Edwards & Ma (1992, pp 250-251) used daily data from January 1985 to March 1989 to fit the equation $R_{Mt} = \alpha+\theta q_t+\varepsilon_t$. They used two index futures (S&P500 and NYSE Composite) to measure q_t, and seven market indices (DJIA, S&P500, NYSE Composite, AMEX, NASDAQ, VLA and the Wiltshire 5000) to measure R_{Mt}. The fourteen estimates of θ ranged from 0.47 to 0.80. Since the estimated equation can be rewritten as $q_t = (R_{Mt}-\alpha)/\theta-\varepsilon_t/\theta$, this implies estimates of β_{Fq} of between 1.25 and 2.13.

Bessembinder (1992) used monthly prices from May 1982 to December 1989 on the S&P500 and VLCI index futures and the monthly values of the CRSP value weighted market index to fit the regression equation $q_t = \alpha+\theta R_{Mt}+\varepsilon_t$. The estimated value of β for S&P500 futures was 1.005, while the estimate of beta for the VLCI was 1.1.

UK.　　　　　Antoniou & Holmes (1994) used weekly data to fit the equation q_t

$= \alpha + (R_{Mt} - R_F)\beta_{Fq} + \varepsilon_t$, where q_t represents logarithmic returns over 7 day periods (Wednesday to Wednesday) on FTSE 100 futures and R_{Mt} is logarithmic weekly returns on the FT-A index for the period 1985 to 1990, excluding dividends. For the pre-crash period $\alpha = 0$ and $\beta_{Fq} = 1$, and during the post-crash period $\alpha = 0.002$ (or 0.2% excess return per week) and $\beta_{Fq} = 1.1$. This means that after the crash, not only did the systematic risk of FTSE 100 futures increase, but they earned excess returns. Since the estimates of β_{Fq} are generally different from one, this adjustment is worthwhile.

Example 1. The GoGo Fund has a share portfolio which is worth £29.24 million and has a beta value of 2.2 with respect to the market portfolio. The fund wishes to hedge the risk of this portfolio between now and 5th April. The beta value of the June FTSE 100 contract is $\beta_F = 1.1$. The current spot price on 4th January of the shares underlying the FTSE 100 is $2{,}720 \times 25 = £68{,}000$. Therefore the risk-minimizing hedge ratio is $(2.2/1.1) = 2$, and the Fund should trade $(29{,}240{,}000 /68{,}000) \times 2 = 860$ contracts short.

Example 2. Itchen Ltd. has a share portfolio currently worth £20.7 million and a beta value of 1.3 with respect to the market portfolio. Itchen desires to hedge the risk of this portfolio until 31st December. The risk-minimizing hedge ratio is simply 1.3. If the current price of the basket of shares underlying the FTSE 100 index is $2{,}760 \times 25 = £69{,}000$, then Itchen should sell short $(2{,}070{,}000/69{,}000) \times 1.3 = 39$ contracts.

9.7 Hedging Many Different Risky Positions

A trader may have a number of risky positions in different spot assets (e.g. different shares), and wish to hedge all of them using the same futures contract. If the objective is to find the risk-minimizing hedge, the hedge for each risky asset can be computed separately, and the required trade in the futures contract is the sum of the risk-minimizing hedges for the individual assets. This additive result follows directly from the fact that the hedge ratio depends on a covariance, and covariances are themselves additive. The covariance between the value of a unit of a portfolio of shares and the price of a futures contract (σ_{fs}) can be restated in terms of the covariances of the individual shares with the future's price, i.e. $\sigma_{fs} = w_1\sigma_{1f} + w_2\sigma_{2f} + \ldots + w_n\sigma_{nf}$, where the w_i terms are market value weights (which sum to one) and the σ_{if} terms are the covariances between the current value of a unit of share i and the price of a futures contract on day $t+k$. Therefore, the risk-minimizing hedge ratio for the share portfolio can be rewritten as $b = w_1\sigma_{1f}/\sigma_f^2 + w_2\sigma_{2f}/\sigma_f^2 + \ldots + w_n\sigma_{nf}/\sigma_f^2 = \Sigma b_i w_i$, where b_i is the risk-minimizing hedge ratio for the ith spot asset (e.g. share). This shows that the weighted sum of the individual risk-minimizing hedge ratios gives the risk-minimizing hedge ratio for the portfolio.

Example. The Solent Company has a number of wholly owned subsidiaries, and each subsidiary has an investment in the shares of five to ten other companies. Luke Skywalker is appointed as treasurer of Solent, and decides to hedge the risk of these share holdings for the period between now and 5th September. One unit of each of these share portfolios corresponds to shares with a current value of 2,667×25 = £66,675, where the current value of the index is 2,667 (i.e. $S_t =$ £66,675). The estimated covariances between the price of one FTSE 100 September contract on 5th September and one unit of the shares in each portfolio are denoted by σ_{fs}, and listed in the table below. The variance of the price of the FTSE 100 September contract on 5th September is £5,000. The current value of the share portfolios held by each of the subsidiaries, together with the values of σ_{fs} are set out in table 9.1 This table also shows the computed weights (w_i), the risk-minimizing hedge ratios (b_i) and the aggregate hedge ratio ($\Sigma b_i w_i$).

Table 9.1: Data on the Share Portfolios of Solent Subsidiaries

Subsidiary	Current Value of the Portfolio	σ_{fs}	w_i	b_i	$w_i b_i$
Romsey	£10 million	£6,000	0.1	1.2	0.12
Hamble	£20 million	£5,000	0.2	1.0	0.20
Hythe	£30 million	£4,000	0.3	0.8	0.24
Eastleigh	£40 million	£3,000	0.4	0.6	0.24
Totals	£100 million	-	1.0	-	0.80

Thus, the aggregate hedge ratio is 0.8 and the required hedge is (100 million/66,675)×0.8 = 1200 contracts short.

9.8 Composite Hedges

So far the risk of a single spot asset has been hedged using a single future, but there is no need to restrict hedging in this way, Anderson & Danthine (1980, 1981). For example, a portfolio of US shares might be hedged using a combination of a number of different futures, e.g. S&P500, NYSE Composite, MMI and VLA index futures. There will be benefits from using such a composite hedge, in the form of a hedged position with lower risk, Marshall (1989, pp 214-216). Suppose a share portfolio is to be hedged using two different types of futures contracts (denoted v and w). The two risk-minimizing hedge ratios are $b_v = -X_v/X_s = (\sigma_{sv}\sigma_w^2 - \sigma_{sw}\sigma_{vw})/(\sigma_v^2\sigma_w^2 - \sigma_{vw}^2)$ and $b_w = -X_w/X_s = (\sigma_{sw}\sigma_v^2 - \sigma_{sv}\sigma_{vw})/(\sigma_v^2\sigma_w^2 - \sigma_{vw}^2)$, where b_v is the risk-minimizing hedge ratio for future v when used in conjunction with future w; σ_{vw}, σ_{sv} and σ_{sw} are the covariances between the prices at time $t+k$ of futures v and w, future v and the spot price, and future w and the spot price, respectively. The variance of the price of future v at time $t+k$ is denoted by σ_v^2, while the corresponding term for future w is σ_w^2. The terms for future w are similarly defined. Note that the covariance between the prices at time $t+k$ of the two futures (σ_{vw}) enters both hedge ratios, and that if this covariance is zero the formulae collapse back to the conventional hedge ratio for a single future. It is obvious that when a variety of futures contracts are used to hedge a particular spot position, the hedge ratios are considerably more complex than when a single contract is used. (They are equivalent to the formulae used to compute the coefficients of the multiple regression equation $S_{t+k} = a + b_v F_{v,(t+k)} + b_w F_{w,(t+k)} + \varepsilon_{t+k})$

Example. Jean Brodie, the manager of the Benwell Fund, wishes to hedge a portfolio of US stocks with a market value of $100 million using either S&P500 futures or NYSE Composite futures, or both. Jean estimates the following statistics for the day on which the hedge is planned to end. The correlations are: S&P500 and the portfolio 0.70, NYSE Composite and the portfolio 0.70, and the S&P500 and the NYSE Composite 0.90. The unit of measurement for defining the standard deviations (and hence the hedge ratio) is taken to be the spot price of the shares corresponding to the S&P500 index (i.e. $200,000), and so the portfolio to be hedged corresponds to $(100,000,000/200,000) = 500$ 'units'. The spot price of the shares corresponding to the NYSE Composite index is $120,000. The standard deviations are: S&P500 $6,000, NYSE Composite $3,000 and the portfolio $8,000. Since $\sigma_{ab} = \rho_{ab}\sigma_a\sigma_b$, the covariances per 'unit' are: S&P500 and the portfolio $33.6 million, S&P500 and NYSE Composite $16.2 million, and the NYSE Composite and the portfolio $16.8 million. Therefore, the various possible hedging strategies are as follows. (a) S&P500 alone: $b = \sigma_{fs}/\sigma_f^2 = 33.6/36 = 0.9333$, and so the hedge is $500 \times 0.9333 = 466.65$ S&P500 contracts short. (b) NYSE alone: $b = \sigma_{fs}/\sigma_f^2 = 16.8/9 = 1.8667$, and so the hedge is $500 \times 1.8667 = 933.3$ NYSE Composite contracts short. (c) Composite hedge using the S&P500 and the NYSE Composite: $b_{S\&P} = (33.6 \times 9 - 16.8 \times 16.2)/(36 \times 9 - 16.2^2) = 0.4912$; which implies the hedge is $500 \times 0.4912 = 245.6$ S&P500 contracts short; $b_{NYSE} = (16.8 \times 36 - 33.6 \times 16.2)/(36 \times 9 - 16.2^2) = 0.9825$, and so the hedge is $500 \times 0.9825 = 491.25$ NYSE Composite contracts short.

The variance of the hedged position using a single future is given by $X_s^2(\sigma_s^2 + b^2\sigma_f^2 - 2b\sigma_{fs})$, while the variance for a hedged position using two futures (v and w) is $X_s^2(\sigma_s^2 + b_v^2\sigma_v^2 + b_w^2\sigma_w^2 - 2b_v\sigma_{sv} - 2b_w\sigma_{sw} + 2b_vb_w\sigma_{vw})$. The standard deviation of the hedged position is $2.857 million for S&P500 futures alone, and $2.857 million for NYSE Composite futures alone. The composite hedge is less risky, and has an estimated standard deviation of $2.783 million.

9.9 Generalized Hedging

If the trader has a number of different spot positions to be hedged using a range of different futures contracts, there are $m \times n$ risk-minimizing hedge ratios for this general case of m spot assets and n futures contracts. The equation for calculating these $m \times n$ risk-minimizing hedge ratios is given in Anderson & Danthine (1980) and Lypny (1988). However, when dealing with multiple spot assets and futures contracts, the hedging problem can be viewed as the construction of a portfolio of spot and futures which gives the desired risk-return trade-off, Levy (1987) and Peterson & Leuthold (1987). This portfolio approach permits objectives other than pure risk-minimisation.

Instead of using complicated expressions for the $m \times n$ hedge ratios, quadratic programming can be used to solve the Markowitz portfolio model to give asset proportions in the same way as for portfolios of shares, except for three important differences. First, the usual model of hedging takes the spot positions as given, while the Markowitz model treats the position in every asset as variable. This difference can be overcome by including additional constraints in the model which restrict the size of the spot positions. Second, the feature that financial securities can only be traded in integer amounts is considerably more important for futures contracts than for shares, Duffie (1989, p. 227). In consequence, rounding the continuous solution may not be optimal, and the use of mixed integer quadratic programming to solve the portfolio problem may be necessary, Peterson & Leuthold (1987). Shanker (1993) showed that rounding is only inferior to quadratic integer programming when there are multiple spot and futures positions. An empirical study of foreign currencies found that, for small spot positions, rounding the continuous solution gave the wrong answer 45% of the time, and that allowance for futures indivisibilities substantially reduced the degree of risk reduction achieved by the hedge. Finally, futures can easily be sold short, and so no non-negativity conditions are required.

9.10 Tail Risk and Tailing the Hedge

Earlier in this chapter, when the risk-minimizing hedge ratio was considered, payments or receipts of variation margin were ignored in the computation of the profit on a hedged position. When marking to the market is recognized, there is an additional source of risk because the interest paid and received on the margin payments may not cancel out. Allowance for this 'tail risk' makes the derivation of the risk-minimizing hedge more complicated. A change in the futures price generates an immediate payment or receipt of variation margin. This sum of money must be borrowed or invested for the period until delivery. (For simplicity, it will be assumed that a common borrowing and lending rate applies to such payments, for example, the rate of interest on money in the trader's margin account.) Therefore, a change in the futures price between times t and $t+1$ does not change the cash flow at the end of the hedge (time $t+k$) by just $(F_{t+1}-F_t)$, but by $(F_{t+1}-F_t) \times (1+i)^{k-1}$, where i is the daily compound interest rate. (Note that interest is only paid or received for $k-1$ days.) Assuming that the interest rate over the life of the hedge is constant and that the dividends are known, the profit from the hedged position at time $t+k$ from holding the spot asset until $t+k$ and the hedged position for one day is $P_{t+k}^d = X_s[S_{t+1}-S_t+D^*_{t+k}-b(F_{t+1}-F_t) \times (1+i)^{k-1}]$. The resulting risk-minimizing hedge ratio is $b = (\sigma_{fs}/\sigma_f^2) \times (1/(1+i)^{k-1})$, where σ_{fs} is the covariance of the spot and futures prices at time $t+k$ and σ_f^2 is the variance of the futures price at time $t+k$. The daily tailing factor is:-

$$\varphi^d = 1/(1+i)^{k-1}$$

This tailing factor can also be derived by equating the cost of financing any payment of variation margin on the initial hedge position of N futures (less the receipt of variation margin on the tail hedge of n futures) to the profit received at delivery on the tail hedge. Thus $(N-n)(F_{t+1}-F_t)[(1+i)^{k-1}-1] = n(F_{t+1}-F_t)$, which can be rearranged as $(N-n)/N = 1/(1+i)^{k-1}$.

This tailing factor assumes the hedge is retailed daily, i.e. the size of the tail hedge is recomputed each day as k drops, (Duffie, 1989, p. 240; Figlewski, Landskroner & Silber, 1991; Kawaller, 1986; Merrick, 1990, pp 104-105; and Zurack & Dattatreya, 1989). To allow for tail risk, the unadjusted hedge ratio (b) is multiplied by φ^d. The value of φ^d will always be less than one, and so adjustment for tail risk will always reduce the size of the hedge ratio (i.e. lead to a smaller futures position). This is shown in table 9.2, where the values of the daily tailing factor φ^d are illustrated for a range of values of the annual interest rate, $[(1+i)^{365}]$ and the life of the hedge in days (k). This table reveals that the reduction in the number of futures contracts in the hedge to allow for tail risk is small, e.g. 1.27% for a hedge of 50 days when the annual interest rate is 10%.

Table 9.2: Daily Tailing Factors for Various Interest Rates

	Annual Interest Rate			
k	**5%**	**10%**	**20%**	**30%**
10	0.9988	0.9977	0.9955	0.9936
20	0.9975	0.9951	0.9905	0.9864
50	0.9935	0.9873	0.9758	0.9654
100	0.9869	0.9745	0.9517	0.9313
150	0.9803	0.9618	0.9282	0.8984
200	0.9737	0.9494	0.9053	0.8667
250	0.9673	0.9370	0.8830	0.8361
300	0.9608	0.9249	0.8612	0.8066

Example. In an earlier example, Max Bialystock found the risk-minimizing hedge ratio to be 0.56 and decided to take a short position of 560 FTSE 100 contracts to hedge the risk of a share portfolio between 2nd July and 5th September (65 days). If the annual risk free interest rate is 10% and Max Bialystock decides to revise his tail hedge daily, then $\varphi^d = 1/(1.000261)^{64} = 0.9834$. Therefore Max's risk-minimizing hedge ratio (allowing for tail risk) drops to $0.56 \times 0.9834 = 0.5507$, and the required hedge is 551 contracts, i.e. nine fewer contracts than when tail risk was ignored.

Daily rebalancing of the hedge will generate transactions costs, and so a single tailing factor to last throughout the life of the hedge will be derived. The profit from a hedged position between time t and time $t+k$, is $P_{t+k} = X_s[S_{t+1} - S_t + S_{t+2} - S_{t+1} + \ldots + S_{t+k} - S_{t+k-1} + D^*_{t+k}] + X_f[(1+i)^{k-1} \times (F_{t+1} - F_t) + (1+i)^{k-2} \times (F_{t+2} - F_{t+1}) + \ldots + (F_{t+k} - F_{t+k-1})]$. Assume that there is zero correlation between futures price changes on different days, zero correlation between spot price changes on different days and zero correlation between non-contemporaneous changes in futures and spot prices. In addition, assume that dividends are certain, and that the variances of daily futures price changes and daily spot price changes are constant for the period of the hedge. Given these assumptions $Var(P_{t+k}) = X_s^2[k\sigma_s^2 + b^2\sigma_f^2\Phi - 2b\sigma_{fs}\Psi]$, where $\Psi = (1+i)^{k-1} + (1+i)^{k-2} + (1+i)^{k-3} + ... + 1 = [(1+i)^k - 1]/i$ and $\Phi = (1+i)^{2(k-1)} + (1+i)^{2(k-2)} + (1+i)^{2(k-3)} + ... + 1 = [(1+i)^{2k} - 1]/(i(2+i))$. This gives the risk-minimizing hedge ratio $b = (\sigma_{fs}/\sigma_f^2) \times (\Psi/\Phi)$. Therefore, the single tailing factor is:-

$$\varphi^s = (\Psi/\Phi) = [(1+i)^k - 1] \times (2+i)/[(1+i)^{2k} - 1]$$

(This result is different from the equation derived by Duffie, 1989, pp. 239-241.) The value of this tailing factor (φ^s) for various interest rates and lives is shown in table 9.3.

Table 9.3: Single Tailing Factors for Various Interest Rates

k	\multicolumn{4}{c}{Annual Interest Rate}			
	5%	10%	20%	30%
10	0.9994	0.9988	0.9978	0.9968
20	0.9987	0.9975	0.9953	0.9932
50	0.9967	0.9936	0.9878	0.9824
100	0.9934	0.9871	0.9753	0.9644
150	0.9900	0.9805	0.9628	0.9465
200	0.9867	0.9740	0.9503	0.9286
250	0.9834	0.9675	0.9378	0.9107
300	0.9800	0.9610	0.9254	0.8929

Example. Suppose Max Bialystock decides to use a single tailing factor, then $\varphi^s = 2.000261 \times (1.000261^{65} - 1)/(1.000261^{130} - 1) = 0.9916$. Therefore, the risk-minimizing hedge ratio is revised downwards to $0.56 \times 0.9916 = 0.5553$, and Max need take a short position of only 555 contracts; 5 fewer than when tail risk was ignored, and 4 larger than when a daily tailing factor is used.

While the single tailing factor (φ^s) is slightly smaller than the equally weighted average of the daily tailing factors ($\Sigma\varphi^d/k$), the difference is very small. Thus, if $k = 10$ and the annual interest rate is 30%, the daily tailing factors for day ten to day one are, in order, 0.9936, 0.9943, 0.9950, 0.9957, 0.9964, 0.9971, 0.9978, 0.9986, 0.9993, 1. The equally weighted average of these daily tailing factors is 0.9968, and the single tailing factor is also 0.9968. If k is increased to 100, the average of the daily tailing factors is 0.9653, while the single tailing factor is slightly smaller at 0.9644. The relationship between the single and daily tailing factors is illustrated in figure 9.4.

One way to avoid tail risk is to use forward contracts. For example, if the objective is to lock in today the price that will be paid at a later date this can be done by taking a long position in a forward contract. However, forward contracts are subject to a number of problems (see chapter 2) that do not exist for stock indices. The potential exists for the creation of a new form of futures contract which avoids the problem of tail risk. Cox, Ingersoll & Ross (1981) and Jarrow & Oldfield (1981) have proposed a 'quasi-futures contract'. This is the same as a futures contract, except that the payments of variation margin do not involve the full daily price change. Instead, the trader pays (or receives) each day only the present value of the daily price change if it were paid on delivery day; i.e. a smaller sum. Such a quasi-future is superior both to a forward contract (because, through daily marking to the market, the risk of default is reduced), and to a futures contract (because 'tail risk' is avoided).

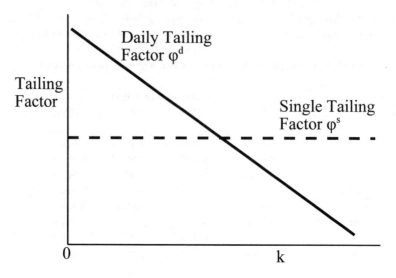

Figure 9.4: Relationship Between Single and Daily Tailing Factors

9.11 Dividend Risk

Above it was assumed that dividends were certain, and so there was no need to hedge dividend risk. A possible alternative approach is to assume, as did Rendleman (1993), that the terminal value of the dividends received over the hedge period is a certain proportion (c) of the value of the index basket at the end of the hedge. In which case, it is possible to hedge dividend risk because it is the same as spot risk. The profit from a hedge held from time t to time $t+k$ is $P_{t+k} = X_s(S_{t+k} - S_t + S_{t+k}c) + X_f(F_{t+k} - F_t)$. Letting $b \equiv -X_s/X_f$, this becomes $P_{t+k} = X_s[S_{t+k}(1+c) - S_t - b(F_{t+k} - F_t)]$. Therefore, since the values of S_t and F_t are known, $Var(P_{t+k}) = X_s^2[(1+c)^2 Var(S_{t+k}) + b^2 Var(F_{t+k}) - 2(1+c)bCov(S_{t+k}, F_{t+k})]$. Differentiating with respect to b, and setting the result equal to zero gives $\delta Var(P_{t+k})/\delta b = 2bX_s^2\sigma_f^2 - 2(1+c)X_s^2\sigma_{fs} = 0$, and so the risk-minimizing hedge ratio is $b = (1+c)\sigma_{fs}/\sigma_f^2$. Thus, in order to hedge dividend risk the number of futures contracts is increased by the proportion $(1+c)$.

9.12 Hedging and the Value of the Firm

There are two basic questions - should the risks of a company be hedged, and, if so, should such hedging be performed by the company or its shareholders? The answer to both of these questions is determined by the presence or absence of market imperfections.

Should the firm hedge?   In a competitive capital market shares are priced according to their risk and return. In the context of a company holding only a diversified portfolio of shares, hedging with index futures will tend to reduce the company's systematic risk (measured by beta) to zero. In consequence, the company's rate of return will fall towards the risk free rate. Thus, hedging by the firm or its shareholders converts a high risk-high return investment into a low risk-low return investment, at the rate given by the market price of risk. Similarly, using an arbitrage argument similar to that of Modigliani & Miller (1958), if capital markets are perfect and shareholders can hedge the firm's risks for themselves, hedging by the firm cannot add value. However, this irrelevancy result relies on an absence of market imperfections, and there are a number of reasons why hedging by the firm or shareholders (after allowing for the transactions costs of hedging) may be beneficial.

Who should do the hedging?   The firm possesses better information on the nature and duration of its risks than do the shareholders so that hedging by the firm is preferable, DeMarzo & Duffie (1991). In addition, futures contracts are 'lumpy' and the individual shareholders will encounter greater indivisibility problems than the firm. Furthermore, the transactions costs for one trade by the firm will be less than the combined cost of many separate hedge transactions by the shareholders.

There are a number of reasons why a financially weak firm faces additional costs, which can be avoided if the firm hedges its risks:-

1. Firms typically exhibit non-trivial bankruptcy costs (Smith & Stulz, 1985, Nance, Smith & Smithson, 1993), and hedging by the firm reduces the risk of incurring these costs, while hedging by the shareholders does not.

2. When a levered firm is close to bankruptcy, the shareholders may have an incentive to undertake highly risky investments, while the debt holders do not. This is because the shareholders are protected by limited liability from losing more than the current value of their stake in the firm, and they receive all the benefits of a successful investment. To compensate for the risk of such investments being made, the cost of debt will be higher than otherwise. Hedging by the firm can avoid this conflict of interest between debt and share holders, and lower the cost of debt. Consider a project which might suffer a disaster. Given such a disaster, the firm can choose to make a further riskless investment which has a positive NPV to restore the project. However, if the value of the firm after a disaster, including the value of this discretionary investment, is less than the value of the firm's outstanding debt, the firm is bankrupt. In which case the shareholders will refuse to make this positive NPV investment that will reduce the losses of the debt holders, which they would have made in the absence of any debt finance. (This assumes the debt holders are unable to immediately take control of the firm and undertake the investment.) Because of this possibility, the use of debt finance lowers the value of the firm. Provided the firm can ensure that its value (including the positive NPV from any disaster recovery investment) is never below the value of the debt, this problem will not occur, and the use of debt will not lower the

firm's value. Hedging by the firm is one way such losses may be avoided, Mayers & Smith (1987).

3.   Customers and suppliers may be reluctant to deal with a company that is likely to go bankrupt. This problem can be reduced if the firm hedges its risks.

4.   The firm may offer some form of after sales service, and potential customers may fear that this will cease on bankruptcy. Hedging by the firm, which reduces the risk of bankruptcy, increases the value of the after sales service, Sercu & Uppal (1995).

5.   The firm may be unable to undertake attractive but risky new investments due to debt covenants which cannot be renegotiated. Hedging by the firm may ensure that such debt covenants are not breached, enabling the project to proceed.

6.   If the firm faces various transactions costs in raising additional finance to cover unexpected losses, hedging by the firm makes its cash flows more predictable, and these transactions costs can be avoided.

7.   Firms subject to rate regulation experience regulatory lag, i.e. a delay between a change in their costs and their prices. Kolb, Morin & Gay (1983) suggested that such firms could hedge this risk using futures markets, so reducing their cost of capital. A response to the problem of regulatory lag has been the fuel adjustment clause, which allows US utilities to pass on increases in fuel costs to their customers. Lien & Liu (1996) argued for the replacement of the fuel adjustment clause by the utilities hedging this risk using natural gas futures. This would remove the distortions introduced into the behaviour of the utilities by the fuel adjustment clause, and prevent customers bearing the risk of fuel price increases, which they have difficulty in hedging for themselves.

If there is a progressive corporate taxation system, hedging by the company will stabilize its profits over time, so reducing cumulative tax payments, Smith & Stulz (1985). Hedging for this reason must be done by the firm. If losses are treated less favourably by the taxation system than profits (e.g. the tax relief on losses is delayed until subsequent profits have been made against which they can be offset), then hedging will reduce losses and be beneficial, Eytan (1990). Nance, Smith & Smithson (1993) found some empirical evidence supporting this explanation of corporate hedging. Hedging for this reason must be done by the firm.

Smith & Stulz (1985) have argued that, if managerial rewards are linked to the firm's profits (e.g. profit-linked pay, share options), hedging by the firm can reduce the risks attached to the remuneration of managers, and may mean that they are prepared to work for a lower, but more certain, income. (It may also prevent managers rejecting attractive projects because they are highly risky.) Thus, managers have an incentive to hedge the firm's risks, and this may mean a reduction in the firm's salary costs, although there may also be a reduction in the incentive effects of profit-related pay. The managers may choose to hedge away only those risks which are beyond their control, so that the bonus more correctly reflects their efforts. Hedging to reduce the risks of managerial reward schemes must be done by the firm.

If the hedging transfers the risk outside the capital market over which the shareholders are diversified (Fite & Pfleiderer, 1995), a net reduction in total risk is experienced by well diversified shareholders. The availability of such hedging opportunities depends on an absence of fully integrated capital markets, e.g. between countries. Hedging for this reason can be conducted by the firm or its shareholders.

If some investors do not have well diversified portfolios (e.g. they have a large holding in the family firm), then hedging the risks of the company will be of benefit to them, but not to well diversified shareholders. This suggests that any hedging for this reason is done by shareholders, rather than the firm. If the hedging is done by the firm, it is redundant for those shareholders who are already well diversified.

Thus, there are a variety of motives for hedging a firm's risks, and all but the last two of these require the hedging to be performed by the firm. Overall, if there are market imperfections of the type described above, hedging by the firm will raise its share price, and lower its cost of capital, Eckl & Robinson (1990), Fite & Pfleiderer (1995) and Kolb, Morin & Gay (1983).

9.13 Estimation of the Risk-minimizing Hedge Ratio

The usual method of estimating the risk-minimizing hedge ratio is to use ordinary least squares (OLS) regression. The risk-minimizing hedge ratio, b, can be estimated by regressing the prices (or price changes) of the asset whose risk is to be hedged (e.g. a portfolio of shares) on the prices (or price changes) of the futures contract to be used for the hedge (e.g. a stock index future). This involves fitting OLS regression equations of the form $S_t = a + bF_t + \varepsilon_t$ [or $(S_{t+k} - S_t) = a + b(F_{t+k} - F_t) + \varepsilon_t$]. The slope coefficient of this regression equation gives an estimate of b, the risk-minimizing hedge ratio. Stoll & Whaley (1993, pp. 59-60) point out that hedge duration is independent of the differencing interval. For a composite hedge, multiple regression is required, with the slope coefficients providing estimates of the corresponding risk-minimizing hedge ratios, Duffie (1989, pp. 221-225), Stoll & Whaley (1993, p. 57).

When spot returns and proportionate futures price changes are used to specify the hedge ratio, an estimate of σ_q/σ^2_q can be obtained by regressing spot returns (r) on proportionate changes in the futures price (q), i.e. $(S_{t+k} - S_t + D^*_{t+k})/S_t = a + c(F_{t+k} - F_t)/F_t + \varepsilon_t$. Multiplying the slope coefficient of this regression (c) by S_t/F_t gives an estimate of b, the risk-minimising hedge ratio. Alternatively spot returns can be regressed on the change in the futures price, divided by the spot price (Q); i.e. $(S_{t+k} - S_t + D^*_{t+k})/S_t = a + b(F_{t+k} - F_t)/S_t + \varepsilon_t$, and the risk-minimizing hedge ratio is given directly by the slope coefficient, b.

Since dividends are assumed to be certain, they can be included or excluded from price changes or returns and, in theory, the estimates of b will be unaffected. Since the risk-minimising hedge ratio (b) can be estimated in three different ways (levels, changes or returns), the choice of variables is made on the basis of statistical considerations.

A practical difficulty with this method of estimating the hedge ratio for a portfolio manager is that every time the composition of the share portfolio changes, the hedge ratio must be re-estimated. This involves calculating a new time series of prices for the portfolio using the current set of portfolio weights, and then re-running the regression. The suggestion by Figlewski, John & Merrick (1986, p. 134), is that the hedge ratios be estimated separately for each share. These can then be aggregated using the chosen portfolio weights to get the risk-minimising hedge ratio for the share portfolio. This avoids having to construct a time series of prices for the new portfolio and rerun the regression. Since the risk-minimising hedge ratio for a number of different spot assets is just the weighted sum of the individual hedge ratios, this procedure is mathematically equivalent to re-estimating the portfolio's hedge ratio directly. However, in practice there will be differences in the statistical results due to the presence of disturbance terms.

The identity of the shares in the index changes, and so the precise nature of the index changes over time. Since, the return on the index appears in the definition of all the various beta values (i.e. β, β_F and β_{Fq}), historic estimates of these beta values may need some slight adjustment if they are to be used in computing hedge ratios.

A decision must be made on how far back in time to collect data for use in the regression. If the hedge ratio is stable over time, the longer the estimation period, the better will be the estimate of the hedge ratio. However, if the hedge ratio changes over time, the use of data from some time ago may degrade the estimates of the current hedge ratio.

The use of OLS regression to estimate the risk-minimizing hedge ratio (as described in the previous paragraphs of this section) has been subject to a number of criticisms, and these can be divided into two main groups. First, a distinction can be drawn between estimating the risk-minimizing hedge ratio and estimating the slope coefficient of a regression equation. The formulae of the risk-minimizing hedge ratio and the regression coefficient are only identical when OLS regression is used. This has implications for the use of advanced econometric techniques to estimate the slope coefficient in the regression equation. Second, there are statistical problems in the estimation of the regression equation (such as intervalling, autocorrelation, simultaneous equations bias, heteroskedasticity, estimation risk and error correction) which can be tackled by using more sophisticated estimation procedures. In the remainder of this section, various statistical problems with performing the regression will be considered, followed by a discussion of the possible dangers of concentrating on efficiently estimating the regression equation.

1. The time interval between price observations is unspecified and, to increase the statistical power of the regression, can be set as short as the data permits. However, if there are price adjustment delays in the spot and futures markets, there will be an intervalling effect, i.e. the slope coefficients estimated from regressing changes in spot prices (or returns) on changes in futures prices (or returns) will be biased, and the magnitude of this bias will be larger, the shorter is the differencing interval. (The slope coefficient will also be biased if price levels are used in the regression.) Grammatikos (1986) presents evidence for currencies that the intervalling effect biases the estimated hedge ratios downwards, and so hedge ratios estimated using short time periods are smaller than those estimated using a longer differencing period. Chen, Lee & Shrestha

(2004) show that, unless one-period price changes are independently, identically distributed, it is inappropriate to use one period price changes to estimate the hedge ratio for a hedge with a longer duration. Lien & Tse (2000b) demonstrate that OLS estimates of the hedge ratio are stable under aggregation, i.e. the hedge ratio is unaffected by the length of hedging horizon, and 1 day returns can be used to estimate the hedge ratio for a 1 month hedge. But this result only applies if all the assumptions underlying the OLS regression are met. Lien & Tse (2000b) show that a similar result applies to hedge ratios estimated using VAR models. If the OLS or VAR model is correctly specified, there is an advantage in using high frequency data. However, error correction models are not stable under aggregation, and so the data frequency should be set equal to the hedging period, even if the EC model is correctly specified.

2. A number of authors have found considerable autocorrelation in the residuals of their OLS regression equations, (e.g. Brown, 1985, Elam, 1991, Herbst, Kare & Caples, 1989, Herbst, Swanson & Caples, 1992, Hill & Schneeweis, 1981) and suggested altering the estimation procedure accordingly, e.g. the use of ARIMA estimation, or generalized least squares.

3. Both the variables (spot and future) in the regression equation are determined jointly. In consequence, if OLS regression is used to compute the risk-minimizing hedge ratio, the estimated slope coefficient is subject to simultaneous equations bias, Bond, Thompson & Lee (1987).

4. The OLS regression approach to estimating the hedge ratio implicitly assumes that the variance of futures prices, futures price changes, or proportionate price changes, and the covariance between futures and spot prices, price changes, or returns are constant throughout the life of the contract. However, the variance is not constant over time (see chapter 7), and so the regression is likely to suffer from the problem of heteroskedasticity. A recent development has been the use of ARCH and GARCH regression models which model the heteroskedasticity in both the spot and futures prices, e.g. Baillie & Myers (1991), Cecchetti, Cumby & Figlewski (1988), Kroner & Sultan (1991) and Myers (1991). However, Wilson, Aggarwal & Inclan (1996) have shown that if there are jumps in volatility which are not allowed for, the use of ARCH models will greatly overstate the volatility persistence. Since basis risk converges to zero at delivery, the covariance between spot and futures prices, price changes or returns will tend to rise over the life of the contract. Therefore, the estimated value of beta will be an average of the true time-varying betas.

5. Spot returns may have an asymmetric response to the arrival of good and bad news. In the context of stochastic volatility modelling, Lien (2005b) showed that, if this asymmetry is ignored, the estimated risk minimizing hedge ratio is biased downwards.

6. The relationship between spot and futures is changed (the constant term shifts) by alteration in the maturity of the futures contract as the interest and dividends for the period until delivery decline. Thus, any regression should control for changes in contract maturity, e.g. by the inclusion of time to maturity as an explanatory variable.

7. Lence & Hayes (1994a, 1994b) have pointed out that, just as the optimal proportions of a stock portfolio are estimated with error, so the optimal proportions

of a portfolio of an underlying asset and futures (e.g. the hedge ratio) are estimated with error. Various techniques have been developed for dealing with this estimation risk (see, for example, Board & Sutcliffe, 1994), including the use of prior information in a Bayesian approach.

8. If the spot and futures prices are cointegrated the regression equation should include an error correction mechanism (ECM), Ghosh (1993b); and ignoring this will result in a futures position that is smaller than optimal (Lien, 1996, 2004).

9. Antoniou, Pescetto & Violaris (2003) have shown that, if cross-country effects on returns and volatility are omitted from an econometric model of a country's spot and futures markets, this alters the estimated hedge ratios.

There are clearly a number of econometric problems with OLS regression in estimating the chosen regression equation, and some of these can be solved by using more complicated estimation procedures. However, such a development risks losing sight of the objective, which is to estimate σ_{fs}/σ_f^2, not the slope coefficient of a regression equation. If the procedure for estimating the regression equation is altered to allow for various statistical problems, the estimated regression coefficient may no longer provide an estimate of the risk-minimizing hedge ratio since the formulae for its computation is no longer σ_{fs}/σ_f^2. For example, even if the relationship between spot and futures prices is non-linear, if regression is used to estimate the hedge ratio, it must be linear as between S_t and F_t, Bell & Krasker (1986). One way of deciding between OLS and the statistically superior methods for estimating the risk-minimizing hedge is to compare their effectiveness, and evidence on this is presented in the next section. However, as Lien (2005a) has shown, measuring effectiveness is problematic and the use of E may bias the results in favour of OLS.

Myers & Thompson (1989) have pointed out that regression need not be used to estimate the components of the risk-minimizing hedge ratio, i.e. σ_{fs} and σ_f^2 can be estimated separately.

As mentioned earlier in this chapter, the estimates of σ_{fs} and σ_f^2 are conditional upon the information available when the hedge ratio is estimated (φ_t). Thus, for the case of price levels, the required regression equation for estimating the risk-minimizing hedge ratio is $S_t = a(\varphi_t) + b(\varphi_t)F_t + \varepsilon_t$, where $a(\varphi_t)$ and $b(\varphi_t)$ represent coefficients that vary with the information set (φ_t). A possible formulation for such a regression equation is $S_t = (a + \gamma Z_t) + (\Gamma + \theta Z_t)F_t + \varepsilon_t$, where the estimate of the hedge ratio is ($\Gamma + \theta Z_t$), and Z_t is a variable that gives information about the hedge ratio. It would be incorrect to run the regression $S_t = a + bF_t + c\varphi_t + \varepsilon_t$, Bell & Krasker (1986). They also point out that, while a correction for heteroskedasticity will make the estimate of the slope coefficient more efficient, unless the correction for heteroskedasticity is based on information known when the hedge ratio is estimated, a correction for heteroskedasticity will bias the regression coefficient as an estimate of the hedge ratio. In consequence, there may be a trade-off between efficiency and bias when the regression procedure is altered to overcome statistical problems, such as heteroskedasticity.

Information that may be helpful in forecasting the value of σ_{fs}/σ_f^2 at the end of the hedge includes the maturity of the contract at time $t+k$. This follows from chapter 7, where evidence was provided that σ_f^2 tends to rise as maturity approaches. Another piece of relevant information is the number of days between the end of the hedge and the delivery date of the futures contract. In the absence of basis risk, the risk-minimizing hedge ratio is $b = 1/(1+i)^{T-k}$, where T is the delivery date of the futures contract, and k is the date on which the hedge is planned to end. While constant for a given hedge, this hedge ratio differs from hedge to hedge, depending on the values of T and k. Therefore, even in this simplified situation, $T-k$ may be useful in predicting the hedge ratio.

The usual approach to estimating hedge ratios is simplistic, and rests on assumptions which are clearly violated in reality. Therefore, it is likely that more sophisticated methods for calculating hedge ratios will be developed and applied. These may move away from risk minimisation and incorporate returns, allow for the maturity of the contract when the hedge ends, and adjust for tail risk.

9.14 Empirical Studies

There has been a steady flow of studies of hedging share portfolios using index futures. In most cases OLS regression has been used to estimate the risk-minimizing hedge ratio and appraise hedging effectiveness. There has also been a small number of studies of the extent to which actual hedging behaviour accords with the portfolio model, although none of these studies has been concerned with index futures. These will be considered after the studies of estimating the hedge ratio and appraising hedging effectiveness for index futures.

9.14.1 Hedging Share Portfolios with Index Futures

Most of these studies are for US index futures, although there is an increasing number of non-US studies. Almost all of the US studies have used the S&P500 index future. There are a number of aspects of hedging that have been examined empirically: hedge duration, the maturity of the futures contract, the spot asset to be hedged, the objective of the hedge ratio (risk-minimizing, utility maximizing etc), the statistical technique used in estimating the hedge ratio, the use of price levels, price changes or returns, the inclusion of dividends, whether the hedge ratio is estimated using past data or data for the period of the hedge (which is only possible when backtesting) and the frequency with which the hedge ratio is re-estimated. These studies have quantified the effect of variations in these parameters on hedging effectiveness, usually measured by E, and the hedge ratio.

USA. Hill & Schneeweis (1984) studied Friday closing prices (spot and future) for 1982-3 for three US indices: S&P500, NYSE Composite and VLCI. They found that the risk-minimizing hedge ratio was about 0.70, while the measure of effectiveness (E) was about 0.8.

Figlewski (1984a) investigated the use of S&P500 futures to hedge the risk of five portfolios of shares. These portfolios consisted of the shares in five US stock indices: S&P500, NYSE Composite, DJIA, NASDAQ and the AMEX Composite. Instead of prices, Figlewski (1984a) used arithmetic rates of return, defined as $(F_{t+1} - F_t)/S_t$ and $(S_{t+1} - S_t + D^*_{t+1})/S_t$, where the returns were calculated over one week periods, dividends were included in the computation of the spot return for 1982-3. The risk-minimizing hedge ratios (b) were calculated by regressing portfolio returns on futures returns. While this hedging strategy worked well in reducing risk for the S&P500, NYSE and DJIA portfolios, it was much less successful in hedging the risk of those share portfolios which contained smaller companies, i.e. NASDAQ and the AMEX Composite. Hedging effectiveness was measured by comparing the standard deviations of returns on the hedged and unhedged portfolios. Figlewski concluded that, unless the portfolio of shares whose risk is to be hedged is similar in composition to that of the index whose futures contracts are used for the hedging, there will be only a limited reduction in risk. The portfolio betas were calculated by regressing the portfolio returns on the returns (including dividends) of the S&P500 index, and were used as hedge ratios. The results from using these beta values to estimate the hedge ratio were similar, and slightly inferior, to those from using b as the hedge ratio.

Figlewski then investigated the sensitivity of his results for b to variations in dividends, holding period and contract maturity. When dividends were omitted from the calculation of returns on the S&P500 index, the results were little changed. Figlewski found that shortening the holding period of the hedge from one week to one day altered its effectiveness, although lengthening the holding period to four weeks had little effect. Finally, varying the maturity of the contract from below to above two months had a small effect on hedging effectiveness.

Nordhauser (1984) investigated the hypothetical performance of VLCI futures in hedging two US mutual funds for 1962-81. Since VLCI index futures did not exist during this period, movements in the futures price were proxied by changes in the underlying index. Using a hedge ratio of one-to-one, he found that hedging led to a substantial reduction in risk, and a lesser reduction in returns. However, he did not directly measure hedging effectiveness.

Figlewski (1985b) used data for 1982 on three US index futures (S&P500, NYSE Composite and VLCI) and studied their effectiveness in hedging five US indices; S&P500, NYSE Composite, AMEX Composite, NASDAQ and the DJIA. He examined the effectiveness of hedges with a duration of between one day and three weeks using the standard deviation of the hedged position, divided by the standard deviation of the unhedged position, as the measure of hedging effectiveness (rather than E). He computed the hedge ratio in two different ways. Assuming constant dividends, he regressed the weekly returns of each of the five indices on the returns of the indices underlying the three futures. Returns were calculated in the same way as Figlewski (1984a). This gave fifteen beta estimates which were used as the hedge ratios (even though the delivery dates of the futures contracts concerned did not coincide with the end of the hedge). He also used daily data to compute the ex-post risk-minimizing hedge ratios (i.e. $b = \sigma_{fs}/\sigma_f^2$). In nearly every case $b < \beta$, and the use of *b* led to a substantial improvement in measured hedging effectiveness. For both types of hedge ratio (*b* and *β*) Figlewski found that hedges under a week were not very effective, and suggested this may be due to the use of 'stale' prices in computing the five indices. He also found that hedging was more effective for the S&P500, NYSE Composite and the DJIA, than for NASDAQ and AMEX Composite.

Junkus & Lee (1985) used daily closing prices (spot and future) for 1982-3 for three US indices: S&P500, NYSE Composite and VLCI. They investigated the effectiveness of various hedging strategies, including the minimum risk and the one-to-one hedge ratios. This was done for each index using data for a month to compute the hedge ratio used during that same month in hedging the spot value of the corresponding index. The risk-minimizing hedge ratios were computed by regressing changes in the spot price on changes in the futures price. The average risk-minimizing hedge ratio was 0.50, while the average effectiveness (as measured by *E*) was 0.72 for the S&P500 and the NYSE Composite, and 0.52 for the VLCI. The effectiveness of the one-to-one hedge ratio was poor, leading to an *increase* in risk for the VLCI and the NYSE Composite, and an effectiveness measure (*E*) of 0.23 for the S&P500. There was little relationship between contract maturity and effectiveness.

Capital investment decisions by firms rely on an estimate of the cost of capital for use in net present value computations. There is a delay between the decision to proceed with an investment project and actually issuing the equity and debt required to finance the project. By hedging with a combination of index futures and interest rate futures (depending on the debt-equity ratio), the cost of capital can 'locked in' at the time the decision is made to proceed with the investment. Sholund (1985) tested this possibility using data for IBM and General Electric, three different debt-equity ratios, and the S&P500 and treasury bond futures. Using weekly data, he found rather low *E* measures, ranging from 0.75 to 0.20. The *E* measures were particularly poor for situations involving substantial amounts of equity finance, in line with the results of Figlewski (1984a, 1985b) that S&P500 futures are poor at hedging the risks of portfolios that have a substantially different composition from the S&P500.

Peters (1986) studied the use of S&P500 futures to hedge three share portfolios; the NYSE Composite, the DJIA and the S&P500 itself. Using data for 1984-5, he regressed daily futures returns on daily spot returns to estimate the risk-minimizing hedge ratio (*b*). He also regressed the daily returns for each index on the S&P500 index to get a beta estimate for each portfolio, which was also used as a hedge ratio. For each of the portfolios, *b* gave a hedged position with a lower risk than did beta.

Hill & Schneeweis (1986) used monthly data for 1982-4 to study the potential effectiveness of the international cross hedging of well diversified share portfolios. To investigate the possible benefits to a US investor who owns a portfolio of shares in a foreign country, they computed the correlations between returns on the S&P500 and NYSE Composite index futures and the US$ returns (excluding dividends) on the Capital International Perspective (CIP) stock market indices for the UK, Canada, Japan and West Germany. For Canada and the UK the correlations were over +0.5. Hill & Schneeweis also investigated the potential for foreign investors to hedge their domestic share portfolios using US index futures. This was done by expressing the previous correlations for the NYSE Composite index future in terms of the relevant domestic currency. Again, the correlations for Canada and the UK were above +0.5.

Grieves (1986) examined the effectiveness of hedging US treasury, industrial and utility bonds using a composite hedge of S&P500 futures and US treasury bond futures. Using monthly data for 1982-5, he regressed the price relatives for each type of bond on the price relatives of treasury bond and S&P500 futures. For the industrial bonds the use of S&P500 futures, in addition to treasury bond futures, led to more effective hedges, as measured by E.

Lee, Bubnys & Lin (1987). Their study of the S&P500, NYSE Composite and VLCI index futures found that the risk-minimizing hedge ratio (estimated using regression) rose as the delivery date of the futures contract used in the hedge approached. This provides empirical support for the view that the hedge ratio depends on the maturity of the contract used in the hedge.

Junkus (1987) investigated whether risk-minimizing hedge ratios are different in rising or falling stock markets. Friday closing prices for 1982-5 for three index futures (S&P500, NYSE Composite and VLCI) were used to compute weekly returns. Junkus also computed weekly returns (including dividends) for seven share portfolios (NASDAQ Composite, MMI, Coca Cola, IBM, General Motors, US Steel and Sears). Including a dummy variable in the regression to represent a rising market, she concluded that there was no systematic difference in the hedge ratio in rising as opposed to falling markets.

For some traders there are taxation advantages in capturing dividends, i.e. buying shares shortly before they go ex-dividend, and selling them shortly after the ex-dividend date, see Posen & Collins (1989). During this short period the trader is exposed to the risk of changes in the share price for reasons unconnected with the ex-dividend event. Dubofsky (1987) investigated the benefits of using index futures to hedge this risk. He selected twenty ex-dividend dates during 1985-6 for the fifty largest companies in the S&P500 index. He investigated the performance of the following trading strategy: purchase a value weighted portfolio of shares five days before their ex-dividend date, hedge this portfolio by a short position in S&P500 index futures, and liquidate the positions in shares and futures immediately the shares go ex-dividend. The hedge ratio used was simply the beta value of the share portfolio (which outperformed the one-to-one hedge ratio). He found that the value of E was 0.45, and concluded that hedging small portfolios (two to six shares) for only five days produced worthwhile risk reductions.

Dubofsky & Kannan (1993) analyzed the performance of S&P500 futures in hedging the dividends of all stocks traded on the NYSE and AMEX for 1983-8. Each stock was purchased six days before it went ex-dividend, and sold at the close on the ex-dividend day. There was never less than twenty stocks in the portfolio to be hedged. The amount invested in stocks was equal to the value of the S&P500 index basket (i.e. a one-to-one hedge ratio). The stock portfolios were constructed using both equal and market value weights. The reduction in risk (E) from hedging with one short S&P500

futures contract, computed over five-day periods, was 76% for the equally weighted portfolio, and 84% for the value weighted portfolio.

Graham & Jennings (1987) classified US companies into nine categories according to their betas and dividend yield. For each beta-dividend yield category, ten equally weighted portfolios of ten shares each were constructed. Weekly returns were computed for each portfolio for 1982-3. They then investigated the performance of S&P500 futures in hedging these portfolios for periods of one, two and four weeks. Three alternative hedge ratios were used: one-to-one, beta and the risk-minimizing hedge ratio. The risk-minimizing hedge ratio (which was estimated using the sample values of σ_{fs} and σ_f^2) produced hedged positions with returns that were about 75% higher than for the other two hedge ratios. The measures of hedging effectiveness (E) ranged from 0.16 to 0.33. For the one and two week hedges, the risk-minimizing hedge ratio was more effective, i.e. had a higher E value. Dividend yield and beta did not appear to cause any clear patterns in hedging effectiveness or returns.

Merrick (1988b) used daily closing prices for the S&P500 index and index future for 1982-6 to study deviations from the no-arbitrage condition (i.e. mispricings). This was done using one day returns on the index and the index future. He found that the risk-minimizing hedge ratio (estimated using regression) for one day hedges rose as delivery approached, and that this rise was larger than implied by the interest rate effect ($1/(1+r_{kT})$). The mispricings tended to revert towards the no-arbitrage condition, and this was found to have hedging implications. While the mispricing at the time the hedge was initiated did not affect the risk-minimizing hedge, it did affect the return on the hedged position. If the future was overpriced, a hedge involving a short position in the future would produce an above average return, and vice versa. This implies that, to some extent, hedging involves an element of profit seeking as well as risk avoidance.

Morris (1989) investigated the performance of S&P500 futures in hedging the risk of a portfolio of the largest firms on the NYSE (which accounted for 10% of the NYSE capitalization). The data was monthly for 1982-7. The risk-minimizing hedge ratio was estimated using data for the entire period, and gave an E value of 0.91.

Malliaris & Urrutia (1991) investigated the stability of the estimated hedge ratio and hedging effectiveness for the S&P500 and NYSE Composite indices (and for four currencies). Using fortnightly price change data for 1984-8, moving window regressions were estimated for a one year period, rolled forwards by three months. The slope coefficients from these linear regressions were used to estimate the risk-minimizing hedge ratios (b) and the effectiveness measures (E). The Dickey-Fuller and variance-ratio tests both accepted the hypothesis that the estimates of the risk-minimizing hedge ratio, and hedging effectiveness for a two week hedging horizon followed a random walk. This result contradicts the assumption that the hedge ratio and effectiveness are stable over time, at least for two week periods.

Lindahl (1991) considered hedging the spot S&P500 portfolio using S&P500 index futures. For weekly data for 1983-8, she used her two part effectiveness measure (described earlier in this chapter) to study the performance of hedges with a hedge ratio of unity. Hedges for one, two and four weeks were judged to be inferior to selling the shares and investing the proceeds in the risk free asset. However, hedges for thirteen weeks offered results that were reasonably close to the risk free rate.

Lindahl (1992) used the Friday closing prices from 1985 to 1989 for the MMI, and for 1983-9 for the S&P500, to examine the stability of the hedge ratio. In each case the basket of shares in the index were hedged using the corresponding index future. OLS regression was used to estimate b, the risk-minimizing hedge ratio, using non-overlapping price changes over one, two and four week periods for the entire data period. She found that b was generally less than one, and that as the time when the hedge was lifted got closer to delivery, b rose towards one. (There was no clear pattern in E, the measure of hedging effectiveness.) This implies that, rather then set an initial hedge ratio which is held for the life of the hedge, hedgers should increase their hedge ratio as delivery approaches. Lindahl also found that b and E tended to increase as the duration of the hedge increased from one to four weeks. However, since longer duration hedges were lifted closer to delivery, part of this duration effect may have been due to b rising as delivery approached.

Kolb & Okunev (1992) considered daily data for 1989 on the S&P500, and compared the risk-minimizing hedge ratio with extended mean Gini hedge ratios computed using a wide range of risk aversion parameters. For low levels of risk aversion, there was little difference between the risk-minimizing and extended mean Gini hedge ratios. However, as risk aversion was increased, while the risk-minimizing hedge ratio was unchanged at 0.94, the extended mean Gini hedge ratio rose to 1.01. Kolb & Okunev also investigated the stability of the hedge ratios over time by using a moving window of the past fifty days to estimate the current hedge ratios. While the risk-minimizing hedge ratio was fairly stable throughout 1989, the extended mean Gini hedge ratio (for a high degree of risk aversion) was not. This implies that a hedger using the extended mean Gini approach would have had to continually adjust their hedge ratio.

Ghosh (1993b) compared two different regression models for estimating the risk-minimizing hedge ratio. He used daily data for 1990-1 on S&P500 futures to hedge three different spot portfolios: the S&P500 basket, the NYSE Composite basket and the DJIA basket. Since S&P500 futures prices were found to be cointegrated with the prices of each of the three spot portfolios, the incorporation of an ECM in the regression equation was indicated. Bivariate OLS regression using price changes was compared with a regression model of price changes which incorporated an ECM; and the ECM approach was found to be statistically superior. The estimated hedge ratios for the DJIA and the S&P500 portfolios were all similar at about 0.89. For the NYSE Composite, the ECM gave a hedge ratio of 0.86, while the bivariate OLS regression produced 0.84.

Lien & Luo (1993c) used weekly data on MMI, NYSE Composite and S&P500 futures for 1984-8 to hedge the underlying index baskets for durations of 1 to 9 weeks. They fitted an ECM model to estimate risk-minimizing hedge ratios using weekly price changes. These averaged 0.98 for the MMI, 0.96 for the NYSE Composite and 0.89

for the S&P500. They also investigated using MMI and NYSE Composite futures to hedge the NYSE Composite index basket (i.e. a composite hedge). The average composite hedge ratios were 0.01 for MMI futures and 0.96 for NYSE Composite futures.

Bera, Bubnys & Park (1993) used daily data for 1982-5 to compute hedge ratios for the S&P500, NYSE Composite and VLCI. Each of the three futures was used to hedge its underlying index basket. Risk-minimizing hedge ratios were estimated by applying OLS regression to price changes, and by fitting an ARCH(1) model to price changes. There was very little difference between the average OLS and ARCH hedge ratios, and the OLS ratios were 0.59 for the S&P500, 0.37 for the NYSE Composite and 0.50 for the VLCI. They found that when the data was partitioned by time to maturity, for each index and estimation method, there was a small increase in the hedge ratio as the time to maturity decreased.

Stoll & Whaley (1993, pp. 58-59) used daily data on S&P500 futures and the corresponding index basket for 1989 to investigate the effect of varying the differencing interval on the OLS estimate of the risk-minimizing hedge ratio (b) and hedging effectiveness (E). Using daily price changes, b was 0.80 and E was 84%. When the differencing interval was increased to two weeks, b rose to 1.00, and E rose to 99%. In each case the hedge duration was one calendar year. Thus, variation in the differencing interval can have an important influence on both the estimated hedge ratio and hedging effectiveness.

Park & Switzer (1995a) used weekly data on S&P500 futures for 1988-91 to hedge the S&P500 basket, including dividends. They used one-to-one and risk-minimizing hedge ratios. The risk-minimizing hedge ratios were obtained by applying three different regression models to changes in the logarithm of spot and futures prices. The alternative regression models used were OLS, ECM and bivariate GARCH (1,1) with an ECM. They used a moving window to generate a hedge ratio for use during the subsequent week. Hedging effectiveness (E) for all four hedge ratios was 98%, which indicates that each type of hedge ratio was highly effective.

Hancock & Weise (1994) analyzed daily data on S&P500 futures for 1987-9 to hedge the S&P500 basket. They applied OLS regression to spot and futures returns to estimate the risk-minimizing hedge ratio (b). This was done using a 90 day moving window to compute b for the next day, and b had an average value of 0.95. Returns on the hedged portfolio were not significantly different from the risk free rate, which is consistent with hedging reducing the systematic risk of the portfolio to zero. However, no results on the reduction in risk for the hedged portfolios were given.

Geppert (1995) investigated the performance of S&P500 futures in hedging the underlying index basket using weekly data for 1990-3. He assumed that spot and futures prices were cointegrated, and decomposed their movements into permanent and transitory components. Estimates of these permanent and transitory components from the first half of the data were then used to estimate b and E for hedges of between one and twelve weeks duration, and these were compared with estimates of b and E produced using OLS regression. Geppert found that for both approaches, hedge ratios increased from about 0.96 for one week hedges to 0.97 or unity for twelve week hedges, while E increased from 97% to over 99%. These hedge ratios were then applied to the data for the second half of the sample period, and the variances of the hedged portfolio returns compared. For hedge durations of 2 to 7 weeks, and also for 9 week hedges, the decomposition procedure had a lower variance than did OLS, while for hedges of 1, 8 and 10-12 weeks duration the reverse was the case.

Benet & Luft (1995) used transactions data on S&P500 futures for 1986-8 to hedge the underlying index basket. The risk-minimizing hedge ratio was estimated by applying weighted least squares regression (to allow for the differences in the length of the return periods) to transactions returns for 30 months, and gave a value of 0.985, while E was 87%. When the analysis was repeated for four non-overlapping 90 day hedge periods, the average hedge ratio was 0.92, while the average E was 81%.

Chang, Chang & Fang (1996) derived a risk-minimizing hedge ratio for the situation where interest rates (and hence the basis) are mean-reverting: $b = (\sigma_{fs}+z)/\sigma_f^2$, where z can be positive or negative. Using data on the S&P500 index and futures for 1992-3, they used weekly log returns over a moving window of a quarter to estimate a hedge ratio for the following week. The 38 estimated values of z (apart from one week) were positive and small, and allowance for mean-reverting interest rates raised the hedge ratio from an average of 0.95 to 1.00, while the effectiveness measure (E) fell from an average of 0.990 to 0.987. These results indicate that, for the S&P500, allowance for mean-reversion in interest rates has little effect.

Lien & Shaffer (1999) examined the performance of the Shalit (1995) estimator of the minimum extended Gini coefficient, which is employed as a risk measure by some hedge ratios. They used daily data on the S&P500, Nikkei 225, Topix, Hang Seng, KOSPI and Ibex indices for 1982-96, and found that, on average, using the Shalit estimator reduced hedging effectiveness by about 8%.

Lien, Tse & Tsui (2002) used daily data on the S&P500 and Nikkei 225 indices for 1988-98. They found that CC-GARCH is a satisfactory model for both indices, but that the out-of-sample hedging effectiveness for hedges of one day duration is slightly better for rolling window OLS, than for rolling window CC-GARCH.

Poomimars, Cadle & Theobald (2003) considered weekly data on the S&P500, Nikkei 225 and FTSE 100 for 1990-8. They used 11 different methods for estimating the risk-minimizing hedge, including models with an asymmetric dynamic covariance (ADC) matrix. The out-of-sample hedging effectiveness was modestly improved by the use of ADC models. The authors than applied a Bayesian adjustment to the hedge ratios by shrinking them towards the static OLS hedge ratio, which gave a further modest improvement in hedging effectiveness.

Chen, Lee & Shrestha (2004) studied daily data on seven futures: S&P500, TSE 35, Nikkei 225, TOPIX, FTSE 100, CAC 40 and the SPI. for 1982-97. They found that as the length of the hedge duration is increased, the risk-minimizing hedge ratio increases towards one, as does hedging effectiveness. This implies that, for long duration hedges, the naive hedge ratio of 1:1 is optimal.

Miffre (2004) analyzed monthly data on the S&P500 and NYSE Composite for

1982-2003. She compared the out-of-sample performance of five different ways of estimating the risk-minimizing hedge ratio - naive 1:1, static OLS, dynamic OLS, bivariate GARCH (1,1) and conditional OLS. The (static) conditional OLS approach allowed the hedge ratio and the basis to vary over time due to changes in exogenous variables, particularly the lagged basis. The conditional OLS estimates of the hedge ratio produced substantially more effective hedges.

Alizadeh & Nomikos (2004) allowed the hedge ratio to switch between two alternative values, depending on the average lagged basis. Out-of-sample, these hedge ratios were superior to those estimated using GARCH, VECM and OLS regression for the FTSE 100, but not for the S&P500.

Brooks, Davies & Kim (2004) considered the out-of-sample hedging effectiveness of 97 US individual stock futures in hedging 438 US stocks using daily data for 2003-4. The hedge ratio was estimated by rolling window OLS. The hedging instrument for each stock was determined in three different ways - the correlation of returns, the similarity of firm characteristics (earnings per share, beta and size), and a mixture of both criteria. The most effective hedges were based on using both criteria to choose the hedging instrument. Composite hedging using two or three individual stock futures, or choosing the hedging instrument from the same industrial classification further improved hedging performance, as did including S&P500 futures as a hedging instrument, along with an individual stock future.

Canada.　　　　Deaves (1994) used weekly data on TSE 300 futures for 1984-7 to hedge the TSE 300 basket, and for TSE 35 futures for 1987-9 to hedge the TSE 35 basket. He used three alternative hedge ratios: one-to-one, and the risk-minimizing hedge ratio (b) computed in two different ways. First, he used OLS regression with spot and futures returns to estimate b. Second, he explicitly estimated the mispricing risk, which varied with maturity, and allowed for the effect of maturity on the riskless interest rate in estimating b. Thus the hedge ratios varied with maturity. Hedging effectiveness (E) for one week hedges was very similar at about 98% for the three different hedge ratios and for both futures, which suggests that E is not very sensitive to maturity effects.

Park & Switzer (1995a) replicated their study of the S&P500 for the TSE 35, using data for exactly the same period. Hedging effectiveness (E) for the one-to-one hedge was 73%, for the OLS and ECM hedges E was 75%, and for bivariate GARCH with an ECM it was 77%. Thus, there was a small improvement in effectiveness from using more sophisticated regression procedures.

Gagnon & Lypny (1997) applied the bivariate GARCH (1,1) model to weekly data on the TSE 35 for 1987-93. Compared with the static OLS and naive hedge ratios, the use of GARCH (1,1) hedge ratios leads to a small improvement in hedging effectiveness.

Japan.　　　　Bailey (1989) used daily data on the Nikkei 225 traded on SGX for 1986-7, and on the Osaka 50 Kabusaki from June to October 1987. The period of each hedge was one day. He used two different hedge ratios: the risk-minimizing ratio estimated using regression, and the derivative of the no-arbitrage futures price, with respect to the spot price, i.e. $\delta F/\delta S = exp(h(\pi - \omega))$, where h, π and ω are as defined in chapter 5.10. The hedging performance was modest, with reductions in the standard deviation of returns of between 3% and 45%.

Yau, Hill & Schneeweis (1990) studied daily returns on the Nikkei 225 for 1986-7. Hedge ratios were computed in three different ways: the risk-minimizing ratio (b), the Howard & D'Antonio ratio (b^*, see chapter 9.3), and a portfolio approach that seeks to maximize utility when holdings of both shares and futures are variable. They found that hedging the Nikkei portfolio with Nikkei 225 futures reduced risk by about 67% (as measured by E) for daily returns, and by 81% for weekly returns. This effectiveness was largely unchanged when the hedge ratios estimated using the last period's data were applied to the current period. The other two methods of calculating hedge ratios indicated that futures can improve a portfolio's risk-return trade-off when the hedge is computed using the actual data for the period of the hedge. However, when the hedge ratio is computed from last period's data is applied to the current period, risk-return performance may worsen.

Chou, Denis & Lee (1996) used weekly data on the Nikkei 225 for 1989-94. Risk-minimizing hedge ratios were estimated using static OLS and an ECM model using data for 1 to 5 week periods. Out-of-sample, the hedging effectiveness of the ECM model was about 2% better than for the OLS model. As the differencing interval moved from 1 to 5 weeks, the hedge ratio tended towards one, hedging effectiveness improved and the superiority of ECM increased.

Ghosh & Clayton (1996) considered daily data for 1990-2 on the Nikkei 225, FTSE 100, CAC 40 and DAX. Using an ECM rather than a static OLS model, improved out of sample hedging effectiveness by between 1% and 11%.

Lien & Tse (1998) used daily data on the Nikkei 225 for 1989-96 to investigate lower partial moment (LPM) hedge ratios. The bivariate asymmetric power ARCH in means (APARCH-M) model was used to estimate the LPM hedge ratios for four values of n, and seven target returns; and compare it with the minimum variance hedge ratio. The correlation between the two alternative hedge ratios is lowest (0.13) for high values of n and high target returns.

Lien & Tse (2000a) analyzed daily data on the Nikkei 225 for 1988-96 to study the hedge ratios which minimize the LPM. They found that these hedge ratios are very different from the minimum variance hedge ratios estimated using OLS.

Lien & Tse (1999) compared the out-of-sample hedging effectiveness of the fractionally integrated error correction (FIEC), ECM, VAR and OLS models in estimating the risk minimizing hedge ratio using daily data on the Nikkei 225 for 1989-97. In addition, GARCH was included in each of the models to allow for autocorrelation in the variances. ECM with GARCH was the best approach, and incorporating FIEC did not lead to a superior performance.

Since the basis is affected by maturity effects, Low, Muthuswamy, Sakar & Terry (2002) argued that this should be allowed for when setting risk-minimizing hedge ratios. Using weekly data on the Nikkei 225 for 1986-96, they compared the out-of-sample hedging effectiveness of their cost-of-carry approach (which incorporates maturity effects), OLS, ECM and GARCH. They found that their cost-of-carry model was slightly better than OLS and ECM; and greatly superior to GARCH. Hedging effectiveness increased with hedge duration.

Choudhry (2003) studied the Nikkei 225, Hang Seng, SPI, FTSE 100, DAX 30 and the JSE Industrial 25 using daily data for 1990-9. He compared the out-of-sample hedging effectiveness of three methods: bivariate MA(1)-GARCH (1,1), bivariate MA(1)-GARCH (1,1)-X, OLS and 1:1. The GARCH models produced similar results, and outperformed OLS by between 1% and 14%.

Lien & Tse (2000b) considered daily data on the Nikkei 225 for 1989-97. Using OLS, VAR and EC hedge ratios, the hedge ratio increased towards one as the sampling interval lengthened; while the out-of-sample effectiveness of hedge ratios estimated using 1 day returns worsened as hedge duration increased.

Choudhry (2004) investigated hedging effectiveness for the Nikkei 225, SPI and Hang Seng using weekly data for 1990-2000. He compared the out-of-sample effectiveness of three alternative ways of estimating the risk-minimizing hedge ratio - 1:1, minimum variance and bivariate GARCH (1,1). The results were mixed, but time varying GARCH hedge ratios tended to be more effective than the other two methods. *Hong Kong.* Lam & Yu (1992) analyzed the performance of Hang Seng futures for 1986-91 in hedging the Hang Seng basket. An OLS regression using price changes was used to estimate the risk-minimizing hedge ratio (b). They found that, as hedge duration increased from 1 to 3 weeks, hedging effectiveness (E) rose from 94% to 97% for the post 1987 crash period, and b rose from 0.90 to 0.91.

Yau (1993) studied data on Hang Seng futures for 1986-92 to examine the effectiveness of these futures in hedging the Hang Seng basket. OLS regression, with an adjustment for serial correlation, was used to fit a relationship to daily spot and futures returns. The risk-minimizing hedge ratio (b) and hedging effectiveness (E) varied as between the 25 sub-periods, but averaged 0.87 and 86% respectively. Using the hedge ratio estimated for the previous period had little effect on E, and hedge ratios were found to be stable over time. Yau also investigated the Howard & D'Antonio hedge ratio (b^*, see chapter 9.3) using the Chang & Shanker (1986) effectiveness measure of $\Theta/(r-c) - 1$, where Θ is the slope of the line from the risk free asset to the hedged position in standard deviation-return space, c is the risk free rate of interest and r is the expected spot return. In some cases the hedge ratio (b^*) was either infinity or zero. Yau also used the hedge ratio (b^*) estimated for the previous period, and found that b^*, unlike b, varied considerably over time.

Kofman & McGlenchy (2004) studied daily data on three indices (Hang Seng, Hang Seng Commerce and Industry, Hang Seng Finance) for 1994-2003. They compared the out-of-sample hedging performance of five risk-minimizing hedge ratio estimators - static regression, expanding window regression, rolling window regression, exponential weighted regression and regression using a window since the most recent structural break. In each case the data were cleaned of GARCH (1,1) ARMA(1,1) effects before the application of OLS regression. The hedging effectiveness of all of these techniques was very similar, and allowance for structural breaks was only the best for the Hang Seng Finance index.

Korea.   Sim & Zurbruegg (2001b) analyzed daily data on the Kospi 200 for 1996-9 to investigate the effectiveness of different ways of estimating the hedge ratio. An EC-GARCH (1,3) model was used to estimate dynamic hedge ratios. The resulting hedge ratios were more effective than the constant hedge ratios estimated using price changes without any allowance for GARCH and cointegration. However, in the period after the Asian financial crisis, the superiority of the dynamic hedge ratios over the constant hedge ratios was reduced.

Taiwan.   Wang & Low (2003) considered hedging the MSCI Taiwan index, which is traded in Taiwan in new Taiwan dollars; and MSCI Taiwan futures, which are traded in Singapore in US$. Ruling out hedging the currency risk separately, they derive different risk-maximizing hedge ratios for Taiwanese and foreign investors. Using daily data for 1997-2000 they compare the out-of-sample hedging effectiveness of the trivariate GARCH (1,1)-X model, 1:1, OLS, and OLS with an error correction term. The results were broadly similar for domestic and international investors, with GARCH-X about 19% better than the conventional OLS hedge.

Demirer, Lien & Shaffer (2005) studied daily data for 1998-2002 on four index futures: TAIEX, mini-TAIEX, TSE Electronics, and TSE Banking and Insurance. They compared the hedging performance of three different hedge ratios - minimum variance, extended Gini and lower partial moment in hedging the underlying indices. They discovered that extended Gini and lower partial moment hedge ratios with a long futures position had a superior performance to hedges with a short futures position. They also found that extended Gini hedge ratios tended to produce a better out-of-sample hedging performance than minimum variance and lower partial moment hedges.

Australia.   Hodgson & Okunev (1992) examined hedging the basket of shares in the Australian AOI with All Ordinaries futures. For daily data for 1985-6, they computed the hedge ratio for each contract using data for the previous contract. As well as computing the variance-minimizing hedge ratios, they used the extended mean Gini coefficient (together with a specified level of risk aversion) to compute alternative hedge ratios. They found differences between the variance-minimizing and extended mean Gini hedge ratios, which led to differences in the returns on the hedged position. They also investigated dynamic hedge ratios, where the ratio was continually re-estimated using data for the previous sixty days, and found substantial changes in the extended mean Gini hedge ratios during the life of a contract.

Seelajaroen (2000) considered weekly data for 1992-8 on the SPI. He used a decision rule based on Working's profit maximization objective, and also the dynamic OLS risk minimizing hedge ratio, relative to the 1:1 hedge. The Working rule was able to generate profits, above those of a 1:1 hedge, while the out-of-sample effectiveness of the OLS hedge ratio was 92%,

Yang (2001) analyzed daily data for 1988-2000 of the SPI. He compared the out-of-sample hedging effectiveness of four methods for estimating the risk-minimizing hedge ratio: bivariate VAR, ECM, multivariate GARCH and static OLS. For a hedge duration of one day, there was little difference between the four models; but for 20-day hedges, the M-GARCH was about 20% better than the other three methods.

Moosa (2003) investigated monthly data for 1987-97 on the SPI. He estimated the risk-minimizing hedge ratio using OLS and price levels, OLS and price changes, a simple EC model and a general EC model. Although OLS applied to price levels produced a higher hedge ratio, all the in-sample Ederington effectiveness measures were very similar.

UK. Theobald & Yallup (1993) analyzed daily data on FTSE 100 futures for 1984-91, and used OLS regression to estimate the risk-minimizing hedge ratio (b) for this period. Since b changes with maturity (see chapter 9.2), they included a time variable in the regression, and this was statistically significant. To allow for the futures market closing price occurring 20 minutes before the stock market closing price and for stale prices; they also included the preceding and subsequent futures returns in the regression. However, Dawson (1993) criticized this rationale for the inclusion of these one day leads and lags. The estimated values of b ranged from 0.34 for the USM, to 0.84 for the FTSE 100. The $\overline{R}^2$ for their regressions, which give an indication of the effectiveness (E) of using FTSE 100 futures to hedge three different stock portfolios, were 84% for the FTSE 100, 86% for the FT-A All Share (86%) and 40% for the USM. To allow for mispricings and for stock exchange account effects, they repeated the analysis using the no-arbitrage futures prices computed with an allowance for the settlement effect inherent in stock exchange accounts to compute the hedge ratios for the FTSE 100 index basket. The value of $\overline{R}^2$ was 83%, which is only 1% different from that when the actual futures prices were used to estimate b.

Lee (1994) studied the performance of FTSE 100 futures in hedging three spot portfolios: the FTSE 100 basket, an equal investment in 10 high beta FTSE 100 stocks, and an equal investment in 10 low beta FTSE 100 stocks, using weekly data for 1984-94. Ignoring dividends, he used OLS regression with price changes (and also the logarithm of price changes) to estimate the risk-minimizing hedge ratio (b). A period of 100 weeks was used to estimate the hedge ratio for the next 12 weeks, and then a new non-overlapping period of 100 weeks (e.g. weeks 113 to 212) to estimate a new set of hedge ratios for use in weeks 213 to 224, etc. He investigated hedges with a duration of 1, 2 and 4 weeks. Hedging effectiveness (E) was greatest for the FTSE 100 portfolio (94% for 1 week hedges), and lowest for the low beta portfolio (44% for 1 week hedges). E increased with hedge duration, e.g. for the low beta portfolio E rose from 44% for 1 week hedges to 89% for 4-week hedges.

Holmes (1995) used weekly data for 1984-92 to examine the effectiveness of FTSE 100 futures in hedging the FTSE 100 portfolio of shares. He examined the performance of the one-to-one hedge ratio, and the risk-minimizing ratio (b) computed using OLS regression in three different ways. First, he used data for each year to compute the hedge ratio to be used during that same year. Second, he used data for each year to compute the hedge ratio to be used during the following year. Finally, he used data for each of the j weeks immediately preceding the hedge period to compute the hedge ratio. He examined hedges lasting one and two weeks. The risk-minimizing hedge ratio was, on average, 0.925 for one-week hedges, rising to 0.944 for two-week hedges. There was little difference in hedging effectiveness (E) for the four different ways of estimating the hedge ratios. This study shows that the use of data from a prior period to estimate the hedge ratio led to only a small reduction in E, which averaged about 95% for one-week hedges, rising to 98% for two week hedges.

Holmes (1996b) used weekly data on FTSE 100 futures for 1984-92 to study hedging the FTSE 100 index basket (ignoring dividends). He estimated the risk-minimizing hedge ratio for this period using three alternative regression procedures: OLS, ECM and GARCH (1,1). Hedging effectiveness (E) was similar for the three different methods, and so Holmes used OLS to study hedge duration, contract maturity and hedge ratio stability. As the duration of the hedge was increased from 1 to 4 weeks E rose from 95% to 99%, while the OLS hedge ratio (b) rose from 0.91 to 0.96. There was evidence that b increased with contract maturity, as predicted in chapter 9.2. Finally, while b varies over time, Holmes found it has a stationary distribution, and so using values of b estimated for past periods provides a good estimate of b for the current period.

Butterworth & Holmes (2000) considered weekly data for 1994-6 on 37 spot assets to be hedged (5 UK stock indices and 32 investment trusts), and two hedging instruments (FTSE 100 and FTSE Mid 250 futures). They found that in-sample and out-of-sample hedging effectiveness for hedge ratios estimated using dynamic OLS (rolling windows) were similar when the spot position was an index. They were also more similar when the rolling window was longer. However, for short windows and spot assets that are not indices, it is important to measure hedging effectiveness out-of-sample.

Butterworth & Holmes (2001) used daily data for 1994-6 on 36 spot assets (4 indices and 32 investment trusts), and two hedging instruments (FTSE 100 and FTSE Mid 250 futures). They examined the in-sample performance of four risk-minimizing hedge ratios: 1:1, OLS, least trimmed squares and the CAPM beta. In addition to a single hedging instrument, they also examined the performance of pre-set combinations of the two hedging instruments (composite hedging). The most effective single hedges used OLS (as least trimmed squares was slightly inferior), while the best overall in-sample effectiveness was for the composite hedges.

Market indices, particularly those that use the price of the last trade, are prone to the problem of non-synchronous prices, and estimators have been developed to allow for this problem. Theobald & Yallup (1997) showed that, if there are leads and lags between the spot and futures markets, these estimators give covariance estimates that are biased upwards. Out-of-sample hedging effectiveness for the FTSE 100 and FT All Share indices using daily data on FTSE 100 futures for 1985-95 found that, despite these problems, OLS is preferred to the Scholes-Williams and Stoll-Whaley estimators.

Sim & Zurbruegg (2001a) analyzed daily data on the FTSE 100 for 1992-9. They found that the in-sample effectiveness of hedge ratios estimated using GARCH-X was slightly superior to that of static OLS hedge ratios.

Brooks, Henry & Persand (2002) analyzed daily data on the FTSE 100 for 1985-99. They compared the performance of 1:1 hedge ratios with those estimated using a multivariate VECM-GARCH (1,1) model with the BEKK parameterization. This BEKK model was estimated with either a symmetric or an asymmetric covariance matrix. Both BEKK models were superior to the 1:1 hedge, with very similar out-of-sample hedging effectiveness. The authors then evaluated hedging performance using a Value at Risk approach; and the minimum capital risk requirement for the asymmetric BEKK model was substantially lower than for the symmetric model, particularly over short horizons.

Harris & Shen (2003) used daily data on the FTSE 100 for 1984-2002. They compared the hedging effectiveness of rolling OLS regression and rolling exponentially weighted moving average estimation of the hedge ratio with that of robust versions of these two estimators. These robust estimators are much less sensitive to extreme values. The out-of-sample hedging effectiveness of the two non-robust estimators was similar, while the switch to robust estimation led to a marginal improvement in hedging effectiveness of about 2% in each case. The main advantage from using robust estimation was the 5%-30% reduction in the variance of the hedge ratio, so reducing the transactions costs of rebalancing a dynamic hedging strategy.

Laws & Thompson (2005) analyzed weekly data on the FTSE 100 and FTSE Mid 250 for 1995-2001. They examined the ability of two hedging instruments (FTSE 100 and FTSE Mid 250 futures) to hedge 17 investment trusts and the FTSE 100 and FTSE Mid 250 indices. They used 1:1, static OLS, rolling window OLS, GARCH and EWMA to estimate the hedge ratios; and the out-of-sample hedging effectiveness of the EWMA hedge ratio was generally a few percent better than the rolling OLS estimate.

Spain.   Lafuente & Novales (2003) considered hourly data on the Ibex 35 for 1993-6. They used a bivariate GARCH-X model to estimate the out-of-sample effectiveness of risk-minimizing hedge ratios. The hedge duration was one week, and Ederington's effectiveness measure had a median value of 58%, which was very similar to that of the 1:1 hedge ratio..

Switzerland.   Stulz, Wasserfallen & Stucki (1990) studied weekly prices for Swiss Market Index futures traded on an OTC market run by the Leu Bank in 1989. OLS regression was used to calculate the risk-minimizing hedge ratios for 5 different assets - the SMI index, an index of about 450 Swiss companies, an equally weighted portfolio of 6 large Swiss companies, shares in the Union Bank of Switzerland and Rückversicherung participation certificates. The effectiveness of these hedges, as measured by E, was high for the 3 portfolios (about 0.90), but was lower for the individual shares. The results were similar for hedge ratios estimated using data for the period of the hedge and those estimated using only data for the period before the hedge began.

Italy.   Pattarin & Ferretti (2003) examined daily data on the MIB 30 for 1994-2002. They investigated the hedging effectiveness of five different ways of estimating the risk minimizing hedge ratio: 1:1, OLS, ECM, CC-GARCH and EWMA.

They found that EWMA produced the best out-of-sample performance.

Greece.   Floros & Vougas (2004) considered daily data on the FTSE-ASE 20 and FTSE-ASE Mid 40 indices for 1999-2001. They found that hedge ratios estimated by multivariate GARCH-X exceeded those estimated using OLS, which exceeded those estimated by ECM or VECM.

Conclusions.   In evaluating the empirical results, it should be remembered that many of these studies examined a hedge duration of only one day, and longer duration hedges will perform somewhat differently. The studies indicate that hedging a well diversified portfolio with index futures can reduce risk by about 50% to over 90%. Hedging portfolios that differ markedly in composition from the basket of shares underlying the index future produces lower, but still worthwhile, reductions in risk. Where a comparison was made between using the estimated values of b and beta as the hedge ratio, b was found to produce the greater reduction in risk. However, there do not appear to be substantial differences in hedging effectiveness as the estimation method of the risk-minimizing ratio is changed from OLS to GARCH, to ECM, or from a static model with a fixed window, to expanding windows, to rolling windows, to windows based on structural breaks, etc. However, as Lien (2005a) showed, this result may be because it is inappropriate to use E to compare OLS hedge ratios with hedge ratios estimated in other ways.

The risk-minimizing hedge ratio was generally found to be less than one ($b < 1$). Since $b = \rho_{FS}\sigma_S/\sigma_F$, and $\sigma_S \approx \sigma_F$; then $b \approx \rho_{FS}$, where $-1 \leq \rho_{FS} \leq 1$. Hence $-1 \leq b \leq 1$, and the risk minimizing ratios tend to be less than one. If the date when the hedge is lifted is moved closer to delivery, b also moves closer to 1. Figure 9.5 shows that if the date when the hedge is lifted moves from time A to time B, basis risk is lower, and so ρ_{FS} (and hence b) is closer to 1. The risk-minimizing hedge ratio rises as the duration of the hedge lengthens. This may be because longer hedges tend to end closer to delivery, at which time basis risk is lower and ρ_{FS} (and hence b) is higher. The longer is the duration of the hedge, the greater its effectiveness in reducing risk. This is because market risk increases with hedge duration, while basis risk does not, as shown in figure 9.6. Finally, there is evidence that lengthening the differencing interval of the data increases the hedge ratio and hedging effectiveness.

9.14.2 Is Actual Hedging Mean-Variance Efficient?

The portfolio approach requires that hedgers locate somewhere on their mean-variance efficiency frontier, as illustrated in figure 9.1. This includes the risk-minimizing (M) and profit-maximizing (C) hedges as special cases. However, it does not include points inside the frontier, such as point I in figure 9.1. A few studies (none of index futures) have examined whether actual hedging decisions accord with mean-variance efficiency. Negative results may just indicate inefficient hedging, or they may suggest that the mean-variance model of hedging is incorrect.

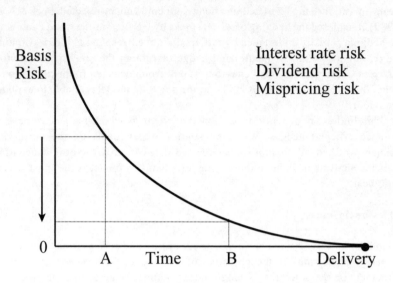

Figure 9.5: The Hedge Ratio and the Date the Hedge is Lifted

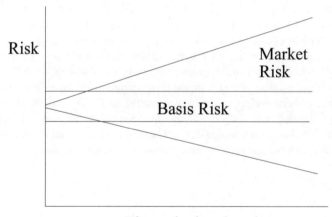

Figure 9.6: Basis Risk Versus Market Risk

Rutledge (1972) studied the hedging decisions of soyabean processors and found that mean-variance models were able to explain the hedging of their raw materials (soyabeans), but were less successful in explaining the hedging of their outputs (soyabean oil and soyabean meal). Hartzmark (1988) studied trading in oat and wheat futures by large commercial US traders and concluded, with some reservations, that the mean-variance model of hedging behaviour could not be rejected. Peck & Nahmias (1989) considered the hedging of wheat stocks by US flour millers, and concluded that the hedging actually undertaken by millers did not correspond to the risk-minimizing hedge, nor to the utility-maximizing hedge (assuming the level of wheat stocks is variable). Thus, the hedging behaviour of this group does not fit the portfolio model. Either they were acting suboptimally, or the portfolio model is unable to explain their behaviour.

This limited evidence is mixed on the extent to which hedgers choose mean-variance efficient hedges. While no studies are available on the mean-variance efficiency of hedged positions in shares and index futures, the dominance of mean-variance analysis in finance theory suggests that this model is the most reasonable hypothesis.

9.15 Conclusions

A fundamental requirement in devising hedge ratios and in measuring the effectiveness of hedging decisions is the objective of the hedge. Because there is no general agreement on the objective of hedging, there cannot be agreement on either a single formula for the hedge ratio, or on a single effectiveness measure. The extent of the agreement is that any hedged position should be mean-variance efficient. Because of its simplicity, much of the literature has focused on the risk-minimizing hedge. However, it may be that real world hedging is not aimed solely at risk-minimisation, and a more general portfolio analysis is required. For equities, both systematic and unsystematic risk can be controlled. Portfolio diversification will remove unsystematic risk, while systematic risk can be removed by hedging. While there are problems in choosing how to estimate the risk-minimizing hedge ratio, the empirical evidence indicates that hedging effectiveness is insensitive to the estimation method used, although this finding may be due to the way in which hedging effectiveness is measured. This evidence also suggests that hedging can lead to substantial reductions in risk, but that risk-minimizing hedging does not eliminate all risk.

Chapter 10

The Uses of Stock Index
Futures by Fund Managers

Introduction

It is shown in this chapter that index futures can be very useful to fund managers. The use of index futures for arbitrage has already been considered in chapters 3, 4 and 5, basis speculation and spreads was discussed in chapter 6, while the use of index futures for hedging was considered in chapter 9. There are many additional ways in which index futures can be used by fund managers, and these are considered in this chapter.

10.1 Two Basic Properties of Index Futures

Most of the uses of index futures by fund managers are based on two properties of index futures: controlling the beta value of a portfolio, and varying the size of the investment in the market, Kon (1984).

10.1.1 Control Beta

The beta value of a portfolio of assets is the weighted sum of the betas of the underlying assets:-

$$\beta_p = \sum_{i=1}^{n} \beta_i x_i \qquad \text{where } \sum_{i=1}^{n} x_i = 1$$

If the investor has borrowed money to invest in shares, there will be a difference between the total sum of money invested in shares and the net value of the portfolio. In this case the weights relate to the net value of the portfolio. Apart from trading share options, there are three ways in which a fund manager can attempt to control the beta value of his or her portfolio.

(a) Trade Shares. The fund manager can trade shares with high or low individual beta values, as appropriate. Thus, the beta value of a portfolio is raised by selling shares with a low beta and buying shares with a high beta. This method of controlling beta has a number of drawbacks. Trading shares because of their estimated beta values may result in a poorly diversified portfolio, i.e. not all unsystematic risk may have been diversified away. Thus, the portfolio will be moving away from the

market portfolio, and will offer an inferior risk-return combination. In figure 10.1 R_FMA is the capital market line, $CMNB$ is the efficiency frontier in the absence of lending or borrowing and M is the market portfolio. If the portfolio of shares is moved away from M to N, the new locus of efficient portfolios (R_FMNB) is inferior to the previous locus (R_FMA). Trading shares to control beta may also generate substantial transactions costs due to buying and selling many shares in different companies. The estimated beta values for individual shares may be unstable over short periods of time, so making it difficult to achieve a target beta value for the portfolio in the short run.

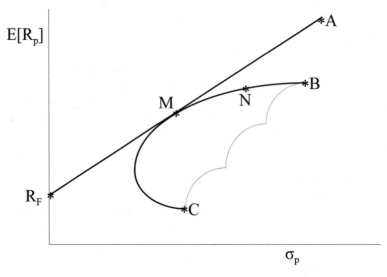

Figure 10.1: Loss of Efficiency by Trading Only Shares to Adjust Beta

Since shares with a low or negative beta are uncommon, it may prove difficult to get the beta value of the portfolio down to low levels while still avoiding unsystematic risk. In theory it is possible to achieve a negative portfolio beta by short selling shares with a high beta. However, in practice, short selling shares is difficult and expensive, and it is uncommon for fund managers to take a short position in shares. Indeed, it has been shown by Board & Sutcliffe (1994) that superior performance is achieved when short selling is ruled out. Hence, there is a lower limit to the portfolio beta that can be obtained in this way. There is also an upper limit on the portfolio beta that can be achieved by trading shares. This is the beta of a well diversified portfolio of high beta shares, e.g. not far above one. Thus beta can be moved between about a half to roughly one and a half. Finally, this strategy may require selling shares which the fund manager expects to outperform the market, and buying shares which the manager expects to underperform the market, purely because they have the requisite beta values.

Example. The Southumbria Fund owns shares in ten companies, with 10% of the total value of the fund invested in each.

Table 10.1: Beta Values for the Southumbria Example

Share	β	Share	β
Bassett	0.4	Portswood	0.9
Bitterne	0.5	Shirley	.1.0
Chilworth	0.6	Swaythling	1.1
Highfield	0.7	Totton	1.2
Netley	0.8	Woolston	1.3

The present portfolio has a beta of 0.85. Charles Foster Kane, the fund manager, wishes to raise the portfolio beta to one. One way of accomplishing this is to sell all of the holding in Bassett and 75% of the holding in Bitterne, and use the proceeds to buy shares in Woolston. This produces a portfolio with no investment in Bassett, 2.5% of the funds in Bitterne, 27.5% in Woolston and 10% in each of the other assets.

(b) Borrow or Lend and Trade Shares.   The fund manager can engage in borrowing or lending at the risk free rate of interest, as well as trading shares. Since investment in the risk free asset has a beta value of zero, the higher the proportion of the portfolio invested in the risk free asset, the lower is the portfolio beta. This strategy of selling shares and investing the proceeds in the risk free asset can push the portfolio beta down to zero. If the aim is to raise the portfolio beta, the fund manager can liquidate existing holdings of the risk free asset, or borrow money at the risk free rate, and invest the proceeds in shares.

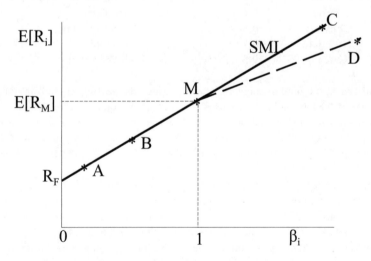

Figure 10.2: The Security Market Line

In diagrammatic terms, this strategy involves the fund moving up and down the line

$R_F ABMC$ in figure 10.2, which is the security market line. Points on this line between R_F and M represent situations when some of the fund's assets are invested in the risk free asset, while points above M, such as C, imply that the fund has borrowed money at the risk free rate and invested the proceeds in a well diversified portfolio of shares.

This approach to managing beta involves either buying or selling shares, depending on whether money is being invested or borrowed at the risk free rate. Therefore it raises the problems of transactions costs, loss of stock selection skills and maintaining the diversified nature of the portfolio. The beta for a well diversified portfolio of high beta shares places an upper limit on the beta that can be achieved. Once all the holdings of the risk free asset have been liquidated, the fund must borrow at the risk free rate to invest in shares. It is likely that a higher rate of interest than R_F must be paid to borrow money, the two fund separation theorem has broken down, and an inferior risk-return trade-off must be accepted to increase the portfolio's beta, e.g. the line MD in figure 10.2. In addition, there may be some upper limit on total borrowing. Therefore, using just shares and the risk free asset, portfolio betas can be manipulated between zero and not far above one.

Example. The Westumbria Fund has invested equal amounts of money in nine shares and the risk free asset.

Table 10.2: Beta Values for the Westumbria Fund

Security	β	Security	β
Riskless Asset	0	Portswood	0.9
Bitterne	0.5	Shirley	1.0
Chilworth	0.6	Swaythling	1.1
Highfield	0.7	Totton	1.2
Netley	0.8	Woolston	1.3

Cal Trask, the fund manager, wishes to reduce the portfolio beta from its present value of 0.81 to 0.62. He chooses to accomplish this by selling all the shares in Woolston and 50% of the shares in Totton, and lending the proceeds at the riskless rate of interest. The resulting portfolio has no investment in Woolston, 5% of the funds in Totton, 25% of the funds in the risk free asset and 10% in each of the other securities.

Example. Jacques Clouseau, the manager of the Moramax Fund, has carefully constructed a portfolio of four shares, see table 10.3. This portfolio is designed both to outperform the market and to have low unsystematic risk. This portfolio has a beta value of 1.6, and Jacques wishes to raise it to 2.0. He wishes to achieve this without changing the importance of individual companies within the equity portfolio so as not to reduce the benefits of diversification. Therefore, he borrows money at the risk free rate and uses it to increase the fund's holdings of each of the four shares by a common percentage. This percentage is given by the ratio of the desired beta to the initial beta, i.e. $2.0/1.6 = 1.25$, or a 25% increase. Thus, Jacques borrows 25% of the value of the fund, and increases the fund's investment in each of the four shares by 25% to produce a fund with a beta value of 2.0.

Table 10.3: Beta Values for the Moramax Fund

Security	β	w_1	βw_1	w_2	βw_2
Highfield	0.7	0.1	0.07	0.125	0.0875
Woolston	1.3	0.2	0.26	0.250	0.3250
Thornhill	1.7	0.3	0.51	0.375	0.6375
Freemantle	1.9	0.4	0.76	0.500	0.9500
Risk free asset	0	0	0	−0.250	0
Portfolio Beta				1.600	2.0000

(c) Trade Index Futures. The fund manager can buy or sell index futures to adjust the portfolio beta. This method for altering a portfolio's beta does not require trading shares or the risk free asset, and overcomes the inability of investors to borrow at the risk free rate, Fabozzi, Fabozzi & Peters (1989). However, it will be necessary to rollover the futures position and to fund the initial margin payment (about 4% for FTSE 100 futures) and any payments of variation margin. If the fund has no unallocated cash, this money could be found by reducing the investment in the risk free asset. Because index futures do not require any investment, it is more meaningful to compute the beta value for a portfolio of shares and futures. The beta value of a portfolio of securities and futures (β_2) can be calculated as the sum of two terms: the beta value of the securities (β_1), and a term representing the systematic risk of the futures position. If the index future has a beta value of one, i.e. $\beta_F = 1$, this is the number of futures contracts (X_f) (positive sign for a long position and negative sign for a short position), divided by the number of index baskets (X_s); where X_s is the value of the share portfolio divided by the value of shares in one index basket. Therefore, $\beta_2 = \beta_1 + X_f/X_s$.

Consider a portfolio of shares worth £100 million, with portfolio weights equivalent to those of the market portfolio. If the fund buys FTSE 100 futures corresponding to shares with a spot value of £100 million (ignoring margin payments) and the price of this future moves with the market portfolio, the portfolio beta rises to two, while if the fund sells FTSE 100 futures worth £100 million, the portfolio beta drops to zero. Using index futures has the advantage of easily achieving a negative portfolio beta, if required, and also very large positive betas. Since no shares are traded, the transactions costs are low, the portfolio of shares remains well diversified and shares expected to outperform the market need not be sold. However, there will be rollover costs and risks, margin payments, and a possible mismatch between the composition of the portfolio of shares and the index basket.

It is quite likely that the index on which the future is based has a different composition from the market portfolio. In this case $\beta_F \neq 1$, and the systematic risk of the futures position must be adjusted, and so $\beta_2 = \beta_1 + \beta_F(X_f/X_s)$, where β_F is the beta value of the index future with respect to the market portfolio. The number of index futures required to change the beta value of a portfolio from β_1 to β_2 is given by:-

$$X_f = X_s(\beta_2 - \beta_1)/\beta_F$$

(see Clarke, 1992). The returns or price changes are measured over the desired investment period. Note that β_F relates excess return, not total return, to the return on a futures contract.

Example. The Eastumbria Fund has invested equal amounts of money in ten securities, and the fund has a beta value of 0.81.

Table 10.4: Beta Values for the Eastumbria Fund

Security	β	Security	β
Riskless Asset	0	Portswood	0.9
Bitterne	0.5	Shirley	1.0
Chilworth	0.6	Swaythling	1.1
Highfield	0.7	Totton	1.2
Netley	0.8	Woolston	1.3

Barney Rubble, the fund manager, wishes to increase the portfolio beta to 1.5. The current market value of the fund is £60 million, while the current value of the FTSE 100 index is 4,800. The value of β_F is 1.2, and so $X_f = (60,000,000/48,000)\times(1.5-0.81)/1.2 = 718.75$. Therefore, he needs to take a long position in 719 FTSE 100 futures contracts. This will require a margin payment of $719\times1,500 = £1,078,500$ which can be obtained by using some of the £6 million invested in the risk free asset.

The omission of margins from the calculation of X_f is irrelevant. If the cash balances required to make the margin payments are included in the initial portfolio (and β_1 and β_2 are adjusted accordingly), the resulting value of X_f is unchanged.

10.1.2 Vary the Size of Investment in the Market

A fund manager can easily increase (decrease) the size of his or her investment in the stock market by buying (selling) index futures. If the manager wishes to invest more money in the stock market, e.g. because he or she thinks the market is about to rise, index futures can be bought. If the manager wishes to invest less money in the stock market, e.g. because he or she thinks the market is about to fall, index futures can be sold. Individual shares need only be purchased because they are thought likely to outperform the market.

There are a number of reasons why a fund manager might prefer to use index futures rather than buying or selling shares. Since the margin requirements are low, (for £1 million he or she can 'invest' about £25 million), futures give very high leverage. Taking a short position to profit from a drop in the market is easy with index futures, but not with shares. The transactions costs are low for futures, while the liquidity is high, and no excess returns due to stock selection skills are lost. However, there will be rollover costs and risks, margin payments, and a possible mismatch between the composition of the portfolio of shares and the index basket.

Example. There is to be a general election on Thursday 3rd May. On Wednesday 2nd May, Ebenezer Scrooge, who manages the Hexham Fund which has an investment in UK equities of £60 million, forms the view that the Conservative Party will win the election and that this will lead to an immediate rise in the UK stock market. Ebenezer decides to increase the exposure of his fund to changes in the level of UK stock prices so as to increase the gain from the rise which will follow a Conservative victory. He decides to do this quickly and cheaply by immediately taking a long position in 1,000 FTSE 100 index futures, where the value of the FTSE 100 index is 4,800. If the beta value of his share portfolio is one and β_F is 0.8, this will increase the beta value of the fund from one to $\beta_F X_f / X_s + \beta_1 = 1.64$. Thus, if returns on the market rise by 5%, returns on the fund will increase by $5 \times 1.64 = 8.2\%$. After the election result is declared, Ebenezer closes out this futures position on the morning of Friday 5th May.

R. Miller (1990) has suggested that the increased use of index futures by fund managers will tend to diminish the charge of short-termism, see chapter 12.

10.2 Uses of Index Futures by Fund Managers

A wide variety of ways in which these two properties of trading index futures (manage beta and vary the investment) can be used in fund management will now be considered, Stoll & Whaley (1988a).

10.2.1 Separation of Stock Selection from Timing Decisions

The performance of a portfolio can be disaggregated into stock selection and market timing. Stock selection relates to the ability of the fund managers to identify particular shares which are mispriced. In the context of the CAPM this implies buying shares with a positive alpha (underpriced) and selling those with a negative alpha (overpriced), where α_i is given by $E[R_i] = \alpha_i + R_F + (E[R_M] - R_F)\beta_i$, and $E[R_i]$ is the expected return on share i, α_i is the alpha of the ith share, R_F is the risk free rate of interest, β_i is the beta value of the ith share and $E[R_M]$ is the expected rate of return for the stock market as a whole. If the CAPM applies, α_i should be zero because a portfolio with no systematic risk, i.e. $\beta_i = 0$, should produce only the riskless rate of return. Thus, α_i measures abnormal returns, and the inclusion of α_i permits a test for the absence of abnormal returns. A possible situation is illustrated in figure 10.3, where α_i is negative.

Aggregating across all assets gives a corresponding equation for the entire fund: $E[R_p] = \Sigma \alpha_i x_i + R_F + (E[R_M] - R_F)\Sigma \beta_i x_i$, where x_i is the proportion of the fund invested in the ith asset and $E[R_p]$ is the expected return on the fund. It can be seen that increasing any α_i (where $x_i > 0$) has a direct effect on the fund's expected return.

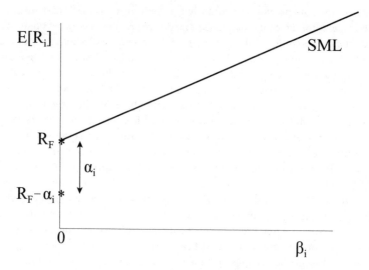

Figure 10.3: Security Market Line and a Negative Alpha Asset

Market timing is concerned with the manager's skill in forecasting movements in the return on the stock market less the risk free rate, i.e. $(E[R_M] - R_F)$, and in varying the beta value of the portfolio accordingly. In the absence of index futures, situations may arise where there is a conflict between stock selection and market timing decisions. For example, a fund manager may be aware of a share that is considerably underpriced. However, this share has a high beta, and the fund manager expects the market to fall. Thus, stock selection indicates the purchase of this share, while market timing suggests otherwise. Such interactions between stock selection and market timing make it difficult to delegate these decisions to separate groups, or to measure the performance of each group if such delegation does take place.

Index futures permit a portfolio's beta to be changed without altering the stock selection decision, Figlewski & Kon (1982), Kon (1986). The beta value of a portfolio can be altered in three ways; the first is to buy shares with a high (low) beta and sell shares with a low (high) beta. Such trading may alter the extent to which the portfolio is well diversified. The beta value of a portfolio can also be altered by changing the allocation of the fund between different classes of asset, e.g. domestic equities, foreign equities, domestic fixed interest, foreign fixed interest, domestic property etc. Finally, index futures can be used to change a portfolio's beta. Altering the composition of a fund using share sales and index futures is compared in the following example.

Example. Fred Flintstone is the manager of the Howdon Fund, which has £100 million invested in a well diversified portfolio of domestic equities. This portfolio is expected to give a return 1% above that on the stock market, due to the skilled selection of its constituent stocks, but to have the same risk as the market, i.e. $\beta_p = 1$. Fred Flintstone expects the stock market to fall, and wishes to reduce the beta value of the portfolio to 0.5. The beta value (and the size of the investment in the stock market) of this portfolio could be halved by selling half of each share holding and putting the funds in the risk free asset, i.e. government debt. While the new portfolio of shares would still be well diversified, this strategy would halve the expected excess returns from 1% to 0.5% of the total value of the fund. An alternative strategy is to sell index futures to reduce the fund's beta value to the desired level of 0.5. If $\beta_F = 1$, the required spot value of the shares corresponding to the index futures to be purchased is £100 million times $(1.0-0.5)/1.0 = £50$ million, while if $\beta_F = 1.25$, the required spot value of the shares corresponding to the index futures to be purchased is £100 million times $(1.0-0.5)/1.25 = £40$ million. If index futures are used to reduce the beta value of the portfolio, there will be no reduction in the expected excess returns on the portfolio, i.e. they will remain at £1 million. Hence, by using index futures, the selection and market timing activities have been separated.

The use of index futures has the advantages of lower transactions costs, no diminution of the benefits from any stock selection skills the manager may possess, and facilitates the delegation of stock selection.

10.2.2 Changing the Asset Allocation

The allocation of funds between different types of asset, e.g. domestic equities, foreign equities, fixed interest securities, property and cash, can be the major determinant of the returns on a fund, with the choice of particular shares etc being of secondary importance. For example, the main determinant of investment performance for UK and US pension funds is asset allocation, rather than asset selection (Blake, Lehmann & Timmermann, 1999; Brinson, Hood & Beebower, 1986; Brinson, Singer & Beebower, 1991; and Ibbotson & Kaplan, 2000). If the managers of a fund wish to make a substantial alteration to the asset allocation decision this can be effected immediately by means of futures, also called a futures overlay. Later, the underlying assets in the portfolio can gradually be altered to reflect the new policy, and the relevant futures contracts closed out. This procedure is, in effect, two hedges. The existing spot asset position which it is desired to end is hedged until it can be liquidated, while the spot asset position which it is desired to acquire is hedged until the spot assets can be traded. It has the advantages of speed and low market impact.

Example. The Paramount Trust, which is managed by Joe Lampton, had total funds of £500 million, of which £300 million were invested in UK shares, £150 million was in UK government debt and £50 million was directly invested in UK property. When Universal were appointed as the new fund managers, they wished to shift to a new allocation of assets: £350 million in UK equities, £40 million in US equities, £60 million in UK gilts and £50 million in UK property. This new asset allocation was implemented immediately by using financial futures. Paramount bought FTSE 100 index futures corresponding to shares with a spot value of £50 million, and S&P500 index futures corresponding to a spot value of £40 million (assuming β_F

is unity for each future). To lower their exposure to gilts, Paramount sold futures in UK government debt corresponding to £90 million. Subsequently, as Paramount purchased UK and US equities and sold UK government debt, the relevant futures were closed out.

10.2.3 Rebalancing the Asset Allocation

The managers of a fund may set targets for the proportions of the fund invested in different classes of asset to give a balanced portfolio. For example, the Pensions Act, 1995 sets a minimum requirement for the proportion of the pensions fund in fixed interest securities. Once such a balanced portfolio is achieved, unless the value of all asset classes changes by the same proportion, it will become unbalanced, i.e. the proportions will deviate from the targets. As the relative values of the various asset classes change, futures can be used to rebalance the fund.

Example. Fred Kite manages the Wembley fund, which has set the targets of 70% of the fund in UK equities, and the remaining 30% in gilts. Fred achieved these proportions, but during the next two months the value of UK equities rose by 10%, while the value of gilts fell by 5%. In consequence, the value of the fund invested in equities rose to $70 \times 1.1/(70 \times 1.1 + 30 \times 0.95) = 73\%$, while that in gilts fell to 27%. Fred decided to rebalance the portfolio by selling FTSE 100 index futures, and buying interest rate futures. In another few months, a further rebalancing may be required.

10.2.4 Anticipating Cash Inflows

The fund may know that a substantial cash inflow will occur within the next few months. Instead of waiting until the cash is received before investing in the stock market, the fund managers may choose to take a long position in the market now via index futures. For example, a survey of 47 UK life assurance companies found that they use index futures for pre-investing their cash inflows, KPMG Peat Marwick, 1994. If existing holdings of government debt are used as the initial margins, the only additional capital required is a reserve for variation margin payments.

10.2.5 Accumulating Money for Investment

Funds often have a small, regular net inflow of money which requires investment. This may be payments into a pension fund, or just dividends from the existing investments. If the fund wishes to maintain a well diversified portfolio, each new sum of money must be spread across a wide range of shares. However, this generates considerable transactions costs. An alternative approach is to initially invest the inflows of money in short term government debt, and to buy index futures with a value corresponding to the amount of the new money (adjusted for β_F). In this way the new money is accumulated until the amount is large enough for direct investment in a wide range of shares. At this time the corresponding futures are closed out.

Example. The Phantom Fund, which is managed by Virgil Tibbs, has a net cash flow of £1 million per month. This fund wishes to hold a well diversified portfolio of the top 500 UK shares. The total transaction costs to the Phantom Fund of buying shares in each of these companies is £150 per purchase, plus 1% of the sum invested. The transaction costs of £150 per trade include the cost of the staff time in placing the order to purchase, checking that the instructions have been executed, paying fees to the custodian for holding the shares, paying for the shares, recording the date and price of the transaction, and checking that the custodian is holding the shares and that the payment has been made. The transaction cost of buying any number of FTSE 100 futures is £150, plus 0.1% of the underlying shares, while lending any sum of money at the riskless rate costs £150. Over a year the transaction costs of immediately investing the net cash inflow in the portfolio of 500 shares are:

Fixed costs (12 months ×500×£150)	£900,000
Variable costs (£12 million ×0.01)	£120,000
Total transaction costs per year	£1,020,000

+Alternatively, the Phantom Fund can buy FTSE 100 futures corresponding to £1 million for the first five months and invest the cash inflow at the risk free rate. In the sixth month, the fund can liquidate these futures and loans and, together with the £1 million cash inflow in that month, invest in the top 500 shares. The annual transaction costs from this strategy are:

Fixed costs - futures (10 months ×£150)	£3,000
Variable costs - futures (£12 million ×0.001)	£12,000
Fixed costs - loans (10 months ×£150)	£3,000
Fixed costs - shares (2 months ×500×£150)	£150,000
Variable costs - shares (£12 million ×0.01)	£120,000
Total transaction costs per year	£288,000

This constitutes a saving of £732,000 per year, or 6.1% of the annual sum invested.

10.2.6. Uncertain Cash Outflows

A fund may be required to make an instant cash payment at an uncertain time. Instead of just keeping the money on short term deposit, the fund may also wish to hold a matching long position in index futures. This is equivalent to having invested the money in the basket of shares underlying the index, except that the position can be instantly liquidated. If the fund is attempting to track the index, this strategy avoids the tracking error that would result from just keeping some of the funds in cash, Tucker, Becker, Isimbabi & Ogden (1994).

10.2.7. Reduced Exchange Risk for Foreign Investors

If an investor buys a widely diversified portfolio of shares in another country this foreign investment is subject to two sources of risk: market risk in the foreign country, and foreign exchange risk. When the investment is liquidated, the entire sum is converted to the home currency of the foreign investor at the prevailing exchange rate. This rate is uncertain when the investment is made. Index futures can be used to greatly reduce the exchange risk of such investments (Jorion & Roisenberg, 1993). If a long (or short) position is taken in index futures of the foreign country, the exchange risk is confined to the margin payments and receipts; usually much smaller than the initial value of the shares in the portfolio.

Example. The Enterprise Fund, which is managed by Montgomery Scott, of the UK wishes to invest £20 million in a widely diversified portfolio of US shares for a period of six months. This can be achieved by converting the £20 million into dollars at the current exchange rate of $1.5 per £1, i.e. $30 million, and buying US shares. Six months later the shares are sold for $31 million, while the terminal value of the dividend payments on these shares is $1 million. The total proceeds of $32 million are converted to sterling at the prevailing exchange rate in six months time of $1.6 per £1, i.e. £20 million. In this example all the money was subject to foreign exchange risk, and the gain on the portfolio of US shares was eliminated by the adverse exchange rate movement.

Alternatively, the fund could buy US index futures (e.g. the S&P500) corresponding to a long position of £20 million. This assumes that, for the desired portfolio of US shares and the S&P500 index future, the beta value equals one. If the current value of the S&P500 index is 1,200, the Enterprise Fund must purchase $(\$20,000,000 \times 1.5)/(1,200 \times \$250) = 100$ S&P500 contracts. This requires the payment of an initial margin of $\$20,000 \times 100 = \$2,000,000$. Assuming the riskless rate of interest in the US is 5% per six months, the current no-arbitrage price of each index futures contract is $1,200 \times \$250 \times 1.05 - 1,000,000/100 = \$305,000$. To pay the initial margin and cover subsequent margin calls, Enterprise converts £2 million into dollars at $1.5 per £1 to produce $3 million. (For simplicity, it is assumed that this money does not earn interest.) The remaining money (£18 million) is invested in UK government debt at 5% per six months, to give an interest payment of £900,000 in six months time. At delivery the price of the relevant S&P500 futures contract has risen to $310,000. Therefore the Enterprise Fund makes a gain of $100(\$310,000 - \$305,000) = \$500,000$ on its futures contracts. (For simplicity, it is assumed the entire rise in the price of the futures contract takes place on the final day. This rules out the complication of earning interest on the gains made during the six month period.) Thus, at the end of the six months the fund has $3.5 million to convert into sterling at $1.6 per £1, producing £2,187,500. The total increase in the value of the fund is £900,000 + £187,500 = £1,087,500. Therefore, by limiting the foreign exchange exposure to the margin money and the gain or loss on the US market, the Enterprise Fund has not seen the gains in the US market wiped out by adverse exchange rate movements. The result is an increase in the value of the fund of over £1 million.

Other strategies exist for reducing exchange risk. One possibility is that, at the same time as the US shares are purchased, a futures contract is entered into to supply dollars in exchange for sterling. The quantity of dollars to be supplied could allow for the expected dividends and capital gains on the US shares. Alternatively, the investor could borrow the dollars to be invested in US shares in the US. The only sum of money subject to foreign exchange risk is the capital gain plus dividends, less the interest payments on the dollar loan. The CME trades Nikkei 225 futures with a contract multiplier of $US5, and so it is possible for Americans to take a position in the Japanese market with zero currency risk.

The removal of foreign exchange risk may be seen by some fund managers as a disadvantage. Many funds do not hedge away their foreign exchange risk, and so the performance of the average fund reflects exchange rate changes, as well as movements in share prices. For a fund manager whose performance is judged against other funds, the removal of foreign exchange risk is a risky strategy. His or her relative performance is now affected by exchange rate changes, whereas the relative performance of an unhedged fund is not.

10.2.8 Investment in Foreign Equities

Funds usually wish to invest some of their money in a range of foreign equity markets. Direct investment in foreign equities encounters a number of difficulties: the presence of foreign exchange risk, higher transactions costs than for the domestic market and problems in obtaining exposure to general movements in a foreign market with only a small investment. However, these difficulties can be reduced or eliminated by the use of index futures, where they exist, as the way in which a fund invests in foreign markets.

Index futures have the advantage that taking short positions is easy, quick and cheap; relative to short selling stocks. So & Tse (2001) investigated this in the context of international diversification. Using monthly returns in $US for 1992-9 for nine countries (Australia, Canada, France, Germany, Hong Kong, Japan, UK and the USA), they computed the efficient portfolio corresponding to the return on the US market. When short sales were ruled out, the efficient portfolio was 100% US stocks. However, when short sales were permitted, every country was traded; with Australia, Hong Kong, France and Canada held short. The risk of this unconstrained portfolio was 12% lower than for the constrained portfolio. Therefore, if the use of index futures facilitates taking short positions in foreign markets which would not be undertaken using shares, it can offer substantial benefits.

10.2.9 Create an Index Fund

An increasingly popular form of passive fund management is the index fund. Such funds aim to replicate the performance of a chosen market index. An index fund can be established by buying all the shares in the index in proportion to their index weights. Alternatively, shares in a smaller number of companies can be purchased so that the performance of the resulting portfolio is expected to closely but not exactly replicate that of the chosen market index, i.e. there will be tracking error. In each case there are transactions costs associated with the initial purchase of the shares in many different companies, the reinvestment of dividends and new monies in a way that retains the index tracking property, and the rebalancing of the fund when the constituents or weights of the index change.

An alternative approach is to use index futures and government debt to construct a portfolio with the same performance as the chosen market index, Fabozzi & Garlicki (1984), Carpenter (1991, pp. 131-132). The change in the value of an index fund of shares over some period is given by the capital gain or loss, plus the terminal value of the dividends, i.e. $(S_T - S_0) + D(1+r)$. A long position in index futures and an investment in a riskless asset produces a gain or loss on the futures position of $(S_T - F_0)$, as well as interest on the money available for investment of rS_0. If the no-arbitrage condition currently applies, then $F_0 = (S_0 - D)(1+r)$, and so $(S_T - F_0) + rS_0 = (S_T - S_0) + D(1+r)$, which is the same change in value as if the money had been invested in the index basket of shares.

Example. The Trantor Fund, which is managed by Lawrence Bourne III, has £100 million to invest, and could use this money to buy a portfolio of shares, thereby receiving the change in the value of the index as a capital gain (or loss) and the dividends on the shares in the index. The dividends over the next six months on these shares have a present value of £2 million. Alternatively, the £100 million could be invested in government debt for six months to yield the risk-free rate of interest, say £5 million at the end of the six months. At the same time a long position could be taken in index futures for the index it is desired to track, for instance the FTSE 100. If the spot value of the FTSE 100 index is 4,800, the desired number of contracts for delivery in six months time to be purchased now is $100,000,000/(4,800 \times £10) \approx 2,083$. The current price of a futures contact, assuming that the no-arbitrage condition applies, is $(S - D)(1+r) = (4,800 \times £10 - 2,000,000 /2,083) \times 1.05 = £49,392$. Let the value of the index at delivery in six months' time be 5,000. Ignoring transactions costs and taxes, and assuming that throughout the period the portfolio of shares is identical in composition to the index, the terminal values of these two alternative strategies are identical:-

(a) The capital gain on the shares in the index is £100 million times $(5,000 - 4,800)/4,800 = £4,167,000$. Dividends on the shares in the index have a terminal value of £2 million $\times 1.05 = £2,100,000$, and so the total increase in the value of the Trantor Fund is £6,267,000.

(b) The interest received on the investment of £100 million in government debt is £5 million. The gain on the futures contracts is $(5,000 \times 10 - £49,392) \times 2,083 = £1,267,000$. This gives a total increase in the value of the Trantor Fund of £6,267,000.

This result is independent of the particular numbers chosen for the example. The use of index futures has two important advantages over the use of shares when creating an index fund: the transactions costs are much lower than for acquiring and maintaining a broadly diversified portfolio of shares (although the costs of rolling over the futures position every few months will mount up), and, if the no-arbitrage condition applies, the performance of the portfolio using the index futures exactly mirrors that of the chosen index. However, index futures require the establishment of a liquidity reserve for variation margin payments, and there are no stock lending opportunities (and revenues).

The futures are subject to a number of sources of risk, and so may fail to precisely replicate the performance of the basket of shares corresponding to the index. The futures may not be priced in accordance with the no-arbitrage condition when the position is opened, closed or rolled over, and this pricing risk will lead to gains or losses, relative to the index portfolio. The rollovers can be timed to benefit from mispricings between the near and far contracts. Watsham (1996) found that for 257 days in 1995-6, on 207 it was possible to roll forwards at a small gain (on average 4.35 index points, or £108.75). Futures are marked to the market, and so any capital gain or loss is received or paid before the terminal date when the index portfolio is liquidated. When the market is rising, the holder of a long futures position will receive margin payments, and this money can be invested to earn extra interest. When the market is falling, such an investor must borrow money to finance the margin payments they must make. These interest receipts or payments will cause the performance of the synthetic index fund to diverge from that of the index portfolio. The dividends that accrue during the life of a futures contract are uncertain. If they are higher than expected, the futures position will underperform, while if they are lower than expected, the futures position will over perform. The risk free interest rate may be unpredictable, and this will affect the calculation of the appropriate no-arbitrage futures price (see chapter 5), leading to either under or over performance, relative to the index portfolio.

The tax payments generated by using index futures to create an index fund may well differ from those when shares are used. In some countries, such as the US, capital gains are only payable on shares when they are sold, and so there is a 'tax timing option'. Futures do not offer this tax timing option, as any gains are assessed in the current tax year. Dividends and interest received are both subject to taxation in the current period.

An investor may wish to create a fund to track an index on which an index future is not traded. Assuming that both index baskets are well diversified, unsystematic risk is not relevant, leaving systematic risk. If the beta value of the index future, with respect to the index to be tracked is β_T, the investor should buy index futures corresponding to $1/\beta_T$ of the sum to be invested in the index fund.

Example. Elaine Robinson has just been appointed to manage the Trantor Fund considered above, and decides to track the IBROX index, on which no futures are traded, using FTSE 100 futures. The data for the situation facing the Trantor Fund is the same as in the previous example. The beta value of FTSE futures, with respect to the IBROX index basket is 0.9. The desired number of FTSE 100 contracts for delivery in six months time to be purchased now is (£100,000,000 ×0.9)/(4,800×£10) = 1,875 contracts. The terminal values of the two alternative strategies for creating a fund tracking the IBROX index are identical:-

(a)   Over the period, the actual rate of return on the FTSE 100 share basket was
      6.267%. Assuming that CAPM applies and $R_i = R_F + (R_M - R_F)\beta_T$, it follows
      that the rate of return on the IBROX basket of shares is given by $R_T = 5 +$
      $(6.267-5)0.9 = 6.1403\%$. Therefore, the increase in the value of £100
      million invested in the IBROX index basket is £6,140,000.

(b)   The interest received from investing £100 million in government debt for the
      period is £5 million. The gain on the FTSE 100 futures contracts is (5,000
      × £10−£49,392)× 1,875 = £1,1400,000. This gives a total gain for the
      Trantor Fund of £6,140,000.

In some situations an index future is traded on a sub-set of the basket of shares it
is desired to track. For example, in the UK index futures are traded on the top 350
shares (the FTSE 100 plus the FTSE Mid 250); while the most popular benchmark for
index tracking is the FT-All Share index, which includes roughly another 500 smaller
companies. In this case, an alternative to using a beta adjustment is to adopt a mixed
strategy. The performance of the top 350 shares is replicated using index futures, while
the performance of the remaining smaller companies is matched by purchasing a
portfolio of shares in these companies. In countries, such as the USA, with index
futures on indices with overlapping constituent stocks, it may be possible to create new
synthetic stock indices, see chapter 6.13.

10.2.10 Tilt a Fund

A fund manager may wish to increase or decrease the exposure of their fund to a
particular sector of the market for a short period of time, and it may be possible to
accomplish this at low cost using index futures, CBOT (1991). For example, if a US
fund manager thinks that, in the short run, large companies will underperform smaller
companies, he or she can take a short position in MMI futures. This effectively tilts the
fund away from large companies, with the degree of tilt governed by the number of
futures contracts traded. It is also possible to tilt a fund towards or away from
particular countries, industrial sectors, growth stocks, value stocks etc, if futures are
traded on the relevant index.

10.2.11 Avoid Restrictions

Some countries restrict the ownership of certain shares, while others restrict capital
flows in or out of the country. For these reasons, it may be impossible for investors to
construct a truly representative share portfolio for some countries. However, it may be
feasible to trade futures on an index which comprises restricted shares, and to trade
index futures for countries where capital movements are restricted, Jorion &
Roisenberg (1993). The remaining cash is invested in the domestic riskless asset.

10.2.12 Indirectly Buying or Short Selling Shares

Investors may wish to conceal that they are trading in the shares of a particular company. This can be done by 'mirror trading'. Suppose an investor wishes to short sell shares in company X, which is a constituent of the Y index. The investor sells a futures contract on the Y index, and buys the index basket of shares, but excluding shares in company X. Assuming the no-arbitrage condition applies, these trades are equivalent to short selling the shares in company X in the index basket, Scott-Quinn, Shyy & Walmsley (1995). However, where company X is a tiny proportion of the index basket, basis risk may mean that the replication is subject to considerable tracking error, while transactions costs will become larger for each £1 of company X's shares that are replicated.

Example. Emory Leeson wishes to short sell 80,000 shares in Brixton Bricks over the next four months, but is unable to do so. The Lurex index contains just three shares: Brixton Bricks, Carshalton Cars and Newington News. On 26th February the Lurex index basket comprised 40,000 shares in Brixton Bricks, 20,000 shares in Carshalton Cars and 30,000 shares in Newington News. Mirror trading will accomplish the desired result, and Emory sold two Lurex index futures, and bought 40,000 shares in Carshalton Cars and 60,000 shares in Newington News. The effect was:

	Sell 2 Lurex Futures	Share Purchases	Net Position
Brixton Bricks	-80,000 shares	0	-80,000 shares
Carshalton Cars	-40,000 shares	40,000 shares	0
Newington News	-60,000 shares	60,000 shares	0

Thus the direct short sale is successfully replicated by mirror trading. However, the transparency of the mirror trade is much lower.

10.2.13 Global Diversification

If a fund wishes to invest globally in equities this can be achieved by buying shares in all the major countries. However, this will expose the fund to exchange risk on the full amount of the investment. It will also require the use of specialist stock selectors for each country, and this may raise costs. It may involve investment in stock markets with a rather low level of liquidity. The creation of a well diversified portfolio may be difficult, either within each country, or across all countries. Finally, there will be additional costs and delays in processing international equity trades and holding foreign securities. Alternatively, the fund can use index futures to create a synthetic index fund for each of the countries concerned. This will reduce the foreign exchange risk, remove the requirement for stock selection skills, ensure a reasonably liquid market, ensure good diversification and involve faster and cheaper execution. Jorion & Roisenberg (1993) have shown that a portfolio of index futures for the UK, Japan,

France, USA and Australia provides a good substitute for an international share portfolio (as measured by the MSCI World index).

10.2.14 Portfolio Insurance

The aim of portfolio insurance is to place a floor on the value of a portfolio, while enabling the portfolio to increase in value as the market rises, see Sharpe & Alexander (1990, pp 580-587) for further explanation of portfolio insurance. Insurance companies are unwilling to insure portfolios of shares because this entails bearing systematic risk, and this cannot be diversified away by insuring the share portfolios of many other investors. There are two different types of portfolio insurance - options and constant proportion.

a. Options-Based Portfolio Insurance.   An obvious way to place a floor on the value of a share portfolio is to buy put options, i.e. a protective put (Figlewski, Chidambaran & Kaplan, 1993). Options-based portfolio insurance can be accomplished in three different ways (a) trading options, (b) replicating options by dynamically trading shares, and (c) replicating options by dynamically trading futures.

Options are traded on many individual stocks and stock indices, e.g. since 3rd May 1984 American style options have been traded on the FTSE 100 index, while European style options have been traded on this index since 1st February 1990. Options can be used to insure a portfolio by trading either put or call options. The use of put options on the market index to insure a well diversified portfolio is illustrated in figures 10.4 and 10.5, which show the profit or loss at expiration. If the index drops below the strike price of the option (K), the gains on exercising the put option exactly offset the losses on the share portfolio (excluding the cost of the option). If the index is above the strike price, the put option is not exercised, and the rise in value of the shares is retained.

An alternative way of using options to insure the value of an investment in the stock market is to sell the shares, invest the money at the riskless rate and buy call options on these shares with a strike price equal to the desired floor, i.e. a fiduciary call or a cash-call fund. The put-call parity for European style options of $C = P+S-K/(1+r)$, where C is the call price, S is the share price, K is the strike price and r is the riskless interest rate between now and expiry. This shows the equivalence between holding the share portfolio and buying put options; and liquidating the share portfolio and investing the proceeds in the riskless asset and buying call options, i.e. $S+P = C+K/(1+r)$. If the market rises, the call options are exercised to give the rise in market value, while if the market drops below the strike price of the call options they are not exercised, but the money invested at the riskless rate is secure.

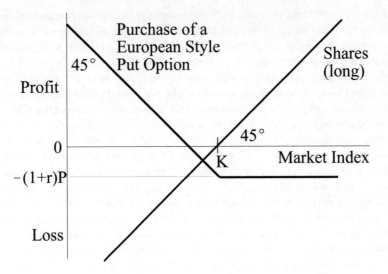

Figure 10.4: Payoffs from a Share Holding and a Purchased Put Option

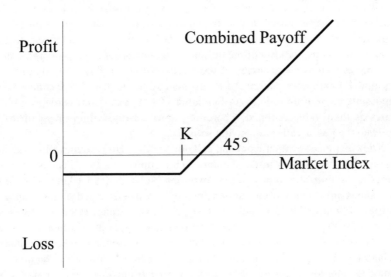

Figure 10.5: Net Payoffs from a Share Holding and Purchased Put Option

The use of equity options, rather than index options has the advantage of no mismatch between the shares in the portfolio and those underlying the options strategy; so that any stock selection skills are retained, although transactions costs and execution lag will be higher. Options-based portfolio insurance has the advantages that it can be conducted independently of the fund manager; and it is guaranteed to work, even when there is a stock market crash. There is a number of problems in using options for portfolio insurance - position limits (although these were relaxed in the US after the 1987 Crash), an illiquid market, high transactions costs, the short time to expiry, the fixed expiry date of the options, missing strike prices, American not European style options (thereby paying for the unwanted right to exercise early), and the requirement to pay the premium (or price) when the options are taken out. However, the use of flex and OTC options can overcome some of these problems, In addition, Tian (1996) has argued that a large number of strike prices will be suitable for use in portfolio insurance, and a combination of these different strike prices can be used to reduce any liquidity problems. In addition, these feasible strike prices will probably include out-of-the-money puts which are cheaper, so reducing the costs.

An alternative to trading options is a dynamic strategy involving shares and investment at the riskless rate to replicate purchased put or call options. Dynamic replication overcomes many of the problems with option-based portfolio insurance. For example, it provides a wide range of feasible strike prices, a perfect match between the shares in the portfolio and those covered by the synthetic option, no need to pay a premium at the start, no position limits, no limit on the horizon date of the insurance and a generally more liquid market.

However, there are a number of disadvantages to using a dynamic replication strategy with shares, rather than a static options strategy. The continuous adjustment of the share position can be costly in terms of management time and transactions costs. It also relies on the validity of the option valuation model used to compute the stock position, as well as the accuracy of the forecast of underlying spot volatility used in this model. Finally, the continuous adjustment of the stock or futures position may be impossible e.g. during the crash of October 1987 it was not possible to trade out of shares as their value dropped. Therefore, dynamic replication may fail to exactly replicate the put or call options, and so is risky.

The creation of synthetic put and call options can also be achieved by substituting index futures for shares in the dynamic replication strategy. This assumes that the shares in the portfolio to be insured correspond to the index basket, and requires the continuous adjustment of the futures position, i.e. dynamic hedging, (Chance, 1991; Duffie, 1989, pp. 290-296; Stoll & Whaley, 1988b; Strong, 1993, pp. 450-452; and Watsham, 1992, 1993, pp. 373-376.) To replicate a put option when the index falls, the size of the short position in index futures is increased, and when the index rises, the short position in index futures is reduced. The futures position is liquidated at the end of each period and the profit or loss invested or borrowed at the riskless rate. To replicate a call option the share portfolio is sold and the money invested in the riskless asset. Then a long position in index futures is opened which is increased when the market rises and reduced when it falls. The use of index futures rather than shares has the advantages of lower transactions costs, greater liquidity and faster execution, but the disadvantages of a mismatch between the index and the portfolio to be insured and the presence of mispricing risk.

The cost of portfolio insurance achieved by buying a put or call option is given in advance by the option premium, although the cost of subsequent rollovers is unknown at the start of the strategy. The cost of portfolio insurance accomplished by dynamic replication is unknown in advance. When the index rises, shares or index futures are purchased, and when the index falls, shares or index futures are sold. Thus, the replication of a purchased put requires buying shares or futures at higher prices than those at which they are sold. The resulting cost depends on the actual price volatility of the equity market during the period.

Loria, Pham & Sim (1991) analyzed daily data on SPI futures for 1984-9. They studied the performance of portfolio insurance with put options, replicated using index futures. For five different rebalancing strategies, each failed on occasion to prevent the value of the portfolio dropping below the floor. In addition, the delivery date of the index future may differ from the horizon date of the insurance, and so the riskless interest rate applicable to pricing the future may differ from that until the horizon date, exposing the portfolio insurance to interest rate risk.

Merrick (1988a) examined the effects of the mispricing of index futures on the performance of futures-based portfolio insurance which seeks to replicate a put option. Using daily data for the S&P500 for 1982-6, he found that ignoring the initial mispricing was suboptimal, and concluded that mispricings decrease the attractiveness of futures-based portfolio insurance. A study by Hill, Jain & Wood (1988) concluded that the impact of mispricings on the cost of futures-based portfolio insurance was relatively small, and extreme realized volatility had a much larger effect on the costs of futures-based portfolio insurance. A simulation study by Rendleman & O'Brien (1990) found that the misestimation of spot volatility can have an important effect on the performance of portfolio insurance using synthetic put options.

Portfolio insurance was invented in 1976, and expanded during the early 1980's using dynamic replication with index futures. However, the stock market crash of 1987 demonstrated that this form of portfolio insurance was flawed - just when it was needed, it failed to work, Clowes (2000).

b. Constant Proportion Portfolio Insurance.   An alternative approach to portfolio insurance is constant proportion portfolio insurance (CPPI), Black & Jones (1987, 1988), Perold & Sharpe (1988). CPPI does not involve replicating a put or call option, and this gives it a number of advantages over portfolio insurance based on options. It does not require continuous trading according to a complex option valuation formula, it does not have a specified horizon date (e.g. the expiry date of the option), no premium is payable at the start, it largely avoids position limits, it does not require forecasts of the volatility of share returns, and the passage of time does not require trading (i.e. the shortening maturity of the option). CPPI can be conducted using shares or index futures. Shares removes mismatch risk and rollover risk, but introduces higher transactions costs, execution lag and less liquid markets.

CPPI may be summarized in the equation: $e = m(a-f)$, where $m \geq 1$ and e is the investment in shares (or index futures), m is a multiplier set by the trader, a is the total value of the portfolio, and f is the floor value of the portfolio, which is set by the trader and must initially be less than a. Some investors may wish the floor to grow over time, e.g. at the riskless rate, so that $f_t = f(1+r)^t$. The term $(a-f)$ has been called the 'cushion', and represents the amount by which the value of the portfolio exceeds the floor. A multiple of this cushion is invested in equities (or index futures), with the remainder, $(a-e)$, in a riskless investment. As the stock market rises by $x\%$, the required investment in equities rises by $mx\%$, while a fall in the stock market leads to a drop in the required investment in equities of $mx\%$. This rule produces a somewhat different set of payoffs from those of an option-based strategy, as illustrated in figure 10.6. Figure 10.7 shows the movements over time of the equity and bond holdings for a fund with $m = 2$. If $m = 1$, the strategy is simply buy-and-hold, with a floor equal to the value of the riskless investment. If share prices suddenly drop by more than the proportion $1/m$ (for example, during a crash), the value of the portfolio will fall below its floor and the insurance will fail (as does dynamic option-based portfolio insurance). At times, the required equity investment may exceed the value of the fund. In which case, the equity investment is constrained to the value of the fund, i.e. $e \le a$.

The share holdings required by CPPI can be replicated by a combination of index futures and debt, as in the creation of an index fund in chapter 10.2.9. Instead of trading the shares in the portfolio, the equity position is left unchanged and index futures and debt are traded instead. A futures position replicates the risky return on the shares, while the risk-free asset replicates the riskless component of share returns. Thus, shares can be replicated by long positions in futures and debt, while debt can be replicated by a long position in shares and a short position in futures. When replicating the purchase of £x million of shares, as well as buying futures, it is necessary to assign £x million of the riskless asset to share replication. Similarly, when replicating the sale of £x million of shares, as well as selling futures, an additional investment of £x million in the riskless asset is created. The futures position is assumed to be liquidated at the end of each period, and the resulting gain or loss added to, or subtracted from, the riskless investment. It is possible that the beta value of the portfolio of shares (β) is not one, and that the beta value of the index futures (β_F) with respect to the market portfolio, differs from one. In which case the value of index futures to be traded is the proportion β/β_F of the equity investment. Even after allowing for different beta values, the index futures may not exactly replicate the risky return of the share portfolio due to mispricings, mismatch etc.

Example. Sir Larry Wildman is the manager of the Scotswood Fund, which has a total value on 1st March of £100 million. Sir Larry wishes to place a floor of £80 million on the value of this portfolio, and chooses a multiplier of two. His initial investments are $2(100-80) = £40$ million in equities and $(£100m-£40m) = £60$ million invested at the risk free rate. The subsequent stock market movements and Sir Larry's response are set out in table 10.5. Interest received on the debt is ignored for simplicity.

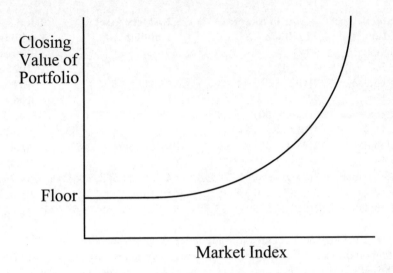

Figure 10.6: Payoffs for Constant Proportion Portfolio Insurance

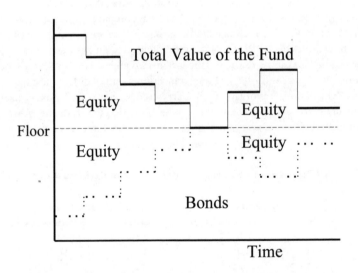

Figure 10.7: Movements in Equity and Bond Holdings Over Time for m = 2

Table 10.5: Constant Proportion Portfolio Insurance Using Shares

Stock Market	Value of Shares £ million	Riskless Asset £ million	Total £ million
Initial	40	60	100
+5%	40×1.05 = 42	60	102
Rebalance	2(102−80) = 44	102−44 = 58	102
+10%	44×1.10 = 48.4	58	106.4
Rebalance	2(106.4−80) = 52.8	106.4−52.8 = 53.6	106.4
−15%	48.4×0.85 = 44.88	53.6	98.48
Rebalance	2(98.48−80) = 36.96	98.48−36.96 = 61.52	98.48
−10%	44.88×0.90 = 33.264	61.52	94.784
Rebalance	2(94.784−80) = 29.568	94.784−29.568 = 65.216	94.784
−10%	33.264×0.90 = 26.6112	65.216	91.8272
Rebalance	2(91.8272−80) = 23.654	91.8272−23.654 = 68.173	91.8272

Sir Larry now decides to trade index futures to conduct his CPPI. In table 10.6 (at the end of this chapter) he continues to hold his initial share portfolio, and the subsequent values of these shares are shown in the second column. The third column shows the futures positions (long positions are positive, and short positions are negative), while the fourth column contains the cumulative profit or loss on the futures positions which are added to, or subtracted from, the riskless investment. The fifth column gives the riskless investment (excluding that due to futures profits or losses, which appear in column four). The final column presents the total value of the Scotswood Fund, which is exactly the same as when Sir Larry uses shares and debt to conduct his CPPI. In constructing table 10.6 it has been assumed that the index futures exactly replicate the price movements of Sir Larry's equity portfolio with a beta ratio (β/β_F) of one, and futures indivisibilities are ignored.

The transactions involved if Sir Larry trades shares or index futures are shown in table 10.7. This reveals that, since $(\beta/\beta_F)=1$, the trades in shares and index futures are of equal size, and that the use of index futures is associated with a much smaller level of trading in the riskless asset.

Table 10.7: Trades in Shares, Futures and the Riskless Asset

Stock Market	Trade Shares		Trade Index Futures	
	Shares	Riskless Asset	Futures	Riskless Asset
+5%	+2.0	−2.0	+2.0	0
+10%	+4.4	−4.4	+4.4	+0.2
−15%	−7.92	+7.92	−7.92	−0.99
−10%	−3.696	+3.696	−3.696	+0.231
−10%	−2.9568	+2.9568	−2.9568	+0.5775

Do & Faff (2004) investigated the performance of the synthetic protective put and CPPI; in each case comparing the use of stocks and debt with index futures and debt. They employed quarterly data on SPI futures for 1987-2002, and concluded that, for daily rebalancing, there was no great difference between the performance of the synthetic put and CPPI strategies, and that futures-based implementation was robust across a range of market conditions.

10.2.15 No Disruption to the Income Stream

If a fund temporarily changes its beta value by switching out of riskless investment and into shares, and then back again; the income stream previously received by the fund is disrupted, e.g. regular and predictable interest payments stop, and unpredictable dividends are received instead. Using index futures to alter the fund's beta avoids this problem (Clarke, 1992).

10.2.16 Form of the Increase in Value

A portfolio of shares produces dividend income, and capital gains (or losses) when the shares are sold. A futures contract and government debt generate capital gains (or losses) on the futures contract (paid under the mark to market procedures), and interest receipts on the money that would have been invested in the shares. Since the capital gains (or losses) on the futures contract are assessed in the current tax year, and it is likely that the interest payments on the government debt exceed the dividends on the shares, the interim cash flows generated by using index futures will probably be larger than for investment in shares. This may be an advantage to some types of investor, e.g. pension funds who have to make regular payments to pensioners. The change in the type of income may also be of benefit to investors who reap tax advantages from receiving the increase in value in a different form, Herbst & Ordway (1984). A specific example of this is hedged dividend capture, which is considered in chapter 10.2.20.

10.2.17 Delaying Taxation

Index futures can be used to delay the realization of capital gains on an equity portfolio, and so postpone the payment of capital gains tax. The investor benefits by earning the riskless rate of interest on the amount of the capital gains tax liability during the period that payment is deferred. Suppose an investor owns an equity portfolio that has risen in value by 50% since it was purchased, and is thought to be currently overvalued by 10%. If the equities are sold now and repurchased later when they have fallen in value, the investor will presently incur a liability to pay capital gains tax on the 50% gain. If the investor hedges the equity position using a short position in index futures, no capital gain on the equities is payable until they are sold, although the investor will incur a tax liability for the gain of 10% on the short position in index futures. Thus, the payment of taxation on the long term gain on the equities is delayed until later by the use of index futures. However, there may be cross-hedging risk if the share portfolio differs form the index basket, and the investor does not receive any money from selling the shares until they are actually sold.

10.2.18 Decentralization of Risk Management

Instead of trying to construct a global portfolio of assets with the desired risk-return characteristics, the use of index futures allows each division of a company to control their own risk exposure. This adjustment of risk can be done independently of the decisions made by the other parts of the same institution, Silber (1985). There is no need for a global risk manager to have detailed knowledge of the asset portfolios of each of the divisions so that risk can be managed centrally. Of course, the centre may still wish to monitor the risk exposure choices made by the divisions.

10.2.19 Hedging Equity Index Swaps

An investor who owns an interest-bearing asset may prefer to receive the returns on the basket of shares comprising the FTSE 100, i.e. capital gains and dividends. However, this investor may be blocked from selling their interest-bearing asset and buying shares, and from trading index futures and options. In which case, the investor may choose to enter into an equity index swap with a counterparty, e.g. a financial institution. By this over the counter (OTC) swap, the investor receives the returns on the FTSE 100, and in return pays the institution a specified interest rate, e.g. LIBOR ± a spread. In effect, the investor has a long position in the FTSE 100 basket of shares, while the institution has a long position in a LIBOR yielding asset, and a short position in the FTSE 100 basket. The institution may wish to remove its exposure to the FTSE 100, and this can be done either by buying the index basket of shares, or by buying FTSE 100 index futures. For the reasons given in chapter 2, futures are usually preferable for hedging this risk, although they do not hedge the dividend risk, Tranter (1994). By hedging, the financial institution can achieve a profit of roughly the spread charged above LIBOR. Any difference will be due to factors such as a mispricing of the index futures at the start or end of the position, and the actual dividends and interest rate for the period differing from the values used in setting the no-arbitrage futures price.

Example. Marty McFly has inherited the income from a trust, whose only asset is an investment of £10 million in gilts. Marty wishes to invest the £10 million in the UK stock market, but is unable to alter the assets of the trust. Therefore, on 17th June he entered a £10 million equity swap with Tilehurst plc. Under this agreement Marty pays LIBOR plus 2% per annum to Tilehurst, and Tilehurst pays the capital gain and dividends on the FTSE 100 index to Marty. Tilehurst hedged this equity swap by buying FTSE 100 index futures. On 17th June the price of September futures was 5,048 index points, while the index was 5,000, and so Tilehurst bought

10,000,000/(5,000×£10) = 200 contracts. During the three months to 16th September, LIBOR was 8% per annum (or 2% for the three months), the FTSE 100 index rose to 5,200 and the terminal value of the dividends for this three months was 1% of the index on 16th September. Thus, on 16th September Marty has to pay interest to Tilehurst of (8+2)/4 = 2.5% on £10 million, or £250,000. Tilehurst has to pay the capital gains of (5,200/5,000−1)£10,000,000 = £400,000, and the dividends of 0.01(5,200/5,000) ×£10,000,000 = £104,000, i.e. a net payment by Tilehurst to Marty of £504,000−£250,000 = £254,000. Tilehurst's long position in index futures gives a profit of 200(5,200−5,048)£10 = £304,000, and so Tilehurst makes a net profit of £304,000−£254,000 =£50,000. Tilehurst's net profit is equal to the spread charged above LIBOR, which is 10,000,000(2/4) = £50,000.

10.2.20 Hedged Dividend Capture

Some investors, e.g. charities, pension schemes etc, may find it advantageous, for tax reasons, to receive (or capture) dividends. This can be achieved by buying shares before they go ex-dividend, and selling them shortly afterwards. Such investors then claim back the tax on these dividends. However, while the shares are held, the investor is exposed to price risk. A possible approach to hedged dividend capture is for the investor to buy the index basket of shares and sell a corresponding value of index futures. The resulting position has a beta value of zero and will give the risk free rate of return, in addition to the tax gain.

Example. The taxation position of the Proteus fund, which is managed by Alexandra Medford, makes it beneficial for the fund to engage in dividend capture. In January, Alexandra withdrew £9 million from an investment in a riskless asset, and invested this money in the index basket of the FTSE 100. Since the FTSE 100 index stood at 4,600 in January and assuming that $\beta_F = 1$, she bought £9,000,000/(4,600×£10) ≈ 196 index baskets. At the same time, Alexandra sold 196 June FTSE 100 futures to fully hedge her long position in stock. The riskless interest rate until the end of June was 4%, while the net value in January of the dividends expected on the index basket over the period until the end of June was £3,000. Since the standard no-arbitrage condition applied, the price in January of a June futures contract was (4,600×£10−3,000)1.04 = £44,720. At the end of June Alexandra unwound her positions. The fund had received (or was due to receive) dividends with a net value at the end of June of 3,000×1.04×196 = £611,520. At the end of June the FTSE 100 was still 4,600, and so the Proteus Fund made a net loss on the futures hedge of 196(£44,720−£46,000) = £250,880, making a total income of £611,520−£250,880 = £360,640. This is the same income as the fund would have received if the £9 million had been left invested in the riskless asset at 4% (the difference of £640 is due to rounding error). Thus, the Proteus fund has converted £360,000 of interest receipts into £611,520 of net dividends, and a net loss on trading futures of £250,880. In addition, Alexandra can now claim back the tax deducted on the dividends of £611,520 she has received.

10.2.21 Guaranteed Funds

Some futures funds guarantee that at a specified date, the value of an investment in the fund will never be less than the initial investment, while offering the possibility of substantial asset growth. This can be achieved by (a) a third party providing a guarantee, (b) the use of a '90/10 fund' or (c) options (portfolio insurance, see chapter 10.2.14). In the case of a 90/10 fund, a sum is invested in fixed interest securities to provide the initial investment at the due date (e.g. 90% of the money), and the remainder (e.g. 10%) is used to trade futures. More generally, if the interest rate for the period of the guarantee is r and the initial investment is I, the futures fund invests $I/(1+r)$ in fixed interest securities to guarantee I at the end. The remaining money is used to trade futures. Such 90/10 funds are not certain to honour the guarantee because losses on futures trading may exceed the sum initially set aside for this activity. Guaranteed funds usually offer reduced participation in increases in value, in exchange for the removal of downside risk. In figure 10.8, where S^* is the terminal value of the equity market, the investor swaps the payoffs given by the solid line for those given by the dotted line, i.e. they sacrifice B in exchange for A.

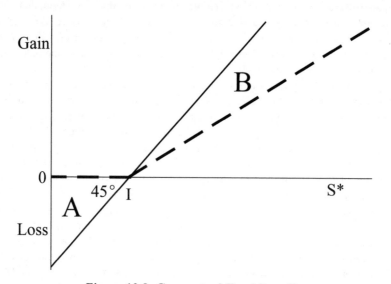

Figure 10.8: Guaranteed Fund Payoffs

Example. The Tottenham Fund decided to guarantee investors the return of their initial investment, in exchange for paying 70% of any increase in the index (excluding dividends). This offer raised £50 million from the public by 1st May. The riskless interest rate over the eight months to the end of December is 8%, and so an investment of $I/(1+r)$ = £50 million/1.08 = £46,296,296 is required in the riskless asset on 1st May to produce £50 million at the end of December. This leaves £3,703,703 free for trading index futures. Norman Bates, the fund manager, has decided that cash should be available to cover 10% of the nominal value of any futures position, and it is assumed that Norman receives 8% interest on this money. On 1st May the price of December FTSE 100 futures was 4,659 points, or £46,590. Thus, Norman can buy £3,703,703/(0.10×£46,590) = 795 December FTSE 100 futures, and invest £46,296,296 at the riskless rate. At delivery in December the FTSE 100 index was 5,000, and investors in the guaranteed fund receive £50 million +0.70[(5,000/4,600)−1]£50 million = £53,043,478 from Tottenham. The Tottenham Fund is able to pay this sum because they have £50 million from the riskless investment, plus the payoff from the futures contracts of 795(5,000 −4,659)£10 = £2,710,950, plus the return of the margin money with interest of £3,703,703(1.08), giving £56,710,950. Thus Tottenham have made a profit of £56,710,950−£53,043,478 = £3,667,472. This strategy does not completely guarantee the return of the initial investment. If the FTSE 100 index in December falls below 4,156 Tottenham will have less than £50 million, and may default on its guarantee to investors.

10.2.22 Alpha Funds

The aim of an alpha fund is to create a portfolio that captures the stock selection skills of its managers, but which has no market (or systematic) risk, i.e. the beta value equals zero, Elton & Gruber (1991, pp. 632-633), Dubofsky (1992, p. 433), Siegel & Siegel (1990, p. 196), Tucker, Becker, Isimbabi & Ogden (1994) and Chance (1989, pp. 438-439). By selling index futures contracts, it is possible to reduce the beta value of the fund to zero. The return on such a fund will be the risk-free rate plus any additional return due to the stock selection skills. The risk of this portfolio will be just the unsystematic risk of the portfolio of selected shares. Provided the selected shares form a reasonably well diversified portfolio, which may not be the case, this unsystematic risk can be diversified away. Apart from capitalizing on stock selection skills, there is little reason to buy or sell actual shares.

Example. The Aquatic Fund, worth £100 million and managed by Wanda Gerschwitz, holds investments of equal value in five companies that Wanda expects to outperform the market. These shares are set out in Table 10.8, together with their expected returns according to the SML and Wanda. The expected return over the next six months on the market portfolio is 6%, while the risk free rate of interest for this period is 3%. The value of the FTSE 100 index is 4,600, while the value of β_F is 1.1.

To reduce the beta value of the fund to zero, Wanda sells (100,000,000×1.16) /(4,600×£10 ×1.1) = 2,292.49 FTSE 100 contracts. The alpha fund has an expected return of 3.0+8.6−6.48 = 5.12% and risk equal to the unsystematic risk of the portfolio of five shares. If everything happens as expected and there is no unsystematic risk, the return on the shares will be £8.6 million. The loss on the futures position will be $S_T - F_t = S_t(R_M - R_F)\beta_F = 46,000(0.06 - 0.03)1.1 = £1,518$ per contract. This gives a total loss of 1,518×2,292.49 = £3.48 million. Therefore, the overall return on the alpha fund is 8.6-3.48 = £5.12 million, i.e. £3 million risk free interest and £2.12 million excess return on the five shares.

Table 10.8: Beta Values and Expected Returns for the Example

Company	β	Expected Return SML	Expected Return Wanda
Battersea	2.0	9.0%	12.0%
Chelsea	1.5	7.5%	10.0%
Hackney	1.0	6.0%	8.0%
Putney	0.8	5.4%	7.0%
Bermonsey	0.5	4.5%	6.0%
Portfolio	1.16	6.48%	8.6%

10.3 Usage of Index Futures

This section documents the sharp difference in the usage of index futures between financial and non-financial companies, and discusses some factors that initially restricted the use of index futures.

10.3.1 Non-Financial Companies

A survey of the non-financial companies in the FTSE 100 by Touche Ross (1995) found that 8% used equity derivatives. Mallin, Ow-Yong & Reynolds (2001) surveyed all quoted UK non-financial companies in 1997 and found that only 2% used equity derivatives. Bailly, Browne, Hicks & Skerrat (2003) also investigated the usage of equity derivatives by quoted UK non-financial companies, and discovered that 4% used equity derivatives in 1998. In 1997 De Ceuster, Durinck, Laveren & Lodewyckx (2000) found that 8% of large non-financial companies operating in Belgium used equity derivatives; while Alkebäck & Hagelin (1999) and Alkebäck, Hagelin & Pramborg (2003) discovered that 9% of Swedish non-financial quoted companies used equity derivatives in 1996; as compared with 10% in 1996. In 1996 6% of these Swedish companies traded equity futures, while the corresponding figure for 2003 was 3%. These results indicate that the usage of index futures by non-financial companies is very low, and this is to be expected because such companies do not hold or trade equities as part of their normal business.

10.3.2 Financial Institutions

Block & Gallagher (1988) surveyed large US bank trust departments in 1987 and found that 11.3% used stock index futures and options, while Block & Gallagher (1990) surveyed large US non-trust money managers in 1987, and discovered that

32.6% used stock index futures and options. Hoyt (1989) estimated that in 1987 about 10% of US life insurers were using index futures. In the UK, the rules governing the use of futures by insurance companies were revised on 1st July 1994 giving them greater freedom to make use of derivatives. A survey of 47 UK life assurance companies (KPMG Peat Marwick, 1994) found that almost 40% were using index futures, and that the prospective usage (in the light of the new regulations) was almost 60%.

In October 1994, a survey of the 103 UK local authority pension funds was conducted by Liffe (1995b). It found that the use of futures and options was permitted on 98.2% of the total funds under management, and that futures and options were used on 42% of the total funds under management. Grant & Marshall (1997) studied the usage of equity derivatives by all the companies in the FTSE 250 index, including the financial companies. In 1994 this was 15%, while in 1995 it was 7%. In comparison with the results for non-financial companies in chapter 10.3.1, this indicates that financial companies are considerably more likely than non-financial companies to use index futures. In 1998 Levich, Hayt & Ripston (1999) surveyed US pension schemes, and university and private foundations. For their sample, about 54% were using foreign equity derivatives, and 56% were using domestic equity derivatives. The nominal value of these equity derivative positions corresponded to 5% of the holding of foreign equities, and 8% for domestic equities. Index futures were about twice as popular as the next type of equity derivative, which was exchange traded options. The main reasons given for trading derivatives by US pension schemes and foundations were (in decreasing order of importance): hedging, asset allocation, increasing the returns on the fund, market timing, increasing the leverage of the fund, accessing markets and tax reduction.

As expected, the usage of index futures by organizations that trade equities is much greater than for non-financial companies. These results show that the use of index futures has become widespread amongst institutional investors; although there is still scope for further growth.

10.3.3 Factors Restricting Use

Some of the factors restricting the use of index futures by funds in the UK will now be considered. Prior to July 1990 authorised unit trusts, pension funds, and investment trusts were exempt from capital gains tax on futures transactions for investment purposes, but were thought liable to pay tax on any trading income, Redhead (1990). The fear of being deemed to be trading (rather than investing) in futures contracts, and so liable to taxation, may have deterred such institutions from using futures as part of their investment strategy. To clarify this situation, *all* futures trades (investment and trading) conducted after 26th July 1990 by pension funds and authorised unit trusts were exempted from taxation by the Finance Act 1990.

The approval of trustees (and possibly alteration of the trust deeds) is required to permit trading in index futures, and the trustees may be unfamiliar with index futures

332

Stock Index Futures

and impose limits on the proportion of the fund that can be invested in derivatives. (In some countries mutual funds are banned from using futures.) A 1991 survey found that 82% of UK fund managers were not permitted to use financial futures, Pope & Walmsley (1992). If index futures are used, the procedures for measuring the performance of the fund managers must be modified. In 1992 Liffe and LTOM (1992) published guidelines, endorsed by the National Association of Pension Funds and the two largest independent performance measurement organizations in the UK (Combined Actuarial Performance Services Limited (CAPS) and World Markets Company plc (WM)), for the performance measurement of financial futures. These provide an agreed method for including financial futures in the performance measurement calculations of investment portfolios. Finally, the legalization in the UK of futures and options funds (FOR) and geared futures and options funds (GFOF) in 1991 allowed the creation of additional vehicles which fund managers can use for investment in index futures.

10.3.4 Diversification

The manager of a broadly diversified portfolio may wish to invest in commodities, in addition to shares, property and government debt. One way of participating in movements in commodity prices that does not involve holding stocks of the commodity is to trade commodity futures, Meaden & Fox-Andrews (1991). A number of studies have found that including either US futures funds or individual futures (where index futures form no more than a tiny fraction of the position in futures) in share portfolios can improve the mean-variance efficiency frontier, Baratz & Eresian (1992a, 1992b), Bodie (1983), Bodie & Rosansky (1980), Chance (1994a, pp.18-21), Edwards & Park (1996), Fischmar & Peters (1991), Fortenbery & Hauser 1990), Herbst & McCormack (1987, 1992), Irwin & Brorsen (1985), Irwin & Landa (1987), Jensen, Johnson & Mercer (2000), Lam (1994), Lintner (1992), Oberuc (1992), Orr (1992) and Schneeweis, Savanayana & McCarthy (1992).This improvement in the efficiency frontier from including commodity futures is illustrated in figure 10.9. Peters (1992b) found that this conclusion is robust to the way in which risk is measured. In general, the futures funds studied have had very little investment in index futures, and so the correlation between the returns on the market index (and also on bonds) with those of the futures has been low (i.e. $\beta \approx 0$), making futures funds an attractive diversification.

However, the conclusion that diversification into futures funds improves the risk-return trade off has been questioned. Elton, Gruber & Rentzler (1987, 1990) found that adding futures funds to a share portfolio did not improve the efficiency frontier, as did Irwin, Krukemyer & Zulauf (1993). Schneeweis, Savanayana & McCarthy (1991) found that investing in futures via private commodity pools and commodity trading advisers improved the mean-variance efficiency of share and bond portfolios, while publicly traded futures funds had little beneficial effect, (except when no risk free asset was assumed). Irwin (1992) and Peters (1992a) have explained this result in two ways.

The conclusion that diversification into futures funds is beneficial, is sensitive to both the time period analyzed and to the costs involved in running the futures fund. Irwin (1992) estimated that the annual costs for a small investment in a futures fund were about 18% of the total assets, while they were only about 11% for a large institutional investment. Therefore, the use of futures funds may be beneficial to institutional investors, but not to small investors. Irwin, Krukemyer & Zulauf (1992) showed that if the operating costs of public commodity pools are used, futures are an unattractive diversification, while if the operating costs of institutional commodity pools are used, futures become an attractive diversification. A similar conclusion is reached by Edwards & Park (1996). There is also some evidence that the benefits are sensitive to the data period

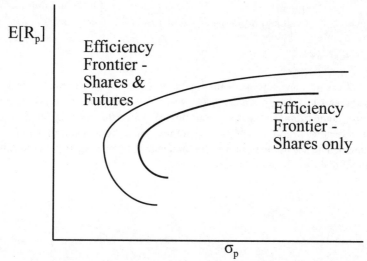

Figure 10.9: Improvement in the Efficiency Frontier from Commodity Futures

10.4 Other Users of Index Futures

Index futures are used by an number of other traders, besides fund managers. Underwriters, market makers, block positioners, OTC traders, equity issuers and index options traders use index futures to hedge their exposure, Dawson & Gemmill (1990), Lee & Nayar (1993), Silber (1985), Stoll & Whaley (1988a and 1988b) and Tosini & Moriarty (1982). This hedging of market risk leads to a reduction in the fees charged. Sarkar & Tripathy (2002) employed daily data on 2,495 NASDAQ stocks for 1977-87. After the introduction of the Value Line, S&P500 and NYSE Composite futures in 1982, NASDAQ bid-ask spreads dropped. In addition, spreads became less sensitive to market risk, and the reduction in spreads was largest during periods of high market volatility. This evidence is consistent with NASDAQ market makers hedging their inventory risk with index futures.

The BIS (1992) has produced estimates of open interest (average of the long and short positions) in domestic index futures as at the end of 1991 for domestic and foreign banks in the USA and France based on 'large trade' data. Table 10.9 indicates that 22% of the open interest in USA index futures was held by banks, while the corresponding figure for French index futures was 50%, which demonstrates that banks are major users of index futures.

Table 10.9: Open Interest in Domestic Index Futures in 1991 ($ billion)

	USA	France
Domestic Banks	5.15	0.2
Foreign Banks	1.65	0.7
Others	24.20	0.9
Total Open Interest	31.00	1.8

10.5 Conclusions

The usefulness of index futures to fund managers is becoming apparent. In addition to arbitrage and hedging, there are many ways in which fund managers can benefit from trading index futures, e.g. the separation of market timing from stock selection, creating an index fund, portfolio insurance and the decentralization of risk management. The use of index futures by fund managers appears to be increasing, and is expected to show considerable growth.

Table 10.6: Constant Proportion Portfolio Insurance Using Futures

Stock Market	Shares £ million	Futures £ million	Cumulative Futures Profit £ million	Riskless Asset £ million	Total £ million
Initial	40	0	0	60	100
+5%	40×1.05=42	0	0	60	102
Rebalance	42	2(102−80)−42=2	0	60−2=58	102
+10%	42×1.10=46.2	2×1.10=2.2	0	58	106.4
Rebalance	46.2	2(106.4−80)−46.2=6.6	0+2×0.10=0.2	60−6.6=53.4	106.4
−15%	46.2×0.85=39.27	6.6×0.85=5.61	0.2	53.4	98.48
Rebalance	39.27	2(98.48−80)−39.27=−2.31	0.2−6.6×0.15=−0.79	60+2.31=62.31	98.48
−10%	39.27×0.90=35.343	−2.31×0.90=−2.079	−0.79	62.31	94.784
Rebalance	35.343	2(94.784−80)−35.343=−5.775	−0.79+2.31×0.10=−0.559	60+5.775=65.775	94.784
−10%	35.343×0.90=31.8087	−5.775×0,90=−5.1975	−0.559	65.775	91.8272
Rebalance	31.8087	2(91.8272−80)−31.8087=−8.1543	−0.559+5.775×0.10=0.0185	60+8.1543=68.1543	91.8272

PART 5

OTHERS

Chapter 11

The Design and Regulation
of Futures Contracts

Introduction

This chapter examines in more detail a number of the aspects of futures contracts which were mentioned in chapter 2. The futures exchange, clearing house or regulator must set margins, price limits, trading hours, minimum price movements, contract multipliers and contract maturities; while the trader must calculate the cash balance required to cover margin payments. Various approaches to selecting numerical values for these variables are considered. There is also a discussion of default risk, the taxation of futures trading, the choice of the underlying index, the dual listing of futures, trading mechanisms, the dual capacity of futures traders, the manipulation of the final settlement price and the determinants of successful futures contracts; which are matters that concern both exchanges and regulators, as well as traders.

11.1 Choice of Initial and Maintenance Margins

There are two different views on setting margins. One view is that the purpose of margins on futures is to guarantee that the contract will be honoured. Therefore, margins are set primarily to produce an acceptable level of default risk, after allowing (where relevant) for any adverse effects on volume, open interest, liquidity and volatility. The other view is that the size of futures margins is a regulatory tool for controlling price volatility, particularly spot volatility. These alternative views of the objective of margin setting, which are based on differing views of the effect of margins on price volatility, will be considered in sequence.

11.1.1 Reducing Default Risk

Guaranteeing that the contract will be honoured is an important problem because, at the delivery date, one of the parties to an index future always has an incentive not to fulfill their obligations under the contract. If the delivery price is below the settlement price of the contract on the day before the delivery price is determined, the buyer has an incentive to renege on the final payment, while if yesterday's settlement price is higher than the delivery price, the seller has an incentive to renege. It should be noted that the daily marking to the market greatly reduces the default problem, as the trader may choose to honour a contract today in the hope that the price of the contract will subsequently move in his or her favour. For those futures where the maintenance margin is below the initial margin, what matters for these purposes is the maintenance margin, Moser (1993).

When there is an adverse price movement and a trader is required to pay a margin call, they can choose either to make the payment, or to default on their contract. Fishe & Goldberg (1986) assumed that, if a trader chooses to default, the balance on their margin account is forfeit. Hence, the higher are the margin requirements, the higher is the cost of defaulting, the lower are the expected profits from defaulting, and the lower are the expected profits from taking a position in a future. This will tend to lower the number of futures traded with the intention of being held overnight, i.e. the size of the closing open interest will decline, and will probably be associated with a drop in volume.

Telser (1981) also argued that higher margins will raise the cost of trading in futures, but for different reasons. Margins use up part of the trader's precautionary balances, and this money is no longer available to deal with unexpected events. This increase in the cost of trading then leads to lower open interest and trading volume. Telser went on to argue that this lower volume results in a less liquid market, which leads to a rise in price volatility. Similar views have been expressed by Figlewski (1984c), Hartzmark (1986b) and Tomek (1985). The drop in volume may be exacerbated by a shift in trading on competing exchanges. The higher transactions costs will also widen the no-arbitrage band, which may reduce the volume of arbitrage trading. They may also lead to an increase in basis risk, which will decrease the attractiveness of the future for hedging purposes.

If futures margins are set too low, defaults will increase. These defaults will lead to the liquidation of the corresponding futures positions. When prices rise, short positions are in danger of default and liquidation, and closing out such short positions requires buying futures. This will tend to push the price up further, leading to additional defaults by short positions. Conversely, when prices fall, there may be defaults by long positions, leading to the selling of futures contracts, and further downward pressure on prices. Gennotte & Leland (1994) have argued that, if even a few traders (e.g. locals) are aware that these liquidating trades are informationless, they will be willing to act as counterparty without changing the price. In this case low margins will not lead to an increase in the volatility of futures returns, nor will raising margins reduce volatility.

Hartzmark (1986a) concluded that higher futures margins, and the resulting increase in transactions costs, leads to a decrease in open interest. He went on to argue that such higher costs changes the composition of futures traders. Traders with price expectations closest to the current market price tend to exit the market, leaving those traders who expect a large price movement. It is possible that this change in the composition of traders may result in a change in futures price volatility, but the direction of any change is theoretically indeterminate.

France (1991) pointed out that, since higher margins decrease the probability of default, an increase in margins may result in lower charges by brokers etc, so tending to reduce transactions costs and raise volume. Even if the net effect of higher margins is to increase transactions costs, the effect on volume may differ as between the short and the long run. Initially, volume may rise as traders adjust their positions, while in the long run it drops. Thus, the effect of margins on volume is an empirical issue.

When setting margins, a trade-off must be made between the costs of margins that are too low and too high. Low margins lead to the risk of default by traders when a daily adverse price movement exceeds the balance in the trader's margin account. High margins increase the sum of money that the trader must deposit in their margin account, so increasing transactions costs. There is also the issue that, to the extent that volume is reduced, high margins damage the profits of members of the exchange. The selection of margins is usually done by the clearing house, in consultation with the futures exchange, and there is a problem in specifying the objective of the clearing house when making this collective decision.

If the clearing house is controlled by its members, making the trade-off between the costs of high and low margins requires the use of an aggregate utility function for exchange members, assuming margins are set with respect to the utility of the members of the futures exchange. One way in which this problem may be overcome in theory is if members of the exchange have single-peaked preferences (Gay, Hunter & Kolb, 1986), while Hunter (1986) overcomes the problem by assuming a negative exponential utility function. Lam, Sin & Leung (2004) argue that members are concerned with protecting the clearing house against default, and with avoiding the imposition of direct and indirect costs on members, e.g. by high margins reducing trading volume. If the clearing house is a profit maximizing company it will set margins to maximize its profits. As well as minimizing default, it will also be interested in increasing volume, as clearing house revenues are tied to the volume of trades cleared. However, the clearing house will not be directly concerned with the cost of capital tied up in margins, liquidity, volatility, etc.

A clearing house can set a superior set of margins if margins can be differentiated according to the individual trader's incentives not to renege; e.g. a large trader who uses the futures market frequently may wish to preserve his or her reputation, and lower margins may be appropriate in such a case. However, setting margins which allow for differences between individuals requires information about particular traders, which is not available. The trader's overall position (i.e. portfolio) can affect the optimal margins, e.g. a spread has much lower risk than a single position in a future because price movements on the two legs of the spread will largely cancel out. This is recognized, and much lower margins are payable for standard and verifiable positions, such as spreads. However, a particular trader may hold a position in both a future and some other asset whose price movements are negatively correlated with those of the future. While this situation results in much less risk to the trader, it will require considerable effort by the margin authorities to verify the other asset holding and to set a special margin requirement. There is also the problem that, since the other asset is beyond the control of the futures exchange, the trader may still choose to default on the contract if it shows a large loss, even though he has simultaneously made a large profit on the other asset. For these reasons, margins do not take a detailed account of the overall risk exposure of the trader. In consequence, margins differ between only a few broad categories of trader (e.g. exchange members and others), and between a few standard categories of position (e.g. spreads or hedges and speculative positions).

A very important factor in setting margins is the price volatility of the futures contract concerned, particularly the probability of an extreme adverse daily price movement which results in the balance on a trader's margin account becoming negative. Daily price movements are relevant because marking to the market usually takes place daily. In chapter 7 it was found that, for many futures, price volatility increases as delivery approaches. This implies that the margin should also increase as delivery approaches if the risk of a daily price movement exceeding the margin is to remain constant. However, futures markets do not vary their margin requirements as the time to delivery declines, although the initial margin is varied in response to general market volatility. Futures exchanges in the US and the UK have the power to instantly change margins, and this power is occasionally used. For example, on Tuesday 21st October 1987 (during the stock market crash of 1987) the initial margin for FTSE 100 contracts was increased from £1,500 to £5,000, while on 2nd November 1987 it was again increased from £5,000 to £7,500. On 16th November 1987 the initial margin was decreased from £7,500 to £5,000, Quality of Markets Unit (1987-8). Similarly, the initial margin on the S&P500 future was doubled in October 1987.

The finding that the variance of futures returns varies over time (e.g. GARCH) implies that the appropriate margin to give a constant risk of default shifts over time, Siegelaer (1992). In addition, since futures returns are leptokurtic after allowing for GARCH effects, if the computation of the margin uses a normal distribution, the margins will be set too low. Kofman (1993), Longin (1994) and others considered below have also argued that, since daily futures returns have a leptokurtic distribution, the use of the normal distribution is inappropriate.

The no-arbitrage futures price includes an allowance for default risk. This will tend to reduce the price that a trader is prepared to pay for a long position, and increase the price required for a short position. An increase in margins will reduce the risk of default, so reducing the size of this premium and narrowing the no-arbitrage band. However, if higher margins result in less liquidity, bid-ask spreads may rise and the no-arbitrage band widen.

11.1.2 Reducing Price Volatility

Proponents of increased margins argue that the low margins in the futures markets allow highly levered futures positions to be acquired. This permits destabilizing speculation which, through the linkages with the spot market, increases the price volatility of equities. Higher futures margins reduce the ability of traders to take extreme speculative positions and, through linkages with the spot market, limit spot price movements, Brady (1988) and SEC (1988). High margins will also raise the costs of default, and this will tend to deter speculation. This reverses the causality considered in the previous section, in which volatility was argued to be a major determinant of margins. It is now argued that higher margins reduce speculative activity, which leads to a drop in futures volume, open interest and volatility. This *drop* in price volatility then feeds through to the equity market. This argument differs from the conclusions reached in chapter 11.1.1, where an increase in margins causes a drop in futures volume and open interest, but a *rise* in volatility. The validity of these predictions will be considered in chapter 11.1.3, where the available empirical evidence is presented.

There has been criticism of raising futures margins to reduce spot volatility, e.g. to the same level as those in the stock market. Miller (1988) suggests that proposals for an increase in futures margins should be viewed with caution for a number of reasons. Futures margins have different functions from share margins. Despite having the same name, margins serve a completely different purpose in stock and futures markets, and therefore there is no obvious implication that two different concepts should be 'made consistent'. The margin on a future is a good faith deposit, while the margin on a share is a down payment with credit being given for the remaining cost of the share. If futures margins were high, large investors would be reluctant to deposit very large sums with a single institution because of the low interest rates payable and because of the risk of collapse. With high futures margins, investors would seek alternatives to futures, leading to a reduction of liquidity in the futures market. The asset underlying an index future is a well diversified portfolio of shares and so has very low unsystematic risk, while a single share is not diversified and is subject to unsystematic risk. Even if margins did serve the same purpose in futures and stock markets, index futures would be expected to have lower margins because they are less risky. Finally, as Ginter (1991) pointed out, futures margins are paid within one day, while for shares the period is much longer (e.g. seven days). To compensate for this, share margins need to be about $\sqrt{7} = 2.65$ times larger than futures margins. Malkiel (1988) also rejects interfering with the existing futures margin arrangements.

Moser (1992) has pointed out that the argument that low margins leads to destabilizing speculation is open to a number of objections. Traders are risk averse, and so are reluctant to speculate unless the expected rewards give sufficient compensation, futures brokers and exchanges are risk averse, and so are unwilling to let traders engage in reckless speculation, and traders can circumvent high margins by borrowing the money to pay them.

11.1.3 Empirical Evidence

The empirical studies of the linkages between margins and price volatility can be divided into three broad groups - (a) the adequacy of existing futures margins in coping with default risk, (b) the effects of futures margins on futures volume, open interest and price volatility, and (c) finding which factors explain the level of futures margins. When studying margin changes, there is a problem over the direction of causality. If a positive relationship is found between margins and spot volatility (in accordance with Telser and others), this may be because (a) higher expected price volatility causes the authorities to increase the margins (i.e. stabilizing), rather than (b) higher margins causing higher price volatility (i.e. destabilizing). However, if there is a negative relationship between margins and price volatility (as suggested by Brady and others), the interpretation is more straightforward, and this is that a rise in margins leads to a decrease in spot volatility (i.e. stabilizing). It is not sensible to argue that, when a decrease in volatility is expected, margins are increased, Kupiec (1993). The various possibilities are illustrated in table 11.1, where the outcomes on the leading diagonal correspond to the Telser et al view, while the off-diagonal elements correspond to the Brady et al view.

Table 11.1: Interpretation of Margin-Volatility Relationships

Margin Change	Observed Volatility Change	
	Up	Down
Up	a. Higher expected volatility led to a rise in margins (*stabilizing*) b. Higher margins caused a rise in volatility (*destabilizing*)	Higher margins caused a fall in volatility (*stabilizing*)
Down	Lower margins caused a rise in volatility (*stabilizing*)	a. Lower expected volatility led to a fall in margins (*stabilizing*) b. Lower margins caused a fall in volatility (*destabilizing*)

a. Default Risk.   The first group of empirical studies accepts that the primary purpose of futures margins is to reduce default risk to an acceptable level, and have investigated the adequacy of existing index futures margins. Some of these studies have also considered the additional costs that higher margins impose on traders.
USA.   Figlewski (1984c) formulated the problem of calculating the probability of a negative balance on the margin account as first calculating the probability of the balance dropping to the maintenance level; and second calculating the probability of the balance becoming negative within the period of time allowed for the payment of a margin call. In order to do this Figlewski assumed that the logarithms of futures prices follow a Wiener process. He then estimated the probability of a negative balance on the margin account for a given size of maintenance margin for three stock index futures: S&P500, NYSE Composite and VLCI. He concluded that the maintenance margins for these contracts appeared to provide adequate coverage against default, while not being excessively large.

Warshawsky (1989) investigated the size of maintenance margins required to give only a 1% chance of the price movement exceeding the margin. The probability distribution of futures prices used was not assumed, as did Figlewski (1984c), but was estimated from actual data. Using US data for 1986-8 for the S&P500 and NYSE Composite indices, he found that margins of about 2.5% were required, while for 75 individual NYSE stocks he found that margins of around 20% were necessary. These much larger margins for shares are accounted for by the grace period of five days given to share owners, and by the greater volatility of individual share prices (since they bear unsystematic as well as systematic risk). The actual margins on US index futures and shares are just a bit larger than the numbers calculated by Warshawsky, and so fit well with this default-based approach to margin setting.

Craine (1992, 1997) pointed out that each time there is a margin call, the trader has the option to default. Traders are argued to default if, prior to paying the margin call, the net value of the futures position and the balance in the margin account is negative. This option to default possessed by the trader can be viewed as a purchased put option for long positions, and a purchased call option for short positions. This default option is supplied for free by the clearing house, and a prudent margin system will increase margins so that the value of this option is zero. Craine used daily data for S&P500 futures during October 1987 and October 1989 to examine the value of the default option. He estimated the daily futures volatilities using the Garman & Klass high-low estimator. For October 1987 these volatility estimates were much larger than those implied by the prices of S&P500 futures options. The calculations used the hedging maintenance margin (which was lower than the speculative maintenance margin), and assumed daily settlement (although intra-day settlement actually occurred in 1989 and for three days in 1987), in order to maximize the estimated value of the default option. Despite this, the value of the default option given by the Black formulae was zero throughout October 1989, and positive for only a few days in October 1987. This indicates that S&P500 margins were adequate.

Baer, France & Moser (1996) computed the coverage ratio for 18 futures - this is the average margin, divided by the standard deviation of futures prices estimated using the implied volatility from the options price. The highest ratio (10.2) was for S&P500 futures, while the lowest (4.0) was for live cattle futures. These ratios imply a very low probability of default, e.g. well under 1%, for all 18 futures, with the margins for S&P500 futures being particularly cautious.

Kupiec (1994) used daily data for 1988-92 to examine the frequency with which S&P500 futures margins were exceeded by daily price movements. For naked futures positions this occurred only three times, or 0.3% of the time. For calendar spreads, the margin was exceeded 8.3% of the time, and Kupiec concluded that the margins for calendar spreads appeared rather low.

Longin (1994) argued that what matters when setting margins to give a specified probability of default, is the distribution of extreme values (the maximum and minimum values which occur during a specified period of time) rather than the entire distribution. Longin used data on daily returns (including dividends) on the S&P500 index for 1975-90 and found that the best fit for the extreme values of this data was the Fréchet distribution. For a given probability of default, the margins set using the normal and Fréchet distributions were compared. It was found that the margins assuming normality were considerably smaller than those set using the Fréchet distribution. For example, for a 5% probability of default during a 60 day period, the margin using normality was 3.1% (long) and 3.2% (short), while that using the Fréchet distribution was 6.1% (long) and 4.4% (short). Longin then compared the observed probabilities of default during the 16 years with those implied by the Fréchet distribution, and found a close correspondence, e.g. for a 5% probability of default the observed frequency was 6.3% (long) and 3.9% (short). There were slightly more large price falls than large price rises, and so the margins required for long positions were larger than those for short positions.

Edwards & Neftci (1988) highlighted the existence of interdependencies between the probability distributions of extreme price changes for different futures. Extreme price changes were defined as those which resulted in a negative balance on the relevant margin account. They argued that, if such dependencies are ignored, the resulting margins may be inappropriate for traders who simultaneously hold positions in more than one futures contract, i.e. too high if the correlation of extreme price changes is negative, and too low if this correlation is positive. Edwards & Neftci (1988) examined the daily settlement prices for nine US futures, including S&P500 index and NYSE Composite index futures, for five years. They found significant correlations (both positive and negative) between the extreme price movements of some of these futures, indicating that, ideally, some account should be taken of the portfolio of futures contracts held by a trader when setting margins. They also found that the correlations of extreme price changes differed from the correlations of all price changes, so that specific estimation of the correlation of extreme price changes is necessary if correct allowance is to be made for this effect. However, as pointed out earlier, there are considerable problems in having margins which vary according to the trader's particular portfolio.

Dewachter & Gielens (1999) argued that the optimal margin is a positive function of the default cost (τ), and a negative function of the liquidity costs induced by a margin (ρ); with the optimal margin given by ρ/τ. Using daily NYSE Composite index quotes for 1982-90, and assuming that daily returns follow the Fréchet distribution, they compared the actual margins with those given by their model. Lacking information on ρ/τ (which is the probability of the loss exceeding the margin), it was set equal to 0.5%. They found that optimal margins were much more volatile than actual margins. In addition, large negative returns appeared more common than large positive returns, and so the distribution of returns was skewed. This implies that long positions should be subject to larger margins than short positions.

If default risk is a major determinant of margins, changes in default risk will require changes in the margin. In order to implement such a policy, the margin setters must monitor the volatility of futures prices, looking for changes. Wilson, Aggarwal & Inclan (1996) proposed an iterative CUSUM procedure for spotting jumps in the variance of a returns series. They applied this technique to daily data on S&P500

index for 1984-92, and found 10 jumps for the variance of S&P500 index returns.

Hong Kong. A severe test of the adequacy of index margins to prevent default was provided by the stock market crash of October 1987. During the 1987 crash the margin system for index futures served its purpose; in that there were no failures of clearing houses, members of clearing houses or futures brokers, Tosini (1988). However, the Hang Seng index fell by 69% in a week, and the Hong Kong clearing house would have defaulted if it had not been rescued by the Hong Kong government, Freris (1991, p 151) and Slayter & Carew (1993, p. 78).

Lam, Sin & Leung (2004) analyzed daily returns for Hang Seng futures for 1986-2001. The variance of returns was estimated in three different ways:- simple moving average (MA), exponentially weighted moving average (EWMA) and GARCH(1,1). The resulting margins were compared using three criteria: the actual probability of default, the actual average default and the actual average overcharge (or margin- loss). The first two criteria focus on default; while the third is concerned with opportunity costs. For a given level of default, the actual average overcharge for margins set using the GARCH variance forecasts was lower than for the EWMA forecasts, which was in turn lower than for the simple MA forecasts.

Europe. Cotter (2001) considered daily closing quotes for 12 European index futures (Belgium, Denmark, France, Germany, Italy, Netherlands, Norway, Portugal, Spain, Sweden, Switzerland and the UK) for 1984-99. The Fréchet distribution fitted the futures returns, and was used to compute the probability of the margin being exceeded by the loss, for a range of margin values. This revealed some substantial differences in risk, e.g. between Portugal and Switzerland, which supports using different margins for different stock indices. He found that large negative price movements were more likely than large positive movements, and so margins should be bigger for long, than for short positions. This is particularly true for Norway. The use of the normal distribution to set margins was shown to lead to much smaller margins than the Fréchet distribution.

UK. Knott & Polenghi (2004) fitted an AR(1)-GARCH(1,1) model to daily FTSE 100 futures returns for 1998-2002. They then fitted four different distributions (historic, normal, Student's *t* and extreme value) to the standardized residuals to derive margins for a given risk of default, and these showed differences. The margins were then adjusted to incorporate the conditional volatility from the GARCH model, and these conditional margins revealed considerable variation over time (although the variation due to different distributional assumptions was small). On average, the actual FTSE 100 margins covered losses 99.86% of the time. They also investigated the capital reserves needed by the clearing house to cover any losses, which requires a knowledge of the size of the defaults. This capital reserve was estimated at £14 million to £250 million.

Cotter (2004) used 5 minute returns on FTSE 100 futures for 1996-9, and found the rescaled returns (daily return/daily standard deviation of returns) were approximately normally distributed. The resulting distribution was used in a Value at Risk type analysis to set margins and minimum capital requirements for financial firms holding portfolios of futures positions. The margins for long positions were smaller than those for short positions.

Germany.   Broussard & Booth (1998) studied trade data on DAX futures for 1992-4, and showed that the maximum intraday price changes followed a Fréchet distribution. They computed some margin violation probabilities, and argued that the Fréchet distribution could be used to set intraday margins.

Finland.   Booth, Broussard, Martikainen & Puttonen (1997) analyzed daily returns on FOX index futures for 1988-9, and found they fitted the Fréchet distribution. They then use this distribution to assign probabilities of default to FOX futures margins.

South Africa.   Roth & Smit (2000) studied daily returns on the South African All Share index for 1986-98, and showed that maximum returns fitted the Fréchet distribution. They used three distributions to set margins - normal, Fréchet and historical, and concluded that the normal distribution led to inadequate margins, while the Fréchet distribution was satisfactory.

Conclusions.   These empirical studies support the view that index futures margins are set to protect against default, and usually do so with a high probability of success. They also support the use of the Fréchet distribution when setting margins. There is also evidence that margins for long positions should be larger than margins for short positions.

b. Effects on Volume, Open Interest and Volatility.   The second group of empirical studies have examined the effects of higher futures margins on futures volume, open interest and price volatility. The competing theories both predict a negative effect on futures volume and open interest, but make opposite predictions about the effect on price volatility.

USA.   Furbush & Poulsen (1989) studied the effect of margin changes on S&P500 futures volume. Between 1982 and 1988 there were only nine margin changes, and four of these occurred during the 1987 Crash. Measuring futures volume relative to spot volume, they compared futures volume for the fifteen days before a margin change with that for the fifteen days after the change. The results are mixed and, if anything, support a positive relationship between margins and volume. They also used the Garman & Klass estimator and the square of the logarithm of the daily price relatives to compute two alternative sets of daily futures volatilities for the fifteen days before and after a change in S&P500 speculative margins. There were only five such changes, of which three occurred during the 1987 Crash. The mean daily volatilities before and after a change in speculative margins were compared, and little evidence of a change in futures price volatility was found. Given the very small number of observations, many of which occurred during a highly unusual period (the 1987 Crash), these results are, at best, only indicative.

Kalavathi & Shanker (1991) presented theoretical arguments about the effect of increasing futures hedging margins on the demand for futures contracts by hedgers. Higher margins increase the costs of hedging and so, provided the hedgers are not pure risk minimizers, they will reduce their hedge ratios and their demand for futures contracts. Kalavathi & Shanker went on to consider daily data for the S&P500 for 1982-8. During this period there were eight changes in the hedging margin (of which six occurred in 1987). On the basis of this data they estimated that increasing futures margins to 50% of contract value would decrease the hedging demand for futures by roughly 11%. However, this estimate is subject to a considerable degree of error.

Moser (1992) used daily prices of S&P500 futures for 1982-9. During this period there were 19 changes in the initial margin for S&P500 futures. Moser used an iterative regression procedure in which the daily volatility of returns was explained by margin changes in the previous and subsequent twelve days, as well as by lagged volatility and the month of the year. There was no evidence that margin changes during the previous twelve days had a negative effect on volatility, e.g. that an increase in margins leads to a decrease in volatility. Moser (1992) also looked at whether margin changes in the subsequent twelve days had a positive effect on volatility. This tested whether margins are increased after an increase in volatility. Again, the results were insignificant.

Moser (1993) studied daily data on the S&P500 futures for 1982-9. He used four different types of margin: initial speculative and hedging margins, and maintenance speculative and hedging margins. Moser found that changes in the four types of margin had no effect on the volatility of futures and spot returns for 12 days before and after the margin change. Similarly, there were no effects on spot volume, futures volume, open interest and the volatility of open interest. However, margins did have a positive effect on the volatility of open interest for the two or three days after the margin change. Margins also had a significant negative effect on the basis $(F-S)$.

Kupiec (1993) studied the link between the initial hedging margin on S&P500 futures and spot volatility for 1982-9. Spot volatility for each month was measured as the standard deviation of the daily returns on the index (corrected for the effects of non-synchronous trading) during that month. During this period there were nine different levels of hedging margin. The monthly spot volatilities were regressed on the current percentage margin and the lagged volatility. Kupiec found a significant positive relationship between margins and spot volatility. He then used the Parkinson high-low estimator to give daily spot volatility estimates for 1987-9. Spot volatility was regressed on the current percentage margin, the percentage margins for the previous four days and the volatilities for the previous five days. The only margin variable to be statistically significant was the current margin, which had a positive effect.

Duffee, Kupiec & White (1992) have suggested that a positive relationship between spot volatility and margins may be due to share price volatility rising in bear markets because of a leverage (or gearing) effect. At the same time, the fall in the share (and futures) price will automatically lead to a rise in the percentage margin. Kupiec allowed for this effect by regressing spot volatility on the current percentage margin, the volatilities for the previous five days and spot returns for the previous five days, where spot returns were included to control for the possibility that spot volatility rises when returns are negative. However, after controlling for this effect, current margins still had a significant positive association with spot volatility. There are three possible interpretations for Kupiec's finding of a positive association between spot volatility and futures margins: margins are raised by the exchange when expected spot volatility increases, or an increase in margins reduces liquidity in the futures market and this increases spot volatility, or the regression equation is misspecified and the finding of a positive association is spurious.

Dutt & Wein (2003a) argued that most previous studies of the effect of a margin change on volume did not control for margin increases (decreases) being caused by a rise (fall) in volatility. Since there is evidence that increases in volume tend to be associated with increases in volatility; if a rise in volatility leads to margins being raised, it may appear that raising margins results in a rise in volume. They regressed daily DJIA futures volume on (margin/standard deviation of daily settlement prices), and some control variables. The regressions used data for 40 day windows centered on each of the eight margin changes over the period 1997-2000. Deflating margins by price volatility controlled for changes in risk, and margin increases had a highly significant negative effect on DJIA futures volume.

Japan.   Ohk & Lee (1994) used daily data on Nikkei 225 futures traded in Osaka for 1990-2 to investigate the effects of the four margin increases that occurred during this period. They found that the volatility of futures returns was the same for the 30 days after a margin change as it was before. Two of the margin increases were followed by a fall in futures volume in the subsequent 30 days. while another margin increase led to a rise in open interest.

Ito & Lin (2001) considered daily data on Nikkei 225 futures traded in both Osaka and SGX for 1988-94. After controlling for day of the week and month of the year effects, they found that three of the four margin increases at Osaka lowered Osaka volume; while three of the five margin decreases at SGX increased SGX volume. These volume changes appear to have been mostly an alteration in the location of trading, rather than a rise or fall in market-wide volume. Margin changes had little effect on returns volatility. Finally, volatility increases (decreases) tended to precede margin increases (decreases).

Chng (2004b) analyzed daily data on Nikkei 225 futures traded in Osaka and Singapore for 1990-3. He found that margins in Osaka have a negative contemporaneous association with volume and volatility in Osaka, and a positive association with volume in Singapore. Price reversals indicate that an increase in Osaka margins strengthens the price discovery role of Singapore. These results indicate that an increase in Osaka margins causes trading activity to switch to Singapore, and this strengthens Singapore's price discovery role.

Other Studies.   Pliska & Shalen (1991) built a mathematical model which they used to simulate the effects of changing the futures margin. They found that an increase in margins lowered liquidity, leading to a drop in open interest and volume, and a slight rise in futures price volatility.

Salinger (1989) reviewed the evidence on the effect of changing share margins on the volatility of share prices, and concluded that this provides no justification for increasing futures margins to reduce spot price volatility. Similarly, after reviewing the evidence for both share margins and futures margins, Chance (1990) concluded that futures margins cannot be used to control volatility because they do not influence volatility. Kupiec (1998) reviewed the US evidence of the effect of margins on volatility for both the stock market and a range of futures markets. He also reviewed the evidence on the effects of introducing futures and options trading on spot volatility (see chapter 12). Again, he concluded that there is no substantial evidence to support the view that margins can be used to control stock market volatility; although higher margins do tend to reduce open interest.

Conclusions.   The empirical evidence summarized above does not provide clear evidence of a link between futures margins and volatility. However, there is some support for a negative relationship between margins and volume, and margins and open interest.

c. Setting Margins.   The final group of empirical studies have sought to discover the factors determining the level of futures margins. While it is possible conceptually to distinguish between the causes and effects of margin changes, this is very difficult empirically because expectations of subsequent events may be used to change the current margins, so altering the actual outcomes away from the expectations. Therefore, while this section considers studies which investigated the determinants of margins, it is also possible to reinterpret some of these studies in terms of the effects of margins. Similarly, some of the studies of the effects of margin changes may be reinterpreted as studies of the determinants of margins.

USA.   Fenn & Kupiec (1993) pointed out there is a trade-off between the size of margins and the length of time between each marking to the market. The longer is this time period, the higher must margins be to maintain the same probability of default. Fenn & Kupiec developed two alternative models of margin setting activity. In the first model the number of settlements per day is fixed in advance, while in the second model this is not the case, and the exchange initiates a marking to the market whenever a price change threatens to exhaust the balance on traders' margin accounts. Provided there are no jumps in futures prices, margin payments (or non-payments) are instantaneous and the position of a non-payer can be closed out immediately, default in the second model is theoretically impossible.

Fenn & Kupiec argue that, for a given policy on the number of settlements per day, the exchange will set margins so as to minimize contracting costs. These are the opportunity costs to the trader of providing the margin, the administrative costs to the trader and the exchange of the settlements during the day and (for the first model only) the costs to the exchange of default by a trader. For a fixed number of settlements per day (i.e. the first model), the minimisation of contracting costs requires that the initial margin is set so that the marginal cost of the margin is equal to the marginal cost of default. In which case the ratio of the margin to the instantaneous volatility of the futures price is constant. Thus, as the price volatility of the future changes over time, the minimisation of contracting costs requires an equal proportionate change in margins. If the number of settlements per day is endogenous (i.e. the second model) and there is no possibility of default, the minimization of contracting costs requires that, as futures price volatility rises, the margin-volatility ratio falls. For example, as volatility rises, margins rise by a smaller proportionate amount.

Fenn & Kupiec (1993) tested these two alternative models of margin setting using data for the S&P500, NYSE Composite and MMI futures from inception to 1990. For all three futures there was very considerable variation in the margin to volatility ratio due to the small number of margin changes, and this is inconsistent with the first model. The number of settlements per day of these three futures was varied only in the post-crash period, and so the second model was not applied to the pre-crash data. For the post-crash period, there was a negative relationship between price volatility and the margin to volatility ratio for all three futures, which is a prediction of the second model. However, the lack of much variation in the number of settlements per day is inconsistent with this model. Therefore, the data is consistent with neither model.

Fenn & Kupiec suggested three possible explanations for these results. First, there may be substantial costs associated with altering the initial margin, so leading to static margins and variations in the margin-volatility ratio. Second, the opportunity cost of putting up margin money may be small, and the risk of default by clearing house members may be low, so that initial margins are irrelevant. In consequence their level is arbitrary, and there is no need to keep adjusting margins for changes in volatility. Finally, Fenn & Kupiec suggested that initial margins may have been set at a high level because of political pressures, as in the USA. The resulting margins would not be adjusted for changes in volatility.

Baer, France & Moser (1996) studied time series data for S&P500 futures. The coverage ratio (margin/volatility) tended to be mean reverting, which suggests that as well as raising margins when volatility rose, exchanges also lowered margins when volatility fell. They also analyzed data on 18 futures (including the S&P500), and discovered that when the opportunity cost of providing margin funds rose, margins tended to be reduced.

Japan.   Ohk & Lee (1994) used daily data on Nikkei 225 futures traded in Osaka for 1990-2 to investigate the factors determining the four margin increases during this period. Volatility was not found to be an important determinant of margin changes. For three margin increases, futures volume rose in the preceding 30 days, and for all four margin increases, open interest rose during the preceding 30 days. This result conflicts with the view that higher volume and open interest reflect increased liquidity and lower risk; leading to lower margins. Ohk & Lee concluded that the Japanese authorities were operating inconsistent criteria for setting margins.

Conclusions.   The available evidence on setting margins has not found clear support for any particular theory.

d. Conclusions.   There is empirical support for the view that index futures margins are positively linked to long run return volatility, that margins are set at an appropriate levels, and that the use of a fat tailed distribution (e.g. the Fréchet) is worthwhile. While it is not generally done in practice, there is empirical support for larger margins for long positions. There is no substantial evidence that margins can be used to control volatility, although there is some support for higher margins leading to lower volume and open interest. Finally, there is no clear empirical support for any of the possible the determinants of margin changes.

11.2 Liquidity Requirements and Variation Margin

Fielitz & Gay (1986) considered the amount of cash that must be earmarked when a futures position is opened to meet the consequent payments of variation margin. They expressed this sum as a function of the variance of the price of the future, the level of the futures price, the selected horizon period, the chosen probability of exhausting the sum earmarked and the size of the futures position. They presented some illustrative tables for the S&P500 index future of percentages of the nominal value of the futures position that must be set aside, and these ranged from 2.3% to 34.6%.

11.2.1 Kolb, Gay & Hunter Model

Kolb, Gay & Hunter (1985a, 1985b) derived an expression for the relationship between the sum of money that is earmarked for meeting payments of variation margin ($£M$), the length of time the position will be held (T days), the standard deviation of daily changes in the futures prices ($£\sigma$) and the acceptable probability of exhausting the sum of money per contract made available for variation margin payments (P). In deriving their model, Kolb, Gay & Hunter assumed that the futures price is not expected to change (i.e. zero risk premium), any changes in futures prices that do occur have a constant variance and are normally distributed (see chapter 2.6 for a discussion of the distribution of changes in futures prices, and the evidence that the variance changes over time and the distribution is leptokurtic), and that futures prices follow a continuous process. The resulting model is $P = 2[1 - \Phi(M/\{\sigma T^{0.5}\})]$, where $\Phi(.)$ denotes the cumulative distribution function for a standardized normal variate. The only parameter in this equation that requires estimation is σ; as the other three variables can be specified by the trader, i.e. P, M and T. Given decisions about any two of these variables, the required value of the third can be calculated from the equation.

Example 1. Randolph Duke is considering taking a position (short or long) in ten FTSE 100 futures, and plans to hold the position for twenty days (i.e. $T = 20$). He estimates that the daily standard deviation of price changes in the FTSE 100 future is £475, (i.e. $\sigma = 475$). He now wishes to calculate the probability that the variation margin payments on these contracts will exhaust the £20,000 he has available. $P = 2[1 - \Phi(2,000/\{475 \times 20^{0.5}\})] = 0.3464$. Thus the chance of being unable to meet the variation margin payments is about one in three.

Example 2. Randolph Duke decides that he must be able to meet the variation margin payments with a 95% probability (i.e. $P = 5\%$), and wishes to know how long he can expect to be able to hold the position open. P is therefore specified, and T is now the dependent variable. Solving $0.05 = 2[1 - \Phi(2,000/\{475 \times T^{0.5}\})]$ gives $T = 4.61$ days. The planned holding period is only 4.6 days.

Example 3. Randolph Duke now decides that he must hold the position open for twenty days, (i.e. $T = 20$), and he is only willing to accept a 5% probability of default, (i.e. $P = 0.05$). He wishes to know the implied sum of money required to be set aside for variation margin payments. $0.05 = 2[1 - \Phi(M/\{475 \times 20^{0.5}\})]$, and $M = £4,164$. Therefore, Randolph Duke requires £41,640 for a position of ten contracts.

The Kolb, Gay & Hunter model applies to positions in a single future. If the trader holds open positions in a number of different futures, unless the variation margin payments on all of these futures are perfectly positively correlated, the separate application of this model will overestimate the sum of money required to avoid default. This situation can be dealt with by applying the Kolb, Gay & Hunter model to the portfolio as a whole, although, as Figlewski (1985a) pointed out, the distributional assumptions used in deriving the formula for a single futures position may not apply to a portfolio. There is another reason why the Kolb, Gay & Hunter model will tend to overestimate the sum of money required. The derivation of the model assumes that margins are paid continuously, while in reality they may be paid only once per day, and so intraday price variations do not matter, Figlewski (1985a). Figlewski has shown that the Kolb, Gay & Hunter model can be extended to allow for a non-zero risk premium, which increases its applicability to index futures.

11.2.2 Blank Model

Blank (1990) and Blank, Carter & Schmiesing (1991, appendix 9) have presented a different approach to calculating the initial cash required to meet variation margin payments. This consists of short and long run conditions, both of which must be met. It makes weaker assumptions about the stochastic process generating futures prices than previous approaches.

The short run condition is that the initial capital must be capable of withstanding a run of N losing days, where N is set by the trader to reflect the acceptable probability (P) of exhausting the available capital. Thus, the initial capital required is $H_s = NL$, where L is the average amount lost per contract per losing day (i.e. the average variation margin payment). Letting α be the estimated probability of a futures position losing money during any day then, assuming α is constant over time, the probability of a run of N losing days is α^N. Therefore, the trader selects an integer value of N such that $N \geq log(P)/log(\alpha)$.

Example. Ted Striker, the manager of the Jarrow Fund, decides that the acceptable probability of exhausting his liquidity reserve (P) is 5%. The estimated average loss per contract per day (L) is £50, while the estimated probability of losing money on any particular day (α) is 0.5. $N \geq log(0.05)/log(0.5) = 4.32$, which is rounded up to five days. Thus $H_s = 50 \times 5 = £250$, and the initial capital required to withstand a run of five losing days is £250. Such a run will occur only $\alpha^N = 0.5^5 = 3.1\%$ of the time.

The long run condition accepts that the trader may lose money every day the position is held. The expected value of the loss (D) on a position held open for T days is $E[D] = L\Sigma(ta^t)$, where the summation is over T days, i.e. $t = 1...T$. If the position is expected to be kept open for an infinite period of time, it can be shown that $E[D] = L\{a/(1-\alpha) +[a/(1-\alpha)]^2\}$.

Example. Continuing with the Ted Striker example, if he sets T equal to ten days then $E[D] = 50\times1.99 = £99.50$, while if T is set to infinity $E[D] = 50\times2 = £100$. This shows that the expected loss is insensitive to variations in T, and Ted needs to have about £100 to cover the expected loses from this position.

Blank then argues that the required initial capital is the larger of H_s and $E[D]$. For Ted Striker, this is £250. Blank goes on to analyze the initial capital requirements of a hedger, and considers the extent to which profits on the spot position being hedged can be liquidated to meet margin calls, and also whether the hedger can liquidate those futures contracts whose margin calls cannot be met. Liquidating the spot position may be impossible, while liquidating part of the spot and futures positions may be undesirable. Blank (1992) points out that, if the aim of the hedge is not solely risk minimisation, the creation of a liquidity reserve will increase the cost of hedging, so reducing the optimal hedge ratio.

Blank (1991b) applied his model to determining the capital required by a speculator who plans to hold the position for N days, and who limits losses using stop-loss orders. The short term capital requirement per contract is $H = NL+M$, where L is the average amount lost per contract on each unprofitable trade, and M is the maintenance margin per contract. The long term capital requirement is $E[D] = L\Sigma(ta^t)+M$, where the summation is over N days. The capital requirement is the larger of the short and the long term figures. Since the futures positions may not be held simultaneously, Blank (1991b) argues that any benefits from diversification should be ignored.

Example. Otis B. Driftwood plans to hold a speculative position of ten Keinik index futures for five days. The estimated probability of a losing trade is 0.4802, while the expected loss on a losing trade is £493. Finally, the maintenance margin for Keinik futures is £700 per contract. Otis's short term capital requirement is $H = NL+M = 5\times493+700 = £3,165$ per contract. The long term capital requirement is $E[D] = L\Sigma(ta^t)+M = 493\times1.6139+700 = £1,496$ per contract, where the summation is over five days. (For an infinite number of days $\Sigma(ta^t) =1.7772$, and the long term capital requirement is £1,576 per contract.) Therefore, the capital requirement is max(£3,165, £1,496) = £3,165 per contract, i.e. £31,650 in total.

11.2.3 Other Considerations

Hsieh (1993) pointed out that, if the volatility of futures returns changes over time, this will affect the required liquidity reserve; and that smaller reserves are required for long than for short positions because the latter can generate an unlimited loss, while losses on long positions are bounded by a price of zero.

It should be noted that the models of the initial capital required to meet margin calls ignore any interest on the money that may accrue while it is held in reserve.

11.3 Price Limits

Most markets do not have artificial constraints on daily price movements, and so futures markets are unusual in this respect. The imposition of daily price limits can delay futures markets reaching an equilibrium price. Such limits also generate enforcement costs, as well as restricting liquidity by preventing trading, Kolb & Gay (1985, p. 9). Since the settlement price is constrained, price limits provide an interest free loan to those who would otherwise have had to pay extra margin, from those who would have received these margin payments. Unless price limits are co-ordinated between markets, traders may find that profits in one market are unavailable to pay losses in another. So what are the offsetting benefits generated by price limits?

There are a number of differing views on the purpose of price limits. It has been suggested that the purpose of price limits is to prevent panic and speculation causing large price movements, or to place an upper bound on the daily liability of traders for variation margin payments. Daily price limits may prevent a trader who has made huge losses during the day due to large price changes, trying to speculate his or her way out of financial ruin before trading ceases for the day and their losses are revealed. Daily price limits may also reduce the benefits of price manipulation, and allow lower margin requirements, Khoury & Jones (1984), Kyle (1988). Price limits may reduce the risks of trading. New information may arrive after an investor has decided to trade and before the order is submitted (implementation risk). This risk is largest when markets are most volatile, and price limits are beneficial because they place an upper bound on this risk, Kodres & O'Brien (1994). Brennan (1986) argued that price limits have the same purpose as margins; to reduce the incentive of traders to renege on their obligations under a futures contract; and Chen (2002) presented cross-section evidence (including S&P500 futures) supporting this view.

11.3.1 Brennan

In Brennan's model the maintenance margin is equal to the initial margin, and so every adverse daily price change generates a corresponding payment of variation margin. This is the situation for FTSE 100 index futures. At the end of each day, those traders required to pay variation margin must decide whether to pay or renege on their futures. Honouring the contract will require the payment of that day's decline in the value of the future, i.e. $(F_{t+1} - F_t)$ for a short position (where F_t is the closing futures price on day t), while reneging will mean the loss of the initial margin (m) and of the trader's reputation (valued at r). If he or she reneges there may also be a lawsuit which, allowing for the probability of losing, is valued by the trader at w. In the absence of price limits, a trader with a short position will renege if $(F_{t+1} - F_t) > G$, where $G \equiv m + r + w$.

If a maximum price change of L is introduced and this limit is exceeded, at the time the payment of variation margin is required the trader does not know the current equilibrium price of his or her asset (F_{t+1}). In this case, if $G>L$, the trader is not certain that $(F_{t+1}-F_t)>G$. There are two possibilities for a trader with a short position: if $G>(F_{t+1}-F_t)>L$, honour the contract, and if $(F_{t+1}-F_t)>G>L$, renege on the contract. (For a trader with a long position $(F_{t+1}-F_t)$ is replaced by (F_t-F_{t+1}).) The key requirement for price limits to reduce the incentive for a trader with a short position to renege is for the current price of the contract used by the trader in his or her decision $(\bar{F}_{t+1})$ to be lower than the closing price that would have been observed if trading had not been halted, i.e. F_{t+1}. In particular, if $F_{t+1}>(F_t+G)$, while $\bar{F}_{t+1}<(F_t+G)$, the decision to renege will have been altered by the presence of price limits. However, the reverse is also possible. Thus if $F_{t+1}<(F_t+G)$, while $\bar{F}_{t+1}<(F_t+G)$, the presence of price limits will have altered the decision from honouring the contract to reneging.

The question of why price limits exist in many, but not all, futures markets has been considered by Brennan (1986). In some futures markets, even though trading has been halted, very good information is available from which to estimate F_{t+1}, the current equilibrium price of the contract. For index futures, the price of the future can be estimated from the prices of the constituent shares, while for interest rate and foreign currency futures, very accurate estimates of the current equilibrium futures price can be made from the corresponding spot markets. For metals, the spot price may also be a good guide to the equilibrium futures price. Price limits will be of little benefit for such futures because $\bar{F}_{t+1} \approx F_{t+1}$, and any limit will have little effect on the decision about honouring the futures contract. Therefore, Brennan's theory predicts an absence of price limits for such futures markets where good information is available on the equilibrium price.

The FTSE 100 does not have daily price limits. Up to 1988 the S&P500 index future also had no price limits. However, following the stock market crash of October 1987, a complicated system of shock absorber and circuit breaker limits was imposed on S&P500 index futures as from 20th October 1988. These price limits started at $25 for the first ten minutes of trading, rising to $150 after the first thirty minutes of trading, Duffie (1989). When a price limit is hit, the market is closed for only a short period of time (two minutes to two hours), rather than closed for the rest of the day. These short trading halts may not affect the settlement price, and so have no influence on margin payments.

For agricultural futures it is not usually possible to use the spot price to accurately estimate the current equilibrium price of the future. Therefore, Brennan predicts that price limits will be effective mainly in agricultural futures markets, which he finds to be the case. Since price limits prevent all the relevant information from being incorporated into the futures price, their presence can destroy any intertemporal independence of futures price changes. Thus, if the futures price rises during the day to hit the upper limit, it is expected that the price will continue to rise when the market opens the following morning.

Chou, Lin & Yu (2000) extended the Brennan model to the two period case. A very large price adjustment may lead to the operation of the price limit for a succession of days, as a very large price rise or fall is accommodated. This complicates the problem, and Brennan's results may not follow. Chou, Lin & Yu (2003) extended the Brennan model to consider the presence of price limits in the spot, as well as the futures market. Their theoretical analysis shows that spot limits further lowers default risk, spot limits are a partial substitute for futures limits, and equal spot and futures price limits result in lower futures margin requirements. Hall & Kofman (2001) investigates the effects of fat-tailed distributions and time varying volatility on the Brennan model.

11.3.2 Chance Model

Chance (1994b) examined the theoretical effects of price limits on futures prices when the price is not limit up or limit down, and there is marking to the market. If the price were to become limit up, holders of long futures positions would not receive all their gains until later, while if the price were limit down, holders of long positions would benefit from the delay in paying their losses. Thus, if a price limit is operative, it alters the gains and losses of holding a futures position. Chance argued that there is only one futures price at which these costs and benefits exactly offset. When the price is close to its upper limit the probability of hitting this limit and delaying the receipt of the gains by long positions is very high; while the probability of hitting the lower limit and delaying payment of losses by long positions is very low. Therefore, in this case, the costs of price limits outweigh the benefits, and this lowers the no-arbitrage futures price below what would otherwise have been the case, e.g. below $F = (S-D)(1+r)$. Similarly, for a futures price that is close to the lower price limit, the benefits of price limits will outweigh the costs, and the no-arbitrage futures price will be above what it would otherwise have been. Hence, the possibility that price limits may be triggered affects the current no-arbitrage futures price, as illustrated in figure 11.1. Chance could not obtain an exact solution for the size of the effect of price limits on the no-arbitrage price, but estimated that it might be over 1% of the futures price about one third of the time.

The introduction of price limits has a number of effects, even if the limits are never operative. The variance of futures prices within each settlement period is reduced, and this alters hedge ratios, with more futures contracts required to hedge a given spot position. There is also a change in the shape of the distribution of share prices, e.g. to a chi-squared distribution, with parameters that change over time. Harel, Harpaz & Yagil (2005) developed a model for predicting the distribution of futures returns in the presence of price limits. The presence of price limits means that some new variables affect the futures price. An increase in futures price volatility increases the chances of hitting the nearest limit more than it increases the chances of hitting the more distant limit, so increasing the effect of price limits on the no-arbitrage price. A lengthening of the settlement period (with the size of the price limits unchanged) gives more time for the price limits to be hit, so increasing the effect on the no-arbitrage price.

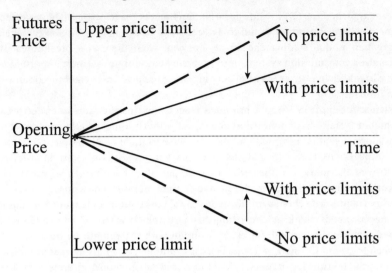

Figure 11.1: Effect of Price Limits on the No-Arbitrage Price

11.3.3 Circuit Breakers

When established trading processes threaten to run out of control, it may be wise to activate various pre-established mechanisms which alter the procedures and pace of trading. Such mechanisms usually include a trading halt, and may involve the wider dissemination of information. Moser (1990) identified three main ways in which circuit breakers are triggered: (a) a big imbalance between buy and sell orders that will create a problem for market makers, (b) volume that is high enough to overwhelm the back-office procedures, and (c) large price changes. Circuit breakers tend to be associated with trading halts in equity markets, and price limits in futures markets. The difference between price limits and trading halts is that price limits do not stop all trading, only trading at prices outside the price limits (usually for the remainder of that day). In contrast, a trading halt bans trading at any price, often for a period of ten minutes to a few hours.

Circuit breakers have been supported by Brady (1988), Greenwald & Stein (1988) and Stoll & Whaley (1988b). The triggering of circuit breakers means that, for a period of time, trading between willing buyers and sellers is impossible – an extreme form of market failure. Such market closure will hinder arbitrage, portfolio insurance and hedging strategies, and investors will be prevented from liquidating their positions. Such restrictions may mean that trading moves to substitutes, e.g. index futures rather than shares, and to other markets, e.g. abroad.

Academics are usually against closing markets involving willing buyers and sellers unless it can be shown that one of the parties to the trade is at a substantial disadvantage (e.g. under legal age, or insane), or lacks knowledge of some highly relevant information (e.g. inside information) or the trade has a negative effect on others who were not party to the trade (e.g. vote selling). The main argument for a trading halt is that trading should be stopped when there is a breakdown of the information transmission system, or to give the market time to digest important news. Such a breakdown may or may not accompany large price movements, Greenwald & Stein (1988).

Kumar & Seppi (1994) have provided a theoretical justification for circuit breakers in which arbitrage is temporarily banned, but other trading is allowed to continue. They suppose that uninformed traders, who wish to trade in a liquid market with low price impact, base their expectations of the market liquidity for a current order on the liquidity of the market in the previous time period. They further suppose that the market was highly illiquid in the previous time period. The consequence is that liquidity traders will choose not to trade, so fulfilling their forecast of low liquidity, and the market is stuck in a low liquidity position. If arbitrageurs are temporarily banned, market makers will be happy to trade with the remaining traders, who are assumed to be uninformed, in what is now a liquid market. This market liquidity then encourages uninformed traders to continue trading in future periods. The ban on arbitrage can now be lifted. Thus, a particular form of circuit breaker is seen as a solution to an illiquid market.

Empirical Evidence.   There is some empirical evidence for index futures on the effectiveness of circuit breakers in reducing price volatility.

USA.   Kuhn, Kuserk & Locke (1991) studied transactions data on the S&P500 and MMI for 13th and 16th October 1989 (the mini-crash). During 13th October there were two trading halts in S&P500 futures. They hypothesized that if trading halts merely delay the price discovery process, spot and futures price volatility when trading resumes will be no lower than it was before the halt, while if a trading halt gives the market time to adjust to some form of market failure, spot and futures price volatility will be reduced after the halt. For the two halts on 13th October, there was no evidence of a reduction in volatility after the halts, implying that they merely delayed the price discovery process. They also found some evidence that, when trading was halted in S&P500 futures, the increased volatility transferred to MMI futures, which continued to trade.

McMillan (1991) analyzed minute-to-minute price changes in S&P500 index futures during October 1989. He found evidence in support of the view that the futures price is attracted towards the level at which a trading halt is triggered. This gravitational or magnet effect may be due to scalpers and day traders withdrawing from the market as the futures price approaches the threshold at which the trading halt is triggered. Such traders withdraw because they are unwilling to hold a risky position through a trading halt. The withdrawal of traders who normally provide liquidity to the market means that someone who wishes to execute a trade before any market closure will tend to move the price more than would otherwise have been the case. As the price gets closer to the threshold price, the size of this effect tends to increase.

Santoni & Liu (1993) considered the effects of the circuit breakers introduced after the 1987 crash. These measures may be divided into those triggered by large movements in the DJIA, and those triggered by movements in the price of S&P500 futures, and may operate on either the stock market or the index futures market. Those which operate on the NYSE and are triggered by large movements in the DJIA are (a) restrictions on the use of DOT for index arbitrage, which came into force as NYSE rule 80a from 4th May 1988, and are triggered by an upward or downward movement of more than 50 points from yesterday's DJIA close (the collar), (b) NYSE rule 80b, which introduced a trading halt in equities as from 20th October 1988 when the DJIA falls 250 points below yesterday's close, and (c) the amendment to rule 80a on 31st July 1990, so that if the 50 point DJIA 'collar' is breached, index arbitrage orders to sell shares can only be executed on an uptick for the stock, and index arbitrage orders to buy shares can only be executed on a down tick for the stock. Those circuit breakers triggered by price movements in S&P500 futures prices were trading halts in S&P500 futures as from 28th March 1988, revised 1st April 1988, 20th October 1988 and 13th December 1990. In addition, a revision to rule 80a on 20th October 1988 introduced the use of the 'sidecar' for index arbitrage via DOT when the S&P500 futures price falls by a set percentage from its previous day's close.

Using daily data on the S&P500 index for 1962-91, Santoni & Liu (1993) found that, while spot volatility was higher after the 1987 crash, none of the changes in spot and futures market circuit breakers had a significant effect on spot market volatility, as measured by the conditional variance in a GARCH regression to explain spot returns. They also considered minute to minute returns for the 16 days when the amended rule 80a, which blocked arbitrage when the last price movement of a share in an arbitrage transaction was in the wrong direction, was triggered. These days were compared with 10 days from the first six months of 1990, when the rule would have been triggered if it had been in force. The found that when the rule was actually triggered, it led to a 34% drop in the variance of returns, while for the control sample, after the hypothetical triggering of the rule, the variance of returns increased by 30%. However, in the ten minutes immediately surrounding the trigger points, there was no significant change in the variance of returns for the test or control samples. This suggests that the triggering of rule 80a and the restriction of index arbitrage did not immediately lead to a fall in spot volatility.

Kuserk, Locke & Sayers (1992) conducted an event study of the 14 days when the amended rule 80a which blocked arbitrage was operative in August, September and October 1990 using transactions data for S&P500 futures. They failed to find evidence that the operation of rule 80a delinked the spot and futures markets, while the operation of this rule led to a slight increase in futures price volatility, and a minor reduction in the liquidity of the futures market. Thus, while rule 80a does not appear to have caused serious damage to the spot and futures markets, it does not seem to have fulfilled its objective of promoting market stabilization.

Overdahl & McMillan (1998) considered S&P500 tick data for 1990-3. When rule 80a was operative, arbitrage volume was much reduced. However, arbitrage opportunities were still removed, but more slowly than otherwise. Triggering rule 80a had no significant effect on futures volatility.

Chen (1998) used daily data on S&P500 futures for 1982-94 to examine the average price for the day after a limit up or limit down closing price the previous day. There was no evidence of price reversals, and therefore no evidence that price limits restricted short term over-reaction to news.

Japan.   Berkman & Steenbeek (1998) investigated the gravitational or magnet effect of price limits on Nikkei 225 futures in 1992. Since these futures are traded in both Osaka and Singapore, gravitational effects on one exchange caused a switch in volume to the other exchange (which is not close to its price limit); but there was no gravitational influence on prices.

Martens & Steenbeek (2001) studied the effects of trading halts on Nikkei 225 futures in Osaka, while Nikkei 225 futures continued to be traded in Singapore. Using tick data for 1991-2, they found that during a trading halt in Osaka, volume switched to Singapore; while price volatility remained high during a trading halt. Therefore, in the special case of a dual listing, trading halts are ineffective in reducing volatility.

Conclusions.   The studies of trading halts indicate that they do not lead to a reduction in spot volatility, nor to a delinking of the spot and futures markets. There is some evidence that futures prices are attracted to the price at which a trading halt is triggered (except for dual listed futures).

11.4 Trading Hours

Futures exchanges can choose their trading hours, and the extent to which these match those of the exchange on which the underlying shares are traded. While riskless arbitrage requires simultaneous trading in both the spot and futures markets, some futures exchanges have trading hours that are slightly different from those of the spot market. Usually the futures market opens earlier and/or closes later than the spot market. The extension of trading hours has been encouraged by the introduction of screen-based futures trading, with its ability to offer liquidity in other time zones during their business hours. A number of empirical studies have investigated the effects of the futures market being open when the spot market is closed.

USA.   Chang, Jain & Locke (1995) analyzed transactions data for S&P500 futures for 1982-90. The spot market closed 15 minutes earlier than the futures market. With the exception of Fridays, they found that futures returns were high in the last 15 minutes of trading, and futures volatility had a U-shaped pattern during the final 15 minutes.

Japan.   Hiraki, Maberly & Takezawa (1995) studied Nikkei 225 futures returns for the 10 or 15 minute period after the spot market had closed. They found a very high variance at the end of the day for the period for 1988-91.

Hong Kong.   For 1993-7 Hang Seng futures continued to trade for 5 or 15 minutes after the spot market closed. Using trade data, Ho & Lee (1998) found that immediately after the spot market closed there was a drop in futures returns, volume and volatility; and that these variables exhibited a U-shaped pattern for the period of extended trading.

On 20th November 1998, Hang Seng futures started trading 15 minutes earlier, and stopped trading 15 minutes later than the spot market. The effects of this extension of futures trading time are reported in four papers.

Cheng & Cheng (2000) found that after November 1998 return volatility for the first 15 minutes of trading in the morning for both the futures and spot markets was reduced. This was attributed to the futures market performing an efficient price discovery process with respect to the information that arrived overnight, in the absence of over-reaction and noise from the spot market.

Fong & Frino (2001) considered trade and quote data on the Hang Seng futures and shares for 1998-9. After the extension of trading time, futures volatility and the number of futures trades during the first and last 15 minutes fell. The volatility of the index during the first and last 15 minutes of spot trading also fell, while the futures bid-ask spread fell during the last 15 minutes of trading. The authors pointed out that if volatility is measured using trade prices, it is biased upwards by bid-ask bounce. After allowing for this bias, they argued there was still a rise in futures volatility when spot trading began. and a drop in futures volatility when spot trading ended.

Chan (2002) analyzed Hang Seng futures trade data for 1998-9, and found that after November 1998 futures volume moved to the first 15 minutes after the open, volatility during this period was lower than before, and pricing errors were reduced. This is consistent with improved price discovery during the opening 15 minutes. Closing the market 15 minutes later had no significant effect on futures volume, volatility or pricing errors in the final 15 minutes.

Cheng, Jiang & Ng (2004) used Hang Seng trade and quote data for 1998-2000. They found that after November 1998 the first 15 minutes of futures trading was dominated by informed traders (i.e. predominantly price discovery). This was not the case for the last 15 minutes of futures trading; although some price discovery still took place during this period.

Conclusions. Extensions to the trading hours of both futures and spot markets are likely as markets become screen-based and more global in their customer base. This process often involves a mismatch between the trading hours of the spot and futures exchanges, which can have consequences for price discovery, arbitrage, volatility and volume for both markets.

11.5 Taxation of Futures Trading

In 1993 Japan was the only country with a major futures market that had a transactions tax (at the rate of 0.001%) on futures trading, Edwards (1993). He considered the arguments for introducing a tax on futures trading. These include reducing the volatility of spot and futures prices, reducing the cost of capital, reducing short-termist behaviour by managers, reducing the volume of futures trading so that resources are released for more productive uses elsewhere in the economy and raising revenue for the government. Each of these arguments will be considered.

The reduction in volatility is argued to be caused by the futures tax leading to a drop in speculative futures trading. However, there is no reason to expect the futures tax to reduce speculative trading rather than other types of trading. Even if the tax succeeded in reducing speculative trading, this may not lead to a reduction in price volatility. A cross-section study of sixteen futures for 1989 by Edwards (1993) found no association between speculative futures trading and spot and futures price volatility. A reduction in the cost of capital is argued to be caused by a tax-induced reduction in price volatility (if any). However, a futures tax may impose greater transactions costs on traders, resulting in an increase in the required rate of return to cover these transactions costs, and therefore an increase in the cost of capital.

Information asymmetries between managers and shareholders may mean that shareholders are poorly informed about the firm's long term prospects, and so tend to concentrate on the firm's short term performance. A futures tax will not eliminate this information asymmetry, and so will not eliminate short-termism. A futures tax will reduce the volume of futures trading, and so release some of the resources devoted to futures trading for other uses. However, the resources released will be slight. This reduction in volume may be associated with other effects which have adverse economic effects. To the extent that information traders are discouraged, a futures tax may lead to a reduction in the price discovery role of futures markets. While if the tax discourages speculators, this may increase the risk premium payable by hedgers.

A futures tax of any size will probably lead to a large reduction in volume. This is because trading may switch to foreign exchanges, particularly if the future has a dual listing (see chapter 11.11), or to substitute instruments. In consequence, a futures tax may raise very little revenue for the government. Edwards (1993) concludes that there is no sound argument for introducing a tax on futures trading.

Futures traded on Taifex are subject to a tax of 0.025% of the value of the trade. Until 1st May 2000 the tax rate was 0.050%. Chung, Liu, Wu & Yang (2003) investigated the effects of this tax reduction using intraday data for Taiwan index futures for 2000. There was improved liquidity, higher volume, lower price volatility, smaller mispricings, and a small increase in tax revenues. A study by Chou & Lee (2002) of the effects of this tax reduction on leads and lags between Taiwan and Singapore is considered in chapter 6.6.3. These empirical results are consistent with theoretical expectations.

11.6 Minimum Price Movement and Price Clustering

Each future has a minimum price movement set by the exchange, and for the FTSE 100 future this is £5.00. The restriction goes further, in that price movements of say £8.00 are not allowed because all price changes have to be exact integer multiples of the minimum price movement. Thus, the price of FTSE 100 futures can change by £5.00, £10.00, £15.00, £20.00, £25.00 etc; but not by any of the intermediate numbers. Ball, Torous & Tschoegl (1985) suggested this restriction has the benefit of facilitating the trading process by reducing the requirement for close attention when recording the transaction prices. But it means that market prices cannot be exactly equal to the equilibrium market clearing price, unless the equilibrium price just happens to coincide with one of the permitted prices. This may lead to reduced volumes, with those who consider the futures contract marginally adversely priced not trading. The minimum price movement determines both the minimum non-zero bid-ask spread, and also the increments in which the spread can increase.

If the minimum price movement is set at a low level, traders may choose to use a larger tick size by avoiding some numbers. For example, they may prefer prices which end in zero or five; even though the minimum price movement permits the use of intermediate numbers. This gives rise to the phenomenon of price clustering. Thus the *de facto* smallest price movement may be higher than the minimum price movement, but can never be lower.

Brown, Laux & Schachter (1991) set out to examine the factors determining the optimal tick size. They found that the optimal tick size was increased by: (a) a high customer volume (due to an increase in the costs to floor traders of bargaining on behalf of their customers); (b) high price volatility (because the information available is insufficient to permit greater price resolution, and because the costs of delay may be increased); (c) a large proportion of trades experience a clearing delay until at least the next morning (as trades at odd prices are more likely to produce an out trade); (d) a low proportion of spread trades (because small price differences are more important in such trades) and (e) a decrease in the average number of contracts per trade (because the benefits of bargaining are greater for larger trades). They argued that the extra transactions costs of a small tick size must be weighed against the drop in trading from a large tick size which rules out a mutually agreeable price.

The imposition of discrete price changes on a random sequence of prices can lead to the rejection of randomness because it may introduce a small amount of negative autocorrelation, Harris (1990b). Gottlieb & Kalay (1985) argued that it can also bias upwards the estimates of the variance. For futures with a low price and a small variance of price changes, this upward bias can be very large, e.g. 200%. Since the variance drops as the time period over which price changes are computed is shortened, the upward bias is accentuated when daily or hourly price data is used. (Using a different, and less realistic, theoretical model, Marsh & Rosenfeld (1986) showed that there is no bias.) According to Gottlieb & Kalay (1985) and Ball (1988), the restriction of a minimum price change introduces (or accentuates) kurtosis in the distribution of price changes, particularly when changes over short time intervals are being considered. They suggest this may account for the leptokurtic distributions for price changes over short periods of time. Volatility estimators which correct for the upward bias in the variance have been suggested by Ball (1988), Cho & Frees (1988), Ederington & Lee (1995) and Harris (1990b).

Empirical Evidence. In the last few years empirical studies have appeared for a few countries. (Some studies considered in chapter 11.7 also deal with changes in the minimum price movement, but in conjunction with a change in the contract multiplier.)

USA.   Schwartz, Van Ness & Van Ness (2004) studied price clustering for S&P500 futures in 1999-2000. They found that over 40% of trade prices ended in a zero or five, although the other decimals were used to a limited extent. Price clustering increased with volatility, and decreased as volume increased.

Kurov & Zabotina (2005) considered trade data for S&P500 and Nasdaq 100 futures and the corresponding E-mini futures for 2002. The E-mini futures have contract multipliers that are one fifth those for the full-size contracts, and only trade electronically on GLOBEX. There was evidence of price clustering for the full size contracts, but not for the E-mini contracts. This is consistent with the minimum price movement placing a binding lower bound on price movements. For the E-mini contracts the mean bid-ask spread is just above the minimum price movement, and this implies it is a binding constraint on reducing the bid-ask spread. They concluded that the minimum price movement for these E-mini futures should be reduced.

UK.   Ap Gwilym, Clare & Thomas (1998) analyzed trades and quotes for FTSE 100 futures for 1992-5, and found that over 98% of trades and quotes were at full index points, i.e. the *de facto* tick size was £10. They also found that the size of trades at odd index values was three times larger than for trades at even index values.

Henker (1998) considered trade and quote data on FTSE 100 futures for 1994-6, and showed that over 99% of the quotes were at full index points. He also found a preference for even index values.

Ap Gwilym & Alibo (2003) studied quotes and trades for FTSE 100 futures for 1997-9. On 10th May 1999 trading moved from the floor to screens, and this was accompanied a drop in price clustering at full index points from over 99% of quotes, to 68.2%, with a similar reduction for trade prices. This change may reflect the price priority rules of the screen trading system, with small price improvements ensuring priority, or it may be because screen trading reduces the disadvantages of a smaller tick size.

Lee, Gleason & Mathur (1999) plotted futures returns at time t against futures returns at time $t+1$ for 13 index futures from the Netherlands, Hong Kong, USA, UK, France, Spain and New Zealand. For daily data, none of these index futures exhibited the compass rose pattern (evenly spaced rays radiating from the origin), which may be generated by the discreteness introduced by the minimum price movement. However, 5 minute returns both the MMI and S&P500 futures exhibited the compass rose pattern, and this probably reflects the greater relative importance of the tick size for 5 minute returns, than for daily returns.

Conclusions.   These studies indicate that price clustering is a common feature, and that too large a minimum price movement can inhibit reductions in the bid-ask spread.

11.7 Contract Multiplier

For each index future, the exchange must select a contract multiplier, e.g. £10 for the FTSE 100. In some cases an exchange has established two index futures on the same underlying index, but with different contract multipliers. The KCBT traded both maxi and mini futures on the Value Line Arithmetic index. The mini contract had a multiplier of $100 and a minimum price movement of $5, while the maxi contract had a multiplier of $500 and a minimum price movement of $25. Now only the mini contract is traded. The original MMI future had a multiplier of $100, and in August 1985 a maxi version was introduced with a multiplier of $250. In September 1986 the original (mini) MMI contract was discontinued. The contract multiplier for FTSE 100 futures was reduced from £25 to £10 for the June 1998 contract onwards, while in July 1998 the CAC 40 futures multiplier dropped from FF 200 to FF 50.

A large contract multiplier exacerbates indivisibility problems when the trader is engaged in intercommodity spreads, hedging, etc. It also deters small traders who might only have the resources to trade half a contract, (Huang & Stoll, 1998). However, since exchange fees, commissions and brokers fees are all per contract, reducing contract size increases transactions costs, at least in the short run.

USA. The S&P500 futures contract multiplier was reduced from $500 to $250 on 3rd November 1997. At the same time the minimum price movement was increased from 0.05 to 0.10 index points (i.e. $25 to $25), and so its monetary value was unchanged, although it doubled in percentage terms. Bollen, Smith & Whaley (2003) considered trade data for S&P500 futures for 1996-8. The redesign of this future led to an increase in price clustering, accompanied by a widening of the effective bid-ask spread and a 20% decrease in volume; with little sign of more retail volume. To achieve positions with the same value, investor transactions costs rose due to the larger bid-ask spread, and the need to trade more contracts with largely unchanged fees per contract. Therefore, while market makers and intermediaries gained, investors did not. Chen & Locke (2004) analyzed transactions data for 1995-2001 and found that these changes in the S&P500 led to an increase in the effective bid-ask spread (measured in index points). There was no increase in either customer volume, nor the total revenue of floor traders. Karagozoglu, Martell & Wang (2003) also studied the effects of the reduction in the S&P500 futures multiplier in November 1997 using trade data for 1996-7. After the change more public customers traded S&P500 futures, the average trade size was slightly reduced, volume was lower, and price volatility was unchanged.

Ates & Wang (2003) investigated the effects of the introduction of the E-mini S&P500 and Nasdaq 100 contracts in September 1997 and June 1999 respectively. Using trade data for 1995-2000, they found that the introduction of the E-mini contracts did not significantly increase the bid-ask spread of the full size contracts, while the volume of the full size S&P500 contracts dropped, and that of the full size Nasdaq 100 contract rose. Price volatility rose for both the S&P500 and the Nasdaq 100 futures. The E-mini contracts attracted smaller investors, with 75% of trades being for just one contract.

Australia. On 11th October 1993 the contract multiplier for SPI futures was reduced from $100 to $25. At the same time the minimum price movement was increased from $10 to $25. Karagozoglu & Martell (1999) discovered that these changes led to an increase in volume, and no consistent effect on the bid-ask spread.

Brown (2001) found these changes resulted in an increase in both volume and the bid-ask spread, and argued that the new situation was beneficial to most market participants.

Conclusions.   The effects of a change in the contract multiplier (and either the absolute or proportionate bid-ask spread) on the bid-ask spread and volume are varied, and may, in part, be due to a simultaneous change in the minimum price movement.

11.8 Contract Delivery Months

Every futures contract has a schedule which determines when each new contract starts trading, and when it will be delivered. For example, a new FTSE 100 futures contract is initiated every three months, and each contract has a life of twelve months. This means that, at any moment, traders have a choice of four different maturities, with three month differences between their maturities. What factors determine such patterns?

The main motives for trading futures contracts appear to be hedging and arbitrage. Arbitrage is unimportant in determining the pattern of contract maturities as it is concerned with price discrepancies, rather than their maturity. This leaves hedging as the main determinant of the demand to trade contracts of a particular maturity. As stated in chapter 9, if there is no dividend or interest rate risk and the no-arbitrage condition applies at all times, the choice of contract maturity for use in a hedge is arbitrary. For any contract maturity, the hedge is riskless and, if there are no costs in rolling over a position, there is no reason to prefer one maturity to another. Traders will be indifferent between a contract with a maturity of one day and another with a maturity of one hundred years. Therefore, there need be only one outstanding contract at any one time, and its maturity is irrelevant, Grant (1982a). Since this model does not fit reality, its assumptions will be relaxed to see if this produces a more realistic outcome.

If rollover transactions costs are introduced, this will favour choosing a contract with a very long maturity, as it reduces the number of times the position must be rolled over. Thus, there will be a single outstanding contract with a long maturity, e.g. many years. If there is dividend uncertainty, assuming that dividend risk drops as the delivery date approaches, basis risk will be lower for contracts with a short maturity. Similarly, if interest rates are uncertain, it is likely that basis risk from this source declines as delivery approaches, again favouring a short maturity. (Interest rate risk could be removed by hedging with interest rate futures.) If mispricing risk is also introduced, rolling a position forwards will also involve rollover risk, i.e. the risk that the relative prices of the two futures contracts are mispriced at the time of the rollover. This increases the costs of rolling over a position, so favouring long maturity contracts. However, as has been argued in chapter 6, it seems reasonable to expect mispricing risk to decrease as maturity approaches. In which case, short maturity contracts would be favoured.

There is a trade-off between factors favouring a long contract maturity (rollover transactions costs and rollover risk), and factors favouring a short maturity (basis risk due to dividend, interest rate and mispricing risk). If most hedgers have a short horizon (e.g. less than the maturity of the near contract), rollover costs and risk (even for a futures contract with a short maturity) will be zero, and hedgers will favour a contract with a short maturity. However, those who want to maintain their position for a long time may prefer contracts with a long maturity. The maturity problem could be solved by having a very large number of outstanding contracts, each with a different maturity, but this raises the issue of liquidity.

Traders always prefer to use a liquid market with low bid-ask spreads and minimal price impact for large trades. If many different contracts were traded, each with a different maturity, the liquidity of each of these contracts would tend to be reduced. So, to maintain liquidity, only a few delivery dates can be traded at any one time. The higher is total volume, the larger is the number of outstanding maturities that can be supported.

Neuberger (1997) proposed that the needs of long term hedgers could be met by a perpetual futures contract, i.e. a futures contract that is never delivered. Such a future would remove rollover risk and costs, and maximize liquidity by concentrating this demand in a single contract.

11.9 Manipulation of the Final Settlement Price

It is possible, at least in theory, to manipulate the final settlement price of an index futures contract by trading in the spot market during the time when this price is determined. A manipulator first establishes a long (short) position in index futures, and then buys (sells) shares to push the final settlement price up (down). Such a strategy has been called 'punching the settlement price'. After delivery of the futures contract, the resulting spot position is liquidated at the subsequent unmanipulated spot price. Provided the futures position is larger than the spot position, the profit on the futures contracts exceeds the loss on the spot position, and the expected gross profit to such a strategy is positive.

Such manipulation may be inhibited by the transactions costs exceeding the expected profits, or by the risk aversion of the manipulator. In addition, the manipulator's spot position must be large enough to move the price by at least one tick, and this may be prevented by wealth constraints; while the futures position may be prevented from exceeding the required spot position by position limits. If manipulation is attractive, after allowing for these inhibiting factors, many traders will attempt to manipulate the final settlement price. But Kumar & Seppi (1992) show that, as the number of manipulators grows towards infinity, their manipulative activity will tend to cancel out, and the expected profit from manipulation drops to zero.

The FTSE 100 EDSP is based on quotations not trades, and so it may be possible for a market maker in most of the FTSE 100 shares to manipulate the EDSP by changing their quotations. The only spot trades required by this strategy would be those done under the market maker's obligation to deal at their SEAQ quotes. The alleged manipulation of the EDSP for the FTSE 100 June 1990 contract took this form. It has been claimed attempts were made by two banks (Goldman Sachs & Barclays de Zoete Wedd) to affect the EDSP of the June 1990 FTSE 100 futures and options contracts. A subsequent investigation cleared both banks of quoting unrealistic prices for shares in the index at which they were unwilling to deal during the period of the calculation of the EDSP, Quality of Markets Unit (1990).

Cita & Lien (1992) considered the problem of how best to convert a set of prices into a settlement price when these prices may be subject to manipulation and errors. They concluded that the average of all the prices is superior to an average from which the highest and lowest prices have been excluded, and to the median price (which is an average from which the maximum possible number of high and low prices have been excluded). Cita & Lien (1997) proposed that the number of excluded observations is determined by the data using the bootstrap procedure.

11.10 Choice of Index

An important decision in the design of a new index future is the selection of the index on which the future is based. There are a number of factors involved in this choice, where the underlying objective is usually to maximize the volume of trading in the resulting index future.

Hedging will probably be the most important source of trading activity. Therefore, any new index future should be an attractive hedging instrument for typical institutional investors. Since the average portfolio is the market portfolio, this suggests basing the index future on a market value weighted index of the larger companies. If movements in the index are to track those of a buy and hold stock portfolio, it should be an arithmetic index. Kook, Kwon, Lee & Choe (1992) simulated the hedging performance of eight Korean indices to guide the choice of index for a Korean index future, while Tay & Tse (1991) simulated the performance of five Singapore stock indices to indicate the most suitable index on which to base an index future. Because no futures prices exist, such simulations have to rely on the assumption of a stable relationship between the value of each index and the price of a future based on that index.

A related problem is whether the index is designed to reflect the movement of share prices for companies from a particular country, or whether the index covers the movement in prices of companies from a number of countries, e.g. the Eurotop 100. In the latter case it may be necessary to specify a common currency for use in the computation of the index.

The facility for easy arbitrage between the spot and futures markets is important in ensuring that the futures price correctly reflects the underlying reality. Arbitrage can also be a useful source of volume. A necessary prerequisite for arbitrage is that deviations from the no-arbitrage price can be recognized at the time. This suggests the use of an arithmetic, rather than a geometric index, the use of market value weights or price weights rather than equal weights, and the computation of the index using current quotations, rather than (stale) transactions prices. Indeed, index futures are only traded on indices that are arithmetic, with market capitalization or price weights. Once a mispricing has been identified, the arbitrageur must be capable of rapidly trading the basket of shares in the index. Therefore, all the shares in the index must be actively traded, and it is preferable if short selling these shares is easy. Once a basket of shares has been traded to establish an arbitrage position, the definition of the index should not change, as this will necessitate an alteration in the basket of shares.

Trading the index basket of shares is facilitated if there are only a few shares in the index, and this can conflict with the objective of using an index which represents the market portfolio (i.e. all shares). Table 11.2 lists a number of indices on which index futures have been traded, together with the number of stocks in the index. This reveals an enormous range; from the 5 stocks in the Dutch Top Five, to the 2,000 stocks in the Russell 2,000. The median value for the index futures considered in table 11.2 is 50 stocks.

Table 11.2: Number of Stocks in Various Stock Indices

Index	Number	Index	Number
Dutch Top Five	5	Fifty Leaders	50
ATX	18	ISEQ	76
SMI	19	FTSE 100	100
Bel-20	20	TSE-100	100
MMI	20	Eurotop 100	100
PSI-20	20	FTSE Eurotrack 100	100
FOX	25	KLSE CI	100
EOE	25	JSE All Share	143
KFX	25	NYSE Utilities	191
OBX	25	Nikkei 225	225
DAX	30	Wilshire SmallCap	250
MIB-30	30	FTSE Mid 250	250
OMX	30	TSE 300	300
Hang Seng	33	Nikkei 300	300
Ibex-35	35	All Ordinaries	305
Toronto-35	35	S&P MidCap 400	400
MSCI Hong Kong	36	S&P500	500
CAC-40	40	Topix	1,200
Forty	40	NYSE Composite	1,700
Osaka 50 Kabusaki	50	Value Line Arithmetic	1,700
		Russell 2000	2,000

If the objective is to choose an index which is heavily traded, provides high profits to insiders and minimizes the losses of liquidity traders, Lien & Luo (1993b) surprisingly argue that a geometric index is superior to an arithmetic index. They conclude that the KCBT was wrong to replace the geometric VLCI with the arithmetic VLA in 1988. However, since then, no futures have been traded on a geometric stock index anywhere in the world.

Since the value of the index at delivery is used to calculate the final settlement price for an index futures contract, the index should not be capable of manipulation. This suggests that the index should cover a reasonably large number of shares in companies with a substantial market capitalization. Finally, the index must be capable of being computed very rapidly (e.g. every fifteen seconds). With the use of computers, this is generally not an important constraint on the choice of index.

11.11 Dual Listing

For some stock indices, index futures are (or have been) traded on more than one exchange, e.g. the Nikkei 225 (OSE, SGX and CME), Eurotop 100 (FTA and Comex), FTSE 100 (Euronext-Liffe and CME). The SGX future on the Nikkei 225 has a number of advantages over the Japanese-based trading on the OSE: lower transactions costs, no exchange tax, no suspension of trading for a lunch break, open for 15 minutes longer than the OSE and the ability to trade other futures quoted on SGX, Semkow (1989). The futures in such dual (or triple) listings may not be perfect substitutes because they are settled in different currencies or trade in different time zones, and so the introduction of a dual listing may create extra volume. However, it is possible that a dual listing splits an unchanged total volume between the two exchanges, leading to lower liquidity for each future than would be the case for a single future. Given the importance of liquidity to traders, this could lead to the failure of the future on one of the exchanges. All the empirical studies to date have been of the Nikkei 225.

Vila & Sandmann (1995) compared the trading of Nikkei 225 futures in Osaka and Singapore using transactions data for 65 days in 1993. The value of a trade in Osaka was almost 7 times larger than in Singapore, while the number of trades in Osaka was only 46% of the number in Singapore. They found that the volatility of minute-to-minute returns was greater in Osaka, while the volatility of daily returns was similar. The bid-ask spread in Osaka was about 3 times larger than in Singapore. Returns in Singapore led those in Osaka by roughly 4-6 minutes, and the minute-to-minute volatility showed greater persistence in Singapore. These differences between Osaka and Singapore may, in part, be due to the larger trade size, lower trade frequency and greater minimum price movement in Osaka, as well as the different trading systems.

Bacha & Vila (1994) studied the effect of the dual listing of the Osaka and CME contracts on the Nikkei 225 on the volatility of the corresponding SGX future. For the 30 and 60 days on either side of the introduction of the Osaka contract, SGX volatility declined, while the introduction of the CME contract had no effect on SGX volatility.

Arbitrage arguments suggest that the prices of essentially the same index future on two exchanges will be linked together so that, in effect, they become one market. In this case liquidity may not be reduced by dual listing, except to the extent there are transactions costs in switching business between the two markets. Indeed, arbitrage transactions exploiting any price discrepancies between the two markets (spread arbitrage) will tend to raise volume and liquidity in both markets.

Example. Suppose that identical FTSE 100 futures contracts are traded in both

London and Edinburgh. On 26th June the price of the September contract was 4,800 in London and 4,790 in Edinburgh, each with a contract multiplier of £10. Dr. Hugo Z. Hackenbush, an arbitrageur undertook the following transactions on 26th June: sell ten contracts in London at 4,800, and buy ten contracts in Edinburgh at 4,790. At delivery in September the FTSE 100 index was 'x' (its value is irrelevant to the arbitrage profit). Hugo's gross profit was $[(4,800-x)+(x-4,790)]\times10\times10 = £1,000$.

Board & Sutcliffe (1996a) studied the dual listing of the Nikkei 225 in Osaka and Singapore, both of which are traded in Japanese yen and have the same final settlement value of the index. In this case the no-arbitrage relationship between these two futures is $F_t^o = (m^o/m^s)F_t^s$, where m^o and m^s are the contract multipliers in Osaka and Singapore, and F_t^o and F_t^s are the futures prices in Osaka and Singapore in Japanese yen at time t. Using daily opening and closing prices from September 1988 to June 1993, the mispricings from a spread between the Osaka and SGX futures were small, and got smaller over time. They did not decrease in size as delivery approached, presumably because there was no reduction in dividend and interest rate risk, since these risks are irrelevant to such spread arbitrage. The mispricings were symmetrical, indicating no systematic under or over pricing, which may be because selling futures is as easy as establishing long positions. The daily mispricings were not autocorrelated, and there was little evidence that mispricings for a given contract tended to change sign. This may be because, since no shares are traded, the very low transactions costs are similar for both establishing a new arbitrage position and for an early unwinding.

Lim, Loo & Tan (1998) analyzed one minute data for 15 days in both 1995 and 1996 for Nikkei 225 futures traded in both Osaka and Singapore. They examined four spread arbitrage strategies and found that, after allowing for transactions costs of 130 yen per trade, each trade made an average profit of about 2 to 5 yen. These net profits are very small, and would probably be eliminated by an allowance for execution risks or slightly higher transactions costs.

Spread arbitrage between Nikkei 225 futures on SGX and the OSE was conducted by Barings Futures (Singapore) and their employee Nick Leeson, who called this activity 'switching'. In 1994 Barings thought the bank had made about £11.9 million from such trading, although at least some of Barings reported profits from this activity were thought to have been due to speculation, not arbitrage, BoBS (sections 3.41 and 3.65, 1995). This is because Leeson might have lifted one leg of the arbitrage position before the other, so leaving a short term speculative position. These arbitrage positions were meant to be closed out by the end of each business day, BoBS (section 3.46, 1995). Two reasons were given to explain the temporary (and highly profitable) differences in price between Osaka and Singapore which this arbitrage was designed to exploit (BoBS, sections 3.28 and 3.29, 1995). First, the Osaka market tends to attract Japanese business, while the Singapore market attracts offshore business. In consequence, different demand and supply factors are at work in the two markets, leading to temporary price differences. Second, the Osaka market is screen-based, while the Singapore market is open outcry (although screen trading has been possible since 1st November 2004), and so the Osaka market reacts more slowly than does SGX. Barings' reported spread arbitrage positions for the Nikkei 225 were very large. On 17th February 1995 Barings believed it was US$3.536 billion long in Osaka and US$3.536 billion short on SGX (equivalent to 38,188 SGX futures), BoBS (section 3.47, 1995). Other traders, besides Barings (and Leeson), were engaged in spread arbitrage, BoBS (section 3.40, 1995).

The reality was very different from the reports by Leeson to Barings in London. In fact, Leeson was not engaged in such spread arbitrage, and on 24th February 1995 he held a long position of 61,039 Nikkei 225 index futures, (15,056 Osaka contracts, multiplied by 2 giving 30,112 to be comparable with SGX contracts, and 30,927 contracts on SGX), BoBS (section 4.18, 1995). During just two months (January and February 1995), Barings lost £308 million from trading in Nikkei 225 futures. Thus, Leeson was not making about £1 million a month from spread arbitrage of the Nikkei 225, as he reported to London. This absence of profits is consistent with the empirical results of Board & Sutcliffe (1996a), who found very few spread arbitrage opportunities between Osaka and SGX.

Board & Sutcliffe (1996a) also studied the dual listing of the Nikkei 225 in Osaka and Chicago using daily opening and closing prices for 1990-93. Although both contracts are based on the same final settlement value of the index, the Osaka contract is denominated in Japanese yen, while the Chicago contract is in US dollars. The no-arbitrage relationship is $F_t^o = R(F_t^c - I_T m^c)c_T + I_T m^o$, where F_t^c and m^c are the Chicago futures price and contract multiplier in US dollars, and I_T is the Nikkei index at delivery. R is the spread ratio, allowing for the difference in currencies, where $R = m^o/(m^c c_T)$ Chicago futures for every one Osaka future, and the size of R depends on the US dollar-Japanese yen exchange rate at delivery (c_T). Riskless arbitrage is not possible for two reasons: the Osaka and Chicago markets are never open synchronously, and a forecast of the exchange rate at delivery (c_T) is required in setting the spread ratio (R). If c_T is known with certainty at the start of the arbitrage, the no-arbitrage condition reduces to that for arbitrage between futures with contract multipliers in the same currency. Board & Sutcliffe (1996a) found that the mispricings were small, symmetrical, and unaffected by contract maturity. There was modest positive autocorrelation in the daily mispricings, and this was partly due to persistence in the errors in forecasting the final exchange rate. Finally, there was little persistence in the sign of the mispricing for a given contract.

Conclusions   Spread arbitrage provides another way in which markets are linked, and the results for Nikkei 225 futures in Osaka, Singapore and Chicago indicate that international futures markets are highly integrated, despite the time gaps and currency risk between Osaka and Chicago. Indeed, since the transactions costs for spread arbitrage are very low, the price linkage is even tighter than between the spot and futures markets.

11.12 Trading Mechanisms

Index futures are traded both by open outcry (e.g. S&P500, NYSE Composite, etc) and by screen-based systems (e.g. FTSE 100, DAX, SMI, OMLX, ATX, FOX, MIB 30, KLSE, PSI 20, Kospi 200, Forty, Ibex etc). Domowitz (1995) suggested that the trading mechanism which is adopted when an exchange is established has a first mover advantage. In consequence, even though screen trading may be chosen by new exchanges, it remains sensible for existing exchanges to continue with floor trading. Many of the existing open outcry exchanges have introduced a limited amount of screen trading as a way of extending the trading hours of pit-traded futures, and as an incubator for new products; while other established exchanges (e.g. Euronext-Liffe, Matif, Hong Kong, SAFEX) have switched fully from floor to screen..

Khan & Ireland (1993) identified a number of differences between screen and floor trading (see also Board, Sutcliffe & Wells, 2002, pp. 105-116).

a. Liquidity. Screen trading is unattractive to locals, which means that floor trading is claimed to be more liquid than screen trading, as the liquidity supplied by locals is absent.

b. Transparency. The computer running a screen-based system contains full information on the price and quantities of all the bids, offers, limit orders, trades and the identities of the traders. Therefore a very high degree of transparency is possible for screen trading. However, exchanges usually choose not to release all of this information. For example, a survey by Domowitz (1993b) found that only 5% of screen-based systems for futures and options trading displayed personal identifiers for quotes, and no information on the identities of traders was supplied to the public. However, screen-based systems usually provide information on the limit order book which is not available for open outcry. With floor trading, the exchange has less information on the order flow. However, the process of open outcry necessitates the availability of some information, including the price and quantity of all trades and the identity and behaviour of the floor traders involved in the bids, offers and trades.

c. Trade Publication. Because the process is automated, screen-based markets can publish trade prices and quantities almost instantly.

d. Trading Procedure. Screen trading can take place according to rules and procedures that may be difficult to implement with floor trading, e.g. the way in which orders are filled.

e. Costs. For screen trading, one person can replace an office broker, a floor broker and a pit trader. In addition, a screen trader can switch between trading a number of different futures, while a pit trader tends to remain in the same pit. As well as requiring fewer people, screen traders tend to have lower salaries than pit traders. A screen-based system avoids the costs of a building to house the trading floor, while it requires both hardware and software, and office space to accommodate the traders and the central computer.

f. Data Entry. With screen trading, the information needed for recording the trades and disseminating prices is captured within the central computer. Floor trading requires this information to be entered manually, with the consequences of unmatched trades and higher costs.

g. Distance. Screen traders can be located anywhere, and this may avoid the need for brokers to maintain a presence in another town or country. Locating the trader in the firm's office, rather than the exchange, permits the trader to be integrated into the firm's operations.

h. Other Information. Information on trading in other markets may be more easily available to a screen trader, and this may make spread trading easier.

i. Space. Introducing a new contract which is traded using open outcry requires that space be found for an additional pit, and this may be a problem. Screen trading requires only a modification of the software to accommodate a new contract.

j. Supervision. Since screen trading takes place in a computer, it is easy to write software to supervise this process. However, since screen traders are not observed by the supervisors, they may indulge in activities such as pre-arranged trading. Floor trading is observed, but less information is captured on computer.

k. Out Trades. Since all trading information is captured by the computer, out trades are prevented by screen-based trading; while erroneous trades may be less common as the relevant information is displayed on a screen rather than signalled in a pit.

k. Human. The nature of screen trading is very different from floor trading, and this leads to a requirement for different skills from those of a floor trader.

l. Volume. It is claimed that screen trading is unsuitable for large volumes of trading and for fast-moving markets. For example, placing limit orders on screen may be particularly costly when volatility is high.

It appears that screen trading is most attractive for a new exchange in a country without a dominant financial centre, that does not expect a large volume of trading in any single future.

USA.   On 20th September 1993, the Chicago Mercantile Exchange listed all its stock index futures on Globex. Thus, by 1996 Globex listed eight CME index futures (S&P500, S&P MidCap 400, Russell 2000, MMI, S&P500/Barra Growth, S&P500/Barra Value, Nasdaq 100 and the IPC) as well as the CAC 40 of Matif.

Domowitz (1993a) compared the Globex system with two types of open outcry using a range of criteria including convergence speed, volatility of transactions prices, bid-ask spread, liquidity and trader surplus. He concluded that on some criteria the Globex system was superior, while on other criteria open outcry was preferable. Overall, he found that Globex was as competitive as open outcry. Bollerslev & Domowitz (1991) used simulation to compare Globex with open outcry, and found that Globex returns exhibited strong ARCH effects, while those for open outcry did not.

Coppejans & Domowitz (1996) used trade data for 1994 on S&P500 futures to compare trading on Globex and the CME floor. Quoted spreads were larger on Globex, and this was attributed to increased adverse selection. There was no significant price clustering on the floor, but some evidence of clustering on Globex, while Globex had much larger ARCH effects than the floor.

Hong Kong.   Fung, Lien, Tse & Tse (2005) investigated the move from floor to screen in June 2000 using trade data for 1999-2000. They discovered that the bid-ask spread narrowed, the proportion of price discovery by the futures market, relative to the spot, increased, and the effect of spot volatility on futures volatility weakened.

Aitken, Frino, Hill & Jarnecic (2004) employed trade and quote data for 1999-2000 on Hang Seng, FTSE 100 and SPI futures and found that the move to screen trading significantly narrowed the bid-ask spread for the Hang Seng and SPI, while the drop in FTSE 100 spreads was not significant. Screen trading also meant that the bid-ask spread widened during periods of increased volatility for all three futures. For Hang Seng and SPI futures, price volatility dropped with the move to screen trading.

Cheng, Fung & Tse (2005) studied trade and quote data on Hang Seng futures and options for 1999-2001. After documenting price clustering for both futures and options, they find that the switch in June 2000 of futures and options to electronic trading reduced their bid-ask spreads, lowered the size of the average futures-options arbitrage opportunity and reduced the time required for mispricings to disappear.

Taiwan.   Huang (2003) compared the performance of screen trading in Taiwan, and floor trading in Singapore of index futures on the Taiwan Stock Market. Using trades and quotes for 2001, bid-ask spreads were found to be lower in Taiwan, and the adverse information component of spreads was lower in Taiwan. Expected and unexpected volume changes had a smaller effect on price changes in Taiwan than in Singapore, which implies greater market depth in Taiwan.

Australia.   Wang (1999) considered SPI futures, which were floor traded during the day, and screen traded in the evenings. Using quote and trade data for 1994, he found that for screen trading the bid-ask spread was more sensitive to market volatility than for floor trading, the adverse information component of the bid-ask spread was higher, while the order processing cost component was lower. These results suggest that screen trading makes it harder to distinguish liquidity traders from informed traders.

In October 1999 trading in SPI futures became screen based, and Anderson & Vahid (2001) analyzed trade data before and after this switch. They discovered that before the change the responses of the futures price to mispricings was nonlinear; while after the move to screen trading this relationship became less non-linear, and more like the response of the screen based stock market to mispricings. Bortoli, Frino & Jarnecic (2004) studied trade and quote data on the SPI for 1998-2001, and found that the switch to screen trading was associated with a decline in commissions, trade size, bid-ask spreads and price volatility.

UK.   Tse & Zabotina (2001) studied quotes and trades on FTSE 100 futures surrounding May 1999, when trading moved from the floor to the CONNECT screen-based system. This move was associated with lower quoted bid-ask spreads, the disappearance of price clustering for quotes, a higher variance for pricing errors (particularly on days with a large number of trades), a drop in the information content of trades, lower open interest and a greater importance of the inventory control motive for trading. Since executing a trade is slower using screens, and limit orders are hard to adjust; the floor is preferable when volume and volatility are high. In other periods, screens work well. Therefore, rather than being rivals, it is concluded that floor and screen trading are complements.

Chng (2004a) analyzed quote and trade data for FTSE 100 futures in 1998-9, before and after the move to screen trading. Contrary to Tse and Zabotina (2001), he found that screen trades were much more informative than floor trades.

Copeland, Lam & Jones (2004) investigated trade data on the FTSE 100, CAC 40, DAX 30 and Kospi-100 futures for 1994-2001. The first two futures switched to screen trading in May 1999 and June 1998, respectively; while the other two futures have always been screen traded. Before the move to screens, in both the UK and France the price process was a random walk. However, for screen trading, a random walk was rejected for both markets. A random walk was also rejected for the screen-traded DAX and the KOSPI futures. These results indicate that screen trading leads to a drop in efficiency, and this drop is due to an excess of daily high and low prices just after the open.

South Africa. Beelders & Massey (2002) examined the switch from floor to screen in June 1996 of futures on the all share index, the gold index and the industrial index. Using daily data for 1990-2000, they concluded that (apart from the gold contract which was delisted) screen trading led to quicker information transmission between the spot and futures markets, a higher contemporaneous correlation, and a reduction in the size and asymmetry of volatility spillovers between these two markets.

Conclusions. The move to screen trading usually lowers bid-ask spreads, and can affect many other aspects of the market:- the response to mispricings, depth, price discovery, price clustering, price volatility, adverse information, market efficiency, volatility spillovers etc. There is a view that screen trading is best when volume and volatility are low or normal; but that floor trading is superior when volume is high and prices are volatile.

11.13 Dual Capacity

Dual capacity exists when a floor trader can both execute trades on their own account, and also act as a floor broker for customers. Stanley (1981) considered the costs and benefits of banning dual trading in futures markets. Requiring traders to have single capacity, i.e. be exclusively either principals or agents, would cause a reduction in regulatory costs and the elimination of any conflict of interest for floor traders (e.g. the use of information from their customers; and front running, which occurs when brokers trade on their own behalf, ahead of their customers' orders). It would also reduce the informational advantage of dual traders over customers. However, since traders would no longer be able to switch between broking and speculating, at times of heavy trading activity market liquidity and the quality of the broking service may decline due to insufficient capacity, e.g. delayed execution. Alternatively, if sufficient brokerage capacity exists to cope with peaks in demand, brokerage fees will be higher because no profits can be made from speculation.

Röell (1990) has argued that information-based traders have an incentive to conceal this fact from the market so that the price does not move against them, while informationless traders have an incentive to reveal this fact to ensure no price impact. If a trader with dual capacity has a client whom they know to be uninformed, the dual trader may themselves take the other side of part of the order, while the remainder is filled by other traders. This will be beneficial for the dual trader, as the price at which the remaining part of the order is filled will rise to incorporate an unnecessary allowance for an information-based trade. The client benefits because, since only part of their order is exposed to the market, the price impact is smaller. However, in total, the presence of dual capacity will reduce the amount of informationless trading on the market, so increasing the price impact of the remaining, largely information-based, orders.

Sarkar (1995) argued that dual capacity reduces the volume of trading by informed customers because the broker mimics their trades, so reducing their profits. The reduction in volume by informed customers is argued to offset the increase in volume by the own account trading of dual traders, so that dual capacity leaves total volume unchanged. Because they trade less, dual capacity reduces the profits of informed customers. Sarkar also argues that dual capacity has no effect on the price impact of uninformed trades.

Chakravarty (1994) suggests that, when about ten or more dual traders are engaged in front running, competition among them will drive the expected profits from front running to zero. Therefore, it is unnecessary to ban dual capacity in actively traded futures markets to prevent front running. This theoretical argument is consistent with the lack of evidence of front running. However, dual traders would attempt to conceal any front running and, as Grossman & Miller (1986) have argued, even with trades timed to the nearest minute, front running is hard for supervisors to detect.

About 12% to 25% of the profits of floor traders come from trading on their own account (US Congress, 1990b, p. 74). Most futures traders are heavily specialized, and 90% of traders conduct either 90% of their trades for customers, or 90% for themselves. As from 22nd June 1987 the CME implemented rule 541. This states that 'a member who has executed an S&P500 futures contract order while on the top step of the S&P500 futures pit shall not thereafter on the same day trade S&P500 futures contracts for his account'. This rule restricted traders on the top step to acting each day as either as agents or proprietary traders (US Congress, 1990b, p. 75). From 20th May 1991, the CME restricted dual trading in all liquid and mature contracts under rule 552, which included S&P500 futures. Rule 552 banned dual trading, except for spread trading, trades cancelling errors, and trades for customers who are exchange members, or who have given their written permission. In addition, own account trading was permitted prior to the first customer trade of the day, and the ban only related to dual capacity for specified contract months - the liquid months. Thus, a trader might have single capacity for the near (say March) and middle (say June) contracts, but dual capacity for the far (say September) contract. Furthermore, rule 552 only applied to a particular contract month, and so this trader could act for customers in the March contract, and simultaneously trade on their own account in the June contract, even though dual trading in both these contracts was restricted, Chang, Locke & Mann (1994).

Empirical Evidence.   There are two main types of empirical study of the effects of dual trading: comparisons of the trades by dual traders with contemporaneous trades by single capacity traders (brokers and locals); and before and after studies of restrictions on dual trading. All the available studies are of US markets.

Park, Sarkar & Wu (1994) studied the performance of dual traders in S&P500 and yen futures using transactions data for 15 days in 1987 (all before the top step rule became operative). They found that customer trades in S&P500 futures were executed by dual traders at a price that was about 18 cents better than that obtained by single capacity brokers for their customers. These results imply that if dual capacity is restricted; as it was by the top step rule just after the end of the data period of this study, there is likely to be an increased cost for customers. Park, Sarkar & Wu also considered the benefits of being a dual trader. They found that dual traders in S&P500 futures made higher profits on their own account trading than did locals; possibly from having access to information on the order flow. Dual traders in S&P500 futures were found to mimic the trades of their customers (piggy backing); although there was no evidence of front running. In addition, deals by S&P500 dual traders on their own account were at prices some 10 cents better than those they obtained for their customers. Part of this price improvement may be compensation to dual traders for supplying market making services (i.e. the traded bid-ask spread).

In a study of MMI futures using half-hour data from 1988, Walsh & Dinehart (1991) found evidence that, when dual traders were active, the bid-ask spread tended to drop. This is consistent with dual traders using their spare capacity to supply liquidity at near marginal cost, which lowers the bid-ask spread. It may also be because, as a broker, they acquire information concerning customer trading patterns which is of benefit to them as a speculator.

Chakravarty & Lai (2003a, 2003b) examined 1992 trade data for S&P400 futures, in which unrestricted dual trading is permitted. When dual traders are informed, they will choose to trade on their own account, and these trades will be more profitable than when they act as a broker for others. Using data for one S&P400 dual trader, there was no evidence of private information, nor was there evidence of piggy backing or front running. However, there was evidence that this dual trader tended to trade in the opposite direction to their customers, i.e. supplied liquidity; and that own-account trading was to rebalance their inventory. These results show that dual trading is beneficial (supplying liquidity), with no evidence of malign behaviour (front running and piggy backing).

Top Step Rule.   The top step of the S&P500 pit is where a high proportion of the trades are executed, and so the introduction of the top step rule in June 1987 was likely to have an important effect on dual trading. While half of the volume in February 1987 was executed by dual traders, this had dropped to only 11% of volume by September 1987.

Park & Sarkar (1992) studied transactions data on the S&P500 for 1986-8, during which time the top step rule was introduced. Apart from a small reduction of 7% in the volume of dual trading, they could find no evidence that this rule had any effects. In particular, there was no effect on mispricings; nor was market depth (as measured by the price impact of large trades) altered.

Smith & Whaley (1994b) analyzed transactions data for S&P500 futures for 1983-7, giving 78 trading days after the top step rule became operative. They regressed the daily estimate of the traded bid-ask spread on a top step rule dummy, daily volume and a daily estimate of the implied volatility of S&P500 futures. The spread decreased with volume and increased with risk, as found in prior studies. The introduction of the top step rule led to an increase in the traded bid-ask spread by about 20%. This supports the view that imposing regulatory restrictions adds to the costs of trading. As a control, Smith & Whaley also investigated MMI futures, which were not subject to any restrictions on dual capacity at this time. After the introduction of the top step rule, there was a significant drop in S&P500 futures volume, relative to MMI futures volume. This is consistent with limits on dual capacity reducing broking capacity and market liquidity. After the top step rule was introduced, the S&P500 futures traded bid-ask spread widened, relative to that of MMI futures, but this result was not statistically significant.

Locke, Sarkar & Wu (1999) studied transactions data for S&P500 futures for 1987, with the top step rule becoming operative roughly half way through this period. The numbers of floor traders who were active during the periods before and after the introduction of the top step rule, and their share of total S&P500 futures volume are shown in table 11.3. This indicates a very substantial reduction in the volume of business conducted by dual traders (from 48% of total volume down to 12%), and a big rise for brokers, and to a lesser extent locals. In addition, average daily volume for the market was over 17% lower after the introduction of the top step rule, and so the reduction in the level of activity of dual traders was even more severe than indicated by the percentage reduction in their share of business. After controlling for trade direction (buy or sell), net volume and the number of locals in the pit; Locke, Sarkar & Wu found that the introduction of the top step rule had no effect on the price impact of customer trades; i.e. market depth. However, the top step rule did lead to a very substantial reduction in the profits of floor traders: 84% down for dual traders on days when they acted in both capacities, 79% down on days when dual traders only traded for their own account, and 57% down for locals. There was also a 10% reduction in the total number of floor traders.

Locke, Sarkar & Wu (1999) also examined the trading skills of dual traders who quit as floor traders in S&P500 futures after the introduction of the top step rule. If they had superior trading skills they should have earned above average profits on their own trades, and executed their customer trades with below average price impact. Relative to traders who continued to act as dual traders after the operation of the top step rule, dual traders who quit the S&P500 pit made significantly higher own account profits (on non-dual days) prior to 22nd June 1987. However, there was no difference in the price impact of customer trades between the continuing and quitting dual traders. This suggests that the top step rule tended to drive out dual traders who were more skilled in trading on their own account.

Table 11.3: Types of S&P500 Futures Floor Traders and Volume Shares in 1987

	Number of Traders		% of Volume	
	Before	After	Before	After
Dual capacity traders	252	197	-	-
• own account	-	-	27%	7%
• customers	-	-	21%	5%
Locals - own account	484	477	40%	54%
Brokers - customers	205	176	12%	34%
Totals	941	850	100%	100%

Conclusions.   The evidence on the effects of dual trading is mixed. The costs of trading for customers have been found to rise, fall or remain unchanged when dual capacity is restricted. Some studies support the view that dual traders make money from their own account trading because they have access to information on their customers' trades, while other studies do not. Finally, it appears that restricting dual trading leads to lower market volume and lower profits for locals.

11.14 Determinants of Success

Barclay & Noll (1992) considered the factors that may be important in determining the success of a market in equity derivatives (futures and options). Their first task was to define 'success'. Somewhat arbitrarily, this was defined as when the turnover in exchange-traded equity derivatives in a country exceeds the turnover in the country's underlying equity markets. There were three factors, which were thought to be important in determining success, on which they did not present any data. The first factor was the costs of trading derivatives relative to the costs of trading the underlying equities. If derivatives present a low cost-alternative to trading equities, derivatives markets are more likely to be successful. The second factor was the extent of foreign participation in the spot market. Foreign investors may be more willing to use derivatives in implementing a global investment strategy. The final factor was the price volatility of the spot market. Derivatives are more attractive if the spot market is volatile.

Three factors, which are largely beyond the control of the markets, were shown to be associated with the success of equity derivatives markets. The first factor was the ratio of spot turnover to spot market capitalization. The higher is this ratio, the greater is the potential demand for derivatives. The second factor was spot market capitalization. The demand for derivatives must be of a sufficient absolute size to cover the fixed costs of establishing the derivatives exchange. The final factor was the growth in the ratio of spot market capitalization to GDP. Assuming GDP is not declining, rapid growth in this ratio suggests that the size of the spot market is growing, and this may well lead to an increased need for risk management tools, such as derivatives.

Barclay & Noll (1992) also considered three factors which are largely within the control of the markets concerned. These factors facilitate arbitrage between the spot and derivatives markets, so helping to ensure that these markets are correctly priced, relative to each other. They were also found to be associated with the success of equity derivative markets. The first factor was spot transparency. The more transparent is the spot market, the better is the information available to traders, and the closer will be the links between markets. The second factor was the computation of the final settlement price of the derivative. If the settlement price is the market price at a point in time, rather than an average over time, it is possible to close out arbitrage positions at exactly the settlement price. This reduces the risk in arbitrage transactions. The final factor was that arbitrage will be eased by an ability to trade baskets of shares, to short sell shares and to cross-margin between derivative and spot positions.

Finally, Barclay & Noll (1992) found that a country with successful derivatives markets had usually established both futures and options markets. A number of other possible determinants of success mentioned earlier in this chapter, all of which are under the control of the derivatives exchange, were not considered: the definition of the index on which the index futures and options are based, the size of margins, the imposition of price limits, the minimum price movement, the size of the contract multiplier, the contract maturities and the trading mechanism.

A new literature is growing on the determinants of the success of individual futures contracts. According to Tashjian (1995) these include a strong hedging demand. Hedging demand will be increased if the price of the asset is volatile, there are substantial holdings of the asset to be hedged, the owners of the asset to be hedged are highly risk averse, and there is a high correlation between the futures price and the price of the asset to be hedged.

Holland & Fremault Vila (1997) investigated the factors determining success (as measured by volume) using data for 16 futures contracts first listed by Euronext-Liffe in 1982-94. Success was positively associated with the size of the underlying spot market, liquidity (measured by volume ÷ open interest), being the first exchange to list a future, and negatively associated with competition from a dual listing on an exchange with non-overlapping trading hours. Surprisingly, hedging effectiveness and spot volatility were not found to be linked with success.

Holder, Tomas & Webb (1999) studied 90 cases of competition between exchanges listing equivalent futures contracts (including 15 for index futures). They found that the winning exchange tended to be the first to list the contract, relatively larger than their rivals, and located in the same country as the spot market. However, the use of open outcry or screens had no effect on success.

11.15 Conclusions

There are a considerable number of design features for futures contracts; and the evidence is that these choices can have important effects on market performance. Many of these choices are made by the exchange; while others are made by the clearing house, the index compilers, other exchanges and the government. There are no simple rules for designing a successful contract, and some trial and error is involved. Exchanges also adjust the design features under their control in response to changing circumstances, with the aim of producing a more successful contract.

Chapter 12

Further Topics in Index Futures

Introduction

This chapter focuses on a number of regulatory issues connected with index futures. A major interest of regulators is whether index futures have increased the volatility of the stock market, and this is addressed in section 1. A related issue is the role which portfolio insurance has played in amplifying stock market volatility; and this is discussed in section 2. In section 3, some other effects of the existence of index futures are considered. Finally, brief consideration is given to the ways in which the equity and futures markets are linked.

12.1 Index Futures and Share Price Volatility

The stock market crash of October 1987 led to considerable concern about the connection between the recently created markets in index futures and the extreme volatility the spot market exhibited during October 1987, Hazen (1992). Four issues are of interest when considering the relationship between futures markets and share price volatility: the relative volatility of futures prices and the price of the underlying asset, the effect of creating a futures market on the price volatility of the underlying asset, the influence of programme trading (much of which is due to the existence of a futures market) on the price volatility of the underlying asset, and the effect of a futures market on the systematic risk of the shares in the index. Each of these issues will be considered in turn.

12.1.1 Relative Volatility

The relative volatility of the spot and futures markets depends, in part, on how volatility is measured. For returns, if the condition for an absence of arbitrage opportunities (the no-arbitrage condition) is met, and interest rates and dividends are certain; the variance of returns on the index computed using an input frequency (the time period over which the returns are computed) of a day or shorter will be the same as the futures variance. As the input frequency lengthens, the volatility of futures returns will tend to be less than the spot volatility, but only by a very small amount. For example, the variance of futures returns measured with an input frequency of one year, will be only about 10% less than the spot variance. For prices and price changes, if the no-arbitrage condition is met and dividends and interest rates are certain, the futures variance will be slightly larger than the spot variance. The theory predicts an extra volatility of approximately 3% for a futures contract with three months to delivery.

If the dividend yield or interest rate is uncertain, then as long as they do not have a strong negative correlation with the spot price, the volatility of futures returns, prices or price changes, relative to the corresponding spot measure, will increase. However, no numerical estimates of the size of the increase in futures volatility are available. The major theoretical results mentioned above are explained more fully in Board & Sutcliffe (1995a). Amihud & Mendelson (1989) have developed a partial adjustment model which also predicts that, if futures prices adjust faster than spot prices, futures volatility will exceed spot volatility.

Empirical studies for the US, Japan, UK, Switzerland, Germany, Finland and Hong Kong have investigated the relative price volatility of index futures and the index, and established that index futures prices are substantially more volatile than the underlying index. These studies may be divided into those that examined price levels or changes, and those which looked at returns.

USA.   Bortz (1984) used daily data for the first six months of trading in S&P500 futures, and found the fortnightly or monthly volatility of futures prices exceeded that of the index. Volatility was computed as $\sigma^2 = \Sigma(P_{t+1} - P_t)^2/n$.

Cornell (1985a) compared the variance of daily futures price changes with the variance of the theoretical futures price changes given by his model, for the S&P500 for 1982-3. He found that the variance of actual changes in closing prices was about 47% higher than the theoretical figure, while the corresponding figure for opening prices was 30%.

Kawaller, Koch & Koch (1990) considered the S&P500 index and, using transactions data for the fourth quarters of 1984-6, found the minute-to-minute variance of futures price changes was five times greater than the corresponding variance of changes in the index.

Miller, Muthuswamy & Whaley (1994) studied transactions data on the S&P500 for 1982-91. They computed price changes over 15, 30 and 60 minute intervals for each futures contract and found that futures volatility was considerably higher than was index volatility.

Japan.   Brenner, Subrahmanyam & Uno (1989b) analyzed daily price changes for 1986-8 for the Nikkei 225 traded on SGX. They found the future had a substantially higher variance than the spot.

Hong Kong.   Mak, Tang & Choi (1993) used daily closing prices on the Hang Seng for the 17 months before the 1987 Crash, and the 16 months afterwards. They found that the variance of futures prices was 15% larger before the Crash, and 50% larger after the Crash.

The results of these studies of price levels or changes are in accordance with the prediction that futures prices would be more volatile than the index, although the sizes of the differences found by many of these authors were considerably larger than the few percent expected.

For returns, the expectation is an equality of variances for futures and the index. However, the available studies have usually found that the variance of futures returns exceeds that for the index.

USA. Chu & Bubnys (1990) studied daily futures and spot data for the S&P500 and the NYSE Composite indices for 1982-8. For both indices the volatility of the natural logarithm of the daily futures price relatives clearly exceeded that of the logarithm of the daily price relatives of the index.

Harris, Sofianos & Shapiro (1994) found the volatility of returns computed over one and five minute intervals for the S&P500 for 1989-90 was much higher for futures than for the index.

For daily returns on the S&P500 for 1982-9, Schwert (1990) reported that the monthly variance for futures was higher than that for the index, but did not state the size of the difference.

Using minute-to-minute data on the S&P500 for 1982-7, MacKinlay & Ramaswamy (1988) found greater volatility for changes in the logarithms of futures prices than for changes in the logarithm of the index.

Cheung & Ng (1990) analyzed 15 minute returns on the S&P500 for 1983-7. Computing the variance separately for each contract, on average the variance of futures returns was about 53% larger than the variance of spot returns.

Morse (1988) considered the S&P500, NYSE Composite and MMI indices for 1986-8, and found that, for each index the variance of returns on the future exceeded the variance of returns on the index.

Park (1993) analyzed transactions data for 1984-6 for the MMI. In contrast to the other studies, he found that the variance of daily spot returns was slightly larger than the variance of futures returns. When volatility was measured as the variance of 30 minute returns, this difference between spot and futures volatilities increased in magnitude. For the first three hours of trading each day, the index was more volatile than the futures price; while there was little difference in volatility for the rest of the day. Park also used a different volatility measure (the length of time required for the price, or index value, to move outside a preset price interval), and found that for 30 minute periods, futures prices were considerably more volatile than the index throughout the day. These results indicate that the way volatility is measured can alter the conclusions.

Japan. Japan might be an exception to the general pattern that index futures volatility exceeds that of the spot market. Brenner, Subrahmanyam & Uno (1990b) studied daily closing data on the Nikkei 225 (traded on both the OSE and SGX) and Topix. For 1988-9, the volatility of daily spot arithmetic returns exceeded that for the corresponding futures. This conflicts with the earlier finding by Brenner, Subrahmanyam & Uno (1989b) that SGX Nikkei 225 futures were more volatile than Osaka Nikkei 225 futures.

Using returns over five minute periods in 1988-9, Lim (1992a & 1992b) also found that the Nikkei index was more volatile that the futures traded on SGX.

Lim & Muthuswamy (1993) studied 5 minute data on Nikkei 225 futures traded on

SGX for 1981-91 and found that the daily spot variance of returns was higher than for futures. These contrary results may be due to the short sample period, but the authors do not offer any suggestions as to why Japanese indices (and futures traded in Singapore) should have a reverse pattern of relative volatilities to that found in other markets.

Brenner, Subrahmanyam & Uno (1994) used daily closing prices to conduct an analysis of the effects of variations in the input and output (the time period for which the variance of a set of returns is computed) periods on the relative volatilities of the Nikkei 225 and Topix indices and the corresponding index futures. They found that, for the period after the 1987 Crash, futures were less volatile than the corresponding spot index.

Bacha & Vila (1994) analyzed daily high, low and closing prices for Nikkei 225 futures traded in Osaka, Singapore and Chicago for 1986-91. Volatility was measured in two different ways: the standard deviation of daily returns, and the mean of the daily volatility estimates produced using the Parkinson high-low estimator. The variances of daily returns were of broadly similar size for the spot and the three futures contracts. For the high-low estimator the only substantial difference was that the futures volatility was 47% lower than for the spot.

Iihara, Kato, & Tokunaga (1996) used 5-minute log returns for 1989-91 to compare the variance of returns on Nikkei 225 futures traded in Osaka with the variance of returns on the index. They split their data into three sub-periods, and found that for two of the sub-periods the spot variance exceeded the futures variance.

Hong Kong.   Yau, Schneeweis & Yung (1990) found a higher variance for the natural logarithm of daily price relatives for futures than for the Hang Seng index, particularly after the October 1987 crash.

Tang & Lui (2002) studied 15 minute data on the Hang Seng for 1994-6. For returns computed over both 24 hours and 15 minutes, futures returns were more volatile than spot returns; except at the open when the spot returns were more volatile than futures returns. The higher spot volatility at the open was attributed to noise traders.

Australia.   Hodgson (1994) compared the variance of returns on the AOI with those of the corresponding SPI futures using 15 minute returns for 1992-3. He found that the futures volatility was 175% higher.

UK.   Yadav & Pope (1990) compared the volatility of daily returns for spot and futures for the FTSE 100 using data for 1984-8. The variances were computed using close to close returns, open to open returns and the Parkinson high-low estimator. The higher futures volatilities, which are given in table 12.1, are all significant at the 5% level.

Board, Goodhart & Sutcliffe (1992) and Board & Sutcliffe (1992, 1995a) studied hourly data for the FTSE 100 for 1984-91. They compared the spot and futures volatilities for three input and three output frequencies using five alternative definitions of volatility, giving a total of thirty comparisons. In all cases futures volatility was higher than spot volatility, and all the numbers given in table 12.1 are statistically significant at the 1% level, apart from the last (i.e. 18%), which is significant at the 5% level. The extra futures volatility was higher, the shorter was the input frequency. There was also some tendency for the extra volatility to decline as the output frequency became longer. They concluded that the evidence was inconsistent with six of the possible explanations: dividend and interest rate risk, a maturity effect in futures volatility, default risk, a double auction market for futures, the weekend effect and the high transactions costs for spot trading. However, the results were consistent with four of the possible explanations: stale prices, trades outside the touch, futures bid-ask bounce and noise traders in futures. These explanations are considered further in this section.

Strickland & Xu (1993) studied hourly on the FTSE 100 for 1988-9.They found that the variance of percentage price changes was 45% larger for futures than for spot. *Germany.* Grünbichler & Callahan (1994) used 5, 15 and 30 minute returns on the DAX index and DAX futures for 1990-1. They discovered that the variance of futures returns was higher than that of the corresponding spot returns, and that this extra futures volatility declined as the differencing interval was lengthened, e.g. 27% for 5 minute returns, and 18% for 30 minute returns.

For returns over one, two and five days, Grünbichler, Longstaff & Schwartz (1994) found that the increase in the spot variance was less than for the futures variance; which is consistent with the extra futures volatility continuing to decline as the differencing interval is lengthened from minutes to days.

Finland. Martikainen & Puttonen (1994a, 1994b) studied daily returns on the FOX index and FOX futures for 1988-90. They found that the variance of futures returns was 60% larger than that for spot returns, while Martikainen, Perttunen & Puttonen (1995a) found that the figure was 80% larger.

Switzerland. Stulz, Wasserfallen & Stucki (1990) studied daily data on Swiss Market Index futures traded in an OTC market run by the Leu Bank for 1989. For two output periods of 3 and 9 months, they found that the variance of futures returns was 3% higher than the variance of spot returns.

Details of the extra volatility of futures price changes and returns found by these studies are set out in table 12.1, where extra volatility is the futures variance divided by the spot variance times 100. CC denotes close to close data, OC is open to close data, while OO is open to open data.

Table 12.1: Empirical Studies of the Extra Volatility of Index Futures Prices and Returns

Study	Index	Input Frequency	Output Frequency	Extra Volatility
Price Changes				
Kawaller, Koch & Koch (1990)	S&P500	1 min	30 min	732%
Kawaller, Koch & Koch (1990)	S&P500	1 min	Day	630%
Bortz (1984)	S&P500	Day OC	Mth	51%
Miller, Muthuswamy & Whaley (1994)	S&P500	15 min	9 yrs	83%

Miller, Muthuswamy & Whaley (1994)	S&P500	30 min	9 yrs	58%
Miller, Muthuswamy & Whaley (1994)	S&P500	60 min	9 yrs	45%
Miller, Muthuswamy & Whaley (1994)	VLCI	15 min	9 yrs	659%
Miller, Muthuswamy & Whaley (1994)	VLCI	30 min	9 yrs	431%
Miller, Muthuswamy & Whaley (1994)	VLCI	60 min	9 yrs	269%
Brenner, Subrahmanyam & Uno (1989b)	Nikkei-SGX	Day CC	24 mths	63%
Mak, Tang & Choi (1993)	Hang Seng	Day CC	17 mths[f]	15%
Mak, Tang & Choi (1993)	Hang Seng	Day CC	16 mths[g]	50%

Returns

Harris, Sofianos & Shapiro (1994)	S&P500	1 min	2 yrs	359%
Harris, Sofianos & Shapiro (1994)	S&P500	5 min	2 yrs	91%
MacKinlay & Ramaswamy (1988)	S&P500	15 min	3 mths	56%
MacKinlay & Ramaswamy (1988)	S&P500	30 min	3 mths	26%
MacKinlay & Ramaswamy (1988)	S&P500	60 min	3 mths	16%
MacKinlay & Ramaswamy (1988)	S&P500	2 hrs	3 mths	13%
MacKinlay & Ramaswamy (1988)	S&P500	Day OC	3 mths	17%
Cheung & Ng (1990)	S&P500	15 min	3 mths	53%
Chu & Bubnys (1990)	S&P500	Day CC	Day[a]	64%
Chu & Bubnys (1990)	S&P500	Day CC	Day[b]	81%
Chu & Bubnys (1990)	S&P500	Day CC	Day[c]	76%
Morse (1988)	S&P500	Day CC	14 mths	4%
Morse (1988)	NYSE	Day CC	14 mths	4%
Chu & Bubnys (1990)	NYSE	Day CC	Day[a]	90%
Chu & Bubnys (1990)	NYSE	Day CC	Day[b]	213%
Chu & Bubnys (1990)	NYSE	Day CC	Day[c]	203%
Morse (1988)	MMI	Day CC	14 mths	3%
Park (1993)	MMI	Day CC	2 yrs	-3%
Park (1993)	MMI	Day OO	2 yrs	-4%
Park (1993)	MMI	30 min	2 yrs	-12%
Park (1993)	MMI	30 min	2 yrs[h]	403%
Brenner, Subrahmanyam & Uno (1990b)	Nikkei-SGX	Day CC	12 mths	-19%
Bacha & Vila (1994)	Nikkei-SGX	Day CC	3 mths	6%
Bacha & Vila (1994)	Nikkei-SGX	Day	3 mths[i]	5%
Lim (1992b)	Nikkei-SGX	5 min	Day	-30%
Lim & Muthuswamy (1993)	Nikkei-SGX	5 min	Day	-16%
Brenner, Subrahmanyam & Uno (1994)	Nikkei-SGX	6 days CC	23 mths[f]	82%
Brenner, Subrahmanyam & Uno (1994)	Nikkei-SGX	3 days CC	23 mths[f]	32%
Brenner, Subrahmanyam & Uno (1994)	Nikkei-SGX	2 days CC	23 mths[f]	15%
Brenner, Subrahmanyam & Uno (1994)	Nikkei-SGX	Day CC	23 mths[f]	28%
Brenner, Subrahmanyam & Uno (1994)	Nikkei-SGX	Day CC	Mth[f]	22%
Brenner, Subrahmanyam & Uno (1994)	Nikkei-SGX	6 days CC	14 mths[g]	-21%
Brenner, Subrahmanyam & Uno (1994)	Nikkei-SGX	3 days CC	14 mths[g]	-33%
Brenner, Subrahmanyam & Uno (1994)	Nikkei-SGX	2 days CC	14 mths[g]	-21%
Brenner, Subrahmanyam & Uno (1994)	Nikkei-SGX	Day CC	14 mths[g]	-20%
Brenner, Subrahmanyam & Uno (1994)	Nikkei-SGX	Day CC	Mth[g]	0%
Brenner, Subrahmanyam & Uno (1990b)	Nikkei-OSE	Day CC	12 mths	-24%
Bacha & Vila (1994)	Nikkei-OSE	Day CC	3 mths	-8%

Bacha & Vila (1994)	Nikkei-OSE	Day	3 mths[i]	-14%
Brenner, Subrahmanyam & Uno (1994)	Nikkei-OSE	6 days CC	14 mths[g]	-49%
Brenner, Subrahmanyam & Uno (1994)	Nikkei-OSE	3 days CC	14 mths[g]	-50%
Brenner, Subrahmanyam & Uno (1994)	Nikkei-OSE	2 days CC	14 mths[g]	-35%
Brenner, Subrahmanyam & Uno (1994)	Nikkei-OSE	Day CC	14 mths[g]	-29%
Brenner, Subrahmanyam & Uno (1994)	Nikkei-OSE	Day CC	Mth[g]	-27%
Iihara, Kato & Tokunaga (1996)	Nikkei-OSE	5 min.	10 mths	-28%
Iihara, Kato & Tokunaga (1996)	Nikkei-OSE	5 min.	8 mths	35%
Iihara, Kato & Tokunaga (1996)	Nikkei-OSE	5 min.	6 mths	-6%
Bacha & Vila (1994)	Nikkei-CME	Day CC	3 mths	3%
Bacha & Vila (1994)	Nikkei-CME	Day	3 mths[i]	-47%
Brenner, Subrahmanyam & Uno (1990b)	Topix	Day CC	12 mths	-9%
Brenner, Subrahmanyam & Uno (1994)	Topix	6 days CC	14 mths[g]	-34%
Brenner, Subrahmanyam & Uno (1994)	Topix	3 days CC	14 mths[g]	-40%
Brenner, Subrahmanyam & Uno (1994)	Topix	2 days CC	14 mths[g]	-18%
Brenner, Subrahmanyam & Uno (1994)	Topix	Day CC	14 mths[g]	0%
Brenner, Subrahmanyam & Uno (1994)	Topix	Day CC	Mth[g]	3%
Yau, Schneeweis & Yung (1990)	Hang Seng	Day CC	18 mths[f]	14%
Yau, Schneeweis & Yung (1990)	Hang Seng	Day CC	14 mths[g]	54%
Hodgson (1994)	All Ord.	15 min	1 yr	175%
Board & Sutcliffe (1995a)	FTSE 100	60 min	Day	101%
Board & Sutcliffe (1995a)	FTSE 100	60 min	Mth	85%
Board & Sutcliffe (1995a)	FTSE 100	60 min	Quarter	82%
Board & Sutcliffe (1995a)	FTSE 100	Day CC	Mth	46%
Board & Sutcliffe (1995a)	FTSE 100	Day CC	Quarter	42%
Board & Sutcliffe (1995a)	FTSE 100	Week	Quarter	18%
Strickland & Xu (1993)	FTSE 100	60 mins	2 yrs	46%
Yadav & Pope (1990)	FTSE 100	Day CC	3 mths[d]	15%
Yadav & Pope (1990)	FTSE 100	Day CC	3 mths[e]	33%
Yadav & Pope (1990)	FTSE 100	Day OO	3 mths[d]	18%
Yadav & Pope (1990)	FTSE 100	Day OO	3 mths[e]	43%
Yadav & Pope (1990)	FTSE 100	Day OC	3 mths[d]	47%
Yadav & Pope (1990)	FTSE 100	Day OC	3 mths[e]	175%
Stulz, Wasserfallen & Stucki (1990)	SMI	Day CC	6 mths	3%
Grünbichler & Callahan (1994)	DAX	5 min	10 mths	27%
Grünbichler & Callahan (1994)	DAX	5 min	10 mths	19%
Grünbichler & Callahan (1994)	DAX	30 min	10 mths	18%
Martikainen & Puttonen (1994a, 1994b)	FOX	Day CC	2 yrs	60%
Martikainen, Perttunen & Puttonen (1995a)	FOX	Day CC	2 yrs	80%

a = Classical volatilities ($\ln(P_{t+1}/P_t)$), b = Garman-Klass volatilities, c = Ball-Torous volatilities, d = Pre Big Bang, e = Post Big Bang, f = Pre 1987 crash, g = Post 1987 Crash, h = Cho & Frees (1988) volatility estimator, i = Parkinson variance estimator.

Most of the extra volatilities in table 12.1 are much larger than the theoretical predictions of a few percent for price changes, and zero for returns. This result appears to be common across all the indices investigated. The table indicates that (excluding the more recent Japanese results) the extra futures volatility is higher, the shorter is the input frequency, as shown in figure 12.1. For volatilities computed with an input frequency of a day, the extra volatility for futures is small. However, during a day, minute to minute futures volatility can be very much greater than that of the index, e.g. several times larger. Explanations for the higher volatility of futures prices may be split into measurement problems and economic factors omitted from the no-arbitrage condition. The measurement problems will be presented first, followed by a discussion of the economic explanations.

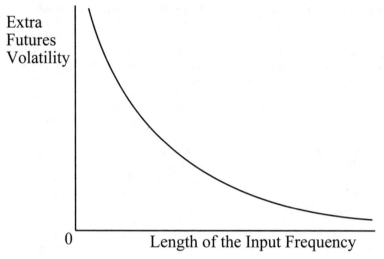

Figure 12.1: Extra Futures Volatility and Input Frequency

Stoll & Whaley (1988b) argued that, even if index futures and the spot prices of individual shares are equally volatile, the spot index will exhibit less volatility than the index futures price because the calculated index in the US is an average over time of the true index, due to the use of transactions (i.e. stale) prices in computing the index. In this case the futures price volatility more accurately reflects the volatility of the spot market than does the volatility of the index. Lengthening the input frequency used to compute the price changes should reduce the difference in volatility as the stale price effect will reduce in importance.

MacKinlay & Ramaswamy (1988) analyzed data on the S&P500 for 1982-7. They found that there was little autocorrelation in futures returns (the logarithms of the price relatives over fifteen minute intervals), while the returns on the index for 15-minute periods exhibited positive first-order autocorrelation of around 0.20. To examine the role played by stale prices in creating this positive autocorrelation in the index, the differencing interval was increased to 30 minutes, one hour, two hours and one day. The first order autocorrelation for returns on the index declined sharply from about 0.20 for fifteen minutes, to around 0.08 for thirty minutes, about 0.06 for an hour, 0.10 for two hours and roughly 0.06 for a day. These results suggest that most of the stale prices effect is removed by differencing over one or two hours, although some unexplained positive autocorrelation remained in the index. Thus, stale prices cannot fully account for the difference in volatility between futures prices and the index. However, based on their model and empirical results for the S&P500, Miller, Muthuswamy & Whaley (1994) suggest that stale prices may lead to an understatement of the variance of price changes over 15 minutes by 23%. When they removed the estimated stale price effect from the index, Miller, Muthuswamy & Whaley found that extra futures volatility for 15 minute S&P500 price changes fell from 83% to 23%.

In the UK, until the introduction of SETS on 20th October 1997, the method of calculating the index was different from that used for the major US indices, and raised different problems. The UK was a quote-driven market, and the FTSE 100 index was based on the mid touch prices for each of the constituent shares (i.e. the average of the best ask and bid quotations). Thus, unlike the major US indices, the FTSE 100 index could move when market makers changed their views, even though no trading had taken place. Consequently, any stale price effect should have been substantially smaller in the UK than for the major US indices; although to the extent that there was a delay before market makers updated their quotes, the UK index may have been affected by an equivalent phenomenon. Large trades in the UK can occur at prices outside the best bid and ask quotations (i.e. outside the touch), and the index would be unchanged. As a result, the volatility of the FTSE 100 index may have understated the real volatility of spot prices. Therefore, measurement problems leading to an understatement of spot volatility were likely to be present in the UK, but for somewhat different reasons than in the US.

Economic factors, which have been omitted from the theoretical model, may explain why futures volatility is greater than spot volatility. Harris, Sofianos & Shapiro (1994) suggested that bid-ask bounce may cause increased futures volatility (relative to the spot). Smith & Whaley (1994b) found that over 80% of the variance of changes in S&P500 futures transactions prices was due to bid-ask bounce. The index is based on midquotes in the UK, while in the US some of the previous transactions will have been at the ask price and others at the bid price, and so the index is less prone to the effects of bid-ask bounce than is the price of the index future. However, in an empirical study of the S&P500, Miller, Muthuswamy & Whaley (1994) suggest that bid-ask bounce can only explain a 0.1% increase in the variance of futures price changes over 15 minute periods. Schwert (1990) suggested the explanation may be that 'noise traders' (traders who do not have correct information about the value of the securities they trade) are more active in the futures than the spot market.

Much higher transactions costs for trading the basket of shares corresponding to the index, coupled with the price discovery role of futures, may mean that the futures price responds to new (market-wide) information without any movement in the index. Only when the mispricing is sufficiently large to cover the transactions costs of trading shares and futures will arbitrage pull the two prices together again. In consequence, the futures price will have many small movements which are not reflected in the index. The Samuelson hypothesis (see chapter 7) is that futures price volatility increases as delivery approaches, and a maturity effect (positive or negative) will create fluctuations in futures volatility. Park (1990) suggested that the volatility of futures prices may exceed that of the index because futures prices are set by a double auction market, while shares are traded via market makers. Dividend and interest rate uncertainty and default risk for the futures may also account for some of the extra futures volatility. If the weekend effects in spot and futures returns are of a different magnitude, this may induce differences in volatility.

12.1.2 Effect of Index Futures on Share Price Volatility

It has been a major source of concern for regulators that the existence of index futures leads to an increase in the price volatility of the underlying asset market. Such concerns over the effects of a futures market on spot volatility are not new. On 28th August 1958 the US Congress passed the Onion Futures Act (Public Law 85-839) which banned trading in onion futures because it was thought to destabilize the spot market, although subsequent empirical studies by Gray (1963) and Working (1960a and 1963) found that onion futures tended to stabilize the spot market, while Johnson (1973) found no evidence for destabilization. In the 1960s there was a failed attempt in the US to outlaw potato futures because, amongst other things, they were claimed to increase spot volatility.

The outcome of theoretical investigations of the effects of introducing a futures market on the volatility of the spot market have been ambiguous. Cass & Shell (1983) proposed a theoretical model of the effects of the existence of a futures market on the volatility of spot prices. Although the creation of a futures market will result in equal values of winnings and losses (i.e. since futures markets are a zero sum game), there will be a change in the distribution of wealth. This shift in the wealth distribution leads to a change in the pattern of demand for the underlying asset, and hence to changes in spot prices (i.e. spot price volatility increases). However, as Green (1986) argued, this model is unlikely to be of major significance for index futures because there is no reason to expect much change in the pattern of demand as wealth flows from the losing to the winning traders (because the participants will have similar patterns of demand).

Subrahmanyam (1991) constructed a theoretical model of shares and index futures, and concluded that the effect of introducing index futures on spot volatility is ambiguous. A similar conclusion has also been reached by Kawai (1983), Turnovsky (1983) and Weller & Yano (1987). The simulation approach of Turnovsky & Campbell (1985) found that, for the specific model considered, the existence of a futures market reduced spot volatility. Chari & Jagannathan (1990) and Chari, Jagannathan & Jones (1990) demonstrated that, while it is possible to construct theoretical models that show that the existence of a futures market leads to a decrease in spot volatility, small changes in the model produce the reverse conclusion. Thus, this issue cannot be decided on theoretical grounds. Chari & Jagannathan also question the view that an increase in spot price volatility is necessarily bad, and show that a decrease in volatility may make some groups in society worse off. This differential welfare effect was also found by Turnovsky & Campbell (1985), who suggested it may account for the opposition to futures markets by some groups, even though social welfare is increased.

Antoniou, Holmes & Priestley (1998) argued that the introduction of index futures may change the way the spot market responds to news, and that such changes might be beneficial. Thus, even if the existence of index futures increases spot volatility, this must be weighed against any beneficial effects the introduction of a futures market may have on the response of the spot market to news.

In recent years there have been a number of empirical studies of the effects of index futures on the volatility of the underlying index, and they generally support the view that index futures do not increase the long run volatility of the spot price. There are four main ways of testing the hypothesis that a futures market increases spot volatility: experimental studies, a comparison of the volatility before and after the introduction of the index future, a cross section (or relative) analysis which compares the volatility of the underlying asset with the volatility of similar assets for which no futures contract was introduced, and a time series analysis that attempts to explain variations in spot volatility using variables such as futures volume. These will be discussed in turn.

a. Experimental Studies.   There have been a few experimental studies of the effects of introducing a futures market on spot volatility. Friedman, Harrison & Salmon (1983, 1984) conducted a laboratory study of Californian students and found that futures markets improved the speed of convergence to equilibrium (i.e. price discovery), and that spot prices tended to be less volatile when a futures market existed. Forsythe, Palfrey & Plott (1984) also conducted a laboratory study of Californian students and found that, because it improved the price discovery process, the introduction of a futures market increased spot volatility. They concluded that the increase in spot volatility represented an efficiency gain, and did not mean that policy makers should intervene in futures markets to stabilize spot prices. Harrison (1992) studied students from South Carolina, and reached the same conclusions as Forsythe, Palfrey & Plott (1984) when a single long-dated future is introduced. When there are futures of varying maturities, the increase in volatility is much reduced. Porter & Smith (1995) studied undergraduate students, principally from the University of Arizona, and found that the introduction of a futures market greatly reduced the bubbles in the spot price. These experimental studies show that the introduction of a futures market can increase or decrease spot volatility, as well as improve price discovery.

b. Before and After Studies.   These studies have compared spot volatility before and after the introduction of index futures.

USA.   Santoni (1987) considered daily and weekly data on the S&P500 index for 1975-86, and found no difference in the variance of changes in the index before and after the introduction of index futures in April 1982. Santoni also analyzed the daily values of $\Lambda = (high-low)/close$ for the index, and found a statistically significant drop in the average value for the period after the introduction of index futures. Finally, Santoni studied the correlations for the post-futures period between the daily volume in S&P500 futures contracts and three measures of volatility: daily percentage changes in the index, the absolute values of daily percentage changes in the index and the daily values of Λ. The only significant result was a negative correlation between futures volume and Λ, suggesting that an increase in futures trading does not lead to an increase in the volatility of the index.

Edwards (1988a and 1988b) studied the volatility of the S&P500 and the VLCI indices before and after the introduction of the corresponding futures using daily data for 1973-87. He found that the daily volatility of the underlying asset (measured in a variety of ways) was not increased by the existence of futures trading.

Becketti & Roberts (1990) argued that what matters is not volatility, but jump volatility; i.e. daily changes in the index of over 1.75%. (Miller, 1991, has suggested that market participants interpret volatility as large price movements, particularly large negative price movements). Using daily data for 1962-90 on the S&P500, they found that the frequency of these large price changes dropped after the introduction of a futures contract on this index, while the average magnitude of these jumps was unchanged. They concluded that there is little or no relationship between the existence of index futures and stock market jump volatility.

Lockwood & Linn (1990) studied daily opening and closing values of the DJIA for 1964-89. They divided their data into various sub-periods using the dates of events thought likely to alter the volatility of the natural logarithm of the daily price relatives. The pre-futures period began in May 1975, when fixed commissions were abolished in the US, and ended in February 1982, when trading began in VLCI index futures. The post-futures period began in February 1982 and ended in February 1988, when larger margins were introduced for index futures. They found that the variance for the post-futures period computed using close to close prices was 120% larger (and highly statistically significant) than for the pre-futures period, and 66% larger than the variance for the entire data period. However, when daily open to open price changes were used, the variance for the post-futures period was only 44% larger (and not statistically significant) than for the pre-futures period, and 35% larger than the variance for the entire period.

Baldauf & Santoni (1991) studied the S&P500 index using daily closing prices for 1975-89. Initially, they compared the variance of daily percentage changes in the index before and after April 1982 (when a futures contract was introduced on the S&P500 index). They found that, after the introduction of index futures, there was a significant increase in volatility. However, they argued that such a test is inadequate because it does not allow for the positive autocorrelation in the size of the percentage price changes (i.e. large price movements tend to follow large price movements, and small movements tend to follow small movements). To deal with this problem they used an ARCH model, and concluded that there was no significant increase in volatility (measured by the daily squared differences between the logarithm of the daily price relatives and their mean value for the entire data period) after the introduction of index futures.

Brorsen (1991) has suggested that the speed with which new information is reflected in the spot price is reduced if there is an increase in the frictions encountered when trading in this market (e.g. higher transactions costs, increased margins, limitations on arbitrage etc). He presented a simple model in which a reduction in the delay of the adjustment of the spot market to new information produces both a drop in the autocorrelation of spot returns, and an increase in short run spot volatility. Using data on daily closing prices for the S&P500 for 1962-86, he defined returns as the logarithm of the daily price relatives. Brorsen found that the autocorrelation in returns only lasted for about one day (i.e. the series was AR(1)), and that it decreased after April 1982. There was a significant increase in the variance of daily returns after the introduction of S&P500 futures in April 1982, but not for returns computed over five or twenty days. Thus, stock index futures appear to reduce the frictions to incorporating new information in share prices. In consequence, the spot price responds more sharply, and its variance increases. However, over longer periods of five or more days, the variance is unchanged because the spot price will have fully responded to new information, and reducing the frictions has no effect on this longer term volatility.

Kamara, Miller & Siegel (1992) considered daily closing values of the S&P500 index for 1976-88. They found that after trading in futures began, the variance of daily returns increased, while that of monthly returns did not. Since the variance of daily returns was found to change over time, this increase in daily volatility was not attributed to the introduction of index futures.

Pericli & Koutmos (1997) analyzed daily data on the S&P500 for 1953-94 index. After allowing for the 1987 Crash and the flexible exchange rate period in their EGARCH model, they found that volatility persistence increased after the introduction of futures trading, but volatility did not.

Rahman (2001) examined the introduction of DJIA futures in October 1997 using quote data on the 30 index constituents for 1997-8. He fitted a GARCH (1,1) model separately to each company for the periods before and after futures were traded, and found no significant changes in the parameters of the conditional variance equation. This indicates that futures trading did not increase spot volatility.

Japan. Chan & Karolyi (1991) studied daily returns on the Nikkei 225 for 1985-7. They fitted a GARCH-M regression model, which included dummy variables in the volatility process. These dummies allowed the volatility process to change in September 1986, when a future on the Nikkei began trading on SGX. They concluded that volatility was not changed by the existence of an index future. However, the volumes on SGX were modest, and the authors did not test whether the introduction of trading in Nikkei 225 futures on the OSE in September 1988 affected spot volatility.

Bacha & Vila (1994) compared the volatility of the Nikkei 225 for the 30 and 60 days before and after the introduction of futures trading in Singapore, Osaka and Chicago. Volatility was measured using the standard deviation of daily returns and the daily Parkinson high-low estimator. No changes in volatility were found.

Brenner, Subrahmanyam & Uno (1994) used daily closing prices to compare the volatilities of the Nikkei 225 and the Topix indices before and after the introduction of index futures. While acknowledging that a variety of other factors will have caused spot volatility to change, they conclude that there is no evidence that futures trading increased spot volatility in Japan.

Chen, Jarrett & Rhee (1992) used daily data on a random sample of 100 Japanese stocks for the year before and after the introduction of Topix futures in September 1988 (which was also the date of the introduction of Nikkei 225 futures in Osaka). Daily volatility was measure in four different ways: the monthly average of squared daily returns, the standard deviation of daily price changes within each month, the monthly average of the daily high-low range divided by the opening price, and the Parkinson high-low estimator. For both the year and the month before and after the introduction of Topix futures, there was no change in the volatility of the 100 stocks in the sample.

Hong Kong.   Freris (1990) looked at the effect of the existence of Hang Seng index futures in Hong Kong from May 1986. Using daily data for 1984-7, he studied the standard deviation of daily arithmetic returns and found the introduction of the index future was associated with a drop in the standard deviation of returns on the index. Freris concluded that the existence of index futures had no measurable effect on the volatility of the Hang Seng index.

Australia.   Hodgson & Nicholls (1991) considered the introduction of a futures contract on the Australian AOI in February 1983. Using daily data for 1981-7, they computed the natural logarithm of the Wednesday weekly price relatives. They concluded that volatility after February 1983 was not significantly different from volatility before that date, and so the existence of futures did not affect the volatility of the Australian stock market.

France and Denmark   Reyes (1996) studied weekly data on the French and Danish market indices for the three years before and after trading began in CAC 40 and KFX futures. An EGARCH $(1,1)$-MA(1) regression found that French spot volatility was lowered, while Danish spot volatility was unchanged.

USA, Japan, Hong Kong, Australia and the UK.   Lee & Ohk (1992a) considered the introduction of index futures in five countries - Australia, Hong Kong, Japan, UK and USA. They analyzed daily returns on an index in each country for two years before and two years after the start of trading in index futures. These indices were the All Ordinaries, the Hang Seng, Topix, the FT Ordinary and the NYSE Composite. The variance of returns for various periods (100 days, 250 days and 500 days) before the introduction of index futures was compared with that for the same period after the introduction. They found a significant increase in volatility in Japan. Depending on the period chosen, there were also volatility increases in the UK and the USA, and a volatility decrease in Hong Kong. There was no change in volatility in Australia.

There is a difficulty in such 'before and after' tests because only one observation is available: the change in volatility when the index future is introduced, and this observation may be contaminated by the effects of other uncontrolled variables, e.g. macro economic and other variables which affect the general level of market volatility (as has been found in the studies of the effect of the introduction of interest rate futures). There is also a causality problem: index futures may tend to be listed when spot volatility is high. For the UK there is an additional problem - FTSE 100 futures and American style FTSE 100 options began trading on the same day, and so before and after studies cannot distinguish between the effects of these two events.

Schwert (1989) found that, using US data for 1857-1987, stock market volatility was influenced by four factors: financial leverage, recessions, spot volume and the volatility of interest rates; while Schwert (1990) also considered operating leverage and share margins as possible determinants of spot volatility. Grossman (1990) suggested that developments in information technology in recent years have enabled market participants to acquire information more quickly and to react faster, leading to increased volatility. Maberly, Allen & Gilbert (1989) have shown that, depending on the data period selected from 1963-88, it is possible to demonstrate that the existence of S&P500 futures increased, decreased or had no effect on the volatility of the daily returns of the underlying S&P500 index. Thus, the methodology of these before and after studies is open to question.

c. Cross Section Studies. These studies have tried to control for other influences on spot volatility by examining the change in spot volatility, relative to that of equities not affected by index futures.

USA. The first study of index futures to use the relative volatility (or cross section) approach to this question was Aggarwal (1988). He used daily data for 1981-7 to study whether the existence of index futures affected the volatility (measured as the standard deviation of returns) of the S&P500 index and the DJIA. To control for other influences, he used the volatility of a composite OTC index (on which there was not an active futures market). He discovered that, while the volatility of the S&P500 and DJIA rose after the introduction of the futures, it declined relative to that of the OTC index. He concluded that the existence of index futures did not increase the price volatility of the underlying index. Aggarwal also investigated the effect of introducing futures on the volume volatility of the DJIA (relative to the OTC market), and found a clear increase in volume volatility after the introduction of the MMI future.

Harris (1989b) used daily data for 1975-87 for shares which were both in the S&P500 and quoted on the NYSE. Each calendar year he compared these shares with a matched sample of similar NYSE shares not included in this index. Returns were computed over a number of differencing intervals from one to twenty days. He adjusted the volatility of each share to remove the effects of a range of other factors, and then compared the adjusted volatility of the S&P500 shares with that of the shares in the control group. Prior to 1982, there was little difference in volatility, while in 1985, 1986 and 1987 the volatility of the S&P500 shares was significantly larger than that of the control group. However, the size of this increase was small, e.g. a 7% increase in the standard deviation for a daily differencing period. For longer differencing periods the increase in volatility was less. Harris's results may be due to a number of factors which changed in the early 1980s, e.g. the growth in foreign ownership of US equities (which is concentrated in the S&P500 shares), or the growth of index funds. Harris suggests that the small increase in relative short run volatility he found is due to either insufficient market liquidity to absorb the trades generated by index arbitrage etc in the short run, or the presence of a futures market speeding up the response of prices of shares in the index to new information (e.g. via index arbitrage). Harris pointed out that, since traders can arbitrage between shares when they construct portfolios, if index futures do increase the volatility of S&P500 shares, some of this increased volatility will have been transmitted to non-S&P500 shares. If this is the case, the results of cross section studies (such as those of Harris, 1989b), will understate the effect on the volatility of S&P500 shares.

Damodaran (1990) considered data for the five year period before the introduction of S&P500 futures on 21st April 1982, and the five years afterwards. He analyzed daily returns on the 378 companies that were in the S&P500 index throughout this ten year period, and the 699 firms that were quoted on the NYSE throughout this period and were never part of the S&P500 index. For each day, he computed two returns: the average unweighted return for the S&P500 stocks and for the other stocks. After the introduction of the S&P500 future, there was an insignificant rise in the variance of the unweighted daily average returns for the S&P500 shares, and a statistically significant fall in the corresponding variance for the non-index stocks. Thus, relative to other stocks, the variance of returns on S&P500 shares rose after the introduction of S&P500 futures.

Laatsch (1991) used daily returns on the shares in the MMI for 1982-6, and for two control groups of twenty shares each. The first control group contained matched shares (largely in other indices on which futures were already traded), and the second was a random selection of shares. The pre-futures data was used to fit the market model (i.e. $R_{jt} = \alpha_j + \beta_j R_{Mt} + \varepsilon_{jt}$) to each of the sixty shares. The prediction errors from each of these equations for the post-futures period were then analyzed. Laatsch found no evidence that the existence of a futures contract altered the beta values of the MMI shares or the control shares (i.e. systematic risk), nor that it increased the variance of these prediction errors (i.e. unsystematic risk).

Koch & Koch (1993) compared the volatilities of the shares in the S&P500 and MMI indices on eight days in 1987-8 with the volatilities on the same days of matched shares that were not in these indices. Volatility was measured as the natural logarithm of the ratio of daily highest price to the daily lowest price, and also by the daily price range. They found that when volatility was measured by the natural logarithm of the ratio of daily high and low prices, there was no evidence of a difference in volatility between index and non-index shares.

Gerety & Mulherin (1991) computed the returns on the Dow Jones using hourly and daily data. For each calendar year for 1974-89, they calculated the variances of these returns. Finally, they plotted the ratios of these annual variances against time. They reasoned that if the introduction of index futures in the US in 1982 led to an increase in intraday volatility, while interday volatility remained constant, this should show up as a jump in the variance ratios. Since the test uses the ratio of hourly and daily volatilities, any increase or decrease in general market volatility will cancel out. What they found was a secular trend in this ratio, with no jump in 1982. Therefore, they concluded that the existence of index futures did not create an increase in intraday spot volatility.

Kamara, Miller & Siegel (1992) considered daily closing values of the S&P500 index for 1976-88. They regressed monthly spot returns on five explanatory variables, and then examined the variance of the residuals before and after the introduction of futures trading. Including the 1987 Crash, there was an increase, while excluding the Crash, there was no change. Since futures have not been shown to cause the Crash, the authors concluded that futures trading did not increase the volatility of spot monthly returns.

Galloway & Miller (1997) investigated the introduction of S&P400 futures in February 1991 using daily data for 1990-2. They compared the change in volatility of the S&P400 index with that of a control sample of 100 medium sized US firms and another sample of 100 large US firms. There was no increase in the relative volatility of the S&P400 index, nor was there a relative change in beta or the volume of trading.

USA, Japan, Hong Kong, Australia and UK. Lee & Ohk (1992a) tried to control for the influence of other factors on volatility in a rather different way. They examined the introduction of index futures in five countries (Australia, Hong Kong, Japan, UK and USA) using daily data for the two years before and two years after the start of trading in index futures. To eliminate the effects of other sources of volatility they centered their data on the date when trading began in index futures, which differed between countries. They then constructed equally weighted and value weighted portfolios of the index values from the five spot markets for the four year period. The variance of daily returns on these five country portfolios before and after the introduction of futures trading were compared, and there was a significant increase when index futures existed. A GARCH model, with dummies for the existence of index futures, was fitted to the daily portfolio returns, and it was concluded that there was a significant rise in volatility after index futures were introduced. There was also a significant change in the autocorrelation structure of volatility; implying that shocks were more quickly absorbed into the indices.

Japan. Chang, Cheng & Pinegar (1999) analyzed daily data on 122 Japanese shares (95 shares in the Nikkei 225 index, and 27 other Japanese shares as a control sample) for 1982-91 to study the effects of the introduction of Nikkei 225 futures in Osaka and Singapore. They disaggregated the volatility of the two spot portfolios into cross-sectional volatility, and the average volatility of shares in the portfolio. The only change that occurred was when futures were introduced in Osaka, was this an increase in Nikkei 225 spot portfolio volatility and a drop in Nikkei 225 cross-sectional volatility relative to average volatility. This indicated that trading Nikkei 225 futures in Osaka led to a small increase in spot volatility.

USA, Japan, UK and Germany. Cohen (1999) used variance ratios for 1, 2, 5 and 20 days to examine whether the introduction of futures trading affected volatility and price discovery for the S&P500, Nikkei 225, FTSE 100 and DAX. He found that, although futures trading resulted in an increase in the standard deviation of spot returns in the USA, Japan and Germany; the variance ratios (2/1, 5/1 and 20/1 days) all declined, but not so much as to indicate negative autocorrelation. This provides a rejection of the view that futures trading destabilized the spot, while the lower variance ratios are consistent with improved price discovery.

d. Time Series Studies.   Some studies have used a fourth approach to study the effect of futures on spot volatility. This is to build a model which uses a variety of economic variables to explain spot volatility, and see if this requires the use of futures volume, open interest or volatility as explanatory variables. This approach assumes that any causality is from the futures market to increased volatility in the spot market, and not vice versa. It also moves away from studying the effect of the discrete event of introducing a futures market, and considers variables representing the level of activity of the futures market. Schwert (1990) mentions that, when spot volatility for the S&P500 is high, spot and futures volumes are also high, while Smith (1989) found that S&P500 futures volume had no effect on changes in the volatility of S&P500 spot returns.

USA.   Bessembinder & Seguin (1992) studied daily data on the S&P500 for 1978-89. Using an iterative procedure developed by Schwert, they studied the determinants of the conditional volatility of spot returns. They argued that the arrival of information can be proxied using spot volume, and disaggregated daily spot volume into a long run time trend (using a 100 day moving average), expected changes (using an ARIMA (0,1,10) model), and unexpected (residual) changes in volume. They allowed for the existence of futures trading by including dummy variables to accommodate shifts in the constant term and the slope coefficients of the three spot volume variables. Unexpected volume and the long run trend in volume were found to increase spot volatility, and these effects were reduced when futures were traded. Bessembinder & Seguin also found that futures trading reduced the constant term (that is, unconditional volatility). In addition, they examined the effect of the level of futures trading (disaggregated into long run, expected and unexpected changes, in the same way as spot volume), on spot volatility. Spot volume (long run, expected and unexpected) had a positive effect on spot volatility and unexpected futures volume also had a positive effect, while expected and long run futures volume had a negative effect. In addition, long run open interest had a negative effect on spot volatility. They concluded that futures trading appears to have caused a decline in spot volatility because it resulted in a deeper and more liquid equity market.

Brown-Hruska & Kuserk (1995) used daily data on S&P500 futures and the NYSE for 1982-90, and so all their data is after the commencement of S&P500 futures trading. They used Schwert's iterative procedure to examine the effects of the value of spot trading, futures trading and the ratio of these two values on the conditional variance of spot returns (measured using the S&P500 index). (They point out that no 'correct' ratio has been established in the literature for the relative volumes of spot and futures trading.) Using an ARIMA (0,0,10) model, each of these three explanatory variables was split into its expected and unexpected components. They found that unexpected spot and futures trading had a positive effect on spot volatility, which is consistent with the arrival of information affecting all three variables. Increases in the expected value of futures trading, relative to the value of spot trading, had a negative effect on spot volatility, while an increase in unexpected futures trading, relative to spot trading, had no effect on spot volatility. These results are not consistent with increases in futures trading destabilizing the spot market. Indeed, they suggest the reverse.

Darrat & Rahman (1995) studied hourly data on the S&P500 index for 1982-91. They investigated whether monthly futures volume or open interest was positively linked with monthly jump spot volatility (the number of hourly index returns whose absolute value exceeded a threshold.) The lagged variance of the term structure and the OTC index (purged of any effects already captured by futures volume or open interest) had a positive effect on spot jump volatility. However, neither lagged changes in futures volume, nor lagged changes in open interest affected spot jump volatility.

Choi & Subrahmanyam (1994) regressed the daily standard deviation of the bid-ask midpoints for the stocks in the MMI during 1984 on their price level, a time trend and variables to control for market wide changes in volatility. They found that the introduction of MMI futures had no effect on spot volatility.

Change, Chou & Nelling (2000) examined the effects of increased futures volatility on the hedging and speculative demand for futures. Using daily data on S&P500 futures for 1984-90, they regressed the long and short open interest of large hedgers on a number of variables, including expected and unexpected futures price volatility. This exercise was repeated for the long and short open interest held by large speculators and small traders. They found that, while an increase in unexpected volatility increased the demand for open positions by hedgers and speculators, hedging demand was dominant. This result indicates that when there is unexpected volatility, hedging (which is generally a stabilizing activity) and not speculation, is the dominant form of trading. This supports the view that futures do not destabilize the spot market.

Hong Kong. Kan (1997) studied daily data on 28 stocks in the Hang Seng index, and a control group of 30 other stocks for 1983-9. The daily variance of each stock was regressed on a Hang Seng constituent dummy, the stock's beta, the inverse of the share price, log of the market value of the company and the stock's trading volume. After allowing for these other influences on volatility, before futures trading began there was no difference in volatility between index and non-index shares; but the volatility of index shares was relatively lower once futures trading commenced.

Korea. Bae, Kwon & Park (2004) analyzed the introduction of Kospi 200 futures in May 1996 using daily data on the stocks in the index and a control group of non-index stocks for 1990-8. They regressed the standard deviation of each firm on the firm's beta risk, market value, inverse stock price and foreign exchange exposure, and concluded that the introduction of Kospi futures led to an increase in spot volatility, and an increase in the speed of adjustment to information.

Australia. Gannon (1995) used 15 minute returns on the All Ordinaries for 1992 to study the effect of futures volatility on spot volatility. This was done in two different ways. First, he fitted a GARCH (1,1) model to spot returns, with futures volatility (measured by the logarithms of the squared changes in futures prices) in the conditional variance equation. The inclusion of non-dummy variables in the conditional variance equation of a GARCH model makes interpreting the coefficients on such variables difficult. This is because the GARCH conditional variance equation involves a recursive relationship between the dependent and independent variables. Therefore, including current volume in this equation effectively includes all lagged values of volume, with an implied set of declining weights, Board, Sandmann & Sutcliffe (2001). The results of this study should be interpreted in the light of this problem. Second, he fitted a regression equation containing an ECM to spot volatility. Both of these analyses reached the conclusion that futures volatility had a positive effect on spot volatility, and also that spot volatility was higher in the first hour of trading. Thus he demonstrated that, as expected, both markets were volatile at the same time, and this does not constitute evidence that one market is destabilizing the other.

UK.   Board, Goodhart & Sutcliffe (1992) and Board & Sutcliffe (1992) studied daily data for the Financial Times All (FT-A) share index for 1978-91, and hourly data on the FTSE 100 index and future for 1984-91. Using daily data for the FT-A, they regressed various measures of spot volatility on a variety of explanatory variables, including a dummy for the existence of futures trading. They found no evidence of a rise in spot volatility following the introduction of futures trading. Using hourly data since 1984, they regressed various measures of spot volatility on a number of explanatory variables, including the volume of trading in index futures. They found an association between spot volatility and contemporaneous futures volume, but attributed this to the arrival of information affecting both markets, rather than futures trading increasing spot volatility. They also studied the effects of futures volume on spot volume volatility, where daily data was used to compute the monthly variances of spot volume for 1987-91. It was found that movements in futures volume were positively associated with movements in the volatility of spot volume, and this was attributed to both markets being affected by the arrival of information.

Antoniou & Holmes (1995b) used daily closing values for the FT 500 index for 1980-91 to compute daily logarithmic returns. They found that GARCH (1,1) was superior to other forms of GARCH (p,q), and that it was also preferable to GARCH-M (p,q). They included returns on the Unlisted Securities Market in the means equation as a proxy for market wide movements, as well as dummies for the 1987 Crash and the 1986 Big Bang. When a dummy for the existence of trading in FTSE 100 futures was included in the conditional variance equation it had a significantly positive coefficient, indicating that futures trading increased the volatility of daily spot returns. They also estimated the GARCH model separately for the periods before and after the introduction of trading in index futures. The unconditional variance rose after the introduction of index futures, indicating that futures trading increased spot volatility. The degree of autocorrelation in the unconditional variances also rose, while the effect of past values of the conditional variance fell slightly. These results were interpreted by Antoniou & Holmes as indicating that the increase in spot volatility after May 1984 was due to an increase in the flow of information, and not to the destabilizing effects of futures trading. They also found that before the introduction of index futures the spot market was integrated (shocks had a permanent effect on the variance), while after May 1984 the spot market was stationary (shocks had only a temporary effect on the spot variance).

Robinson (1994) considered daily data on the FT-A for 1980-93 to study the effect of the introduction of FTSE 100 futures in May 1984. He estimated an ARCH-M regression model for daily log returns, where the conditional variance equation included four dummy variables to allow for changes in monetary regime and a Big Bang dummy, as well as dummies on the constant and the ARCH variables to allow for the introduction of index futures. He found that two of the monetary regime dummies and the shift in the constant due to the introduction of index futures had a significant effect on the conditional variance. Big Bang had no effect on the conditional volatility, while the introduction of index futures did not have a significant effect on the coefficients of the ARCH variables. The conditional variance did not have a significant effect on returns, and this may be because risk should be measured by systematic rather than total risk. Robinson concluded that the introduction of futures trading led to a 17% decrease in spot volatility.

Holmes (1996a) examined the effects of the introduction and then delisting of FTSE Eurotrack futures on the volatility of the underlying FTSE Eurotrack index. He did this by fitting a GARCH (1,1) model to spot returns for the three sub-periods: before, during and after futures trading. To control for general changes in the level of market volatility, he included returns on the Morgan Stanley Capital International Europe index in the returns equation. Using daily closing values for 1990-4 (FTSE Eurotrack futures were traded from June 1991 to June 1992), he found that when futures were traded information was more quickly impounded into spot prices (α_1 increased and β_1 decreased), and when futures ceased to be traded the speed of information incorporation reverted to its slower pre-futures level.

Kyriacou & Sarno (1999) studied daily data on the FTSE 100 for 1992-5 using a simultaneous equations model. After controlling for the effect of FTSE 100 options trading; daily futures volume divided by open interest had a negative effect on daily spot volatility measured using the daily range; and a positive effect when volatility was measured using GARCH. When volatility was measured in two other ways, futures trading had no effect on spot volatility.

Hwang & Satchell (2000) investigated the introduction of FTSE 100 futures using daily data for 1984-96. A stochastic volatility model was used to split total spot volatility into fundamental volatility and transitory or noise volatility. They found that futures trading had a positive effect on fundamental volatility, and a negative effect on noise volatility, with no change in total volatility.

Board, Sandmann & Sutcliffe (2001) considered daily data on the FTSE 100 for 1988-95. Their methodology, which employed a stochastic volatility model, overcame the problems of the inclusion of non-dummy variables in the conditional variance equation, simultaneity bias and problems with the construction of the activity variables. After adjusting for the effects of information arrival and time trends, contemporaneous futures volume did not destabilize the spot market. They also demonstrated that using inappropriate estimation techniques can lead to incorrect conclusions concerning the effect of futures trading on spot volatility.

Spain.   Illueca & Lafuente (2003a) analyzed hourly data on the Ibex 35 for 1993-6 and found that total futures volume had no effect on contemporaneous spot volatility.

Using 15 minute data for 2000-2, Illueca & Lafuente (2003b) found that spot volatility increased with unexpected futures volume, but not with expected futures volume. This supports the price discovery role of futures markets, and the view that futures do not destabilize the spot market.

In November 2001 trading began in Ibex 35 mini futures, and Illueca & Lafuente (2004) analyzed 15 minute returns for 2001-2. The introduction of the mini futures may increase trading by small investors, who may be predominantly noise traders, leading to an increase in spot volatility. Illueca & Lafuente found no connection between Ibex 35 expected mini futures volume and spot volatility, and so mini futures did not destabilize the spot market. However, unexpected mini futures volume was positively associated with spot volatility, which is consistent with improved price discovery due to the introduction of mini futures.

Meneu & Torró (2003) analyzed daily returns data on the Ibex 35 for 1994-2001. After fitting a multivariate GARCH model with an asymmetric covariance matrix, they found that shocks in the futures market had a smaller effect on both spot and futures volatility than shocks in the spot market; while the response of the spot variance to shocks was larger than the response of futures volatility. They concluded that the futures market was a stabilizing influence, and that the main source of volatility was the spot market.

Switzerland.   Braund & Gibson-Asner (1998) examined daily data on the SMI for 1985-94, and found that the introduction of futures trading in November 1990 led to a reduction in spot return volatility.

Clerc & Gibson (2000) considered weekly data on the SMI for 1988-92, and discovered that the introduction of futures and options trading reduced the volatility of spot returns. It also led to a lowering of the Swiss risk premium.

USA, Japan, UK, Germany, Spain, Switzerland.   Antoniou, Holmes & Priestley (1998) studied the introduction of six index futures: S&P500, Nikkei 225 (in Osaka), FTSE 100, DAX, Ibex 35 and SMI. They used a GARCH (1,1) model, but with an additional term in the conditional variance equation to measure any asymmetric response to good and bad news. As well as the ARCH term involving lagged squared deviations, their model again included the lagged squared deviations, but only when the deviation was negative. The returns equation included day of the week dummies. They used daily data for the three years before and after the introduction of futures trading (and for the UK this required the use of the FT-A All Share index). They placed a dummy variable for the existence of index futures in the conditional variance equation, and estimated their GARCH model for each of the six countries using the six years of data. They found that the introduction of index futures decreased spot volatility in Germany and Switzerland, and had no effect on spot volatility in the USA,

UK, Japan and Spain. They then investigated the effects of the existence of a futures market on the asymmetric response of spot volatility to good and bad news. Fitting the GARCH model with the asymmetric term (but not the futures dummy) to data for the three years before the existence of futures trading, they found strong asymmetries for Germany, Japan, Spain and Switzerland, but not the USA and UK. In each case, bad news had a larger effect on spot volatility than did good news. The asymmetric response is consistent with the leverage effect in which good news increases spot prices, so decreasing leverage. This leads to lower volatility and a lower required rate of return (so tending to raise prices further). The reverse applies for bad news and, for the same size of price change, the effect on the rate of return will be larger than for good news. They then repeated this analysis for the three years after the introduction of index futures, and found that the significant asymmetric response remained only for Japan and Spain, while the effect was not quite significant in Switzerland. They conclude that index futures trading altered the way in which the spot market responds to news. The disappearance of the asymmetric response, particularly in Germany, is inconsistent with the leverage effect which is unaffected by the trading of index futures. Finally, they fitted the GARCH model with the asymmetric term to the three years of futures data after the introduction of futures, and found that bad news had a significantly larger effect on the conditional variance of futures returns in Japan, Spain and Switzerland; the same countries with an asymmetric response for spot volatility during this period.

USA, Japan, Hong Kong and UK. Lee & Ohk (1992b) analyzed the introduction of index futures in the UK (FTSE 100), USA (NYSE Composite), Japan (Topix) and Hong Kong (Hang Seng). Data for the four years before, and the three years after, the introduction of index futures was used in time series regressions. (It is not clear how the pre-futures index values in the UK were obtained, as the FTSE 100 began in the same year that the index futures were introduced.) Spot volatility was measured in two different ways using monthly and daily index values, while monthly values of seven macro-economic variables were used to control for other influences on spot volatility. Bayesian vector autoregression was used, and for both monthly and daily measures of monthly volatility, and for all four countries, there was no evidence that the introduction of index futures affected spot volatility. Lee & Ohk (1992b) also conducted a simple before and after comparison of spot volatilities for each of the four countries using volatilities computed from monthly and daily data. For Japan they found a significant rise in the volatility computed using daily data, while for the UK there was a significant fall in this figure, showing the dangers of not controlling for other potential influences on spot volatility.

US, Canada, Japan, UK, France and Germany. Antoniou, Koutmos & Pericli (2005) studied daily data for 1969-96 on the S&P500, Toronto 300, Nikkei 225, FTSE All Share, CAC Industrial and Frankfurt Commerzbank indices. The creation of a futures market may attract positive feedback traders, with the resulting high volatility in the futures market transmitted to the spot market via arbitrage links. Alternatively, a futures market may attract rational traders who tend to stabilize futures trading, and hence the spot market via arbitrage links. In all countries studied, except for the USA, there was a significant drop in positive feedback trading following the introduction of futures, and in no country did spot volatility increase. Positive feedback trading in the USA was not reduced by the introduction of futures, because it did not exist. Therefore, futures trading does not destabilize the spot market.

25 Countries.   Gulen & Mayhew (2000) considered daily data for 1973-97 on the stock indices in 25 different counties. Using a bivariate GARCH model, which allows the conditional covariance for each country with the world index to vary over time, they found that the introduction of the corresponding index future increased spot volatility in five counties (Finland, Germany, Hungary, Japan, and Spain), decreased spot volatility in eleven countries (Australia, Canada, Chile, Denmark, Malaysia, Netherlands, Norway, S. Africa, Sweden, Switzerland and the UK), and left spot volatility unchanged in nine counties (Austria, Belgium, France, Hong Kong, Israel, Italy, Korea, Portugal and the USA). For 17 countries they added expected and unexpected futures volume and open interest to the conditional variance equation of a GJR-GARCH model, and concluded that expected futures volume had a positive effect on spot volatility for Denmark, Germany and Hong Kong, and a negative effect for Austria and the UK. (Note the objections of Board, Sandmann & Sutcliffe, 2001, to including a non-dummy variable in the conditional variance equation; see chapter 12.1.2.)

The empirical studies of the existence of index futures on spot volatility are summarized in table 12.2. This reveals that over three quarters of the studies have found that trading in index futures did not result in an increase in spot price volatility.

Table 12.2: Effect of Index Futures on Spot Volatility

Study	Index	Period	Volatility Increase	No Change	Volatility Decrease
Experimental					
Friedman et al (1983, 1984)	None	None	–	–	✓
Forsythe, Palfrey & Plott (1984)	None	None	✓	–	–
Harrison (1992)	None	None	✓	–	–
Porter & Smith (1995)	None	None	–	–	✓
Before and After					
Santoni (1987)	S&P500	1975-86	–	✓	–
Becketti & Roberts (1990)	S&P500	1962-90	–	✓	–
Kamara, Miller & Siegel (1992)	S&P500	1976-88	–	✓	–
Baldauf & Santoni (1991)	S&P500	1975-89	–	✓	–
Brorsen (1991)	S&P500	1962-86	✓	✓	–
Maberly et al (1989)	S&P500	1963-88	✓	✓	✓
Edwards (1988a, 1988b)	S&P500, VLCI	1973-87	–	✓	–
Cohen (1999)	S&P500	1970-83	–	✓	–
Pericli & Koutmos (1997)	S&P500	1953-94	–	✓	–
Lee & Ohk (1992a)	NYSE Comp.	1980-84	✓	-	–
Lee & Ohk (1992b)	NYSE Comp.	1978-85	–	✓	–

Lockwood & Linn (1990)	DJIA	1964-89	✓	✓	–
Rahman (2001)	DJIA	1997-8	–	✓	–
Chan & Karolyi (1991)	Nikkei -SGX	1985-7	–	✓	–
Bacha & Vila (1994)	Nikkei -SGX	1986	–	✓	–
Brenner et al (1994)	Nikkei -SGX	1984-9	✓	–	–
Bacha & Vila (1994)	Nikkei -Osaka	1988	–	✓	–
Brenner et al (1994)	Nikkei -Osaka	1984-9	–	–	✓
Bacha & Vila (1994)	Nikkei -CME	1990	–	✓	–
Cohen (1999)	Nikkei - SGX	1972-89	–	✓	–
Lee & Ohk (1992a)	Topix	1986-90	✓	–	–
Brenner et al (1994)	Topix	1984-9	–	–	✓
Lee & Ohk (1992b)	Topix	1984-91	✓	–	–
Chen, Jarrett & Rhee (1992)	Topix	1987-9	–	✓	–
Freris (1990)	Hang Seng	1984-7	–	✓	–
Lee & Ohk (1992a)	Hang Seng	1984-8	–	–	✓
Lee & Ohk (1992b)	Hang Seng	1980-91	–	✓	–
Hodgson & Nicholls (1991)	All Ordinaries	1981-7	–	✓	–
Lee & Ohk (1992a)	All Ordinaries	1981-5	–	✓	–
Lee & Ohk (1992a)	FTSE 100	1982-6	–	✓	–
Lee & Ohk (1992b)	FTSE 100	1978-89	–	–	✓
Cohen (1999)	FTSE 100	1975-98	–	✓	–
Cohen (1999)	DAX	1970-91	–	✓	–
Reyes (1996)	CAC 40	1985-91	–	–	✓
Reyes (1996)	KFX	1986-92	–	✓	–
Cross Section					
Harris (1989b)	S&P500	1975-87	✓	–	–
Damodaran (1990)	S&P500	1977-87	✓	–	–
Kamara, Miller & Siegel (1992)	S&P500	1976-88	–	✓	–
Aggarwal (1988)	S&P500, DJIA	1981-7	–	✓	–
Koch & Koch (1993)	S&P500, MMI	1987-8	–	✓	–
Gerety & Mulherin (1991)	DJIA	1974-89	–	✓	–
Laatsch (1991)	MMI	1982-6	–	✓	–
Galloway & Miller (1997)	S&P400	1990-2	–	✓	–
Chang, et al. (1999)	Nikkei - Osaka	1982-91	✓	–	–
Chang, et al. (1999)	Nikkei - SGX	1982-91	–	✓	–
Lee & Ohk (1992a)	Five countries	1980-8	✓	–	–
Time Series					
Bessembinder & Seguin (1992)	S&P500	1978-89	–	–	✓
Darrat & Rahman (1995)	S&P500	1982-91	–	✓	–
Brown-Hruska & Kuserk (1995)	S&P500	1982-90	–	✓	–
Antoniou et al (1998)	S&P500	1979-85	–	✓	–
Change, Chou & Nelling (2000)	S&P500	1984-90	–	✓	–
Choi & Subrahmanyam (1994)	MMI	1984	–	✓	–
Antoniou et al (1998)	Nikkei-Osaka	1985-91	–	✓	–
Kan (1997)	Hang Seng	1983-9	–	–	✓
Bae, Kwon & Park (2004)	Kospi 200	1990-8	✓	–	–
Board et al (1992)	FTSE 100	1977-91	–	✓	–
Antoniou & Holmes (1995b)	FTSE 100	1980-91	✓	–	–

Robinson (1994)	FTSE 100	1980-93	–	–	✓
Antoniou et al (1998)	FTSE 100	1981-7	–	✓	–
Hwang & Satchell (2000)	FTSE 100	1984-96	–	✓	–
Kyriacou & Sarno (1999)	FTSE 100	1992-5	✓	✓	✓
Board, et al. (2001)	FTSE 100	1988-95	–	✓	–
Antoniou et al (1998)	DAX	1987-93	–	–	✓
Antoniou et al (1998)	Ibex 35	1989-95	–	✓	–
Illueca & Lafuente (2003a)	Ibex 35	1993-6	–	✓	–
Illueca & Lafuente (2003b)	Ibex 35	2000-2	–	✓	–
Illueca & Lafuente (2004)	Ibex 35	2001-2	–	✓	–
Meneu & Torró (2003)	Ibex 35	1994-2001	–	✓	–
Antoniou et al (1998)	SMI	1987-93	–	–	✓
Braund & Gibson-Asner (1998)	SMI	1985-94	–	–	✓
Lee & Ohk (1992b)	4 countries	1980-8	–	✓	–
Gulen & Mayhew (2000)	25 countries	1973-97	5	9	11
Antoniou et al (2005)	6 countries	1969-96	–	6	–

The studies of the introduction of futures trading have generally used the date on which trading commenced, rather than the earlier date when the future was announced. This is consistent with the view that it is the process of futures trading that has an effect. Many of these studies have ignored the simultaneous or subsequent introduction of trading of options on the index, although it is possible that this could have affected spot volatility..

Due to the newness of index futures, most of the empirical studies of spot volatility have placed considerable reliance on data for the period immediately after the introduction of index futures. However, because of the low futures volume and the inexperience of traders, data from this initial period may be atypical. Therefore, the results of the empirical studies reported above are questionable. However, the finding that futures do not increase spot price volatility is not confined to index futures. Evidence for other futures indicates it is the usual outcome of introducing a futures market.

When considering volatility from a regulatory perspective, it may be useful to distinguish three different types of volatility: fundamental volatility, transactions-induced volatility and noise-induced volatility, Harris (1989c). Fundamental volatility is caused by uncertainty over the value of the underlying assets (e.g. the arrival of information), and so is necessary if market prices are to correctly reflect fluctuations in the value of the underlying assets. Transactions-induced volatility is caused by the trading process, e.g. bid-ask bounce or short term order imbalances, and is undesirable. Noise-induced volatility is created by people who trade for pleasure, or on information that they believe is valuable, but which in fact is useless. Noise traders increase volatility, but their uninformed trading creates profits for the informed traders with whom they deal, so increasing the returns to becoming informed. The resulting increase in informed traders may lead to more informative prices, and so it is not clear that noise trading is undesirable.

To the extent that index futures have caused an increase in measured spot volatility via a price discovery role and a reduction in the stale prices effect, fundamental volatility is more accurately exhibited in the spot price, and this is beneficial. Thus, it is not sufficient to establish that index futures have led to a rise in spot volatility. Any such increase has to be analyzed into desirable and undesirable components. Regulators may wish to minimize transactions-induced volatility, irrespective of whether total spot volatility has increased or decreased, and to accept an increase in fundamental volatility even though total volatility has also increased. The previous academic literature summarized above has dealt only with total spot volatility.

Individual stock futures are traded in Australia, and studies by Dennis & Sim (1999), Lee & Tong (1998) and McKenzie, Brailsford & Faff (2001) considered the effect of the introduction of these equity futures on the returns' volatility of the underlying stocks. All of these studies found that futures trading did not increase spot volatility.

12.1.3 Influence of Programme Trading on Share Price Volatility

Some of the critics of index futures have argued that the programme trading associated with index arbitrage and portfolio insurance may be responsible for increasing the volatility of equity prices, Brady (1988). However, Miller (1990b) rejected index arbitrage as a destabilizing influence on share prices in the long run, although he did accept that it may cause an increase in minute-to-minute price volatility. For example, as suggested by Harris (1989b), if index arbitrage creates short term liquidity problems in the stock market, there will be a small rise in the short term price volatility of shares in the index. This effect will die out as new liquidity flows into the market.

Fremault (1991) constructed a theoretical model of the effects of index arbitrage on the volatility of spot and futures prices, and concluded that no clear theoretical predictions can be made about the effects. Spot price volatility may raise or fall, and futures price volatility may also rise or fall, so that the change in relative price volatility is unpredictable. She did find that index arbitrage can make some traders worse off, so providing a rationale for some groups to oppose programme trading.

Programme trading may increase the volatility of an index computed from the prices of the last trade in each share. Usually, roughly equal numbers of shares in the index were last traded at the bid and at the ask prices. In consequence, the bid-ask spread tends to cancel out, and the value of the index is equivalent to that which would have been computed if midquote prices at the time of the last trade had been used. However, just after a programme trade to buy (sell) many shares, most of the prices used in the index calculation will be ask (bid) prices. In consequence, the movement in the index will be exaggerated by about half the bid-ask spread. In addition to this bid-ask effect, a programme trade temporarily ensures that most of the last trade prices are recent or 'fresh', so removing the 'stale' price effect. Therefore, as a result of a programme trade, most share prices reflect their current, rather than historic, values. This will also tend to increase the volatility of an index computed using transactions prices as it reduces the reduction in measured volatility due to the use of stale prices.

USA.   Furbush (1989) used data for five minute intervals on the S&P500 index for 14th, 15th, 16th, 19th and 20th October 1987 - the period of the stock market crash and the few days just before. He concluded that on 14th, 15th and 16th, programme trading explained about half of the variation in the index, while on 19th and 20th (the days of the crash) programme trading explained only 5-10% of index variation. Thus programme trading was not a major player in the 1987 crash.

Harris, Sofianos & Shapiro (1994) analyzed the effects of programme trading on the volatility of the S&P500 index. To examine the bid-ask spread effect, they constructed two new indices, equivalent to the S&P500 but based on the current midquote prices (QC), and the midquote prices at the time of the last trade of the stock concerned (QL). This enabled them to disaggregate the current value of the S&P500 index which is based on the last trade prices (I), into a bid-ask bounce component ($I-QL$), a stale price component ($QL-QC$), and the true index (QC). Thus $I = (I-QL) +(QL-QC)+QC$. They found that the variance of one minute price changes in the S&P500 index (I) for June 1989 was 140% larger than for price changes in the midquote index (QL). Thus, fluctuations in the last trade prices due to switching between the bid and ask prices led to a considerable increase in measured spot volatility. The variance of current midquote prices (QC) was about 20% larger than that of midquotes at the time of the last trade (QL), indicating that the use of stale prices to compute the index led to a reduction in the measured variance. Thus, the increase in measured volatility for one minute returns due to bid-ask bounce considerably exceeded the decrease in measured volatility due to stale prices. Since programme trades refresh stale prices and induce a bid-ask effect, they are expected to increase the variance by 160%. Harris, Sofianos & Shapiro (1994) did not find price reversals in the 30 minutes after index arbitrage trades, and interpret this as evidence that such trades did not cause short term liquidity problems, leading to excess spot volatility.

Using daily data for 1987, Grossman (1988d) found no relationship between the daily volatility of the S&P500 index and the intensity of programme trading on the NYSE. Price volatility was measured in two different ways: the natural logarithm of H/L and $(H-L)/L$, where H is the daily high and L is the daily low. The intensity of programme trading was also measured in two different ways: the number of programme orders (purchases plus sales, measured in shares) divided by total NYSE orders (i.e. twice the daily volume), and the number of programme orders divided by the number of DOT orders. However, Grossman found a positive relationship between daily S&P500 volatility and the intensity of non-programme trading. There were statistically significant correlations between daily volatility and both DOT orders divided by NYSE orders, and non-programme DOT orders divided by NYSE orders.

Sultan, Hogan & Kroner (1995) used daily data on the S&P500 for 1988-91 to analyze the effects of programme trading on spot and futures volatility. They fitted a bivariate GARCH (1,1) model to spot and futures returns, with various measures of the volume of programme trading as additional explanatory variables in the conditional variance equation. (Note the objections of Board, Sandmann & Sutcliffe (2001) to including a non-dummy variable in the conditional variance equation; see chapter 12.1.2). The daily volume of programme trading was disaggregated into buy trades and sell trades, expressed as a proportion of the daily non-programme trading volume. Sultan, Hogan & Kroner found that the proportion of buy programme trades had a negative effect on the daily volatility of both spot and futures returns, while the proportion of sell trades had a positive effect. They interpreted this as consistent with a leverage effect in which buy programme trades increase spot prices, so decreasing leverage, and this leads to lower volatility. The reverse applies for sell programme trades. Finally, they found that the volume of non-programme trades was positively associated with spot and futures volatility, and interpret this as due to information arrival stimulating both price movement and trading.

Hogan, Kroner & Sultan (1997) studied daily data for 1988-91 on the S&P500. They used a bivariate GARCH (1,1) model with error correction terms, spot volume and day of the week effects in the means equations. They also included buy, sell, programme and non-programme volume variables in the conditional variance equations (see Board, Sandmann & Sutcliffe, 2001, concerning the problems this causes). They concluded that programme trading, particularly sell trades, is associated with higher spot and futures volatility. Since arbitrage trades pull both the spot and futures prices towards equilibrium, an increase in spot and futures volatility at these times is to be expected.

An SEC study in 1989, reported in Duffee, Kupiec & White (1992), also examined the effects of programme trading on the volatility of the NYSE and came to different conclusions from those of Grossman. Using data for 1988-9, they disaggregated programme trading into that due to three different motives: index arbitrage, asset allocation and other strategies (which included portfolio insurance). Both the total level of programme trading on the NYSE and that due to index arbitrage were significantly positively correlated with spot volatility, as measured by the daily standard deviation of hourly returns. Programme trading for 'other strategies' was marginally positively correlated with spot intraday volatility, while programme trading for asset allocation was not correlated with spot volatility.

Thosar & Trigeorgis (1990) argued that, once a share is included in an index on which an index future is based, it is subject to the effects of programme trading. They compared the volatility of shares before and after inclusion in the S&P500 index as a test of the effects of programme trading on spot volatility. They used data on 86 shares added to the S&P500 in 1982-6, and computed the standard deviations of daily returns for the 60 (and also 150) trading days before and after inclusion in the index. They found a statistically significant increase in volatility of about 6% following inclusion in the index, and they interpreted this result as due to some types of programme trading - portfolio insurance and certain kinds of asset allocation strategy.

Chan & Chung (1993) considered the relationships between the size of the spot-futures mispricing and the volatility of futures and spot prices. They used transactions data for the MMI index for 1984-5. Measuring volatility by the absolute values of five minute returns, they found that an increase in the absolute mispricing led to an increase in spot and futures volatility five minutes later. This finding is consistent with an increase in index arbitrage activity leading to a rise in the volatility of spot and futures prices. There was also some evidence that, when the mispricing requires short selling shares, the arbitrage response is weaker. An increase in spot and futures volatility led to a decline in the absolute mispricing five minutes later. Chan & Chung suggested this may be because higher volatility leads to an increase in the supply of arbitrage services, which results in a reduction in the mispricing. It should be noted that Chan & Chung used VAR as their estimation technique, and when Koch (1993) used SEM, most of these results were altered.

Conclusions.   There is evidence of a positive link between the volume of programme trading and spot volatility, but this is due to the bid-ask effect refreshing stale prices, and to arbitrage trades correcting mispricings. There is no evidence that programme trades destabilize the spot market.

12.1.4 Effect of Index Futures on Systematic Risk

Besides investigating the effect of index futures on total spot volatility, a number of studies have investigated the effects on part of volatility - systematic risk.

USA.   Martin & Senchack (1989) analyzed monthly returns for the shares comprising the MMI for 1976-87 using a 'before and after' methodology. They found that the average beta value of the twenty shares in this index rose by over 50% after the introduction of the index future in July 1984, while the average systematic risk as a proportion of total risk (i.e. $\beta_i^2 \sigma_M^2 / \sigma_i^2$), for the twenty shares in the MMI increased from 24% to 49%, i.e. a 100% increase.

A subsequent study by Martin & Senchack (1991) and Senchack & Martin (1990) used daily data on the twenty shares in the MMI for 1980-7. Since other index futures (where the index included the twenty MMI shares) commenced from February 1982 onwards, they analyzed the data for the transition period of February 1982 to July 1984 separately. They compared the change in the proportion of total risk that was systematic for the twenty MMI shares with that for a control group of twenty smaller shares not included in any index for which a futures or options contract existed (i.e. a cross section methodology). The systematic risk percentage rose by an average of 14% for the twenty MMI shares, but did not increase for the twenty non-index shares.

Martin & Senchack (1991) and Senchack & Martin (1990) argue that this increase in the proportion of risk that is systematic may be due to programme trading in the MMI shares associated with the creation of index futures involving these shares. To test this, following Grossman (1988d), they divided the trading days in 1987 into those with a high level of programme trading, and other days. They then calculated separately the average correlation between the returns on the MMI shares for the days with high and low levels of programme trading. This correlation was 66% higher on days with a high intensity of programme trading than on the other days. For the non-index control group, the average correlation fell by 16% when programme trading was intense. This suggests that the increase in the proportion of systematic risk for the

MMI shares is associated with being part of programme trades.

Damodaran (1990) considered daily returns on 378 firms in the S&P500 index and 699 non-index firms for 1977-87. He fitted the market model to each firm for the five year period before the introduction of S&P500 futures on 21st April 1982, and the five years afterwards. There was a statistically significant increase in the estimated betas after April 1982 for the S&P500 firms, while there was no significant change in the betas of the non-index stocks. This significant increase in S&P500 betas confirms the findings of Martin & Senchack (1989). Damodaran then investigated whether variables, other than the existence of S&P500 futures, could account for the rise in the beta values of the S&P500 firms. He considered five possible firm specific characteristics that may account for the higher betas: dividend yield, debt/equity ratio, cash/total assets ratio, book value of assets and repurchases/equity ratio. He concluded that none of the variables could account for the rise in the betas of S&P500 shares.

As reported earlier in this chapter, Laatsch (1991) for the MMI and Galloway & Miller (1997) for the S&P400 found no evidence that futures trading altered the beta values of the shares in the index.

Hong Kong. Kan & Tang (1999) studied daily data for 1980-92 on shares in the Hang Seng index, together with a control sample of non-index shares. They concluded there was no evidence that trading in Hang Seng futures increased the beta values of the stocks in the index.

Conclusions.. The US empirical studies have generally found that the importance of systematic risk for index shares has increased since the introduction of index futures, and that this effect is positively associated with the intensity of programme trading. However there are also some studies that have not found any change in beta.

12.2 Portfolio Insurance and Share Price Volatility

It has been argued that one form of programme trading (portfolio insurance) is especially responsible for large increases in equity price volatility, such as the stock market crash of October 1987, Brady (1988), Gammill & Marsh (1988) and Stoll & Whaley (1988b). If there is a demand for portfolio insurance (e.g. creating a synthetic put option by trading index futures and debt), there will be an increase in the volatility of share prices, Grossman (1988a, 1988b, 1988c). This is because portfolio insurers wish to sell when prices fall and buy when prices rise, so amplifying price movements, i.e. they are momentum rather than value traders (or positive rather than negative feedback traders).

Grossman (1988a, 1988b, 1988c) drew a distinction between the consequences of trading real securities and their synthetic equivalents. In particular, he considered the different effects of portfolio insurance using put options and using dynamic hedging strategies (trading stocks and/or index futures) designed to replicate a put option. He argued that buying put options informs the market about the trader's intention to sell shares if the price falls below the exercise price. Thus, the price of put options brings into balance the plans of portfolio insurers to sell shares, and of other traders to buy shares, when the price is low. If portfolio insurers use a synthetic strategy the market is not informed in advance of their intention to sell shares if the price drops. Such unexpected trades in futures and shares tend to exhaust the capital capacity (i.e. liquidity) of these markets. They may also appear to convey bad news about expected returns, so reducing the willingness of traders to buy from the portfolio insurers. As a result, share prices will fall further, so increasing the price volatility of shares and futures. This is the 'cascade theory' of the stock market crash of October 1987, i.e. a fall in stock market prices led portfolio insurers to sell index futures, resulting in a drop in their price, and, via index arbitrage, a further fall in stock market prices etc.

This explanation of the crash was tested by Santoni (1988), who examined two implications of the cascade theory: positive autocorrelation in futures returns, and spot returns leading futures returns. Using minute to minute data for the S&P500 for the 16th, 19th and 20th October 1987, he found no evidence in favour of the cascade theory. Neal (1993a) tested Grossman's hypothesis by examining the relationship between the volume of US programme trading for synthetic portfolio insurance and conditional spot volatility during the 1987 Crash. Using data for five minute periods and the volume of portfolio insurance for the contemporaneous and three preceding and subsequent five minute periods, he found no connection between volatility and portfolio insurance trades, and so rejected Grossman's hypothesis.

During the stock market crash of October 1987 Brady (1988) reported that relatively few investors were involved in insurance-based transactions, but those that were involved traded very heavily, with three insurers accounting for $2bn of stock sales and $2.8bn of futures sales. Portfolio insurance accounted for 21% of the volume of selling in US index futures markets on Friday 16th October. There was evidence that on Monday 19th October some US investors tried to pre-empt the expected NYSE fall by selling in London before the NYSE opened (one investor sold stock worth $95m). Leland & Rubinstein (1988) argued that, as portfolio insurance in the US accounted for at most 2% of market capitalization just before the crash, it could not be held responsible for a 20% fall in price. In the UK, portfolio insurance trading accounted for only about 5% of the trading in FTSE 100 index futures in the week of the crash, corresponding to only 1.5% of the trading in equities that week, Quality of Markets Unit (1987-8). Miller (1988) suggested there is no need for regulation to restrict portfolio insurance activity. The reasons he gave for this conclusion are that portfolio insurance, although large in absolute terms, was small in relative terms during the crash; the effect of the crash was of similar magnitude in countries without derivatives markets; there is no evidence that the timing of portfolio insurance sales was unduly influential; and the drawbacks of portfolio insurance are now obvious and the scale of such activity has declined dramatically of its own accord.

A suggested way of dealing with any adverse effects of synthetic portfolio insurance is 'sunshine trading'. This is the public announcement by a particular investor that they will initiate a trade of a given size at a specified time in the future. This would permit investors to distinguish between trades motivated by new information and those produced by activities such as portfolio insurance; and thereby increase the willingness of investors to trade with portfolio insurers (because it eliminates any suspicions of information imbalances between participants). However, sunshine trading is currently ruled out in the US.

Kodres (1994) looked for the presence of momentum (or positive feedback) traders in S&P500 futures using transactions data for 1989. Portfolio insurance is one possible reason for being a momentum trader. Momentum trading was defined as buying (selling) in the 15 minutes after a price rise (fall) of at least 0.25 index points during the previous 15 minutes. She found that about 16% to 20% of all active traders were classified as predominantly momentum or positive feedback traders. (A broadly similar proportion of active traders was classified as predominantly value, or negative feedback, traders.) The positive feedback traders accounted for 12% to 17% of the volume of trading by all active traders. Most of the positive feedback traders were customers, rather than locals or clearing members. Note that if traders break up large orders into a sequence of smaller orders, this could appear to be momentum trading. In October 1989 (the month of the mini-crash of Friday 13th October) there was a decline in the volume of momentum trading, suggesting that such trading was not a contributory factor to the mini-crash. To test the effects of feedback trading on futures volatility, Kodres estimated futures volatility in three different ways: the Parkinson high-low estimator, the Schwert iterative procedure and ARCH(1). Regressing estimated volatility for 15 minute periods on the trading volume of positive and negative feedback traders, as a proportion of total volume for the same 15 minute periods, she found mixed results. There was some weak evidence that, when both positive and negative feedback traders were more active, volatility was higher. Momentum traders were most active when futures volume was high, i.e. the futures market was 'thick'. Finally, Kodres found that after a 15 minute period when momentum traders accounted for an unusually large proportion of total volume, there was no tendency for price reversals during the subsequent 30 minutes, nor was there evidence that momentum traders lost money (at least over this 30 minute horizon). Overall, it appears that momentum traders do not have the damaging effects on volatility that theory predicts.

Conclusions. While synthetic portfolio insurance has the potential to destabilize the spot market, the available evidence suggests it was not responsible for the 1987 Crash,

12.3 Other Effects of the Existence of Index Futures

The introduction of index futures might affect a number of other aspects of the spot market besides its volatility; and a number of these possibilities have been investigated empirically.

12.3.1 Spot Quoted Bid-Ask Spread

Jegadeesh & Subrahmanyam (1993) looked at the impact of the introduction of trading in S&P500 index futures in April 1982 on the size of bid-ask spreads on the NYSE. The existence of index futures may lead to some informationless traders (e.g. hedgers) migrating from the spot to the futures market to take advantage of the much lower transactions costs. There are two reasons why this will cause an increase in spot bid-ask spreads. First, there will be a higher proportion of informed traders in the spot market, and spot bid-ask spreads will rise to protect market makers against information asymmetries. Second, the lower spot volumes will mean that the fixed costs of market makers must be recovered from a smaller number of trades, again leading to a rise in spot bid-ask spreads. However, the introduction of index futures also provides an opportunity for spot market makers to hedge the systematic risks involved in holding an inventory of shares, and this will lead to lower spot bid-ask spreads. Thus, the effect of introducing index futures on the size of the bid-ask spreads of the underlying spot market is an empirical issue.

The empirical analysis conducted by Jegadeesh & Subrahmanyam (1993) used end-of-the-month quoted bid-ask spreads for shares in the S&P500 index over the six months before and after the introduction of S&P500 index futures, and for a control sample of non-S&P500 shares traded on the NYSE. After controlling for the effects of changes in the variance of spot returns, the level of spot prices and spot volume, the proportionate spot quoted bid-ask spreads showed a statistically significant (though economically insignificant) rise after the introduction of S&P500 index futures. This suggests that the effects of the migration of informationless traders from the spot to the futures market dominated the effect of hedging by market makers, and this is consistent with the evidence that equity market makers do not hedge their inventory using equity options, Board & Sutcliffe (1995b, 1998).

The effect of the introduction of futures trading on spot quoted bid-ask spreads was also studied by Choi & Subrahmanyam (1994). In addition to the effects of the migration of uninformed traders to the futures market and the use of futures for hedging by equity market makers considered by Jegadeesh & Subrahmanyam (1993); they considered that a futures market may stimulate additional trading on market-wide information. Such informed futures trading may then spill over into the spot market via index arbitrage, leading to a widening of the spot bid-ask spread and an increase in spot volume. Thus, they had three distinct hypotheses: (a) the migration of uninformed traders to the futures market increases spot bid-ask spreads and decreases spot volume, (b) the use of futures for hedging reduces spot bid-ask spreads and leaves spot volume unchanged, and (c) trading on market-wide information in the futures market widens the spot bid-ask spread and increases spot volume. They used quote data on stocks for 1984 (seven months before the introduction of the MMI future, and five months afterwards) to test these hypotheses. They controlled for the effects on the bid-ask spread of the price level, spot returns volatility, spot volume and market-wide factors unconnected with the existence of index futures. The regression results indicated that the introduction of MMI index futures led to a statistically significant increase in the quoted bid-ask spread for the 20 constituent stocks of the MMI. However, this increase was under one cent, and may be viewed as economically insignificant, which is the same conclusion reached by Jegadeesh & Subrahmanyam (1993).

12.3.2 Spot Volume

Damodaran (1990) studied daily returns and the daily value of shares traded (relative to market capitalization) for 378 shares in the S&P500 index and 699 non-index shares for the five years before and after the introduction of S&P500 futures in 1982. In the later five year period, the value of the S&P500 shares traded (relative to market capitalization), rose by 98%, while the value of non-index shares traded (relative to market capitalization), rose by only 42%. Compared with the non-index stocks, there was a statistically significant increase in the value of shares traded (relative to market capitalization) for the S&P500 shares. This may be due to the introduction of S&P500 index futures, although it could also be due to the rapid growth of index funds in the early 1980s.

12.3.3 Variance Ratios

Damodaran (1990) also studied, for each firm, the variance of returns computed over twenty days, divided by the variance of daily returns multiplied by twenty. If share prices fully adjust to new information and returns are independent over time, this variance ratio should be one. For the S&P500 shares, the unweighted average variance ratio fell by 2.9% to 0.9661 after the introduction of futures trading, while the corresponding figure for non-index shares rose by 0.5% to 0.9321. He interpreted this result as indicating a rise in information noise due to the introduction of index arbitrage and portfolio insurance. However, other interpretations are possible, e.g. an increase in the bid-ask spread for S&P500 shares (as found by Jegadeesh & Subrahmanyam, 1993).

12.3.4 Trade Duration

Taylor (2004a) used the autoregressive conditional duration (ACD) model to investigate the determinants of the length of the time gaps between adjacent spot trades; termed trade duration. For the stocks in the FTSE 100 for 1998 trade duration exhibited an inverted U-shape, with duration lowest at the open and close. Therefore it could be explained by the bid-ask spread and trade volume; both of which have a strong daily U-shape. In addition, Taylor found that trade duration dropped when there are spot-futures mispricings. This relationship was non-linear, with a substantial increase in trade duration occurring only when the mispricing exceeded arbitrage transaction costs. Taylor then argues that modelling trade duration is equivalent to modelling the inverse of the instantaneous conditional spot return volatility. Therefore, the bid-ask spread, trade volume and arbitrage opportunities are determinants of spot volatility.

12.3.5 Spot Day of the Week Effects

Hiraki, Maberly & Taube (1998) analyzed daily data on the Nikkei 225 index for 1976-96. They found that, after the introduction of trading in Nikkei 225 index futures in Singapore in 1986, the Tuesday effect in the Japanese stock market disappeared. This is attributed to the major structural changes in the Japanese equity markets at this time, of which trading index futures was one.

12.4 Linkages between Equity and Futures Markets

The introduction of markets in index futures from the early 1980's onwards has led both to interactions between the spot and futures markets, and to an interest by regulators in controlling any possible harmful influences of this new derivative instrument on the established equities markets, Board, Goodhart & Sutcliffe (1991). The stock market crash of October 1987 has been blamed on index futures, and this led to a number of regulatory changes in the US to deal with this supposed problem. This section will first consider linkages between the spot and futures markets that are generally accepted to be beneficial and worthy of encouragement. Second, various potentially harmful linkages will be discussed.

12.4.1 Beneficial Linkages

Most of the beneficial linkages between spot and futures markets have been considered at length elsewhere in this book, and so will only be briefly mentioned here.

a. Hedging.   The use of hedging to reduce risk is a major reason for trading index futures. A key factor in the effectiveness of hedging is the stability of the basis, i.e. the current futures price minus the spot price, (see chapter 9). The usefulness of index futures for hedging is improved by stabilizing the relationship between the futures and spot prices. One aspect of promoting this stability is the removal of arbitrage opportunities by facilitating the arbitrage process. The introduction of index futures provided a vehicle for market makers to hedge their share holdings, and this risk reduction for market makers may have resulted in a drop in the bid-ask spread in the spot market, Kling (1986).

b. Arbitrage.   Arbitrage ties the spot and futures markets together, so stabilizing the basis. Arbitrage also adds liquidity and risk-bearing capacity to the spot and futures markets, Fremault (1991). Holden (1995) developed a model in which arbitrage is likened to market making. Market makers supply liquidity to traders in a single security who arrive at different times, while arbitrageurs supply liquidity to traders in different securities who arrive at the same time. Thus, arbitrage activity is seen as a normal feature of well functioning markets, rather than as a manifestation of inefficiency.

A number of empirical studies has looked for departures from arbitrage-free pricing for index futures (see chapter 4). The results are not clear cut, but they generally support the view that, although the futures and spot prices are highly correlated, some arbitrage opportunities have existed in all the countries studied, even after allowing for transactions costs. A study of the size effect over the turn-of-the-year in US shares returns (i.e. small firms have higher returns than large firms around the 1st January) by Maberly and Maris (1991) found that this anomaly is much reduced since the introduction of index futures in 1982. They suggest this may be due to futures facilitating the exploitation of the difference in returns between large and small firms at the turn-of-the-year, for instance, by selling S&P500 futures and buying Value Line futures. The changes in futures prices induced by this trading will then feed through to the stock market via stock index arbitrage.

c. Liquidity. The creation of markets in index futures attracts additional traders and new capital into trading equity-based securities. This creates extra liquidity which makes it easier for the stock market to absorb large trades, such as programme trades, without a substantial price impact (Grossman & Miller, 1988). The low transactions costs per trade of index futures means that large trades can be split into a number of smaller transactions, so reducing the demands on market liquidity (since no single investor is required to act as counterparty to the large trade), Grossman (1988a).

d. Spot Volume. The existence of index futures allows traders who wish to participate in movements in the market as a whole to do this more effectively through index futures than by buying shares (e.g. by creating a synthetic index fund using index futures and debt, see chapter 10.2.9). This diverts trading volume away from the stock market. However, the existence of index futures also allows index arbitrage, which increases volume in both the stock and futures markets. In addition, the use of futures markets to hedge the risk of a portfolio of shares can increase the volume in both markets. On Monday 13th April 1992 trading on the CME was halted at noon for the rest of the day because of flooding of the exchange from the Chicago loop tunnel. Kuserk & Locke (1994) found that NYSE volume fell during this closure of the CME, and the size of this fall exceeded that attributable to index arbitrage. Thus, it appears that the closure of the futures market discouraged spot trading. The index futures markets may have a substantial effect on the average volume of shares traded, and also on the variability of volume. If futures trading increases equity volume this will also increase stock market liquidity, and reduce the price effect of large trades.

e. Information and Price Discovery. The futures prices can reflect additional information, over and above that already reflected in the spot price, and so can serve as a leading indicator for the spot price, see chapter 6. US studies suggest that the prices of index futures lead the corresponding market index by a few minutes.

f. New Financial Instruments. The existence of index futures has given rise to index arbitrage, which has created a need to trade baskets of shares corresponding to the shares in the index. To this demand from arbitrageurs to trade baskets of shares must be added that from portfolio insurers and others. This has led to proposals for new equity products, e.g. warehouse receipts, securitized open-ended mutual funds, package trading, super shares and index participations (these were initially blocked in the US by regulatory disputes, but index participations in the Toronto 35 index have been actively traded since 9th March 1990), Harris (1990a), Kupiec (1990), Rubinstein (1989) and Stoll (1987). Index participations are now widely traded in many countries under the name exchange traded funds. It is possible that, for some purposes, these new equity instruments will replace index futures (e.g. in the creation of an index fund).

g. Trading Facilities.   The need for the rapid execution of programme trades in connection with index arbitrage and other strategies has encouraged the development of equity trading facilities such as DOT in the US.

h. Short-termism.   R. Miller (1990) has argued that, as fund managers increasingly use index futures, the charge of short-termism against City institutions may be reduced. Without the use of index futures, implementing the timing decisions of a fund requires the purchase or sale of shares in many companies for reasons largely unconnected with the performance of that company. This can give the appearance that funds are short term investors, as they repeatedly buy and sell shares. However, if timing decisions can be implemented using stock index futures, the long term investment of the fund in chosen companies will become more apparent. Such a development would mean a transfer of volume from the equity market to index futures, and so the equity market will become less liquid. This would lead to higher market impact costs, so widening the band within which futures and equity prices can fluctuate before arbitrage is triggered.

12.4.2 Potentially Harmful Linkages

Most of the potentially harmful linkages involve the introduction of distortions into the behaviour of spot prices by the trading of index futures.

a. Price Volatility.   It has been alleged that the existence of a futures market increases the price volatility of the underlying asset. While this is theoretically possible, the empirical studies indicate that futures do not increase the price volatility of the corresponding spot market, see chapter 12.1.

b. Expiration.   There is some US and Canadian evidence of a short term increase in the price volatility of the index when index futures are delivered (e.g. the 'triple witching hour'), but this is small in magnitude, Chamberlain, Cheung & Kwan (1989), Edwards (1988a, 1988b), Feinstein & Goetzmann (1988), Hancock (1993), Herbst & Maberly (1990, 1991), Merrick (1989), Santoni (1987), Sofianos (1994), Stoll (1986, 1988), Stoll & Whaley (1987a, 1987b, 1990a, 1991) and Whaley (1986). There is also an increase in volume for both shares and futures at this time.

USA.   Chen & Williams (1994) found that the switch on 19th June 1987 in the settlement time for S&P500 futures and NYSE Composite futures and options from the Friday close to the Friday open did not reduce the daily volatility for the final Friday, but did result in less volatility at the Friday close, and more volatility at the

Friday open. For S&P500 index options introduced after July 1992, settlement is at the Friday open, rather than the Friday close.

The increase in volatility at delivery may be due to the use of cash rather than physical settlement, Petzel (1989, p. 104). With physical delivery, every position that remains open requires a physical transaction at expiration, while with cash settlement some positions may just be cash settled. Arbitrageurs will usually try to undertake an offsetting transaction in the spot market, rather than accept cash settlement of their futures position. Therefore, it is harder to predict the trades in the underlying spot market at delivery if there is cash settlement.

Hancock (1991) studied the effect of the expiration of S&P500 index futures options on the volatility of the underlying S&P500 index future, and found some evidence of an increase in volatility.

Sultan, Hogan & Kroner (1995) used daily data on the S&P500 for 1988-91 to December 1991 to look for a change in the volatility of spot and futures returns on the expiry day and during the expiry week. Using a bivariate GARCH (1,1) model, they found that expiration had no effect on volatility. This finding may be because the study used daily rather than 5-minute returns, and because the data is all post 1987.

Hong Kong. Chow, Yung & Zhang (2003) studied the expiration effects of Hang Seng futures using 5 minute returns for 1990-9. The EDSP is computed as the average price over the entire last trading day. From 1993, Hang Seng index options also expired on the same day as index futures. On the expiration day there was no change in returns or spot volume. However, there was a modest increase in spot return volatility, relative to the previous day.

UK. In a study of the FTSE 100, Karakullukcu (1992) found little evidence of an increase in price volatility or volume at the time the EDSP was calculated. This may be because the settlement price in the UK is calculated in the middle of the morning, rather than at the close of trading.

Germany. Schlag (1996) used data on the DAX for 1991-4. The EDSP of DAX futures is computed on Fridays, using the opening prices of the stocks in the index. He found that on expiration Fridays, volume in the DAX stocks was over three times higher than normal, while there was an increase in the delay in the opening of many index stocks. However, there was no increase in price volatility for the first hour of trading on Fridays.

Futures expiration can lead to an increase in the price volatility of equities, but is a minor problem which can easily be dealt with by ensuring that the expiration times of the various derivatives are non-synchronous.

c. Portfolio Insurance. By selling index futures (or shares) when share prices fall, portfolio insurance has the potential to be destabilizing. However, it has been rejected as a prime cause of the stock market crash of October 1987, Leland & Rubinstein (1988) and Miller (1988).

d. Relative Share Prices. The creation of a future on an index which covers only a selection of the shares quoted on a stock market has the potential to alter the prices of shares in the index, relative to non-index shares. Damodaran (1990) considered the effect of introducing index futures on the returns of shares in the index. He found that, in the five year period after April 1982, the unweighted average daily return on the S&P500 shares rose by 88%, while that for the non-index shares rose by only 38%. In consequence, although there was no significant difference between the average returns before April 1982, after this date the S&P500 shares had significantly higher returns than the non-index shares. This may be because the demand for shares in the index was increased in the first half of the 1980's by the growth of index funds, rather than because of the introduction of index futures.

A number of studies have looked at a slightly different question. These papers, which have analyzed the effect on the price of a share of inclusion in the S&P500 index, are summarized in chapter 1 of Sutcliffe (1997). In some of these papers the results can be disaggregated into those before and after the introduction of a future on the S&P500 index. This event appears to have had no effect on the results.

There has also been a study of relative share prices during the stock market crash of October 1987. Blume, MacKinlay & Terker (1989) investigated the relative price changes of shares in the S&P500 index and non-S&P500 shares of equivalent market capitalization during the stock market crash of October 1987. After recomputing the S&P500 index to adjust for 'stale' prices, they found the S&P500 stocks declined by 7% more (i.e. -20% not -13%) than the non-S&P500 stocks on Monday 19th October and, in the early trading on Tuesday 20th October, recovered almost all of this loss. After controlling for differences in market capitalization, volume was consistently higher for the S&P500 stocks throughout these two days. Measuring buying pressure for a given period of time as the dollar volume at the ask price, selling pressure as the volume at the bid price, and order imbalance as buying pressure minus selling pressure, they found a strong positive correlation between order imbalance and returns for both the S&P500 index and the non-S&P500 index. When Blume, MacKinlay & Terker (1989) conducted a cross section analysis of the relationship between the returns and order imbalance for individual stocks, they also found a positive correlation. They interpreted these results as consistent with the hypothesis that the S&P500 shares fell more on Monday 19th October because the market was unable to absorb the heavy selling pressure on these shares. Such selling pressure may have been induced by index-related strategies, such as portfolio insurance. However, on the following day, the prices of these shares bounced back. Thus, for a brief period, the relative prices of shares in the S&P500 index and other NYSE shares were distorted. (Kleidon & Whaley, 1992, have rejected this price pressure hypothesis, see chapter 6.7.)

Board, Goodhart & Sutcliffe (1992) and Board & Sutcliffe (1992) examined the effect of FTSE 100 futures volume on the level of the FTSE 100 index, after controlling for market wide movements (as measured by the level of the FT-A index). Using daily data for 1984-91, they found a very small, but statistically significant, positive relationship between futures volume and the FTSE 100 index. This may be due to a 'large firm' effect, an increased demand for index stocks due to arbitrage and a rise in liquidity, or to the growth of index funds.

e. Competition for Capital. US regulators were concerned that the existence of index futures would divert scarce risk capital from investment in shares to investment in futures. However, the simplistic view that the total supply of investment funds will be reduced is now widely rejected, Jaffee (1984), Stein (1986). The purchase or sale of a future involves the payment of initial margin and variation margin, and the setting aside of a sum of money to cover margin calls. None of these amounts is lost to the capital market. The money received by the clearing house as initial margin earns interest for either the relevant member of the clearing house, or the clearing house itself. Variation margins are a zero sum game and the precautionary balances held by the trader to meet margin calls can be invested to earn interest. Thus, all of the capital involved in futures trading is lent out to earn interest. Powers & Castelino (1991) have suggested that, by allowing banks and brokers to hedge their risks, and by enabling the development of new savings products, futures have increased the level of capital formation.

A more sophisticated concern is that index futures might absorb capital that would otherwise go to finance high risk ventures. If this were true, the existence of index futures will change the distribution of investment away from risky investment and towards safer investments. However, futures permit the reallocation of risk between traders, with hedgers reducing their overall risk. Such investors may now be prepared to invest in risky projects, whereas previously they were not. Therefore, although there is no reason to expect a decline in the amount of risk capital available, the suppliers of such capital may change and, because of differences in preferences, the relative costs of debt and equity may alter.

f. The EDSP. If an open position in index futures is held until delivery, the holder has an incentive to influence the exchange delivery settlement price (EDSP). The manipulation of the EDSP was considered in chapter 11.9.

12.5 Conclusions

Apart from portfolio insurance and expiration effects, the available evidence supports the view that index futures do not have an adverse effect on the spot market. Portfolio insurance (as practiced in the first half of the 1980's) was seriously damaged by the 1987 Crash, and is unlikely to be a problem in the future; while the increase in volatility at expiration is a small problem that has been reduced in the US by altering the timing of the calculation of the EDSP. While other negative effects from index futures are possible, they have not occurred in practice. Index futures bring many benefits which, although hard to quantify, are substantial.

Questions

1   Enrico (Ratzo) Rizzo wishes to diversify his portfolio internationally, but he is concerned about exchange risk.
    a   Explain how he could reduce his foreign exchange exposure by trading stock index futures rather than shares.
    b   Discuss the advantages and disadvantages of the strategy used in part (a).

2   Explain the benefits and costs of using stock index futures in the management of a large investment fund.

3   'Index futures can, with advantage, replace a well diversified portfolio of shares'. Discuss.

4   Discuss the case for launching a successful global index futures contract (i.e. a future based on some international index of equity markets).

5   Explain how the possibilities of early unwinding or rollover affect the arbitrage decision in stock index futures.

6   How does the early unwinding and rollover of index futures positions:-
    a.   tend to prevent mispricings from changing sign.
    b.   reduce the size of the no-arbitrage band.
    c.   tend to reduce any increase in volatility at delivery.

7   How do futures markets differ from forwards markets?

8   Explain how it is possible to insure the value of a share portfolio, and discuss the usefulness to fund managers of such strategies.

9   Hedging is merely portfolio theory applied to spot assets and futures contracts? Discuss.

10   How might the effectiveness of a hedge using stock index futures be measured? What factors affect hedging effectiveness?

11   Should hedging be performed by firms rather than shareholders? Give reasons for your answer.

12   "Firms are exposed to foreign currency risk, interest rate risk, commodity price risk, energy price risk, stock market risk etc. With the development of derivatives

(e.g. futures markets) these risks can be hedged away." As the newly appointed chairman of Branson Brothers Ltd (a publicly quoted company), explain which one of the following hedging strategies you would follow and why:- (a) hedge all risks, (b) hedge some risks (which ones), or (c) hedge no risks.

13 How might the risk-minimising hedge ratio be estimated? Explain various ways of estimating this number, and consider their advantages and disadvantages.

14 "Stock index futures are merely a derivative product that does not provide any additional useful functions not already available by combining existing financial instruments." Discuss.

15 Explain how an investor can use stock index futures to achieve the following:
    a   control the risk of a stock portfolio
    b   create constant proportion portfolio insurance
    c   alter the allocation of funds across major asset classes.
    d   Rebalance a fund to maintain the target allocation of funds between different classes of asset.

16 Explain how an investor can use stock index futures to achieve each of the following:-
    a   Separation of stock selection from market timing decisions
    b   Indirect purchase or short sale of shares
    c   Creation of an index fund
    d   Reduction of foreign exchange risk when investing overseas.

17 Explain how an institutional investor or investment bank can use stock index futures to achieve each of the following:-
    a   Delay paying capital gains taxation
    b   Hedge equity index swaps
    c   Accumulate money for investment
    d   Decentralise risk management

18 Explain how an investor can use stock index futures to achieve each of the following:
    a   Anticipating cash inflows into an investment fund.
    b   Investment in foreign equities.
    c   Hedged dividend capture, i.e. the receipt of dividends by tax exempt institutions.
    d   Create a guaranteed funds, i.e. a fund which guarantees to repay at least the initial investment.
    e   Alpha funds, i.e. funds with a positive alpha and zero beta.

19 Explain how an investor can use stock index futures to achieve each of the following:-
   a   Tilt a fund towards or away from a particular market sector or country
   b   Avoid restrictions on investing in particular shares or countries
   c   Global diversification
   d   Alter the form of the increase in value, e.g. capital gains, dividends, interest

20 a   Explain how the establishment of an arbitrage position in stock index futures contains an embedded option to unwind early or rollover.
   b   How does the presence of this embedded option affect arbitrage activity?
   c   How might an arbitrageur seek to value this embedded option?

21 Explain how options can be used in each of the following situations:-
   a   Laura Burney wishes to make money from her forecast that the volatility of returns on shares in Brixham Bricks will be much higher than usual over the next 2 months.
   b   Billy Caufield wishes to profit from his forecast that dividend announcements for the top 100 UK companies will be substantially lower than expected over the next 4 months.
   c   Edward Lewis wishes to hedge the risk of a share holding in Catford Catering over the next fortnight.
   d   Kevin McCallister wishes to short sell shares in Millwall Milk for the next 4 weeks, but is not allowed to sell shares short.

22 Rick Blaine inherits a 5% holding in Blaine Industries, that is currently worth £2 billion. The estimated beta value of Blaine Industries is 1.0, and Rick's investment objective is to receive the market rate of return with minimum risk. What investment advice would you give to Rick and why, in each of the following situations:-
   a.   He can sell his holding in Blaine Industries, although he cannot short sell any shares in the company.
   b.   The terms of his inheritance prevent him from selling his holding in Blaine Industries.

23 Explain the following concepts in hedging using futures contracts:-
   a   Hedging effectiveness.
   b   Hedge ratio.
   c   Cross-hedge.
   d   Basis risk.

24 a   What is the difference between an arbitrage opportunity and a mispricing?
   b   How do the size, frequency, and direction of mispricings change with contract maturity?

   c   What is an arbitrage portfolio, and what are its advantages and
        disadvantages?
   d   In the context of arbitrage, distinguish between computer trading and
        programme trading.

25 Explain the following terms used in derivatives markets:-
   a   Initial margin and variation margin.
   b   Price limits and position limits.
   c   Open interest and volume.
   d   Clearing house and delivery.

26 Explain the following terms used in derivatives markets:-
   a   Contract multiplier and tick size.
   b   Scalping and day trading.
   c   Mispricings and arbitrage opportunities.
   d   Double auction markets and continuous markets.

27 a   Explain what is meant by an exchange traded fund (ETF), and how an ETF
        resembles and differs from an index future.
   b   How can ETFs be used by traders and investors to replace trading in shares
        and futures?

28 a   Rayette Dipesto is the finance director of 5EP Ltd, and has hedged all the
        firm's foreign exchange exposure using foreign exchange futures. About half
        of these trades resulted in the company being worse off than if there had been
        no hedging. This indicates there is plenty of room for improvement in
        Rayette's financial management. Discuss.
   b   Rayette now considers using options for this hedging. What effect is this
        likely to have on hedging costs and benefits?

29 a   'Stock index futures play a useful 'price discovery' role as futures prices lead
        share prices'.
   b   'Arbitrage between stock index futures and shares ensures the no-arbitrage
        pricing condition is met'. Discuss these contrasting views of the relationship
        between futures and share prices.

30 a   Would you expect to find negative, positive or zero first order
        autocorrelation between price changes for (i) index futures and (ii) a stock
        market index? Give reasons for your answer.
   b   Describe a situation in which autocorrelation in share returns is consistent
        with market efficiency.

31 Most indices underlying stock index futures are arithmetic capitalization-weighted

price indices. What are the reasons for this dominance?

32 Many empirical studies of stock index futures have found that arbitrage opportunities have existed. What conclusions might be drawn?

33 a   What types of spread trade are possible using index futures?

    b   Explain the alternative rules a trader may use for setting spread ratios.

34 a   Explain a low risk trading strategy using both index futures and the index basket of shares designed to profit from each of the following forecasts:

        i   You expect that in 6 weeks time the Government will announce a change in the law which will lead to an increase in dividends.

        ii   While economic commentators strongly expect the Monetary Policy Committee of the Bank of England to announce a rise in interest rates in 4 weeks time; you expect interest rates to be unchanged.

        iii   The stock market index will drop sharply in about 8 weeks time.

        iv   In 5 weeks time, instead of an average delay of 70 days between a dividend being announced and paid, this will drop to 50 days.

    b   Explain why your trading strategies in part (a) are low risk, and outline higher risk trading strategies using either index futures or the index basket which are designed to profit from each of the situations described in part (a).

35 a   Explain a trading strategy for Janet Colgate using both index futures for a particular delivery date and the index basket to profit from each of the following forecasts:-

        i   Tomorrow the riskless interest rate will be cut.

        ii   Later this week, the UK stock market is expected to rise, when the government announces that the UK is to adopt the euro.

        iii   Next week, the government will announce a change in the tax system which will encourage companies to declare much higher dividends.

    b   Explain a trading strategy for Janet Colgate using just index futures for two or more different delivery dates to profit from each of the following forecasts:-

        i   Tomorrow the riskless interest rate will be cut.

        ii   Later this week, the UK stock market is expected to rise, when the government announces that the UK is to adopt the euro.

        iii   Next week, the government will announce a change in the tax system which will encourage companies to declare much higher dividends.

Glossary

90/10 fund. A sum is invested in fixed interest securities to guarantee the initial investment at a specified date (e.g. 90% of the money), and the remainder (e.g. 10%) is used to trade futures.

Anticipatory hedge. A trader expects to make a spot transaction at a future date and opens a futures position now to protect against a change in the spot price.

Arbitrage. The simultaneous purchase of one asset against the sale of the same or equivalent asset from zero initial wealth to create a riskless profit due to price discrepancies.

Arbitrage band. The band around the no-arbitrage price within which arbitrage transactions are not worthwhile.

Arbitrage channel. See arbitrage band.

Arbitrage risk. While the arbitrage transaction is riskless in theory, in practice, some risk may be present.

Ask price. The price at which a market maker is willing to sell. Also called the offer price.

Back contract. See deferred contract.

Backwardation. This occurs when the spot price exceeds the current price of a futures contract. The opposite of contango.

Basis. The difference between the cash price of a financial instrument and the price of a particular futures contract relating to that instrument. Also known as a crude basis or simple basis.

Basis risk. The possibility that the value of the basis will change over time.

Bear market. A market in which prices are falling.

Bear spread. A calendar spread designed to profit in a bear market.

Beta. A measure of the responsiveness of a security or portfolio to movements in the stock market as a whole. Measures systematic risk.

Bid–ask bounce. In the absence of new information, the transaction prices for a security will fluctuate between the bid and the ask prices, depending on whether the trade was initiated by a buyer or a seller.

Bid–ask spread. The difference between the ask price and the bid price.

Bid price. The price at which a market maker is willing to buy.

Broker. A person who acts as an agent for others in buying and selling futures contracts in return for a commission.

Brownian motion. A random variable which is normally distributed with zero mean.

Bull market. A market in which prices are rising.

Bull spread. A calendar spread designed to profit from a bull market.

Butterfly spread. When the price of the middle contract is out of line with that of the near and far contracts, a bull (bear) spread in the near and middle contracts is matched by a bear (bull) spread in the middle and far contracts.

Buy-and-hold. A passive strategy in which a trader buys a security (or portfolio), which is then held for a period of time without revision.

Buying in. See liquidation.

Calendar spread. The simultaneous purchase and sale of futures contracts for different delivery months of the same financial instrument. Also called an intracommodity spread, a horizontal spread or a time spread.

CAPM. Capital Asset Pricing Model. The equilibrium expected return on an asset depends on the riskless interest rate, the expected return on the market and the asset's beta (β) value.

Carrying charges. The total cost of carrying an asset forwards in time, including storage, insurance and financing costs.

Cascade theory. The stock market crash of October 1987 was caused by a fall in stock market prices, which led portfolio insurers to sell index futures, resulting in a drop in their price, and, via index arbitrage, a further fall in stock market prices, etc.

Cash and carry. An arbitrage transaction where the trader holds a long position in the underlying asset and a short position in the corresponding futures contract.

Cash market. In commodities markets this term is used to refer to the market in a particular grade and location of the underlying asset. For index futures there is only one underlying grade and location, and so the cash market is synonymous with the spot market.

Cash price. See spot price.

Cash settlement. At delivery time, instead of the physical transfer of the underlying asset, there is a final marking to the market at the EDSP and the positions are closed out.

CFTC. Commodity Futures Trading Commission. An independent US federal agency which has regulated futures trading since 21 April 1975.

Cheap. See underpriced.

Circuit breaker. A trading halt when the price movement exceeds some preset limit.

Clearing house. An organization connected with a futures exchange through which all contracts are reconciled, settled, guaranteed and later either offset or fulfilled through delivery or cash settlement. Its function is to manage the margin and delivery systems, as well as to guarantee exchange traded contracts.

Clearing member. A member of the clearing house.

Close. The time period at the end of the trading session during which that day's settlement price is determined.

Close out. See liquidation.

Closing price. The last price of the trading period for a security.

Collars. When the NYSE moves up or down by more than some preset limits, programme traders were required to execute their orders manually, rather than use Super DOT.

Commission. A fee charged by a broker to a customer when a position is liquidated. See round trip.

Commodity pool. See futures fund.

Commodity pool operator. The firm managing a commodity pool.

Commodity trading adviser. Professional traders who conduct individually managed accounts on behalf of investors.

Composite hedge. A single spot position is hedged using a number of different futures.

Condor spread. A bull (bear) calendar spread in two different maturities is matched by a bear (bull) calendar spread in another two maturities. This requires there to be at least four outstanding maturities.

Contagion. Mistakes in setting prices in one market are transmitted to another.

Contango. This exists when the spot price is less than the current price of a futures contract. The opposite of backwardation.

Continuous compounding. Interest is paid continuously rather than at discrete intervals. The interest is assumed to be added to the capital sum and so interest is then payable on the interest received.

Contract. The standard unit of trading for futures markets.

Contract for differences. This is an OTC futures contract on an individual equity. Under a short contract for differences the investor receives the reduction in value of the shares. Typically, the investor in a short contract for differences pays the counterparty an initial margin based on the value of the shares. They then receive interest on the value of the shares, probably at an agreed discount to LIBOR. Under a long contract for differences the investor pays the counterparty an initial margin based on the value of the shares, and then pays interest on the value of the shares at an agreed premium above LIBOR. Such contracts are marked to market at least once per week, and the expiry date is entirely at the choice of the investor. Besides permitting short sales, such contracts have the advantage of avoiding stamp duty.

Contract month. See delivery month.

Contract multiplier. The monetary value that is multiplied by the index value to determine the market value of the futures contract.

Contract specification. The definition of the futures contract to be traded, e.g. trading times, delivery procedures.

Convergence. The movement to equality of the spot and futures prices as the delivery date approaches.

Corner. A few people gain control of all available supplies of the underlying asset.

Cost of carry. The costs of holding a stock of the underlying asset e.g. the costs of storing, insuring and financing the asset.

Cost of carry price. The futures price given by the cost of carrying an equivalent spot position until delivery.

Counterparty. The other party (buyer or seller) to a transaction.

Counterparty risk. The risk that the counterparty will not fulfil the terms of the contract.

Covering. See liquidation.

Cross hedge. Hedging a risk in one asset by initiating a position in a different but related asset.

Crossing. A situation where a broker acts for both the buyer and the seller. All cross trades must be transacted on the trading floor, or through the screen market.

Crowd. The group of people standing in the futures pit.

Crude basis. See basis.

Cum dividend. A share is cum dividend when the purchaser receives the next dividend payment.

Day order. An order to trade futures contracts that automatically expires at the end of that day's trading session.

Day trades. Trades that are opened and closed on the same day.

Deck. The orders for the purchase or sale of futures contracts held in the hands of a floor broker.

Default risk. The risk that a counterparty will fail to meet their obligations under a contract.

Deferred contract. Futures contracts other than the near contract.

Delivery. The transfer of ownership of an actual financial instrument, or final cash payment in lieu thereof, in settlement of a futures contract under the specific terms and procedures established by the exchange.

Delivery day. The day on which the futures contract matures.

Delivery month. The calendar month in which a futures contract matures, resulting in delivery or cash settlement of the specified financial instrument.

Delivery price. The price fixed by the clearing house at which deliveries on futures contracts are invoiced.

Derivative. A financial instrument designed to replicate an underlying security for the purpose of transferring risk.

Derivative overlay. The inclusion of derivatives in a portfolio to alter its overall exposure.

Discrete compounding. Interest payments are made periodically. The interest is assumed to be added to the capital sum and so interest is then payable on the interest received.

DOT. Designated Order Turnaround. An electronic order routing system for the NYSE. It was introduced in 1976 and improved and renamed Super DOT in November 1984.

Double auction market. This occurs when the price is determined by competitive bidding between both buyers and sellers, as in futures markets.

Dual capacity. A floor trader is allowed to trade on his or her own behalf, as well as an agent for others.

Dual listing. Futures contracts on the same underlying asset are traded on more than one exchange.

Dynamic hedge. An investment strategy in which a long position in shares is hedged by selling futures. The futures position is adjusted frequently so that it replicates a purchased put option.

Efficient frontier. Feasible combinations of expected profit and risk which, for each level of risk, have maximum profit.

Eligible margin. The cash or other collateral which may be accepted as cover for margin obligations.

EDSP. Exchange Delivery Settlement Price. This is the price at which the delivery or cash settlement takes place, expressed in index points.

Equity swap. A contract between two parties by which they swap the returns from an equity portfolio and an investment at a fixed or variable interest rate.

Excess return. The return on a security beyond that which could have been earned on the riskless asset.

Ex-dividend. A share is ex-dividend when the purchaser does not receive the next dividend payment.

Execution risk. The risk that prices may move between the time an order is initiated and executed.

Expiration. The date that any futures contract (or option) ceases to exist.

Expiration month. See delivery month.

Fair value. The no-arbitrage price of a futures contract. Also known as the theoretical value.

Fair value range. See arbitrage band.

Far contract. The future that is furthest from its delivery month i.e. has the longest maturity.

Fill or kill order. An order to trade futures contracts which must be executed immediately. If not it is cancelled.

Financial engineering. The process of designing new financial instruments, especially derivative securities.

Float capitalization. The value of that portion of the firm's equity that is available for trading, and so excludes shares in the hands of controlling investors.

Floor trader. A person on the floor of an exchange who executes orders.

Forced liquidation. A customer's open positions in futures contracts are offset by the brokerage firm holding the account, usually after the customer fails to meet margin calls.

Forward contract. An agreement between two parties to trade an asset at a specified future date and price.

Forward months. Futures contracts other than the near contract.

Front month. See near contract.

Front running. Brokers trade on their own behalf, ahead of their customers' orders. This was only banned in Japan in December 1992.

Fundamental analysis. The application of economic analysis to publicly available information to predict price movements.

Futures contract. A legal, transferable standardized contract that represents an agreement to buy or sell a quantity of a standardized asset at a predetermined delivery date.

Futures funds. They raise money from investors and pool this capital into a fund which is invested in futures contracts. A popular form is a 90/10 fund.

Futures and options fund. UK unit trusts that can invest up to 10 per cent of their funds in futures and options. They must cover exposures with holdings of underlying securities.

Futures option. An option written on a futures contract.

Geared futures and options fund. UK unit trusts that can invest up to 20 per cent of their funds in futures and options and have the potential to lose all the money in the fund.

Generalized hedge. A number of different spot positions are hedged using a variety of different futures.

Globex. GLOBal EXchange. Screen-based system for futures trading developed by the CME, CBOT and Reuters, which was launched on 25 June 1992. As from 21 May 1994, CBOT ceased to be a member. In addition to the CME futures and options, Matif listed some of their futures on Globex.

Heat Wave. Information (and increased volatility) affects one part of the Earth, but not others.

Hedge. A spread between a spot asset and a futures position that reduces risk.

Hedge portfolio. The portfolio of shares whose risk is being hedged away.

Hedge ratio. The number of futures contracts bought or sold divided by the number of spot contracts whose risk is being hedged.

Hedging. The purchase or sale of futures contracts to offset possible changes in the value of assets or cost of liabilities currently held, or expected to be held at some future date.

Holding period. The time period over which an investment is held.

Horizontal spread. See calendar spread.

Implementation risk. The risk that new information may arrive after an investor has decided to trade and before the order is submitted.

Implied volatility. The variance of returns on an asset that is implied by equating the observed and theoretical prices of an option on that asset.

Index fund. An institutional investment portfolio that aims to replicate the performance of a chosen market index.

Index option. An option written on a stock index.

Index participations. The trading of baskets of shares corresponding to those in some specified market index. The buyer of the index participation pays immediately in exchange for a promise by the seller to deliver the shares (or their cash equivalent) at one of a number of subsequent dates, chosen by the buyer.

Infrequent trading. If trading is not continuous, it is infrequent. Infrequent trading may be either non-synchronous trading or non-trading.

Initial margin. The 'good faith' deposit of cash or securities which a user of futures markets must make with his or her broker when purchasing or selling futures contracts, as a guarantee of contract fulfilment.

Inside information. Private and confidential information, usually acquired through a position of trust, that is likely to have an impact on security prices when made public.

Insider trading. Dealing on the basis of inside information.

Intercommodity spread. The simultaneous purchase and sale of futures contracts in different financial instruments.

Interdelivery spread. See calendar spread.

Intermarket spread. A spread involving futures contracts traded on different exchanges.

Intermonth spread. See calendar spread.

Intracommodity spread. See calendar spread.

Intramarket spread. A spread involving futures contracts traded on the same exchange.

Inverted market. A market in which the price of a stock index futures contract is higher the closer is the contract to delivery.

January effect. See turn-of-the-year effect.

Kerb trading. Unofficial trading when the market has closed.

Leg. One of the two positions constituting a spread.

Leverage effect. When the price of a share rises, and the value of the firm's outstanding debt is fixed, the ratio of debt to equity falls, i.e. its leverage (or gearing) falls. This makes returns on the share less risky. A reverse argument applies for price falls.

Lifting a leg. Liquidating one side of a spread or arbitrage position prior to liquidating the other side. Also called 'legging out'.

Limit down. This occurs when the futures price has moved down to the lower price limit.

Limit move. The price has increased or decreased by the maximum amount permitted by the price limits.

Limit order. An order to buy or sell at a specific price (or better), to be executed when and if the market price reaches the specified price.

Limit order book. A list of the outstanding limit orders.

Limit price. See price limit.

Limit up. This occurs when the futures price has moved up to the upper price limit.

Liquidation. Any transaction that offsets or closes out a previously established long or short position; also known as buying in or covering.

Liquidity. The degree to which a market can accommodate a large volume of business without moving the price, i.e. market impact.

Local. A floor trader who executes trades on his or her own account.

Long. A market position established by buying one or more futures contracts not yet closed out through an offsetting sale; the opposite of short.

Long hedge. A hedge involving a long futures position and a short spot position.

Long the basis. The purchase of the underlying asset and sale of contracts in the corresponding futures contract.

Lot. See contract.

Macro hedging. A firm hedges the combined exposure of all its assets and liabilities. See also micro hedging.

Maintenance margin. The minimum amount which a person is required to keep in their margin account.

Margin. A deposit of funds to provide collateral for an investment position. See also initial margin, variation margin and maintenance margin.

Margin call. A request for the payment of additional funds into a person's margin account.

Market capitalization. This is calculated by multiplying the number of a company's shares issued by the share price.

Market efficiency. The degree to which current prices reflect a set of information.

Market-if-touched order. An order to buy futures contracts which becomes a market order if the market reaches a specified price below the current price, or to sell if the market price reaches a specified level above the current price. Opposite of a stop order.

Market impact. See liquidity.

Market maker. A dealer who makes firm bids and offers at which he or she will trade.

Market-on-close order. An order to buy or sell at a price as close as possible to the closing price for that day.

Market-on-open. A market order to be executed during the opening.

Market order. An order to buy or sell for immediate execution at the best obtainable price.

Market portfolio. A market value weighted portfolio consisting of every share traded on the exchange.

Market risk. The possibility of gain or loss due to movements in the general level of the stock market.

Marking to the market. The daily revaluation of open positions to reflect profits and losses based on closing market prices at the end of the trading day.

Matching. The process by which buy and sell transactions are reconciled, before being passed to the clearing house.

Maturity. The length of time before delivery.

Meteor shower. Information (and increased volatility) arrives on the Earth like a meteor shower, e.g. it rains on the Earth as it turns so that information (and increased volatility) which arrives in New York subsequently arrives in Tokyo.

Micro hedging. A firm hedges only specific transactions rather than all its assets and liabilities. See also macro hedging.

Minimum price movement. The smallest possible price change. See also point and tick size.

Mirror trading. Trading asset x indirectly by trading two or more securities, at least one of which subsumes asset x, so that the net position amounts to trading asset x.

Mispricing. It usually refers to the actual less the no-arbitrage futures price, and may be deflated by either the spot price or the no-arbitrage futures price. In a few cases the mispricing incorporates transactions costs.

Momentum trader. A trader who sells when the market falls and buys when the market rises. This behaviour tends to amplify price movements. Also known as a positive feedback trader.

Mutual fund. This is a type of US investment company. It sells its shares to the public and uses the proceeds to invest in other companies.

National Futures Association. A self-regulating US body which registers those employed in the futures brokerage industry.

Naïve hedge ratio. A one-for-one hedge ratio.

Near contract. The future that is nearest to its delivery month, i.e. has the shortest maturity.

Net position. The difference between the long and short open positions in any one future held by an individual or group.

Noise trader. A trader who trades for pleasure, or who trades on information that they believe is valuable but which is useless.

Non-synchronicity. Stocks trade at least once every interval, but not necessarily at the close of each interval. See non-trading.

Non-trading. Stocks do not trade during every interval. See non-synchronicity.

Normal backwardation. This occurs when the expected price of a futures contract at delivery exceeds the current price of the future.

Normal market. A market in which the price of a stock index futures contract is lower the closer is the contract to delivery.

Novation. The legal word for the conversion of a futures contract between a buyer and seller into two separate contracts, each with the clearing house as counterparty.

Odd lot. A quantity of shares that does not correspond to that in which trading normally takes place.

Offer price. See ask price.

Offset. See liquidation.

Open interest. The cumulative number of either long or short contracts which have been initiated on an exchange, and have not been offset.

Open outcry. The method of trading on many futures exchanges whereby bids and offers are audible to all other participants on the floor of the exchange (or pit) in a competitive public auction.

Open positions. Contracts which have been initiated and are not yet offset by a subsequent sale or purchase, or by making or taking delivery.

Original margin. The initial margin required to cover a new futures position.

Out trade. A trade for which there is not a matching record by the two parties. This may be because the price, quantity, maturity, counterparty or side (long–short) fail to match.

Overbought. A view that the market price has risen too steeply in relation to the underlying fundamental factors.

Overnight trade. A trade which is not liquidated on the same day in which it was established.

Overpriced. The actual futures price exceeds the no-arbitrage futures price.

Oversold. A view that the market price has declined too steeply in relation to the underlying fundamental factors.

Over-the-counter market. A securities market where dealing does not take place at an organized exchange.

Perfect hedge. A hedge where the change in the value of the futures contracts is identical to the change in the value of the other asset or liability.

Physical delivery. Settlement of a futures contract by the supply or receipt of the asset underlying the contract.

Pit. An octagonal or hexagonal area on the trading floor of an exchange, surrounded by a tier of steps upon which traders and brokers stand while executing futures trades.

Point. This can mean the minimum permissible price change, or it can mean a price change of 100 basis points. For index futures, index points are simply the units of measurement of the index. Currently for the FTSE 100 the minimum price movement is 0.5 index points.

Portfolio insurance. An investment strategy employing various combinations of shares, options, futures and debt that is designed to provide a minimum or floor value to the portfolio.

Position. A market commitment.

Position limit. A restriction on the maximum number of contracts that can be held by a single trader at any one time.

Position trading. A trading strategy in which a position is held for longer than one day.

Positive feedback trader. See momentum trader.

Price discovery. The process by which a market (usually the futures market) reflects new information before another related market (usually the spot market).

Price limits. The maximum and minimum prices, as specified by the exchange, between which transactions may take place during a single trading session.

Price range. The difference between the highest and lowest prices during a given period.

Price relative. The price at time $t+1$ divided by the price at time t.

Programme trading. The simultaneous trading of a basket of shares as part of a plan or strategy. The NYSE definition requires the simultaneous trading of at least fifteen stocks with a total value of over $1 million.

Project A. A screen-based order-matching system developed by the CBOT for trading unconventional products during normal trading hours. It began trading on 23 October 1992, and on 20 October 1994 began trading after hours.

Punching the settlement price. A manipulator first establishes a long (short) position in index futures, and then buys (sells) shares to push the final settlement price up (down).

Pyramiding. The use of profits on a previously established position as margin for adding to that position.

Quasi-futures contract. This is the same as a futures contract, except that the payments of variation margin do not involve the full daily price change. Instead, the trader pays (or receives) each day only the present value of the daily price change if it were paid on delivery day; a smaller sum.

Queue. The sequence of potential arbitrageurs, in order of increasing transactions costs.

Random walk. The theory that changes in the variable (for example, share returns) are at random; that is, they are independently and identically distributed over time.

Realized bid–ask spread. The difference between the prices at which scalpers have bought and sold.

Reportable position. The number of futures contracts above which one must report daily to the exchange or the CFTC the size of the position by delivery month and purpose of trading.

Reverse cash and carry. An arbitrage transaction where the trader holds a short position in the underlying asset and a long position in the corresponding futures contract.

Rich. See overpriced

Ring. See pit.

Risk premium. The additional return risk-averse investors require for assuming risk.

Roll over. The liquidation of a futures position, and the establishment of a similar position in a more distant delivery month. This is also called a switch. When a hedger switches their futures position to a more distant delivery month this can be called 'rolling the hedge forwards'.

Round lot. A quantity of shares that corresponds to that in which trading normally takes place.

Round trip. The purchase (sale) of a futures contract and the subsequent offsetting sale (purchase). Transactions costs are normally quoted on a 'round trip' basis.

Round turn. See round trip.

Rule 80a. When the NYSE moves down (up) by more than some preset limit, selling (buying) shares (not just short selling) as part of an index arbitrage transaction can be executed only if the last price movement was up (down). This rule was introduced in 1990.

Scalp. To trade for small gains, normally by establishing and liquidating a futures position quickly, often within minutes, but always within the same day.

Scanning range. The largest price movement in the underlying security for which the clearing house requires cover.

Seat. Membership of a securities exchange.

SEC. Securities and Exchange Commission. A federal agency charged with the regulation of all US equity and options markets.

Security market line. A line showing the relationship between a security's beta and its expected return.

Settlement. The process by which clearing members close positions.

Settlement date. See delivery date.

Settlement effect. Due to the system of stock exchange accounts that prevailed on the LSE until 18 July 1994, the period of interest free credit when shares are purchased varied, depending on when in the account the deal took place.

Settlement price. The price which the clearing house uses to determine the daily variation margin payments. It may differ from the price of the last transaction.

Sharpe's ratio. A measure of the risk-adjusted performance of an investment. It is calculated as the excess return on the investment divided by the standard deviation of investment returns.

Short. A market position established by selling one or more futures contracts not yet closed out through an offsetting purchase in anticipation of falling prices; the opposite of long.

Short hedge. A hedge involving a short futures position and a long spot position.

Short sale. A trader sells shares he or she does not own. This is equivalent to a negative holding of the share.

Short the basis. The purchase of a futures contract as a hedge against a commitment to sell the underlying asset.

Sidecar. This is the procedure by which, when the S&P500 futures price falls by more than some preset limit, for the next 5 minutes retail orders have priority over programme trades on Super DOT.

Simple basis. See basis.

Size effect. This exists when the returns for small firms exceed the risk-adjusted returns predicted by the CAPM.

SPAN. Standard Portfolio Analysis of Risk. This is a system for calculating initial margins on portfolios of options and futures developed by the CME, and used by them since 16 December 1988, and by LIFFE from 2 April 1991.

Special expiration index. The final settlement price for US index futures computed from non-synchronous opening prices.

Specialist. A floor trader charged with the duty of making a fair and orderly market in particular shares or options.

Speculation. Trading on anticipated price changes, where the trader does not hold another position which will offset any such price movements.

Spiders. Standard and Poor's Depositary Receipts (SPDRs) were introduced on 29 January 1993 by AMEX. They represent shares in a trust consisting of a basket of shares that is designed to track the S&P500 index. The trust has a life of 25 years, at which point it will be distributed to share holders.

Spot market. The market in which the asset underlying the futures contract is traded e.g. the stock market.

Spot month. See delivery month.

Spot price. A derivation of 'on the spot', usually referring to the cash market price of a financial instrument available for immediate delivery.

Spread. The simultaneous purchase of one futures contract and sale of another, in the expectation that the price relationship between the two will change so that the subsequent offsetting sale and purchase will yield a net profit.

Spread basis. The difference in the prices of the near and far contracts in a spread.

Spread margin. A reduced margin payment for the holder of a spread position.

Spread ratio. The number of futures contracts bought, divided by the number of futures contracts sold.

Stack hedge. A large position in an existing futures contract is partly rolled over into a later contract month, possibly several times. This procedure may be used to hedge a series of payments or receipts.

Stale prices. A price is stale if it refers to the price of a trade that took place some time ago. See infrequent trading.

Stock exchange account. These were two (or occasionally three) week periods, and all shares purchased on the LSE during a particular account were paid for on the same day. This ceased on 18 July 1994.

Stop order. A market order to buy when the market price has touched a specified level above the current price, or a market order to sell when the market price has touched a specified level below the current price. Also known as a stop-loss order. Opposite of a market-if-touched order.

Straddle. For futures contracts, this is a synonym for a spread.

Strengthening of the basis. This occurs when the futures price declines relative to the spot price.

Strike price. See exercise price.

Strip hedge. A trader takes the same position (long or short) in a future for a series of delivery dates. This may be used to hedge a series of payments or receipts.

Sunshine trading. The announcement by a particular investor that they will initiate a trade of a given size at a specified time in the future.

Switch. See roll over.

Synthetic futures. A combination of a long call option and a short put option, or debt and the underlying asset, that replicates the behaviour of a long futures contract.

Systematic risk. Risk inherent in the market as a whole which cannot be diversified away. It is measured for each firm by a 'beta' value.

Tail risk. The risk created by marking to the market.

Tailing factor. The correction factor by which the hedge ratio is multiplied to allow for tail risk.

Tailing the hedge. Correcting the size of a hedge to allow for the risks of marking to the market.

Tax timing option. Capital gains (losses) on shares are taxable when realized. The tax timing option refers to the fact that the owner can choose when to liquidate his or her position in the shares, and hence when the tax liability (or tax loss) occurs.

Technical analysis. The prediction of prices by examining past prices, volume and open interest.

Term structure of futures prices. The relationship between futures prices on the same underlying asset, but with a different time to maturity.

Texas hedge. A long position in both the spot and futures markets or a short position in both the spot and futures markets.

Theoretical basis. No-arbitrage futures price minus the spot price.

Theoretical value. See fair value.

Thin market. A market with few trades.

Tick size. Minimum permitted movement in the price.

Tick value. See minimum price movement.

Time spread. See calendar spread.

Tracking error. The deviations between a portfolio's performance and that of the portfolio whose performance it is desired to mimic.

Trading lag. The time delay between when an order is initiated and executed.

Trading limit. The maximum number of contracts that a person can trade in a single day.

Triple witching hour. That time every 3 months when four different contracts reach maturity – stock index futures contracts, stock index options, options on index futures and some options on individual stocks.

Turn-of-the-month effect. This occurs when returns are higher on the last trading day of the calendar month, and the first half of the next calendar month.

Turn-of-the-year effect. This exists when returns are higher for the end of December and the first few days of January.

Underlying asset. The security, stock, commodity or index on which a futures contract is based.

Underpriced. The actual futures price is less than the no-arbitrage futures price.

Unsystematic risk. Risk due to events which affect individual companies, not the market as a whole. It can be removed by holding a well diversified portfolio.

Unwind. See liquidation.

Uptick. An increase of one tick in the price of a security.

Value basis. The actual futures price less the no-arbitrage futures price.

Value trader. A trader who buys when assets look underpriced, and sells when assets look overpriced. Such a trader tends to buy when there is a large drop in prices, and sell when there is a large rise, and so tends to stabilize prices.

Variation margin. The gains or losses on open contracts, which are calculated by reference to the settlement price at the end of each trading day and are credited or debited by the clearing house to the clearing member's margin accounts and by those members to or from the appropriate customers' margin accounts.

Volatility. A market is volatile when it is changeable and lively. Academics often choose to measure the volatility of a variable by its variance or standard deviation.

Volume. The number of transactions in a futures contract during a specified period of time.

Weakening of the basis. This occurs when the futures price rises relative to the spot price.

Weekend effect. This exists when returns over the weekend are lower than for the rest of the week.

Zero-sum game. This is when the gains (losses) of the long positions are exactly equal to the losses (gains) of the short positions.

References

Abhyankar, A.H. (1995) Return and volatility dynamics in the FTSE 100 stock index and stock index futures markets, *Journal of Futures Markets*, 15(4), pp. 457-488.

Abhyankar, A.H. (1998) Linear and nonlinear Granger causality: evidence from the UK stock index futures market, *Journal of Futures Markets*, 18(5), pp. 519-540.

Abhyankar, A.H., Copeland, L.S. & Wong, W. (1999) LIFFE cycles: intraday evidence from the FTSE 100 stock index futures market, *European Journal of Finance*, 5(2), pp. 123-139.

Acar, E., Lequeux, P. & Ritz, S. (1996) Timing the highs and lows of the day, *Liffe Equity Products Review*, 2nd Quarter, pp. 1-3.

Adachi, T. & Kurasawa, M. (1993) Stock futures and options markets in Japan. In *Japanese Capital Markets: New Developments in Regulations and Institutions*, ed. by S. Takagi, Blackwell Publishers, pp. 405-425.

Adams, K.J. & Van Deventer, D.R. (1992) Comment on intraday arbitrage opportunities and price behaviour of the Hang Seng futures, *Review of Futures Markets*, 11(3), pp. 431-445.

Admati, A.R. & Pfleiderer, P. (1988) A theory of intraday patterns: volume and price variability, *Review of Financial Studies*, 1(1), pp. 3-40.

Aggarwal, R. (1988) Stock index futures and cash market volatility, *Review of Futures Markets*, 7(2), pp. 290-299.

Aggarwal, R. & Park, Y.S. (1994) The relationship between daily US and Japanese equity prices: evidence from spot versus futures markets, *Journal of Banking and Finance*, 18(4), pp. 757-773.

Ahn, D.H., Boudoukh, J., Richardson, M. & Whitelaw, R.F. (2002) Partial adjustment or stale prices? Implications from stock index and futures return autocorrelations, *Review of Financial Studies*, 15(2), pp. 655-689.

Aitken, M.J., Frino, A., Hill, A.M. & Jarnecic, E. (2004) The impact of electronic trading on bid-ask spreads: evidence from futures markets in Hong Kong, London and Sydney, *Journal of Futures Markets*, 24(7), pp. 675-696.

Aitken, M.J., Frino, A. and Jarnecic, E. (1997) Intraday returns and the frequency of trading at the ask on the Sydney Futures Exchange: a research note, *Abacus*, 33(2), pp. 228-235.

Akin, R.M. (2003) Maturity effects in futures markets: evidence from eleven financial futures markets, Working paper, University of California, Santa Cruz, 42 pages.

Alexander, S.S. (1961) Price movements in speculative markets: trends or random walks, *Industrial Management Review*, 2(2), pp. 7-26.

Alexander, S.S. (1964) Price movements in speculative markets: trends or random walks, no. 2. *Industrial Management Review*, vol. 5, Spring, pp. 338-372.

Alexakis, P., Kavussanos, M. & Visvikis, I. (2002) An investigation of the lead-lad relationship in returns and volatility between cash and stock index futures: the case of Greece, Working paper, Athens University of Economics and Business, 28 pages.

Alizadeh, A. & Nomikos, N. (2004) A Markov regime switching approach for hedging stock indices, *Journal of Futures Markets*, 24(7), pp. 649-674.

Alkebäck, P. & Hagelin, N. (1999) Derivative usage by non-financial firms in Sweden with an international comparison, *Journal of International Financial Management and Accounting*, 10(2), pp. 105-120.

Alkebäck, P., Hagelin, N. & Pramborg, B. (2003) Derivatives usage by non-financial firms in Sweden 1996 and 2003: what has changed? Working paper, Stockholm University, 26 pages.

Allen, R.D.G. (1975) *Index Numbers in Theory and Practice*, Macmillan.

Allingham, M. (1985) Futures markets and economic efficiency: a theoretical perspective, *Resources Policy*, 11(1), pp. 43-48.

Amihud, Y. & Mendelson, H. (1989) Index and index futures returns, *Journal of Accounting, Auditing and Finance*, vol. 4, pp. 415-431.

422222222222222222.

Andersen, T.G. & Bollerslev, T. (1997) Intraday periodicity and volatility persistence in financial markets, *Journal of Empirical Finance*, 4(2-3), pp. 115-158.

Anderson, H.M. & Vahid, F. (2001) Market architecture and nonlinear dynamics of Australian stock and futures indices, *Australian Economic Papers*, 40(4), pp. 541-566.

Anderson, R.W. & Danthine, J.P. (1980) Hedging and joint production: theory and illustrations, *Journal of Finance*, 35(5), pp. 487-498.

Anderson, R.W. & Danthine, J.P. (1981) Cross hedging, *Journal of Political Economy*, 89(6), pp. 1182-1196.

Anderson, R.W. & Danthine, J.P. (1983) The time pattern of hedging and the volatility of futures prices, *Review of Economic Studies*, 50(2), no. 161, pp. 249-266.

Antoniou, A. & Garrett, I. (1989) Long run equilibrium and short run dynamics: the case of the FTSE 100 share index and futures contract. Brunel University, Working paper 89-06, 32 pages.

Antoniou, A. & Garrett, I. (1992) Are financial markets effectively functioning? Some evidence from the UK stock index futures markets. Brunel University, Working paper 92-05, 32 pages.

Antoniou, A. & Garrett, I. (1993) To what extent did stock index futures contribute to the October 1987 stock market crash?, *Economic Journal*, vol. 103, no. 421, pp. 1444-1461.

Antoniou, A. & Holmes, P. (1994) Systematic risk and returns to stock index futures contracts: international evidence, *Journal of Futures Markets*, 14(7), pp. 773-787.

Antoniou, A. & Holmes, P. (1995a) Futures market efficiency, the unbiasedness hypothesis and variance bounds tests: the case of the FTSE 100 futures contract. Brunel University, Working paper 95-12, 23 pages.

Antoniou, A. & Holmes, P. (1995b) Futures trading, information and spot price volatility: evidence for the FTSE 100 stock index futures contract using GARCH, *Journal of Banking and Finance*, 19(1), pp. 117-129.

Antoniou, A., Holmes, P. & Priestley, R. (1998) The effects of stock index futures on stock index volatility: an analysis of the asymmetric response of volatility to news, *Journal of Futures Markets*, 18(2), pp. 151-166.

Antoniou, A., Koutmos, G. & Pericli, A. (2005) Index futures and positive feedback trading: evidence from major stock exchanges, *Journal of Empirical Finance*, 12(2), pp. 219-238.

Antoniou, A., Pescetto, G. & Violaris, A. (2003) Modelling international price relationships and interdependencies between the stock index and stock index futures markets of three EU countries: a multivariate analysis, *Journal of Business Finance and Accounting,* 30(5-6), pp. 645-667.

ap Gwilym, O. & Alibo, E. (2003) Decreased price clustering in FTSE 100 futures contracts following a transfer from floor to electronic trading, *Journal of Futures Markets*, 23(7), pp. 647-659.

ap Gwilym, O., Brooks, C., Clare, A. & Thomas, S. (1999) Tests of non-linearity using LIFFE futures transactions price data, *The Manchester School*, 67(2), pp. 167-186.

ap Gwilym, O. & Buckle, M. (2001) The lead-lag relationship between the FTSE 100 stock index and its derivative contracts, *Applied Financial Economics*, 11(4), pp. 385-393.

ap Gwilym, O., Buckle, M. & Thomas, S. (1999) The intra-day behaviour of key market variables for LIFFE derivatives. In *Financial Markets Tick by Tick* ed. by P. Lequeux, John Wiley & Sons, pp. 151-189.

ap Gwilym, O., Clare, A. & Thomas, S. (1998) Extreme price clustering in the London equity index futures and options markets, *Journal of Banking and Finance*, 22(9), pp. 1193-1206.

ap Gwilym, O., McMillan, D. & Speight, A. (1999) The intraday relationship between volume and volatility in LIFFE futures markets, *Applied Financial Economics*, 9(6), pp. 593-604.

ap Gwilym, O., & Sutcliffe, C.M.S. (1999) *High-Frequency Financial Market Data: Sources, Applications and Market Microstructure*, Risk Books, London.

ap Gwilym, O., & Sutcliffe, C.M.S. (2001) Problems encountered when using high frequency financial market data: suggested solutions, *Journal of Financial Management and Analysis*, vol. 14, no. 1, January-June 2001, pp. 38-51.

Aragó, V., Corredor, P. & Santamaría, R. (2003) Transaction costs, arbitrage and volatility spillover: a note, *International Review of Economics and Finance*, 12(3), pp. 399-415.

Arai, T., Akamatsu, T. & Yoshioka, A. (1993) Stock index futures in Japan: problems and prospects, *NRI Quarterly*, 2(1), pp. 28-57. A slightly edited version of the final section appears in the *Journal of*

International Securities Markets, vol. 7, Autumn, 1993, pp. 159-164.

Arditti, F.D., Ayaydin, S., Mattu, R.K. & Rigsbee, S. (1986) A passive futures strategy that outperforms active management, *Financial Analysts Journal*, 42(4), pp. 63-67.

Arnott, R.D., Hsu, J. & Moore, P. (2005) Fundamental indexation, *Financial Analysts Journal*, 61(2), pp. 83-99.

Arnott, R.D. & Vincent, S.J. (1986) S&P additions and deletions: a market anomaly, *Journal of Portfolio Management*, 13(1), pp. 29-33.

Arrow, K.J. (1981) Futures markets: some theoretical perspectives, *Journal of Futures Markets*, 1(2), pp. 107-115.

Arshanapalli. B. & Doukas, J. (1994) Common volatility in S&P500 stock index and S&P500 index futures prices during October 1987, *Journal of Futures Markets*, 14(8), pp. 915-925.

Arshanapalli. B. & Doukas, J. (1997) The linkages of S&P500 stock index and S&P500 stock index futures prices during October 1987, *Journal of Economics and Business*, 49(3), pp. 253-266.

Atchison, M.D., Butler, K.C. & Simonds, R.R. (1987) Non-synchronous security trading and market index autocorrelation, *Journal of Finance*, 42(1), pp. 111-118.

Ates, A. & Wang, G.H.K. (2003) When size matters: the case of equity index futures, Working paper, CFTC, 50 pages.

Ates, A. & Wang, G.H.K. (2005) Information transmission in electronic versus open outcry trading systems: an analysis of US equity index futures markets, *Journal of Futures Markets*, 25(7), pp. 679-715.

Bacha, O. & Vila, A.F. (1994) Futures markets, regulation and volatility: the case of the Nikkei stock index futures markets, *Pacific Basin Finance Journal*, 2(2-3), pp. 201-225.

Bae, K.H., Chan, K. & Cheung, Y.L. (1998) The profitability of index futures arbitrage: evidence from bid-ask quotes, *Journal of Futures Markets*, 18(7), pp. 743-763.

Bae, S.C., Kwon, T.H. & Park, J.W. (2004) Futures trading, spot market volatility and market efficiency: the case of the Korean index futures markets, *Journal of Futures Markets*, 24(12), pp. 1195-1228.

Baer, H.L., France, V.G. & Moser, J.T. (1996) Opportunity cost and prudentiality: an analysis of futures clearing house behaviour. Office of Futures and Options Research, University of Illinois at Urbana-Champaign, OFOR Working Paper no. 96-01, 45 pages.

Bailey, W. (1989) The market for Japanese stock index futures: some preliminary evidence, *Journal of Futures Markets*, 9(4), pp. 283-295.

Bailey, W. & Ng, E. (1991) Default premiums in commodity markets: theory and evidence, *Journal of Finance*, 46(3), pp. 1071-1093.

Baillie, R.T. & Myers, R.J. (1991) Bivariate GARCH estimation of the optimal commodity futures hedge, *Journal of Applied Econometrics*, 6(2), pp. 109-124.

Bailly, N., Browne, D., Hicks, E. & Skerrat, L. (2003) UK corporate use of derivatives, *European Journal of Finance*, 9(2), pp. 169-193.

Baker, W.E. (1984) Floor trading and crowd dynamics. In *The Social Dynamics of Financial Markets*, ed. by P.A. Adler & P. Adler, JAI Press, pp. 107-128.

Balbás, A., Longarela, I.R. & Pardo, A. (2000) Integration and arbitrage in the Spanish financial markets: an empirical approach, *Journal of Futures Markets*, 20(4), pp. 321-344.

Baldauf, B. & Santoni, G.J. (1991) Stock price volatility: some evidence from an ARCH model, *Journal of Futures Markets*, 11(2), pp. 191-200.

Ball, C.A. (1988) Estimation bias induced by discrete security prices. *Journal of Finance*, 43(4), pp. 841-865.

Ball, C.A. & Torous, W.N. (1986) Futures options and the volatility of futures prices, *Journal of Finance*, 61(4), pp. 857-870.

Ball, C.A., Torous, W.N. & Tschoegl, A.E. (1985) The degree of price resolution: the case of the gold market, *Journal of Futures Markets*, 5(1), pp. 29-43.

Bamberg, G. & Röder, K. (1994a) The intraday ex ante profitability of DAX futures arbitrage for institutional investors in Germany: the case of early and late transactions, *Financial Markets and Portfolio Management* (Austria), 8(1), pp. 50-62.

Bamberg, G. & Röder, K. (1994b) Seasonality in ex ante German stock index futures arbitrage; where do reverse cash and carry arbitrage profits in Germany come from? Paper presented to the Seventh Annual

European Futures Research Symposium, Chicago Board of Trade, Bonn.

Bank for International Settlements. (1992) Derivative financial instruments and banks' involvement in selected off-balance-sheet business, *International Banking and Financial Market Developments*, May, pp. 15-29.

Bank for International Settlements. (1995) *65th Annual Report: 1st April 1994-31st March 1995*, Bank for International Settlements, June.

Bank of England. (1988) The equity market crash, *Bank of England Quarterly*, February, pp. 51-58.

Baratz, M.S. & Eresian, W. (1992a) The role of managed futures accounts in an investment portfolio (I). In *Managed Futures: Performance, Evaluation and Analysis of Commodity Funds, Pools and Accounts*, ed. by C.C. Peters, Probus Publishing Co., pp. 189-205.

Baratz, M.S. & Eresian, W. (1992b) The role of managed futures accounts in an investment portfolio (II). In *Managed Futures: Performance, Evaluation and Analysis of Commodity Funds, Pools and Accounts*, ed. by C.C. Peters, Probus Publishing Co., pp. 347-366.

Barclay, W.J. & Noll, E.W. (1992) The creation of equity derivative markets: learning from experience, Paper presented at the Pacific Basin Capital Markets Research Centre Conference, Hong Kong, 1992, 26 pages.

Barkoulas, J.T., Labys, W.C. & Onochie, J.I. (1999) Long memory in futures prices, *The Financial Review*, 34(1), pp. 91-100.

Bassett, G.W., France, V.G. & Pliska, S.R. (1989) The MMI cash-futures spread on October 19, 1987, *Review of Futures Markets*, 8(1), pp. 118-146.

Bassett, N.F. (1987) Financial futures markets: London regulatory framework. In *Current Developments in International Securities Commodities and Financial Futures Markets*, ed. by K.K. Lian, H.H.M. Chan, H.P. Kee & P.N. Pillai, Butterworths, pp. 330-348.

Bear, R.M. (1972) Margin levels and the behaviour of futures prices, *Journal of Financial and Quantitative Analysis*, 7(4), pp. 1907-1930.

Beaulieu, M.C. (1998) Time to maturity in the basis of stock market indices: evidence from the S&P500 and the MMI, *Journal of Empirical Finance*, 5(3), pp. 177-195.

Beaulieu, M.C., Ebrahim, S.K. & Morgan, I.G. (2003) Does tick size influence price discovery? Evidence from the Toronto Stock Exchange, *Journal of Futures Markets*, 23(1), pp. 49-66.

Becker, K.G., Finnerty, J.E. & Friedman, J. (1995) Economic news and equity market linkages between the US and UK, *Journal of Banking and Finance*, 19(7), pp. 1191-1210.

Becker, K.G., Finnerty, J.E. & Tucker, A.L. (1993) The overnight and daily transmission of stock index futures prices between major international markets, *Journal of Business Finance and Accounting*, 20(5), pp. 699-710.

Beckers, S. (1983) Variances of security price returns based on high, low and closing prices, *Journal of Business*, 56(1), pp. 97-112.

Becketti, S. & Roberts, D.J. (1990) Will increased regulation of stock index futures reduce stock market volatility?, *Federal Reserve Bank of Kansas City Economic Review*, November-December, pp. 33-46.

Beelders, O. & Massey, J. (2002) The relationship between spot and futures index contracts after the introduction of electronic trading on the Johannesburg Stock Exchange, Working paper, Emory University, 23 pages.

Bell, D.E. & Krasker, W.S. (1986) Estimating hedge ratios, *Financial Management*, 15(2), pp. 34-39.

Beneish, M.D. & Gardner, J.C. (1995) Information costs and liquidity effects from changes in the Dow Jones Industrial Average list, *Journal of Financial and Quantitative Analysis*, 30(1), pp. 135-157.

Benet, B.A. & Luft, C.F. (1995) Hedge performance of SPX index options and S&P500 futures, *Journal of Futures Markets*, 15(6), pp. 691-717.

Benninga, S., Eldor, R. & Zilcha, I. (1983) Optimal hedging in the futures market under price uncertainty, *Economics Letters*, 13(2-3), pp. 141-145.

Benninga, S., Eldor, R. & Zilcha, I. (1984) The optimal hedge ratio in unbiased futures markets, *Journal of Futures Markets*, 4(2), pp. 155-159.

Bera, A., Bubnys, E.L. & Park, H.Y. (1993) ARCH effects and efficient estimation of hedge ratios for stock index futures. In *Advances in Futures and Options Research*, vol. 6, ed. by D.M. Chance & R.R Trippi, JAI Press Inc., pp. 313-328.

Berglund, T. & Kabir, R. (1994) What explains the difference between the futures' price and its "fair value"? Evidence from the European Options Exchange, Working paper, Tilburg University, Netherlands, 20 pages.

Bernanke, B.S. (1990) Clearing and settlement during the crash, *Review of Financial Studies*, 3(1), pp. 133-151.

Berkman, H., Brailsford, T. & Frino, A. (2005) A note on execution costs for stock index futures: information versus liquidity effects, *Journal of Banking and Finance*, 29(3), pp. 565-577.

Berkman, H. & Steenbeek, O.W. (1998) The influence of daily price limits on trading in Nikkei futures, *Journal of Futures Markets*, 18(3), pp. 265-279.

Bessembinder, H. (1992) Systematic risk, hedging pressure and risk premiums in futures markets, *Review of Financial Studies*, 5(4), pp. 637-667.

Bessembinder, H., Coughenour, J.F., Seguin, P.J. & Smoller, M.M. (1995a) Mean reversion in equilibrium asset prices: evidence from the futures term structure, *Journal of Finance*, 50(1), pp. 361-375.

Bessembinder, H., Coughenour, J.F., Seguin, P.J. & Smoller, M.M. (1995b) Futures price volatility and spot price stationarity: reevaluating the Samuelson hypothesis, Working paper, University of Massachusetts-Boston, 1995, 24 pages.

Bessembinder, H. & Seguin, P.J. (1992) Futures-trading activity and stock price volatility, *Journal of Finance*, 47(5), pp. 2015-2034.

Bhar, R. (2001) Return and volatility dynamics in the spot and futures markets in Australia: an intervention analysis in a bivariate EGARCH-X framework, *Journal of Futures Markets*, 21(9), pp. 833-850.

Bhatt, S. & Cakici, N. (1990) Premiums on stock index futures - some evidence, *Journal of Futures Markets*, 10(4), pp. 367-375.

Billingsley, R.S. & Chance, D.M. (1988) The pricing and performance of stock index futures spreads, *Journal of Futures Markets*, 8(3), pp. 303-318.

Bilson, C., Brailsford, T. & Evans, T. (2005) The international transmission of arbitrage information across futures markets, *Journal of Business Finance and Accounting*, 32(5-6), pp. 973-1000.

Binns, W.G. (1989) Pension funds, program trading and stock index futures. In *Handbook of Stock Index Futures and Options*, ed. by F.J. Fabozzi and G.M. Kipnis, Dow Jones-Irwin, pp. 258-272.

Black, F. (1976) The pricing of commodity contracts, *Journal of Financial Economics*, 3(1), pp. 167-179.

Black, F. & Jones, R. (1987) Simplifying portfolio insurance, *Journal of Portfolio Management*, 14(1), pp. 48-51.

Black, F. & Jones, R. (1988) Simplifying portfolio insurance for corporate pension plans, *Journal of Portfolio Management*, 14(4), pp. 33-37.

Blake, D. (1990) *Financial Market Analysis*, McGraw-Hill, ch. 8 and 12.

Blake, D., Lehmann, B.N. & Timmermann, A. (1999) Asset allocation dynamics and pension fund performance, *Journal of Business*, 72(4), pp. 429-461.

Blank, S.C. (1990) Determining futures 'hedging reserve' capital requirements, *Journal of Futures Markets*, 10(2), pp. 169-177.

Blank, S.C. (1991a) 'Chaos' in futures markets? A nonlinear dynamical analysis, *Journal of Futures Markets*, 11(6), pp. 711-728.

Blank, S.C. (1991b) Futures market risk capital requirements for speculative survival. In *Advances in Futures and Options Research*, vol. 5, ed. by F.J. Fabozzi, JAI Press Inc., pp. 279- 287.

Blank, S.C. (1992) The significance of hedging capital requirements, *Journal of Futures Markets*, 12(1), pp. 11-18.

Blank, S.C., Carter, C.A. & Schmiesing, B.H. (1991) *Futures and Options Markets: Trading in Commodities and Financials*, Prentice-Hall.

Block, S.B. & Gallagher, T.J. (1988) How much do bank trust departments use derivatives?, *Journal of Portfolio Management*, 15(1), pp. 12-15.

Block, S.B. & Gallagher, T.J. (1990) The use of stock index futures and options by non-trust professional money managers. In *Managing Institutional Assets*, ed. by F.J. Fabozzi, Harper & Row, pp. 633-639.

Blume, M.E., MacKinlay, A.C. & Terker, B. (1989) Order imbalances and stock price movements on October 19 and 20, 1987, *Journal of Finance*, 44(4), pp. 827-848.

Board, J.L.G., Goodhart, C.A.E., & Sutcliffe, C.M.S. (1991) *Equity and Derivatives Markets: Linkages and Regulatory Implications*, The Securities and Investments Board, 45 pages.

Board, J.L.G., Goodhart, C.A.E., & Sutcliffe, C.M.S. (1992) *Inter-Market Linkages: The London Stock*

Exchange and London International Financial Futures Exchange, The Securities and Investments Board, 121 pages.

Board, J.L.G., Sandmann, G. & Sutcliffe, C.M.S. (2001) The Effect of Futures Market Volume on Spot Market Volatility, *Journal of Business Finance and Accounting*, 28(7-8), pp. 799-819.

Board, J.L.G. & Sutcliffe, C.M.S. (1985) Optimal portfolio diversification and the effects of differing intra sample measures of return, *Journal of Business Finance and Accounting*, 12(4), pp. 561-574.

Board, J.L.G. & Sutcliffe, C.M.S. (1988) The weekend effect in UK stock market returns, *Journal of Business Finance and Accounting*, 15(2), pp. 199-213.

Board, J.L.G. & Sutcliffe, C.M.S. (1990) Information, volatility, volume and maturity: an investigation of stock index futures, *Review of Futures Markets*, 9(3), pp. 532-549.

Board, J.L.G. & Sutcliffe, C.M.S. (1991) Risk and income tradeoffs in regional policy: a portfolio theoretic approach, *Journal of Regional Science*, 31(2), pp. 191-210.

Board, J.L.G. & Sutcliffe, C.M.S. (1992) Stock market volatility and stock index futures, *Stock Exchange Quarterly with Quality of Markets Review*, Summer edition, pp. 11-14.

Board, J.L.G. & Sutcliffe, C.M.S. (1994) Estimation methods in portfolio selection and the effectiveness of short sales restrictions: UK evidence, *Management Science*, 40(4), pp. 516-534.

Board, J.L.G. & Sutcliffe, C.M.S. (1995a) The relative volatility of the markets in equities and index futures, *Journal of Business Finance and Accounting*, 22(2), pp. 201-223.

Board, J.L.G. & Sutcliffe, C.M.S. (1995b) *The Effects of Trade Transparency in the London Stock Exchange: A Summary*, Financial Markets Group Special Paper No. 67, London School of Economics, 30 pages.

Board, J.L.G. & Sutcliffe, C.M.S. (1996a) The dual listing of stock index futures: arbitrage, spread arbitrage and currency risk, *Journal of Futures Markets*, 16(1), pp. 29-54.

Board, J.L.G. & Sutcliffe, C.M.S. (1996b) Trade transparency and the London Stock Exchange, *European Financial Management*, 2(3), pp. 355-365.

Board, J.L.G. & Sutcliffe, C.M.S. (1998) Options Trading When the Underlying Market is Not Transparent, *Journal of Futures Markets,* 18(2), pp. 225-242

Board, J.L.G., Sutcliffe, C.M.S. & Wells, S. (2002) *Transparency and Fragmentation: Financial Market Regulation in a Dynamic Environment*, Palgrave, London.

Board, J.L.G. & Sutcliffe, C.M.S. (2005a) Futures and Forwards. In *The Blackwell Encyclopedia of Management,* second edition, volume 4, edited by Ian Garrett, Blackwell Publishers, Oxford, 2005, pp. 86-7.

Board, J.L.G. & Sutcliffe, C.M.S. (2005b) Program Trading. In *The Blackwell Encyclopedia of Management,* second edition, volume 4, edited by Ian Garrett, Blackwell Publishers, Oxford, 2005, pp. 159-160.

Board of Banking Supervision (1995) *Report of the Board of Banking Supervision Inquiry into the Circumstances of the Collapse of Barings*, HMSO, 1995.

Bodie, Z. (1983) Commodity futures as a hedge against inflation, *Journal of Portfolio Management*, 9(3), pp. 12-17.

Bodie, Z. & Rosansky, V.I. (1980) Risk and return in commodity futures, *Financial Analysts Journal*, 36(3), pp. 27-39.

Bollen, N.P.B., Smith, T. & Whaley, R.E. (2003) Optimal contract design: for whom?, *Journal of Futures Markets*, 23(8), pp. 719-750.

Bollerslev, T. & Domowitz, I, (1991) Price volatility, spread variability and the role of alternative market mechanisms, *Review of Futures Markets*, 10(1), pp. 78-106.

Bond, G.E., Thompson, S.R. & Lee, B.M.S. (1987) Application of a simplified hedging rule, *Journal of Futures Markets*, 7(1), pp. 65-72.

Booth, G.G., Broussard, J.P., Martikainen, T. & Puttonen, V. (1997) Prudent margin levels in the Finnish stock index futures markets, *Management Science*, 43(8), pp. 1177-1188.

Booth, G.G., Chowdhury, M. & Martikainen, T. (1996) Common volatility in major stock index futures markets, *European Journal of Operations Research*, 95(3), pp. 623-630.

Booth, G.G., Chowdhury, M., Martikainen, T. & Tse, T. (1997) Intraday volatility in international stock index futures markets: meteor showers or heat waves? *Management Science*, 43(11), pp. 1564-1576.

Booth, G.G., Lee, T.H. & Tse, Y. (1996) International linkages in Nikkei stock index futures markets,

Pacific Basin Finance Journal, 4(1), pp. 59-76.

Booth, G.G., Martikainen, T. & Puttonen V. (1993) The international lead-lag effect between market returns: comparison of stock index futures and cash markets, *Journal of International Financial Markets, Institutions and Money*, 3(2), pp. 59-71.

Booth, G.G., So, R.W. & Tse, Y. (1999) Price discovery in the German equity index derivatives markets, *Journal of Futures Markets*, 19(6), pp. 619-643.

Bortoli, L.G., Frino, A. & Jarnecic, E. (2004) Differences in the cost of trade execution services on floor-based and electronic futures markets, *Journal of Financial Services Research*, 26(1), pp. 73-87.

Bortz, G.A. (1984) Does the treasury bond futures market destabilize the treasury bond cash market?, *Journal of Futures Markets*, 4(1), pp. 25-38.

Bowers, J. & Twite, G. (1985) Arbitrage opportunities in the Australian share price index futures contract, *Australian Journal of Management*, 10(2), pp. 1-29.

Bradbery, A. (1992) Norway ready to break out, *Futures and Options World*, no. 252, pp. 37-40.

Brady, N.F. (Chairman). (1988) *Report on the Presidential Task Force on Market Mechanisms*, US Government Printing Office, 320 pages.

Braga, B.S. (1995) Derivatives markets in Brazil: an overview, Working paper, Comissão de Valores Mobiliários, Rio de Janeiro, 23 pages.

Brailsford, T.J., Corrigan, K. & Heaney, R. (2001) A comparison of measures of hedging effectiveness: a case study using the Australian All Ordinaries share price index futures contract, *Journal of Multinational Financial Management*, 11(4-5), pp. 465-481.

Brailsford, T.J. & Cusack, A.J. (1997) A comparison of futures pricing models in a new market: the case of individual share futures, *Journal of Futures Markets*, 17(5), pp. 515-541.

Brailsford, T.J., Frino, A., Hodgson, A. & West, A. (1999) Stock market automation and the transmission of information between spot and futures markets, *Journal of Multinational Financial Management*, 9(3-4), pp. 247-264.

Braund, M. & Gibson-Asner, R. (1998) The effects of newly listed derivatives in a thin stock market, *Review of Derivatives Research*, 2(1), pp. 59-86.

Brealey, R.A. (1970) The distribution and independence of successive rates of return from the British equity market, *Journal of Business Finance*, 2(2), pp. 29-40.

Brennan, M.J. (1986) A theory of price limits in futures markets, *Journal of Financial Economics*, 16(2), pp. 213-233.

Brennan, M.J. & Schwartz, E.S. (1988) Optimal arbitrage strategies under basis variability, *Studies in Banking and Finance*, vol, 5, pp. 167-180.

Brennan, M.J. & Schwartz, E.S. (1990) Arbitrage in stock index futures, *Journal of Business*, 63(1), part 2, pp. S7-S31.

Brenner, M., Subrahmanyam, M.G. & Uno, J. (1989a) Stock index futures arbitrage in the Japanese markets, *Japan and the World Economy*, 1(3), pp. 303-330.

Brenner, M., Subrahmanyam, M.G. & Uno, J. (1989b) The behaviour of prices in the Nikkei spot and futures markets, *Journal of Financial Economics*, 23(2), pp. 363-384.

Brenner, M., Subrahmanyam, M.G. & Uno, J. (1990a) The Japanese stock index futures markets: the early experience. In *Japanese Capital Markets: Analysis and Characteristics of Equity, Debt and Financial Futures Markets*, ed. by E.J. Elton & M.J. Gruber, Harper and Row (Ballinger), pp. 301-334.

Brenner, M., Subrahmanyam, M.G. & Uno, J. (1990b) Arbitrage opportunities in the Japanese stock and futures markets, *Financial Analysts Journal*, 46(2), pp. 14-24.

Brenner, M., Subrahmanyam, M.G. & Uno, J. (1994) The volatility of the Japanese stock indices: evidence from the cash and futures markets. In *Japan, Europe and International Financial Markets: Analytical and Empirical Perspectives*, ed. by R. Sato, R.M. Levich & R.V. Ramachandran, Cambridge University Press, pp. 176-196.

Brinson, G.P., Hood, L.R. & Beebower, G.L. (1986) Determinants of portfolio performance, *Financial Analysts Journal*, 42(4), pp. 39-44.

Brinson, G.P., Singer, B.D. & Beebower, G.L. (1991) Determinants of portfolio performance II: an update, *Financial Analysts Journal*, 47(3), pp. 40-48.

Brock, W.A. & Kleidon, A.W. (1992) Periodic market closure and trading volume: a model of intraday bids and asks, *Journal of Economic Dynamics and Control*, 16(3-4), pp. 451-489.

454 *Stock Index Futures*

Brooks, C., Davies, R.J. & Kim, S.S. (2004) Reducing basis risk for stocks by cross hedging with matched futures, Working paper, City University, 31 pages.

Brooks, C., Garrett, I. & Hinich, M.J. (1999) An alternative approach to investigating lead-lag relationships between stock and stock index futures markets, *Applied Financial Economics*, 9(6), pp. 605-613.

Brooks, C., Henry, O.T. & Persand, G. (2002) The effect of asymmetries on optimal hedge ratios, *Journal of Business*, 75(2), pp. 333-352.

Brooks, C., Rew, A.G. & Ritson, S. (2001) A trading strategy based on the lead-lag relationship between the spot index and futures contract for the FTSE 100, *International Journal of Forecasting*, 17(1), pp. 31-44.

Brooks, R.D. (1994) The unbiased prediction hypothesis in futures markets: a varying coefficient approach, Working paper no. 1994-11, RMIT, Australia.

Brooks, R.D. & Hand, J. (1988) Evaluating the performance of stock portfolios with index futures contracts, *Journal of Futures Markets*, 8(1), pp. 33-46.

Brooks, R.D. & Lee, J.H.H. (1997) The stability of ARCH models across Australian financial futures markets, *Applied Financial Economics*, 7(4), pp. 347-359.

Brooks, R.D. & Michaelides, P.S. (1995) Autocorrelations, returns and Australian financial futures, *Applied Economics Letters*, 2(10), pp. 323-326.

Brorsen, B.W. (1991) Futures trading, transactions costs and stock market volatility, *Journal of Futures Markets*, 11(2), pp. 153-163.

Brorsen, B.W. & Irwin, S.H. (1985) Examination of commodity fund performance, *Review of Research in Futures Markets*, 4(1), pp. 84-94.

Brorsen, B.W. & Lukac, L.P. (1990) Optimal portfolios for commodity futures funds, *Journal of Futures Markets*, 10(3), pp. 247-258.

Broussard, J.P. & Booth. G.G. (1998) The behaviour of extreme values in Germany's stock index futures: an application to intra-daily margin setting, *European Journal of Operational Research*, 104(3), pp. 393-402.

Brown, C.A. (2001) The successful re-denomination of a futures contract: the case of an Australian All Ordinaries share price index futures contract, *Pacific-Basin Finance Journal*, 9(1), pp. 47-64.

Brown, S.L. (1985) A reformulation of the portfolio model of hedging, *American Journal of Agricultural Economics*, 67(3), pp. 508-512.

Brown, S., Laux, P. & Schachter, B. (1991) On the existence of an optimal tick size, *Review of Futures Markets*, 10(1), pp. 50-72.

Brown-Hruska, S. & Kuserk, G. (1995) Volatility, volume and the notion of balance in the S&P500 cash and futures markets, *Journal of Futures Markets*, 15(6), pp. 677-689.

Buckle, M., ap Gwilym, O., Thomas, S.H. & Woodhams, M.S. (1998) Intraday empirical regularities in interest rate and equity index futures markets and the effect of macroeconomic announcements, *Journal of Business Finance and Accounting*, 25(7-8), pp. 921-944.

Buckle, M. Clare, A. & Thomas, S. (1999) Developing a trading rule from the FTSE 100 stock index futures contract: evidence in support of the EMH, *Journal of Business Finance and Accounting*, 26(1-2), pp. 249-260.

Bühler, W. & Kempf, A. (1994) The value of the early unwind option in futures contracts with an endogenous basis, Working paper no. 94-2, University of Mannheim, 28 pages.

Bühler, W. & Kempf, A. (1995) DAX index futures: mispricing and arbitrage in German markets, *Journal of Futures Markets*, 15(7), pp. 833-859.

Burton, J. (1990) Divide and rule, *Futures and Options World*, no. 230, pp. 55-56.

Butterworth, D. & Holmes, P. (2000) Ex ante hedging effectiveness of UK stock index futures contracts: evidence for the FTSE 100 and FTSE Mid 250 contracts, *European Financial Management*, 6(4), pp. 441-457.

Butterworth, D. & Holmes, P. (2001) The hedging effectiveness of stock index futures: evidence for the FTSE 100 and FTSE Mid 250 indices traded in the UK, *Applied Financial Economics*, 11(1), pp. 57-68.

Butterworth, D. & Holmes, P. (2002) Inter-market spread trading: evidence from UK index futures markets, *Applied Financial Economics*, 12(11), pp. 783-790.

Cakici, N. & Chatterjee, S. (1991) Pricing stock index futures with stochastic interest rates, *Journal of*

Futures Markets, 11(4), pp. 441-452.

Cakici, N., Harpaz, G. & Yagil, J. (1990) The inefficiency of the Value Line futures market. In *Advances in Futures and Options Research: A Research Annual*, vol. 4, ed. by F.J. Fabozzi, JAI Press Inc., pp. 237-251.

Canina, L. & Figlewski, S. (1995) Program trading and stock index arbitrage. In *Finance*, ed. by R.A. Jarrow, V. Maksimovic & W.T. Ziemba, Handbooks in Operations research and Management Science, vol. 9, Elsevier Science B.V. pp. 315-339.

Cargill, T.F. & Rausser, G.C. (1975) Temporal price behaviour in commodity futures markets, *Journal of Finance*, 30(4), pp. 1043-1053.

Carlton, D.W. (1984) Futures markets: their purpose, their history, their growth, their successes and failures, *Journal of Futures Markets*, 4(3), pp. 237-271.

Carpenter, A. (1991) *Inside the International Financial Futures and Options Markets*, Woodhead-Faulkner, Simon and Schuster.

Carroll, B.L. (1989) *Financial Futures Trading*, Butterworths.

Cass, D. & Shell, K. (1983) Do sunspots matter?, *Journal of Political Economy*, 91(2), pp. 193-227.

Castelino, M.G. (1992) Hedge effectiveness: basis risk and minimum-variance hedging, *Journal of Futures Markets*, 12(2), pp. 187-201.

Castelino, M.G. & Francis, J.C. (1982) Basis speculation in commodity futures: the maturity effect, *Journal of Futures Markets*, 2(2), pp. 195-206.

Castelino, M.G. & Vora, A. (1984) Spread volatility in commodity futures: the length effect, *Journal of Futures Markets*, 4(1), pp. 39-46.

Cecchetti, S.G., Cumby, R.E. & Figlewski, S. (1988) Estimation of the optimal futures hedge, *Review of Economics and Statistics*, 70(4), pp. 623-630.

Chakravarty, S. (1994) Should actively traded futures contracts come under the dual trading ban?, *Journal of Futures Markets*, 14(6), pp. 661-684.

Chakravarty, S. & Lai, K. (2003a) A Bayesian analysis of dual trader informativeness in futures markets, *Journal of Empirical Finance*, 10(3), pp. 355-371.

Chakravarty, S. & Lai, K. (2003b) An examination of own account trading by dual traders in futures markets, *Journal of Financial Economics*, 69(2), pp. 375-397.

Chalk, D.C.H. (1993) An Event Study of the Effect of Base Rate Changes on FTSE 100 Index Futures. MSc Dissertation, University of Southampton, 51 pages.

Chamberlain, T.W. (1989) Maturity effects in futures markets: some evidence from the City of London, *Scottish Journal of Political Economy*, 36(1), pp. 90-95.

Chamberlain, T.W., Cheung, C.S. & Kwan, C.C.Y. (1988) Cash versus futures prices and the weekend effect: the Canadian evidence. In *Advances in Futures and Options Research: A Research Annual*, vol. 3, ed. by F.J. Fabozzi, JAI Press Inc., pp. 329-339.

Chamberlain, T.W., Cheung, C.S. & Kwan, C.C.Y. (1989) Expiration-day effects of index futures and options: some Canadian evidence, *Financial Analysts Journal*, 45(5), pp. 67-71.

Chan, K. (1992) A further analysis of the lead-lag relationship between the cash market and stock index futures market, *Review of Financial Studies*, 5(1), pp. 123-152.

Chan, K., Chan, K.C. & Karolyi, G.A. (1991) Intraday volatility in the stock index and stock index futures markets, *Review of Financial Studies*, 4(4), pp. 657-684.

Chan, K. & Chung, Y.P. (1993) Intraday relationships among index arbitrage, spot and futures price volatility, and spot market volume: a transactions data test, *Journal of Banking and Finance*, 17(4), pp. 663-687.

Chan, K. & Chung, Y.P. (1995) Vector autoregression or simultaneous equations model? The intraday relationship between index arbitrage and market volatility, *Journal of Banking and Finance*, 19(1), pp. 173-179.

Chan, K.C. & Karolyi, G.A. (1991) The volatility of the Japanese stock market: evidence from 1977 to 1990. In *Japanese Financial Market Research*, ed. by W. Ziemba, W. Bailey & Y. Hamao, North-Holland, pp. 121-144.

Chan, Y.C. (2002) Volatility, volume and pricing efficiency in the stock index futures market when the underlying cash market does not trade, Working paper, Hong Kong Polytechnic University, 29 pages.

Chance, D.M. (1990) *The Effect of Margins on the Volatility of Stock and Derivative Markets: A Review of the Evidence*, Salomon Centre, Leonard N. Stern School of Business, New York University, Monograph Series in Finance and Economics, No. 1990-2, 65 pages.

Chance, D.M. (1991) *An Introduction to Options and Futures*, Dryden Press, Second edition.

Chance, D.M. (1994a) *Managed Futures and Their Role in Investment Portfolios*, Research Foundation of the Institute of Chartered Financial Analysts.

Chance, D.M. (1994b) Futures pricing and the cost of carry under price limits, *Journal of Futures Markets*, 14(7), pp. 813-836.

Chang, C.W., Chang, J.S.K. & Fang, H. (1996) Optimum futures hedges with jump risk and stochastic basis, *Journal of Futures Markets*, 16(4), pp. 441-458.

Chang, C.W., Chang, J.S.K., Loo, J.C.H. & Fang, H. (1991) Marking to market and futures-forward price differential: further evidence from the foreign exchange markets. In *Pacific Basin Capital Markets Research*, vol. 2, ed. by S.G. Rhee & R.P. Chang, North Holland, pp. 453-475.

Chang, E.C. Cheng, J.W. & Pinegar, J.M. (1999) Does futures trading increase stock market volatility? The case of the Nikkei stock index futures market, *Journal of Banking and Finance*, 23(5), pp. 727-753.

Chang, E., Chou, R.Y. & Nelling, E.F. (2000) Market volatility and the demand for hedging in stock index futures, *Journal of Futures Markets*, 20(2), pp. 105-125.

Chang, E.C., Jain, P.C. & Locke, P.R. (1995) Standard and Poor's 500 index futures volatility and price changes around the New York Stock Exchange close, *Journal of Business*, 68(1), pp. 61-84.

Chang, E.C., Locke, P.R. & Mann, S.C. (1994) The effect of CME rule 552 on dual traders, *Journal of Futures Markets*, 14(4), pp. 493-510.

Chang, E.C., Pinegar, J.M. and Schachter, B. (1997) Interday variations in volume, variance and participation of large speculators, *Journal of Banking and Finance*, 21(6), pp. 797-810.

Chang, J.S.K. & Fang, H. (1990) An intertemporal measure of hedging effectiveness, *Journal of Futures Markets*, 10(3), pp. 307-321.

Chang, J.S.K., Loo, J.C.H. & Chang, C.C.W. (1990) The pricing of futures contracts and the arbitrage pricing theory, *Journal of Financial Research*, 13(4), pp. 297-306.

Chang, J.S.K. & Shanker, L. (1986) Hedging effectiveness of currency options and currency futures, *Journal of Futures Markets*, 6(2), pp. 289-304.

Chang, J.S.K. & Shanker, L. (1987) A risk-return measure of hedging effectiveness: a comment, *Journal of Financial and Quantitative Analysis*, 22(3), pp. 373-376.

Chari, V.V. & Jagannathan, R. (1990) The simple analytics of commodity futures markets: do they stabilize prices? Do they raise welfare?, *Federal Reserve Bank of Minneapolis Quarterly Review*, 14(3), pp. 12-24.

Chari, V.V., Jagannathan, R. & Jones, L. (1990) Price stability and futures trading in commodities, *Quarterly Journal of Economics*, 105(2), pp. 527-534.

Chatrath, A., Christie-David, R., Dhanda, K.K. & Koch, T.W. (2002) Index futures leadership, basis behaviour and trader selectivity, *Journal of Futures Markets*, 22(7), pp. 649-677.

Chen, C. & Williams, J. (1994) Triple witching hour, the change in expiration timing and the stock market reaction. *Journal of Futures Markets*, 14(3), pp. 275-292.

Chen, H. (1998) Price limits, overreaction, and price resolution in futures markets, *Journal of Futures Markets*, 18(3), pp. 243-263.

Chen, H. (2002) Price limits and margin requirements in futures markets, *The Financial Review*, 37(1), pp. 105-121.

Chen, J. & Locke, P.R. (2004) Splitting the S&P500 futures, *Journal of Futures Markets*, 24(12), pp. 1147-1163.

Chen, N.F., Cuny, C.J. & Haugen, R.A. (1995) Stock volatility and the levels of the basis and open interest in futures contracts, *Journal of Finance*, 50(1), pp. 281-300.

Chen, S.K., Jarrett, J.E. & Rhee, S.G. (1992) The impact of futures trading on cash market volatility: evidence from the Tokyo Stock Exchange, PACAP Research Centre, University of Rhode Island, Working paper 92-05, 20 pages.

Chen, S.S., Lee, C.F. & Shrestha, K. (2003) Futures hedge ratios: a review, *Quarterly Review of Economics and Finance*, 43(3), pp. 433-465.

Chen, S.S., Lee, C.F. & Shrestha, K. (2004) An empirical analysis of the relationship between the hedge ratio and hedging horizon: a simultaneous estimation of the short and long run hedge ratios, *Journal of Futures Markets*, 24(4), pp. 359-386.

Chen, Y.J., Duan, J.C. & Hung, M.W. (1999) Volatility and maturity effects in the Nikkei index futures, *Journal of Futures Markets*, 19(8), pp. 895-909.

Cheng, K. & Cheng, L.T.W (2000) Trading hour extension in futures markets reduces cash market volatility, Hong Kong Futures Exchange, Educational article no. 8, 3 pages.

Cheng, K.H.K., Fung, J.K.W. & Tse, Y. (2005) How electronic trading affects bid-ask spreads and arbitrage efficiency between index futures and options, *Journal of Futures Markets*, 25(4), pp. 375-398.

Cheng, L.T.W., Fung, J.K.W. & Chan, K.C. (2000) Pricing dynamics of index options and index futures in Hong Kong before and during the Asian financial crisis, *Journal of Futures Markets*, 20(2), pp. 145-166.

Cheng, L.T.W., Fung, J.K.W. & Pang, C. (1998) Early unwinding strategy in index options-futures arbitrage, *Journal of Financial Research*, 21(4), pp. 447-467.

Cheng, L.T.W., Jiang, L. & Ng, R.W.Y. (2004) Information content of extended trading for index futures, *Journal of Futures Markets*, 24(9), pp. 861-886.

Cheng, L.T.W. & White, J. (2003) Measuring pricing inefficiencies under stressful market conditions, *Journal of Business Finance and Accounting*, 30(3-4), pp. 383-411.

Chetverikov, V.M. (2000) Arbitrage possibilities in Russian spot and future markets, Working paper, Economics Education & Research Consortium.

Cheung, C.S., Kwan, C.C.Y. & Yip, P.C.Y. (1990) The hedging effectiveness of options and futures: a mean-Gini approach, *Journal of Futures Markets*, 10(1), pp. 61-73.

Cheung, Y.W. & Ng, L.K. (1990) The dynamics of S&P500 index and S&P500 futures intraday price volatilities, *Review of Futures Markets*, 9(2), pp. 458-486.

Chiang, M.H. (2003) Price discovery and changes in regimes for stock index futures, *Global Finance Journal*, 14(3), pp. 287-301.

Chiang, R. & Fong, W.M. (2001) Relative informational efficiency of cash, futures and options markets: the case of an emerging market, *Journal of Banking and Finance*, 25(2), pp. 355-375.

Chicago Board of Trade. (1989) *Stock Index Futures and Dividend Seasonality*. MMI Trading Strategy Series, CBOT.

Chicago Board of Trade. (1990) *Stock Index Futures: A Home Study Course*, Chicago Board of Trade.

Chicago Board of Trade. (1991) *Major Market Index Futures and Options Reference Guide*, Chicago Board of Trade.

Chng, M.T. (2004a) A model of price discovery and market design: theory and empirical evidence, *Journal of Futures Markets*, 24(12), pp. 1107-1146.

Chng, M.T. (2004b) The trading dynamics of close-substitute futures markets: evidence of margin policy spillover effects, *Journal of Multinational Financial Management*, 14(4-5), pp. 463-483.

Chng, M.T. & Gannon, G. (2003) Contemporaneous intraday volume, option and futures volatility transmissions across parallel markets, *International Review of Financial Analysis*, 12(1), pp. 49-68.

Cho, D.C. & Frees, E.W. (1988) Estimating the volatility of discrete stock prices, *Journal of Finance*, 43(2), pp. 451-466.

Choi, H. & Subrahmanyam, A. (1994) Using intraday data to test for effects of index futures on the underlying stock market, *Journal of Futures Markets*, 14(3), pp. 293-322.

Chou, P.H., Lin, M.C. & Yu, M.T. (2000) Price limits, margin requirements and default risk, *Journal of Futures Markets*, 20(6), pp. 573-602.

Chou, P.H., Lin, M.C. & Yu, M.T. (2003) The effectiveness of coordinating price limits across futures and spot markets, *Journal of Futures Markets*, 23(6), pp. 577-602.

Chou, R.K. & Chung, H. (2004) Decimalization, trading costs and information transmissions between ETFs and index futures, Working paper, National Central University at Taiwan.

Chou, R.K. & Lee, J.H. (2002) The relative efficiencies of price execution between the Singapore Exchange and the Taiwan Futures Exchange, *Journal of Futures Markets*, 22(2), pp. 173-196.

Chou, W.L., Denis, K.K.F. & Lee, C.F. (1996) Hedging with the Nikkei index futures: the conventional model versus the error correction model, *Quarterly Review of Economics and Finance*, 36(4), pp. 495-505.

Chou, W.L., Denis, K.K.F. & Lee, C.F. (1996) Hedging with the Nikkei index futures: the conventional model versus the error correction model, *Quarterly Review of Economics and Finance*, 36(4), pp. 495-505.

Choudhry, T. (1997) Short run deviations and volatility in spot and futures stock returns: evidence from Australia, Hong King and Japan, *Journal of Futures Markets*, 17(6), pp. 689-705.

Choudhry, T. (2003) Short-run deviations and optimal hedge ratio: evidence from stock futures, *Journal of Multinational Financial Management*, 13(2), pp. 171-192.

Choudhry, T. (2004) The hedging effectiveness of constant and time-varying hedge ratios using three Pacific Basin stock futures, *International Review of Economics and Finance*, 13(4), pp. 371-385.

Chow, Y.F., Yung, H.H.M. & Zhang, H. (2003) Expiration day effects: the case of Hong Kong, *Journal of Futures Markets*, 23(1), pp. 67-86.

Chu, C.C. & Bubnys, E.L. (1990) A likelihood ratio test of price volatilities: comparing stock index spot and futures, *The Financial Review*, 25(1), pp. 81-94.

Chu, Q.C., Hsieh, W.G. & Tse, Y. (1999) Price discovery on the S&P500 index markets; an analysis of spot index, index futures and SPDRs, *International Review of Financial Analysis*, 8(1), pp. 21-34.

Chung, H., Liu, M.Y., Wu, S. & Yang, F.J. (2003) Transactions costs and trading activity in the index futures market: the case of the transaction tax reduction in Taiwan, Working paper, Chines Culture University, 41 pages.

Chung, Y.P. (1991) A transaction data test of stock index futures market efficiency and index arbitrage profitability, *Journal of Finance*, 46(5), pp. 1791-1809.

Chung, Y.P., Kang, J.K. & Rhee, S.G. (1994a) The lead-lag relationship between the stock market and stock index futures market in Japan. PACAP Research Centre, University of Rhode Island, Working paper, 27 pages.

Chung, Y.P., Kang, J.K. & Rhee, S.G. (1994b) Index arbitrage in Japan. PACAP Research Centre, University of Rhode Island, Working paper, 35 pages.

Chung, Y.P., Kang, J.K. & Rhee, S.G. (2003) Index-futures arbitrage in Japan. In *The Japanese Finance: Corporate Finance and Capital Markets in Changing Japan*, ed. by J.J. Choi & T. Hiraki, Elsevier, pp. 173-197.

Cinar, E.M. & Vu, J.D. (1991) Seasonal effects in the Value Line and Standard and Poor's 500 cash and futures returns, *Review of Futures Markets*, 10(2), pp. 282-295.

Cita, J. & Lien, D.D. (1992) Constructing accurate cash settlement indices: the role of index specifications, *Journal of Futures Markets*, 12(3), pp. 339-360.

Cita, J. & Lien, D.D. (1997) Estimating cash settlement price: the bootstrap and other estimators, *Journal of Futures Markets*, 17(6), pp. 617-632.

Clare, A. & Miffre, J. (1995) A note on forecasting the CAC 40 and DAX stock index futures, *Applied Economics Letters*, 2(10), pp. 327-330.

Clark, P.K. (1973) A subordinated stochastic process model with finite variance for speculative prices, *Econometrica*, 41(1), pp. 135-159.

Clark, R. & Ziemba, W.T. (1987) Playing the turn of the year effect with index futures, *Operations Research*, 35(6), pp. 799-813.

Clarke, R.G. (1992) Asset allocation using futures markets. In *Active Asset Allocation: State-of-the Art Portfolio Policies, Strategies and Tactics*, ed. by R.D. Arnott & F.J. Fabozzi, Probus Publishing Co., pp. 303-326.

Clerc, N. & Gibson, R. (2000) Do newly listed derivatives affect the market risk premium in a thin stock market, *European Finance Review*, 4(2), pp. 97-127.

Clowes, M.J. (2000) *The Money Flood: How Pension Funds Revolutionized Investing*, John Wiley & Sons, chapter 12.

Cohen, B.H. (1999) Derivatives, volatility and price discovery, *International Finance*, 2(2), pp. 167-202.

Cohen, L.R. (1993) A futures market in cadaveric organs: would it work?, *Transplantation Proceedings*, 25(1), pp. 60-61.

Commodity Futures Trading Commission. (1995) *Commitments of Traders in Futures*, Commodity Futures Trading Commission.

Conrardy, R.T. (1993) The intra day effects of program trading on stock returns, *Review of Futures Markets*, 12(1), pp. 167-173.

Cooper, I. & Mello, A.S. (1990) Stock index futures: the case for markets in baskets of securities. In

Advances in Futures and Options Research: A Research Annual, vol. 4, ed. by F.J. Fabozzi, JAI Press Inc., pp. 23-38.

Cootner, P.H. (1966) Stock market indexes: fallacies and illusions, *Commercial and Financial Chronicle*, 29th September.

Copeland, L., Lam, K. & Jones, S.A. (2004) The index futures markets: is screen trading more efficient?, *Journal of Futures Markets*, 24(4), pp. 337-357.

Copeland, T.E. (1976) A model of asset trading under the assumption of sequential information arrival, *Journal of Finance*, 31(4), pp. 1149-1168.

Copeland, T.E. & Weston, J.F. (1988) *Financial Theory and Corporate Policy*, Addison-Wesley, Third edition, Ch. 9.

Coppejans, M. & Domowitz, I. (1996) Automated trade execution and open outcry trading: a first look at the GLOBEX trading system. Working paper, Duke University, 49 pages.

Cornell, B. (1981) The relationship between volume and price variability in futures markets, *Journal of Futures Markets*, 1(3), pp. 303-316.

Cornell, B. (1985a) Taxes and the pricing of stock index futures: empirical results, *Journal of Futures Markets*, 5(1), pp. 89-101.

Cornell, B. (1985b) The weekly pattern in stock returns: cash versus futures: a note, *Journal of Finance*, 40(2), pp. 583-588.

Cornell, B. & French, K.R. (1983a) The pricing of stock index futures, *Journal of Futures Markets*, 3(1), pp. 1-14.

Cornell, B. & French, K.R. (1983b) Taxes and the pricing of stock index futures, *Journal of Finance*, 38(3), pp. 675-694.

Corner, D. & Takenashi, T. (1992) New Japanese index futures contracts: a comparison with US and UK contracts. In *Risk, Portfolio Management and Capital Markets*, ed. by T.E. Cooke, J. Matatko & D.C. Stafford, Macmillan, pp. 130-157.

Cornew, R.W. (1988) Commodity pool operators and their pools: expenses and profitability, *Journal of Futures Markets*, 8(5), pp. 617-637.

Cotter, J. (2001) Margin exceedences for European stock index futures using extreme value theory, *Journal of Banking and Finance*, 25(8), pp. 1475-1502.

Cotter, J. (2004) Minimum capital requirement calculations for UK futures, *Journal of Futures Markets*, 24(2), pp. 193-220.

Covey, T. & Bessler, D.A. (1995) Asset storability and the informational content of inter-temporal prices, *Journal of Empirical Finance*, 2(2), pp. 103-115.

Covrig, V., Ding, D.K. & Low, B.S. (2004) The contribution of a satellite market to price discovery: evidence from the Singapore exchange, *Journal of Futures Markets*, 24(10), pp. 981-1004.

Cox, C.C. (1976) Futures trading and market information, *Journal of Political Economy*, 84(6), pp. 1215-1237.

Cox, J.C., Ingersoll, J.E. & Ross, S.A. (1981) The relation between forward prices and futures prices, *Journal of Financial Economics*, 9(4), pp. 321-346.

Craig, A., Dravid, A. & Richardson, M. (1995) Market efficiency around the clock: some supporting evidence using foreign-based derivatives, *Journal of Financial Economics*, 39(2-3), pp. 161-180.

Craine, R. (1992) Are futures margins adequate? University of California at Berkeley, Working paper no. 92-192, 29 pages.

Craine, R. (1997) Valuing the futures market performance guarantee, *Macroeconomic Dynamics*, 1(4), pp. 701-719.

Crato, N. & Ray, B.K. (2000) Memory in returns and volatilities of futures contracts, *Journal of Futures Markets*, 20(6), pp. 525-543.

Cuthbertson, K., Hall, S.G. & Taylor, M.P. (1992) *Applied Econometric Techniques*, Harvester Wheatsheaf, Hemel Hempstead.

Deaves, R. (1994) Naïve versus conditional hedging strategies: the case of Canadian stock index futures, *Canadian Journal of Administrative Sciences*, 11(3), pp. 264-270.

Daigle, K. & Schachter, B. (1992) Clearing houses in futures markets. In *The New Palgrave Dictionary of Money and Finance*, ed. by P. Newman, M. Milgate & J. Eatwell, Macmillan, vol. 1, pp 367-369.

Daigler, R.T. (1990) The S&P500 index futures: a hedging contract, *CME Financial Strategy Paper*,

CME, 6 pages.

Daigler, R.T. (1993a) *Financial Futures Markets: Concepts, Evidence and Applications*, Harper Collins College Publishers.

Daigler, R.T. (1993b) *Managing Risk with Financial Futures: Hedging, Pricing and Arbitrage*, Probus Publishing Co.

Daigler, R.T. (1997) Intraday futures volatility and theories of market behaviour, *Journal of Futures Markets*, 17(1), pp. 45-74.

Daigler, R.T. & Wiley, M.K. (1999) The impact of trader type on the futures volatility-volume relation, *Journal of Finance*, 54(6), pp. 2297-2316.

Damodaran, A. (1990) Index futures and stock market volatility, *Review of Futures Markets*, 9(2), pp. 442-457.

Darrat, A.F. & Rahman, S. (1995) Has futures trading activity caused stock price volatility? *Journal of Futures Markets*, 15(5), pp. 537-557.

Darrat, A.F. & Rahman, S. (1999) The long-run relationship between spot and futures prices of the S&P500 index: evidence from cointegration tests, *Advances in Investment Analysis and Portfolio Management*, vol. 6, ed. by C.F. Lee, JAI Press, pp. 47-54.

Darrat, A.F., Rahman, S. & Zhong, M. (2002) On the role of futures trading in spot market fluctuations: perpetrator of volatility or victim of regret?, *Journal of Financial Research*, 25(3), pp. 431-444.

Dawson, P. (1993) Stock index futures hedging ratios: fair values, temporal effects and lead-lad relationships - commentary, *Review of Futures Markets*, 11(1), pp. 11-12.

Dawson, P. & Gemmill, G. (1990) Returns to market making on the London Traded Options Market, *Review of Futures Markets*, 9(3), pp. 666-680.

De Ceuster, M.J.K., Durinck, E., Laveren, E. & Lodewyckx, J. (2000) A survey into the use of derivatives by large non-financial forms operating in Belgium, *European Financial Management*, 6(3), pp. 301-318.

DeMarzo, P.M. & Duffie, D. (1991) Corporate financial hedging with proprietary information, *Journal of Economic Theory*, 53(2), pp. 261-286.

De Jong, F. & Donders, M.W.M. (1997) Intraday lead-lag relationships between the futures, options and stock market, *European Finance Review*, vol. 1(3), pp. 337-359.

De Jong, F. & Nijman, T. (1997) High frequency analysis of lead-lag relationships between financial markets, *Journal of Empirical Finance*, 4(2-3), pp. 259-277.

Demirer, R., Lien, D.D. & Shaffer, D.R. (2005) Comparisons of short and long hedge performance: the case of Taiwan, *Journal of Multinational Financial Management*, 15(1), pp. 51-66.

Dennis, S.A. & Sim, A.B. (1999) Share price volatility with the introduction of individual share futures on the Sydney Futures Exchange, *International Review of Financial Analysis*, 8(2), pp. 153-163.

De Roon, F.A., Nijman, T.E. & Veld, C. (2000) Hedging pressure effects in futures markets, *Journal of Finance*, 55(3), pp. 1437-1456.

Dewachter, H. & Gielens, G. (1999) Setting futures margins: the extremes approach, *Applied Financial Economics*, 9(2), pp. 173-181.

Dhillon, U. & Johnson, H. (1991) Changes in the Standard and Poor's list, *Journal of Business*, 64(1), pp. 75-85.

Diamond, B.B. & Kollar, M.P. (1989) *24-Hour Trading: The Global Network of Futures and Options Markets*, John Wiley & Sons.

Dimson, E. (editor). (1988) *Stock Market Anomalies*, Cambridge University Press.

Ding, D.K. & Charoenwong, C. (2003) Bid-ask spreads, volatility, quote revisions and trades of thinly traded futures contracts, *Journal of Futures Markets*, 23(5), pp. 455-486.

Do, B.H. & Faff, R.W. (2004) Do futures-based strategies enhance dynamic portfolio insurance?, *Journal of Futures Markets*, 24(6), pp. 591-608.

Domowitz, I. (1993a) Equally open and competitive: regulatory approval of automated trade execution in the futures markets, *Journal of Futures Markets*, 13(1), pp. 93-113.

Domowitz, I. (1993b) A taxonomy of automated trade execution systems, *Journal of International Money and Finance*, 12(6), pp. 607-631.

Domowitz, I. (1995) Electronic derivatives exchanges: implicit mergers, network externalities and standardization, *Quarterly Review of Economics and Finance*, 35(2), pp. 163-175.

Draper, P. & Fung, J.K.W. (2002) A study of arbitrage efficiency between the FTSE 100 index futures and options contracts, *Journal of Futures Markets*, 22(1), pp. 31-58.

Draper, P. & Fung, J.K.W. (2003) Discretionary government intervention and the mispricing on index futures, *Journal of Futures Markets*, 23(12), pp. 1159-1189.

Drummen, M. & Zimmermann, H. (1991) European stock market indices: hedging and tracking performance, *Journal of International Securities Markets*, vol. 5, Summer, pp. 19-28.

Dubofsky, D.A. (1987) Hedging dividend capture strategies with stock index futures, *Journal of Futures Markets*, 7(5), pp. 471-481.

Dubofsky, D.A. (1992) *Options and Financial Futures: Valuation and Uses*, McGraw-Hill.

Dubofsky, D.A. & Kannan, S. (1993) Hedged dividend capture and ex-day returns: an empirical update, *Journal of Business Finance and Accounting*, 20(5), pp. 725-735.

Duffee, G., Kupiec, P. & White. A.P. (1992) A primer on program trading and stock price volatility: a survey of the issues and the evidence. In *Research in Financial Services: Private and Public Policy*, vol. 4, ed. by G.G. Kaufman, JAI Press Inc., pp. 21-49.

Duffie, D. (1989) *Futures Markets*, Prentice-Hall.

Duffie, D. (1990) The risk-neutral value of the early arbitrage option: a note. In *Advances in Futures and Options Research*, vol. 4, ed. by F.J. Fabozzi, JAI Press Inc., pp. 107-110.

Dumas, B., & Allaz, B. (1995) *Financial Securities: Market Equilibrium and Pricing Methods*, Chapman & Hall.

Dusak, K. (1973) Futures trading and investor returns: an investigation of commodity market risk premiums, *Journal of Political Economy*, 81(6), pp. 1387-1406.

Dutt, H.R. & Wein, I.L. (2003a) Revisiting the empirical estimation of the effect of margin changes on futures trading volume, *Journal of Futures Markets,* 23(6), pp. 561-576.

Dutt, H.R. & Wein, I.L. (2003b) On the adequacy of single stock futures margining requirements, *Journal of Futures Markets*, 23(10), pp. 989-1002.

Dwyer, G.P., Locke, P.R. & Yu, W. (1996) Index arbitrage and nonlinear dynamics between the S&P500 futures and cash, *Review of Financial Studies*, 9(1), pp. 301-332.

Dybvig, P.H. & Ross, S.A. (1992) Arbitrage. In *The New Palgrave Dictionary of Money and Finance*, ed. by P. Newman, M. Milgate & J. Eatwell, Macmillan, 1992, vol. 1, pp 43-50.

Dyl, E.A. & Maberly, E.D. (1986a) The daily distribution of changes in the price of stock index futures, *Journal of Futures Markets*, 6(4), pp. 513-521.

Dyl, E.A. & Maberly, E.D. (1986b) The weekly pattern in stock index futures: a further note, *Journal of Finance*, 41(5), pp. 1149-1152.

Dyl, E.A. & Maberly, E.D. (1988) A possible explanation of the weekend effect, *Financial Analysts Journal*, 44(3), pp. 83-84.

Eagle, D. & Nelson, E. (1991) Index arbitrage and the concentration effect, *Review of Futures Markets*, 10(2), pp. 212-247.

Eckl, S. & Robinson, J.N. (1990) Some issues in corporate hedging policy, *Accounting and Business Research*, vol. 20, no. 80, pp. 287-298.

Ederington, L.H. (1979) The hedging performance of the new futures markets, *Journal of Finance*, 34(1), pp. 157-170.

Ederington, L.H. & Lee, J.H. (1993) How markets process information: news releases and volatility, *Journal of Finance*, 48(4), pp. 1161-1191.

Ederington, L.H. & Lee, J.H. (1995) The short run dynamics of the price adjustment to new information, *Journal of Financial and Quantitative Analysis*, 30(1), pp. 117-134.

Edwards, F.R. (1984) The clearing association in futures markets: guarantor and regulator. In *The Industrial Organization of Futures Markets*, ed. by R.W. Anderson, Lexington Books, pp. 225-259.

Edwards, F.R. (1988a) Does futures trading increase stock market volatility?, *Financial Analysts Journal*, 44(1), pp. 63-69.

Edwards, F.R. (1988b) Futures trading and cash market volatility: stock index and interest rate futures, *Journal of Futures Markets*, 8(4), pp. 421-439.

Edwards, F.R. (1993) Taxing transactions in futures markets: objectives and effects, *Journal of Financial Services Research*, 7(1), pp. 75-91.

Edwards, F.R. & Ma, C.W. (1992) *Futures and Options*, McGraw-Hill.

Edwards, F.R. & Neftci, S.N. (1988) Extreme price movements and margin levels in futures markets, *Journal of Futures Markets*, 8(6), pp. 639-655.

Edwards, F.R. & Park, J.M. (1996) Do managed futures make good investments?, *Journal of Futures Markets*, 16(5), pp. 475-517.

Ekman, P.D. (1992) Intraday patterns in the S&P500 index futures market, *Journal of Futures Markets*, 12(4), pp. 365-381.

Elam, E. (1991) Reduction in hedging risk from adjusting for autocorrelation in the residuals of a price level regression, *Journal of Futures Markets*, 11(3), pp. 371-384.

Eldridge, R.M., Peat, M. & Stevenson, M. (2003) The role of intraday and interday data effects in determining linear and nonlinear Granger causality between Australian futures and cash index markets, Working paper no. 22, University of Technology Sydney, 33 pages.

Elton, E.J. & Gruber, M.J. (1991) *Modern Portfolio Theory and Investment Analysis*, John Wiley & Sons, Fourth edition, Ch. 21.

Elton, E.J., Gruber, M.J. & Rentzler, J.C. (1984) Intra-day tests of the efficiency of the treasury bill futures market, *Review of Economics and Statistics*, 62(1), pp. 129-137.

Elton, E.J., Gruber, M.J. & Rentzler, J.C. (1987) Professionally managed publicly traded commodity funds, *Journal of Business*, 60(2), pp. 175-199.

Elton, E.J., Gruber, M.J. & Rentzler, J.C. (1990) The performance of publicly offered commodity funds, *Financial Analysts Journal*, 46(4), pp. 23-30.

Epps, T.W. & Epps, M.L. (1976) The stochastic dependence of security price changes and transaction volumes: implications for the mixture of distributions hypothesis, *Econometrica*, 44(2), pp. 305-321.

Eytan, T.H. (1990) Corporate taxes and hedging with futures, *Journal of Futures Markets*, 10(5), pp. 535-540.

Eytan, T.H. & Harpaz, G. (1986) The pricing of futures and options contracts on the Value Line index, *Journal of Finance*, 41(4), pp. 843-855.

Fabozzi, F.J., Fabozzi, T.D. & Peters, E.E. (1989) Applications of stock index futures to index fund management. In *Handbook of Stock Index Futures and Options*, ed. by F.J. Fabozzi & G.M. Kipnis, Dow Jones-Irwin, pp. 244-257.

Fabozzi, F.J. & Garlicki, T.D. (1984) Creating an index fund. In *Stock Index Futures*, ed. by F.J. Fabozzi & G.M. Kipnis, Dow Jones-Irwin, pp. 199-209.

Fabozzi, F.J., Ma, C.K. & Briley, J.E. (1994) Holiday trading in futures markets, *Journal of Finance*, 49(1), pp. 307-324.

Fabozzi, F.J. & Peters, E.E. (1989) Hedging with stock index futures. In *Handbook of Stock Index Futures and Options*, ed. by F.J. Fabozzi & G.M. Kipnis, Dow Jones-Irwin, pp. 188-222.

Fama, E.F. (1991) Efficient capital markets: II, *Journal of Finance*, 46(5), pp. 1575-1617.

Farrell, C.H. & Olszewski, E.A. (1993) Assessing inefficiency in the S&P500 futures market, *Journal of Forecasting*, 12(5), pp. 395-420.

Federation of European Stock Exchanges (1995) *Annual Report*.

Feinstein, S.P. & Goetzmann, W.N. (1988) The effect of the triple witching hour on stock market volatility, *Federal Reserve Bank of Atlanta Economic Review*, vol. 73, September-October, pp. 2-18.

Fenn, G. & Kupiec, P. (1993) Prudential margin policy in a futures-style settlement system, *Journal of Futures Markets*, 13(4), pp. 389-408.

Fielitz, B.D. & Gay, G.D. (1986) Managing cash flow risks in stock index futures, *Journal of Portfolio Management*, 12(2), pp. 74-78.

Figlewski, S. (1984a) Hedging performance and basis risk in stock index futures, *Journal of Finance*, 39(3), pp. 657-669.

Figlewski, S. (1984b) Explaining the early discounts on stock index futures: the case for disequilibrium, *Financial Analysts Journal*, 40(4), pp. 43-47.

Figlewski, S. (1984c) Margins and market integrity: margin setting for stock index futures and options, *Journal of Futures Markets*, 4(3), pp. 385-416.

Figlewski, S. (1985a) Liquidity and capital requirements for futures market hedges: comment, *Review of Research in Futures Markets*, 4(1), pp. 26-28.

Figlewski, S. (1985b) Hedging with stock index futures: theory and application in a new market, *Journal of Futures Markets*, 5(2), pp. 183-199.

Figlewski, S. (1987) The interaction between derivative securities on financial instruments and the underlying cash markets: an overview, *Journal of Accounting, Auditing and Finance*, 2(3), pp. 299-318.

Figlewski, S. (1988) Arbitrage-based pricing of stock index options, *Review of Futures Markets*, 7(2), pp. 250-270.

Figlewski, S., Chidambaran, N.K. & Kaplan, S. (1993) Evaluating the performance of the protective put strategy, *Financial Analysts Journal*, 49(4), pp. 46-69.

Figlewski, S., John, K. & Merrick, J. (1986) *Hedging with Financial Futures for Institutional Investors: From Theory to Practice*, Ballinger Publishing Co.

Figlewski, S. & Kon, S.J. (1982) Portfolio management with stock index futures, *Financial Analysts Journal*, 38(1), pp. 52-60.

Figlewski, S., Landskroner, Y. & Silber, W.L. (1991) Tailing the hedge: why and how, *Journal of Futures Markets*, 11(2), pp. 201-212.

Figlewski, S. & Urich, T. (1983) Optimal aggregation of money supply forecasts: accuracy, profitability and market efficiency, *Journal of Finance*, 38(3), pp. 695-710.

Fink, R.E. & Feduniak, R.B. (1988) *Futures Trading: Concepts and Strategies*, New York Institute of Finance (Simon and Schuster).

Finnerty, J.E. & Park, H.Y. (1987) Stock index futures: does the tail wag the dog?, *Financial Analysts Journal*, 43(2), pp. 57-61.

Finnerty, J.E. & Park, H.Y. (1988a) How to profit from program trading, *Journal of Portfolio Management*, 14(2), pp. 40-46.

Finnerty, J.E. & Park, H.Y. (1988b) Intraday return and volatility patterns in the stock market: futures versus spot. In *Advances in Futures and Options Research: A Research Annual*, vol. 3, ed. by F.J. Fabozzi, JAI Press Inc., pp. 301-317.

Fischmar, D. & Peters, C. (1991) Portfolio analysis of stocks, bonds and managed futures using compromise stochastic dominance, *Journal of Futures Markets*, 11(3), pp. 259-270.

Fishe, R.P.H. & Goldberg, L.G. (1986) The effects of margins on trading in futures markets, *Journal of Futures Markets*, 6(2), pp. 261-271.

Fite, D. & Pfleiderer, P. (1995) Should firms use derivatives to manage risk?. In *Risk Management: Problems and Solutions*, ed. by W.H. Beaver & G. Parker, McGraw-Hill, pp. 139-169.

Fitzgerald, M.D.(1993) *Financial Futures*, Euromoney Books, Second Edition.

Fleming, J., Kirby, C. & Ostdiek, B. (1998) Information and volatility linkages in the stock, bond and money markets, *Journal of Financial Economics*, 49(1), pp. 111-137.

Fleming, J., Ostdiek, B. & Whaley, R.E. (1996) Trading costs and the relative rates of price discovery in stock, futures and option markets, *Journal of Futures Markets*, 16(4), pp. 353-387.

Flesaker, B. (1991) The relationship between forward and futures contracts: a comment, *Journal of Futures Markets*, 11(1), pp. 113-115.

Floros, C. & Vougas, D.V. (2004) Hedge ratios in Greek stock index futures market, *Applied Financial Economics*, 14(15), pp. 1125-1136.

Followill, R.A. & Rodriguez, A.J. (1991) The estimation and determinants of bid-ask spreads in futures markets, *Review of Futures Markets*, 10(1), pp. 1-11.

Fong, K. & Frino, A. (2001) Stock market closure and intraday stock index futures market volatility: "contagion", bid-ask bias or both?, *Pacific-Basin Finance Journal*, 9(3), pp. 219-232.

Fong, K. & Martens, M. (2002) Overnight futures trading: now even Australia and US have common trading hours, *Journal of International Financial Markets, Institutions and Money*, 12(2), pp. 167-182.

Fong, K. & Zurbruegg, R. (2003) How much do locals contribute to the price discovery process?, *Journal of Empirical Finance*, 10(3), pp. 305-320.

Forsythe, R., Palfrey, T.R. & Plott, C.R. (1984) Futures markets and informational efficiency: a laboratory examination, *Journal of Finance*, 39(4), pp. 955-981.

Fortenbery, T.R. & Hauser, R.J. (1990) Investment potential of agricultural futures contracts, *American Journal of Agricultural Economics*, 72(3), pp. 721-726.

France, V.G. (1991) The regulation of margin requirements. In *Margins and Market Integrity*, ed. by the Mid America Institute, Probus Publishing Co., pp. 1-47.

Francis, J.C. (1991) *Investments: Analysis and Management*, McGraw-Hill, Fifth edition, Ch. 24.

Fremault, A. (1991) Stock index futures and index arbitrage in a rational expectations model, *Journal of Business*, 64(4), pp. 523-547.

Freris, A.F. (1990) The effects of the introduction of stock index futures on stock prices: the experience of Hong Kong 1984-1987. In *Pacific Basin Capital Markets Research*, ed. by S.G. Rhee & R.P. Chang, North Holland, pp. 409-416.

Freris, A.F. (1991) *The Financial Markets of Hong Kong*, Routledge.

Friedman, D., Harrison, G.W. & Salmon, J.W. (1983) The informational role of futures markets: some experimental evidence. In *Futures Markets: Modelling, Managing and Monitoring Futures Trading*, ed. by M.E. Streit, Basil Blackwell, pp. 124-164.

Friedman, D., Harrison, G.W. & Salmon, J.W. (1984) The informational efficiency of experimental asset markets, *Journal of Political Economy*, 92(3), pp. 349-408.

Frino, A., Harris, F.H.D., McInish, T.H. & Tomas, M.J. (2004) Price discovery in the pits; the role of market makers on the CBOT and the Sydney Futures Exchange, *Journal of Futures Markets*, 24(8), pp. 785-804.

Frino, A. & Hill, A. (2001) Intraday futures market behaviour around major scheduled macroeconomic announcements: Australian evidence, *Journal of Banking and Finance*, 25(7), pp. 1319-1337.

Frino, A. & McKenzie, M.D. (2002) The pricing of stock index futures spreads as contract expiration, *Journal of Futures Markets*, 22(5), pp. 451-469.

Frino, A. & McKenzie, M.D. (2003) Screen trading and the link between cash and futures prices: evidence from UK index markets, Proceedings of the IASTED International Conference on Financial Engineering and Applications, Banff, pp. 103-112.

Frino, A., Walter, T. & West, A. (2000) The lead-lad relationship between equities and stock index futures markets around information releases, *Journal of Futures Markets*, 20(5), pp. 467-487.

Frino, A. & West, A. (1999) The lead-lag relationship between stock indices and stock index futures contracts: further Australian evidence, *Abacus*, 35(3), pp. 333-341.

Frino, A. & West, A. (2003) The impact of transaction costs on price discovery: evidence from cross-listed stock index futures contracts, *Pacific-Basin Journal of Finance*, 11(2), pp. 139-151.

Froot, K.A., Gammill, J.F. & Perold, A.F. (1990) New trading practices and the short-run predictability of the S&P500. In *Market Volatility and Investor Confidence*, New York Stock Exchange, Appendix G1.

Froot, K.A. & Perold, A.F. (1995) New trading practices and short run market efficiency, *Journal of Futures Markets*, 15(7), pp. 731-765.

FTSE Actuaries Share Indices Steering Committee (1995) *FTSE Actuaries Share Indices: Guide to Calculation Methods*, Indices Unit, London Stock Exchange, Version 2, 33 pages.

Fung, A.K.W. & Lam, K. (2004) Overreaction of index futures in Hong Kong, *Journal of Empirical Finance*, 11(3), pp. 331-351.

Fung, A.K.W., Mok, D.M.Y. & Lam, K. (2000) Intraday price reversals for index futures in the US and Hong Kong, *Journal of Banking and Finance*, 24(7), pp. 1179-1201.

Fung, H.G., Leung, W.K. & Xu, X.E. (2001) Information role of US futures trading in a global financial market, *Journal of Futures Markets*, 21(11), pp. 1071-1090.

Fung, H.G. & Lo, W.C. (1993) Memory in interest rate futures, *Journal of Futures Markets*, 13(8), pp. 865-872.

Fung, H.G., Lo, W.C. & Peterson, J.E. (1994) Examining the dependency in intra-day stock index futures, *Journal of Futures Markets*, 14(4), pp. 405-419.

Fung, J.K.W. & Chan, K.C. (1994) On the arbitrage-free pricing relationship between index futures and index options: a note, *Journal of Futures Markets*, 14(8), pp. 957-962.

Fung, J.K.W., Cheng, L.T.W. & Chan, K.C. (1997) The intraday pricing efficiency of Hong Kong Hang Seng index options and futures markets, *Journal of Futures Markets*, 17(7), pp. 797-815.

Fung, J.K.W. & Draper, P. (1999) Mispricing of index futures contracts and short sales constraints, *Journal of Futures Markets*, 19(6), pp. 695-715.

Fung, J.K.W. & Fung, A.K.W. (1997) Mispricing of index futures contracts: a study of index futures versus index options, *Journal of Derivatives*, 5(2), pp. 37-45.

Fung, J.K.W. & Jiang, L. (1999) Restrictions on short-selling and spot-futures dynamics, *Journal of Business Finance and Accounting*, 26(1-2), pp. 227-248.

Fung, J.K.W., Lien, D.D., Tse, Y. & Tse, Y.K. (2005) Effects of electronic trading on the Hang Seng index futures market, *International Review of Economics and Finance*, forthcoming.

Fung, J.K.W., & Mok, M.K. (2001)Index options-futures arbitrage: a comparative study with bid-ask and transaction data, *The Financial Review*, 36(1), pp. 71-94.

Fung, J.K.W., & Mok, M.K. (2003) Early unwinding of options-futures arbitrage with bid-ask quotations and transaction prices, *Global Finance Journal*, 14(2), pp. 121-133.

Furbush, D. (1989) Program trading and price movement: evidence from the October 1987 market crash, *Financial Management*, 18(3), pp. 68-83.

Furbush, D. & Poulsen, A. (1989) Harmonizing margins: the regulation of margin levels in stock index futures markets, *Cornell Law Review*, 74(5), pp. 873-901.

Gagnon, L. & Lypny, G. (1997) The benefits of dynamically hedging the Toronto 35 stock index, *Canadian Journal of Administrative Science*, 14(1), pp. 69-78.

Galloway, T.M. & Kolb, R.W. (1996) Futures prices and the maturity effect, *Journal of Futures Markets*, 16(7), pp. 809-828.

Galloway, T.M. & Miller, J.M. (1997) Index futures trading and stock return volatility: evidence from the introduction of MidCap 400 index futures, *Financial Review*, 32(3), pp. 845-866.

Gammill, J.F. & Marsh, T.A. (1988) Trading activity and price behaviour in the stock and stock index futures markets in October 1987, *Journal of Economic Perspectives*, 2(3), pp. 25-44.

Gannon, G.L. (1994) Simultaneous volatility effects in index futures, *Review of Futures Markets*, 13(4), pp. 1027-1068.

Gannon, G.L. (1995) Volatility spillovers and transmission effects: currency futures and equity index futures. Working paper no. 1995-4, RMIT, Australia, 48 pages.

Gannon, G.L. (2005) Simultaneous volatility transmissions and spillover effects: US and Hong Kong stock and futures markets, *International Review of Financial Analysis*, forthcoming.

Gannon, G.L. & Au-Yeung, S.P. (2004) Structural effects and spillovers in HSIF, HSI and S&P500 volatility, *Research in International Business and Finance,* 18(3), pp. 305-317.

Gannon, G.L. & Choi, D.F.S. (1998) Structural models: intra-inter day volatility transmission and spillover persistence of the HSI, HSIF and S&P500 futures, *International Review of Financial Analysis*, 7(1), pp. 19-36.

Gao, A.H. & Wang, G.H.K. (1999) Modelling nonlinear dynamics of daily futures price changes, *Journal of Futures Markets*, 19(3), pp. 325-351.

Garbade, K.D. & Silber, W.L. (1983a) Price movements and price discovery in futures and cash markets, *Review of Economics and Statistics*, 65(2), pp. 289-297.

Garbade, K.D. & Silber, W.L. (1983b) Cash settlement of futures contracts: an economic analysis, *Journal of Futures Markets*, 3(4), 4, pp. 451-472.

Gardner, B.L. (1989) Rollover hedging and missing long-term futures markets, *American Journal of Agricultural Economics*, 71(2), pp. 311-318.

Garman, M. & Klass, M. (1980) On the estimation of security price volatilities from historical data, *Journal of Business*, 53(1), pp. 67-78.

Garrett, I. & Taylor, N. (2001) Intraday and interday basis dynamics: evidence from the FTSE 100 index futures market, *Studies in Nonlinear Dynamics and Econometrics*, 5(2), pp. 133-152.

Gastineau, G. & Madansky, A. (1983) S&P500 stock index futures evaluation tables, *Financial Analysts Journal*, 30(6), pp. 68-76.

Gay, G.D. & Kim, T.H. (1987) An investigation into seasonality in the futures market, *Journal of Futures Markets*, 7(2), pp. 169-181.

Gay, G.D., Hunter, W.C. & Kolb, R.W. (1986) A comparative analysis of futures contract margins, *Journal of Futures Markets*, 6(2), pp. 307-324.

Gay, G.D. & Jung, D.Y. (1999) A further look at transaction costs, short sale restrictions and futures market efficiency: the case of Korean stock index futures, *Journal of Futures Markets*, 19(2), pp. 153-174.

Geiss, C.G. (1995) Distortion-free futures price series, *Journal of Futures Markets*, 15(7), pp. 805-831.

Gemmill, G. (1994) Margins and the safety of clearing houses, *Journal of Banking and Finance*, 18(5), pp. 979-996.

Gennotte, G. & Leland, H. (1994) Low margins, derivative securities and volatility, *Review of Futures*

Markets, 13(3), pp. 709-754.

Geppert, J.M. (1995) A statistical model for the relationship between futures contract hedging effectiveness and investment horizon length, *Journal of Futures Markets*, 15(7), pp. 507-536.

Gerety, M.S. & Mulherin, J.H. (1991) Patterns in intraday stock market volatility, past and present, *Financial Analysts Journal*, 47(5), pp. 71-79.

Ghosh, A. (1993a) Cointegration and error correction models: intertemporal causality between index and futures prices, *Journal of Futures Markets*, 13(2), pp. 193-198.

Ghosh, A. (1993b) Hedging with stock index futures: estimation and forecasting with error correction model, *Journal of Futures Markets*, 13(7), pp. 743-752.

Ghosh, A. & Clayton, R. (1996) Hedging with international stock index futures: an intertemporal error correction model, *Journal of Financial Research*, 19(4), pp. 477-491.

Ginter, G.D. (1991) Toward a theory of harmonized margins. In *Margins and Market Integrity*, ed. by the Mid America Institute, Probus Publishing Co., pp. 49-53.

Gjerde, Ø. (1987) Measuring hedging effectiveness in a traditional one-period portfolio framework, *Journal of Futures Markets*, 7(6), pp. 663-674.

Goldenberg, D.H. (1988) Trading frictions and futures price movements, *Journal of Financial and Quantitative Analysis*, 23(4), pp. 465-481.

Goldenberg, D.H. (1989) Memory and equilibrium futures prices, *Journal of Futures Markets*, 9(3), pp. 199-213.

Gordon, J.D., Moriarty, E.J. & Tosini, P.A. (1987) Stock index futures: does the tail wag the dog?, *Financial Analysts Journal*, 43(6), pp. 72-73.

Gottlieb, G. & Kalay, A. (1985) Implications of the discreteness of observed stock prices, *Journal of Finance*, 40(1), pp. 135-153.

Gould, F.J. (1988) Stock index futures: the arbitrage cycle and portfolio insurance, *Financial Analysts Journal*, 44(1), pp. 48-62.

Graham, D. & Jennings, R. (1987) Systematic risk, dividend yield and the hedging performance of stock index futures, *Journal of Futures Markets*, 7(1), pp. 1-13.

Grammatikos, T. (1986) Intervalling effects and the hedging performance of foreign currency futures, *The Financial Review*, 21(1), pp. 21-36.

Grammatikos, T. & Saunders, A. (1986) Futures price variability: a test of maturity and volume effects, *Journal of Business*, 59(2), pp. 319-330.

Grant, D. (1982a) Market index futures contracts: some thoughts on delivery dates, *Financial Analysts Journal*, 38(3), pp. 60-63.

Grant, D. (1982b) A market index futures contract and portfolio selection, *Journal of Economics and Business*, vol. 34, pp. 387-390.

Grant, J.L., Wolf, A. & Yu, S. (2005) Intraday price reversals in the US stock index futures market: a 15 year study, *Journal of Banking and Finance*, forthcoming.

Grant, K. & Marshall, A.P. (1997) Large UK companies and derivatives, *European Financial Management*, 3(2), pp. 191-208.

Gray, R.W. (1963) Onions revisited, *Journal of Farm Economics*, vol. 45, May, pp. 273-276.

Green, C.J. & Joujon, E. (2000) Unified tests of causality and cost of carry: the pricing of the French stock index futures contract, *International Journal of Finance and Economics*, 5(2), pp. 121-140.

Green, E.J. (1986) Financial futures and price-level variability. In *Financial Futures and Options in the US Economy: A Study by the Staff of the Federal Reserve System*, ed. by M.L. Kwast, Board of Governors of the Federal Reserve System, pp. 79-89.

Greenwald, B. & Stein, J. (1988) The task force report: the reasoning behind the recommendations, *Journal of Economic Perspectives*, 2(3), pp. 3-23.

Greer, T.V. & Brorsen, B.W. (1989) Execution costs for a public futures fund. In *Applied Commodity Price Analysis, Forecasting and Market Risk Management*, Proceedings of the NCR-134 Conference, Chicago, 20-21 pp. 147-160.

Gressis, N., Vlahos, G. & Philippatos, G.C. (1984) A CAPM based analysis of stock index futures, *Journal of Portfolio Management*, 10(3), pp. 47-52.

Gribbin, D.W., Harris, R.W. & Lau, H.S. (1992) Futures prices are not stable Paretian distributed, *Journal of Futures Markets*, 12(4), pp. 475-487.

Grieves, R. (1986) Hedging corporate bond portfolios, *Journal of Portfolio Management*, 12(4), pp. 23-25.

Grossman, S.J. (1977) The existence of futures markets, noisy rational expectations and informational externalities, *Review of Economic Studies*, 44(3), pp. 431-449.

Grossman, S.J. (1986) An analysis of the role of 'insider trading' on futures markets, *Journal of Business*, 59(2), Part 2, pp. S129-S146.

Grossman, S.J. (1988a) An analysis of the implications for stock and futures price volatility of program trading and dynamic hedging strategies, *Journal of Business*, 61(3), pp. 275-298.

Grossman, S.J. (1988b) Program trading and stock and futures price volatility, *Journal of Futures Markets*, 8(4), pp. 413-419.

Grossman, S.J. (1988c) Insurance seen and unseen: the impact on markets, *Journal of Portfolio Management*, 14(4), pp. 5-8.

Grossman, S.J. (1988d) Program trading and market volatility: a report on interday relationships, *Financial Analysts Journal*, 44(4), pp. 18-28.

Grossman, S.J. (1990) Institutional investing and new trading technologies. In *Market Volatility and Investor Confidence*, New York Stock Exchange, Appendix G2.

Grossman, S.J. & Miller, M.H. (1986) Economic costs and benefits of the proposed one minute time bracketing regulation, *Journal of Futures Markets*, 6(1), pp. 141-166.

Grossman, S.J. & Miller, M.H. (1988) Liquidity and market structure, *Journal of Finance*, 43(3), pp. 617-633.

Grudnitski, G. & Osburn, L. (1993) Forecasting S&P and gold futures prices: an application of neural networks, *Journal of Futures Markets*, 13(6), pp. 631-643.

Grünbichler, A. & Callahan, T.W. (1994) Stock index futures arbitrage in Germany: the behaviour of the DAX index futures price, *Review of Futures Markets*, 13(2), pp. 661-694.

Grünbichler, A., Longstaff, F.A. & Schwartz, E.S. (1994) Electronic screen trading and the transmission of information: an empirical examination, *Journal of Financial Intermediation*, 3(2), pp. 166-187.

Gulen, H. & Mayhew, S. (2000) Stock index futures trading and volatility in international equity markets, *Journal of Futures Markets*, 20(7), pp. 661-685.

Habeeb, G., Hill, J.M. & Rzad, A.J. (1991) Potential rewards from path-dependent index arbitrage with S&P500 futures, *Review of Futures Markets*, 10(1), pp. 180-203.

Hall, A.D. & Kofman, P. (2001) Regulatory tools and price changes in futures markets, *Australian Economic Papers*, 40(4), pp. 520-540.

Hall, J.A., Brorsen, B.W. & Irwin, S.H. (1989) The distribution of futures prices: a test of the stable Paretian and mixture of normals hypothesis, *Journal of Financial and Quantitative Analysis*, 24(1), pp. 105-116.

Hammer, J.A. (1988) Hedging and risk aversion in the foreign currency market, *Journal of Futures Markets*, 8(6), pp. 657-686.

Hammer, J.A. (1990) Hedging performance and hedging objectives: tests of new performance measures in the foreign currency market, *Journal of Financial Research*, 13(4), pp. 307-323.

Han, L.M. & Misra, L. (1990) The relationship between the volatilities of the S&P500 index and futures contracts implicit in their call option prices, *Journal of Futures Markets*, 10(3), pp. 273-285.

Hancock, G.D. (1991) Futures option expirations and volatility in the stock index futures market, *Journal of Futures Markets*, 11(3), pp. 319-330.

Hancock, G.D. (1993) Whatever happened to the triple witching hour?, *Financial Analysts Journal*, 49(3), pp. 66-72.

Hancock, G.D. (2005) A text book treatment of calculating returns on non-traditional portfolios, *Review of Financial Economics*, forthcoming.

Hancock, G.D. & Weise, P.D. (1994) Competing derivative equity instruments: empirical evidence on hedged portfolio performance, *Journal of Futures Markets*, 14(4), pp. 421-436.

Harel, A., Harpaz, G. & Yagil, J. (2005) Forecasting futures returns in the presence of price limits, *Journal of Futures Markets*, 25(2), pp. 199-210.

Harris, L. (1987) Transaction data tests of the mixture of distributions hypothesis, *Journal of Financial and Quantitative Analysis*, 22(2), pp. 127-141.

Harris, L. (1989a) The October 1987 S&P500 stock-futures basis, *Journal of Finance*, 44(1), pp. 77-90.

Harris, L. (1989b) S&P500 cash stock price volatilities, *Journal of Finance*, 44(5), pp. 1155-1175.

Harris, L. (1989c) The dangers of regulatory overreaction to the October 1987 crash, *Cornell Law Review*, 74(5), pp. 927-942.

Harris, L. (1990a) The economics of cash index alternatives, *Journal of Futures Markets*, 10(2), pp. 179-194.

Harris, L. (1990b) Estimation of stock price variances and serial covariances from discrete observations, *Journal of Financial and Quantitative Analysis*, 25(3), pp. 291-306.

Harris, L. & Gurel, E. (1986) Price and volume effects associated with changes in the S&P500 list: new evidence for the existence of price pressures, *Journal of Finance*, 41(4), pp. 815-829.

Harris, L., Sofianos, G. & Shapiro, J.E. (1994) Program trading and intraday volatility, *Review of Financial Studies*, 7(4), pp. 653-685.

Harris, R.D.F. & Shen, J. (2003) Robust estimation of the optimal hedge ratio, *Journal of Futures Markets*, 23(8), pp. 799-816.

Harrison, G.W. (1992) Market dynamics, programmed traders and futures markets: beginning the laboratory search for a smoking gun, *Economic Record*, Supplement, pp. 46-62.

Hartzmark, M.L. (1986a) The effects of changing margin levels on futures market activity, the composition of traders in the market and price performance, *Journal of Business*, 59(2), Part 2, pp. S147-S180.

Hartzmark, M.L. (1986b) Regulating futures margin requirements, *Review of Research in Futures Markets*, 5(3), pp. 242-260.

Hartzmark, M.L. (1987) Returns to individual traders of futures: aggregate results, *Journal of Political Economy*, 95(6), pp. 1292-1306.

Hartzmark, M.L. (1988) Is risk aversion a theoretical diversion?, *Review of Futures Markets*, 7(1), pp. 1-26.

Hartzmark, M.L. (1991) Luck versus forecast ability: determinants of trader performance in futures markets, *Journal of Business*, 64(1), pp. 49-74.

Hasbrouck, J. (1996) Order characteristics and stock price evolution: an application to program trading, *Journal of Financial Economics*, 41(1), pp. 129-149.

Hasbrouck, J. (2003) Intraday price formation in US equity index markets, *Journal of Finance*, 58(6), pp. 2375-2399.

Hazen, T.L. (1992) Rational investments, speculation or gambling? - Derivative securities and financial futures and their effect on the underlying capital markets, *Northwestern University Law Review*, 86(4), pp. 987-1037.

He, Y. & Wu, C. (2001) Further evidence on mean reversion in index basis changes, *The Financial Review*, 36(1), pp. 95-124.

Heaney, R. (1990) Australian All Ordinaries share price index futures and random walks, *Australian Journal of Management*, 15(1), pp. 129-149.

Heifner, R.G. (1972) Optimal hedging levels and hedging effectiveness in cattle feeding, *Agricultural Economics Research*, 24(2), pp. 25-36.

Helms, B.P. & Martell, T.F. (1985) An examination of the distribution of futures price changes, *Journal of Futures Markets*, 5(2), pp. 259-272.

Hemler, M.L. & Longstaff, F.A. (1991) General equilibrium stock index futures prices: theory and empirical evidence, *Journal of Financial and Quantitative Analysis*, 26(3), pp. 287-308.

Henker, T. (1998) The bid-ask spread of the FTSE 100 futures contract, Working paper, University of Massachusetts, 30 pages.

Henker, T. & Martens, M. (2005) Index futures arbitrage before and after the introduction of sixteenths on the NYSE, *Journal of Empirical Finance*, 12(3) pp. 353-373.

Hensel, C.R., Sick, G.A. & Ziemba, W.T. (1994) The turn-of-the-month effect in the US stock index futures markets, 1982-1992, *Review of Futures Markets*, 13(3), pp. 827-860.

Hensel, C.R. & Ziemba, W.T. (2000) Anticipation of the January small firm effect in the US futures markets. In *Security Market Imperfections in Worldwide Equity Markets*, ed. by D.B. Keim and W.T. Ziemba, Cambridge University Press, pp. 179-202.

Herbst, A.F., Kare, D.D. & Caples, S.C. (1989) Hedging effectiveness and minimum risk hedge ratios in the presence of autocorrelation: foreign currency futures, *Journal of Futures Markets*, 9(3), pp. 185-197.

Herbst, A.F., Kare, D.D. & Marshall, J.F. (1993) A time varying convergence adjusted minimum risk futures hedge ratio. In *Advances in Futures and Options Research*, vol. 6, ed. by D.M. Chance & R.R Trippi, JAI Press Inc., pp. 137-155.

Herbst, A.F. & Maberly, E.D. (1987) Shoes and ships and sealing wax, cabbages and kings: now tail-wagged dogs and stock index futures, *Financial Analysts Journal*, 43(6), pp. 73-75.

Herbst, A.F. & Maberly, E.D. (1990) Stock index futures, expiration day volatility, and the 'special' Friday opening: a note, *Journal of Futures Markets*, 10(3), pp. 323-325.

Herbst, A.F. & Maberly, E.D. (1991) An alternative methodology for measuring expiration day price effects at Friday's close: the expected price reversal - a note, *Journal of Futures Markets*, 11(6), pp. 751-754.

Herbst, A.F. & Maberly, E.D. (1992) The informational role of end-of-the-day returns in stock index futures, *Journal of Futures Markets*, 12(5), pp. 595-601.

Herbst, A.F. & McCormack, J.P. (1987) An examination of the risk/return characteristics of portfolios combining commodity futures contracts with common stocks, *Review of Futures Markets*, 6(3), pp. 416-425.

Herbst, A.F. & McCormack, J.P. (1992) A further examination of the risk/return characteristics of portfolios combining commodity futures contracts with common stocks. In *Managed Futures: Performance, Evaluation and Analysis of Commodity Funds, Pools and Accounts*, ed. by C.C. Peters, Probus Publishing Co., pp. 287-304.

Herbst, A.F., McCormack, J.P. & West, E.N. (1987) Investigation of a lead-lag relationship between spot stock indices and their futures contracts, *Journal of Futures Markets*, 7(4), pp. 373-381.

Herbst, A.F. & Ordway, N.O. (1984) Stock index futures contracts and separability of returns, *Journal of Futures Markets*, 4(1), pp. 87-102.

Herbst, A.F., Swanson, P.E. & Caples, S.C. (1992) A redetermination of hedging strategies using foreign currency futures contracts and forward markets, *Journal of Futures Markets*, 12(1), pp. 93-104.

Hicks, J.R. (1946) *Value and Capital*, Clarendon Press, Second edition.

Hietala, P., Jokivuolle, E. & Koskinen, Y. (2000) Informed trading, short sales constraints and futures pricing, Working paper, Bank of Finland, 34 pages.

Hill, J.M., Jain, A. & Wood, R.A. (1988) Insurance: volatility risk and futures mispricing, *Journal of Portfolio Management*, 14(2), pp. 23-29.

Hill, J.M. & Schneeweis, T. (1981) A note on the hedging effectiveness of foreign currency futures, *Journal of Futures Markets*, 1(4), pp. 659-664.

Hill, J.M. & Schneeweis, T. (1984) Reducing volatility with financial futures, *Financial Analysts Journal*, 40(6), pp. 34-40.

Hill, J.M. & Schneeweis, T. (1986) International risk reduction with financial and foreign currency futures. In *Advances in Futures and Options Research: A Research Annual: Futures*, ed. by F.J. Fabozzi, vol. 1, Part B, JAI Press, pp. 113-135.

Hiraki, T., Maberly, E.D. & Takezawa, N. (1995) The information content of end of the day index futures returns: international evidence from the Osaka Nikkei 225 futures contract, *Journal of Banking and Finance*, 19(5), pp. 921-936.

Hiraki, T., Maberly, E.D. & Taube, P.M. (1998) The impact of index futures trading on day of the week effects in Japan, *Pacific-Basin Finance Journal*, 6(5), pp. 493-506.

Ho, R.Y.K., Fang, J.Z. & Woo, C.K. (1992) Intraday arbitrage opportunities and price behaviour of the Hang Seng index futures, *Review of Futures Markets*, 11(3), pp. 413-445.

Ho, R.Y.K. & Lee, R.S.K. (1998) Market closure effects on return, volatility and turnover patterns in the Hong Kong index futures market, *Journal of International Financial Markets, Institutions and Money*, 8(3-4), pp. 433-451.

Hodgson, A. (1994) The evolution of intraday prices and information shocks, Working paper, Strathclyde University, 25 pages.

Hodgson, A., Keef, S.P. & Okunev, J. (1993) Mean reversion in futures prices: some empirical evidence, *Review of Futures Markets*, 12(3), pp. 551-575.

Hodgson, A., Kendig, C. & Tahir, M. (1993) Intraday price movements in related markets: futures and cash prices, Working paper, Australian National University, 25 pages.

Hodgson, A., Masih, A.M.M. & Masih, R. (2005) Futures trading volume as a determinant of prices in different momentum phases, *International Review of Financial Analysis*, forthcoming.

Hodgson, A. & Nicholls, D. (1991) The impact of index futures markets on Australian share market volatility, *Journal of Business Finance and Accounting*, 18(2), pp. 267-280.

Hodgson, A. & Okunev, J. (1992) An alternative approach for determining hedge ratios for futures contracts, *Journal of Business Finance and Accounting*, 19(2), pp. 211-224.

Holden, C.W. (1995) Index arbitrage as cross sectional market making, *Journal of Futures Markets*, 15(4), pp. 423-455.

Hogan, K.C., Kroner, K.F. & Sultan, J. (1997) Program trading, non-program trading and market volatility, *Journal of Futures Markets*, 17(7), pp. 733-756.

Holder, M.E., Tomas, M.J. & Webb, R.I. (1999) Winners and losers: recent competition among futures exchanges for equivalent financial contract markets, *Derivatives Quarterly*, 6(2), pp. 19-27.

Holland, A. & Fremault Vila, A. (1997) Features of a successful contract: financial futures on LIFFE, *Bank of England Quarterly*, 37(2), pp. 181-186.

Holmes, P. (1995) Ex ante hedge ratios and the hedging effectiveness of the FTSE 100 stock index futures contract, *Applied Economic Letters*, 2(3), pp. 56-59.

Holmes, P. (1996a) Spot price volatility, information and futures trading: evidence from a thinly traded market, *Applied Economics*, 3(1), pp. 63-66.

Holmes, P. (1996b) Stock index futures hedging: hedge ratio estimation, duration effects, expiration effects and hedge ratio stability, *Journal of Business Finance and Accounting*, 23(1), pp. 63-78.

Holmes, P. & Rougier, J. (2001) Trading volume and contract rollover in futures contracts, *Journal of Empirical Finance*. 12(2), pp. 317-338.

Holmes, P. & Tomsett, M. (2004) Information and noise in UK futures markets, *Journal of Futures Markets*, 24(8), pp. 711-731.

Hong, H. (2000) A model of returns and trading in futures markets, *Journal of Finance*, 55(2), pp. 959-988.

Hooker, R.H. (1901) The suspension of the Berlin produce exchange and its effects upon corn prices, *Journal of the Royal Statistical Society*, 64(4), pp. 574-613.

Houthakker, H.S. (1957) Can speculators forecast prices? *Review of Economics and Statistics*, 39(2), pp. 143-151.

Houthakker, H.S. (1961) Systematic and random elements in short term price movements, *American Economic Review*, 51(2), pp. 164-172.

Houthakker, H.S. (1968) Normal backwardation. In *Value, Capital and Growth: Papers in Honour of Sir John Hicks*, ed. by J.N. Wolfe, Edinburgh University Press, pp. 193-214.

Houthakker, H.S. (1982) The extension of futures trading to the financial sector, *Journal of Banking and Finance*, 6(1), pp. 37-47.

Houthakker, H.S. (1994) Samuelson's conjecture holds for commodity futures but not for financial futures, Harvard Institute of Economic Research, Working paper no. 1682, 12 pages.

Howard, C.T. & D'Antonio, L.J. (1984) A risk-return measure of hedging effectiveness, *Journal of Financial and Quantitative Analysis*, 19(1), pp. 101-112.

Howard, C.T. & D'Antonio, L.J. (1987) A risk-return measure of hedging effectiveness: a reply, *Journal of Financial and Quantitative Analysis*, 22(3), pp. 377-381.

Howard, C.T. & D'Antonio, L.J. (1991) Multiperiod hedging using futures: a risk minimisation approach in the presence of autocorrelation, *Journal of Futures Markets*, 11(2), pp. 697-710.

Howard, C.T. & D'Antonio, L.J. (1994) The cost of hedging and the optimal hedge ratio, *Journal of Futures Markets*, 14(2), pp. 237-258.

Hoyt, R.E. (1989) Use of financial futures by life insurers, *Journal of Risk and Insurance*, 56(4), pp. 740-748.

Hsieh, D.A. (1989) Testing for nonlinear dependence in daily foreign exchange rates, *Journal of Business*, 62(3), pp. 339-368.

Hsieh, D.A. (1993) Implications of nonlinear dynamics for financial risk management, *Journal of Financial and Quantitative Analysis*, 28(1), pp. 41-64.

Hsieh, W.G. (2004) Regulatory changes and information competition: the case of Taiwan index futures, *Journal of Futures Markets*, 24(4), pp. 399-412.

Hsin, C.W., Kuo, J. & Lee, C.F. (1994) A new measure to compare the hedging effectiveness of foreign currency futures versus options, *Journal of Futures Markets*, 14(6), pp. 685-707.

Huang, R. & Stoll, H.R. (1998) Is it time to spilt the S&P500 futures contract?, *Financial Analysts Journal*, 54(1), pp. 23-35.

Huang, Y.C. (2002) Trading activity in stock index futures markets: the evidence of emerging markets, *Journal of Futures Markets*, 22(10), pp. 983-1003.

Huang, Y.C. (2003) The market microstructure and relative performance of Taiwan stock index futures: a comparison of the Singapore exchange and the Taiwan futures exchange, *Journal of Financial Markets*, 7(3), pp. 335-350.

Hudson, M.A. Leuthold, R.M. & Sarassoro, G.F. (1987) Commodity futures price changes: recent evidence for wheat, soyabeans and live cattle, *Journal of Futures Markets*, 7(3), pp. 287-301.

Hull, J.C. (2005) *Options, Futures and Other Derivatives,* Prentice-Hall, Sixth edition.

Hung, M.W. & Zhang, H. (1995) Price movements and price discovery in the municipal bond index and the index futures markets, *Journal of Futures Markets*, 15(4), pp. 489-506.

Hunter, W.C. (1986) Rational margins on futures contracts: initial margins, *Review of Research in Futures Markets*, 5(2), pp. 160-173.

Hwang, S. & Satchell, S.E. (2000) Market risk and the concept of fundamental volatility: measuring volatility across asset and derivative markets and testing for the impact of derivatives markets on financial markets, *Journal of Banking and Finance*, 24(5), pp. 759-785.

Ibbotson, R.G. & Kaplan, P.D. (2000) Does asset allocation policy explain 40, 90 or 100 percent of performance?, *Financial Analysts Journal*, 56(1), pp. 26-33.

IG Index. (1989) *IG Index Dealing Handbook*, IG Index, London.

Iihara, Y., Kato, K. & Tokunaga, T. (1996) Intraday return dynamics between the cash and the futures markets in Japan, *Journal of Futures Markets*, 16(2), pp. 147-162.

Illueca, M. & Lafuente, J.A. (2003a) The effect of spot and futures trading on stock index market volatility: a non-parametric approach, *Journal of Futures Markets*, 23(9), pp. 841-858.

Illueca, M. & Lafuente, J.A. (2003b) The effect of futures trading activity on the distribution of spot market returns, Working paper WP-EC 2003-23, Valencian Institute of Economic Research, 24 pages.

Illueca, M. & Lafuente, J.A. (2003c) Return-volume relationship in the Ibex 35 futures market: a non-parametric approach, *Derivatives Use, Trading and Regulation*, 9(2), pp. 150-163.

Illueca, M. & Lafuente, J.A. (2004) Introducing the mini-futures contract in Ibex 35: implications for price discovery and volatility transmission, Working paper WP-EC 2004-13, Valencian Institute of Economic Research, 24 pages.

In, F. & Kim, S. (2003) Hedge ratio and correlation between the stock and the futures markets: evidence from wavelet analysis, Working paper, Monash University, 35 pages.

Irwin, S.H. (1992) The potential role of managed futures in institutional pension portfolios. In *Managed Futures: Performance, Evaluation and Analysis of Commodity Funds, Pools and Accounts*, ed. by C.C. Peters, Probus Publishing Co., pp. 35-54.

Irwin, S.H. & Brorsen, B.W. (1985) Public futures funds, *Journal of Futures Markets*, 5(3), pp. 461-485.

Irwin, S.H., Gerlow, M.E. & Liu, T.R (1994) The forecasting performance of livestock futures prices: a comparison to USDA expert predictions, *Journal of Futures Markets*, 14(7), pp. 861-875.

Irwin, S.H., Krukemyer, T.R. & Zulauf, C.R. (1992) Are public commodity pools a good investment?. In *Managed Futures: Performance, Evaluation and Analysis of Commodity Funds, Pools and Accounts*, ed. by C.C. Peters, Probus Publishing Co., pp. 403-434.

Irwin, S.H., Krukemyer, T.R. & Zulauf, C.R. (1993) Investment performance of public commodity pools: 1979-1990, *Journal of Futures Markets*, 13(7), pp. 799-820.

Irwin, S.H. & Landa, D. (1987) Real estate, futures and gold as portfolio assets, *Journal of Portfolio Management*, 14(1), pp. 29-34.

Irwin, S.H. & Yoshimaru, S. (1999) Managed futures, positive feedback trading and futures price volatility, *Journal of Futures Markets*, 19(7), pp. 759-776.

Ito, T. & Lin, W.L. (2001) Race to the centre: competition for the Nikkei 225 futures trade, *Journal of Empirical Finance*, 8(3), pp. 219-242.

Jabbour, G.M. & Sachlis, J.M. (1993) Hedging risk on futures contracts under stochastic interest rates, *Journal of Futures Markets*, 13(1), pp. 55-60.

Jacques, W.E. (1988) The S&P500 membership anomaly, or would you join this club?, *Financial Analysts Journal*, 44(6), pp. 73-75.

Jaffee, D.M. (1984) The impact of financial futures and options on capital formation, *Journal of Futures Markets*, 4(3), pp. 417-447.

Jain, P.C. (1987) The effect on stock prices of inclusion in or exclusion from the S&P500, *Financial Analysts Journal*, 43(1), pp. 58-65.

Jarrow, R.A. & Oldfield, G.S. (1981) Forward contracts and futures contracts, *Journal of Financial Economics*, 9(4), pp. 373-382.

Jegadeesh, N. & Subrahmanyam, A. (1993) Liquidity effects of the S&P500 index futures contract on the underlying stocks, *Journal of Business*, 66(2), pp. 171-187.

Jensen, G.R., Johnson, R.R. & Mercer, J.M. (2000) Efficient use of commodity futures in diversified portfolios, *Journal of Futures Markets*, 20(5), pp. 489-506.

Jensen, M.C. (1978) Some anomalous evidence regarding market efficiency, *Journal of Financial Economics*, 6(2-3), pp. 95-101.

Jiang, L., Fung, J.K.W. & Cheng, L.T.W. (2001) The lead-lag relation between spot and futures markets under different short-selling regimes, *The Financial Review*, 36(3), pp. 63-88.

Johnson, A.C. (1973) *Effects of Futures Trading on Price Performance in the Cash Onion Market, 1930-1968.* Economic Research Service, U.S. Department of Agriculture, Technical Bulletin no. 1470, 79 pages.

Johnson, J. & Phelan, B. (1990) The weekly pattern of returns in the Australian share price index futures contract, 1983-1989, *Review of Futures Markets*, vol. 9, Supplement, pp. 162-177.

Johnson, L.L. (1960) The theory of hedging and speculation in commodity futures, *Review of Economics and Statistics*, 27(3), pp. 139-151.

Johnson, R. S. & Giaccotto, C. (1995) *Options and Futures: Concepts, Strategies and Applications*, West Publishing Co.

Jones, F.J. (1982) The economics of futures and options contracts based on cash settlement, *Journal of Futures Markets*, 2(1), pp. 63-82.

Jones, F.J. (1984) The uses and users of the stock index futures markets. In *Stock Index Futures*, ed. by F.J. Fabozzi & G.M. Kipnis, Dow Jones-Irwin, pp. 145-166.

Jones, J.D., Nachtmann, R. & Phillips-Patrick, F. (1993) Linkage between S&P and non-S&P stocks on the NYSE, *Applied Financial Economics*, 3(2), pp. 127-144.

Jordan, J.V. & Morgan, G.E. (1990) Default risk in futures markets: the customer-broker relationship, *Journal of Finance*, 45(3), pp. 909-933.

Jorion, P. & Roisenberg, L. (1993) Synthetic international diversification: the case for diversifying with stock index futures, *Journal of Portfolio Management*, 19(2), 2, pp 65-74.

Junkus, J.C. (1986) Weekend and day of the week effects in returns on stock index futures, *Journal of Futures Markets*, 6(3), pp. 397-407.

Junkus, J.C. (1987) Hedge ratios in up and down equity markets. In *Advances in Futures and Options Research: A Research Annual*, vol. 2, ed. by F.J. Fabozzi, JAI Press Inc., pp. 279-289.

Junkus, J.C. & Lee, C.F. (1985) Use of three stock index futures in hedging decisions, *Journal of Futures Markets*, 5(2), pp. 201-222.

Kahl, K.H. (1983) Determination of the recommended hedging ratio, *American Journal of Agricultural Economics*, 65(3), pp. 603-605.

Kalavathi, L. & Shanker, L. (1991) Margin requirements and the demand for futures contracts, *Journal of Futures Markets*, 11(2), pp. 213-237.

Kamara, A. (1982) Issues in futures markets: a survey, *Journal of Futures Markets*, 2(3), pp. 261-294.

Kamara, A. (1984) The behaviour of futures prices: a review of theory and evidence, *Financial Analysts Journal*, 40(4), pp. 68-75.

Kamara, A. (1997) New evidence on the Monday seasonal in stock returns, *Journal of Business*, 70(1), pp. 63-84.

Kamara, A., Miller, T.W. & Siegel, A.F. (1992) The effect of futures trading on the stability of Standard and Poor 500 returns, *Journal of Futures Markets*, 12(6), pp. 645-658.

Kan, A.C.N. (1997) The effect of index futures trading on volatility of HSI constituent stocks: a note, *Pacific-Basin Finance Journal*, 5(1), pp. 105-114.

Kan, A.C.N. & Tang, G.Y.N. (1999) The impact of index futures trading on the betas of the underlying constituent stocks; the case of Hong Kong, *Journal of International Financial Markets, Institutions and Money*, 9(1), pp. 97-114.

Karagozoglu, A.K. & Martell, T.F. (1999) Changing the size of a futures contract: liquidity and microstructure effects, *The Financial Review*, 34(4), pp. 75-94.

Karagozoglu, A.K., Martell, T.F. & Wang, G.K. (2003) The split of the S&P500 futures contract: effects on liquidity and market dynamics, *Review of Quantitative Finance and Accounting*, 21(4), pp. 323-348.

Karakullukcu, M. (1992) Index futures: expiration day effects in the UK and prospects in Turkey, Mimeo, London School of Economics, 36 pages.

Karjalainen, R. (1998) Evolving technical trading rules for S&P500 futures. In *Advanced Trading Rules*, ed. by E. Acar & S. Satchell, Butterworth-Heinemann, pp. 209-230.

Karpoff, J.M. (1987) The relation between price changes and trading volume: a survey, *Journal of Financial and Quantitative Analysis*, 22(1), pp. 109-126.

Karpoff, J.M. (1988) Costly short sales and the correlation of returns with volume, *Journal of Financial Research*, 11(3), pp. 173-188.

Kaufman, P.J. (editor) (1984) *Handbook of Futures Markets: Commodity, Financial, Stock Index, and Options*, John Wiley & Sons.

Kawai, M. (1983) Price volatility of storable commodities under rational expectations in spot and futures markets, *International Economic Review*, 24(2), pp. 435-459.

Kawaller, I.G. (1986) Hedging with futures contracts: going the extra mile, *Journal of Cash Management*, pp. 34-36.

Kawaller, I.G. (1987) A note: debunking the myth of the risk-free return, *Journal of Futures Markets*, 7(3), pp. 327-331.

Kawaller, I.G. (1991) Determining the relevant fair value(s) of S&P500 futures: a case study approach, *Journal of Futures Markets*, 11(4), pp. 453-460.

Kawaller, I.G. (1997) Tailing futures hedges - tailing spreads, *Journal of Derivatives*, Winter, pp. 62-70.

Kawaller, I.G., Koch, P.D. & Koch, T.W. (1987) The temporal price relationship between S&P500 futures and the S&P500 index, *Journal of Finance*, 42(5), pp. 1309-1329.

Kawaller, I.G., Koch, P.D. & Koch, T.W. (1988) The relationship between the S&P500 index and S&P500 index futures prices, *Federal Reserve Bank of Atlanta Economic Review*, vol. 73, May-June, pp. 2-10.

Kawaller, I.G., Koch, P.D. & Koch, T.W. (1990) Intraday relationships between volatility in S&P500 futures prices and volatility in the S&P index, *Journal of Banking and Finance*, 14(2-3), pp. 373-397.

Kawaller, I.G., Koch, P.D. & Koch, T.W. (1993) Intraday market behaviour and the extent of feedback between S&P500 futures prices and the S&P500 index, *Journal of Financial Research*, 16(2), pp. 107-121.

Kawaller, I.G., Koch, P.D. & Peterson, J.E. (1994) Assessing the intraday relationship between implied and historical volatility, *Journal of Futures Markets*, 14(3), pp. 323-346.

Kawaller, I.G., Koch, P.D. & Peterson, J.E. (2001) Volume and volatility surrounding quarterly redesignation of the lead S&P500 futures contract, *Journal of Futures Markets*, 21(12), pp. 1119-1149.

Keim, D.B. & Smirlock, M. (1987) The behaviour of intraday stock index futures prices. In *Advances in Futures and Options Research: A Research Annual*, vol. 2, ed. by F.J. Fabozzi, JAI Press Inc., pp. 143-166.

Keim, D.B. & Smirlock, M. (1989) Pricing patterns in stock index futures. In *Handbook of Stock Index Futures and Options*, ed. by F.J. Fabozzi & G.M. Kipnis, Dow Jones-Irwin, pp. 142-157.

Kempf, A. (1998) Short selling, unwinding and mispricing, *Journal of Futures Markets*, 18(8), pp. 903-923.

Kempf, A. & Korn, O. (1998) Trading systems and market integration, *Journal of Financial Intermediation*, 7(3), pp. 220-239.

Kessler, J.R. (1992) Risks in the clearing and settlement systems of markets for financial futures and option. In *Risk Management in Financial Services*, OECD, pp. 59-104.

Keynes, J.M. (1923) Some aspects of commodity markets, *The Manchester Guardian Commercial*, Reconstruction Supplement, 29th March.

Keynes, J.M. (1930) *A Treatise on Money, Volume Two - The Applied Theory of Money*, Macmillan, ch. 29.

Khan, B. & Ireland, J. (1993) The use of technology for competitive advantage: a study of screen v floor trading, City Research Project, London Business School, Subject Report 4, Corporation of London, 82 pages.

Khoury, S.J. & Jones, G.L. (1984) Daily price limits on futures contracts: nature, impact and justification, *Review of Research in Futures Markets*, 3(1), pp. 22-39.

Kilcollin, T.E. & Frankel, E.S. (1993) Futures and options markets: their new role in Eastern Europe, *Journal of Banking and Finance*, 17(6), pp. 869-881.

Kim, J., Ko, K. & Noh, S.K. (2002) Time-varying bid-ask components of Nikkei 225 index futures on SIMEX, *Pacific-Basin Finance Journal*, 10(2), pp. 183-200.

Kim, M., Szakmary, A.C. & Schwarz, T.V. (1999) Trading costs and price discovery across stock index futures and cash markets, *Journal of Futures Markets*, 19(4), pp. 475-498.

King, M.A. & Wadhwani, S. (1990) The transmission of volatility between stock markets, *Review of Financial Studies*, 3(1), pp. 5-35.

Kipnis, G.M. & Tsang, S. (1984a) Classical theory, dividend dynamics, and stock index futures pricing. In *Stock Index Futures*, ed. by F.J. Fabozzi & G.M. Kipnis, Dow Jones-Irwin, pp. 80-98.

Kipnis, G.M. & Tsang, S. (1984b) Arbitrage. In *Stock Index Futures*, ed. by F.J. Fabozzi & G.M. Kipnis, Dow Jones-Irwin, pp. 124-141.

Kirzner, E. (1995) Index participation units. In *The Handbook of Equity Derivatives*, ed. by J.C. Francis, W.W. Toy & J.G. Whittaker, Irwin, pp. 100-121.

Kleidon, A.W. (1992) Arbitrage, non-trading and stale prices: October 1987, *Journal of Business*, 65(4), pp. 483-507.

Kleidon, A.W. & Whaley, R.E. (1992) One market? Stocks, futures and options during October 1987, *Journal of Finance*, 47(3), pp. 851-877.

Klemkosky, R.C. & Lee, J.H. (1991) The intraday ex post and ex ante profitability of index arbitrage, *Journal of Futures Markets*, 11(3), pp. 291-311.

Kling, A. (1986) Futures markets and transactions costs. In *Financial Futures and Options in the US Economy: A Study by the Staff of the Federal Reserve System*, ed. by M.L. Kwast, Board of Governors of the Federal Reserve System, pp. 41-54.

Knott, R. & Polenghi, M. (2004) Assessing central counterparty margin coverage on futures contracts using GARCH models, Working paper, Bank of England, 39 pages.

Kobayashi, T. & Yamada, H. (2000) Publicly listed parent-subsidiary pairs: benchmarking to TOPIX and market distortion, Working Paper, University of Tokyo, 16 pages.

Kocagil, A.E. & Shachmurove, Y. (1998) Return-volume dynamics in futures markets, *Journal of Futures Markets*, 18(4), pp. 399-426.

Koch, P.D. (1993) Reexamining intraday simultaneity in stock index futures markets, *Journal of Banking and Finance*, 17(6), pp. 1191-1205.

Koch, P.D. & Koch, T.W. (1993) Index and non-index stock price volatilities around the 1987 market crash, *Journal of Business Research*, 26(2), pp. 189-199.

Kodres, L.E. (1994) The existence and impact of destabilizing positive feedback traders: evidence from the S&P500 index futures market, Working paper, International Monetary Fund, 42 pages.

Kodres, L.E. & O'Brien, D.P. (1994) The existence of Pareto superior price limits, *American Economic Review*, 84(4), pp. 919-932.

Kofman, P. (1993) Optimizing futures margins with distribution tails. In *Advances in Futures and Options Research*, vol. 6, ed. by D.M. Chance & R.R Trippi, JAI Press Inc., pp. 263-278.

Kofman, P. & Martens, M. (1997) Interaction between stock markets: an analysis of the common trading hours at the London and New York stock exchange, *Journal of International Money and Finance*, 16(3), pp. 387-414.

Kofman, P. & McGlenchy, P. (2004) Structurally sound dynamic index futures hedging, Working paper, University of Melbourne, 31 pages.

Kolb, R.W. (1988) *Understanding Futures Markets*, Second edition, Scott Foreman and Co., Illinois. Appendix to chapter 9.

Kolb, R.W. & Gay, G.D. (1985) *Interest Rate and Stock Index Futures and Options: Characteristics, Valuation and Portfolio Strategies*, Financial Analysts Research Foundation, Monograph no. 18.

Kolb, R.W., Gay, G.D. & Hunter, W.C. (1985a) Liquidity and capital requirements for futures market hedges, *Review of Research in Futures Markets*, 4(1), pp. 1-25.

Kolb, R.W., Gay, G.D. & Hunter, W.C. (1985b) Liquidity requirements for financial futures investments, *Financial Analysts Journal*, 41(3), pp. 60-68.

Kolb, R.W., Morin, R.A. & Gay, G.D. (1983) Regulation, regulatory lag and the use of futures markets, *Journal of Finance*, 38(2), pp. 405-418.

Kolb, R.W. & Okunev, J. (1992) An empirical evaluation of the extended mean-Gini coefficient for futures hedging, *Journal of Futures Markets*, 12(2), pp. 177-186.

Kolb, R.W. & Okunev, J. (1993) Utility maximizing hedge ratios in the extended mean Gini framework, *Journal of Futures Markets*, 13(6), pp. 597-609.

Kon, S.J. (1984) Active portfolio management. In *Stock Index Futures*, ed. by F.J. Fabozzi & G.M. Kipnis, Dow Jones-Irwin, pp. 210-222.

Kon, S.J. (1986) Optimal market timing and security selection decisions with index futures contracts. In *Advances in Futures and Options Research: A Research Annual: Futures*, ed. by F.J. Fabozzi, vol. 1, Part B, JAI Press, pp. 1-28.

Kook, C.P., Kwon, Y.J., Lee, W.H. & Choe, H.S. (1992) Selection of underlying index for stock index futures in Korea. In *Pacific Basin Capital Markets Research*, vol. 3, ed. by S.G. Rhee & R.P. Chang, North Holland, pp. 427-440.

Koschat, M.A. & Weerahandi, S. (1992) Chow-type tests under heteroskedasticity, *Journal of Business and Economic Statistics*, 10(2), pp. 221-228.

Kostovetsky, L. (2003) Index mutual funds and exchange-traded funds, *Journal of Portfolio Management*, 29(4), pp. 80-92.

Koutmos, G. (2002) Testing for feedback trading in index futures: a dynamic CAPM approach, Working paper, Fairfield University.

Koutmos, G. & Tucker, M. (1996) Temporal relationships and dynamic interactions between spot and futures stock markets, *Journal of Futures Markets*, 16(1), pp. 55-69.

KPMG Peat Marwick (1994) *Use of Derivative Instruments by UK Life Offices: a Survey*, KPMG Peat Marwick, London, 34 pages.

Kroner, K.F. & Sultan, J. (1991) Exchange rate volatility and time varying hedge ratios. In *Pacific Basin Capital Markets Research*, vol. 2, ed. by S.G. Rhee & R.P. Chang, North Holland, pp. 397-412.

Kuhn, B.A., Kuserk, G.J. & Locke, P.R. (1991) Do circuit breakers moderate volatility? Evidence from October 1989, *Review of Futures Markets*, 10(1), pp. 136-175.

Kumar, P. & Seppi, D.J. (1992) Futures manipulation with cash settlement, *Journal of Finance*, 47(4), pp. 1485-1502.

Kumar, P. & Seppi, D.J. (1994) Information and index arbitrage, *Journal of Business*, 67(4), pp. 481-509.

Kuo, C.K. & Chen, K.W. (1995) A risk-return measure of hedging effectiveness: a simplification, *Journal of Futures Markets*, 15(1), pp. 39-44.

Kupiec, P.H. (1990) A survey of exchange-traded basket instruments, *Journal of Financial Services Research*, 4(3), pp. 175-190.

Kupiec, P.H. (1993) Futures margins and stock price volatility: is there any link?, *Journal of Futures Markets*, 13(6), pp. 677-691.

Kupiec, P.H. (1994) The performance of S&P500 futures product margins under the SPAN margining system, *Journal of Futures Markets*, 14(7), pp. 789-811.

Kupiec. P.H. (1998) Margin requirements: volatility and market integrity: what have we learned since the crash?, *Journal of Financial Services Research*, 13(3), pp. 231-255.

Kurov, A.A. & Lasser, D.J. (2002) The effect of the introduction of Cubes on the NASDAQ 100 index spot-futures pricing relationship, *Journal of Futures Markets*, 22(3), pp. 197-218.

Kurov, A.A. & Lasser, D.J. (2004) Price dynamics in the regular and e-mini futures markets, *Journal of Financial and Quantitative Analysis*, 39(2), pp. 365-384.

Kurov, A.A. & Zabotina, T. (2005) Is it time to reduce the minimum tick sizes of the E-mini futures?, *Journal of Futures Markets*, 25(1), pp. 79-104.

Kuserk, G.J. & Locke, P.R. (1993) Scalper behaviour in futures markets: an empirical examination, *Journal of Futures Markets*, 13(4), pp. 409-431.

Kuserk, G.J. & Locke, P.R. (1994) The Chicago loop tunnel flood: cash pricing and activity, *Review of Futures Markets*, 13(1), pp. 115-154.

Kuserk, G.J., Locke, P.R. & Sayers, C.L. (1992) The effects of amendments to rule 80a on liquidity, volatility and price efficiency in the S&P500 futures, *Journal of Futures Markets*, 12(4), pp. 383-409.

Kutner, G.W. & Sweeney, R.J. (1991) Causality tests between the S&P500 cash and futures markets, *Quarterly Journal of Business and Economics*, 30(2), pp. 51-74.

Kyle, A.S. (1988) Trading halts and price limits, *Review of Futures Markets*, 7(3), pp. 426-434.

Kyriacou, K. & Sarno, L. (1999) The temporal relationship between derivatives trading and spot market volatility in the UK: empirical analysis and Monte Carlo evidence, *Journal of Futures Markets*, 19(3), pp. 245-270.

Laatsch, F.E. (1991) A note on the effects of the initiation of Major Market Index futures on the daily returns of the component stocks, *Journal of Futures Markets*, 11(3), pp. 313-317.

Laatsch, F.E. & Schwarz, T.V. (1988) Price discovery and risk transfer in stock index cash and futures markets, *Review of Futures Markets*, 7(2), pp. 272-289.

Lafuente, J.A. (2002) Intraday return and volatility relationships between the Ibex 35 spot and futures markets, *Spanish Economic Review*, 4(3), pp. 201-220.

Lafuente, J.A. & Novales, A. (2003) Optimal hedging under departures from the cost of carry valuation: evidence from the Spanish stock index futures market, *Journal of Banking and Finance*, 27(6), pp. 1053-1078.

Lam, B. (1994) Enter the dragons, *Futures and Options World*, no. 272, pp. 27-28.

Lam, K., Sin, C.Y. & Leung, R. (2004) A theoretical framework to evaluate different margin-setting methodologies, *Journal of Futures Markets*, 24(2), pp. 117-145.

Lam, K. & Yu, P.L.H. (1992) Hedging performance of the Hang Seng index futures contract, *Review of Futures Markets*, 11(3), pp. 447-474.

Lamm, R.M. (1992) Emerging issues and policy options in the US futures industry, *Business Economics*, 27(4), pp. 39-43.

Lamoureux, C.G. & Wansley, J.W. (1987) Market effects of changes in the Standard & Poor's 500 index, *The Financial Review*, 22(1), pp. 53-69.

Lascelles. D. (2002) *Single Stock Futures: The Ultimate Derivative*, Centre for the Study of Financial Innovation, No. 52, February, 23 pages.

Latane, H.A., Tuttle, D.L. & Young, W.E. (1971) Market indices and their implications for portfolio management, *Financial Analysts Journal*, 27(5), pp. 75-85.

Lau, H.S., Gribbin, D.W. & Harris, R.W. (1992) How prevalent are stable Paretian distributed financial variables?, *Decision Sciences*, 23(5), pp. 1240-1250.

Lauterbach, B. & Monroe, M. (1989) A transaction data examination of the weekend effect in futures markets, *Review of Futures Markets*, 8(3), pp. 370-382.

Laux, P.A. & Senchack, A.J. (1992) Bid-ask spreads in financial futures, *Journal of Futures Markets*, 12(6), pp. 621-634.

Laws, J. & Thompson, J. (2005) Hedging effectiveness of stock index futures, *European Journal of Operational Research*, 163(1), pp. 177-191.

Lee, C.F., Bubnys, E.L. & Lin, Y. (1987) Stock index futures hedge ratios: tests on horizon effects and functional form. In *Advances in Futures and Options Research: A Research Annual*, vol. 2, ed. by F.J. Fabozzi, JAI Press Inc, pp. 291-311.

Lee, C.F., Leuthold, R.M. & Cordier, J.E. (1985) The stock market and the commodity futures market: diversification and arbitrage potential, *Financial Analysts Journal*, 41(4), pp. 53-60.

Lee, C.I., Gleason, K.C. & Mathur, I. (2000) Efficiency tests in the French derivatives market, *Journal of Banking and Finance*, 24(5), pp. 787-807.

Lee, C.I. & Mathur, I. (1999) Efficiency tests in the Spanish futures market, *Journal of Futures Markets*, 19(1), pp. 59-77.

Lee, C.I. & Tong, H.C. (1998) Stock futures: the effects of their trading on the underlying stocks in Australia, *Journal of Multinational Financial Management*, 8(2-3), pp. 285-301.

Lee, I.E., Gleason, K.C. & Mathur, I. (1999) A comprehensive examination of the compass rose pattern in futures markets, *Journal of Futures Markets*, 19(5), pp. 541-564.

Lee, J.H. & Linn, S.C. (1994) Intraday and overnight volatility of stock index and stock index futures returns, *Review of Futures Markets*, 13(1), pp. 1-38.

Lee, J.H. & Nayar, N. (1993) A transactions data analysis of arbitrage between index options and index futures, *Journal of Futures Markets*, 13(8), pp. 889-902.

Lee, J.W.C. (1994) An empirical study of the effectiveness of hedging UK share portfolios with FTSE 100 index futures contracts. MSc Dissertation, University of Southampton, 55 pages.

Lee, S.B. & Huh, S.M. (1991) Futures market timing ability with neural networks, *Review of Futures Markets*, 10(3), pp. 534-548.

Lee, S.B. & Ohk, K.Y. (1992a) Stock index futures listing and structural change in time-varying volatility, *Journal of Futures Markets*, 12(5), pp. 493-509.

Lee, S.B. & Ohk, K.Y. (1992b) Does futures trading increase stock market volatility: the US, Japan, the UK and Hong Kong, *Review of Futures Markets*, 11(3), pp. 253-288.

Leland, H. & Rubinstein, M. (1988) Comments on the market crash: six months after, *Journal of Economic Perspectives*, 2(3), pp. 45-50.

Lence, S.H. (1995) On the optimal hedge under unbiased futures markets, *Economics Letters*, 47(3-4), pp. 385-388.

Lence, S.H. & Hayes, D.J. (1994a) The empirical minimum-variance hedge, *American Journal of Agricultural Economics*, 76(1), pp. 94-104.

Lence, S.H. & Hayes, D.J. (1994b) Parameter-based decision making under estimation risk: an application to futures trading, *Journal of Finance*, 49(1), pp. 345-357.

Lequeux, P. (1999) A practical approach to information spillover at high frequency: empirical study of the Gilt and FTSE LIFFE contracts. In *Financial Markets Tick by Tick* ed. by P. Lequeux, John Wiley & Sons, pp. 207-226.

Leuthold, R.M. (1976) On the methodology of testing for independence in futures prices: reply, *Journal of Finance*, 31(3), pp. 984-985.

Leuthold, R.M., Garcia, P. & Lu, R. (1994) The returns and forecasting ability of large traders in the frozen pork bellies futures market, *Journal of Business*, 67(3), pp. 459-473.

Leuthold, R.M., Junkus, J.C. & Cordier, J.E. (1989) *The Theory and Practice of Futures Markets*, Lexington Books.

Levich, R.M., Hayt, G.S. & Ripston, B.A. (1999) 1998 survey of derivatives and risk management practices by US institutional investors, Working paper, New York University, 43 pages.

Levy, A. (1989) A note on the relationship between forward and futures contracts, *Journal of Futures Markets*, 9(2), pp. 171-173.

Levy, H. (1987) Futures, spots, stocks and bonds: multi-asset portfolio analysis, *Journal of Futures Markets*, 7(4), pp. 383-395.

Levy, H., & Sarnat, M. (1984) *Portfolio and Investment Selection: Theory and Practice*, Prentice Hall International.

Li, W. & Lam, K. (2002) Optimal market timing strategies under transactions costs, *Omega*, 30(2), pp. 97-108.

Lien, D.D. (1990) A note on hedging performance and portfolio effects, *Journal of Futures Markets*, 10(2), pp. 201-204.

Lien, D.D. (1992a) A note on the effect of no-arbitrage conditions, *Journal of Futures Markets*, 12(5), pp. 587-593.

Lien, D.D. (1992b) Optimal hedging and spreading in cointegrated markets, *Economics Letters*, 40(1), pp. 91-95.

Lien, D.D. (1993a) Risk-return measures of hedging effectiveness: the case of multiple cash and futures markets, *Managerial and Decision Economics*, 14(1), pp. 71-74.

Lien, D.D. (1993b) The effect of the cointegration relationship on futures hedging: a note, *Journal of Futures Markets*, 16(7), pp. 773-780.

Lien, D.D. (2004) Cointegration and the optimal hedge ratio: the general case, *Quarterly Review of Economics and Finance*, 44(5), pp. 654-658.

Lien, D.D. (2005a) The use and abuse of the hedging effectiveness measure, *International Review of Financial Analysis*, 14(2), pp. 277-282.

Lien, D.D. (2005b) A note on asymmetric stochastic volatility and futures hedging, *Journal of Futures Markets*, 25(6), pp. 607-612.

Lien, D.D. & Liu, L. (1996) Futures trading and fuel adjustment clauses, *Journal of Regulatory*

Economics, 9(2), pp. 157-178.

Lien, D.D. & Luo, X. (1993a) Estimating the extended mean Gini coefficient for futures hedging, *Journal of Futures Markets*, 13(6), pp. 665-676.

Lien, D.D. & Luo, X. (1993b) A theoretical comparison of composite index futures contracts, *Journal of Futures Markets*, 13(7), pp. 821-836.

Lien, D.D. & Luo, X. (1993c) Estimating multiperiod hedge ratios in cointegrated markets, *Journal of Futures Markets*, 13(8), pp. 909-920.

Lien, D.D. & Luo, X. (1993d) A theoretical comparison of composite index futures contracts, *Journal of Futures Markets*, 13(7), pp. 821-836.

Lien, D.D. & Shaffer, D.R. (1999) A note on estimating the minimum extended Gini hedge ratio, *Journal of Futures Market*, 19(1), pp. 101-113.

Lien, D.D. & Tse, Y.K. (1998) Hedging time-varying downside risk, *Journal of Futures Markets*, 18(6), pp. 705-722.

Lien, D.D. & Tse, Y.K. (1999) Fractional cointegration and futures hedging, *Journal of Futures Markets*, 19(4), pp. 457-474.

Lien, D.D. & Tse, Y.K. (2000) Hedging downside risk with futures contracts, *Applied Financial Economics*, 10(2), pp. 163-170.

Lien, D.D. & Tse, Y.K. (2000b) A note on the length effect of futures hedging, *Advances in Investment Analysis and Portfolio Management*, vol. 7, ed. by C.F. Lee, JAI Press, pp. 131-143.

Lien, D.D. & Tse, Y.K. (2002) Some recent developments in futures hedging, *Journal of Economic Surveys*, 16(3), pp. 357-396.

Lien, D.D. & Tse, Y.K. (2005) A survey on physical delivery versus cash settlement in futures contracts, *International Review of Economics and Finance*, forthcoming.

Lien, D.D., Tse, Y.K. & Tsui, A.K.C. (2002) Evaluating the hedging performance of the constant correlation GARCH model, *Applied Financial Economics*, 12(11), pp. 791-798.

Lien. D.D. & Yang, L. (2003a) Contract settlement specification and price discovery: empirical evidence in Australia individual share futures market, *International Review of Economics and Finance*, 12(4), pp. 495-512.

Lien. D.D. & Yang, L. (2003b) Options expiration effects and the role of individual share futures contracts, *Journal of Futures Markets*, 23(11), pp. 1107-1118.

Lien. D.D. & Yang, L. (2004) Alternative settlement methods and Australian individual share futures contracts, *Journal of International Financial Markets, Institutions and Money*, 14(5), pp. 473-490.

Lim, K.G. (1992a) Arbitrage and price behaviour of the Nikkei stock index futures, *Journal of Futures Markets*, 12(2), pp. 151-161.

Lim, K.G. (1992b) Speculative, hedging, and arbitrage efficiency of the Nikkei index futures. In *Pacific Basin Capital Markets Research*, vol. 3, ed. by S.G. Rhee & R.P. Chang, North Holland, pp. 441-461.

Lim, K.G. (1996) Portfolio hedging and basis risks, *Applied Financial Economics*, 6(6), pp. 543-549.

Lim, K.G., Loo, K.C. & Tan, R. (1998) Arbitrage in Nikkei stock average futures across Osaka and Simex, *Accounting Research Journal*, 11(1), pp. 218-232.

Lim, K.G. & Muthuswamy, J. (1993) The impact of transaction costs on Nikkei index futures arbitrage, *Review of Futures Markets*, 12(3), pp. 717-743.

Lin, C.C., Chen, S.Y. & Hwang, D.Y. (2003) An application of threshold cointegration to Taiwan stock index futures and spot markets, *Review of Pacific Basin Financial Markets and Policies*, 6(3), pp. 291-304.

Lin, J.B., Onochie, J.I. & Wolf, A.S. (1999) Weekday variations in short-term contrarian profits in futures markets, *Review of Financial Economics*, 8(2), pp. 139-148.

Lindahl, M. (1989) Measuring hedging effectiveness with R^2: a note, *Journal of Futures Markets*, 9(5), pp. 469-475.

Lindahl, M. (1990) Erratum: measuring hedging effectiveness with R^2: a note, *Journal of Futures Markets*, 10(6), p. 679.

Lindahl, M. (1991) Risk-return hedging effectiveness measures for stock index futures, *Journal of Futures Markets*, 11(4), pp. 399-409.

Lindahl, M. (1992) Minimum variance hedge ratios for stock index futures: duration and expiration effects, *Journal of Futures Markets*, 12(1), pp. 33-53.

Lintner, J. (1992) The potential role of managed commodity-financial futures accounts (and/or) funds in portfolios of stocks and bonds. In *Managed Futures: Performance, Evaluation and Analysis of Commodity Funds, Pools and Accounts*, ed. by C.C. Peters, Probus Publishing Co., pp. 61-100.

Liouliou, A. (1995) Does arbitrage between index futures and index options hold? An empirical analysis. MSc Dissertation, University of Southampton, 93 pages.

Liu, S.M. & Brorsen, B.W. (1995) GARCH-stable as a model of futures price movements, *Review of Quantitative Finance and Accounting*, 5(2), pp. 155-167.

Locke, P.R., Sarkar, A. & Wu, L. (1999) Market liquidity and trader welfare in multiple dealer markets: evidence from dual trading restrictions, *Journal of Financial and Quantitative Analysis*, 34(1(, pp. 57-88.

Locke, P.R. & Sayers, C.L. (1993) Intra-day futures price volatility: information effects and variance persistence, *Journal of Applied Econometrics*, vol. 8, pp. 15-30.

Lockwood, L.J. & Linn, S.C. (1990) An examination of stock market return volatility during overnight and intraday periods, 1964-1989, *Journal of Finance*, 45(2), pp. 591-601.

London International Financial Futures Exchange (1990) *FTSE 100 Index Futures*, LIFFE.

London International Financial Futures Exchange (1991) *Guide to the Liffe FTSE Eurotrack 100 Index Futures Pricing Model*, LIFFE 17 pages.

London International Financial Futures Exchange (1992a) *The Merger of Liffe and LTOM: What Will the Merger Mean to You?*, LIFFE, 8 pages.

London International Financial Futures and Options Exchange (1992b) *Futures and Options: A Guide for UK Fund Managers*, LIFFE, 62 pages.

London International Financial Futures and Options Exchange (1993) *Taxation of Liffe Futures and Options for UK Institutional Investors*, LIFFE, 20 pages.

London International Financial Futures and Options Exchange (1995a) *Investing With Confidence*, LIFFE, 46 pages.

London International Financial Futures and Options Exchange (1995b) Local authority investments, *Liffe Equity Products Review*, 2nd Quarter, pp. 18-19.

London International Financial Futures Exchange & London Traded Options Market (1991) *Eurotrack Futures and Options*, LIFFE & LTOM.

London International Financial Futures Exchange & London Traded Options Market (1992) *The Reporting and Performance Measurement of Financial Futures and Options in Investment Portfolios*, LIFFE, 59 pages.

London Stock Exchange (1994a) *Stock Borrowing and Lending*, London Stock Exchange, 1994, 12 pages.

London Stock Exchange (1994b) *Regulation of Short Selling of UK Equities and Related Securities During Secondary Offers*, London Stock Exchange, 1994, 23 pages.

Longin, F. (1994) Optimal margin level in futures markets: a parametric extreme-based method. Working paper No. 192-94, London Business School, 44 pages.

Loosigian, A.M. (1985) *Stock Index Futures: Buying and Selling the Market Averages*, Addison-Wesley, Reading, Massachusetts.

Loria, S., Pham, T.M. & Sim, A.B. (1991) The performance of a stock index futures-based portfolio insurance scheme: Australian evidence, *Review of Futures Markets*, 10(3), pp. 438-459.

Low, A., Muthuswamy, J., Sakar, S. & Terry, E. (2002) Multiperiod hedging with futures contracts, *Journal of Futures Markets*, 22(12), pp. 1179-1203.

Lukac, L.P. & Brorsen, B.W. (1990) A comprehensive test of futures market disequilibrium, *The Financial Review*, 25(4), pp. 593-622.

Lukac, L.P., Brorsen, B.W. & Irwin, S.H. (1988a) Similarity of computer guided technical trading systems, *Journal of Futures Markets*, 8(1), pp. 1-13.

Lukac, L.P., Brorsen, B.W. & Irwin, S.H. (1988b) A test of futures market disequilibrium using twelve different technical trading systems, *Applied Economics*, 20(5), pp. 623-639.

Luskin, D.L. (1987) *Index Options and Futures: The Complete Guide*, John Wiley & Sons.

Lypny, G.J. (1988) Hedging foreign exchange risk with currency futures: portfolio effects, *Journal of Futures Markets*, 8(6), pp. 703-715.

Ma, C.K., Dare, W.H. & Donaldson, D.R. (1990) Testing rationality in futures markets, *Journal of Futures Markets*, 10(2), pp. 137-152.

Ma, C.K. Mercer, J.M. & Walker, M.A. (1992) Rolling over futures contracts: a note, *Journal of Futures Markets*, 12(2), pp. 203-217.

Maberly, E.D. (1986) The informational content of the interday price change with respect to stock index futures, *Journal of Futures Markets*, 6(3), pp. 385-395.

Maberly, E.D. (1987) An analysis of trading and non-trading period returns for the Value Line Composite Index: spot versus futures: a note, *Journal of Futures Markets*, 7(5), pp. 497-500.

Maberly, E.D., Allen, D.S. & Gilbert, R.F. (1989) Stock index futures and cash market volatility, *Financial Analysts Journal*, 45(6), pp. 75-77.

Maberly, E.D. & Maris, B.A. (1991) The January effect, arbitrage opportunities and derivative securities: has anything changed?, *Journal of Futures Markets*, 11(2), pp. 253-257.

Maberly, E.D., Spahr, R.W. & Herbst, A.F. (1989) An analysis of daily patterns in stock returns across indices: spot versus futures, *Quarterly Journal of Business and Economics*, 28(1), pp. 55-67.

MacKinlay, A.C. & Ramaswamy, K. (1988) Index-futures arbitrage and the behaviour of stock index futures prices, *Review of Financial Studies*, 1(2), pp. 137-158.

Mak, B.S.C., Tang, G.Y.N. & Choi, D.F.S. (1993) Validity of the carrying cost model and long run relationship between futures and spot index prices, *Review of Futures Markets*, 12(3), pp. 687-715.

Malkiel, B.G. (1988) The Brady Commission report: a critique, *Journal of Portfolio Management*, 14(4), pp. 9-13.

Malliaris, A.G. & Urrutia, J.L. (1991) Tests of random walk of hedge ratios and measures of hedging effectiveness for stock indexes and foreign currencies, *Journal of Futures Markets*, 11(1), pp. 55-68.

Mallin, C., Ow-Yong, K. & Reynolds, M. (2001) Derivative usage in UK non-financial companies, *European Journal of Finance*, 7(1), pp. 63-91.

Marks, P. & Stuart, A. (1971) An arithmetic version of the Financial Times Industrial Ordinary Share Index, *Journal of the Institute of Actuaries*, vol. 97, December, pp. 297-324.

Marsh, T.A. & Rosenfeld, E.R. (1986) Non-trading, market making and estimates of stock price volatility, *Journal of Financial Economics*, 15(3), pp. 359-372.

Marshall, J.F. (1989) *Futures and Option Contracting: Theory and Practice*, South-Western Publishing Co.

Marshall, J.F. & Herbst, A.F. (1992) A multiperiod model for the selection of a futures portfolio, *Journal of Futures Markets*, 12(4), pp. 411-428.

Martell, T.F. & Salzman, J.E. (1981) Cash settlement for futures contracts based on common stock indices: an economic and legal perspective, *Journal of Futures Markets*, 1(3), pp. 291-301.

Martell, T.F. & Wolf, A.S. (1987) Determinants of trading volume in futures markets, *Journal of Futures Markets*, 7(3), pp. 233-244.

Martens, M., Kofman, P. & Vorst, T.C.F. (1995) A threshold error correction model for intraday futures and index returns, Working paper, Tinbergen Institute, Rotterdam, 34 pages.

Martens, M. & Steenbeek, O.W. (2001) Intraday trading halts in the Nikkei futures market, *Pacific-Basin Finance Journal*, 9(5), pp. 535-561.

Martikainen, T., Perttunen, J. & Puttonen, V. (1995a) On the dynamics of stock index futures and individual stock returns, *Journal of Business Finance and Accounting*, 22(1), pp. 87-100.

Martikainen, T., Perttunen, J. & Puttonen, V. (1995b) Finnish turn-of-the-month effects: returns, volume and implied volatility, *Journal of Futures Markets*, 15(6), pp. 605-615.

Martikainen, T. & Puttonen, V. (1992) On the informational flow between financial markets: international evidence from thin stock and stock index futures markets, *Economics Letters*, 38(2), pp. 213-216.

Martikainen, T. & Puttonen, V. (1994a) A note on the predictability of Finnish stock market returns: evidence from stock index futures markets, *European Journal of Operational Research*, 73(1), pp. 27-32.

Martikainen, T. & Puttonen, V. (1994b) International price discovery in Finnish stock index futures and cash markets, *Journal of Banking and Finance*, 18(5), pp. 809-822.

Martikainen, T. & Puttonen, V. (1996) Finnish day-of-the-week effects, *Journal of Business Finance and Accounting*, 23(7), pp. 1019-1032.

Martin, J.D. & Senchack, A.J. (1989) Program trading and systematic stock price behaviour, *Financial Analysts Journal*, 45(3), pp. 61-67.

Martin, J.D. & Senchack, A.J. (1991) Index futures, program trading and the covariability of the major market index stocks, *Journal of Futures Markets*, 11(1), pp. 95-111.

Martin, L. (1988) Stock index and financial futures. In *Portfolio Insurance*, ed. by D.L. Luskin, John Wiley & Sons, pp. 138-142.

Mayers, D. & Smith, C.W. (1987) Corporate insurance and the under investment problem, *Journal of Risk and Insurance*, vol. 54, pp. 45-54.

McKenzie, M.D., Brailsford, T.J. & Faff, R.W. (2001) New insights into the impact of the introduction of futures trading on stock price volatility, *Journal of Futures Markets*, 21(3), pp. 237-255.

McMillan, H. (1991) Circuit breakers in the S&P500 futures market: their effects on volatility and price discovery in October 1989, *Review of Futures Markets*, 10(2), pp. 248-281.

Meaden, N. & Fox-Andrews, M. (1991) *Futures Fund Management*, Woodhead-Faulkner, Simon and Schuster.

Meneu, V. & Torró, H. (2003) Asymmetric covariance in spot-futures markets, *Journal of Futures Markets*, 23(11), pp. 1019-1046.

Mercer, J.M. (1997) An alternative specification for intraday simultaneity in spot and futures markets, *Quarterly Review of Economics and Finance*, 37(3), pp. 667-682.

Merrick, J.J. (1987) Volume determination in stock and stock index futures markets: an analysis of arbitrage and volatility effects, *Journal of Futures Markets*, 7(5), pp. 483-496.

Merrick, J.J. (1988a) Portfolio insurance with stock index futures, *Journal of Futures Markets*, 8(4), pp. 441-455.

Merrick, J.J. (1988b) Hedging with mispriced futures, *Journal of Financial and Quantitative Analysis*, 23(4), pp. 451-464.

Merrick, J.J. (1989) Early unwindings and rollovers of stock index futures arbitrage programs: analysis and implications for predicting expiration day effects, *Journal of Futures Markets*, 9(2), pp. 101-111.

Merrick, J.J. (1990) *Financial Futures Markets: Structure, Pricing and Practice*, Harper and Row, Ballinger Division.

Miffre, J. (2001a) Efficiency in the pricing of the FTSE 100 futures contract, *European Financial Management*, 7(1), pp. 9-22.

Miffre, J. (2001b) Economic activity and time variation in expected futures returns, *Economics Letters*, 73(1), pp. 73-79.

Miffre, J. (2004) Conditional OLS minimum variance hedge ratios, *Journal of Futures Markets*, 24(10), pp. 945-964.

Miller, K.D. (1979) The relation between volatility and maturity in futures contracts. In *Commodity Markets and Futures Prices*, ed. by R.M. Leuthold, Chicago Mercantile Exchange, pp. 25-36.

Miller, M.H. (Chairman) (1988) *Final Report of the Committee of Enquiry Appointed by the CME to Examine the Events Surrounding October 19 1987*, Chicago Mercantile Exchange.

Miller, M.H. (1990a) International competitiveness of U.S. futures exchanges, *Journal of Financial Services Research*, 4(4), pp. 387-408.

Miller, M.H. (1990b) Index arbitrage and volatility, *Financial Analysts Journal*, 46(4), pp. 6-7.

Miller, M.H. (1991) Volatility, episodic volatility and coordinated circuit breakers. In *Pacific Basin Capital Markets Research*, vol. 2, ed. by S.G. Rhee & R. P. Chang, North Holland, pp. 23-47.

Miller, M.H. (1992) Volatility, episodic volatility and coordinated circuit breakers: the sequel. In *Pacific Basin Capital Markets Research*, vol. 3, ed. by S.G. Rhee & R.P. Chang, North Holland, pp. 11-21.

Miller, M.H. (1993) The economics and politics of index arbitrage in the US and Japan, *Pacific Basin Finance Journal*, 1(1), pp. 3-11.

Miller, M.H. & Modigliani, F. (1961) Dividend policy, growth and the valuation of shares, *Journal of Business*, 34(4), pp. 411-433.

Miller, M.H., Muthuswamy, J. & Whaley, R.E. (1994) Mean reversion of Standard & Poor's 500 index basis changes: arbitrage induced or statistical illusion?, *Journal of Finance*, 49(2), pp. 479-513.

Miller, R. (1990) Short-termism and the index revolution, *Futures and Options World*, no. 232, pp. 47-48.

Millers, J. (1992) *Stock Index Options and Futures*, McGraw-Hill.

Min, J.H. & Najand, M. (1999) A further investigation of the lead-lag relationship between the spot market and stock index futures: early evidence from Korea, *Journal of Futures Markets*, 19(2), pp. 217-232.

Miskovic, M. (1989) *Futures and Options: A Practical Guide for Institutional Investors*, Longman.

Modest, D.M. (1984) On the pricing of stock index futures, *Journal of Portfolio Management*, 10(4), pp.

51-57.

Modest, D.M. & Sundaresan, M. (1983) The relationship between spot and futures prices in stock index futures markets: some preliminary evidence, *Journal of Futures Markets*, 3(1), pp. 15-41.

Modigliani, F. & Miller, M.H. (1958) The cost of capital, corporation finance and the theory of investment, *American Economic Review*, 48(3), 1958, pp. 261-297.

Mok, D.M.Y., Lam, K. & Li, W. (2000) Using daily high-low time to test for intraday random walk in two index futures markets, *Review of Quantitative Finance and Accounting*, 14(4), pp. 381-397.

Monroe, M.A. (1988) Indeterminacy of price and quantity in futures markets, *Journal of Futures Markets*, 8(5), pp. 575-588.

Moosa, I.A. (2003) The sensitivity of the optimal hedge ratio to model specification, *Finance Letters*, 1(1), pp. 15-20.

Moriarty, E.J., Gordon, J.D., Kuserk, G.J. & Wang, G.H.K. (1990) Statistical analysis of price and basis behaviour: October 12-26, 1987, S&P500 futures and cash. In *The Stock Market: Bubbles, Volatility, and Chaos*, ed. by G.P. Dwyer & R.W. Hafer, Kluwer Academic Publishers, pp. 141-179.

Moriarty, E.J., Phillips, S. & Tosini, P.A. (1981) A comparison of options and futures in the management of portfolio risk, *Financial Analysts Journal*, 37(1), pp. 61-67.

Morris, C.S. (1989) Managing stock market risk with stock index futures, *Federal Reserve Bank of Kansas Economic Review*, 74(6), pp. 3-16.

Morse, J.N. (1988) Index futures and the implied volatility of options, *Review of Futures Markets*, 7(2), pp. 324-333.

Moser, J.T. (1990) Circuit breakers, *Federal Reserve Bank of Chicago Economic Perspectives*, 14(5), pp. 2-13.

Moser, J.T. (1992) Determining margin for futures contracts: the role of private interests and the relevance of excess volatility, *Federal Reserve Bank of Chicago Economic Perspectives*, March-April, pp. 2-18.

Moser, J.T. (1993) Changes in futures margin specifications and the performance of futures and cash markets. In *Research in Financial Services: Private and Public Policy*, vol. 5 ed. by G.G. Kaufman, Jai Press Inc., pp. 95-129.

Moser, J.T. (1994) A note on the crash and participation in stock index futures, *Journal of Futures Markets*, 14(1), pp. 117-119.

Monoyios, M. & Sarno, L. (2002) Mean reversion in stock index futures markets: a non-linear analysis, *Journal of Futures Markets*, 22(4), pp. 285-314.

Murphy, J.A. (1986) Futures fund performance: a test of the effectiveness of technical analysis, *Journal of Futures Markets*, 6(2), pp. 175-185.

Myers, R.J. (1991) Estimating time-varying optimal hedge ratios on futures markets, *Journal of Futures Markets*, 11(1), pp. 39-53.

Myers, R.J. & Thompson, S.R. (1989) Generalized optimal hedge ratio estimation, *American Journal of Agricultural Economics*, 71(4), pp. 858-868.

Najand, M. & Yung, K. (1994) Conditional heteroskedasticity and the weekend effect in S&P500 index futures, *Journal of Business Finance and Accounting*, 21(4), pp. 603-612.

Nance, D.R., Smith, C.W. & Smithson, C.W. (1993) On the determinants of corporate hedging, *Journal of Finance*, 48(1), pp. 267-284.

Neal, R. (1993a) The intra day effects of program trades on stock returns: evidence from October 1987, *Review of Futures Markets*, 12(1), pp. 143-165.

Neal, R. (1993b) Is program trading destabilizing? *Journal of Derivatives*, vol. 1, Winter, pp. 64-77.

Neal, R. (1995) Direct tests of index arbitrage models, Research working paper, Research Division, Federal Reserve Bank of Kansas City, RWP 95-03, 36 pages.

Nelson, R.D. & Collins, R.A. (1985) A measure of hedging's performance, *Journal of Futures Markets*, 5(1), pp. 45-55.

Neuberger, A. (1997) Using futures contracts for corporate hedging: the problem of expiry and a possible solution, *European Financial Management*, 2(3), pp. 263-271.

Ng, N. (1987) Detecting spot price forecasts in futures prices using causality tests, *Review of Futures Markets*, 6(2), pp. 250-267.

Niederhoffer, V. & Zeckhauser, R. (1980) Market index futures contracts, *Financial Analysts Journal*, January-February, pp. 49-55.

Niemeyer, J. (1994) An analysis of the lead-lag relationship between the OMX index forwards and the OMX cash index. Paper presented to the Seventh Annual European Futures Symposium, Bonn, 28 pages.

Nix, W.E. & Nix, S.W. (1984) *The Dow Jones-Irwin Guide to Stock Index Futures and Options*, Dow Jones-Irwin.

Nordhauser, F. (1984) Using stock index futures to reduce market risk, *Journal of Portfolio Management*, 10(3), pp. 56-62.

Norman, A. & Annandale, C. (1991) Index futures or stocks, *FTSE 100 Index Futures Review* (Liffe), Fourth Quarter, pp. 3-4.

Oberuc, R.E. (1992) How to diversify portfolios of Euro-stocks and bonds with hedged U.S. managed futures. In *Managed Futures: Performance, Evaluation and Analysis of Commodity Funds, Pools and Accounts*, ed. by C.C. Peters, Probus Publishing Co., pp. 327-345.

Office of Fair Trading (1995), *Rules of the London Stock Exchange Relating to Market Makers*, Office of Fair Trading, London, 87 pages.

Ohk, K.Y. & Lee, D.H. (1994) Futures margin changes and their impact on Japanese stock index futures markets, *Review of Futures Markets*, 13(4), pp. 1173-1208.

Olszewski, E.A. (1998) Assessing inefficiency in the futures markets, *Journal of Futures Markets*, 18(6), pp. 671-704.

Orr, A.H. (1992) John Lintner and the theory of portfolio management. In *Managed Futures: Performance, Evaluation and Analysis of Commodity Funds, Pools and Accounts*, ed. by C.C. Peters, Probus Publishing Co., pp. 101-119

Östermark, R. & Hernesniemi, H. (1995) The impact of information timeliness on the predictability of stock and futures returns: an application of vector models, *European Journal of Operational Research*, 85(1), pp. 111-131.

Östermark, R., Martikainen, T. & Aaltonen, J. (1995) The predictability of Finnish stock index futures and cash returns by derivatives volume, *Applied Economics Letters*, 2(10), pp. 391-393.

Overdahl, J. & McMillan, H. (1998) Another day, another collar: an evaluation of the effects of NYSE rule 80a on trading costs and intermarket arbitrage, *Journal of Business*, 71(1), pp. 27-53.

Pan, M.S. & Hsueh, P. (1998) Transmission of stock returns and volatility between the US and Japan: evidence from the stock index futures markets, *Asia-Pacific Financial Markets*, 5(3), pp. 211-225.

Pan, M.S., Liu, Y.A. & Roth, H.J. (2003) Volatility and trading demands in stock index futures, *Journal of Futures Markets*, 23(4), pp. 399-414.

Panton, D.B. & Joy, O.M. (1978) Empirical evidence on International Monetary Market currency futures, *Journal of International Business Studies*, vol. 9, Fall, pp. 59-68.

Park, H.Y. (1990) Trading mechanisms and the price volatility: spot versus futures, University of Illinois at Urbana-Champaign, Working paper no. 90-1683, 29 pages.

Park, H.Y. (1993). Trading mechanisms and the price volatility: spot versus futures, *Review of Economics and Statistics*, 75(1), pp 175-179.

Park, H.Y. & Sarkar, A. (1992) Market depth, liquidity and the effect of dual trading in futures markets. University of Illinois at Urbana-Champaign, Working paper 92-0134, 50 pages.

Park, H.Y. & Sarkar, A. (1994) Measuring changes in liquidity of the futures market, Working paper no. 94-09, University of Illinois at Urbana-Champaign, 11 pages.

Park, H.Y., Sarkar, A. & Wu, L. (1994) The costs and benefits of endogenous market making: the case of dual trading, Working paper, Federal Reserve Bank of New York, 30 pages.

Park, H.Y. & Sears, R.S. (1985) Estimating stock index futures volatility through the prices of their options, *Journal of Futures Markets*, 5(2), pp. 223-237.

Park, T.H. & Switzer, L.N. (1995a) Bivariate GARCH estimation of the optimal hedge ratios for stock index futures: a note, *Journal of Futures Markets*, 15(1), pp. 61-67.

Park, T.H. & Switzer, L.N. (1995b) Index participation units and the performance of index futures markets: evidence from the Toronto 35 index participation units market, *Journal of Futures Markets*, 15(2), pp. 187-200.

Parkinson, M. (1980) The extreme value method for estimating the variance of the rate of return, *Journal of Business*, 53(1), pp. 61-65.

Pattarin, F. & Ferretti, R. (2003) The MIB 30 index and futures relationship: econometric analysis and implications for hedging, Working paper, University of Moderna and Reggio Emilia, 16 pages.

Paul, A.B. (1985) The role of cash settlement in futures contract specification. In *Futures Markets: Regulatory Issues*, ed. by A.E. Peck, American Enterprise Institute for Public Policy Research, Washington D.C., pp. 271-328.

Peck, A.E. & Nahmias, A.M. (1989) Hedging your advice: do portfolio models explain hedging?, *Food Research Institute Studies*, 21(2), pp. 193-204.

Pericli, A. & Koutmos, G. (1997) Index futures and options and stock market volatility, *Journal of Futures Markets*, 17(8), pp. 957-974.

Perold, A.F. & Sharpe, W.F. (1988) Dynamic strategies for asset allocation, *Financial Analysts Journal*, 44(1), pp. 16-27.

Peters, C.C. (1992a) Managed Futures - A Performance Perspective. In *Managed Futures: Performance, Evaluation and Analysis of Commodity Funds, Pools and Accounts*, ed. by C.C. Peters, Probus Publishing Co., pp. 3-20.

Peters, C.C. (1992b) A Comparative Analysis of Portfolio Diversification Criteria Using Managed Futures. In *Managed Futures: Performance, Evaluation and Analysis of Commodity Funds, Pools and Accounts*, ed. by C.C. Peters, Probus Publishing Co., pp. 305-326.

Peters, E.E. (1986) Hedged equity portfolios: components of risk and return. In *Advances in Futures and Options Research: A Research Annual: Futures*, ed. by F.J. Fabozzi, vol. 1, Part B, JAI Press, pp. 75-91.

Peterson, P.E. & R.M. Leuthold, R.M. (1987) A portfolio approach to optimal hedging for a commercial cattle feedlot, *Journal of Futures Markets*, 7(4), pp. 443-457.

Petzel, T.E. (1989) *Financial Futures and Options: A Guide to Markets, Applications and Strategies*, Quorum Books.

Phillips-Patrick, F.J. & Schneeweis, T. (1988) The weekend effect for stock indices and stock index futures: dividend and interest rate effects, *Journal of Futures Markets*, 8(1), pp. 115-121.

Pieptea, D.R. & Prisman, E. (1988) The Monday effect and speculative opportunities in the stock index futures market. In *Advances in Futures and Options Research: A Research Annual*, vol. 3, ed. by F.J. Fabozzi, JAI Press Inc., pp. 319-328.

Pizzi, M.A., Economopoulos, A.J. & O'Neill, H.M. (1998) An examination of the relationship between stock index cash and futures markets: a cointegration approach, *Journal of Futures Markets*, 18(3), pp. 297-305.

Pliska, S.R. & Shalen, C.T. (1991) The effects of regulations on trading activity and return volatility in futures markets, *Journal of Futures Markets*, 11(2), pp. 135-151.

Polakoff, M.A. (1991) A note on the role of futures indivisibility: reconciling the theoretical literature, *Journal of Futures Markets*, 11(1), pp. 117-120.

Polakoff, M.A. & Diz, F. (1992) The theoretical source of autocorrelation in forward and futures price relationships, *Journal of Futures Markets*, 12(4), pp. 459-473.

Poomimars, P., Cadle, J. & Theobald, M. (2003) Futures hedging using dynamic models of the variance-covariance structure, *Journal of Futures Markets*, 23(3), pp. 241-260.

Pope, P.F. & Walmsley, J. (1992) Giving trustees an option to trust derivatives, *Professional Investor*, February, pp. 16-19.

Pope, P.F. & Yadav, P.K. (1992) Transaction cost thresholds, arbitrage activity and index futures pricing, 51 pages. Ch. 4 in *Studies on Stock Index Futures Pricing: A UK Perspective*, by P.K. Yadav, PhD Thesis, University of Strathclyde.

Pope, P.F. & Yadav, P.K. (1994) The impact of short sales constraints on stock index futures prices: evidence from FTSE 100 futures, *Journal of Derivatives*, vol. 1, Summer, pp. 15-26.

Porter, D.P. & Smith, V.L. (1995) Futures contracting and dividend uncertainty in experimental asset markets, *Journal of Business*, 68(4), pp. 509-541.

Posen, D.T. & Collins, B.M. (1989) The use of futures and options in dividend capture strategies. In *Handbook of Stock Index Futures and Options*, ed. by F.J. Fabozzi & G.M. Kipnis, Dow Jones-Irwin, pp. 291-309.

Powers, M. & Castelino, M.G. (1991) *Inside the Financial Futures Markets*, Third edition, John Wiley & Sons.

Price, Q. (1988) Stock index arbitrage: should it be encouraged in London?, *Journal of International*

Securities Markets, vol. 2, Summer, pp. 113-116.

Pruitt, S.W. & Wei, K.C.J. (1989) Institutional ownership and changes in the S&P500, *Journal of Finance*, 44(2), pp. 509-513.

Puttonen, V. (1993a) Stock index futures arbitrage in Finland: theory and evidence in a new market, *European Journal of Operational Research*, 68(3), pp. 304-317.

Puttonen, V. (1993b) Short sales restrictions and the temporal relationship between stock index cash and derivatives markets, *Journal of Futures Markets*, 13(6), pp. 645-664.

Puttonen, V. & Martikainen, T. (1991) Short sale restrictions: implications for stock index arbitrage, *Economics Letters*, 37(2), pp. 159-163.

Quality of Markets Unit (1987-1988) Market inter-relationships and derivative products, *Quality of Markets Quarterly*, Winter, pp. 35-44.

Quality of Markets Unit (1989) Index arbitrage, *Quality of Markets Quarterly*, October-December, pp. 25-31.

Quality of Markets Unit (1990) Events of June 29th index expiry, *Quality of Markets Quarterly*, April-June, pp. 14-15.

Quality of Markets Unit (1991) Equity stock lending and borrowing, *Quality of Markets Quarterly*, January-March, pp. 21-24.

Quick Research Institute (1993) The future of futures in Japan, *Journal of International Securities Markets*, Autumn, pp. 149-157.

Racine, M.D. & Ackert, L.F. (2000) Time-varying volatility in Canadian and US stock index and index futures markets: a multivariate analysis, *Journal of Financial Research*, 23(2), pp. 129-143.

Ragunathan, V. & Peker, A. (1997) Price variability, trading volume and market depth: evidence form the Australian futures market, *Applied Financial Economics*, 7(5), pp. 447-454.

Rahman, S. (2001) The introduction of derivatives on the Dow Jones Industrial Average and their impact on the volatility of component stocks, *Journal of Futures Markets*, 21(7), pp. 633-653.

Raj, M. (1995) Cointegration and error correction model based examination of the efficiency of the New Zealand and Hong Kong futures markets, Working paper, University of Waikato, 39 pages.

Raj, M. & Thurston, D. (1996) Effectiveness of simple technical trading rules in the Hong Kong futures markets, *Applied Economics Letters*, 3(1), pp. 33-36.

Rao, R.P. & Ma, C.K. (1991) A comparative analysis of price dependence in the spot and futures markets. In *Advances in Futures and Options Research: A Research Annual*, vol. 5, ed. by F.J. Fabozzi, JAI Press Inc., pp. 267-278.

Redhead, K. (1990) *Introduction to Financial Futures and Options*, Woodhead-Faulkner, Simon and Schuster.

Rendleman, R.J. (1993) A reconciliation of potentially conflicting approaches to hedging with futures. In *Advances in Futures and Options Research*, vol. 6, ed. by D.M. Chance & R.R Trippi, JAI Press Inc., pp. 81-92.

Rendleman, R.J. & O'Brien, T.J. (1990) The effects of volatility misestimation on option-replication portfolio insurance, *Financial Analysts Journal*, 46(2), pp. 61-70.

Rendon, J. & Ziemba, W.T. (2005) Is the January Effect Still Alive in the Futures Markets? Working Paper, University of British Columbia, 38 pages.

Reyes, M.G. (1996) Index futures trading and stock price volatility: evidence from Denmark and France, *Journal of Economics and Finance*, 20(3), pp. 81-88.

Robertson, M.J. (1990) *FTSE 100 Futures and Options*, LIFFE & LTOM.

Robichek, A.A., Cohn, R.A. & Pringle, J.J. (1972) Returns on alternative investment media and implications for portfolio construction, *Journal of Business*, 45(3), pp. 427-443.

Robinson, G. (1994) The effects of futures trading on cash market volatility: evidence from the London Stock Exchange, *Review of Futures Markets*, 13(2), pp. 429-459.

Rockwell, C.S. (1967) Normal backwardation, forecasting and the returns to commodity futures traders, *Food Research Institute Studies*, vol. 7, Supplement, pp. 107-130.

Röell, A. (1990) Dual capacity trading and the quality of the market, *Journal of Financial Intermediation*, 1(2), pp. 105-124.

Roope, M. & Zurbruegg, R. (2002) The intra-day price discovery process between the Singapore Exchange and Taiwan Futures Exchange, *Journal of Futures Markets*, 22(3), pp. 219-240.

Rose, H. (1971) Share price indices and the measurement of investment performance, *Investment Analyst*, no. 31, pp. 3-9.

Roth, C.J. & Smit, E.V.D.M. (2000) Optimal initial margin levels in South African futures markets: an empirical analysis, *Investment Analysts Journal* (S. Africa), 51(1), pp. 5-24.

Rothstein, N.H. & Little, J.M. (editors) (1984) *The Handbook of Financial Futures: A Guide for Investors and Professional Financial Managers*, McGraw-Hill.

Rougier, J. (1996) An optimal price index for stock index futures contracts, *Journal of Futures Markets*, 16(2), pp. 189-199.

Rubinstein, M. (1989) Market based alternatives, *Financial Analysts Journal*, 45(5), pp. 20-29 and 61.

Rubio, F. (2004) Simple trading rules: trading on IBEX at MEFF, Working paper, University de Valparaiso, Chile.

Rutledge, D.J.S. (1972) Hedgers' demand for futures contracts: a theoretical framework with applications to the United States soyabean complex, *Food Research Institute Studies*, 11(3), pp. 237-256.

Rutledge, D.J.S. (1976) A note on the variability of futures prices, *Review of Economics and Statistics*, 58(1), pp. 118-120.

Rutz, R.D. (1988) Clearance, payment and settlement systems in the futures, options and stock markets, *Review of Futures Markets*, 7(3), pp. 346-370.

Salinger, M.A. (1989) Stock market margin requirements and volatility: implications for regulation of stock index futures, *Journal of Financial Services Research*, 3(2-3), pp. 121-138.

Samuelson, P.A. (1965) Proof that properly anticipated prices fluctuate randomly, *Industrial Management Review*, vol. 6, pp. 41-49.

Santoni, G.J. (1987) Has programmed trading made stock prices more volatile?, *Federal Reserve Bank of St. Louis Review*, May, pp. 18-29.

Santoni, G.J. (1988) The October crash: some evidence on the cascade theory, *Federal Reserve Bank of St. Louis Review*, vol. 70, May-June, pp. 18-33.

Santoni, G.J. & Liu, T. (1993) Circuit breakers and stock market volatility, *Journal of Futures Markets*, 13(3), pp. 261-277.

Sarkar, A. (1995) Dual trading: winners, losers and market impact, *Journal of Financial Intermediation*, 4(1), pp. 77-93.

Sarkar, S.K. & Tripathy, N. (2002) An empirical analysis of the impact of stock index futures trading on securities dealers' inventory risk in the NASDAQ market, *Review of Financial Economics*, 11(1), pp. 1-17.

Sarno, L. & Valente, G. (2000) The cost of carry model and regime shifts in stock index futures markets: an empirical investigation, *Journal of Futures Markets*, 20(7), pp. 603-624.

Sarnoff, P. (1985) *Trading in Financial Futures*, Woodhead-Faulkner.

Satyanarayan, S. (1998) A note on a risk-return measure of hedging effectiveness, *Journal of Futures Markets*, 18(7), 867-870.

Scarff, D. (1985). The securities and commodities markets: a case study in product convergence and regulatory disparity. In *Market Making and the Changing Structure of the Securities Industry* ed. by Y. Amihud, T.S.Y. Ho & R.A. Schwartz, Lexington Books, pp. 183-203.

Schlag, C. (1996) Expiration day effects of stock index derivatives in Germany, *European Financial Management*, 1(1), pp. 69-95.

Schneeweis, T., Savanayana, U. & McCarthy, D. (1991) Alternative commodity trading vehicles: a performance analysis, *Journal of Futures Markets*, 11(4), pp. 475-490.

Schneeweis, T., Savanayana, U. & McCarthy, D. (1992) Multi-manager commodity portfolios: a risk-return analysis. In *Managed Futures in the Institutional Portfolio*, ed. by C.B. Epstein, John Wiley & Sons, pp. 81-102.

Schrock, N.W. (1971) The theory of asset choice: simultaneous holding of short and long positions in the futures market, *Journal of Political Economy*, vol. 79, pp. 270-293.

Schwager, J.D. (1984) *A Complete Guide to the Futures Markets: Fundamental Analysis, Trading, Spreads and Options*, John Wiley & Sons.

Schwartz, A.L., Van Ness, B.F. & Van Ness, R.A. (2004) Clustering in the futures market: evidence from S&P500 futures contracts, *Journal of Futures Markets*, 24(5), pp. 413-428.

Schwarz, E.W., Hill, J.M. & Schneeweis, T. (1986) *Financial Futures: Fundamentals, Strategies and*

Applications, Irwin.

Schwarz, T.V. (1991) The relationship between stock indices and stock index futures from 3:00 to 3:15: a clarification, *Journal of Futures Markets*, 11(5), pp. 647-649.

Schwarz, T.V. & Laatsch, F.E. (1991) Dynamic efficiency and price leadership in stock index cash and futures markets, *Journal of Futures Markets*, 11(6), pp. 669-683.

Schwert, G.W. (1989) Why does stock market volatility change over time?, *Journal of Finance*, 44(5), pp. 1115-1153.

Schwert, G.W. (1990) Stock market volatility, *Financial Analysts Journal*, 46(3), pp. 23-34.

Scott-Quinn, B., Shyy, G. & Walmsley, J. (1995) Implications of European equity derivatives for corporate finance: mirror trading, equity swaps and LEPOs, *European Financial Management*, 1(2), pp. 211-216.

Securities and Exchange Commission. (1988) *The October 1987 Market Break: A Report by the Division of Market Regulation*, Securities and Exchange Commission, US Government Printing Office, 850 pages.

Seelajaroen, R. (2000) Hedge ratios and hedging effectiveness of the SPI futures contract, *Accounting Research Journal*, 13(2).

Semkow, B.W. (1989) Emergence of derivative financial products markets in Japan, *Cornell International Law Review*, 22(1), pp. 39-58.

Senchack, A.J. & Martin, J.D. (1990) *Program Trading and Systematic Risk*, Research Foundation of the Institute of Chartered Financial Analysts.

Sercu, P. & Uppal, R. (1995) *International Financial Markets and the Firm*, Chapman & Hall.

Serletis, A. (1992) Maturity effects in energy futures, *Energy Economics*, 14(2), pp. 150-157.

Shalen, C.T. (1989) The optimal maturity of hedges and participation of hedgers in futures and forward markets, *Journal of Futures Markets*, 9(3), pp. 215-224.

Shalit, H. (1995) Mean-Gini hedging in futures markets, *Journal of Futures Markets*, 15(6), pp. 617-635.

Shanker, L. (1993) Optimal hedging under indivisible choices, *Journal of Futures Markets*, 13(3), pp. 237-259.

Sharda, R. & Musser, K.D. (1986) Financial futures hedging via goal programming, *Management Science*, 32(8), pp. 933-947.

Sharpe, W.F. (1966) Mutual fund performance, *Journal of Business*, 39(1), Part 2, pp. 119-138.

Sharpe, W.F. (1970) *Portfolio Theory and Capital Markets*, McGraw-Hill.

Sharpe, W.F. & Alexander, G.J. (1990) *Investments*, Prentice-Hall, Fourth edition.

Sherrick, B.J., Irwin, S.H. & Forster, D.L. (1992) Option-based evidence of the non-stationarity of expected S&P500 futures price distributions, *Journal of Futures Markets*, 12(3), pp. 275-290.

Shiller, R.J. (1993) Measuring asset values for cash settlement in derivatives markets: hedonic repeated measures indices and perpetual futures, *Journal of Finance*, 48(3), pp. 911-931.

Shiyun, W., Guan, L.K. & Chang, C. (1999) A new methodology for studying intraday dynamics of Nikkei index futures using Markov chains, *Journal of International Financial Markets, Institutions and Money*, 9(3), pp. 247-265.

Shleifer, A. (1986) Do demand curves for stocks slope down?, *Journal of Finance*, 41(3), pp. 579-590.

Sholund, J.D. (1985) The impact of financial futures on the firm's cost of capital and investment decisions, *Review of Research in Futures Markets*, 4(1), pp. 36-49.

Shyy, G. & Shen, C.H. (1997) A comparative study on interday market volatility and intraday price transmission of Nikkei-JGB futures markets between Japan and Singapore, *Review of Quantitative Finance and Accounting*, 9(2), pp. 147-163.

Shyy, G., Vijayraghavan, V. & Scott-Quinn, B. (1996) A further investigation of the lead-lag relationship between the cash market and stock index futures market with the use of bid-ask quotes: the case of France, *Journal of Futures Markets*, 16(4), pp. 405-420.

Siegel, D.R. & Siegel, D.F. (1990) *The Futures Markets*, McGraw-Hill, (previously published by Dryden Press, 1990).

Siegelaer, G.C.M. (1992) Dynamic risk management by a futures clearing house, *Review of Futures Markets*, 11(1), pp. 50-71.

Silber, W.L. (1984) Market maker behaviour in an auction market: an analysis of scalpers in futures markets, *Journal of Finance*, 39(4), pp. 937-953.

Silber, W.L. (1985) The economic role of financial futures. In *Futures Markets: Their Economic Role*, ed. by A.E. Peck, American Enterprise Institute for Public Policy Research, Washington D.C., pp. 83-114.

Silk, R. (1986) Hong Kong index futures market, *Asian Monetary Monitor*, 10(4), pp. 1-13.

Sim, A.B., & Zurbruegg, R. (1999) Intertemporal volatility and price interactions between Australian and Japanese spot and futures stock index markets, *Journal of Futures Markets*, 19(5), pp. 523-540.

Sim, A.B., & Zurbruegg, R. (2001a) Optimal hedge ratios and alternative hedging strategies in the presence of cointegrated time-varying risks, *European Journal of Finance*, 7(3), pp. 269-283.

Sim, A.B., & Zurbruegg, R. (2001b) Dynamic hedging effectiveness in South Korean index futures and the impact of the Asian financial crisis, *Asia-Pacific Financial Markets*, 8(3), pp. 237-258.

Simon, D.P. & Wiggins, R.A. (2001) S&P futures returns and contrary sentiment indicators, *Journal of Futures Markets*, 21(5), pp. 447-462.

Slayter, W. & Carew, E. (1993) *Trading Asia-Pacific Financial Futures Markets*, Allen and Unwin.

Smith, C.W. (1989) Market volatility: causes and consequences, *Cornell Law Review*, 74(5), pp. 953-962.

Smith, C.W. & Stulz, R.M. (1985) The determinants of firms' hedging policies, *Journal of Financial and Quantitative Analysis*, 20(4), pp. 391-405.

Smith, T. & Whaley, R.E. (1994a) Assessing the costs of regulation: the case of dual trading, *Journal of Law and Economics*, 37(1), pp. 215-246.

Smith, T. & Whaley, R.E. (1994b) Estimating the effective bid-ask spread from time and sales data, *Journal of Futures Markets*, 14(4), pp. 437-455.

So, R.W., Booth, G.G. & Loistl, O. (1997) An examination of intraday common volatility in the German index derivatives markets, *Journal of Multinational Financial Management*, 7(4), pp. 305-316.

So, R.W. & Tse, Y. (2001) A note on international portfolio diversification with short selling, *Review of Quantitative Finance and Accounting*, 16(4), pp. 311-321.

So, R.W. & Tse, Y. (2004) Price discovery ion the Hang Seng index markets: index, futures and the tracker fund, *Journal of Futures Markets*, 24(9), pp. 887-907.

Sofianos, G. (1991) Potential rewards from path-dependent index arbitrage with S&P500 futures: commentary, *Review of Futures Markets*, 10(1), pp. 204-206.

Sofianos, G. (1993) Index arbitrage profitability, *Journal of Derivatives*, vol. 1, Fall, pp. 6-20.

Sofianos, G. (1994) Expirations and stock price volatility, *Review of Futures Markets*, 13(1), pp. 39-113.

Solnik, B. (1988) *International Investments*, Addison-Wesley, Reading, Massachusetts, Ch. 8.

Speight, A.E.H., McMillan, D.G. & ap Gwilym, O. (2000) Intraday volatility components in FTSE 100 stock index futures, *Journal of Futures Markets*, 20(5).

Stanley, K.L. (1981) Measuring the operational costs of dual trading: an analytical framework, *Journal of Futures Markets*, 1(3), pp. 329-336.

Stein, J.L. (1961) The simultaneous determination of spot and futures prices, *American Economic Review*, 51(5), pp. 1012-1025.

Stein, J.L. (1986) *The Economics of Futures Markets*, Basil Blackwell.

Sternberg, J.S. (1994) A re-examination of put-call parity on index futures, *Journal of Futures Markets*, 14(1), pp. 79-101.

Stoll, H.R. (1986) Expiration-day effects of index futures and options - alternative proposals, *Review of Research in Futures Markets*, 5(3), pp. 309-314.

Stoll, H.R. (1987) Portfolio trading, *Journal of Portfolio Management*, 14(4), pp. 20-24.

Stoll, H.R. (1988) Index futures, program trading, and stock market procedures, *Journal of Futures Markets*, 8(4), pp. 391-412.

Stoll, H.R. (1989) Inferring the components of the bid-ask spread: theory and empirical tests, *Journal of Finance*, 44(1), pp. 115-134.

Stoll, H.R. & Whaley, R.E. (1987a) *Expiration Day Effects of Index Options and Futures*, Monograph Series in Finance and Economics, Monograph 86-3, New York University.

Stoll, H.R. & Whaley, R.E. (1987b) Program trading and expiration day effects, *Financial Analysts Journal*, 43(2), pp. 16-28.

Stoll, H.R. & Whaley, R.E. (1988a) Stock index futures and options: economic impact and policy issues, *Journal of International Securities Markets*, vol. 2, pp. 3-18.

Stoll, H.R. & Whaley, R.E. (1988b) Futures and options on stock indexes: economic purpose, arbitrage, and market structure, *Review of Futures Markets*, 7(2), pp. 224-248.

Stoll, H.R. & Whaley, R.E. (1990a) Program trading and individual stock returns: ingredients of the triple-witching brew, *Journal of Business*, 63(1), Part 2, pp. S165-S192.

Stoll, H.R. & Whaley, R.E. (1990b) The dynamics of stock index and stock index futures returns, *Journal of Financial and Quantitative Analysis*, 25(4), pp. 441-468.

Stoll, H.R. & Whaley, R.E. (1991) Expiration-day effects: what has changed?, *Financial Analysts Journal*, 47(1), pp. 58-72.

Stoll, H.R. & Whaley, R.E. (1993) *Futures and Options: Theory and Applications*, South-Western Publishing Co.

Streeter, D.H. & Tomek, W.G. (1989) Models of the variability of futures prices: specification and evaluation. In *Applied Commodity Price Analysis, Forecasting and Market Risk Management*, Proceedings of the NCR-134 Conference, Chicago, 20-21 pp. 119-136.

Streeter, D.H. & Tomek, W.G. (1992) Variability in soyabean futures prices: an integrated framework, *Journal of Futures Markets*, 12(6), pp. 705-728.

Strickland, C. & Xu, X. (1993) Behaviour of the FTSE 100 basis. *Review of Futures Markets*, 12(2), pp. 459-502.

Strong, R.A. (1993) *Portfolio Construction, Management and Protection*, West Publishing Co.

Strong, R.A. (1994) *Speculative Markets*, second edition, Harper Collins.

Stulz, R.M., Wasserfallen, W. & Stucki, T. (1990) Stock index futures in Switzerland: pricing and hedging performance, *Review of Futures Markets*, 9(3), pp. 576-592.

Subrahmanyam, A. (1991) A theory of trading in stock index futures, *Review of Financial Studies*, 4(1), pp. 17-51.

Sultan, J., Hogan, K. & Kroner, K.F. (1995) The effects of programme trading on market volatility: new evidence. In *New Directions in Finance* ed. by D.K. Ghosh & S. Khaksari, Routledge, pp. 159-180.

Sutcliffe. C.M.S. (1992) The small firm effect. In *The New Palgrave Dictionary of Money and Finance*, ed. by P. Newman, M. Milgate & J. Eatwell, Macmillan, vol 3, pp 464-465.

Sutcliffe, C.M.S. (1993) *Stock Index Futures: Theories and International Evidence*, Chapman & Hall.

Sutcliffe, C.M.S. (1997) *Stock Index Futures: Theories and International Evidence*, Second ed., International Thomson Business Press.

Sutrick, K.H. (1993) Reducing the bias in empirical studies due to limit moves, *Journal of Futures Markets*, 13(5), pp. 527-543.

Swinnerton, E.A., Curcio, R.J. & Bennett, R.E. (1988) Index arbitrage program trading and the prediction of intraday stock index price changes, *Review of Futures Markets*, 7(2), pp. 300-323.

Switzer, L.N., Varson, P.L. & Zghidi, S. (2000) Standard and Poor's depositary receipts and the performance of the S&P500 index futures market, *Journal of Futures Markets*, 20(8), pp. 705-716.

Szakmary, A.C. & Kiefer, D.B. (2004) The disappearing January - turn of the year effect: evidence from stock index futures and cash markets, *Journal of Futures Markets*, 24(8), pp. 755-784.

Tang, G.Y.N. (1990) The informational content of the implied interest rate from stock index futures, *Review of Futures Markets*, vol. 9, Supplement, pp. 180-189.

Tang, G.Y.N. & Lui, D.T.W. (2002) Intraday and intraweek volatility patterns of Hang Seng index and index futures and a test of the wait to trade hypothesis, *Pacific-Basin Finance Journal*, 10(4), pp. 475-495.

Tang, G.Y.N., Mak, S.C. & Choi, D.F.S. (1992) The causal relationship between stock index futures and cash index prices in Hong Kong, *Applied Financial Economics*, 2(4), pp. 187-190.

Tashjian, E. (1995) Optimal futures contract design, *Quarterly Review of Economics and Finance*, 35(2), pp. 153-162.

Tauchen, G.E. & Pitts, M. (1983) The price variability volume relationship on speculative markets, *Econometrica*, 51(2), pp. 485-505.

Tay, A.S.A. & Tse, Y.K. (1991) Selecting an index for a stock index futures contract: an analysis of the Singapore market, *Review of Futures Markets*, 10(3), pp. 412-436.

Taylor, N. (2004a) Trading intensity, volatility and arbitrage activity, *Journal of Banking and Finance*, 28(5), pp. 1137-1162.

Taylor, N. (2004b) A new econometric model of index arbitrage, Working paper, Cardiff University.

Taylor, N., Van Dijk, D., Frances, P.H. & Lucas, A. (2000) SETS, arbitrage activity and stock price dynamics, *Journal of Banking and Finance*, 24(8), pp. 1289-1306.

Taylor, S.J. (1983) Trading rules for investors in apparently inefficient futures markets. In *Futures Markets: Modelling, Managing and Monitoring Futures Trading*, ed. by M.E. Streit, Basil Blackwell, pp. 165-198.

Taylor, S.J. (1985) The behaviour of futures prices over time, *Applied Economics*, 17(4), pp. 713-734.

Taylor, S.J. (1986) *Modelling Financial Time Series*, John Wiley & Sons.

Taylor, S.J. (1992a) Efficiency of the yen futures market at the Chicago Mercantile Exchange. In *Rational Expectations and Efficiency in Futures Markets*, ed. by B.A. Goss, Routledge, pp. 109-128.

Taylor, S.J. (1992b) Rewards available to currency futures speculators: compensation for risk or evidence of inefficient pricing?, *Economic Record*, Supplement, pp. 105-116.

Taylor, S.J. & Tari, A. (1989) Further evidence against the efficiency of futures markets. In *A Reappraisal of the Efficiency of Financial Markets*, ed. by R.M.C. Guimarães, B.G. Kingsman & S.J. Taylor, Springer-Verlag, pp. 577-605.

Terry, E. (2005) Minimum variance futures hedging under alternative return specifications, *Journal of Futures Markets*, 25(6), pp. 537-552.

Telser, L.G. (1960) Returns to speculators: Telser versus Keynes: reply, *Journal of Political Economy*, 68(4), pp 404-415.

Telser, L.G. (1981) Margins and futures contracts, *Journal of Futures Markets*, 1(2), pp. 225-253.

Teweles, R.J. & Jones, F.J. (1987) *The Futures Game: Who Wins? Who Loses? Why?* McGraw-Hill.

Theobald, M.F. & Yallup, P.J. (1993) Stock index futures hedging ratios: fair values, temporal effects and lead-lad relationships, *Review of Futures Markets*, 11(1), 1, pp. 1-12.

Theobald, M.F. & Yallup, P.J. (1996) Settlement, tax and non-synchronous effects in the basis of UK stock index futures, *Journal of Banking and Finance*, 20(9), pp. 1509-1530.

Theobald, M.F. & Yallup, P.J. (1997) Hedging ratios and cash-futures market linkages, *Journal of Futures Markets*, 17(1), pp. 101-115.

Theobald, M.F. & Yallup, P.J. (1998) Measuring cash-futures temporal effects in the UK using partial adjustment factors, *Journal of Banking and Finance*, 22(2), pp. 221-243.

Theobald, M.F. & Yallup, P.J. (2001) Mean reversion and basis dynamics, *Journal of Futures Markets*, 21(9), pp. 797-818.

Thomas, S. (1995) The saga of the first stock index futures contract: was it a case of the market using the wrong model and not learning?, Working paper, Case Western Reserve University, 51 pages.

Thompson, P. & Mercer, V. (1993) *Introduction to Futures and Options: Personal Workbook*, Securities Institute, London.

Thosar, S. & Trigeorgis, L. (1990) Stock volatility and programme trading: theory and evidence, *Journal of Applied Corporate Finance*, vol. 2, Winter, pp. 91-96.

Tian, Y. (1996) A re-examination of portfolio insurance: the use of index put options, *Journal of Futures Markets*, 16(2), pp. 163-188.

Tomek, W.G. (1985) Margins on futures contracts: their economic roles and regulation. In *Futures Markets: Regulatory Issues*, ed. by A.E. Peck, American Enterprise Institute for Public Policy Research, Washington D.C., pp. 143-209.

Tosini, P.A. (1988) Stock index futures and stock market activity in October 1987, *Financial Analysts Journal*, 44(1), pp. 28-37.

Tosini, P.A. & Moriarty, E.J. (1982) Potential hedging use of a futures contract based on a composite stock index, *Journal of Futures Markets*, 2(1), pp. 83-103.

Touche Ross (1995) *Survey of Corporate Use of Derivatives*, Touche Ross, London, 8 pages.

Townsend, R.M. (1978) On the optimality of forward markets, *American Economic Review*, 68(1), pp. 54-66.

Tranter, N. (1994) Hedging index swaps with index futures, *FTSE 100 Index Review*, 1st Quarter, pp. 1-3.

Trippi, R.R. & DeSieno, D. (1992) Trading equity index futures with a neural network, *Journal of Portfolio Management*, 19(1), pp. 27-33.

Tse, Y. & Zabotina, T.V. (2001) Transaction costs and market quality: open outcry versus electronic trading, *Journal of Futures Markets*, 21(8), pp. 713-735.

Tse, Y.K. (1995) Lead-lag relationship between spot index and futures price of the Nikkei Stock Average, *Journal of Forecasting*, 14(7), pp. 553-563.

Tse, Y.K. (1999a) Market microstructure of FTSE 100 index futures: an intraday empirical analysis,

Journal of Futures Markets, 19(1), pp. 31-58.

Tse, Y.K. (1999b) Price discovery and volatility spillovers in the DJIA index and futures markets, *Journal of Futures Markets*, 19(8), pp. 911-930.

Tse, Y.K. (2001) Index arbitrage with heterogeneous investors: a smooth transition error correction analysis, *Journal of Banking and Finance*, 25(10), pp. 1829-1855.

Tsaih, R., Hsu, Y. & Lai, C.C. (1998) Forecasting S&P500 stock index futures with a hybrid AI system, *Decision Support Systems*, 23(2), pp. 161-174.

Tucker, A.L. (1991) *Financial Futures, Options and Swaps*. West Publishing Co.

Tucker, A.L., Becker, K.G., Isimbabi, M.J. & Ogden, J.P. (1994) *Contemporary Portfolio Theory and Risk Management*, West Publishing Co.

Tucker, A.L. Madura, J. & Marshall, J.F. (1994) Pricing currency futures options with lognormally distributed jumps, *Journal of Business Finance and Accounting*, 21(6), pp. 857-874.

Turner, S.C., Houston, J.E. & Shepherd, T.L. (1992) Supplementary information and Markov processes in soyabean futures trading, *Journal of Futures Markets*, 12(1), pp. 61-74.

Turnovsky, S.J. (1983) The determination of spot and futures prices with storable commodities, *Econometrica*, 51(5), pp. 1363-1387.

Turnovsky, S.J. & Campbell, R.B. (1985) The stabilizing and welfare properties of futures markets: a simulation approach, *International Economic Review*, 26(2), pp. 277-303.

Tussing, A.R. & Hatcher, D.B. (1994) Prospects for an electricity futures market, *Resources Policy*, 20(2), pp. 135-141.

Twite, G.J. (1990a) The properties of spot and futures prices, University of New South Wales, Working paper 90-010, 27 pages.

Twite, G.J. (1990b) Seasonality in the share price index and the SPI futures contracts, University of New South Wales, Working paper 90-012, 34 pages.

Twite, G.J. (1991) Effect of a thin trading bias in the share price index on the pricing of SPI futures contracts, University of New South Wales, Working paper 91-009, 31 pages.

Twite, G.J. (1992) The effect of stochastic interest rates on the pricing of SPI futures contracts, *Australian Journal of Management*, 17(2), pp. 259-270.

Twite, G.J. (1998) The pricing of Australian index futures contracts with taxes and transaction costs, *Australian Journal of Management*, 23(1), pp. 57-81.

US Congress, Office of Technology Assessment (1990a) *Trading Around the Clock : Global Securities Markets and Information Technology - Background Paper*, OTA-BP-CIT-66, US Government Printing Office.

US Congress, Office of Technology Assessment (1990b) *Electronic Bulls and Bears: US Securities Markets and Information Technology*, OTA-CIT-469, US Government Printing Office.

Vaidyanathan, R. & Krehbiel, T. (1992) Does the S&P500 futures mispricing series exhibit nonlinear dependence across time?, *Journal of Futures Markets*, 12(6), pp. 659-677.

Vale, S. (1995) Share indices: breaking new ground, *Professional Investor*, May, pp. 36-39.

Varian, H.R. (1987) The arbitrage principle in financial economics, *Economic Perspectives*, 1(2), pp. 55-72.

Venkateswaran, M., Brorsen, B.W. & Hall, J.A. (1993) The distribution of standardized futures price changes, *Journal of Futures Markets*, 13(3), pp. 279-298.

Vila, A.F. (1993) Execution lags and imperfect arbitrage: the case of stock index arbitrage, *Economics Letters*, 43(1), pp. 103-109.

Vila, A.F. & Bacha, O. (1994) Multi-market trading and patterns in volume and mispricing: the case of the Nikkei stock index futures market, Working paper, Boston University, 54 pages.

Vila, A.F. & Bacha, O. (1995) Lead-lag relationships in a multi-market context: the Nikkei stock index futures market. In *New Directions in Finance* ed. by D.K. Ghosh & S. Khaksari, Routledge, pp. 181-193.

Vila, A.F. & Sandmann, G. (1995) Floor trading versus electronic screen trading: an empirical analysis of market liquidity and information transmission in the Nikkei stock index futures market, Financial Markets Group, London School of Economics, Working paper no. 218, 49 pages.

Wahab, M. (1995) Conditional dynamics and optimal spreading in the precious metals markets, *Journal of Futures Markets*, 15(2), pp. 131-166.

Wahab, M. & Lashgari, M. (1993) Price dynamics and error correction in stock index and stock index futures markets: a cointegration approach, *Journal of Futures Markets*, 13(7), pp. 711-742.

Walsh, M.J. & Dinehart, S.J. (1991) Dual trading and futures market liquidity: an analysis of three Chicago Board of Trade contract markets, *Journal of Futures Markets*, 11(5), pp. 519-537.

Wang, C. (2002) Information, trading demand and futures price volatility, *The Financial Review*, 37(2), pp. 295-316.

Wang, C. (2003) Hedging with foreign currency denominated stock index futures: evidence from the MSCI Taiwan index futures market, *Journal of Multinational Financial Management*, 13(1), pp. 1-17.

Wang, G.H.K., Michalski, R.J., Jordan, J.V. & Moriarty, E.J. (1994) An intraday analysis of bid-ask spreads and price volatility in the S&P500 index futures market, *Journal of Futures Markets*, 14(7), pp. 837-859.

Wang, G.H.K., Moriarty, E.J., Michalski, R.J. & Jordan, J.V. (1990) Empirical analysis of the liquidity of the S&P500 stock index futures market during the October 1987 market break. In *Advances in Futures and Options Research: A Research Annual*, vol. 4, ed. by F.J. Fabozzi, JAI Press Inc., pp. 191-218.

Wang, G.H.K. & Yau, J. (1994) A time series approach to testing for market linkage: unit root and cointegration tests, *Journal of Futures Markets*, 14(4), pp. 457-474.

Wang, G.H.K. & Yau, J. (2000) Trading volume, bid-ask spread and price volatility in futures markets, *Journal of Futures Markets*, 20(10), pp. 943-970.

Wang, J. (1999) Asymmetric information and the bid-ask spread: an empirical comparison between automated order execution and open outcry auction, *Journal of International Financial Markets, Institutions and Money*, 9(2), pp. 115-128.

Wang, J. (2000) Trading and hedging in S&P500 spot and futures markets using genetic programming, *Journal of Futures Markets*, 20(10), pp. 911-942.

Wang, S. (2005) Dependence of the intraday Nikkei stock index futures, *Pacific-Basin Finance Journal*, forthcoming.

Warshawsky, M. (1989) The adequacy and consistency of margin requirements: the cash, futures and options segments of the equity market, *Review of Futures Markets*, 8(3), pp. 420-437.

Watsham, T.J. (1992) *Options and Futures in International Portfolio Management*, Chapman & Hall.

Watsham, T.J. (1993) *International Portfolio Management*, Longman.

Watsham, T.J. (1996) Synthetic index funds, *LIFFE Equity Products Review*, 4th Quarter, pp. 1-5.

Weiner, N.S. (1984) *Stock Index Futures: A Guide for Traders, Investors and Analysts*, John Wiley & Sons.

Weller, P. & Yano, M. (1987) Forward exchange, futures trading and spot price variability: a general equilibrium approach, *Econometrica*, 55(6), pp. 1433-1450.

Whaley, R.E. (1986) Expiration-day effects of index futures and options - empirical results, *Review of Research in Futures Markets*, 5(3), pp. 292-308.

White, J.R.C. (1992) *Regulation of Securities and Futures Dealing*, Sweet and Maxwell.

Wiggins, J.B. (1992) Estimating the volatility of S&P500 futures using the extreme value method, *Journal of Futures Markets*, 12(3), pp. 265-273.

Wiley, M.K. & Daigler, R.T. (1998) Volume relationships among types of traders in the financial futures markets, *Journal of Futures Markets*, 18(1), pp. 91-113.

Williams, J. (1986) *The Economic Function of Futures Markets*, Cambridge University Press.

Wilson, B., Aggarwal, R. & Inclan, C. (1996) Detecting volatility changes across the oil sector, *Journal of Futures Markets*, 16(3), pp. 313-330.

Wilson, N. (1995) Trend lines, *The Clearing Business: A Supplement to Futures and Options World*, July, pp. 11-13.

Woolridge, J.R. & Ghosh, C. (1986) Institutional trading and security prices: the case of changes in the composition of the S&P500 index, *Journal of Financial Research*, 9(1), pp. 13-24.

Working, H. (1953) Futures trading and hedging, *American Economic Review*, 43(3), pp. 314-343.

Working, H. (1960a) Price effects of futures trading, *Food Research Institute Studies*, 1(1), pp. 3-31.

Working, H. (1960b) Note on the correlation of first differences of averages in a random chain, *Econometrica*, 28(3), pp. 916-918.

Working, H. (1963) Futures markets under renewed attack, *Food Research Institute Studies*, vol. 4, pp. 13-24.

Wu, C., Li, J. & Zhang, W. (2005) Intraday periodicity and volatility spillovers between international stock index futures markets, *Journal of Futures Markets*, 26(6), pp. 553-585.

Wu, S., Sheu, H. & Lee, C.S. (1990) A risk-tolerance hedging strategy, *Review of Futures Markets*, vol. 9, Supplement, pp. 283-292.

Yadav, P.K. & Pope, P.F. (1990) Stock index futures arbitrage: international evidence, *Journal of Futures Markets*, 10(6), pp. 573-604.

Yadav, P.K. & Pope, P.F. (1992a) Intraweek and intraday seasonalities in stock market risk premia: cash and futures, *Journal of Banking and Finance*, 16(1), pp. 233-272.

Yadav, P.K. & Pope, P.F. (1992b) Stock index futures mispricing: profit opportunities or risk premia?, 62 pages. Ch. 6 in *Studies on Stock Index Futures Pricing: A UK Perspective*, by P.K. Yadav, PhD Thesis, University of Strathclyde.

Yadav, P.K. & Pope, P.F. (1992c) Mean reversion in stock index futures mispricing: evidence from the US and the UK, 44 pages. Ch. 7 in *Studies on Stock Index Futures Pricing: A UK Perspective*, by P.K. Yadav, PhD Thesis, University of Strathclyde.

Yadav, P.K. & Pope, P.F. (1992d) Pricing of stock index futures spreads: theory and evidence, 69 pages. Ch. 8 in *Studies on Stock Index Futures Pricing: A UK Perspective*, by P.K. Yadav, PhD Thesis, University of Strathclyde.

Yadav, P.K. & Pope, P.F. (1994) Stock index futures mispricing: profit opportunities or risk premia?, *Journal of Banking and Finance*, 18(5), pp. 921-953.

Yadav, P.K., Pope, P.F. & Paudyal, K. (1994) Threshold autoregressive modelling in finance: the price differences of equivalent assets, *Mathematical Finance*, 4(2), pp. 205-221.

Yang, S.R. & Brorsen, B.W. (1993) Nonlinear dynamics of daily futures prices: conditional heteroskedasticity or chaos?, *Journal of Futures Markets*, 13(2), pp. 175-191.

Yang, W. (2001) GARCH hedge ratios and hedging effectiveness in Australian futures markets, Working paper, Edith Cowan University, 32 pages.

Yau, J. (1993) The performance of the Hong Kong Hang Seng index futures contract in risk-return management, *Pacific Basin Finance Journal*, 1(1), pp. 381-406.

Yau, J., Hill, J. & Schneeweis, T. (1990) An analysis of the effectiveness of the Nikkei 225 futures contracts in risk-return management, *Global Finance Journal*, 1(4), pp. 255-276.

Yau, J., Savanayana, U. & Schneeweis, T. (1990) The effect of alternative return measures in financial futures research. In *Advances in Futures and Options Research: A Research Annual*, vol. 4, ed. by F.J. Fabozzi, JAI Press Inc., pp. 281-295.

Yau, J., Savanayana, U. & Schneeweis, T. (1992) Alternative performance models in interest rate futures. In *Rational Expectations and Efficiency in Futures Markets*, ed. by B.A. Goss, Routledge, pp. 167-189.

Yau, J., Schneeweis, T. & Yung, K. (1990) The behaviour of stock index futures prices in Hong Kong: before and after the crash. In *Pacific Basin Capital Markets Research*, ed. by S.G. Rhee & R.P. Chang, North Holland, pp. 357-378.

Yeh, S.C. & Gannon, G.L. (2000) Comparing trading performance of the constant and dynamic hedge models: a note, *Review of Quantitative Finance and Accounting*, 14(2), pp. 155-160.

Zeckhauser, R. & Niederhoffer, V. (1983a) The performance of market index futures contracts, *Financial Analysts Journal*, 39(1), pp. 59-65.

Zeckhauser, R. & Niederhoffer, V. (1983b) Predictions fulfilled: the early experience of market index futures contracts. In *Readings in Investment Management*, ed. by F.J. Fabozzi, Richard D. Irwin, pp. 323-329.

Ziemba, W.T. (1990) Seasonality effects in Japanese futures markets. In *Pacific Basin Capital Markets Research*, ed. by S.G. Rhee & R.P. Chang, North Holland, pp. 379-407.

Ziemba, W.T. (1994) Investing in the turn of the year effect in the futures markets, *Interfaces*, 24(3), pp. 46-61.

Zhong, M., Darrat, A.F. & Otero, R. (2004) Price discovery and volatility spillovers in index futures markets: some evidence from Mexico, *Journal of Banking and Finance*, 28(12), pp. 3037-3054.

Zurack, M.A. & Dattatreya, R.E. (1989) Asset allocation using futures contracts. In *Handbook of Stock Index Futures and Options*, ed. by F.J. Fabozzi & G.M. Kipnis, Dow Jones-Irwin, pp. 310-333.

Index